JN123856

英文和訳解説と
参考文例付

実務家のための

外国税額還付の手引書

改訂版

非居住者と外国法人に対する
課税実務と還付事例から学ぶ
外国政府に対する外国税額の
還付申告書の作成ガイド

THE
GUIDEBOOK OF
FOREIGN
TAX REFUND
FOR
PRACTITIONERS

一般財団法人 大蔵財務協会

はじめに

外国人や海外の企業に対し支払うサービス又は技術等の提供の対価には、支払の際に源泉徴収の対象となるものがあります。

実務においては、支払の際に源泉徴収を失念し、後日、税務調査で徴収もれが判明した場合、徴収すべき税金だけでなく、ペナルティも当然に支払うことになりますが、外国人や外国企業に代わって国に納付した税金が海外から回収できないケースもあります。

源泉徴収すべき支払か否の判断に際しては、国内法（所得税法）の理解はもとより、各国との間の租税条約についても正しい理解が必要です。

また、日本の企業が海外から支払を受ける所得については、その所得の発生した国と我が国との間での二重課税を回避するための外国税額控除が税法に規定されています。

しかしながら、外国での税額が軽減又は免除される場合には、軽減額を超える税額又は免除される税額は外国税額控除の対象とはなりません。

米国において、租税条約に基づく税額の免除の手続きがされていない場合には支払額の30%が源泉所得税として課税されることになります。

米国の税額の軽減又は免除は同租税条約に基づく取扱いですが、事後（源泉徴収後）においても、確定申告書の提出により同条約による取扱いが可能であり、源泉徴収された税額の還付を受けることができます。

本書は、我が国から非居住者又は外国法人にサービス又は技術等の提供の対価を支払う際に、課税上、留意すべき事項について事例により解説します。

また、我が国の法人が租税条約の適用を受けないで課税された外国税額について、還付事例を基に還付のための外国政府に提出する外国法人の確定申告書（還付申告書）の作成について解説し、さらに、米国において我が国の個人が租税条約の適用を受けないで課税された外国税額について、還付のための外国政府に提出する非居住者の確定申告書（還付申告書）の作成について解説します。

実務家と経理担当者の皆様方の参考にしていただければ幸いです。

令和５年12月

著者

目　次

課税実務編

還付請求実務編［米国版］

参考法令等

〔凡　　例〕

本書において使用している法令等の略語は以下によっています。

所法……………所得税法
所令……………所得税法施行令
所規則…………所得税法施行規則
所基通…………所得税基本通達
法………………法人税法
法令……………法人税法施行令
法規則…………法人税法施行規則
法基通…………法人税法基本通達
実特法…………租税条約等の実施に伴う所得税法、法人税法及び地方税法の特例等に関する法律
実特令…………租税条約等の実施に伴う所得税法、法人税法及び地方税法の特例等に関する法律の施行に関する省令

（注）本書の内容は令和５年12月31日現在の法令通達等に基づいています。

課税実務編

1　居住者・非居住者の区分と国内源泉所得について

ガイダンス

所得税は、居住者と非居住者に対して課税されることになりますが、居住者と非居住者では、税負担に大きな差が生じます。

したがって、まずは、居住者と非居住者について正しく理解することが大事になります。

日本国内に住所を有する者は、居住者となりますが、住所とは、生活の本拠地をいうわけです。それでは、生活の本拠地はどのような客観的事実により判断するのか。

客観的事実については裁決事例を通じ理解します。

次に、非居住者と居住者に対しては、国内で発生した所得、いわゆる国内源泉所得に対して課税が行われることになります。

つまり、所得の源泉地が国内にある所得が課税対象となります。

この国内源泉所得については所得税法第161条第１項に規定されていますが、租税条約によりその所得の源泉地が国内あるいは国外に置き換えられ、また、所得の区分が国内源泉所得と異なるときがあります。

したがって、国内源泉所得の意義と租税条約の関係を理解することも重要になります。

「居住者・非居住者の区分と国内源泉所得」では、居住者・非居住者の区分を中心に、さらに、国内源泉所得と租税条約の関係を理解していただきます。

特に、居住者・非居住者を区分するためのポイントについては、演習事例を通じて理解します。

⑴　居住者と非居住者の区分

居住者とは国内に住所を有し、又は現在まで引き続いて国内に１年以上居所を有する個人をいいます。

非居住者とは居住者以外の個人をいいます。

居住者か非居住者かの具体的な判定は、次の所令14条及び所令15条の**推定規定**により判断することになります。

	所得税法	所得税法施行令（居住者又は非居住者の推定規定）
居住者	国内に住所を有し、又は現在まで引き続いて国内に１年以上居所を有する個人 **（所法２①三）**	**居住者と推定する場合（所令14）** ⑴　その者が国内において継続して１年以上居住することを通常必要とする職業を有すること ⑵その者が日本国籍を有し、かつ、その者が国内において生計を一にする配偶者その他の親族を有することその他国内におけるその者の職業及び資産の有無等の状況に照らし、その者が国内において継続して１年以上居住するものと推測するに足りる事実があること。
非居住者	居住者以外の個人 **（所法２①五）**	**非居住者と推定する場合（所令15）** ⑴　その者が国外において継続して１年以上居住することを通常必要とする職業を有すること。 ⑵　その人が外国国籍を有し又は外国の法令によりその外国に永住する許可を受けており、かつ、その人が国内において生計を一にする配偶者その他の親族を有しないこと、その他国内におけるその人の職業及び資産の有無等に照らし、その人が再び国内に帰り、主として国内に居住すると推測するに足りる事実がないこと。

演習事例１

居住者・非居住者の判定

当社は、ソフトウエア開発の先進国であるインドから技術者２名を招き、本格的に自社ソフトウエアを開発することになりました。

来日する技術者は、開発スケジュールの都合により、Ａ氏は本年の４月１日から２年の滞在、また、Ｂ氏は10ヶ月の滞在となります。

当社と直接雇用契約を結び、給与等は当社が負担しますが、これら外国人の日本での課税上、居住者と非居住者の取扱いはどうなるのでしょうか。

Ａ氏　　4／1入国 ――――――――――――――――――→ 2年

Ｂ氏　　4／1入国 ――――――――→ 10ヶ月

Ａ氏は入国の日（４／１）から居住者として取り扱われます。

Ｂ氏は入国の日（４／１）から非居住者として取り扱われます。

１　居住形態の判定

○　居住者とは、国内に住所を有し、又は現在まで引き続いて１年以上居所を有する個人をいいます。

○　非居住者とは居住者以外の個人をいいます。

また、その者が国内において、継続して１年以上居住することを通常必要とする職業を有する場合には、その者は「国内に住所を有する者」と推定され、課税上は居住者として取り扱われます。

さらに、その者が国内での滞在期間が契約等によりあらかじめ１年未満であることが明らかである場合には、非居住者として取り扱われます。

２　Ａ氏とＢ氏の場合

ご質問の場合は、Ａ氏は滞在期間が２年の予定ですので日本での滞在が継続して１年以上となりますので、入国の日（４／１）から居住者として取り扱われます。

Ｂ氏は滞在期間が10ヶ月の予定であり、日本での滞在期間が１年未満であることが明らかですので、入国の日（４／１）から非居住者となります。

（根拠法令等：所法２①三・五、所令14・15、所基通３－３）

演習事例２

居住者・非居住者の判定（滞在期間が確定していない場合）

当社の英国本店から日本支店の業務支援のために、社員Ｓが来日し滞在しております。

滞在期間はおおむね１年としておりますが、正確な期間はまだ決まっておりません。

社員Ｓは、居住者か非居住者かどちらに判定するのでしょうか。

社員Ｓは国内での滞在期間が１年未満であることが明らかではありませんので、課税上は居住者として取り扱われます。

解説

１　居住形態の判定

居住者とは、国内に住所を有し、又は現在まで引き続いて１年以上居所を有する個人をいいます。

非居住者とは居住者以外の個人をいいます。

また、その者が国内において、継続して１年以上居住することを通常必要とする職業を有する場合には、その者は「国内に住所を有する者」と推定され、課税上は居住者として取り扱われます。

さらに、国内に居住することになった者の国内での在留期間が契約等によりあらかじめ１年未満であることが明らかである場合を除き、「国内に住所を有する者」と推定され、課税上は居住者として取り扱われます。

（根拠法令等・所法２三、五・所令14・所基通３－３）

２　Ｓ氏の場合

ご質問の場合には、日本での滞在期間がおおむね１年とされてはいますが、正確な期間はまだ、決まっていないということです。

したがって、日本での滞在期間が契約等によりあらかじめ１年未満であることが明らかではありませんので、社員Ｓは居住者になります。

（根拠法令等：所法２①三・五、所令14、所基通３－３）

演習事例3

居住者・非居住者の判定（海外滞在期間が延長された場合）

当社は米国支店の開設準備のために、令和４年４月１日から６ヶ月の予定で社員Ａ氏を派遣しました。

その後、派遣した社員に現地での責任者として働いてもらうために、滞在期間は令和４年10月１日から１年半延長し、２年間となりました。社員の居住者・非居住者の判定はどうなるのでしょうか。

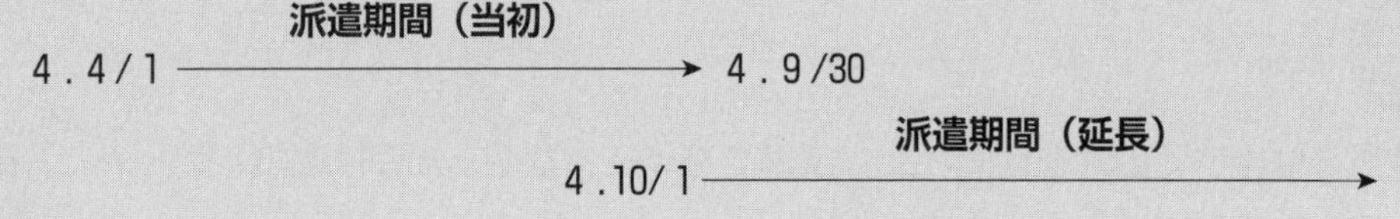

10月１日からは、課税上の取扱いは、非居住者になります。

1　居住形態の判定

国外に居住することとなった個人が、国外において継続して１年以上居住することを通常必要とする職業を有する場合は、その者は「国内に住所を有しない者」と推定され非居住者として取り扱われます。

2　Ａ氏の場合

ご質問の場合には、令和４年４月１日から６ヶ月の予定で海外に滞在していますので、課税上の取扱は居住者となっていました。

その後、令和４年10月１日からは、海外滞在期間がさらに１年半延長されましたので、この時点で、「国外に継続して１年以上居住することを通常必要とする職業を有する」ことになりますので、「国内に住所を有しない者」と推定され非居住者になります。

（根拠法令等：所令15）

演習事例4

居住者・非居住者の判定（国内滞在期間が延長された場合）

当社は米国支店から本店業務応援のために、令和４年４月１日から６ヶ月の予定で社員Ｂ氏の派遣を受けました。

その後、派遣を受けた社員に日本支店の責任者として働いてもらうために、滞在期間は令和４年10月１日から１年半延長し２年になりました。

社員の居住者・非居住者の判定はどうなるのでしょうか。

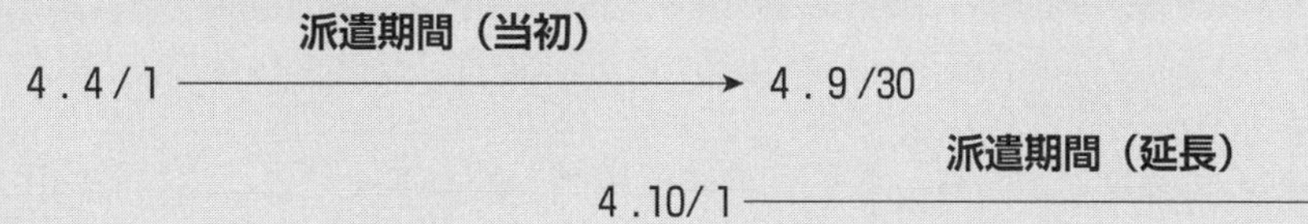

10月１日からは、課税上の取扱は、居住者となります。

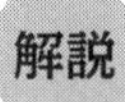

１　居住形態の判定

国内における勤務期間が、契約等においてあらかじめ１年未満の場合は、非居住者に該当することになります。

２　Ｂ氏の場合

ご質問の場合には、当初の滞在は６ヶ月の予定ですので、令和４年４月１日からは課税上の取扱は非居住者となっていました。

その後、令和４年10月１日からは、国内滞在期間がさらに１年半延長されましたので、この時点で、「国内に継続して一年以上居住することを通常必要とする職業を有する」ことになりますので、「国内に住所を有する者」と推定され居住者になります。

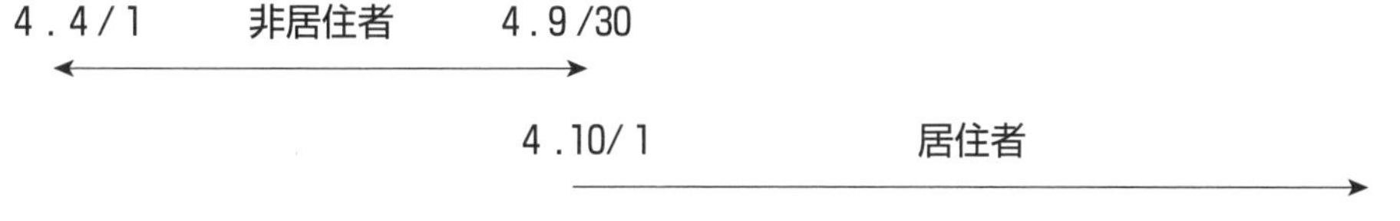

（根拠法令等：所令14）

演習事例 5

生活の本拠地とは

居住者とは、国内に住所を有し、又は現在まで引き続いて１年以上居所を有する個人をいうとされています。

住所とは個人の生活の本拠地をいいます。

生活の本拠地であるかどうかはどのように判定するのでしょうか。

ご教示をお願いいたします。

生活の本拠地であるかどうかは、客観的事実によって判断することとされています。

1　居住者の課税所得の範囲

居住者は非永住者以外の居住者と非永住者に区分されます。

非永住者以外の居住者は、国の内外で生じた全ての所得が課税対象となります。いわゆる**全世界所得課税**となります。

一方、非居住者は、**国内源泉所得のみが課税**となり、限定的な課税が行われますので、税負担に大きな違いがあります。

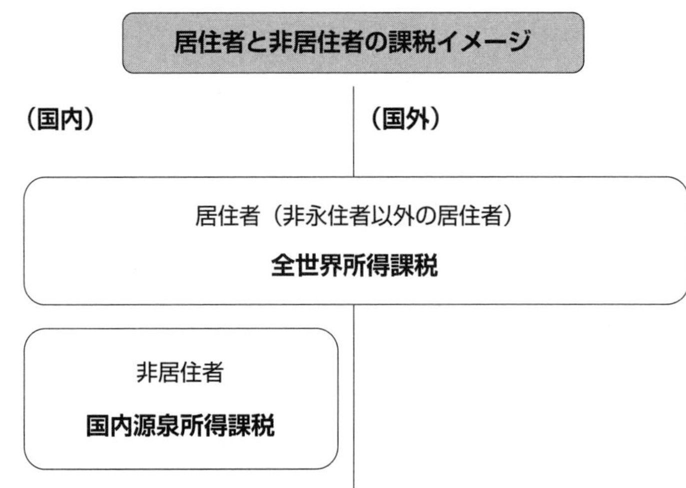

（参考）　納税義務者の区分と課税所得の範囲

（表１）【納税義務者の区分と課税所得の範囲・課税方法の概要】

<table>
<tr><th colspan="3">項　目
納税義務の区分</th><th>課税所得の範囲</th><th>課税方法</th></tr>
<tr><td rowspan="3">個人</td><td rowspan="2">居住者</td><td>非永住者以外の居住者
（所法２①三）</td><td>国の内外で生じた全ての所得（所法５①、７①一）</td><td>申告納税又は源泉徴収</td></tr>
<tr><td>非永住者
（所法２①四）</td><td>国内源泉所得及びこれ以外の所得で国内において支払われ、又は国外から送金された所得（所法５①、７①二）</td><td>申告納税又は源泉徴収</td></tr>
<tr><td colspan="2">非居住者
（所法２①五）</td><td>国内源泉所得（所法５②、７①三）</td><td>申告納税又は源泉徴収</td></tr>
<tr><td rowspan="3">法人</td><td colspan="2">内国法人
（所法２①六）</td><td>国内において支払われる利子等、配当等、定期積金の給付補填金等、匿名組合契約等に基づく利益の分配及び賞金（所法５③、７①四）</td><td>源泉徴収</td></tr>
<tr><td colspan="2">外国法人
（所法２①七）</td><td>国内源泉所得のうち特定のもの（所法５④、７①五）</td><td>源泉徴収</td></tr>
<tr><td colspan="2">人格のない社団等
（所法２①八）</td><td>内国法人又は外国法人に同じ（所法４）</td><td>源泉徴収</td></tr>
</table>

（出典：「国税庁・令和５年版・源泉徴収のあらまし」より）

２　生活の本拠地とは

⑴　国内に住所を有する個人は居住者と判定されることになりますが、住所とは、生活の本拠地をいい、生活の本拠地であるかどうかは、客観的事実により判定することとされています。（所基通２－１）

⑵　客観的事実とは

次の裁決事例から、生活の本拠地を判断する際の客観的事実は、滞在日数のみではなく、次の事項も客観的事実として判断することになります。

○　海外滞在時のビザの資格
○　収入の発生地
○　国内での住宅の有無
○　生計を一にする者（配偶者等）の居住地（海外への出国の状況）
○　海外での滞在場所
○　国外資産の有無
○　国内の社会保険の加入状況
○　国内の確定申告の状況

(3) 裁決事例の紹介

最近の居住者か非居住者かの判断が示された裁決事例を紹介します。

（平成30.１.23の裁決事例・・・・居住者と非居住者の判定）

課税庁の主張

請求人の生活の本拠地は客観的な事実より、国内にあり居住者と認定

請求人の主張

請求人は、インドネシアに250日以上滞在しているので、インドネシアが生活の本拠地であり、所得税法上の非居住者に該当する。

審判所の判断

審判所は、請求人はインドネシアに年250日以上滞在しているが、次の客観的な事実関係を認定し、請求人の生活の本拠地は国内であると判断した。

1　インドネシアに滞在するために取得していたビザは、いわゆるリタイヤメントビザであったこと。
2　本人の収入の大半を日本の証券会社とのインターネットを利用した有価証券取引で得ていたこと。
3　日本に居宅を有していたこと。
4　生計を一にする妻が日本から出国したことがない。
5　インドネシアでの所在地が長期滞在型ホテルの一室であったこと。
6　国外資産をほとんど有していなかった。
7　肩書住所地を住所として国民健康保険に加入し、平成25年分の所得税等の申告書でも自己の住所を同所としていた。

⑵　国内源泉所得とは

イ　所得源泉地とは

所得源泉地とは所得の発生する場所をいいます。

ロ　国内源泉所得の内容

源泉所得税の課税対象となる非居住者及び外国法人の国内源泉所得とは、国内に所得の源泉地がある所得税法第161条第１項第４号から第16号までに掲げる対価等をいいます。

区分	国内源泉所得の内容
非居住者及び外国法人	⑴　国内において行う組合事業から生じる利益の分配 ⑵　国内にある土地等の譲渡による対価 ⑶　国内において人的役務の提供事業を行う者が受けるその役務提供の対価 ⑷　国内にある不動産、船舶、航空機などの貸付けの対価及び地上権などの設定の対価 ⑸　国内にある営業所等に預けられた預貯金の利子等 ⑹　内国法人から受ける剰余金の配当、利益の配当、剰余金の分配又は基金利息等 ⑺　国内において業務を行う者に対するその国内業務に係る貸付金の利子 ⑻　国内において業務を行う者から受けるその国内業務に係る工業所有権、著作権等の使用料又は譲渡の対価 ⑼　①給与その他人的役務の提供に対する報酬のうち、国内において行う勤務に基因するもの、②公的年金等、③退職手当等のうち受給者が居住者であった期間に行った勤務等に基因するもの　**（非居住者のみ対象）** ⑽　国内において行う事業の広告宣伝のための賞金 ⑾　国内にある営業所等を通じて保険業法に規定する生命保険会社、損害保険会社等と締結した保険契約等に基づく年金 ⑿　国内の営業所等が受け入れた定期積金の給付補填金等 ⒀　国内において事業を行う者に対する出資につき、匿名組合契約等に基づいて受ける利益の分配

ハ　租税条約で異なる定めがある場合の所得の源泉地について

源泉徴収の対象となる非居住者又は外国法人の国内源泉所得とは、国内に所得の源泉地がある所得ですが、所得の源泉地について、租税条約で異なる定めがある場合には、租税条約の規定が優先的に適用されますので、所得源泉地の置き換えが行われ、日本国外での役務提供等の対価についても国内源泉所得とみなして課税が行われます。

所法162条に「租税条約において国内源泉所得につき前条（所法161条）の規定と異なる定めがある場合には、その条約の適用を受ける者については、同条の規定にかかわらず、国内源泉所得は、その異なる定めがある限りにおいて、その条約に定めるところに

よる…」と規定しています。

つまり、所得の源泉地に関し、租税条約に国内法と異なる定めがある場合には、租税条約が優先して適用され、国外から国内へと所得の源泉地が置き換えられることになります。

したがって、実務的には相手国との租税条約に異なる定めがあるか確認することになります。異なる定めがある場合とは次の場合をいいます。

異なる定めがある場合とは

1　国内法（所得税法）には日本に所得の源泉はないが、租税条約においては日本に所得の源泉がある場合

2　租税条約で国内法（所得税法）の国内法（所得税法）の各号と異なる所得区分をする場合

源泉徴収の際には、国内法を適用しますので、租税条約の異なる定めにより所得の源泉地が日本国内にある所得を所得税法第161条第１項第４号ないし16号の所得とみなして、租税条約に規定する限度税率により税額計算を行います。

（所法162）

2　租税条約について

ガイダンス

租税条約は、国際的な二重課税の排除と脱税の防止等を目的とする二国間の条約です。

我が国が各国と締結した租税条約は、OECD のモデル条約を基礎に、所得の源泉地を決定するに際しては、OECD モデル条約を参考に、国別に修正が行われています。

海外に支払を行う場合には、相手国との間の租税条約の取扱いについて理解が必要となりますが、まずは、所得源泉地に関する基本的な概念である「使用地主義」と「債務者主義」の理解が必要となります。

「租税条約について」では、「使用地主義」と「債務者主義」について理解し、次に、モデル条約と我が国が締結した租税条約の比較を行い、その違いを理解します。

さらに、英国、イスラエル、マレーシア、シンガポール、エジプト、インド等との間の租税条約により、租税条約の読み方についても理解します。

(1)　租税条約の意義と目的

イ　租税条約とは、国際的な二重課税、脱税の防止等を目的とする国際的な二国間のルールです。

租税条約は次の目的を有しています。

国際的な二重課税の排除	国際的な課税上の紛争の解決
国際的な脱税の防止	発展途上国の経済発展への貢献

ロ　租税条約の適用を受ける手続き

租税条約による軽減又はを受けるためには、支払者経由で支払者を所轄する税務署長に支払日の前日までに「租税条約に関する届出書」を提出しなければなりません。

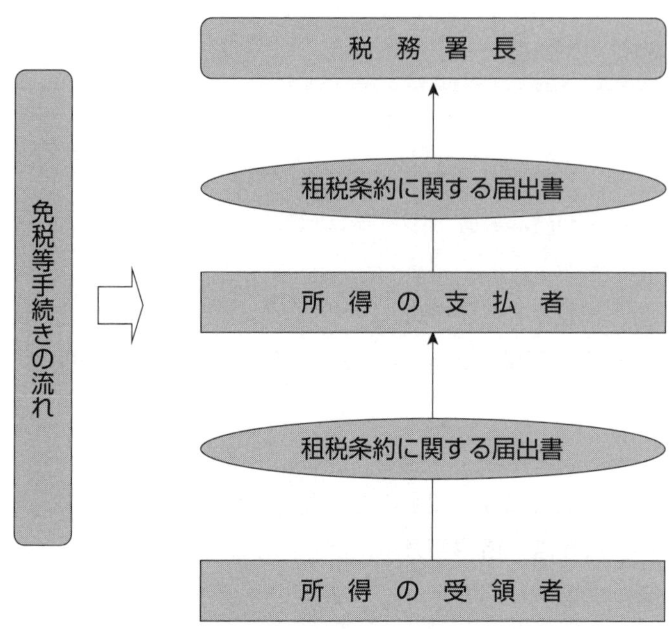

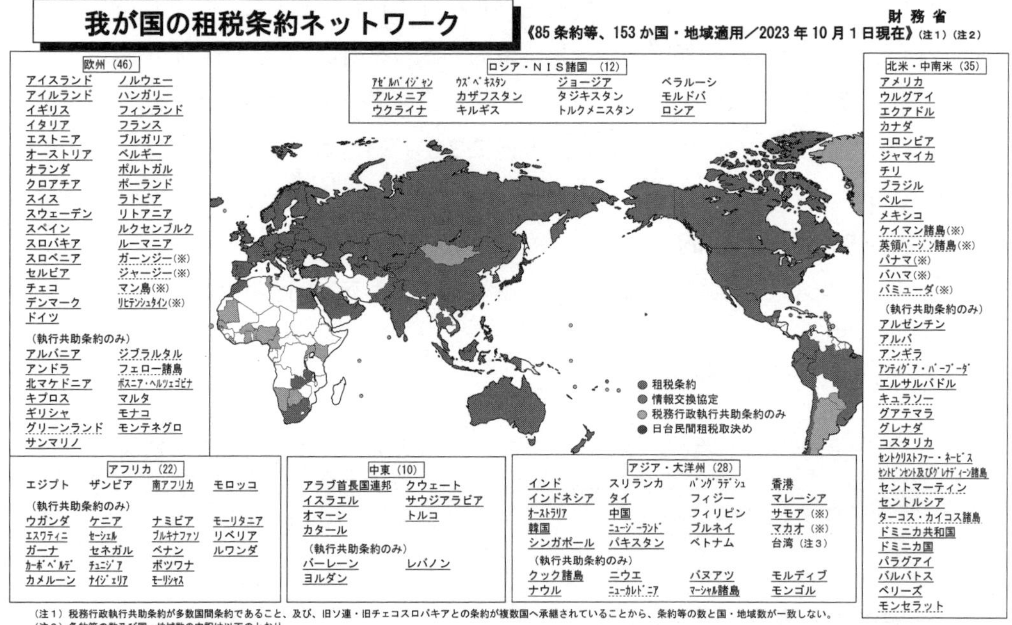

(注1) 税務行政執行共助条約が多数国間条約であること、及び、旧ソ連・旧チェコスロバキアとの条約が複数国へ承継されていることから、条約等の数と国・地域数が一致しない。
(注2) 条約等の数及び国・地域数の内訳は以下のとおり。
・租税条約(二重課税の除去並びに脱税及び租税回避の防止を主たる内容とする条約):72本、79か国・地域
・情報交換協定(租税に関する情報交換を主たる内容とする条約):11本、11か国・地域(図中、(※)で表示)
・税務行政執行共助条約:締約国は我が国を除いて122か国(図中、国名に下線)。適用拡張により140か国・地域に適用(図中、適用拡張地域名に点線)。このうち我が国と二国間条約を締結していない国・地域は62か国・地域。
・日台民間租税取決め:1本、1地域
(注3) 台湾については、公益財団法人交流協会(日本側)と亜東関係協会(台湾側)との間の民間租税取決め及びその内容を日本国内で実施するための法令によって、全体として租税条約に相当する枠組みを構築(現在、両協会は、公益財団法人日本台湾交流協会(日本側)及び台湾日本関係協会(台湾側)にそれぞれ改称されている。)。

(出典:財務省HP「我が国の租税条約ネットワーク」)

(2) モデル条約と我が国が締結した租税条約の比較(所得源泉地)

租税条約には、モデル条約というものがあり、OECDの加盟国である我が国は、

OECD モデル条約を基礎とし、各国と租税条約を締結しています。

項目	モデル条約	日本が締結した租税条約
①対象となる租税	国と地方政府等のために課される所得と財産に対するすべての租税を対象とする	対象税目は限定列挙されている。所得税と法人税が対象である。相手国に地方税がある場合は住民税も対象となる。
②不動産所得課税	不動産から生じる所得は、当該不動産が存在する国で課税される。	モデル条約に同じ
③事業所得課税	企業が相手国内に支店等を有し、その支店等を通じて事業を行う場合にその支店に帰属する部分の所得についてのみ課税される。	モデル条約に同じ
④国際運輸業所得課税	事業所得課税の例外として、国際運輸業を実質的に管理する場所が存在する国で課税される。	モデル条約に同じ
⑤配当所得課税	配当を受領する国（居住地国）での課税が原則であるが、配当が発生する国（源泉地国）でも課税される。	一部の国との間では相互に免税とし、その他の国はモデル条約に同じ
⑥利子所得課税	利子を受領する国（居住地国）での課税が原則であるが、利子が発生する国（源泉地国）でも課税される。	一部の国との間では相互に免税とし、その他の国はモデル条約に同じ
⑦使用料課税	使用料を受領する国においてのみ課税	一部の国との間では相互に免税とし、その他の国は使用料が発生した国（源泉地国）でも課税される。
⑧譲渡所得課税	不動産と事業関連資産等の動産の譲渡による所得は、存在する国で課税され、その他の資産は譲渡者の居住地国で課税される。	モデル条約に同じ
⑨短期滞在者	相手国の滞在が183日以下は免税	モデル条約に同じ
⑩役員報酬	役員である法人の所在地国で課税	モデル条約に同じ
⑪芸能人等	役務提供地国で課税	モデル条約に同じ
⑫教授・学生等	規定なし	教授免税・学生、事業収習生免税

(3) 租税条約の実務（条約の読み方）

イ　使用地主義

所得税法第161条第１項第11号によりますと、工業所有権、著作権、機械、装置及び用具等の使用料（以下「工業所有権等の使用料等」といいます。）の所得源泉地については「国内において業務を行う者から受ける使用料で、国内業務に係るもの」と規定し、その工業所有権等を日本国内で使用した場合にのみ国内に所得源泉地がある（国内源泉所得に該当）ことから課税することとしています。これを**「使用地主義」**といいます。

ロ　債務者主義

所得税法第162条によりますと、租税条約で国内法と異なる所得源泉地を規定している場合には租税条約が国内法に優先するとしています。

日本が締結した多くの租税条約における工業所有権等の使用料の課税上の取扱いによりますと、その工業所有権等の使用料を支払う債務者の居住地で所得が発生するという規定になっています。これを**「債務者主義」**といいます。

したがって、租税条約の規定が国内法（所法161①十一）に優先しますので、工業所有権等の使用料が日本の企業等が負担する契約である場合には、その工業所有権等が日本で使用されるかにかかわらず、**日本国内に所得の源泉がある**ことになり、日本で課税されることになります。

（参考）

債務者主義について

所得の源泉地について債務者主義が適用されるかどうかは、支払先の相手国との間の租税条約を確認する必要があります。

租税条約の中での債務者主義の表現としては、「その支払者が一方の締約国の政府、当該一方の締約国の地方公共団体又は一方の締約国の居住者である場合には、当該一方の締約国内において生じたものとされる。」と規定されます。（下線部分が債務者主義の表現となります。）

ハ　特典条項（日米租税条約の場合）

条約は、真に、適用を受けるものに適用されることから、適用対象者及び対象取引には制限が行われます。

(1) 適用対象者

次に掲げる者が対象とされます。

A　適格者基準の要件を満たす者

① 個人 ……………………………………………………………………………… (第22条1(a))

② 国、地方政府（地方公共団体）、日本銀行、連邦準備銀行
…………………………………………………………………………………………… (第22条1(b))

③ 特定の公開会社、公開会社の関連会社 …………………… (第22条1(c)(i)(ii))

④ 公益団体 ………………………………………………………………………… (第22条1(d))

⑤ 年金基金 ………………………………………………………………………… (第22条1(e))

⑥ 個人以外の者で支配基準と課税ベース浸食基準の両方の要件を満たすもの

B　支配基準の要件を満たす者

個人以外の者でその者の株式等の50%以上が、上記①～⑤の個人、政府等、特定の公開会社、公益団体又は年金基金により直接又は間接に所有されていること。
………………………………………………………………………………… (第22条1(f)(i))

C　課税ベース浸食基準の要件を満たす者

個人以外の者でその者の総所得のうちに第三国の者に直接又は間接に支払われるべきものの額の占める割合が50%未満であること。 ……………………… (第22条1(f)(ii))

D　能動的事業活動基準の要件を満たす者

(1) 能動的事業基準とは、次の三条件を満たす場合である。

① 居住地国で、営業又は事業の活動（投資活動を除く。）に従事していること。

② その取得する所得が上記①の営業又は事業の活動に関連又は付随して取得されるものであること。

③ その取得する所得に関し、個別の条項に別に定める特典を受けるための要件を満たしていること。 ………………………………………………………… (第22条2(a))

(2) さらに、他方の締約国内で支店又は子会社等を通じて営業又は事業活動を行う場合には追加の要件を満たす必要があり、居住地国で行う営業活動等が他方の締約国で行う営業活動等との関係において実質的なものでなければならない。（営業活動等が実質的であるか否かの判断は、すべての事実と状況により判断する。…例えば、居住地国の事業規模と支店等の事業規模の比較、あるいは営業活動全体に対する本店と支店等の貢献度の比較など。） ……………………………………………………… (第22条2(b))

[特典条項に関する付表（米)]

様　式　17-米
FORM 17-US

特典条項に関する付表（米）

ATTACHMENT FORM FOR LIMITATION ON BENEFITS ARTICLE (US)

記載に当たっては、別紙の注意事項を参照してください。
See separate instructions.

1　適用を受ける租税条約の特典条項に関する事項；
Limitation on Benefits Article of applicable Income Tax Convention
日本国とアメリカ合衆国との間の租税条約第 22 条
The Income Tax Convention between Japan and The United States of America, Article 22

2　この付表に記載される者の氏名又は名称；
Full name of Resident this attachment Form

	居住地国の権限ある当局が発行した居住者証明書を添付してください（注5）。 Attach Residency Certification issued by Competent Authority of Country of residence. (Note 5)

3　租税条約の特典条項の要件に関する事項；
AからCの順番に各項目の「□該当」又は「□非該当」の該当する項目に✓印を付してください。いずれかの項目に「該当」する場合には、それ以降の項目に記入する必要はありません。なお、該当する項目については、各項目ごとの要件に関する事項を記入の上、必要な書類を添付してください。（注6）
In order of sections A, B and C , check applicable box "Yes" or "No" in each line. If you check any box of "Yes", in section A to C, you need not fill the lines that follow. Applicable lines must be filled and necessary document must be attached. (Note6)

A

(1)　個人 Individual　　□該当 Yes，□非該当 No

(2)　国、地方政府又は地方公共団体、中央銀行　　□該当 Yes，□非該当 No
Contracting Country, any Political Subdivision or Local Authority, Central Bank

(3)　公開会社（注7）Publicly Traded Company (Note 7)　　□該当 Yes，□非該当 No
（公開会社には、下表のC欄が6％未満である会社を含みません。）（注8）
("Publicly traded Company" does not include a Company for which the Figure in Column C below is less than 6%.)(Note 8)

株式の種類 Kind of Share	公認の有価証券市場の名称 Recognized Stock Exchange	シンボル又は証券コード Ticker Symbol or Security Code	発行済株式の総数の平均 Average Number of Shares outstanding	有価証券市場で取引された株式の数 Number of Shares traded on Recognized Stock Exchange	B/A(%)
			A	B	C %

(4)　公開会社の関連会社 Subsidiary of Publicly Traded Company　　□該当 Yes，□非該当 No
（発行済株式の総数（＿＿＿＿＿株）の 50%以上が上記(3)の公開会社に該当する5以下の法人により直接又は間接に所有されているものに限ります。）（注9）。
("Subsidiary of Publicly Traded Company" is limited to a company at least 50% of whose shares outstanding (＿＿＿＿＿shares) are owned directly or indirectly by 5 or fewer "Publicly Traded Companies" as defined in (3) above.)(Note 9)
＿年＿月＿日現在の株主の状況 State of Shareholders as of (date)＿＿/＿＿/＿＿

株主の名称 Name of Shareholder(s)	居住地国における納税地 Place where Shareholder is taxable in Country of residence	公認の有価証券市場 Recognized Stock Exchange	シンボル又は証券コード Ticker Symbol or Security Code	間接保有 Indirect Ownership	所有株式数 Number of Shares owned
1				□	
2				□	
3				□	
4				□	
5				□	
合　計 Total（持株割合 Ratio (%) of Shares owned）					(　%)

(5)　公益団体（注10）Public Service Organization (Note 10)　　□該当 Yes，□非該当 No
設立の根拠法令 Law for Establishment＿＿＿＿＿　設立の目的 Purpose of Establishment＿＿＿＿＿

(6)　年金基金（注11）Pension Fund (Note 11)　　□該当 Yes，□非該当 No
（直前の課税年度の終了の日においてその受益者、構成員又は参加者の 50%を超える者が日本又はアメリカ合衆国の居住者である個人であるものに限ります。受益者等の50%超が、両締約国の居住者である事情を記入してください。）
"Pension Fund" is limited to one more than 50% of whose beneficiaries, members, or participants were individual residents of Japan or the United States of America as of the end of the prior taxable year. Provide below details showing that more than 50% of beneficiaries etc. are individual residents of either contracting country.

設立等の根拠法令 Law for Establishment＿＿＿＿＿　非課税の根拠法令 Law for Tax Exemption＿＿＿＿＿

Aのいずれにも該当しない場合は、Bに進んでください。If none of the lines in A applies, proceed to B.

B

次の(a)及び(b)の要件のいずれも満たす個人以外の者 Person other than an Individual, and satisfying both (a) and (b) below □該当 Yes , □非該当 No

(a) 株式や受益に関する持分(＿＿＿＿＿＿＿＿)の 50%以上が、Aの(1)、(2)、(3)、(5)及び(6)に該当する日本又はアメリカ合衆国の居住者により直接又は間接に所有されていること(注 12)

Residents of Japan or the United States of America who fall under (1),(2),(3),(5) or (6) of A own directly or indirectly at least 50% of Shares or other beneficial Interests (＿＿＿＿＿＿) in the Person. (Note 12)

＿年＿月＿日現在の株主等の状況 State of Shareholders, etc. as of (date)＿＿/＿＿/＿＿

株主等の氏名又は名称 Name of Shareholders	居住地国における納税地 Place where Shareholders is taxable in Country of residence	Aの番号 Number of applicable Line in A	間接所有 Indirect Ownership	株主等の持分 Number of Shares owned
			□	
			□	
			□	
合　　計 Total (持分割合 Ratio(%) of Shares owned)				(　%)

(b) 総所得のうち、課税所得の計算上控除される支出により、日本又はアメリカ合衆国の居住者に該当しない者（以下「第三国居住者」といいます。）に対し直接又は間接に支払われる金額が、50%未満であること(注 13)

Less than 50% of the person's gross income is paid or accrued directly or indirectly to persons who are not residents of Japan or the United States of America ("third country residents") in the form of payments that are deductible in computing taxable income in country of residence (Note 13)

第三国居住者に対する支払割合 Ratio of Payment to Third Country Residents (通貨 Currency:　　　)

	申告 Tax Return	源泉徴収税額 Withholding Tax		
	当該課税年度 Taxable Year	前々々課税年度 Taxable Year three Years prior	前々課税年度 Taxable Year two Years prior	前課税年度 Prior taxable Year
第三国居住者に対する支払 Payment to third Country Residents	A			
総所得 Gross Income	B			
A/B (%)	C　%	%	%	%

Bに該当しない場合は、Cに進んでください。If B does not apply, proceed to C.

C

次の(a)から(c)の要件を全て満たす者 Resident satisfying all of the following Conditions from (a) through (c) □該当 Yes , □非該当 No

居住地国において従事している営業又は事業の活動の概要(注 14) ; Description of trade or business in residence country (Note 14)

(a) 居住地国において従事している営業又は事業の活動が、自己の勘定のために投資を行い又は管理する活動（商業銀行、保険会社又は登録を受けた証券会社が行う銀行業、保険業又は証券業の活動を除きます。）ではないこと(注 15) : □はい Yes , □いいえ No

Trade or business in country of residence is other than that of making or managing investments for the resident's own account (unless these activities are banking, insurance or securities activities carried on by a commercial bank, insurance company or registered securities dealer) (Note 15) □はい Yes , □いいえ No

(b) 所得が居住地国において従事している営業又は事業の活動に関連又は付随して取得されるものであること(注 16) :

Income is derived in connection with or is incidental to that trade or business in country of residence (Note 16)

(c) （日本国内において営業又は事業の活動から所得を取得する場合）居住地国において行う営業又は事業の活動が日本国内において行う営業又は事業の活動との関係で実質的なものであること(注 17) : □はい Yes , □いいえ No

(If you derive income from a trade or business activity in Japan) Trade or business activity carried on in the country of residence is substantial in relation to the trade or business activity carried on in Japan. (Note 17)

日本国内において従事している営業又は事業の活動の概要 ; Description of Trade or Business in Japan.

D 国税庁長官の認定（注 18）;

Determination by the NTA Commissioner (Note18)

国税庁長官の認定を受けている場合は、以下にその内容を記載してください。その認定の範囲内で租税条約の特典を受けることができます。なお、上記AからCまでのいずれかに該当する場合には、原則として、国税庁長官の認定は不要です。

If you have been a determination by the NTA Commissioner, describe below the determination. Convention benefits will be granted to the extent of the determination. If any of the above mentioned Lines A through to C are applicable, then in principle, determination by the NTA Commissioner is not necessary.

・認定を受けた日 Date of determination ＿＿年＿＿月＿＿日

・認定を受けた所得の種類
Type of income for which determination was given＿＿＿＿＿＿＿＿

二　「導管取引」を規制する規定（日米租税条約の場合）

その取引が「導管取引」であり、真に適用を受けようとする者が条約締結国の者ではなく条約が締結されていない国の者である場合には、日米租税条約12条５（使用料の場合）の規定により租税条約は適用されません。

導管取引の要件

①　一方の締約国の居住者がある無体財産権の使用に関して他方の締約国の居住者から使用料の支払を受ける場合。

②　次に該当する者が、①と同一の無体財産権に関し一方の締約国の居住者から支払を受ける。

○　①の使用料に関し、一方の居住者に対し条約により認められる特典を受ける権利を有しない。

○　いずれの締約国の居住者でもないこと。

⑷　租税条約の規定ぶり（使用料について）

［事例１］使用料を免税としている条約の事例

（日・英租税条約）

所法第161条第１項第11号	日英租税条約第12条
国内において業務を行う者から受ける次に掲げる使用料又は対価で当該業務に係るもの イ　工業所有権その他の技術に関する権利、特別の技術による生産方式若しくはこれらに準ずるものの使用料又はその譲渡による対価 ロ　著作権（出版権及び著作隣接権その他これに準ずるものを含む。）の使用料又はその譲渡による対価 ハ　機械、装置その他政令で定める用具の使用料	１　一方の締約国内において生じ、他方の締約国の居住者が受益者である使用料に対しては、当該他方の締約国においてのみ租税を課することができる。 ２　この条において、「使用料」とは、文学上、芸術上若しくは学術上の著作物（映画フィルム及びラジオ放送用又はテレビジョン放送用のフィルム又はテープを含む。）の著作権、特許権、商標権、意匠、模型、図面、秘密方式若しくは秘密工程の使用若しくは使用の権利の対価として、又は産業上、商業上若しくは学術上の経験に関する情報の対価として受領されるすべての種類の支払金等をいう。 ３　１の規定は、一方の締約国の居住者である使用料の受益者が、当該使用料の生じた他方の締約国内において当該他方の締約国内にある恒久的施設を通じて事業を行う場合において、当該使用料の支払の基因となった権利又は財産が当該恒久的施設と実質的な関連を有するものであるときは、適用しない。この場合には、第７条の規定を適用する。

（租税条約の読み方）

下線部分が使用料を免税としている規定となります。これによりますと、使用料が生じた国ではなく、使用料の受益者の国で課税することになります。

［事例２］使用料の課税を認めている条約の事例
（日・イスラエル租税条約）

所法第161条第１項第11号	日・イスラエル租税条約第12条
国内において業務を行う者から受ける次に掲げる使用料又は対価で当該業務に係るもの イ　工業所有権その他の技術に関する権利、特別の技術による生産方式若しくはこれらに準ずるものの使用料又はその譲渡による対価 ロ　著作権（出版権及び著作隣接権その他これに準ずるものを含む。）の使用料又はその譲渡による対価 ハ　機械、装置その他政令で定める用具の使用料	１　一方の締約国内において生じ、他方の締約国の居住者に支払われる使用料に対しては、当該他方の締約国において租税を課することができる。 ２　１の使用料に対しては、当該使用料が生じた締約国においても、当該締約国の法令に従って租税を課すことができる。その租税の額は、当該使用料の受領者が当該使用料の受益者である場合には、10%を超えないものとする。 ３　この条において、「使用料」とは、文学上、芸術上若しくは学術上の著作物（ソフトウエア、映画フィルム及びラジオ放送用又はテレビジョン放送用のフィルム又はテープを含む。）の著作権、特許権、商標権、意匠、模型、図面、秘密方式若しくは秘密工程の使用若しくは使用の権利の対価として、産業上、商業上若しくは学術上の設備の使用若しくは使用の権利の対価として、又は産業上、商業上若しくは学術上の経験に関する情報の対価として受領するすべての種類の支払金をいう。

（租税条約の読み方）

下線部分が使用料の課税を認めている規定となります。これによりますと、使用料が生じた国でも課税することになります。

[事例3] 債務者主義により使用料の所得源泉地を置き換えている条約の事例

(日・マレーシア租税条約)

所法第161条第1項第11号	日・マレーシア租税条約第12条
国内において業務を行う者から受ける次に掲げる使用料又は対価で当該業務に係るもの イ 工業所有権その他の技術に関する権利、特別の技術による生産方式若しくはこれらに準ずるものの使用料又はその譲渡による対価 ロ 著作権(出版権及び著作隣接権その他これに準ずるものを含む。)の使用料又はその譲渡による対価 ハ 機械、装置その他政令で定める用具の使用料	1 一方の締約国内において生じ、他方の締約国の居住者に支払われる使用料に対しては、当該他方の締約国において租税を課することができる。 2 1の使用料に対しては、当該使用料が生じた締約国においても、当該締約国の法令に従って租税を課すことができる。その租税の額は、当該使用料の受益者が他方の締約国の居住者である場合には、当該使用料の額の10%を超えないものとする。 3 この条において、「使用料」とは、文学上、芸術上若しくは学術上の著作物(ソフトウエア、映画フィルム及びラジオ放送用又はテレビジョン放送用のフィルム又はテープを含む。)の著作権、特許権、商標権、意匠、模型、図面、秘密方式若しくは秘密工程の使用若しくは使用の権利の対価として、産業上、商業上若しくは学術上の設備の使用若しくは使用の権利の対価として、又は産業上、商業上若しくは学術上の経験に関する情報の対価として受領するすべての種類の支払金及び船舶又は航空機の裸用船契約に基づいて受領する料金(第8条で取り扱うものを除く。)をいう。 4 使用料は、その支払者が一方の締約国又は一方の締約国の地方政府、地方公共団体若しくは居住者である場合には、当該一方の締約国内において生じたものとされる。

(租税条約の読み方)

下線部分が債務者主義により所得源泉地を置き換えている規定になります。これにより使用料を支払う国で課税することになります。

[事例４] 著作権等の譲渡を使用料として規定している条約の事例
（日・シンガポール租税条約）

所法第161条第１項第11号	日・シンガポール租税条約第12条
国内において業務を行う者から受ける次に掲げる使用料又は対価で当該業務に係るもの イ　工業所有権その他の技術に関する権利、特別の技術による生産方式若しくはこれらに準ずるものの使用料又はその譲渡による対価 ロ　著作権（出版権及び著作隣接権その他これに準ずるものを含む。）の使用料又はその譲渡による対価 ハ　機械、装置その他政令で定める用具の使用料	1　一方の締約国内において生じ、他方の締約国の居住者に支払われる使用料に対しては、当該他方の締約国において租税を課することができる。 2　1の使用料に対しては、当該使用料が生じた締約国においても、当該締約国の法令に従って租税を課すことができる。その租税の額は、当該使用料の受益者が他方の締約国の居住者である場合には、当該使用料の額の10%を超えないものとする。 3　この条において、「使用料」とは、文学上、美術上若しくは学術上の著作物（ソフトウエア、映画フィルム及びラジオ放送用又はテレビジョン放送用のフィルム又はテープを含む。）の著作権、特許権、商標権、意匠、模型、図面、秘密方式又は・・・・・・【中略】・・・・・・・すべての種類の支払金及び船舶又は航空機の裸用船契約に基づいて受領する料金（第８条で取り扱うものを除く。）をいう。 5　1、2及び4の規定は、文学上、美術上若しくは学術上の著作物（ソフトウエア、映画フィルム及びラジオ放送用又はテレビジョン放送用のフィルム又はテープを含む。）の著作権、特許権、商標権、意匠、模型、図面、秘密方式又は秘密工程の譲渡から生ずる所得についても、同様に適用する。

（租税条約の読み方）

下線部分が著作権等の譲渡を使用料としている規定です。これによりますと著作権等の譲渡から生じる所得も使用料として取り扱われます。

［事例５］著作権等の譲渡を国内法で課税すると規定している条約の事例

（日・エジプト租税条約）

所法第161条第１項第11号	日・エジプト租税条約第10条
国内において業務を行う者から受ける次に掲げる使用料又は対価で当該業務に係るもの イ　工業所有権その他の技術に関する権利、特別の技術による生産方式若しくはこれらに準ずるものの使用料又はその譲渡による対価 ロ　著作権（出版権及び著作隣接権その他これに準ずるものを含む。）の使用料又はその譲渡による対価 ハ　機械、装置その他政令で定める用具の使用料	１　一方の締約国内において生じ、他方の締約国の居住者に支払われる使用料に対しては、当該一方の締約国において、当該使用料の金額の15%を超えない税率で租税を課することができる。 ２　この条において、「使用料」とは、文学上、・・・・・・・【以下省略】・・・・・・・ **日・エジプト租税条約第11条** １　第４条２に定義する不動産の譲渡から生ずる収益に対しては、当該不動産が存在する締約国において租税を課することができる。 ２　一方の締約国の企業が他方の締約国内に有する恒久的施設において使用する事業用資産の一部をなす動産又は一方の締約国の居住者が自由職業を行うため他方の締約国において使用することができる固定的施設に係る動産の譲渡から生じる収益（単独……収益を含む。）に対しては、当該他方の締約国において租税を課することができる。ただし、……。 ３　１及び２にいう財産又は資産以外の財産又は資産の譲渡から生ずる収益に対しては、当該収益が生じた締約国において租税を課することができる。

（租税条約の読み方）

下線部分が著作権等の譲渡を国内法で課税するとする規定です。これによりますと著作権等の譲渡から生じる所得は、譲渡が発生した国で課税することになります。

［事例６］ 人的役務提供の対価を使用料等として規定している条約の事例（日・インド租税条約）

所法第161条第１項第11号	日・インド租税条約第12条
国内において業務を行う者から受ける次に掲げる使用料又は対価で当該業務に係るもの イ　工業所有権その他の技術に関する権利、特別の技術による生産方式若しくはこれらに準ずるものの使用料又はその譲渡による対価 ロ　著作権（出版権及び著作隣接権その他これに準ずるものを含む。）の使用料又はその譲渡による対価 ハ　機械、装置その他政令で定める用具の使用料	1　一方の締約国内において生じ、他方の締約国の居住者に支払われる使用料及び技術上の役務に対する料金に対しては、当該他方の締約国において租税を課すことができる。 2　１の使用料及び技術上の役務に対する料金に対しては、これらが生じた締約国においても、当該締約国の法令に従って租税を課すことができる。その租税の額は、当該使用料又は技術上の役務に対する料金の受領者が当該使用料又は技術上の役務に対する料金の受益者である場合には、当該使用料又は技術上の役務に対する料金の10%を超えないものとする。 3　この条において、「使用料」とは、文学上、・・・・・・・・・【中略】・・・・・・・・・の経験に関する情報の対価として受領するすべての種類の支払金をいう。 4　この条において、「技術上の役務に対する料金」とは、技術者その他の人員によって提供される役務を含む経営的若しくは技術的性質の役務又はコンサルタントの役務の対価としてのすべての支払金（支払者のその雇用する者に対する支払金及び第14条に定める独立の人的役務の対価としての個人に対する支払金を除く。）をいう。

（租税条約の読み方）

下線部分が人的役務提供の対価を使用料とする規定です。これによりますと専門的な役務の提供の対価が著作権等の使用料として取り扱われます。

3　非居住者と外国法人に対する課税実務

(1)　不動産賃借料に対する課税（所法161①７）

ガイダンス

非居住者と外国法人の国内源泉所得の中で、最近、多く登場する不動産賃借料に対する課税を取り上げます。

これは、最近の急激な円安を背景として、外国人が資産運用を目的として都市部のマンションを買い占めるケースがある訳ですが、仮に、企業がその外国人からマンションを借り上げ、賃料を支払う場合には、その外国人は非居住者に該当しますので、賃借料は、所得税法第161条第１項第７号国内源泉所得（不動産の貸付けの対価）に該当し、支払の際には、源泉徴収する必要があります。

「不動産賃借料に対する課税」では、海外に赴任した社員から借り上げた住宅の賃借料の課税に関する演習事例を通じて課税の仕組みを理解していただきます。

演習事例６

非居住者に対する不動産賃貸料の支払

当社は、社員Ａを３年の予定で米国へ派遣しました。

社員Ａは住宅を購入したばかりでしたので、まだ、住宅ローンが多額に残っていますので、会社として、その住宅を借り上げることにしました。

社員Ａに住宅の賃借料を支払う際の日本での課税関係はどうなるのでしょうか。

社員Ａに住宅の賃借料を支払う際には、20.42％の税率により源泉徴収する必要があります。

解説

社員Ａは、３年の予定で海外へ行きますので、出国日の翌日から非居住者となります。

非居住者が国内で土地を貸付け、賃貸料を収受している場合は、その賃貸料は所法161七（国内にある不動産の貸付けの対価）の国内源泉所得に該当しますので、住宅の賃貸料を支払う際に20.42％の税率により源泉徴収する必要があります。

また、日米租税条約第６条によりますと、不動産の直接使用、賃貸その他の形式のすべての形式から生じる所得は「他方の締約国（日本）において租税を課すことができる」と規定しておりますので、不動産が存在する日本での課税となります。

（注）　非居住者が有する家屋の賃貸の対価で、その家屋を自己又はその親族の居住の用に供するために借り受けた個人からの支払われるものについては源泉徴収を要しないこととされています。（所令328二）

○　**確定申告**

非居住者は、その賃貸料について総合課税により確定申告する必要があります。

確定申告する際には、事前に納税管理人を定める必要があります。

（根拠法令等：所法161①七、所法212①、日米租税条約６）

⑵ 使用料に対する課税（所法161①11）

ガイダンス

世界の企業が研究開発にしのぎを削る人工知能（Artificial Inteligence）や、Iot（Internet of things）は、いづれも、プログラムの集合体であるソフトウエアを用いて生み出されるものになります。

ソフトウエアを海外から導入しその対価を支払う場合には、その対価は所法税第161条第１項第十一号の国内源泉所得（著作権の使用料）に該当し、支払の際には、源泉徴収する必要があります。

また、海外の映像又は出版に関する版権を使用し、使用料を支払う場合には、これも著作権等の使用の対価として支払の際に源泉徴収する必要があります。

さらには、海外で器具・備品等を借用し、その使用料を支払う場合には、器具・備品の使用の対価として支払の際に源泉徴収する必要があります。

このように、企業が非居住者や外国法人に日本国内で課税しなければならないものが身近に存在します。

支払いの際に、源泉徴収を失念した場合には、海外から回収することになるわけですが、国内法あるいは租税条約の適用などの理解なしには、問題を解決することはできません。

「使用料に対する課税」では、国内源泉所得である使用料の意義と課税の仕組みについて、租税条約の適用と共に、演習事例を通じて理解します。

演習事例７

海外の企業にソフトウエアの開発費用を支払う場合の税金

当社は海外の企業にソフトウエアの開発を委託し、開発費用を支払うのですが、その開発費用を支払う際には税金が課税されるとのことですが、どのようなことなのでしょうか。

詳しく教えてください。

回答

海外の企業に支払うソフトウエアの開発費用は、著作権の使用料又は譲渡の対価になりますので、日本から支払う際には、支払金額の20.42%を税金として控除し、税務署に納税しなければなりません。

解説

1　ソフトウエアは著作権法上の著作物である

ソフトウエアはプログラムであることから、著作権法上、著作物として取り扱われています。

著作権法第２条第１項第１号（定義）
著作物とは思想又は感情を創作的に表現したものであって、文芸、学術、美術又は音楽の範囲に属するものをいう。

著作権法第２条第１項第10号（定義）
プログラムとは電子計算機を機能させて一の結果を得ることができるようにこれに対する指令を組み合わせたものとして表現したものをいう。

著作権法第10条第１項第９号（著作物の例示）
小説、脚本、論文、講演、音楽の著作物、舞踏、絵画、建築の著作物、 ・・・・・・・・・・・・・・・**プログラムの著作物**他

2　開発費用が著作権等の使用料又は譲渡の対価に該当するか否かの判断のポイント

開発費用が著作権等の使用料又は譲渡の対価に該当するか否かの判断に際しては、海外の企業との間の開発の委託に関する契約書を検討することになります。

⑴　その契約書において著作権等の知的財産権等の発生、使用及び譲渡等の規定がある場合

⇩

知的財産等の発生、使用及び譲渡等の規定がある場合には、開発費用は所得税法第161条第１項第11号ロに規定する著作権の使用料又は譲渡の対価に該当します。

したがって、著作権の使用料又は譲渡の対価に該当する場合には、支払の際に20.42%の税率により源泉徴収する必要があります。

(2)　Ｓ社がＡ社に著作権の使用を許諾する開発契約書の事例

[ソフトウエアの使用許諾を規定する条項]

○契約当事者　ソフトウエア開発委託者……Ａ社（日本）
　　　　　　　ソフトウエア開発受託者……Ｓ社（Ｘ国）

①　第○条・Ｓ社からＡ社へのライセンス付与、制限及び所有権

「作業範囲で指定した特定のプロジェクトに限りＳ社の納品物を使用かつ複製し、また、作業範囲で指定した特定のプロジェクトに限り第三者に提供するための全世界的、非独占的、譲渡不可、永久的なライセンスを付与する。」

②　第○条・知的財産権の所有権

「契約の両当事者は、本開発委託契約の遂行から生じる新規の発見若しくは発明、並びにそれらについての知的財産権すべては別段の合意がない限り、Ｓ社が所有することにつき合意する。…」

3　課税の方法（源泉徴収による課税）

ソフトウエアは著作物として取り扱われますので、その開発費用を支払う際には、海外の企業が日本国内で得た所得の税金として源泉所得税を徴収（支払金額から支払金額の20.42%を控除）し、税務署に納税しなければなりません。

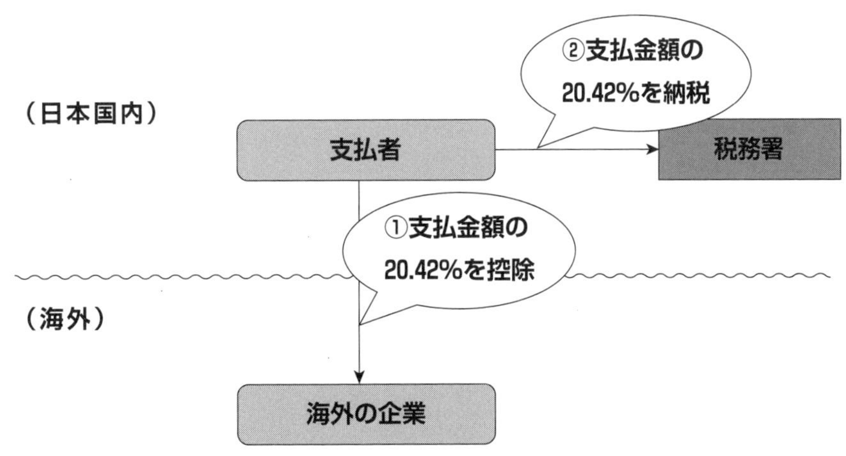

（参考）

所得税法第161条第１項第11号

国内において業務を行う者から受ける次に掲げる使用料又は対価で当該業務に係るもの

イ　工業所有権その他の技術に関する権利、特別の技術による生産方式若しくはこれらに準ずるものの使用料又はその譲渡による対価

ロ　著作権（出版権及び著作隣接権その他これに準ずるものを含む。）の使用料又はその譲渡による対価

ハ　機械、装置その他政令で定める用具の使用

所得税法基本通達161－35

………所得税法第161条第１項第11号ロの著作権の使用料とは、著作物（著作権法第２条第１項第１号（定義）に規定する著作物をいう。以下この項において同じ。）の複製、上演、演奏、放送、展示、上映、翻訳、編曲、脚色、映画化その他の著作物の利用又は出版権の設定につき支払を受ける対価の一切をいうのであるから、これらの使用料には、契約を締結するに当たって支払を受ける頭金、権利金等のほか………

演習事例 8

設計図の対価に対する源泉所得税

旧ソビエト連邦のベラルーシ共和国の法人に工業用精密機械の設計図の作成を依頼しました。その製作対価の支払の際に、留意すべき事項についてご教示をお願いいたします。

特に、何をどのように検討すればよろしいのか検討の際のポイントも合わせてご教示をお願いいたします。

ベラルーシの法人に対する設計図作成の対価が工業所有権等の使用料に該当する場合には、その対価支払の際に20.42%の税率により源泉所得税を徴収し納税しなければなりません。

ただし、日本とベラルーシとの間の租税条約により、ベラルーシの法人が貴社経由で貴社を所轄する税務署長に対しその対価支払の前日までに「租税条約に関する届出書」を提出した場合には、税率は10%に軽減されます。

また、その設計図作成の対価が工業所有権等の譲渡（設計図の所有権が発注者に移転する場合）に該当する場合には、日本とベラルーシとの間の租税条約により、所得の源泉地はベラルーシにあることから、日本では課税できません。

解説

1　国内源泉所得に対する源泉徴収

外国法人に対し、国内源泉所得の支払をする者は、その国内源泉所得の支払の際に源泉徴収する必要があります。（所法212①）

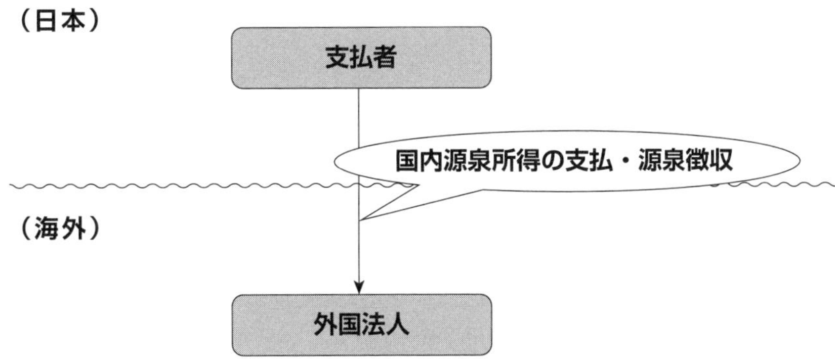

2 国内源泉所得とは

源泉徴収の対象となる国内源泉所得とは次に掲げる所得をいいます。

	国内源泉所得
支払を受ける者・非居住者及び外国法人	(1) 国内において行う組合事業から生じる利益の分配 (2) 国内にある土地等の譲渡による対価 (3) 国内において人的役務の提供事業を行う者が受けるその役務提供の対価 (4) 国内にある不動産、船舶、航空機などの貸付けの対価及び地上権などの設定の対価 (5) 国内にある営業所等に預けられた預貯金の利子等 (6) 内国法人から受ける剰余金の配当、利益の配当、剰余金の分配又は基金利息等 (7) 国内において業務を行う者に対するその国内業務に係る貸付金の利子 (8) 国内において業務を行う者から受けるその国内業務に係る工業所有権、著作権等の使用料又は譲渡の対価 (9) ①給与その他人的役務の提供に対する報酬のうち、国内において行う勤務に基因するもの、②公的年金等、③退職手当等のうち受給者が居住者であった期間に行った勤務等に基因するもの・・・**非居住者のみ対象** (10) 国内において行う事業の広告宣伝のための賞金 (11) 国内にある営業所等を通じて保険業法に規定する生命保険会社、損害保険会社等と締結した保険契約等に基づく年金 (12) 国内の営業所等が受け入れた定期積金の給付補填金等 (13) 国内において事業を行う者に対する出資につき、匿名組合契約等に基づいて受ける利益の分配

（所法161①四～十六）

3 設計図作成の対価が国内源泉所得（工業所有権等の使用料又は譲渡の対価）に該当するか否かのポイント

国内源泉所得に該当するか否かの判断に際しては、外国法人との間の設計図作成に関する契約を検討することになります。

(1) その契約書において特許権、工業所有権等の知的財産権等の発生、使用及び譲渡等の規定がある場合

知的財産等の発生、使用及び譲渡等の規定がある場合には、設計図作成の対価は所得税法第161条第１項第11号イに規定する使用料の対価又は譲渡の対価に該当する可能性があります。

したがって、使用料の対価又は譲渡の対価に該当する場合には、支払の際に20.42%の税率により源泉徴収する必要があります。

所得税法第161条第１項第11号

国内において業務を行う者から受ける次に掲げる使用料又は対価で当該業務に係るもの
イ　工業所有権その他の技術に関する権利、特別の技術による生産方式若しくはこれらに準ずるものの使用料又はその譲渡による対価

(2)　その契約書において設計図作成の対価が、物（設計図）の代金又は人的役務の対価とされている場合

その物又は人的役務の対価が次の①又は②のいずれかに該当する場合には、所得税法第161条第１項第11号イに規定する使用料に該当することになります。

使用料に該当する場合には、支払の際に20.42％の税率により源泉徴収する必要があります。

①　その設計図作成の対価の額が、設計図の使用回数、期間、生産高又はその使用による利益の額に応じて算定されている場合
②　その設計図作成の対価が、設計図作成又は人的役務提供のために要した経費の額に通常の利潤の額を加算した金額に相当する金額を超えるもの
（所基通161－36）

4　ベラルーシ共和国との間の租税条約の取扱い

ベラルーシ共和国は、旧ソ連邦であり、旧ソ連との間の租税条約を引き継ぐことから旧ソ連邦との間の租税条約（以下「租税条約」といいます。）により取扱いを検討することになります。

（参考）　平成９年外務省告示第６号より
ベラルーシ共和国が独立を達成する前に日本国とソヴィエト社会主義共和国連邦との間で締結され、効力を有していた条約その他の国際約束は、日本国がベラルーシ共和国の独立を承認した日から日本国とベラルーシ共和国との間で適用される。

日・ソ連租税条約（抜粋）

第９条
2(a)　文学上、美術上又は学術上の著作物（映画フィルム及びラジオ放送用又はテレビジョン放送用のフィルム又はテープを含む。）の著作権の使用又は使用の権利の対価として受領する使用料については、当該使用料の受益者が他方の締約国の居住者である場合には、当該使用料が生じた一方の締約国において租税を免除する。

日・ソ連租税条約（抜粋）

第９条
２(b) 特許権、商標権、意匠、模型、図面、秘密方式若しくは秘密工程の使用若しくは使用の権利の対価として、産業上、商業上若しくは学術上の設備の使用若しくは使用の権利の対価として、又は産業上、商業上若しくは学術上の経験に関する情報の対価として受領する使用料に対しては、当該使用料が生じた一方の締約国においても、当該一方の締約国の法令に従って租税を課すことができる。その租税の額は、当該使用料の受益者が他方の締約国の居住者である場合には、当該使用料の額の10パーセントを超えないものとする。

日・ソ連租税条約（抜粋）

第９条
４ 使用料は、その支払者が一方の締約国又は当該一方の地方公共団体若しくは居住者である場合には、当該一方の締約国内において生じたものとされる。**（債務者主義）**

５ 課税上の取扱い

設計図作成の対価について工業所有権等の使用料に該当する場合又は工業所有権等の譲渡に該当する場合（設計図の所有権が発注者に移転する場合）について、国内法（所法161①十一）及び租税条約に基づき課税上の取扱いを検討することになります。

・・・・・・・使用料に該当する場合・・・・・・・

設計図作成の対価が所法161⑪イの使用料に該当する場合には租税条約第９条（使用料）２(b)に該当し、工業的使用料として課税となります。さらに、租税条約第９条４の**「債務者主義」**の規定により、設計図の使用場所にかかわらず、設計図の対価の支払者の所在地に所得の源泉地があることになりますので、日本が所得源泉地となり、支払の際に源泉徴収することになります。

ベラルーシ共和国の法人が日本の支払者経由で所轄税務署長に「租税条約に関する届出書」を提出することにより、税率は10％となります。

・・・・・・・譲渡に該当する場合・・・・・・・

設計図作成の対価が所法161⑪イの譲渡に該当する場合には、租税条約第11条（譲渡収益）５に該当し、ベラルーシ共和国に所得の源泉地があることになりますので、日本では課税されません。

日・ソ連租税条約（抜粋）

第11条
５ 一方の締約国の居住者が１から４までに規定する財産以外の財産の譲渡によって取得する収益に対しては、当該一方の締約国においてのみ租税を課すことができる。

演習事例９

英国Ｓ社との間の開発委託契約に関する課税関係

当社は英国法人Ｓ社との間でソフトウエア開発委託契約を締結し、Ｓ社にソフトウエアの開発を委託しました。

その契約書においては、次の事項が記載してあります。

開発費の対価を支払う際に、課税関係について留意すべき事項をご教示願います。

［ソフトウエア開発委託契約（契約条項の一部）

① 第８条　ライセンス付与、制限及び所有権

「作業範囲で指定した特定のプロジェクトに限りＳ社の納品物を使用かつ複製し、また、作業範囲で指定した特定のプロジェクトに限り第三者に提供するための全世界的、非独占的、譲渡不可、永久的なライセンスを付与する。」

② 第９条　知的財産権の所有権

「契約の両当事者は、本開発委託契約の遂行から生じる新規の発見もしくは発明、ならびにそれらについての知的財産権すべては、別段の合意がない限り、Ｓ社が所有することにつき合意する。……」

回答

英国法人Ｓ社に対するソフトウエア開発委託契約の対価が国内源泉所得（著作権等の使用料又は譲渡の対価）に該当する場合には、その対価支払の際に20.42%の税率により源泉所得税を徴収し納税しなければなりません。

ただし、Ｓ社が貴社経由で貴社を所轄する税務署長に対しその対価支払の前日までに「租税条約に関する届出書」を提出した場合には、源泉所得税は免税となります。

解説

1　国内法（所法161）の取扱い

ソフトウエアは、我が国の著作権法上の著作物に該当しますので、その開発の対価が著作権の使用料又は譲渡の対価に該当すれば、**国内源泉所得**（著作権の使用料又はその譲渡による対価）に該当し、支払の際に20.42%の税率により源泉徴収しなければなりません。　（所法161①十一）

2　租税条約の取扱い

英国との間の租税条約第12条第１項によりますと「一方の締約国内（日本）において生じ、他方の締約国（英国）の居住者が受益者である使用料に対しては、当該他方の締

約国内（英国）においてのみ租税を課することができる。」と規定しています。

したがって、上記1の国内法では、日本で著作権の使用料として課税となりますが、日英租税条約によりますと、英国内でのみ課税することができますので、日本では源泉所得税は免税となります。　（日英租税条12①）

3　英国S社の場合

英国S社とのソフトウエア開発委託契約（以下「本契約」といいます。）第8条によりますと、本契約に基づき開発されたソフトウエアの知的財産権（著作権を含む）は、開発受託者である英国S社に帰属し、貴社はその知的財産権（著作権を含む）を使用する権利を認められていると解されますので、英国S社に支払う開発委託費は所法161⑪の国内源泉所得（著作権の使用料）に該当し、開発委託費支払いの際に、20.42%の税率により源泉徴収しなければなりません。

しかし、日英租税条約によりますと、使用料については、英国内でのみ課税することができますので、日本では免税となります。

4　日英租税条約の免税を受けるための手続き

日英租税条約による免税の適用を受けるためには、英国法人S社は貴社経由で、**支払日の前日まで**に、貴社の所轄税務署長に**「租税条約に関する届出書」（様式3）**を提出しなければなりません。

また、日英租税条約の適用を受けるためには、加えて**「特典条項に関する付表（様式17ー英）」**を提出し、これに**英国政府（IRA）が納税者に発行する「居住者証明書」**を添付しなければなりません。

[租税条約に関する届出書（使用料等）]

様式 3
FORM

租税条約に関する届出書
APPLICATION FORM FOR INCOME TAX CONVENTION

（使用料に対する所得税及び復興特別所得税の軽減・免除
Relief from Japanese Income Tax and Special
Income Tax for Reconstruction on Royalties）

この届出書の記載に当たっては、別紙の注意事項を参照してください。
See separate instructions.

税務署受付印

（税務署整理欄
For official use only）

適用；有、無

番号確認　身元確認

□ 限度税率____%
Applicable Tax Rate
□ 免　税（注11）
Exemption (Note 11)

____税務署長殿
To the District Director, ________Tax Office

1　適用を受ける租税条約に関する事項；
Applicable Income Tax Convention
日本国と________との間の租税条約第___条第___項___
The Income Tax Convention between Japan and________, Article____, para.____

2　使用料の支払を受ける者に関する事項；
Details of Recipient of Royalties

氏名又は名称 Full name		
個人番号又は法人番号（有する場合のみ記入） Individual Number or Corporate Number (Limited to case of a holder)		
個人の場合 Individual	住所又は居所 Domicile or residence	（電話番号 Telephone Number）
	国籍 Nationality	
法人その他の団体の場合 Corporation or other entity	本店又は主たる事務所の所在地 Place of head office or main office	（電話番号 Telephone Number）
	設立又は組織された場所 Place where the Corporation was established or organized	
	事業が管理・支配されている場所 Place where the business is managed and controlled	（電話番号 Telephone Number）
下記「4」の使用料につき居住者として課税される国及び納税地（注8） Country where the recipient is taxable as resident on Royalties mentioned in 4 below and the place where he is to pay tax (Note 8)		（納税者番号 Taxpayer Identification Number）
日本国内の恒久的施設の状況 Permanent establishment in Japan □有(Yes) , □無(No) If "Yes", explain:	名称 Name	
	所在地 Address	（電話番号 Telephone Number）
	事業の内容 Details of Business	

3　使用料の支払者に関する事項；
Details of Payer of Royalties

氏名又は名称 Full name		
住所（居所）又は本店（主たる事務所）の所在地 Domicile (residence) or Place of head office (main office)		（電話番号 Telephone Number）
個人番号又は法人番号（有する場合のみ記入） Individual Number or Corporate Number (Limited to case of a holder)		
日本国内にある事務所等 Office, etc. located in Japan	名称 Name	（事業の内容 Details of Business）
	所在地 Address	（電話番号 Telephone Number）

4　上記「3」の支払者から支払を受ける使用料で「1」の租税条約の規定の適用を受けるものに関する事項（注9）；
Details of Royalties received from the Payer to which the Convention mentioned in 1 above is applicable (Note 9)

使用料の内容 Description of Royalties	契約の締結年月日 Date of Contract	契約期間 Period of Contract	使用料の計算方法 Method of Computation for Royalties	使用料の支払期日 Due Date for Payment	使用料の金額 Amount of Royalties

5　その他参考となるべき事項（注10）；
Others (Note 10)

【裏面に続きます（Continue on the reverse）】

6　日本の税法上、届出書の「2」の外国法人が納税義務者とされるが、租税条約の規定によりその株主等である者（相手国居住者に限ります。）の所得として取り扱われる部分に対して租税条約の適用を受けることとされている場合の租税条約の適用を受ける割合に関する事項等（注4）；
Details of proportion of income to which the convention mentioned in 1 above is applicable, if the foreign company mentioned in 2 above is taxable as a company under Japanese tax law, and the convention is applicable to income that is treated as income of the member (limited to a resident of the other contracting country) of the foreign company in accordance with the provisions of the convention (Note 4)

届出書の「2」の外国法人の株主等で租税条約の適用を受ける者の氏名又は名称 Name of member of the foreign company mentioned in 2 above, to whom the Convention is applicable	間接保有 Indirect Ownership	持分の割合 Ratio of Ownership	受益の割合＝ 租税条約の適用を受ける割合 Proportion of benefit = Proportion for Application of Convention
	□	%	%
	□	%	%
	□	%	%
	□	%	%
	□	%	%
合計 Total		%	%

届出書の「2」の欄に記載した外国法人が支払を受ける「4」の使用料について、「1」の租税条約の相手国の法令に基づきその株主等である者の所得として取り扱われる場合には、その根拠法令及びその効力を生じる日を記載してください。
If royalties mentioned in 4 above that a foreign company mentioned in 2 above receives are treated as income of those who are its members under the law in the other contracting country of the convention mentioned in 1 above, enter the law that provides the legal basis to the above treatment and the date on which it will become effective.

根拠法令
Applicable law＿＿＿＿＿＿＿＿　効力を生じる日　年　月　日
Effective date＿＿＿＿＿＿＿＿

7　日本の税法上、届出書の「2」の団体の構成員が納税義務者とされるが、租税条約の規定によりその団体の所得として取り扱われるものに対して租税条約の適用を受けることとされている場合の記載事項等（注5）；
Details if, while the partner of the entity mentioned in 2 above is taxable under Japanese tax law, and the convention is applicable to income that is treated as income of the entity in accordance with the provisions of the convention (Note 5)

他の全ての構成員から通知を受けこの届出書を提出する構成員の氏名又は名称＿＿＿＿＿＿＿＿
Full name of the partner of the entity who has been notified by all other partners and is to submit this form

届出書の「2」に記載した団体が支払を受ける「4」の使用料について、「1」の租税条約の相手国の法令に基づきその団体の所得として取り扱われる場合には、その根拠法令及びその効力を生じる日を記載してください。
If royalties mentioned in 4 above that an entity at mentioned in 2 above receives are treated as income of the entity under the law in the other contracting country of the convention mentioned in 1 above, enter the law that provides the legal basis to the above treatment and the date on which it will become effective.

根拠法令
Applicable law＿＿＿＿＿＿＿＿　効力を生じる日　年　月　日
Effective date＿＿＿＿＿＿＿＿

○　代理人に関する事項　；　この届出書を代理人によって提出する場合には、次の欄に記載してください。
Details of the Agent　;　If this form is prepared and submitted by the Agent, fill out the following columns.

代理人の資格 Capacity of Agent in Japan	氏名（名称） Full name		納税管理人の届出をした税務署名 Name of the Tax Office where the Tax Agent is registered
□ 納税管理人 ※ Tax Agent □ その他の代理人 Other Agent	住所（居所・所在地） Domicile (Residence or location)	（電話番号 Telephone Number）	税務署 Tax Office

※　「納税管理人」とは、日本国の国税に関する申告、申請、請求、届出、納付等の事項を処理させるため、国税通則法の規定により選任し、かつ、日本国における納税地の所轄税務署長に届出をした代理人をいいます。

※ "Tax Agent" means a person who is appointed by the taxpayer and is registered at the District Director of Tax Office for the place where the taxpayer is to pay his tax, in order to have such agent take necessary procedures concerning the Japanese national taxes, such as filing a return, applications, claims, payment of taxes, etc., under the provisions of Act on General Rules for National Taxes.

○　適用を受ける租税条約が特典条項を有する租税条約である場合；
If the applicable convention has article of limitation on benefits

特典条項に関する付表の添付　□有Yes
"Attachment Form for Limitation on Benefits Article" attached　□添付省略Attachment not required
（特典条項に関する付表を添付して提出した租税条約に関する届出書の提出日　年　月　日）
Date of previous submission of the application for income tax convention with the "Attachment Form for Limitation on Benefits Article"

様　式　17-英
FORM 17-UK

特典条項に関する付表(英)

ATTACHMENT FORM FOR LIMITATION ON BENEFITS ARTICLE (UK)

記載に当たっては、別紙の注意事項を参照してください。
See separate instructions.

1　適用を受ける租税条約の特典条項に関する事項；
Limitation on Benefits Article of applicable Income Tax Convention
日本国とグレートブリテン及び北アイルランド連合王国との間の租税条約第 22 条
The Income Tax Convention between Japan and The United Kingdom of Great Britain and Northern Ireland, Article 22

2　この付表に記載される者の氏名又は名称；
Full name of Resident

	居住地国の権限ある当局が発行した居住者証明書を添付してください(注5)。 Please Attach Residency Certification issued by Competent Authority of Country of residence. (Note5)

3　租税条約の特典条項の要件に関する事項；
AからCの順番に各項目の「□該当」又は「□非該当」の該当する項目に✓印を付してください。いずれかの項目に「該当」する場合には、それ以降の項目に記入する必要はありません。なお、該当する項目については、各項目ごとの要件に関する事項を記入の上、必要な書類を添付してください。(注6)
In order of sections A, B and C, check the applicable box in each line as "Yes" or "No". If you check any box as "Yes" in sections A to C, you need not fill in the lines that follow. Only the applicable lines need to be filled in and any necessary documents must be attached. (Note6)

A

(1)　個人 Individual　□該当 Yes，□非該当 No

(2)　適格政府機関(注7)　Qualified Governmental Entity (Note7)　□該当 Yes，□非該当 No

(3)　公開会社又は公開信託財産(注8)　Publicly Traded Company, Publicly Traded Trust (Note8)　□該当 Yes，□非該当 No

主たる種類の株式又は持分証券の別 Principal class of Shares/Units	公認の有価証券市場の名称 Recognised Stock Exchange	シンボル又は証券コード Ticker Symbol or Security Code
□株式 Shares　□持分証券 Units		

(4)　年金基金又は年金計画(注9)　Pension Fund, Pension Scheme (Note9)　□該当 Yes，□非該当 No
直前の課税年度又は賦課年度の終了の日においてその受益者、構成員又は参加者の 50%超が日本又はグレートブリテン及び北アイルランド連合王国(以下「英国」といいます。)の居住者である個人であるものに限ります。受益者等の 50%超がいずれかの締約国の居住者である事情を記入してください。
The "Pension Fund" or "Pension Scheme" is limited to those where more than 50% of beneficiaries, members or participants were individual residents of Japan or the United Kingdom as of the end of the prior taxable year or chargeable period. Please provide details below showing that more than 50% of beneficiaries et al. are individual residents of either Japan or the United Kingdom.

設立等の根拠法令 Law for Establishment　　非課税の根拠法令 Law for Tax Exemption

(5)　公益団体(注 10)　Public Service Organisation (Note10)　□該当 Yes，□非該当 No
設立等の根拠法令 Law for Establishment　設立の目的 Purpose of Establishment　非課税の根拠法令 Law for Tax Exemption

Aのいずれにも該当しない場合は、Bに進んでください。If none of the lines in A are applicable, please proceed to B.

B

(1)　個人以外の者又は信託財産若しくは信託財産の受託者
Person other than an Individual, Trust or Trustee of a Trust　□該当 Yes，□非該当 No
「個人以外の者」の場合、Aの(1)から(5)までの者である日本又は英国の居住者が、議決権の 50%以上に相当する株式その他の受益持分を直接又は間接に所有するものに限ります。また、「信託財産若しくは信託財産の受託者」の場合、日本若しくは英国の居住者であるAの(1)から(5)までの者又はB(2)(a)の「同等受益者」が、その信託財産の受益持分の 50%以上を直接又は間接に所有するものに限ります。(注 11)
The "Person other than an Individual" is limited to the person, where residents of Japan or the United Kingdom who fall under (1),(2),(3),(4) or (5) of A own, either directly or indirectly, shares or other beneficial interests representing at least 50% of the voting power of the person. The "Trust or Trustee of a Trust" is limited to the person, where residents of Japan or the United Kingdom who fall under (1),(2),(3),(4) or (5) of A or "equivalent beneficiaries" of B(2)(a) own, either directly or indirectly, at least 50% of the beneficial interest.(Note11)
年　月　日現在の株主等の状況 State of Shareholders, etc. as of (date)　/　/

株主等の氏名又は名称 Name of Shareholder(s)	居住地国における納税地 Place where Shareholder(s) is taxable in Country of residence	Aの番号又は同等受益者 Number in A, or equivalent beneficiaries	間接保有 Indirect Ownership	株主等の持分 Number of Shares owned
			□	
			□	
			□	
合　計 Total (持分割合 Ratio (%) of Shares owned)				(　%)

B

⑵ 英国の居住者である法人 □該当 Yes，□非該当 No
Company that is a resident of the United Kingdom
次の⒜又は⒝の要件を満たす７以下の者（「同等受益者」といいます。）が、その法人の議決権の 75%以上に相当する株式を直接又は間接に保有する場合に限ります。「同等受益者」に関する事情を記入してください。（注 12）
⒜ 日本との間に租税条約を有している国の居住者であって、次の(aa)から(cc)までの要件を満たすもの
(aa) その租税条約が実効的な情報交換に関する規定を有すること
(bb) その租税条約において、その居住者が特典条項における適格者に該当すること（その租税条約が特典条項を有しない場合には、その条約に日本国と英国との間の租税条約（以下「日英租税条約」といいます。）の特典条項が含まれているとしたならばその居住者が適格者に該当するであろうとみられること）
(cc) 日英租税条約第 10 条３、第 11 条１、第 12 条、第 13 条又は第 21 条に定める所得、利得又は収益に関し、その居住者が日英租税条約の特典が要求されるこれらの規定に定める種類の所得、利得又は収益についてその租税条約の適用を受けたとしたならば、日英租税条約に規定する税率以下の税率の適用を受けるであろうとみられること
⒝ Aの⑴から⑸までの者
The company is limited to those where shares representing at least 75% of the voting power of the company are owned, either directly or indirectly, by seven or fewer persons who meet requirement ⒜ or ⒝ (“equivalent beneficiaries”). Please provide details below regarding equivalent beneficiaries. (Note12)
⒜ The resident of a country that has a convention for avoidance of double taxation between that country and Japan, and meets the following requirements from (aa) through to (cc)
(aa) that convention contains provisions for effective exchange of information
(bb) that resident is a qualified person under the limitation on benefits provisions in that convention (where there are no such provisions in that convention, would be a qualified person when that convention is read as including provisions corresponding to the limitation on the benefits provisions of the Japan-UK Income Tax Convention)
(cc) with respect to an item of income, profit or gain referred to in paragraph 3 of Article 10 or paragraph 1 of Article 11; or in Article 12, 13 or 21 of the Japan-UK Income Tax Convention that resident would be entitled under that convention to a rate of tax with respect to the particular class of income, profit or gain for which the benefits are being claimed under the Japan-UK Income Tax Convention that is at least as low as the rate applicable under the Japan-UK Income Tax Convention
⒝ Person who falls under ⑴, ⑵, ⑶, ⑷, or ⑸ of A

株主の氏名又は名称 Name of Shareholders	居住地国における納税地 Place where Shareholder is taxable in Country of residence	⒜の場合 ⒜			⒝の場合 ⒝	株主等の持分 Number of Shares owned
		(aa)を満たすか Requirement (aa)	(bb)を満たすか Requirement (bb)	(cc)を満たすか Requirement (cc)	Aの番号 Number in A	
		□はい Yes，□いいえ No	□はい Yes，□いいえ No	□はい Yes，□いいえ No		
		□はい Yes，□いいえ No	□はい Yes，□いいえ No	□はい Yes，□いいえ No		
		□はい Yes，□いいえ No	□はい Yes，□いいえ No	□はい Yes，□いいえ No		
		□はい Yes，□いいえ No	□はい Yes，□いいえ No	□はい Yes，□いいえ No		
		□はい Yes，□いいえ No	□はい Yes，□いいえ No	□はい Yes，□いいえ No		
		□はい Yes，□いいえ No	□はい Yes，□いいえ No	□はい Yes，□いいえ No		
		□はい Yes，□いいえ No	□はい Yes，□いいえ No	□はい Yes，□いいえ No		
合計 Total（持分割合 Ratio(%) of Shares owned）						（ %）

Bに該当しない場合は、Cに進んでください。If B does not apply, proceed to C.

C

次の⒜から⒞の要件をすべて満たす者 □該当 Yes，□非該当 No
Resident satisfying all of the following Conditions from ⒜ through to ⒞
居住地国において行う事業の概要(注 13)；Description of business in the country of residence (Note13)

⒜ 居住地国において行う事業が、自己の勘定のために投資を行い又は管理するもの（銀行、保険会社又は証券会社が行う銀行業、保険業又は証券業を除きます。）ではないこと（注 14）： □はい Yes，□いいえ No
The business in the country of residence is other than that of making or managing investments for the resident's own account (unless the business is banking, insurance or a securities business carried on by a bank, insurance company or securities dealer) (Note14)
⒝ 所得等が居住地国において行う事業に関連又は付随して取得されるものであること（注 15）： □はい Yes，□いいえ No
An item of income, profit or gain is derived in connection with or is incidental to that business in the country of residence (Note15)
⒞ （日本国内において行う事業から所得等を取得する場合）居住地国において行う事業が日本国内において行う事業との関係で実質的なものであること（注 16）： □はい Yes，□いいえ No
(If you derive an item of income, profit or gain from a business in Japan) The business carried on in the country of residence is substantial in relation to the business carried on in Japan. (Note 16)

日本国内において行う事業の概要；Description of Business in Japan.

D 国税庁長官の認定（注 17）；
Determination by the NTA Commissioner (Note17)
国税庁長官の認定を受けている場合は、以下にその内容を記載してください。その認定の範囲内で租税条約の特典を受けることができます。なお、上記AからCまでのいずれかに該当する場合には、国税庁長官の認定は不要です。
If you have received authorization from the NTA Commissioner, please describe below the nature of the authorization. The convention benefits will be granted within the range of the authorization. If any of the above mentioned Lines A through to C is applicable, then authorization from the NTA Commissioner is not necessary.

・認定を受けた日 Date of authorization ＿＿年＿＿月＿＿日
・認定を受けた所得の種類
Type of income for which the authorization was received＿＿＿＿＿＿＿＿＿＿

演習事例10

導管取引について

当社は、米国のA社との間で特許権の使用許諾契約（以下、「許諾契約」といいます。）締結する手続きをすすめております。

その手続きの中で、A社はX国のS社から使用許諾を受けた特許権を当社にサブライセンスすることが判明いたしました。

日本とX国との間には租税条約の締結はありません。また、S社は日本及び米国の居住者ではありません。

当社は、許諾契約の相手先が米国の法人ですので、日米租税条約（以下「条約」といいます。）に基づく免税の手続きを行う予定ですが、A社と許諾契約を締結した場合に条約による免税を受けることができるのでしょうか。

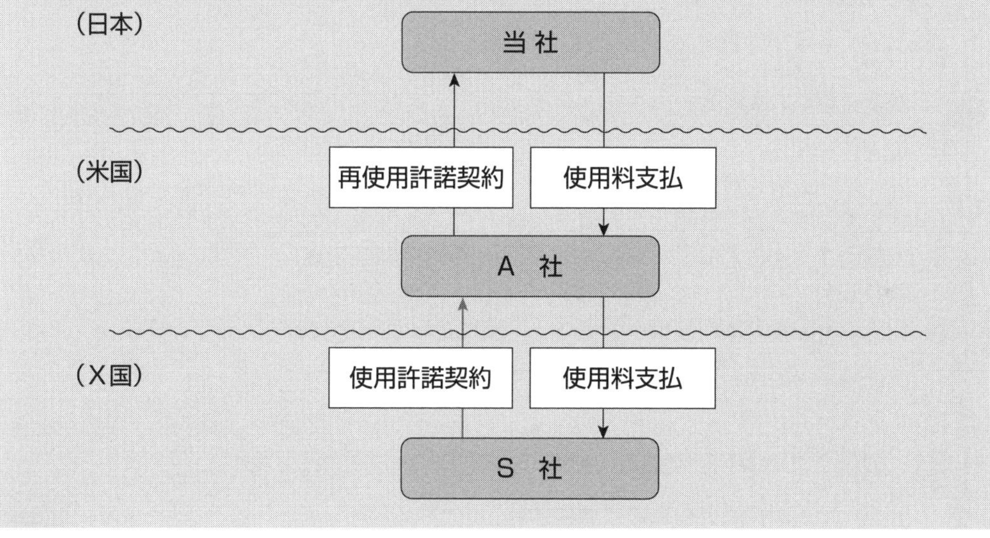

貴社は、米国のA社と許諾契約を締結しますが、X国のS社からのサブライセンスということですので、いわゆる「導管取引」として条約の免税が受けられないと考えられます。

したがって、貴社は、A社に特許権の使用料を支払う際に20.42%の税率により源泉徴収しなければなりません。

1　国内法の取扱い

貴社が米国Ａ社から提供をうける特許権の使用の対価は、国内源泉所得に該当しますので、支払う際には、20.42%の税率により源泉徴収する必要があります。

（所法161①十一・212①）

2　日米条約の取扱い

条約によりますと日本国内で生じた特許権使用の対価は米国でのみ課税できることとされています。　（日米租税条約12①）

3　日米条約の適用対象者

条約は、真に、適用を受けるものに適用されることから、適用対象者及び対象取引には制限が行われております。

⑴　適用対象者

次に掲げる者が対象とされております。

A　適格者基準の要件を満たす者
①　個人・・・・・・・・・・・・・・・・・・・・（第22条１⒜） ②　国、地方政府（地方公共団体)、日本銀行、連邦準備銀行　（第22条１⒝） ③　特定の公開会社、公開会社の関連会社・・・（第22条１⒞（ⅰ）（ⅱ）） ④　公益団体・・・・・・・・・・・・・・・・・・（第22条１⒟） ⑤　年金基金・・・・・・・・・・・・・・・・・・（第22条１⒠） ⑥　個人以外の者で支配基準と課税ベース浸食基準の両方の要件を満たすもの
B　支配基準の要件を満たす者
個人以外の者でその者の株式等の50%以上が、上記①～⑤の個人、政府等、特定の公開会社、公益団体又は年金基金により直接又は間接に所有されていること。
C　課税ベース浸食基準の要件を満たす者
個人以外の者でその者の総所得のうちに第三国の者に直接又は間接に支払われるべきものの額の占める割合が50%未満であること。
D　能動的事業活動基準の要件を満たす者
⑴　能動的事業基準とは、次の三条件を満たす場合である。 ①　居住地国で、営業又は事業の活動（投資活動を除く。）に従事していること。 ②　その取得する所得が上記①の営業又は事業の活動に関連又は付随して取得されるものであること。 ③　その取得する所得に関し、個別の条項に別に定める特典を受けるための要件を満たしていること。 ⑵　さらに、他方の締約国内で支店又は子会社等を通じて営業又は事業活動を行う場合には追加の要件を満たす必要があり、居住地国で行う営業活動等が他方の締約国で行う営業活動等との関係において実質的なものでなければならない。（営業活動等が実質的で

あるか否かの判断は、すべての事実と状況により判断する。…例えば、居住地国の事業規模と支店等の事業規模の比較、あるいは営業活動全体に対する本店と支店等の貢献度の比較など。）

⑵　使用料の「導管取引」を規制する規定

その取引が「導管取引」であり、真に適用を受けようとする者が条約締結国の者ではなく条約が締結されていない国の者である場合には、日米租税条約第12条５の規定により租税条約は適用されません。

導管取引の要件

①　一方の締約国の居住者がある無体財産権の使用に関して他方の締約国の居住者から使用料の支払を受ける場合。

②　次に該当する者が、①と同一の無体財産権に関し一方の締約国の居住者から支払を受ける。

○　①の使用料に関し、一方の居住者に対し条約により認められる特典を受ける権利を有しない。

○　いずれの締約国の居住者でもないこと

4　貴社の場合

ライセンスの原所有者がＸ国のＳ社であり、貴社はサブライセンスを受けていますので、Ｘ国のＳ社は米国のＡ社を通じて租税条約の恩典を受けようとしているものと考えられます。

しかし、日本とＸ国との間には租税条約の締結はありません。また、Ｓ社は日本及び米国の居住者ではありませんので、Ｓ社は租税条約の恩典を受けるものには該当しません。

つまり、日米租税条約第12条５に規定する米国のＡ社が貴社から特許権の使用の対価を受ける場合において、Ｘ国のＳ社が米国のＡ社から特許権の使用料の支払を受けないとしたならば、米国のＳ社が貴社から特許権の使用の対価を受けることはなかったであろう場合に該当することになります。

したがって、貴社は、Ａ社に支払う際に20.42％の税率により源泉徴収しなければなりません。

日米租税条約第12条５（導管取引を規制する規定）

一方の締約国の居住者がある無体財産権の使用に関して他方の締約国の居住者から使用料の支払を受ける場合において、次の(a)及び(b)に該当する者が当該無体財産権と同一の無体財産権の使用に関して当該一方の締約国の居住者から使用料の支払いを受けないとしたならば、当該一方の締約国の居住者が当該無体財産権の使用に関して当該他方の締約国の居住者から使用料の支払を受けることはなかったであろうと認められるときは、当該一方の締約国の居住者は、当該使用料の受益者とはされない。

(a)　当該他方の締約国内において生ずる使用料に関し、当該一方の締約国の居住者に対してこの条約により認められる特典と同等の又はそのような特典よりも有利な特典を受ける権利を有しないこと。

(b)　いずれの締約国の居住者でもないこと。

演習事例11

機械、装置及び用具の使用料と債務者主義

当社は、自動車部品を輸出する会社ですが、昨年、輸出先であるシンガポールで販売代理店を対象とした営業会議を開催しました。

その際に、会議に必要なイス・テーブル・カウンター・DVDプレイヤー等の会議用機材を現地のレンタル会社Ｂ社から賃借しました。

賃借料は、後日、Ｂ社へ海外送金しました。

今回、税務調査があり、この支払については、源泉徴収が必要であるとの指摘を受けました。

昨年の会議はシンガポールで開催したものであり、また、賃借した会議用機材は、すべて同国で使用しておりましたので、日本から支払いする際に源泉徴収することは考えておりませんでした。課税関係について教えてください。

回答

日本とシンガポール共和国との間の租税条約では、会議用機材がどこで使用されたかにかかわらず、使用料の支払者の所在する日本で所得が発生し課税されることになります。

Ｂ社に対する会議用機材の賃借料支払の際に、源泉徴収する必要があります。

なお、支払日の前日までに、Ｂ社が貴社経由で、「租税条約に関する届出書」（様式３）を貴社を所轄する税務署長に提出することにより税率は、10%となります。

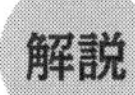

解説

1　外国法人に対する源泉徴収について

外国法人に対する源泉徴収の対象となる所得は、所得税法第161条第１項第４号から第11号まで及び第13号から第16号に規定しています。

国内源泉所得	税率
①　組合契約事業利益の配分　（所法161①四）	20.42%
②　土地等の譲渡の対価　（所法161①五）	10.21%
③　人的役務の提供事業の対価　（所法161①六）	20.42%
④　不動産の賃貸料等（所法161①七）	20.42%
⑤　利子等（所法161①八）	15.315%
⑥　配当等（所法161①九）	20.42%

⑦ 貸付金利子（所法161①十）	20.42%
⑧ 使用料等（所法161①十一）	20.42%
⑨ 給与その他の人的役務の提供に対する報酬（所法161①十二）	20.42%
⑩ 事業の広告宣伝のための賞金（所法161①十三）	20.42%
⑪ 生命保険契約に基づく年金等（所法161①十四）	20.42%
⑫ 定期積金の給付補填金等（所法161①十五）	15.315%
⑬ 匿名組合契約等に基づく利益の分配（所法161①十六）	20.42%

2　会議用機材の賃借料の所得区分

今回の会議に際し賃借した会議用機材の賃借料は上記の国内源泉所得の⑧の使用料等（機械、装置及び用具の使用料）に該当します。

3　租税条約で異なる定めがある場合の所得源泉地

所得税法第161条第１項第11号によりますと、機械、装置及び用具の使用料は「国内において業務を行う者から受ける使用料で、国内業務に係るもの」と規定されております。

つまり、会議用機材を日本国内で使用した場合にのみ国内源泉所得に該当することから使用した場所に所得源泉地があることになります。これを**「使用地主義」**といいます。

また、所得税法第162条によりますと、租税条約で国内法と異なる所得源泉地を規定している場合には租税条約が国内法に優先するとしています。

シンガポールとの間の租税条約によりますと、会議用機材の賃借料は第12条の「産業上、商業上若しくは学術上の設備の使用の対価」として使用料に該当します。

そして、貴社がＢ社へ支払う会議用機材の賃借料の所得源泉地については、その使用料を支払う債務者の居住地で所得が発生するという規定になっております。これを**「債務者主義」**といいます。

租税条約の規定が国内法（所法161①十一）に優先しますので、会議用機材が日本で使用されるかにかかわらず、**日本国内に所得の源泉がある**ことになります。

4　租税条約に基づく軽減税率について

所得税法第212条によりますと、今回の機材の使用料に適用される税率は20.42%ですが、シンガポールとの間の租税条約では、適用される税率は10%となります。

租税条約に基づく軽減税率の適用をうける場合は、Ｂ社が貴社経由で貴社の所轄税務署長に「租税条約に関する届出書」（様式３）を提出する必要があります。

（参考）　債務者主義について

所得の源泉地について債務者主義が適用されるかどうかは、支払先の相手国との間の租税条約を確認する必要があります。

租税条約の中での債務者主義の表現としては、「その支払者が一方の締約国の政府、当該一方の締約国の地方公共団体又は一方の締約国の居住者である場合には、当該一方の締約国内において生じたものとされる。」となっています。

（根拠法令等：所法161①十一、所法212①、日シンガポール租税条約12）

演習事例12

米国の有限責任会社と源泉所得税

当社は、国内で海外の小説を出版する会社ですが、このたび、米国の出版会社であるABCL.L.Cから世界的なベストセラー小説の版権の使用許諾を受け国内で出版する予定です。

使用許諾に際しては3億円を支払います。

ABCL.L.Cは米国の有限責任会社ですが、個人D（持分40%）、個人E（持分50%）及び個人F（持分10%）により構成されているとのことです。

なお、ABCL.L.Cは当社が支払う版権使用料については、米国で構成員課税（個人D、E、Fが納税者となる。）を選択するとの連絡がありました。日米租税条約によりますと、版権の使用料は、日本では非課税であると聞いておりますが、課税関係及び免税の手続きはどのようになるのでしょうか。

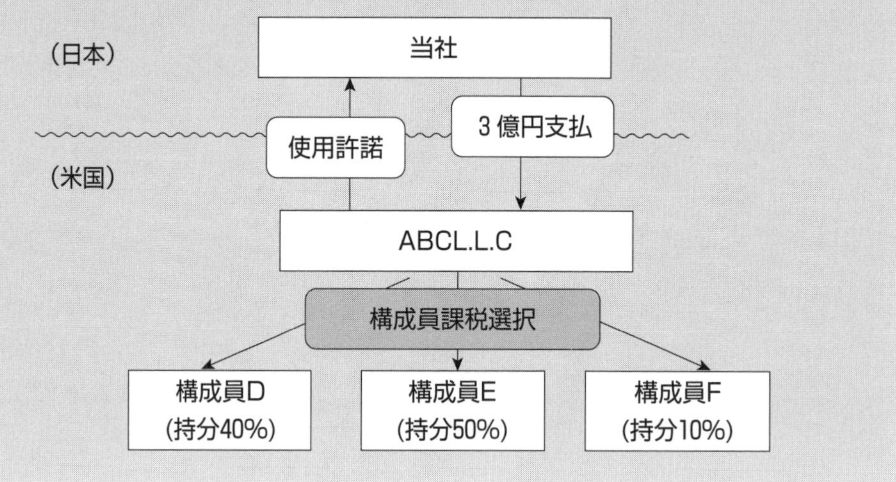

回答

日米租税条約では、版権の使用料は米国でのみ課税されます。

米国ではABCL.L.Cの構成員であるD、E、Fが納税者となることを選択していますので、ABCL.L.Cが貴社を通じ貴社を所轄する税務署長に提出する**「租税条約に関する届出書」（様式3）、「特典条項に関する付表」（様式17）**において、D、E、Fが免税をうける者であることを明らかにすることにより日本では免税となります。

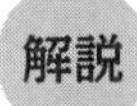

1　版権の使用料の所得区分

小説は、著作権法第２条の著作物に該当しますので、版権の使用の対価は、所得税法第161条第１項第11号のロ「著作権（出版権及び著作隣接権その他これに準ずるものを含む。）の使用料又はその譲渡による対価」に規定する著作権の使用料に該当します。

2　国内法（所法161①十一）による課税の取扱い

米国のL.L.C（有限責任会社）は、我が国の税務上は法人税法第２条第４号の外国法人に該当します。

したがって、ABC L.L.Cは外国法人として取り扱われますので、版権の使用料を支払う際に、所得税法第212条第１項の規定により源泉徴収（税率20.42%）をしなければなりません。

3　日米租税条約による版権の使用料に対する課税の取扱い

日米租税条約によりますと小説の版権の使用料は、同条約第12条の２に規定する「文学上の著作物の著作権の使用若しくは使用の権利の対価」として「使用料」に該当します。

課税の取り扱いについては、同条約第12条の１では「……他方の締約国においてのみ租税を課すことができる。」と規定しています。

他方の締約国とは米国をいいますので、ご質問の米国のABC L.L.Cに支払う小説の版権の使用料は、米国でのみ課税できるものであり、日本では課税されないことになります。

4　日米租税条約による特典（免税）の適用を受ける者について

⑴　日米租税条約により日本では免税となりますが、免税を受ける者については、同条約第４条１では、同条約を適用する「一方の締約国の居住者」とは、「当該一方の締約国の法令の下において………当該一方の締約国において課税を受けるべきものとされる者をいい………」と規定しています。

したがって、同条約の適用を受ける者は、一方の締約国（米国）において納税義務を有する者ということになります。

⑵　米国においては、有限責任会社（L.L.C）やパートナーシップ（P.S）など様々な形態の事業体があることから、これら事業体の事業活動から生じる所得の納税については、L.L.CやP.Sなどの事業体を納税者とするか、あるいは、事業体の出資者やパートナー等の構成員を納税者とするかの選択ができることとされています。

このことを踏まえ、日米租税条約第４条６ⓐにおいては、「……当該一方の締約国の租税に関する法令に基づき当該受益者、構成員又は参加者の所得として取り扱われるか否かにかかわらず、当該他方の締約国の居住者である当該受益者、構成員又は参加者の所得として取り扱われる部分についてのみ、この条約の特典が与えられる。」と規定しています。

つまり、国内法ではABCL.L.Cの所得として取り扱われますが、米国でL.L.Cの構成員課税を選択した場合には、その構成員の所得として取り扱われ、構成員に対してのみ免税の特典を付与するというものです。

したがって、ご質問のABC L.L.Cに対し支払われる版権使用料収入については、居住地国（米国）では、ABC L.L.Cの構成員である個人D、個人E及び個人Fが課税を選択していますので、それぞれが租税条約の免税の特典を受ける居住者となります。

免税に際しては、版権使用料の支払の前日までに、ABCL.L.Cが、貴社経由で貴社の所轄税務署長に**「租税条約に関する届出書」**、**「特典条項に関する付表」**、その他の必要書類を提出しなければなりません。

5　免税対象となる支払金額について

免税対象者	免税対象金額の計算	免税金額
構成員D	3億円×40%（出資割合）	1億2千万円
構成員E	3億円×50%（出資割合）	1億5千万円
構成員F	3億円×10%（出資割合）	3千万円

（根拠法令等：所法161①十一、所法212①、日米租税条約4・22）

⑶　人的役務に対する課税（所法161①７）

ガイダンス

非居住者に対する給与その他人的役務の提供に対する報酬のうち国内において行う勤務に対する報酬は、所得税法第161条第１項第12号の国内源泉所得に該当します。

しかし、短期間の滞在時に支給を受ける報酬等については、課税事務の煩雑による過大な事務負担を軽減するために、短期滞在者に対する免税措置が租税条約に定められています。

したがって、短期滞在者に対する免税措置の要件を理解することが重要になります。

また、非居住者である役員に対する報酬については、その役務提供地にかかわらず、法人の所在地で課税されることになり、支払の際に源泉所得税が課税されることになります。

ただし、内国法人の役員としての勤務であっても、国外での勤務が使用人として常時勤務するものである場合には、支給される報酬については、国内源泉所得としないこととされています。

「人的役務提供に対する課税」では、短期滞在者免税の対象となる短期滞在者の定義と要件、また、内国法人の役員であって、国外での使用人としての業務について演習事例により理解します。

演習事例13

短期滞在者免税（その１）

当社は米国法人Ｘ社の日本子会社Ｙ社です。
現在、親会社から５名の社員（非居住者）が、本年10月１日から翌年２月末までの５ヶ月間の予定で、派遣されております。
給与は親会社である米国が直接社員に支払うとのことです。
社員は、日本で働いていますので、日本で納税の義務があると思うのですが、先日、同業者から短期の日本滞在者であれば、租税条約により免税になるとの話を聞きました。
短期滞在者の免税とはどのような制度なのでしょうか。
親会社から派遣された５名の社員は日本では免税となるでしょうか。

米国法人Ｘから派遣された社員は、「日米租税条約」による短期滞在者となりますので、免税となります。

なお、社員に支払う給与は国内で源泉徴収されませんので、免税に際しては、「租税条約に関する届出書」の提出は必要ありません。

解説

海外支店あるいは子会社への短期出張の際に、滞在国で課税が行われた場合には、滞在国と居住国の双方で課税されることになり、二重課税となり、納税あるいは還付手続きが煩雑になります。

このことを回避するために、租税条約において、滞在国での課税を免除しております。

短期滞在者の免税要件

① 当該課税年度において開始又は終了するいずれかの12ヶ月の期間においても、報酬の受領者が当該他方の締約国内に滞在する期間が合計183日を超えないこと。

② 給与等の支払者が、勤務が行われた締約国の居住者でない雇用者であること、又はその者に代わる者であること。

③ 給与等が、役務提供地にある支店その他の恒久的施設によって負担されないこと。

ご質問の場合には、次の⑴～⑶の日米租税条約の短期滞在者の要件を満たしておりますので免税となります。

⑴　当該課税年度において開始又は終了するいずれかの12ヶ月の期間においても、報酬の受領者が当該他方の締約国内に滞在する期間が合計183日を超えていない。

[イメージ図]

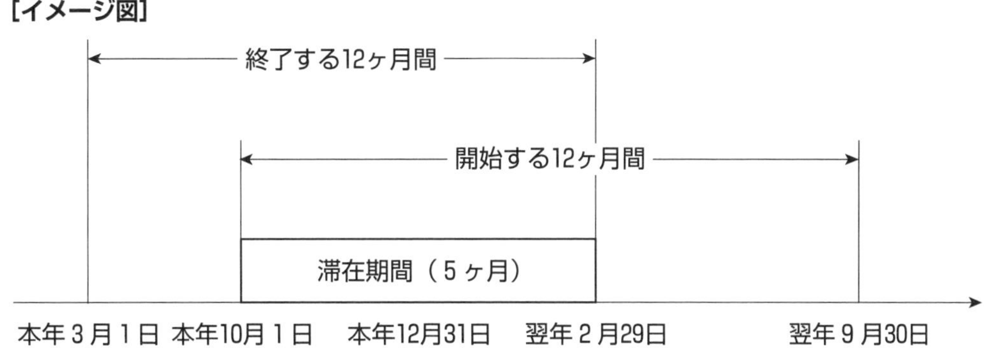

⑵　給与の支払者は米国法人Ｘである。

⑶　米国法人Ｘが給与の負担者となる。

（根拠法令等：所法161①十二、日米租税条約14）

演習事例14

短期滞在者免税（その２）

当社は米国法人Ｓ社の日本支店ですが、本店の社員Ｘは昨年10月１日から本年１月末までの４ヶ月の予定で日本支店に来日し国内の業務に従事しておりました。

社員Ｘの給与はＳ社の本店が負担し、米国内で支払われていましたが、「国内払い」とみなされることから、日米租税条約に基づく「短期滞在者免税の届出書」を税務署へ提出し、源泉所得税の免除を受けておりました。

このたび、日本支店の業務拡大に伴い本年２月１日から滞在期間が３ヶ月間延長され滞在日数が183日を超えることになりました。

短期滞在者の免税の扱いはどうなるのでしょうか。

社員Ｘの国内での滞在期間（当初滞在期間＋延長滞在期間）を日米租税条約に規定する滞在期間で計算しますと、昨年10月から本年４月まで継続する滞在期間の合計期間（７ヶ月）は183日を超えますので、同条約の短期滞在者の免税の要件を満たさなくなります。

社員Ｘに対する給与は、米国内で支払われているとのことですが、米国法人Ｓ社は日本に支店を有していますので、米国内での支払も日本国内で支払うものとみなされ、昨年の10月に遡及して20.42%の税率により所得税を源泉徴収しなければなりません。

解説

1　非居住者に対する課税について

社員Ｘは、１年未満の予定で入国し、Ｓ社日本支店に勤務していますので、勤務の対価は、所得税法第161条第１項第12号に規定する非居住者に対する国内において行う勤務の対価に該当します。

2　源泉徴収について

国外払いの給与であっても、その支払者が日本国内に住所（又は居所）を有し、又は、日本国内に事務所、事業所その他これに準じるものを有するときは、その者がその給与等を国内において支払ったものとみなして、源泉徴収をしなければなりません。

この場合の法定納期限は、支払日の属する月の「翌月末日」となります（所法212②）。

したがって、ご質問の社員Ｘの給与は米国において支払われているとのことですが、米国法人Ｓ社は日本支店を有していますので、米国払いの給与は日本国内において支払ったものとみなされますので、社員Xに対し給与を支払う際に源泉徴収し支払日の属する月の翌月末まで納付しなければなりません。

3　租税条約に基づく短期滞在者免税の要件と滞在日数の計算

海外支店への短期出張者について課税が行われると本国と滞在先での二重課税の問題や納税などの煩雑な様々な問題が生じます。

このため、租税条約においては、次の条件がクリアされた場合には、短期出張者の滞在先での所得を免税としております。

短期滞在者の免税要件

⑴　滞在期間が課税年度又は継続する12ヶ月を通じて183日を超えない。

⑵　給与等の支払者は、勤務が行われた締約国の居住者でない雇用者又はこれに代わるものから支払われるものであること。

⑶　給与等が役務提供地にある支店その他の恒久的施設によって負担されるものでないこと。

短期滞在者免税の滞在日数の計算について

租税条約による短期滞在者免税の要件の一つである滞在日数の183日は各国との間の租税条約の規定に基づき計算することになります。各国との間の租税条約に基づく滞在期間の計算の規定は次のように分類されます。

1　課税年度中の滞在日数が合計183 日を超えないとする条約

{締結国名}　アイルランド、オーストラリア等

{条　　文}　「その報酬の受領者が当該課税年度を通じて合計183日を超えない期間……滞在……」

2　暦年中の滞在日数が183 日を超えないとする条約

{締結国名}　イタリア、インドネシア、ヴェトナム、カナダ等

{条　　文}　「その報酬の受領者がその年（又は当該年）を通じて合計183日を超えない期間……滞在……」

3　継続する12ヶ月を通じて183日を超えないとする条約

{締約国名}　アメリカ、イギリス、オーストラリア、オランダ等

{条　　文}　「当該課税年度において開始又は終了するいずれかの十二箇月のいずれかの期間においても……滞在する期間が合計183日を超えない」

4　本件の検討結果

ご質問の内容から判断しますと、社員Xの給与は本店が負担し、本店が支払うとのことですので、上記の短期滞在者の免税要件のうち⑵及び⑶の要件を満たしています。

短期滞在者の免税要件のうち⑴の国内での滞在日数については、日米租税条約第14条第２項ⓐの規定により計算し、継続する12ヶ月を通じて滞在日数が183日を超えている

かにより判断することになります。

[イメージ図]

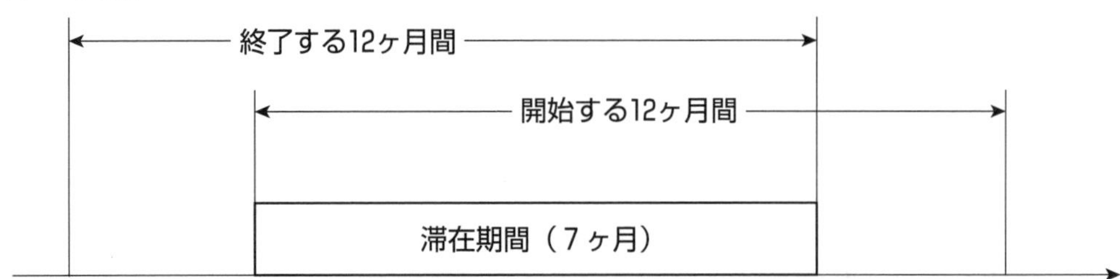

社員Xの滞在期間は昨年10月1日から本年4月30日まで7ヶ月ですので、継続する12ヶ月を通じて滞在日数は183日を超えることになります。

したがって、短期滞在者免税は適用できませんので、昨年の10月1日に遡及して20.42%の税率により所得税を源泉徴収します。

> （参考）
>
> 給与所得者の短期滞在者免税の適用を受けるための「租税条約に関する届出書（様式7）」を税務署長へ提出するケースとしては、源泉徴収が必要となる所得税法第212条第2項に規定する「みなし国内払」給与又は国内払給与（支払事務の委託等により国内で給与が支払われる場合）に限られます。

（根拠法令等：所法161①十二、所法212②、日英租税条約14）

[租税条約に関する届出書（給与等）]

様式 7
FORM

租税条約に関する届出書

APPLICATION FORM FOR INCOME TAX CONVENTION

自由職業者・芸能人・運動家・短期滞在者の報酬・給与に対する所得税及び復興特別所得税の免除
Relief from Japanese Income Tax and Special Income Tax for Reconstruction on Income Earned by Professionals, Entertainers, Sportsmen, or Temporary Visitors

この届出書の記載に当たっては、別紙の注意事項を参照してください。
See separate instructions.

税務署受付印

（税務署整理欄 For official use only）

適用；有、無

番号確認		身元確認	

＿＿＿＿＿税務署長殿
To the District Director, ＿＿＿＿＿＿＿＿Tax Office

1 適用を受ける租税条約に関する事項；
Applicable Income Tax Convention
日本国と＿＿＿＿＿＿＿＿＿＿＿との間の租税条約第＿＿条第＿＿項＿＿
The Income Tax Convention between Japan and＿＿＿＿＿＿＿＿＿＿, Article＿＿, para.＿＿

2 報酬・給与の支払を受ける者に関する事項；
Details of Recipient of Salary or Remuneration

氏名 Full name		
住所 Domicile		(電話番号 Telephone Number)
個人番号（有する場合のみ記入） Individual Number (Limited to case of a holder)		
日本国内における居所 Residence in Japan		(電話番号 Telephone Number)
(国籍 Nationality) (入国年月日 Date of Entry)		(在留期間 Authorized Period of Stay) (在留資格 Status of Residence)
下記「4」の報酬・給与につき居住者として課税される国及び納税地(注6) Country where the recipient is taxable as resident on Salary or Remuneration mentioned in 4 below and the place where he is to pay tax (Note6)		(納税者番号 Taxpayer Identification Number)
自由職業者、芸能人又は運動家の場合（短期滞在者に該当する者を除く。）：日本国内の恒久的施設又は固定的施設の状況 In case of Professionals, Entertainers or Sportsmen (other than Temporary Visitors) : Permanent establishment or fixed base in Japan □有(Yes) , □無(No) If "Yes",explain:	名称 Name	
	所在地 Address	(電話番号 Telephone Number)
	事業の内容 Details of Business	
短期滞在者の場合：以前に日本国に滞在したことの有無及び在留したことのある場合にはその入出国年月日等 In case of Temporary Visitors: Particulars on previous stay □有(Yes) , □無(No) If "Yes",explain:		(以前の入国年月日) Date of Previous Entry (以前の出国年月日) Date of Previous Departure (以前の在留資格) Previous Status Residence

3 報酬・給与の支払者に関する事項；
Details of Payer of Salary or Remuneration

氏名又は名称 Full name		
住所（居所）又は本店（主たる事務所）の所在地 Domicile (residence) or Place of head office (main office)		(電話番号 Telephone Number)
個人番号又は法人番号（有する場合のみ記入） Individual Number or Corporate Number (Limited to case of a holder)		
日本国内にある事務所等 Office, etc. located in Japan	名称 Name	(事業の内容 Details of Business)
	所在地 Address	(電話番号 Telephone Number)

4 上記「3」の支払者から支払を受ける報酬・給与で「1」の租税条約の規定の適用を受けるものに関する事項（注7）；
Details of Salary or Remuneration received from the Payer to which the Convention mentioned in 1 above is applicable (Note 7)

提供する役務の概要 Description of Services performed	役務提供期間 Period of Services performed	報酬・給与の支払期日 Due Date for Payment	報酬・給与の支払方法 Method of Payment of Salary, etc.	報酬・給与の金額及び月額・年額の区分 Amount of Salary, etc. (per month, year)

5 上記「3」の支払者以外の者から日本国内における勤務又は人的役務の提供に関して支払を受ける報酬・給与に関する事項（注8）；
Others Salaries or Remuneration paid by Persons other than 3 above for Personal Services performed in Japan (Note 8)

【裏面に続きます (Continue on the reverse) 】

6　その他参考となるべき事項（注9）；
Others (Note 9)

○　代理人に関する事項　；　この届出書を代理人によって提出する場合には、次の欄に記載してください。
Details of the Agent　;　If this form is prepared and submitted by the Agent, fill out the following columns.

代理人の資格 Capacity of Agent in Japan	氏名（名称） Full name		納税管理人の届出をした税務署名 Name of the Tax Office where the Tax Agent is registered
□　納税管理人　※ Tax Agent □　その他の代理人 Other Agent	住所（居所・所在地） Domicile (Residence or location)	（電話番号 Telephone Number）	税務署 Tax Office

※　「納税管理人」とは、日本国の国税に関する申告、申請、請求、届出、納付等の事項を処理させるため、国税通則法の規定により選任し、かつ、日本国における納税地の所轄税務署長に届出をした代理人をいいます。

※ "Tax Agent" means a person who is appointed by the taxpayer and is registered at the District Director of Tax Office for the place where the taxpayer is to pay his tax, in order to have such agent take necessary procedures concerning the Japanese national taxes, such as filing a return, applications, claims, payment of taxes, etc., under the provisions of Act on General Rules for National Taxes.

○　適用を受ける租税条約が特典条項を有する租税条約である場合；
If the applicable convention has article of limitation on benefits

特典条項に関する付表の添付
"Attachment Form for Limitation on Benefits Article" attached

□有Yes
□添付省略 Attachment not required
（特典条項に関する付表を添付して提出した租税条約に関する届出書の提出日
Date of previous submission of the application for income tax convention with the "Attachment Form for Limitation on Benefits Article"　　　年　　月　　日）

演習事例15

短期滞在者免税と源泉徴収の免除（その３）

当社は、米国に本店を有するＡ社の日本支店です。

この度、新規のプロジェクトを立ち上げたことから本社から本年10月１日から翌年２月末までの５ヶ月間の予定で、応援の社員Ｓ氏が来日することになりました。

日本滞在中の給与については、米国本社が負担し、支払う予定です。

この場合の課税関係はどうなるのでしょうか。海外から短期間で来日する社員には、米国との間の「日米租税条約」に基づき、免税が受けられるとの話を聞いておりますが、社員Ａ氏の場合はどのような取扱いになるのでしょうか。免税の手続きも含めてご教示をお願いいたします。

回答

社員Ｓ氏は短期滞在者免税の要件を満たしています。

ただし、Ａ社は国内に支店を有していますので、給与を米国本社で支払った場合には、日本国内で支払うものとみなされますので、米国本社で支払う際に源泉徴収しなければなりません。

この源泉徴収を免除するためには、社員Ｓ氏は最初の給与の支払の前日まで貴社を通じて、所轄税務署長に**「租税条約に関する届出書・様式７（自由職業者・芸能人・運動家・短期滞在者の報酬・給与に対する所得税及び復興特別所得税の免除）」**及び**「特典条項に関する付表」**を提出しなければなりません。

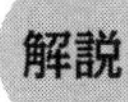

解説

１　国内法の取扱い

⑴　居住形態の判定（居住者か非居住者か）

○居住者とは、国内に住所を有し、又は現在まで引き続いて一年以上居所を有する個人をいいます。

　また、国内に居住することとなった個人が国内において、継続して一年以上居住することを通常必要とする職業を有する場合には、その個人は国内に住所を有する者（居住者）と推定されます。

（所法２①三、所令14①一）

○非居住者とは居住者以外の個人をいいます。　（所法２①五）

⑵ 非居住者に対する課税所得の範囲

非居住者に対しては、次の国内源泉所得のみが課税所得となります。

（所法161①）

支払を受ける者	国内源泉所得
非居住者	⑴ 国内において行う組合事業から生じる利益の分配 ⑵ 国内にある土地等の譲渡による対価 ⑶ 国内において人的役務の提供事業を行う者が受けるその役務提供の対価 ⑷ 国内にある不動産、船舶、航空機などの貸付けの対価及び地上権などの設定の対価 ⑸ 国内にある営業所等に預けられた預貯金の利子等 ⑹ 内国法人から受ける剰余金の配当、利益の配当、剰余金の分配又は基金利息等 ⑺ 国内において業務を行う者に対するその国内業務に係る貸付金の利子 ⑻ 国内において業務を行う者から受けるその国内業務に係る工業所有権、著作権等の使用料又は譲渡の対価 ⑼ ①給与その他人的役務の提供に対する報酬のうち、国内において行う勤務に基因するもの、②公的年金等、③退職手当等のうち受給者が居住者であった期間に行った勤務等に基因するもの ⑽ 国内において行う事業の広告宣伝のための賞金 ⑾ 国内にある営業所等を通じて保険業法に規定する生命保険会社、損害保険会社等と締結した保険契約等に基づく年金 ⑿ 国内の営業所等が受け入れた定期積金の給付補填金等 ⒀ 国内において事業を行う者に対する出資につき、匿名組合契約等に基づいて受ける利益の分配

⑶ みなし国内払いについて

国内源泉所得の支払が国外において行われる場合において、その支払をする者が国内に、住所若しくは居所を有し、又は国内に事務所、事業所その他これに準ずるものを有するときは、その者がその国内源泉所得を国内において支払うものとみなして、その支払いの際、源泉徴収することとされています。

この場合には、源泉所得税の納付期限は「翌月末」となります。

（所法212②）

（注） その支払をする者とは

その支払をするものとは、具体的に支払行為をする者ではなく、国内源泉所得の支払義務を負う者をいいます。

> **（注）　事務所、事業所その他これに準ずるものとは**
> 事務所、事業所その他これに準ずるものとは、内国法人の本店又は主たる事務所及び非居住者又は外国法人が有する恒久的施設（支店等）をいいます。

2　「日米租税条約」に基づく取扱い

⑴　「日米租税条約」に基づく短期滞在者免税について

日米租税条約においては、短期滞在者免税について次のように規定しています。

（一方の締約国を米国、他方の締約国を日本と読み替えた場合）

> 第14条
> 1　次条、第17条及び第18条の規定が適用される場合を除くほか、**米国の居住者**がその勤務について取得する給料、賃金その他これらに類する報酬に対しては、勤務が**日本国内**において行われない限り、**米国**においてのみ租税を課すことができる。
> 勤務が**日本国内**において行われる場合には、当該勤務から生ずる報酬に対しては、**日本**において租税を課すことができる。
> 2　1の規定にかかわらず、**米国の居住者**が**日本国内**において行う勤務について取得する報酬に対しては、次の⒜から⒞までに掲げる要件を満たす場合には、**米国**においてのみ租税を課することができる。
> ⒜　当該課税年度において開始又は終了するいずれか12箇月の期間においても、報酬の受領者が**日本**に滞在する期間が合計183日を超えないこと。
> ⒝　報酬が**日本の居住者**でない雇用者又はこれに代わる者から支払われるものであること。
> ⒞　報酬が雇用者の日本国内に有する恒久的施設によって負担されるものでないこと。

⑵　日本における免税の要件

日米租税条約第14条によりますと次の要件を満たす場合には、米国のみでの課税となりますので、日本では免税となります。

> ①　日本に滞在する期間が合計183日を超えないこと。
> ②　報酬が日本の居住者でない雇用者又はこれに代わる者から支払われる。
> ③　報酬が雇用者の日本国内に有する恒久的施設（支店等）によって負担されるものでない。

5　社員S氏の課税関係

(1)　国内法の取扱い

イ　社員S氏の居住形態の判定

社員S氏は国内での滞在期間が5ヶ月ということですので、1年以上の滞在ではありませんので、入国時から非居住者として取り扱われます。

ロ　社員S氏に支給される給与の課税上の取扱い

社員S氏は非居住者ですので、支給される給与は、国内において行う勤務によるものですので、国内源泉所得に該当します。

また、A氏に対する給与については、米国本社が支払うとのことですが、その給与の支払が国外において行われる場合において、その支払をする者が国内に、住所若しくは居所を有し、又は国内に事務所、事業所その他これに準ずるものを有するときは、その者がその給与を国内において支払うものとみなして、その支払の際、源泉徴収することとされています。

したがって、A社は国内に支店を有していますので、給与を米国本社で支払った場合には、日本国内で支払うものとみなされますので米国本社で支払う際に源泉徴収しなければなりません。

この場合には、源泉所得税の納付期限は支払月の「翌月末」となります。

（所法161①十二、212②）

(2)　日米租税条約の取扱い

上記4の短期滞在者免税について検討すると次のようになります。

イ　社員S氏の日本国内での滞在期間は5ヶ月間であり、183日を超えていません。

[イメージ図]

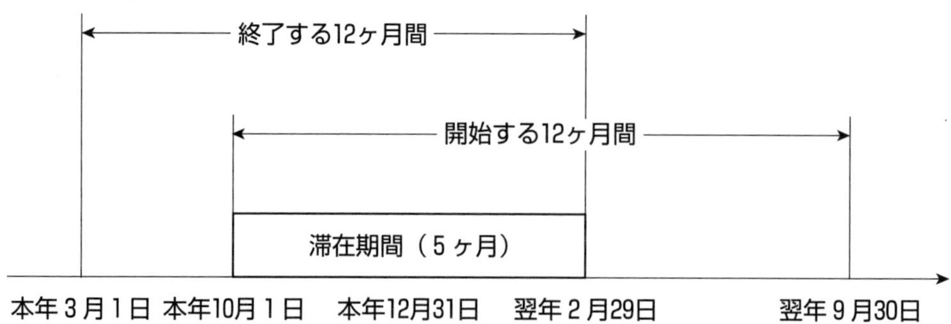

ロ　社員S氏の給与は米国の本社が負担し、支払を行う。

ハ　社員S氏の給与は日本支店によって負担されていない。

したがって、上記イ～ロにより社員S氏は短期滞在者免税の要件を満たしています。

⑶　みなし国内払いと源泉徴収の免除

Ａ社は国内に支店を有していますので、給与を米国本社で支払った場合には、日本国内で支払うものとみなされますので、米国本社で支払う際に源泉徴収しなければなりません。

この源泉徴収を免除するためには、社員Ｓ氏は最初の給与の支払の前日まで貴社を通じて、所轄税務署長に**「租税条約に関する届出書・様式７（自由職業者・芸能人・運動家・短期滞在者の報酬・給与に対する所得税及び復興特別所得税の免除）」**及び**「特典条項に関する付表」**を提出しなければなりません。

演習事例16

内国法人の役員としての国外での勤務

当社はＡ国での事業活動を拡大するために、社長直属の海外事業本部の最高責任者である取締役ＺをＡ国の子会社Ｂ社の代表取締役として、３年間派遣することにいたします。

Ｚ氏の当社の役員報酬については、国内での社会保険料の支払のためにその一部をＺ氏の国内の口座へ支払い、残額は、海外の口座へ支払います。

役員の場合には、国外で勤務しても、役員報酬の支払の際に源泉徴収が必要であると聞いております。

Ｚ氏は出国後、非居住者になりますが、海外勤務期間中の役員報酬の課税関係について教えてください。

Ｚ氏の出国後には、出国前の勤務期間に係る賞与も支払いすることになっております。

また、毎月の取締役会や業務打合わせで来日し、１週間程度、国内に滞在する予定ですが、その際には、役員報酬とは別に、当社から手当を支給する予定です。

出国後に支給する賞与と来日時に国内での勤務に対し支給する手当の課税関係についても合わせて教えてください。

Ｚ氏はＢ社の代表取締役であると同時に、貴社の海外事業本部の最高責任者としての職務も兼務しておりますので、Ｂ社での勤務は貴社の役員としての国外での勤務となります。

したがって、貴社からＺに支給する役員報酬は、所得税法第161条第１項第12号の国内源泉所得に該当しますので、支払の際に、20.42％の税率により源泉徴収し納税することになります。

また、Ｚ氏は出国後、非居住者となりますので、貴社が出国後に支払った出国前の勤務期間の賞与と来日した際に支給される手当は、国内での勤務の対価になりますので、支払の際に、20.42％の税率により源泉徴収し納税することになります。

1　Ｚ氏のＢ社での勤務は、内国法人の役員としての国外での勤務である

所得税法第161条第１項第12号イによりますと、国内において行う勤務その他の人的役務の提供の対価は国内源泉所得と規定しています。

また、内国法人の役員としての国外での勤務その他の政令で定める人的役務の提供を国内源泉所得に含むと規定しています。役員の場合は、役務提供地にかかわらず、日本で課税を行うという規定になります。

ただし、国外に勤務する役員すべてが課税の対象となるのではなく、所得税法施行令第285条第１項第１号によりますと、「その内国法人の使用人として常時勤務を行う場合の当該役員としての勤務を除く」と規定しています。

これは、国外に勤務する内国法人の役員であっても、その勤務内容が内国法人の使用人として常時勤務を行う場合には、課税の対象となる役員から除外することになります。

課税の対象から除外される役員とは、所得税基本通達161－42では、**支店長として常時勤務する場合**を事例として掲げています。また、所得税基本通達161－43では**子会社で内国法人の使用人として勤務する場合**を掲げています。

ご質問の場合、Ｚ氏は、Ｂ社の代表取締役であること、また、貴社では取締役で社長直属の海外事業の最高責任者であること、これらの勤務の内容から、Ｂ社での勤務は貴社の使用人としての勤務ではなく**内国法人の役員としての国外での勤務**となります。

したがって、Ｚ氏に支給する役員報酬は、所得税法第161条第１項第12号の国内源泉所得に該当しますので、所得税法第212条第１項の規定により、非居住者に対する給与として支払の際に源泉徴収し、その徴収の日の属する月の翌月10日までに納付します。

2　Ｚ氏に出国後に支払われる出国前の勤務期間の賞与の課税上の取扱い

Ｚ氏の出国前の勤務期間に係る賞与は国内の勤務の対価で、所得税法第161条第１項第12号の国内源泉所得に該当します。所得税法第212条第１項の規定により、非居住者に対する給与として、支払の際に源泉徴収し、その徴収の日の属する月の翌月10日まで納付します。

3　Ｚ氏が取締役会や業務打合わせで来日の際に支給される手当の取扱い

Ｚ氏が国内へ来日した際に支払う手当は、国内での勤務の対価で、所得税法第161条第１項第12号の国内源泉所得に該当します。所得税法第212条第１項の規定により、非居住者に対する給与として、支払の際に源泉徴収し、その徴収の日の属する月の翌月10日までに納付します。

（根拠法令等：所法161①十二、所令285、所基通161－42・43）

4　租税条約の手続きに関する事例

ガイダンス

租税条約による税額の減免等を受けるためには、「租税条約に関する届出書」を支払の前日までに所轄の税務署長に提出しなければなりませんが、支払後に提出し、税額の減免等を受けられるのかとの疑問があります。

また、租税条約が改正された場合の税額の減免等の適用開始時期はいつか、また、租税条約に基づく減免手続きを適用する場合の還付手続きはどのように行うのでしょうか。

さらに、税務調査による指摘で租税条約の適用ができなく、追徴課税される事例も多いと聞きます。
したがって、租税条約の適用対象となる所得については、正確に理解する必要があります。

「租税条約の手続きに関する事例」では、租税条約に関する届出書」の提出手続き及び還付請求手続き、また、改正時などの課税上の取扱いについて、演習事例により理解します。

演習事例17

税金が軽減又は免除される場合（租税条約の適用）

当社は海外の企業にソフトウエアの開発を委託し、開発費用を支払うのですが、その開発費用を支払う際には20.42%の税率により源泉所得税が課税されるとのことですが、この税率が10%に軽減されたり、免除されたりする場合があると聞いております。どのようなことなのでしょうか。

詳しく教えてください。

日本は海外の多くの国と租税条約を締結していますので、ソフトウエアの開発を委託した企業が租税条約の締結国にある場合には、税率を10%に軽減する規定や免除する規定があります。

したがって、開発を委託する海外の企業がある国との間の租税条約の有無を確認します。

解説

1　ソフトウエアは著作権法上の著作物である

ソフトウエアはプログラムであることから、著作権法上、著作物として取り扱われています。

著作権法第２条第１項第１号（定義）
著作物とは思想又は勘定を創作的に表現したものであって、文芸、学術、美術又は音楽の範囲に属するものをいう。

著作権法第２条第１項第10号（定義）
プログラムとは電子計算機を昨日させて一の結果を得ることができるようにこれに対する指令を組み合わせたものとして表現したものをいう。

著作権法第10条第１項第９号（著作物の例示）
小説、脚本、論文、講演、音楽の著作物、舞踏、絵画、建築の著作物、………**プログラムの著作物**他

2　国内法（所法161）の取扱い

ソフトウエアは、我が国の著作権法上の著作物に該当しますので、その開発の対価が著作権の使用料又は譲渡の対価に該当すれば、**国内源泉所得**（著作権の使用料又はその譲渡による対価）に該当し、支払の際に源泉徴収しなければなりません。

（所法161⑪）

3　税率の軽減又は免除について

日本は海外の多くの国と租税条約を締結していますので、ソフトウエアの開発を委託した企業が租税条約の締結国にある場合には、税率が10%に軽減されたり、免除されたりします。

税率の軽減又は税額の免除がある場合には、**「租税条約に関する届出書」**の提出が必要となります。

4　租税条約の適用を受ける手続き

租税条約による軽減又は免除を受けるためには、その適用を受けようとする者は、支払者経由で支払者を所轄する税務署長に支払日の前日までに**「租税条約に関する届出書」**を提出しなければなりません。

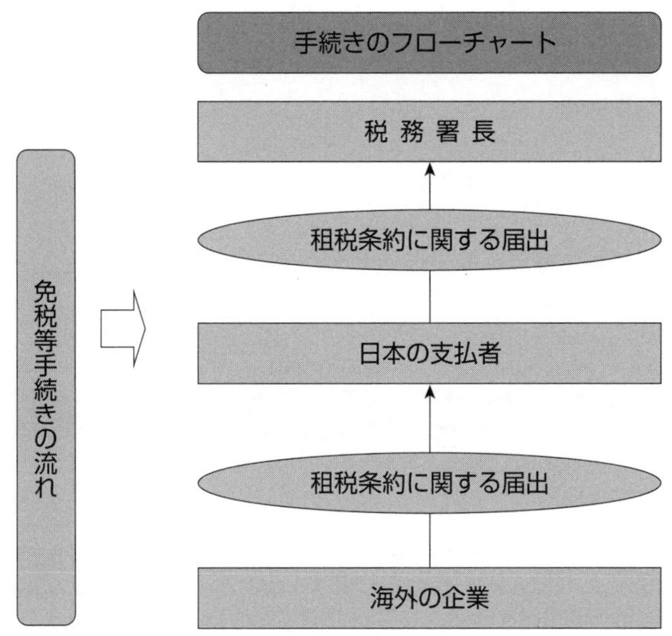

演習事例18

税金が軽減又は免除されない場合（エジプトとの租税条約）

当社は、ソフトウエアの新製品の開発をエジプトのＡ社に委託しました。完成したソフトウエアの権利はＡ社から譲り受ける予定です。

開発費の対価の支払に際し、租税条約による租税の軽減は受けられるのでしょうか。

回答

日・エジプト租税条約においては、著作権の譲渡の対価は同条約第11条第３項の規定により、財産の譲渡による収益として取り扱われており、その収益が発生した日本で課税することとされています。

したがって、ソフトウエアの対価支払の際に、20.42％の税率により源泉所得税を課税しなければなりません。

解説

1　国内法（所法161）の取扱い

ソフトウエアは、我が国の著作権法上の著作物に該当しますので、その開発の対価が著作権の使用料又は譲渡の対価に該当すれば、**国内源泉所得**（著作権の使用料又はその譲渡による対価）に該当し、支払の際に源泉徴収しなければなりません。

（所法161①十一）

所得税法第161条第１項第11号
国内において業務を行う者から受ける次に掲げる使用料又は対価で当該業務に係るもの イ　工業所有権その他の技術に関する権利、特別の技術による生産方式若しくはこれらに準ずるものの使用料又はその譲渡による対価 ロ　著作権（出版権及び著作隣接権その他これに準ずるものを含む。）の使用料又はその譲渡による対価 ハ　機械、装置その他政令で定める用具の使用

2　日・エジプト租税条約上の取り扱い

(1)　著作権の使用料について

日・エジプト租税条約では、著作権の使用料については同条約第10条第１項、第２項の規定により、日本において15％を限度税率として課税されることになります。

日・エジプト租税条約第10条第1項
一方の締約国において生じ、他方の締約国の居住者に支払われる使用料に対しては、当該一方の締約国において、……15%を超えない税率で租税を課することができる。
この条において、「使用料」とは、文学上、芸術上若しくは学術上の著作物の著作権、特許権、商標権、意匠若しくは模型、図面、秘密方式若しくは秘密工程の使用若しくは使用の権利の対価として、産業上、商業上若しくは学術上の設備の使用若しくは使用の権利の対価として、又は産業上、若しくは学術上の経験に関する情報の対価として受けるすべての種類の支払金をいう。

⑵ 著作権の譲渡の対価について

日・エジプト租税条約においては、**著作権の譲渡の対価**は日・エジプト租税条約第11条第3項の規定により、**財産の譲渡による収益**として取り扱われており、**日本で課税**することになります。

日・エジプト租税条約第11条第3項
1及び2にいう財産又は資産以外の財産又は資産の譲渡から生ずる収益に対しては、当該収益が生じた締約国（日本）において租税を課することができる。

⑶ 日本での課税について

ソフトウエアは、我が国の著作権法上の著作物に該当しますので、その開発の対価が著作権の譲渡の対価に該当しますので、支払の際に20.42%の税率により源泉所得税を課税し、税務署に納税することになります。**（租税条約による税額の軽減・免除はありません。）**

演習事例19

「租税条約に関する届出書」を継続して提出する場合の留意事項

当社は、米国のA社との間で技術提携契約を締結し、同社から今後、工業所有権の供与を受け、使用料（以下「ロイヤリティ」といいます。）を支払います。

A社はロイヤリティの支払に際し、「日米租税条約」に基づく免税の恩典を受けたいとの申し出があることから、支払の前日まで「租税条約に関する届出書」の提出をお願いしております。

ロイヤリティは、今後、長期間、支払われる予定ですので、「租税条約に関する届出書」を継続的に提出することになります。

提出に際し留意する事項についてご教示をお願いいたします。

回答

1 「特典条項に関する付表（様式17－米)」を添付した「租税条約に関する届書」（様式3）の提出の省略について

「特典条項に関する付表（様式17－米)」を添付した「租税条約に関する届書」（様式3）については、支払を受ける日の前日以前3年内のいずれかの時において、源泉徴収義務者を経由して所轄の税務署長に提出している場合には提出は省略することができます。

2 「居住者証明書」の有効期限について

「居住者証明書」については、提示の日前1年以内に作成されたものに限ります。

解説

1 税率の軽減又は免除について

日本は米国との間で租税条約を締結していますので、米国の企業にロイヤリティを支払う際には源泉所得税が免除されます。

税額の免除のためには、**「租税条約に関する届出書」**の提出が必要となります。

2 租税条約の適用を受ける手続き

租税条約による税額の免除を受けるためには、その適用を受けようとする者は、支払者経由で支払者を所轄する税務署長に支払日の前日までに**「租税条約に関する届出書」**を提出しなければなりません。

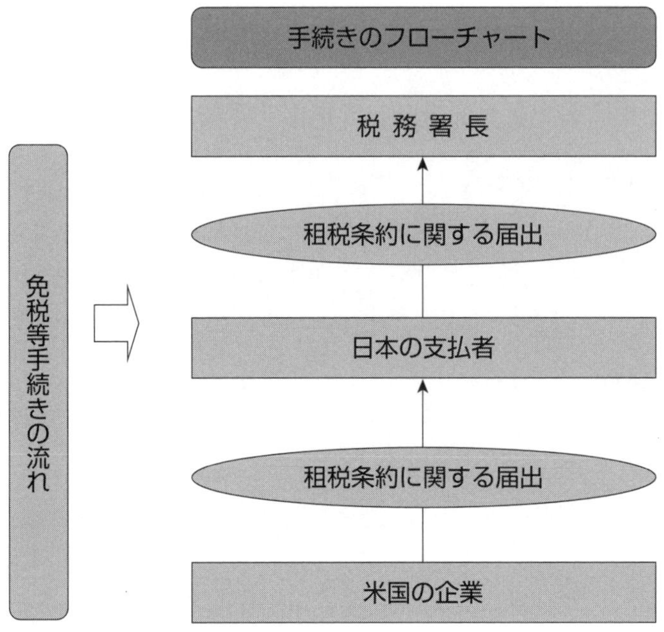

3　日米条約の適用対象者

条約は、真に、適用を受けるものに適用されることから、適用対象者には制限が行われております。

○適用対象者

次に掲げる者が適用対象者とされております。

A　適格者基準の要件を満たす者

① 個人 ………………………………………………………………… (第22条1(a))

② 国、地方政府（地方公共団体)、日本銀行、連邦準備銀行
………………………………………………………………………… (第22条1(b))

③ 特定の公開会社、公開会社の関連会社 ……………………… (第22条1(c)（ⅰ）（ⅱ）)

④ 公益団体 …………………………………………………………… (第22条1(d))

⑤ 年金基金 …………………………………………………………… (第22条1(e))

⑥ 個人以外の者で支配基準と課税ベース浸食基準の両方の要件を満たすもの

B　支払基準の要件を満たす者

個人以外の者でその者の株式等の50%以上が、上記①～⑤の個人、政府等、特定の公開会社、公益団体又は年金基金により直接又は間接に所有されていること。

C　課税ベース浸食基準の要件を満たす者

個人以外の者でその者の総所得のうちに第三国の者に直接又は間接に支払われるべきものの額の占める割合が50%未満であること。

D　能動的事業活動基準の要件を満たす者

⑴　能動的事業基準とは、次の三条件を満たす場合である。

① 居住地国で、営業又は事業の活動（投資活動を除く。）に従事していること。

② その取得する所得が上記①の営業又は事業の活動に関連又は付随して取得されるものであること。

③ その取得する所得に関し、個別の条項に別に定める特典を受けるための要件を満たしていること。

⑵　さらに、他方の締約国内で支店又は子会社等を通じて営業又は事業活動を行う場合には追加の要件を満たす必要があり、居住地国で行う営業活動等が他方の締約国で行う営業活動等との関係において実質的なものでなければならない。（営業活動等が実質的であるか否かの判断は、すべての事実と状況により判断する。……例えば、居住地国の事業規模と支店等の事業規模の比較、あるいは営業活動全体に対する本店と支店等の貢献度の比較など。）

4　日米租税条約の免税を受けるための手続き

日米租税条約による免税の適用を受けるためには、米国Ａ社は支払者経由で、**支払日の前日までに**、支払者の所轄税務署長に**「租税条約に関する届出書」（様式３）**を提出しなければなりません。

また、日米租税条約の適用を受けるためには、加えて**「特典条項に関する付表（様式17－米）」**を提出し、これに**米国政府が納税者に発行する「居住者証明書」**を添付しなければなりません。

5　「租税条約に関する届出書」を継続して提出する場合に留意すべき事項

⑴　「特典条項に関する付表（様式17－米）」を添付した「租税条約に関する届書」（様式３）の提出の省略

「特典条項に関する付表（様式17－米）」を添付した「租税条約に関する届書」（様式３）については、支払を受ける日の前日以前三年内のいずれかの時において、源泉徴収義務者を経由して所轄の税務署長に提出している場合には提出は省略することができます。（支払を受ける国内源泉所得が提出済の国内源泉所得と同一であるものに限ります。）

ただし、**「特典条項に関する付表（様式17－米）」**の記載事項が提出済の**「特典条項に関する付表（様式17－米）」**の記載事項と異なる場合は、この取扱いはありません。

（実特令９の５①②）

⑵　**「居住者証明書」の有効期限**

「居住者証明書」は提示の日前１年以内に作成されたものに限ります。

（実特令９の10③）

演習事例20

改正租税条約により免税となる源泉所得税

当社はＡ国のＳ社から製造に関する技術提供を受けております。

技術使用料として毎月の生産金額の５％を翌月末に支払う契約となっております。

令和５年１月～６月までに発生した技術使用料は翌月末に支払い、支払の際には、租税条約に基づき支払金額の10％を源泉徴収し、納税しております。

今般、Ａ国との間で租税条約の改正が行われ令和５年８月23日に発効することになり、「源泉徴収される租税に関しては、協定が効力を生じる年の翌年一月一日以後に租税を課される額」は免税になるとのことです。

令和５年７月～12月までに発生した技術使用料は資金繰りの都合で翌月末日まで支払うことができないことから未払金として計上し、来年の３月31日に行う予定です。

この場合に、支払時点（令和６年３月31日）では、租税条約が改正されていることから、令和５年７月～12月の期間に発生した技術使用料に課税される源泉所得税については全額が免税の取扱いでよろしいでしょうか。

① 技術使用料の経理処理　　未払金（令和５年７月～12月）
② 改正租税条約発行日　　令和５年８月23日
③ 技術使用料の支払予定日　　令和６年３月31日

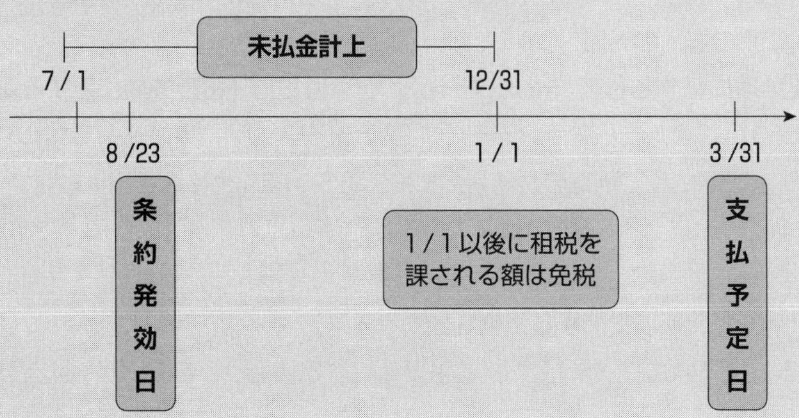

回答

貴社がＡ国のＳ社に支払う令和５年７月分～11月分の技術使用料については、改正後の租税条約は適用されませんので、支払の際には、源泉徴収しなければなりません。

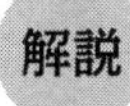

1　改正租税条約により免税となる源泉所得税

改正後の租税条約によりますと、「源泉徴収される租税に関しては、協定が効力を生じる年の翌年１月１日以後に租税を課される額」は免税とすると規定されています。

したがって、技術使用料の支払期日が令和６年１月１日以後であるものについては免税となります。

また、支払期日が定められていない支払については、実際の支払日が令和６年１月１日以後であるものについては免税となります。

2　貴社の場合

貴社の場合には、技術使用料の支払期日は技術使用料の発生月の翌月末とされています。

したがって、支払期日が令和５年12月31日以前であるものについては源泉所得税は課税（税率10％）となりますが、支払期日が令和６年１月１日以後のものについては免税となります。

（技術使用料発生月）	（支払期日）	（免税又は課税）
５年７月分	５年８月末	課税
５年８月分	５年９月末	課税
５年９月分	５年10月末	課税
５年10月分	５年11月末	課税
５年11月分	５年12月末	課税
５年12月分	６年１月末	免税

演習事例21

租税条約に基づく還付請求

当市は米国からALT（外国語指導助手）を公立小中学校の英語能力向上のために採用しております。
ALTの報酬については、給与として毎月源泉徴収しておりましたが、「日米租税条約」により免税であることを、最近、知りました。
「租税条約に関する届出書」は、支払の前日までに所轄の税務署に提出が必要だと聞いておりますが、免税を受けずに源泉徴収し納付した税金については還付請求はできるのでしょうか。

源泉所得税の本税は還付請求することができます。

解説

租税条約による免税を受けるには、「租税条約に関する届出書」を支払日の前日まで、所轄の税務署長に提出することになりますが、租税条約の免税を受けずに納付した源泉所得税は、ALTが市経由で市の所轄税務署長に対し**「租税条約に関する届出書」（様式3）、「租税条約に関する源泉徴収税額の還付請求書」（様式11）**及びその他必要資料を提出し、還付の請求を行うことができます。

その他必要書類については、所轄の税務署に確認してください。

なお、ご質問の場合には、租税条約の相手国が米国ですので、**「特典条項に関する付表」（様式17）**の提出も必要になります。

（根拠法令等：実特省令2⑧、日米租税条約22）

[租税条約に関する届出書（使用料等）・様式３]

様　式　３
FORM

税務署受付印

租税条約に関する届出書

APPLICATION FORM FOR INCOME TAX CONVENTION

（使用料に対する所得税及び復興特別所得税の軽減・免除
Relief from Japanese Income Tax and Special Income Tax for Reconstruction on Royalties）

この届出書の記載に当たっては、別紙の注意事項を参照してください。
See separate instructions.

（税務署整理欄 For official use only）

適用；有、無			
番号確認		身元確認	

□ 限度税率＿＿＿％
Applicable Tax Rate
□ 免　税（注11）
Exemption (Note 11)

＿＿＿＿＿＿税務署長殿
To the District Director, ＿＿＿＿＿＿＿＿Tax Office

1　適用を受ける租税条約に関する事項；
Applicable Income Tax Convention
日本国と＿＿＿＿＿＿＿＿＿＿＿＿＿＿＿＿との間の租税条約第＿＿条第＿＿項＿＿
The Income Tax Convention between Japan and＿＿＿＿＿＿＿＿＿＿＿＿, Article＿＿＿, para.＿＿＿

2　使用料の支払を受ける者に関する事項；
Details of Recipient of Royalties

氏名又は名称 Full name		
個人番号又は法人番号（有する場合のみ記入） Individual Number or Corporate Number (Limited to case of a holder)		
個人の場合 Individual	住所又は居所 Domicile or residence	（電話番号 Telephone Number）
	国籍 Nationality	
法人その他の団体の場合 Corporation or other entity	本店又は主たる事務所の所在地 Place of head office or main office	（電話番号 Telephone Number）
	設立又は組織された場所 Place where the Corporation was established or organized	
	事業が管理・支配されている場所 Place where the business is managed and controlled	（電話番号 Telephone Number）
下記「4」の使用料につき居住者として課税される国及び納税地（注8） Country where the recipient is taxable as resident on Royalties mentioned in 4 below and the place where he is to pay tax (Note 8)		（納税者番号 Taxpayer Identification Number）
日本国内の恒久的施設の状況 Permanent establishment in Japan □有(Yes)，□無(No) If "Yes", explain:	名称 Name	
	所在地 Address	（電話番号 Telephone Number）
	事業の内容 Details of Business	

3　使用料の支払者に関する事項；
Details of Payer of Royalties

氏名又は名称 Full name		
住所（居所）又は本店（主たる事務所）の所在地 Domicile (residence) or Place of head office (main office)		（電話番号 Telephone Number）
個人番号又は法人番号（有する場合のみ記入） Individual Number or Corporate Number (Limited to case of a holder)		
日本国内にある事務所等 Office, etc. located in Japan	名称 Name	（事業の内容 Details of Business）
	所在地 Address	（電話番号 Telephone Number）

4　上記「3」の支払者から支払を受ける使用料で「1」の租税条約の規定の適用を受けるものに関する事項（注9）；
Details of Royalties received from the Payer to which the Convention mentioned in 1 above is applicable (Note 9)

使用料の内容 Description of Royalties	契約の締結年月日 Date of Contract	契約期間 Period of Contract	使用料の計算方法 Method of Computation for Royalties	使用料の支払期日 Due Date for Payment	使用料の金額 Amount of Royalties

5　その他参考となるべき事項（注10）；
Others (Note 10)

【裏面に続きます（Continue on the reverse）】

6　日本の税法上、届出書の「2」の外国法人が納税義務者とされるが、租税条約の規定によりその株主等である者（相手国居住者に限ります。）の所得として取り扱われる部分に対して租税条約の適用を受けることとされている場合の租税条約の適用を受ける割合に関する事項等（注4）；
Details of proportion of income to which the convention mentioned in 1 above is applicable, if the foreign company mentioned in 2 above is taxable as a company under Japanese tax law, and the convention is applicable to income that is treated as income of the member (limited to a resident of the other contracting country) of the foreign company in accordance with the provisions of the convention (Note 4)

届出書の「2」の外国法人の株主等で租税条約の適用を受ける者の氏名又は名称 Name of member of the foreign company mentioned in 2 above, to whom the Convention is applicable	間接保有 Indirect Ownership	持分の割合 Ratio of Ownership	受益の割合＝ 租税条約の適用を受ける割合 Proportion of benefit = Proportion for Application of Convention
	□	%	%
	□	%	%
	□	%	%
	□	%	%
	□	%	%
合計 Total		%	%

届出書の「2」の欄に記載した外国法人が支払を受ける「4」の使用料について、「1」の租税条約の相手国の法令に基づきその株主等である者の所得として取り扱われる場合には、その根拠法令及びその効力を生じる日を記載してください。
If royalties mentioned in 4 above that a foreign company mentioned in 2 above receives are treated as income of those who are its members under the law in the other contracting country of the convention mentioned in 1 above, enter the law that provides the legal basis to the above treatment and the date on which it will become effective.

根拠法令
Applicable law____________________　効力を生じる日 Effective date________ 年　月　日

7　日本の税法上、届出書の「2」の団体の構成員が納税義務者とされるが、租税条約の規定によりその団体の所得として取り扱われるものに対して租税条約の適用を受けることとされている場合の記載事項等（注5）；
Details if, while the partner of the entity mentioned in 2 above is taxable under Japanese tax law, and the convention is applicable to income that is treated as income of the entity in accordance with the provisions of the convention (Note 5)

他の全ての構成員から通知を受けこの届出書を提出する構成員の氏名又は名称____________________
Full name of the partner of the entity who has been notified by all other partners and is to submit this form

届出書の「2」に記載した団体が支払を受ける「4」の使用料について、「1」の租税条約の相手国の法令に基づきその団体の所得として取り扱われる場合には、その根拠法令及びその効力を生じる日を記載してください。
If royalties mentioned in 4 above that an entity at mentioned in 2 above receives are treated as income of the entity under the law in the other contracting country of the convention mentioned in 1 above, enter the law that provides the legal basis to the above treatment and the date on which it will become effective.

根拠法令
Applicable law____________________　効力を生じる日 Effective date________ 年　月　日

○　代理人に関する事項　；　この届出書を代理人によって提出する場合には、次の欄に記載してください。
Details of the Agent　；　If this form is prepared and submitted by the Agent, fill out the following columns.

代理人の資格 Capacity of Agent in Japan	氏名（名称） Full name		納税管理人の届出をした税務署名 Name of the Tax Office where the Tax Agent is registered
□ 納税管理人 ※ Tax Agent □ その他の代理人 Other Agent	住所（居所・所在地） Domicile (Residence or location)	（電話番号 Telephone Number）	税務署 Tax Office

※「納税管理人」とは、日本国の国税に関する申告、申請、請求、届出、納付等の事項を処理させるため、国税通則法の規定により選任し、かつ、日本国における納税地の所轄税務署長に届出をした代理人をいいます。

※ "Tax Agent" means a person who is appointed by the taxpayer and is registered at the District Director of Tax Office for the place where the taxpayer is to pay his tax, in order to have such agent take necessary procedures concerning the Japanese national taxes, such as filing a return, applications, claims, payment of taxes, etc., under the provisions of Act on General Rules for National Taxes.

○　適用を受ける租税条約が特典条項を有する租税条約である場合；
If the applicable convention has article of limitation on benefits
特典条項に関する付表の添付　□有Yes
"Attachment Form for Limitation on Benefits Article" attached　□添付省略Attachment not required
（特典条項に関する付表を添付して提出した租税条約に関する届出書の提出日　年　月　日）
Date of previous submission of the application for income tax convention with the "Attachment Form for Limitation on Benefits Article"

[租税条約に関する源泉徴収税額の還付請求書・様式11]

様式 11
FORM

税務署受付印

租税条約に関する源泉徴収税額の還付請求書

（発行時に源泉徴収の対象となる割引債及び芸能人等の役務提供事業の対価に係るものを除く。）

APPLICATION FORM FOR REFUND OF THE OVERPAID WITHHOLDING TAX OTHER THAN REDEMPTION OF SECURITIES WHICH ARE SUBJECT TO WITHHOLDING TAX AT THE TIME OF ISSUE AND REMUNERATION DERIVED FROM RENDERING PERSONAL SERVICES EXERCISED BY AN ENTERTAINER OR A SPORTSMAN IN ACCORDANCE WITH THE INCOME TAX CONVENTION

この還付請求書の記載に当たっては、裏面の注意事項を参照してください。
See instructions on the reverse side.

（税務署整理欄 For official use only）

通信日付印	・　・
確認	
還付金；有、無	

番号確認		身元確認	

＿＿＿＿税務署長殿
To the District Director, ＿＿＿＿＿＿ Tax Office

1　還付の請求をする者（所得の支払を受ける者）に関する事項；
Details of the Person claiming the Refund (Recipient of Income)

フリガナ Furigana 氏名又は名称（注5） Full name (Note 5)	（納税者番号 Taxpayer Identification Number）
住所（居所）又は本店（主たる事務所）の所在地 Domicile (residence) or Place of head office (main office)	（電話番号 Telephone Number）
個人番号又は法人番号（有する場合のみ記入） Individual Number or Corporate Number (Limited to case of a holder)	

2　還付請求金額に関する事項；
Details of Refund

(1) 還付を請求する還付金の種類；（該当する下記の条項の□欄に✓印を付してください（注6）。）
Kind of Refund claimed; (Check applicable box below (Note 6).)

租税条約等の実施に伴う所得税法、法人税法及び地方税法の特例等に関する法律の施行に関する省令第15条第1項
Ministerial Ordinance of the Implementation of the Law concerning the Special Measures of the Income Tax Act, the Corporation Tax Act and the Local Tax Act for the Enforcement of Income Tax Conventions, paragraph 1 of Article15 ……………………

- □第1号 (Subparagraph 1)
- □第3号 (Subparagraph 3)
- □第5号 (Subparagraph 5)
- □第7号 (Subparagraph 7)

に掲げる還付金
Refund in accordance with the relevant subparagraph

(2) 還付を請求する金額；
Amount of Refund claimed　¥　　　円

(3) 還付金の受領場所等に関する希望；（該当する下記の□欄に✓印を付し、次の欄にその受領を希望する場所を記入してください。）
Options for receiving your refund; (Check the applicable box below and enter your information in the corresponding fields.)

受取希望場所 Receipt by transfer to:	銀行 Bank	支店 Branch	預金種類及び口座番号又は記号番号 Type of account and account number	口座名義人 Name of account holder
□ 日本国内の預金口座 a Japanese bank account				
□ 日本国外の預金口座(注7) a bank account outside Japan(Note 7)				
	支店住所(国名、都市名) Branch Address (Country ,City):		銀行コード(Bank Code)	送金通貨(Currency)
□ ゆうちょ銀行の貯金口座 an ordinary savings account at the Japan Post Bank		―		
□ 郵便局等の窓口受取りを希望する場合 the Japan Post Bank or the post office (receipt in person)			―	―

3　支払者に関する事項；
Details of Payer

氏名又は名称 Full name	
住所（居所）又は本店（主たる事務所）の所在地 Domicile (residence) or Place of head office (main office)	（電話番号 Telephone Number）
個人番号又は法人番号（有する場合のみ記入） Individual Number or Corporate Number (Limited to case of a holder)	

4　源泉徴収義務者の証明事項；
Items to be certified by the withholding agent

(1) 所得の種類 Kind of Income	(2) 所得の支払期日 Due Date for Payment	(3) 所得の支払金額 Amount paid	(4)(3)の支払金額から源泉徴収した税額 Withholding Tax on (3)	(5)(4)の税額の納付年月日 Date of Payment of (4)	(6)租税条約を適用した場合に源泉徴収すべき税額 Tax Amount to be withheld under Tax Convention	(7)還付を受けるべき金額 Amount to be refunded ((4)−(6))
		円 yen	円 yen		円 yen	円 yen

上記の所得の支払金額につき、上記のとおり所得税及び復興特別所得税を徴収し、納付したことを証明します。
I hereby certify that the tax has been withheld and paid as shown above.

年　月　日
Date＿＿＿＿＿＿＿＿＿＿
源泉徴収義務者
Certifier of withholding agent ＿＿＿＿＿＿＿＿＿＿

【裏面に続きます (Continue on the reverse) 】

○ 代理人に関する事項 ；この届出書を代理人によって提出する場合には、次の欄に記載してください。
Details of the Agent ; If this form is prepared and submitted by the Agent, fill out the following columns.

代理人の資格 Capacity of Agent in Japan	氏名（名称） Full name		納税管理人の届出をした税務署名 Name of the Tax Office where the Tax Agent is registered
□ 納税管理人 ※ Tax Agent □ その他の代理人 Other Agent	住所（居所・所在地） Domicile (Residence or location)	（電話番号 Telephone Number）	税務署 Tax Office

※ 「納税管理人」については、「租税条約に関する届出書」の裏面の説明を参照してください。

※ "Tax Agent" is explained on the reverse side of the "Application Form for Income Tax Convention".

注 意 事 項

還付請求書の提出について

1 この還付請求書は、還付を請求する税額の源泉徴収をされた所得の支払者（租税特別措置法第９条の３の２第１項に規定する利子等の支払の取扱者を含みます。以下同じです。）ごとに作成してください。

2 この還付請求書は、上記１の所得につき租税条約の規定の適用を受けるための別に定める様式（様式１～様式３、様式６～様式10及び様式19）による「租税条約に関する届出書」（その届出書に付表や書類を添付して提出することとされているときは、それらも含みます。）とともに、それぞれ正副２通を作成して所得の支払者に提出し、所得の支払者は還付請求書の「４」の欄の記載事項について証明をした後、還付請求書及び租税条約に関する届出書の正本をその支払者の所轄税務署長に提出してください。

3 この還付請求書を納税管理人以外の代理人によって提出する場合には、その委任関係を証する委任状をその翻訳文とともに添付してください。

4 この還付請求書による還付金を代理人によって受領することを希望する場合には、還付請求書にその旨を記載してください。この場合、その代理人が納税管理人以外の代理人であるときは、その委任関係を証する委任状をその翻訳文とともに添付してください。

還付請求書の記載について

5 納税者番号とは、租税の申告、納付その他の手続を行うために用いる番号、記号その他の符号でその手続をすべき者を特定することができるものをいいます。支払を受ける者の居住地である国に納税者番号に関する制度が存在しない場合や支払を受ける者が納税者番号を有しない場合には納税者番号を記載する必要はありません。

6 還付請求書の「2(1)」の条項の区分は、次のとおりです。

□第１号…… 租税条約の規定の適用を受ける人的役務の対価としての給与その他の報酬を２以上の支払者から支払を受けるため、その報酬につき「租税条約に関する届出書」を提出できなかったこと又は免税の金額基準が設けられている租税条約の規定の適用を受ける株主等対価の支払を受けるため、その対価につき「租税条約に関する届出書」を提供できなかったことに基因して源泉徴収をされた税額について還付の請求をする場合

□第３号…… 第１号及び第５号以外の場合で、租税条約の規定の適用を受ける所得につき「租税条約に関する届出書」を提出しなかったことに基因して源泉徴収をされた税額について還付の請求をする場合

□第５号…… 特定社会保険料を支払った又は控除される場合において、当該給与又は報酬につき源泉徴収をされた税額について還付の請求をする場合

□第７号…… 租税条約の規定が遡及して適用されることとなったため、当該租税条約の効力発生前に支払を受けた所得につき既に源泉徴収をされた税額について還付の請求をする場合

7 受取希望場所を「日本国外の預金口座」とした場合は、銀行コード（SWIFT コード、ABA ナンバー等）を記載し、送金通貨を指定してください。
なお、欧州向けの場合は、口座番号欄に IBAN コードを記載してください。

INSTRUCTIONS

Submission of the FORM

1 This form must be prepared separately for each Payer of Income who withheld the tax to be refunded(including Person in charge of handling payment of Interrest or other payment who prescribed in paragraph 1 of Article 9-3-2 of the Act on Special Measures Concerning Taxation; the same applies below).

2 Submit this form in duplicate to the Payer of Income concerned together with the "Application Form for Income Tax Convention" (Forms 1 to 3, 6 to 10 and 19) prepared in duplicate for the application of Income Tax Convention to Income of 1 above (including attachment forms or documents if such attachment and documents are required). The Payer of the Income must certify the item in 4 on this form and then file the original of each form with the District Director of Tax Office for the place where the Payer resides.

3 An Agent other than the Tax Agent must attach a power of attorney together with its Japanese translation.

4 The applicants who wishes to receive refund through an Agent must state so on this form. If the Agent is an Agent other than a Tax Agent, a power of attorney must be attached together with its Japanese translation.

Completion of the FORM

5 The Taxpayer Identification Number is a number, code or symbol which is used for filing of return and payment of due amount and other procedures regarding tax, and which identifies a person who must take such procedures. If a system of Taxpayer Identification Number does not exist in the country where the recipient resides, or if the recipient of the payment does not have a Taxpayer Identification Number, it is not necessary to enter the Taxpayer Identification Number.

6 The distinction of the provisions of the item 2 (1) on this form is as follows:

□Subpara.1… For the refund of tax on salary or other remuneration for personal services withheld to the benefits of the Income Tax Convention which was withheld due to the failure to file the "Application Form for Income Tax Convention" because there are more than two Payers of Income. Alternatively, regarding the payment of stockholder value entitled according to the benefits of the Income Tax Convention, which provides an exemption amounts standard, the failure to file the "Application Form for Income Tax Convention" for the value.

□Subpara.3… For the refund of tax on income entitled to the benefits of the Income Tax Convention which was withheld due to the failure to file the "Application Form for Income Tax Convention" in cases other thanSubpara.1 and Subpara.5.

□Subpara.5… For the refund of tax which was withheld at the source from wages or remuneration with which designated insurance premiums were paid or from which said premiums are deducted.

□Subpara.7… For the refund of tax withheld on income paid before the coming into effect of Income Tax Convention when the Convention became applicable retroactively.

7 If you designate a "bank account outside Japan" as the place to receive of your choice, enter the bank code (Swift code, ABA number, etc.) and specify a currency for remittance.
In the case of accounts in Europe, enter IBAN code in the column for the account number.

様 式 17-米
FORM 17-US

特 典 条 項 に 関 す る 付 表 (米)

ATTACHMENT FORM FOR LIMITATION ON BENEFITS ARTICLE (US)

記載に当たっては、別紙の注意事項を参照してください。
See separate instructions.

1 適用を受ける租税条約の特典条項に関する事項；
Limitation on Benefits Article of applicable Income Tax Convention
日本国とアメリカ合衆国との間の租税条約第22条
The Income Tax Convention between Japan and The United States of America, Article 22

2 この付表に記載される者の氏名又は名称；
Full name of Resident this attachment Form

	居住地国の権限ある当局が発行した居住者証明書を添付してください(注5)。 Attach Residency Certification issued by Competent Authority of Country of residence. (Note 5)

3 租税条約の特典条項の要件に関する事項；
AからCの順番に各項目の「□該当」又は「□非該当」の該当する項目に✓印を付してください。いずれかの項目に「該当」する場合には、それ以降の項目に記入する必要はありません。なお、該当する項目については、各項目ごとの要件に関する事項を記入の上、必要な書類を添付してください。(注6)
In order of sections A, B and C , check applicable box "Yes" or "No" in each line. If you check any box of "Yes", in section A to C, you need not fill the lines that follow. Applicable lines must be filled and necessary document must be attached. (Note6)

A

(1) 個人 Individual　□該当 Yes , □非該当 No

(2) 国、地方政府又は地方公共団体、中央銀行
Contracting Country, any Political Subdivision or Local Authority, Central Bank　□該当 Yes , □非該当 No

(3) 公開会社(注7) Publicly Traded Company (Note 7)　□該当 Yes , □非該当 No
(公開会社には、下表のC欄が6%未満である会社を含みません。)(注8)
("Publicly traded Company" does not include a Company for which the Figure in Column C below is less than 6%.)(Note 8)

株式の種類 Kind of Share	公認の有価証券市場の名称 Recognized Stock Exchange	シンボル又は証券コード Ticker Symbol or Security Code	発行済株式の総数の平均 Average Number of Shares outstanding	有価証券市場で取引された株式の数 Number of Shares traded on Recognized Stock Exchange	B/A(%)
			A	B	C %

(4) 公開会社の関連会社 Subsidiary of Publicly Traded Company　□該当 Yes , □非該当 No
(発行済株式の総数(______株)の 50%以上が上記(3)の公開会社に該当する5以下の法人により直接又は間接に所有されているものに限ります。)(注9)。
("Subsidiary of Publicly Traded Company" is limited to a company at least 50% of whose shares outstanding (______shares) are owned directly or indirectly by 5 or fewer "Publicly Traded Companies" as defined in (3) above.)(Note 9)
___年___月___日現在の株主の状況 State of Shareholders as of (date)___/___/___

株主の名称 Name of Shareholder(s)	居住地国における納税地 Place where Shareholder is taxable in Country of residence	公認の有価証券市場 Recognized Stock Exchange	シンボル又は証券コード Ticker Symbol or Security Code	間接保有 Indirect Ownership	所有株式数 Number of Shares owned
1				□	
2				□	
3				□	
4				□	
5				□	
合　計 Total (持株割合 Ratio (%) of Shares owned)					(%)

(5) 公益団体(注10) Public Service Organization (Note 10)　□該当 Yes , □非該当 No
設立の根拠法令 Law for Establishment　設立の目的 Purpose of Establishment

(6) 年金基金(注11) Pension Fund (Note 11)　□該当 Yes , □非該当 No
(直前の課税年度の終了の日においてその受益者、構成員又は参加者の 50%を超える者が日本又はアメリカ合衆国の居住者である個人であるものに限ります。受益者等の50%超が、両締約国の居住者である事情を記入してください。)
"Pension Fund" is limited to one more than 50% of whose beneficiaries, members, or participants were individual residents of Japan or the United States of America as of the end of the prior taxable year. Provide below details showing that more than 50% of beneficiaries etc. are individual residents of either contracting country.

設立等の根拠法令 Law for Establishment　非課税の根拠法令 Law for Tax Exemption

Aのいずれにも該当しない場合は、Bに進んでください。If none of the lines in A applies, proceed to B.

B

次の(a)及び(b)の要件のいずれも満たす個人以外の者 Person other than an Individual, and satisfying both (a) and (b) below　□該当 Yes, □非該当 No

(a) 株式や受益に関する持分(＿＿＿＿＿＿)の 50%以上が、Aの(1)、(2)、(3)、(5)及び(6)に該当する日本又はアメリカ合衆国の居住者により直接又は間接に所有されていること(注 12)
Residents of Japan or the United States of America who fall under (1),(2),(3),(5) or (6) of A own directly or indirectly at least 50% of Shares or other beneficial Interests (＿＿＿＿＿＿) in the Person. (Note 12)
＿年＿月＿日現在の株主等の状況 State of Shareholders, etc. as of (date)＿＿/＿＿/＿＿

株主等の氏名又は名称 Name of Shareholders	居住地国における納税地 Place where Shareholders is taxable in Country of residence	Aの番号 Number of applicable Line in A	間接所有 Indirect Ownership	株主等の持分 Number of Shares owned
			□	
			□	
			□	
合　計 Total (持分割合 Ratio(%) of Shares owned)				(%)

(b) 総所得のうち、課税所得の計算上控除される支出により、日本又はアメリカ合衆国の居住者に該当しない者（以下「第三国居住者」といいます。）に対し直接又は間接に支払われる金額が、50%未満であること(注 13)
Less than 50% of the person's gross income is paid or accrued directly or indirectly to persons who are not residents of Japan or the United States of America ("third country residents") in the form of payments that are deductible in computing taxable income in country of residence (Note 13)
第三国居住者に対する支払割合　Ratio of Payment to Third Country Residents　(通貨 Currency:　　　)

	申告 Tax Return	源泉徴収税額 Withholding Tax		
	当該課税年度 Taxable Year	前々々課税年度 Taxable Year three Years prior	前々課税年度 Taxable Year two Years prior	前課税年度 Prior taxable Year
第三国居住者に対する支払 Payment to third Country Residents	A			
総所得 Gross Income	B			
A/B (%)	C %	%	%	%

Bに該当しない場合は、Cに進んでください。If B does not apply, proceed to C.

C

次の(a)から(c)の要件を全て満たす者 Resident satisfying all of the following Conditions from (a) through (c)　□該当 Yes, □非該当 No
居住地国において従事している営業又は事業の活動の概要(注 14) ; Description of trade or business in residence country (Note 14)

(a) 居住地国において従事している営業又は事業の活動が、自己の勘定のために投資を行い又は管理する活動（商業銀行、保険会社又は登録を受けた証券会社が行う銀行業、保険業又は証券業の活動を除きます。）ではないこと(注 15)：　□はい Yes, □いいえ No
Trade or business in country of residence is other than that of making or managing investments for the resident's own account (unless these activities are banking, insurance or securities activities carried on by a commercial bank, insurance company or registered securities dealer) (Note 15)　□はい Yes, □いいえ No

(b) 所得が居住地国において従事している営業又は事業の活動に関連又は付随して取得されるものであること(注 16)：
Income is derived in connection with or is incidental to that trade or business in country of residence (Note 16)

(c) （日本国内において営業又は事業の活動から所得を取得する場合）居住地国において行う営業又は事業の活動が日本国内において行う営業又は事業の活動との関係で実質的なものであること(注 17)：　□はい Yes, □いいえ No
(If you derive income from a trade or business activity in Japan) Trade or business activity carried on in the country of residence is substantial in relation to the trade or business activity carried on in Japan. (Note 17)

日本国内において従事している営業又は事業の活動の概要 ; Description of Trade or Business in Japan.

D　国税庁長官の認定(注 18)；
Determination by the NTA Commissioner (Note18)
国税庁長官の認定を受けている場合は、以下にその内容を記載してください。その認定の範囲内で租税条約の特典を受けることができます。なお、上記AからCまでのいずれかに該当する場合には、原則として、国税庁長官の認定は不要です。
If you have been a determination by the NTA Commissioner, describe below the determination. Convention benefits will be granted to the extent of the determination. If any of the above mentioned Lines A through to C are applicable, then in principle, determination by the NTA Commissioner is not necessary.

・認定を受けた日　Date of determination　＿＿年＿＿月＿＿日
・認定を受けた所得の種類
Type of income for which determination was given＿＿＿＿＿＿

演習事例22

租税条約に基づく還付請求をする場合の留意点

当社は、A国のB社との間でソフトウエアのライセンス契約を締結し、使用料の支払をしておりましたが、この度の税務調査において、源泉徴収の課税もれを指摘されました。

追徴された源泉所得税（税率20.42%）については当社が立替払いします。A国との間の租税条約によれば、税率が10%に軽減されることから、使用料の支払後ではありますが、B社に「租税条約の届出書」を当社の所轄の税務署長に提出させることにより税額の軽減を受けることができるのでしょうか。

また、税額の軽減を受けることができる場合、追徴された源泉所得税（税率20.42%）と軽減税率10%適用後の源泉所得税との差額は、税務署から当社に直接還付されるのでしょうか。

ご教示をお願いします。

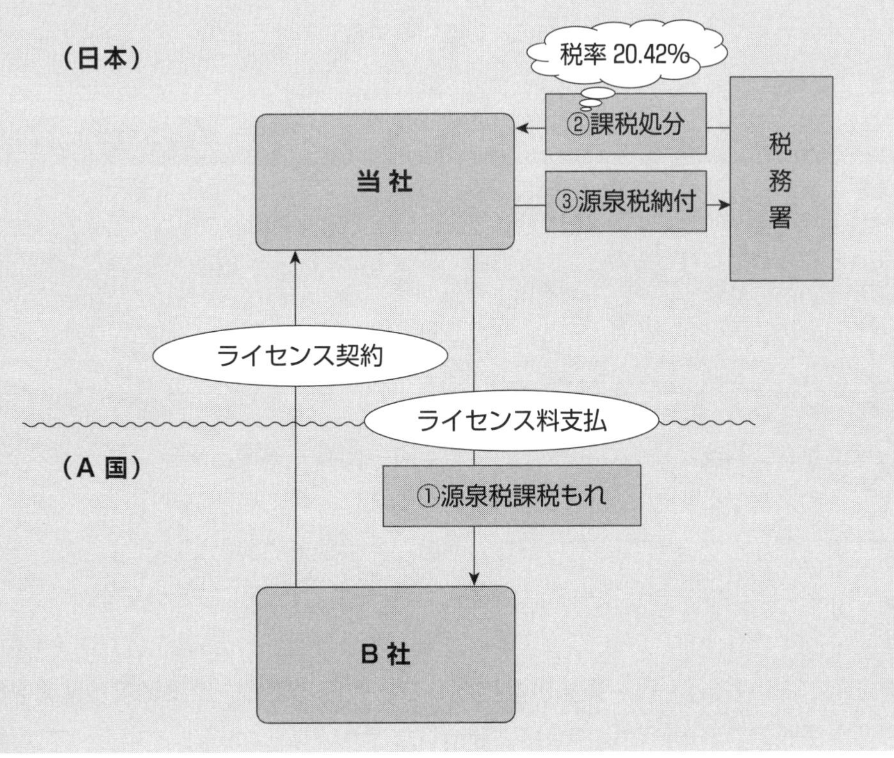

回答

1　B社は「租税条約の届出書」を提出することより税率は10%に軽減することができ

ます。

2　追徴された源泉所得税（税率20.42%）と軽減税率10%適用後の源泉所得税との差額は、税務署から租税条約の適用を受けるB社に還付されますので、貴社が立替払いした源泉所得税としてB社から還付を受けることになります。

解説

1　租税条約による軽減税率の適用について

租税条約を国内の課税上運用する法律として「租税条約の実施に伴う所得税、法人税法及び地方税法の特例等に関する法律」（以下「実特例法」といいます。）があります。

実特例法によりますと、使用料に対する税率は所得税法による税率20.42%から租税条約で定める限度税率に置き換えることとしています。

（実特例法２五・３の２①）

実特例法第２条⑤（限度税率）
限度税率とは、租税条約において相手国居住者等に対する課税につき一定の税率又は一定の割合で計算した金額を超えないものとしている場合におけるその一定の税率又は一定の割合をいう。

実特例法第３条の２①（税率の置換え）
相手国居住者等が支払を受ける配当等のうち、当該相手国居住者等に係る相手国等との間の租税条約の規定において、当該相手国等においてその法令に基づき当該相手国居住者等の所得として取り扱われるものとされるものであって限度税率を定める当該租税条約の規定の適用があるものに対する………の適用については、当該限度税率が等が当該配当等に適用されるこれらの税率以上である場合を除き、これらの税率に代えて、当該租税条約の規定により当該配当等につきそれぞれ適用される限度税率によるものとする。

2　ライセンス料支払後の「租税条約に関する届出書」の提出

租税条約に基づく軽減・免除の届出書については、実特例法第12条（実施規定）において「第二条から前条までに定めるもののほか、租税条約等の実施及びこの法律の適用に関し必要な事項は、総務省令、財務省令で定める。」と規定しています。

上記の規定を受けて租税条約に基づく軽減・免除の届出書については実特例法の省令第２条①において、**「………支払いを受ける日の前日までに、源泉徴収義務者を経由して、源泉徴収義務者の所轄税務署長に提出しなければならない。」**と規定しています。

したがって、「租税条約に関する届出書」を提出しない場合には、支払の際に、20.42%の税率により、源泉徴収されることになります。

その後、租税条約による軽減・免除を受けるには、「租税条約に関する届出書」を後日、提出することにより、源泉徴収税額（20.42%）と限度税率（10%）の差額又は源泉徴収税額（20.42%）の還付を受けることができます。（実特令⑧）

3　源泉所得税の還付手続きと還付先

調査により追徴課税された源泉所得税は、Ａ国のＢ社が貴社経由で貴社の所轄税務署長に対し**「租税条約に関する届出書」（様式３）**、**「租税条約に関する源泉徴収税額の還付請求書」（様式11）**及び**その他必要資料**を提出し、還付の請求を行うことができます。

源泉所得税は、Ａ国のＢ社に対して還付されます。

［還付手続きと還付の流れ］

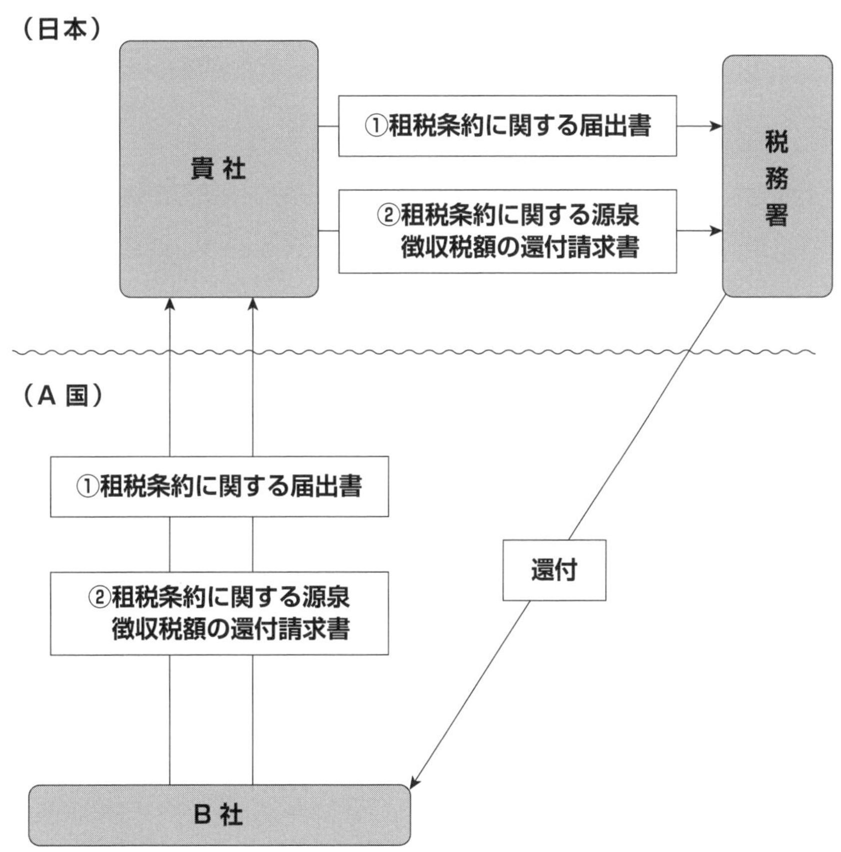

[租税条約に関する届出書（使用料等）・様式3]

様式3
FORM

租税条約に関する届出書
APPLICATION FORM FOR INCOME TAX CONVENTION

（使用料に対する所得税及び復興特別所得税の軽減・免除
Relief from Japanese Income Tax and Special Income Tax for Reconstruction on Royalties）

この届出書の記載に当たっては、別紙の注意事項を参照してください。
See separate instructions.

税務署受付印

（税務署整理欄 For official use only）

適用；有、無

番号確認		身元確認	

□ 限度税率＿＿％ Applicable Tax Rate
□ 免　税（注11） Exemption (Note 11)

＿＿＿＿税務署長殿
To the District Director, ＿＿＿＿Tax Office

1 適用を受ける租税条約に関する事項；
Applicable Income Tax Convention
日本国と＿＿＿＿との間の租税条約第＿＿条第＿＿項＿＿
The Income Tax Convention between Japan and＿＿＿＿, Article＿＿, para.＿＿

2 使用料の支払を受ける者に関する事項；
Details of Recipient of Royalties

氏名又は名称 Full name		
個人番号又は法人番号（有する場合のみ記入） Individual Number or Corporate Number (Limited to case of a holder)		
個人の場合 Individual	住所又は居所 Domicile or residence	（電話番号 Telephone Number）
	国籍 Nationality	
法人その他の団体の場合 Corporation or other entity	本店又は主たる事務所の所在地 Place of head office or main office	（電話番号 Telephone Number）
	設立又は組織された場所 Place where the Corporation was established or organized	
	事業が管理・支配されている場所 Place where the business is managed and controlled	（電話番号 Telephone Number）
下記「4」の使用料につき居住者として課税される国及び納税地（注8） Country where the recipient is taxable as resident on Royalties mentioned in 4 below and the place where he is to pay tax (Note 8)		（納税者番号 Taxpayer Identification Number）
日本国内の恒久的施設の状況 Permanent establishment in Japan □有(Yes)，□無(No) If "Yes", explain:	名称 Name	
	所在地 Address	（電話番号 Telephone Number）
	事業の内容 Details of Business	

3 使用料の支払者に関する事項；
Details of Payer of Royalties

氏名又は名称 Full name		
住所（居所）又は本店（主たる事務所）の所在地 Domicile (residence) or Place of head office (main office)		（電話番号 Telephone Number）
個人番号又は法人番号（有する場合のみ記入） Individual Number or Corporate Number (Limited to case of a holder)		
日本国内にある事務所等 Office, etc. located in Japan	名称 Name	（事業の内容 Details of Business）
	所在地 Address	（電話番号 Telephone Number）

4 上記「3」の支払者から支払を受ける使用料で「1」の租税条約の規定の適用を受けるものに関する事項（注9）；
Details of Royalties received from the Payer to which the Convention mentioned in 1 above is applicable (Note 9)

使用料の内容 Description of Royalties	契約の締結年月日 Date of Contract	契約期間 Period of Contract	使用料の計算方法 Method of Computation for Royalties	使用料の支払期日 Due Date for Payment	使用料の金額 Amount of Royalties

5 その他参考となるべき事項（注10）；
Others (Note 10)

【裏面に続きます（Continue on the reverse）】

6　日本の税法上、届出書の「2」の外国法人が納税義務者とされるが、租税条約の規定によりその株主等である者（相手国居住者に限ります。）の所得として取り扱われる部分に対して租税条約の適用を受けることとされている場合の租税条約の適用を受ける割合に関する事項等（注4）；
Details of proportion of income to which the convention mentioned in 1 above is applicable, if the foreign company mentioned in 2 above is taxable as a company under Japanese tax law, and the convention is applicable to income that is treated as income of the member (limited to a resident of the other contracting country) of the foreign company in accordance with the provisions of the convention (Note 4)

届出書の「2」の外国法人の株主等で租税条約の適用を受ける者の氏名又は名称 Name of member of the foreign company mentioned in 2 above, to whom the Convention is applicable	間接保有 Indirect Ownership	持分の割合 Ratio of Ownership	受益の割合＝租税条約の適用を受ける割合 Proportion of benefit = Proportion for Application of Convention
	□	%	%
	□	%	%
	□	%	%
	□	%	%
	□	%	%
合計 Total		%	%

届出書の「2」の欄に記載した外国法人が支払を受ける「4」の使用料について、「1」の租税条約の相手国の法令に基づきその株主等である者の所得として取り扱われる場合には、その根拠法令及びその効力を生じる日を記載してください。
If royalties mentioned in 4 above that a foreign company mentioned in 2 above receives are treated as income of those who are its members under the law in the other contracting country of the convention mentioned in 1 above, enter the law that provides the legal basis to the above treatment and the date on which it will become effective.

根拠法令
Applicable law＿＿＿＿＿＿＿＿＿＿　効力を生じる日　年　月　日
Effective date＿＿＿＿＿＿＿＿

7　日本の税法上、届出書の「2」の団体の構成員が納税義務者とされるが、租税条約の規定によりその団体の所得として取り扱われるものに対して租税条約の適用を受けることとされている場合の記載事項等（注5）；
Details if, while the partner of the entity mentioned in 2 above is taxable under Japanese tax law, and the convention is applicable to income that is treated as income of the entity in accordance with the provisions of the convention (Note 5)

他の全ての構成員から通知を受けこの届出書を提出する構成員の氏名又は名称＿＿＿＿＿＿＿＿＿＿
Full name of the partner of the entity who has been notified by all other partners and is to submit this form

届出書の「2」に記載した団体が支払を受ける「4」の使用料について、「1」の租税条約の相手国の法令に基づきその団体の所得として取り扱われる場合には、その根拠法令及びその効力を生じる日を記載してください。
If royalties mentioned in 4 above that an entity at mentioned in 2 above receives are treated as income of the entity under the law in the other contracting country of the convention mentioned in 1 above, enter the law that provides the legal basis to the above treatment and the date on which it will become effective.

根拠法令
Applicable law＿＿＿＿＿＿＿＿＿＿　効力を生じる日　年　月　日
Effective date＿＿＿＿＿＿＿＿

○　代理人に関する事項　；　この届出書を代理人によって提出する場合には、次の欄に記載してください。
Details of the Agent　;　If this form is prepared and submitted by the Agent, fill out the following columns.

代理人の資格 Capacity of Agent in Japan	氏名（名称） Full name		納税管理人の届出をした税務署名 Name of the Tax Office where the Tax Agent is registered
□ 納税管理人 ※ Tax Agent □ その他の代理人 Other Agent	住所（居所・所在地） Domicile (Residence or location)	(電話番号 Telephone Number)	税務署 Tax Office

※　「納税管理人」とは、日本国の国税に関する申告、申請、請求、届出、納付等の事項を処理させるため、国税通則法の規定により選任し、かつ、日本国における納税地の所轄税務署長に届出をした代理人をいいます。

※ "Tax Agent" means a person who is appointed by the taxpayer and is registered at the District Director of Tax Office for the place where the taxpayer is to pay his tax, in order to have such agent take necessary procedures concerning the Japanese national taxes, such as filing a return, applications, claims, payment of taxes, etc., under the provisions of Act on General Rules for National Taxes.

○　適用を受ける租税条約が特典条項を有する租税条約である場合；
If the applicable convention has article of limitation on benefits

特典条項に関する付表の添付　□有Yes
"Attachment Form for Limitation on Benefits Article" attached　□添付省略Attachment not required
（特典条項に関する付表を添付して提出した租税条約に関する届出書の提出日　年　月　日）
Date of previous submission of the application for income tax convention with the "Attachment Form for Limitation on Benefits Article"

[租税条約に関する源泉徴収税額の還付請求書・様式11]

様　式　11
FORM

租税条約に関する源泉徴収税額の還付請求書

（発行時に源泉徴収の対象となる割引債及び芸能人等の役務提供事業の対価に係るものを除く。）

APPLICATION FORM FOR REFUND OF THE OVERPAID WITHHOLDING TAX OTHER THAN REDEMPTION OF SECURITIES WHICH ARE SUBJECT TO WITHHOLDING TAX AT THE TIME OF ISSUE AND REMUNERATION DERIVED FROM RENDERING PERSONAL SERVICES EXERCISED BY AN ENTERTAINER OR A SPORTSMAN IN ACCORDANCE WITH THE INCOME TAX CONVENTION

この還付請求書の記載に当たっては、裏面の注意事項を参照してください。
See instructions on the reverse side.

税務署受付印

（税務署整理欄 For official use only）

通信日付印	・　・
確認	
還付金；有、無	

番号確認		身元確認	

＿＿＿＿＿税務署長殿
To the District Director, ＿＿＿＿＿＿ Tax Office

1　還付の請求をする者（所得の支払を受ける者）に関する事項；
Details of the Person claiming the Refund (Recipient of Income)

フリガナ Furigana 氏名又は名称（注5） Full name (Note 5)	（納税者番号 Taxpayer Identification Number）
住所（居所）又は本店（主たる事務所）の所在地 Domicile (residence) or Place of head office (main office)	（電話番号 Telephone Number）
個人番号又は法人番号（有する場合のみ記入） Individual Number or Corporate Number (Limited to case of a holder)	

2　還付請求金額に関する事項；
Details of Refund

(1)　還付を請求する還付金の種類；（該当する下記の条項の□欄に✓印を付してください（注6）。）
Kind of Refund claimed; (Check applicable box below (Note 6).)

租税条約等の実施に伴う所得税法、法人税法及び地方税法の特例等に関する法律の施行に関する省令第15条第1項
Ministerial Ordinance of the Implementation of the Law concerning the Special Measures of the Income Tax Act, the Corporation Tax Act and the Local Tax Act for the Enforcement of Income Tax Conventions, paragraph 1 of Article15 ……………………

- □第1号(Subparagraph 1)
- □第3号(Subparagraph 3)
- □第5号(Subparagraph 5)
- □第7号(Subparagraph 7)

に掲げる還付金
Refund in accordance with the relevant subparagraph

(2)　還付を請求する金額；
Amount of Refund claimed　［ ¥　　　　円 ］

(3)　還付金の受領場所等に関する希望；（該当する下記の□欄に✓印を付し、次の欄にその受領を希望する場所を記入してください。）
Options for receiving your refund; (Check the applicable box below and enter your information in the corresponding fields.)

受取希望場所 Receipt by transfer to:	銀行 Bank	支店 Branch	預金種類及び口座番号又は記号番号 Type of account and account number	口座名義人 Name of account holder
□ 日本国内の預金口座 a Japanese bank account				
□ 日本国外の預金口座(注7) a bank account outside Japan(Note 7)				
	支店住所(国名、都市名)Branch Address (Country ,City):		銀行コード(Bank Code)	送金通貨(Currency)
□ ゆうちょ銀行の貯金口座 an ordinary savings account at the Japan Post Bank		—		
□ 郵便局等の窓口受取りを希望する場合 the Japan Post Bank or the post office (receipt in person)			—	—

3　支払者に関する事項；
Details of Payer

氏名又は名称 Full name	
住所（居所）又は本店（主たる事務所）の所在地 Domicile (residence) or Place of head office (main office)	（電話番号 Telephone Number）
個人番号又は法人番号（有する場合のみ記入） Individual Number or Corporate Number (Limited to case of a holder)	

4　源泉徴収義務者の証明事項；
Items to be certified by the withholding agent

(1) 所得の種類 Kind of Income	(2) 所得の支払期日 Due Date for Payment	(3) 所得の支払金額 Amount paid	(4)(3)の支払金額から源泉徴収した税額 Withholding Tax on (3)	(5)(4)の税額の納付年月日 Date of Payment of (4)	(6)租税条約を適用した場合に源泉徴収すべき税額 Tax Amount to be withheld under Tax Convention	(7)還付を受けるべき金額 Amount to be refunded ((4)−(6))
		円 yen	円 yen		円 yen	円 yen

上記の所得の支払金額につき、上記のとおり所得税及び復興特別所得税を徴収し、納付したことを証明します。
I hereby certify that the tax has been withheld and paid as shown above.

年　月　日　Date＿＿＿＿＿＿＿＿　源泉徴収義務者 Certifier of withholding agent ＿＿＿＿＿＿＿＿

【裏面に続きます (Continue on the reverse) 】

○ 代理人に関する事項 ; この届出書を代理人によって提出する場合には、次の欄に記載してください。
Details of the Agent ; If this form is prepared and submitted by the Agent, fill out the following columns.

代理人の資格 Capacity of Agent in Japan	氏名（名称） Full name		納税管理人の届出をした税務署名 Name of the Tax Office where the Tax Agent is registered
□ 納税管理人 ※ Tax Agent □ その他の代理人 Other Agent	住所（居所・所在地） Domicile (Residence or location)	(電話番号 Telephone Number)	税務署 Tax Office

※ 「納税管理人」については、「租税条約に関する届出書」の裏面の説明を参照してください。

※ "Tax Agent" is explained on the reverse side of the "Application Form for Income Tax Convention".

注意事項

還付請求書の提出について

1 この還付請求書は、還付を請求する税額の源泉徴収をされた所得の支払者（租税特別措置法第9条の3の2第1項に規定する利子等の支払の取扱者を含みます。以下同じです。）ごとに作成してください。

2 この還付請求書は、上記1の所得につき租税条約の規定の適用を受けるための別に定める様式（様式1～様式3、様式6～様式10及び様式19）による「租税条約に関する届出書」（その届出書に付表や書類を添付して提出することとされているときは、それらも含みます。）とともに、それぞれ正副2通を作成して所得の支払者に提出し、所得の支払者は還付請求書の「4」の欄の記載事項について証明をした後、還付請求書及び租税条約に関する届出書の正本をその支払者の所轄税務署長に提出してください。

3 この還付請求書を納税管理人以外の代理人によって提出する場合には、その委任関係を証する委任状をその翻訳文とともに添付してください。

4 この還付請求書による還付金を代理人によって受領することを希望する場合には、還付請求書にその旨を記載してください。この場合、その代理人が納税管理人以外の代理人であるときは、その委任関係を証する委任状をその翻訳文とともに添付してください。

還付請求書の記載について

5 納税者番号とは、租税の申告、納付その他の手続を行うために用いる番号､記号その他の符号でその手続をすべき者を特定することができるものをいいます。支払を受ける者の居住地である国に納税者番号に関する制度が存在しない場合や支払を受ける者が納税者番号を有しない場合には納税者番号を記載する必要はありません。

6 還付請求書の「2(1)」の条項の区分は、次のとおりです。

□第 1 号…… 租税条約の規定の適用を受ける人的役務の対価としての給与その他の報酬を2以上の支払者から支払を受けるため、その報酬につき「租税条約に関する届出書」を提出できなかったこと又は免税の金額基準が設けられている租税条約の規定の適用を受ける株主等対価の支払を受けるため、その対価につき「租税条約に関する届出書」を提供できなかったことに基因して源泉徴収をされた税額について還付の請求をする場合

□第 3 号…… 第1号及び第5号以外の場合で、租税条約の規定の適用を受ける所得につき「租税条約に関する届出書」を提出しなかったことに基因して源泉徴収をされた税額について還付の請求をする場合

□第 5 号…… 特定社会保険料を支払った又は控除される場合において、当該給与又は報酬につき源泉徴収をされた税額について還付の請求をする場合

□第 7 号…… 租税条約の規定が遡及して適用されることとなったため、当該租税条約の効力発生前に支払を受けた所得につき既に源泉徴収をされた税額について還付の請求をする場合

7 受取希望場所を「日本国外の預金口座」とした場合は、銀行コード（SWIFT コード、ABA ナンバー等）を記載し、送金通貨を指定してください。

なお、欧州向けの場合は、口座番号欄に IBAN コードを記載してください。

INSTRUCTIONS

Submission of the FORM

1 This form must be prepared separately for each Payer of Income who withheld the tax to be refunded(including Person in charge of handling payment of Interrest or other payment who prescribed in paragraph 1 of Article 9-3-2 of the Act on Special Measures Concerning Taxation; the same applies below).

2 Submit this form in duplicate to the Payer of Income concerned together with the "Application Form for Income Tax Convention" (Forms 1 to 3, 6 to 10 and 19) prepared in duplicate for the application of Income Tax Convention to Income of 1 above (including attachment forms or documents if such attachment and documents are required). The Payer of the Income must certify the item in 4 on this form and then file the original of each form with the District Director of Tax Office for the place where the Payer resides.

3 An Agent other than the Tax Agent must attach a power of attorney together with its Japanese translation.

4 The applicants who wishes to receive refund through an Agent must state so on this form. If the Agent is an Agent other than a Tax Agent, a power of attorney must be attached together with its Japanese translation.

Completion of the FORM

5 The Taxpayer Identification Number is a number, code or symbol which is used for filing of return and payment of due amount and other procedures regarding tax, and which identifies a person who must take such procedures. If a system of Taxpayer Identification Number does not exist in the country where the recipient resides, or if the recipient of the payment does not have a Taxpayer Identification Number, it is not necessary to enter the Taxpayer Identification Number.

6 The distinction of the provisions of the item 2 (1) on this form is as follows:

□Subpara.1… For the refund of tax on salary or other remuneration for personal services withheld to the benefits of the Income Tax Convention which was withheld due to the failure to file the "Application Form for Income Tax Convention" because there are more than two Payers of Income. Alternatively, regarding the payment of stockholder value entitled according to the benefits of the Income Tax Convention, which provides an exemption amounts standard, the failure to file the "Application Form for Income Tax Convention" for the value.

□Subpara.3… For the refund of tax on income entitled to the benefits of the Income Tax Convention which was withheld due to the failure to file the "Application Form for Income Tax Convention" in cases other thanSubpara.1 and Subpara.5.

□Subpara.5… For the refund of tax which was withheld at the source from wages or remuneration with which designated insurance premiums were paid or from which said premiums are deducted.

□Subpara.7… For the refund of tax withheld on income paid before the coming into effect of Income Tax Convention when the Convention became applicable retroactively.

7 If you designate a "bank account outside Japan" as the place to receive of your choice, enter the bank code (Swift code, ABA number, etc.) and specify a currency for remittance.

In the case of accounts in Europe, enter IBAN code in the column for the account number.

演習事例23

租税条約に基づき課税の免除を受ける給与等がある場合の「法定調書」の記載方法

当社はインドネシアから日本の大学に留学している学生をアルバイトとして雇用しております。

今年の年末調整事務も終わり、現在、法定調書「給与所得の源泉徴収票」を作成中ですが、租税条約に基づき課税の免除を受けている学生については、調書の作成が必要なのでしょうか。

もし、作成が必要であれば、どのように作成するのか教えてください。

給与等が居住者に対するものであれば、インドネシアからの留学生の給与についても「給与所得の源泉徴収票」の作成は必要です。

解説

1　法定調書の作成と提出の義務

居住者に対し国内において給与等の支払をする者は「給与所得の源泉徴収票」を作成し提出しなければなりません。

（所法226①）

インドネシアからの学生は、我が国に１年以上の滞在予定で入国しますので、入国の日から居住者として取り扱われますので、その学生に給与等の支払をする者は「給与所得の源泉徴収票」を作成し提出しなければなりません。

2　免税を受ける給与等に関する「給与所得の源泉徴収票」の具体的な記載方法について

免税の適用を受ける居住者に対する給与等に関する「給与所得の源泉徴収票」の作成に際しては、「摘要」欄に免税に関する事項を記載することとされています。

（所規則別表第六(一)備考２(17)(ワ)）

国内において給与等の支払をする者は「給与所得の源泉徴収票」を次の要領で作成し提出します。

(1)　住所又は居所……「租税条約に関する届出書」を基にし外国における住所を記入

(2)　支払金額……免税所得も含めて記載

(3)　摘要……免税対象金額及び租税条約の該当条項（日〇租税条約〇〇条該当）を赤書き

令和　年分　給与所得の源泉徴収票

支払を受ける者	住所又は居所	①外国における住所	(受給者番号)
			(個人番号)
			(役職名)
		②免税対象金額も含む	(フリガナ)
			氏名

種別	支払金額	給与所得控除後の金額（調整控除後）	所得控除の額の合計額	源泉徴収税額
	内　千　円	千　円	千　円	内　千　円

(源泉)控除対象配偶者の有無等		老人	配偶者(特別)控除の額	控除対象扶養親族の数(配偶者を除く。) 特定		老人			その他		16歳未満扶養親族の数	障害者の数(本人を除く。) 特別		その他	非居住者である親族の数
有	従有		千　円	人	従人	内	人	従人	人	従人	人	内	人	人	人

社会保険料等の金額	生命保険料の控除額	地震保険料の控除額	住宅借入金等特別控除の額
内　千　円	千　円	千　円	千　円

(摘要)

③免税対象金額及び租税条約の該当条項
（日○○租税条約△△条該当）

生命保険料の金額の内訳	新生命保険料の金額	円	旧生命保険料の金額	円	介護医療保険料の金額	円	新個人年金保険料の金額	円	旧個人年金保険料の金額	円

住宅借入金等特別控除の額の内訳	住宅借入金等特別控除適用数		居住開始年月日(1回目)	年　月　日	住宅借入金等特別控除区分(1回目)		住宅借入金等年末残高(1回目)	円
	住宅借入金等特別控除可能額	円	居住開始年月日(2回目)	年　月　日	住宅借入金等特別控除区分(2回目)		住宅借入金等年末残高(2回目)	円

(源泉・特別)控除対象配偶者	(フリガナ) 氏名	区分	配偶者の合計所得	円	国民年金保険料等の金額	円	旧長期損害保険料の金額	円
	個人番号				基礎控除の額	円	所得金額調整控除額	円

控除対象扶養親族			区分	16歳未満の扶養親族			区分	(備考)
1	(フリガナ) 氏名		区分	1	(フリガナ) 氏名		区分	
	個人番号							
2	(フリガナ) 氏名		区分	2	(フリガナ) 氏名		区分	
	個人番号							
3	(フリガナ) 氏名		区分	3	(フリガナ) 氏名		区分	
	個人番号							
4	(フリガナ) 氏名		区分	4	(フリガナ) 氏名		区分	
	個人番号							

未成年者	外国人	死亡退職	災害者	乙欄	本人が障害者 特別	その他	寡婦	ひとり親	勤労学生		中途就・退職 就職	退職	年	月	日	受給者生年月日 元号	年	月	日

支払者	個人番号又は法人番号		(右詰で記載してください。)
	住所(居所)又は所在地		
	氏名又は名称		(電話)

(税務署提出用)

整理欄		

375

国際関係のトピック

租税条約に基づく情報交換協定と税務行政執行共助条約

1　情報交換協定とは

各国の税務当局との間で、主に情報交換を主体とする租税条約です。

⑴　我が国と情報交換協定を締結したタックス・ヘイブン

条約締結の状況

（締結日）		（締約国）
平成22年２月	情報交換協定（新規）	バミューダ
平成23年１月	情報交換協定（新規）	バハマ
平成23年２月	情報交換協定（新規）	ケイマン諸島
平成23年６月	情報交換協定（新規）	マン島
平成23年12月	情報交換協定（新規）	ガンジー
平成23年12月	情報交換協定（新規）	ジャージー
平成24年７月	情報交換協定（新規）	リヒテンシュタイン
平成25年６月	情報交換協定（新規）	サモア
平成26年３月	情報交換協定（新規）	マカオ
平成26年６月	情報交換協定（新規）	英領バージン諸島

⑵　情報交換協定の内容（ケイマン諸島の場合）

我が国とケイマン諸島との間では平成23年２月７日に情報交換協定が締結されており、同協定により、租税の賦課・徴収、**租税債権の回収・執行、租税事案の捜査・訴追に関連する情報等を交換**することが可能となり、また、**海外における調査の立会**も認められています。

したがって、我が国の課税当局が行う任意又は強制の税務調査において、今後は、情報交換協定の活用が予想されます。

情報交換協定のイメージ

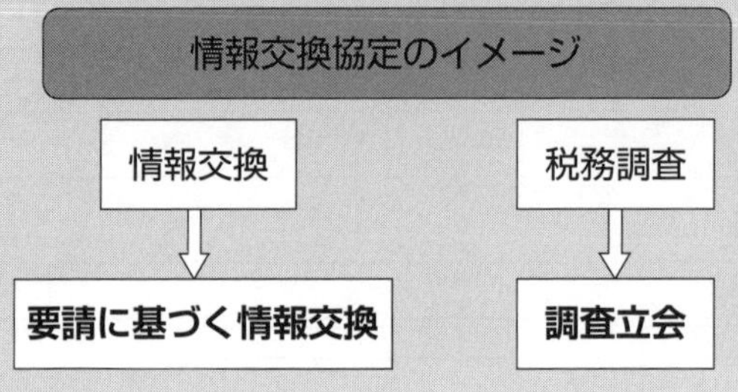

（参考） ケイマン諸島政府との間の情報交換協定

脱税の防止のための情報の交換及び個人の所得についての課税権の配分に関する日本国政府とケイマン諸島政府との間の協定（情報交換協定）

（抜粋）

第二章　情報の交換

第二条　目的及び適用範囲

両締約国の権限のある当局は、この協定の実施又は第四条に規定する租税に規定する租税に関する両締約者の法令の規定の運用及び執行に関連する情報の交換を通じて支援を行う。

そのような情報には、同条に規定する租税の決定、賦課及び徴収、租税債権の回収及び執行並びに租税事案の捜査及び訴追に関連する情報を含む。

第六条　海外における租税に関する調査

被要請者（日本国又はケイマン諸島）の権限ある当局は、要請者（日本国又はケイマン諸島）の権限ある当局の要請があったときは、被要請者における租税に関する調査の適当な部分に要請者の権限のある当局の代表者が立ち会うことを認めることができる。

2　税務行政執行共助条約とは

各国の税務当局との間で、租税に関する**行政支援（情報交換、徴収共助、送達共助）**を相互に行うための条約です。

本条約を締結することにより、国際的な脱税と租税回避に適切に対処していくことが可能であるとされています。

⑴　**共助条約の締結国数**

締結国数……55カ国

⑵　**行政支援の形態**

イ　情報交換……条約締約国間の情報交換（要請によるもの・自発的なもの・自動的なもの）と**税務同時調査、海外の調査立合**

ロ　徴収共助……租税の滞納者の資産が他の条約締約国にある場合、他の条約締約国にその**租税の徴収を依頼**すること

ハ　送達共助……租税に関する文書の名宛人が他の条約締約国にいる場合、他の条約締約国にその**文書の送達を依頼**すること

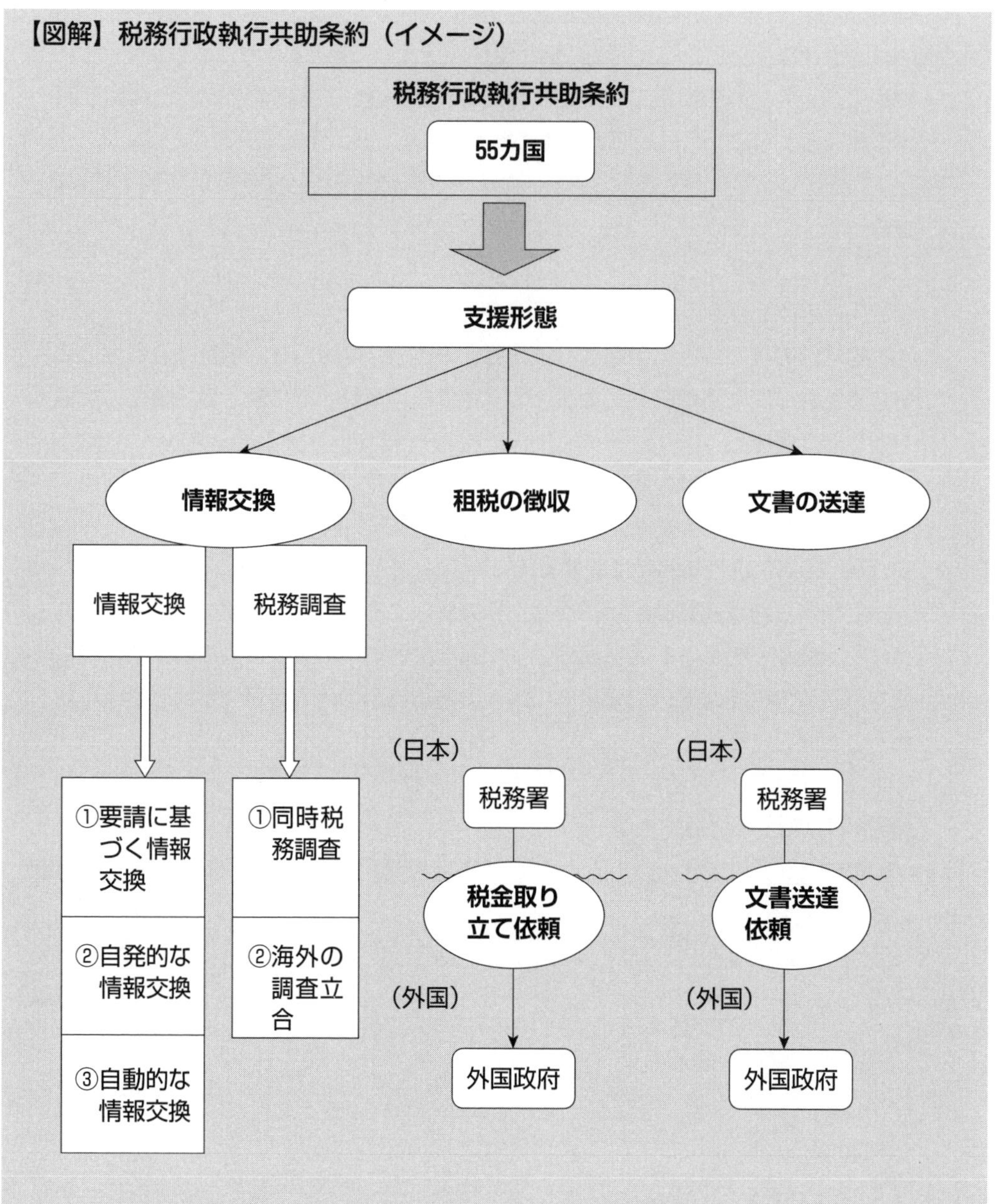
【図解】税務行政執行共助条約（イメージ）
税務行政執行共助条約
55カ国
支援形態
情報交換
租税の徴収
文書の送達
情報交換
税務調査
①要請に基づく情報交換
②自発的な情報交換
③自動的な情報交換
①同時税務調査
②海外の調査立合
（日本）
税務署
税金取り立て依頼
（外国）
外国政府
（日本）
税務署
文書送達依頼
（外国）
外国政府

租税に関する相互行政支援に関する条約の締結内容

租税に関する相互行政支援に関する条約

前文

この条約の署名国である欧州評議会の加盟国及び経済協力開発機構（OECD）の加盟国は、

人、資本、物品及びサービスの国際的な移動の進展が、それ自体は非常に有益であるが、租税回避及び脱税の可能性を高めていることから、税務当局間で一層の協力が必要であることを考慮し、

二国間であるか多数国間であるかを問わず、租税回避及び脱税に国際的に対処するため、近年様々な努力が払われていることを歓迎し、

納税者の権利の適切な保護を確保すると同時にあらゆる種類の租税に関しあらゆる形態の行政支援を促進するため、各国が相互に調整の上努力することが必要であることを考慮し、

納税義務の適切な確定を促進し、及び納税者による自己の権利の確保に資するため、国際協力が重要な役割を果たすことができることを認識し、

全ての国の租税に関し、全ての者が適正な法令上の手続に従って決定される自己の権利及び義務を有するという基本原則が適用されることが認められるべきであること並びに各国が納税者の正当な利益（差別及び二重課税からの適切な保護を含む。）を保護するよう努めるべきであることを考慮し、

よって、各国が、情報の秘密を保護する必要性に留意し、かつ、プライバシー及び個人情報の流れの保護に関する国際的な枠組みを考慮して、自国の法令及び慣行に合致する場合を除くほか、措置をとるべきでなく、又は情報を提供すべきでないことを確信し、

租税に関する相互行政支援に関する条約を締結することを希望して、

次のとおり協定した。

第一章　条約の適用範囲

第１条　条約の目的及び対象となる者

1　締約国は、第四章の規定に従い、租税に関する事項について相互に行政支援を行う。当該行政支援には適当な場合には司法機関がとる措置を含めることができる。

2　行政支援は、次のものから成る。

a　情報の交換（同時税務調査及び海外における租税に関する調査への参加を含む。）

b　徴収における支援（保全の措置を含む。）

c　文書の送達

3　締約国は影響を受ける者が締約国の居住者若しくは国民であるか又は締約国以外の国の居住者若しくは国民であるかにかかわらず、行政支援を行う。

第二条　対象となる租税

1　この条約は、次の租税について適用する。

a　締約国のために課される次に掲げる租税

i　所得又は利得に対する租税

ii　所得又は利得に対する租税とは別に課される譲渡収益に対する租税

iii　純資産に対する租税

b　次に掲げる租税

i　締約国の地方政府又は地方公共団体のために課される所得、利得、譲渡収益又は純資産に対する租税

ii　強制加入の社会保険に係る保険料であって、一般政府又は公法に基づいて設立された社会保障機関に対して支払われるもの

iii　締約国のために課されるその他の区分の租税（関税を除く。）、すなわち、次のAからGまでに掲げるもの

A　遺産税、相続税又は贈与税

B　不動産に対する租税

C　付加価値税、売上税等の一般消費税

D　個別消費税等の物品及び役務に対する特定の租税

E　自動車の使用又は所有に対する租税

F　自動車以外の動産の使用又は所有に対する租税

G　その他の租税

iv　締約国の地方政府又は地方公共団体のために課されるiiiに掲げる区分の租税

2　この条約が適用される現行の租税は、1に規定する区分により、附属書Aに掲げる。

3　締約国は、2の規定により掲げる租税の変更の結果として附属書Aに生ずるいかなる修正も、欧州評議会事務局長又は経済協力開発機構事務総長（以下「寄託者」という。）に通告する。当該修正は寄託者がその通告を受領した日の後三箇月の期間が満了する日の属する月の翌月の初日に効力を生ずる。

4　この条約は、附属書Aに掲げる現行の租税に加えて又はこれに代わって、この条約が締約国について効力を生じた後に当該締約国において課される租税であって、当該現行の租税と同一であるもの又は実質的に類似するものについても、その採用の時から適用する。この場合には、当該締約国は、そのような租税の採用をいずれか一の寄託者に通告する。

5　来日外国人に対する課税

ガイダンス

「出入国管理及び難民認定法」が改正され、新たな外国人材受入れのための「特定技能1号」と「特定技能2号」の在留資格が創設されました。

これにより、従来以上に外国人が、日本で雇用される機会が増えるわけです。

現行の外国人技能実習生の約50%が、この「特定技能1号」に移行するのではないかと予想されています。

それでは、そもそも、外国人技能実習生に対する課税の制度の基本的な仕組みはどのようになっているのか。

また、小学生に対する英語教育は、2020年度から「小学3年生からの必修化、小学5年生からの教科化」が完全実施されることになりました。

従来から我が国の英語教育をサポートする仕組みの一つとして海外からJETプログラムによる外国人英語講師派遣があります。

このJETプログラムの仕組みと来日する外国人に対する課税の制度の仕組みはどのようになっているのか。

この他にも、医療介護の現場を支えるための経済連携協定に基づき受け入れる外国人看護師・介護福祉士候補者など、今後、様々な業界、業種で来日する外国人が増加することが見込まれます。

「来日外国人に対する課税」は、これらの外国人に対する課税上の取扱いについて演習事例により理解していただきます。

演習事例24

中国人留学生に支給するアルバイト賃金

当社は中国から日本の大学に留学している学生をアルバイトとして雇用しております。給料支払いの際に、源泉徴収したところ、本人から中国人留学生の所得税は免税ではないかとの申立てがありました。
日本で働く中国人留学生の課税関係について教えてください。

中国人留学生の給与については支払の際に源泉徴収の対象となりますが、「日中租税条約」によりますと、生計のために受け取る給付又は所得は免税となりますので、「租税条約に関する届出書」を提出することにより、源泉徴収は免除となります。

解説

中国人留学生の給与については、所法183条の規定により支払いの際に源泉徴収の対象となりますが、「日中租税条約」第21条によりますと、教育等のために日本に滞在する学生等で、中国の居住者又は入国の直前に中国の居住者であった者が、生計、教育等のために受け取る給付又は所得は免税となっております。
免税となる「学生」の範囲については、「租税条約実施特例法」省令第８条で「学校教育法第１条に規定する学校の生徒」と規定されています。

ご質問の場合は、中国人留学生のアルバイト代は生計のために受け取る所得となりますので、中国人留学生が貴社を通じ、貴社を所轄する税務署長に**「租税条約に関する届出書」（様式８）**と必要な添付書類を提出することにより、源泉徴収は免除となります。
なお、必要な添付書類については税務署に確認してください。

（根拠法令等：日中租税条約21、条約実特法省令８）

[租税条約に関する届出書（教授、留学生等）・様式8]

様式 8
FORM

租税条約に関する届出書
APPLICATION FORM FOR INCOME TAX CONVENTION

（税務署整理欄 For official use only）

適用；有、無			
番号確認		身元確認	

税務署受付印

（教授等・留学生・事業等の修習者・交付金等の受領者の報酬・交付金等に対する所得税及び復興特別所得税の免除
Relief from Japanese Income Tax and Special Income Tax for Reconstruction on Remunerations, Grants, etc., Received by Professors, Students, or Business Apprentices）

この届出書の記載に当たっては、別紙の注意事項を参照してください。
See separate instructions.

＿＿＿＿＿税務署長殿
To the District Director, ＿＿＿＿＿＿＿Tax Office

1　適用を受ける租税条約に関する事項；
Applicable Income Tax Convention
日本国と＿＿＿＿＿＿＿＿＿＿との間の租税条約第＿＿条第＿＿項＿＿
The Income Tax Convention between Japan and＿＿＿＿＿＿＿＿, Article＿＿, para.＿＿

2　報酬・交付金等の支払を受ける者に関する事項；
Details of Recipient of Remuneration, etc.

氏名 Full name		
日本国内における住所又は居所 Domicile or residence in Japan		（電話番号 Telephone Number）
個人番号（有する場合のみ記入） Individual Number (Limited to case of a holder)		
入国前の住所 Domicile before entry into Japan		（電話番号 Telephone Number）
（年齢 Age）　（国籍 Nationality）　（入国年月日 Date of Entry）　（在留期間 Authorized Period of Stay）　（在留資格 Status of Residence）		
下記「4」の報酬・交付金等につき居住者として課税される国及び納税地（注6） Country where the recipient is taxable as resident on Remuneration, etc., mentioned in 4 below and the place where he is to pay tax (Note 6)		（納税者番号 Taxpayer Identification Number）
日本国において教育若しくは研究を行い又は在学し若しくは訓練を受ける学校、事業所等 School or place of business in Japan where the Recipient teaches, studies or is trained	名称 Name	
	所在地 Address	（電話番号 Telephone Number）

3　報酬・交付金等の支払者に関する事項；
Details of Payer of Remuneration, etc.

氏名又は名称 Full name		
住所（居所）又は本店（主たる事務所）の所在地 Domicile (residence) or Place of head office (main office)		（電話番号 Telephone Number）
個人番号又は法人番号（有する場合のみ記入） Individual Number or Corporate Number (Limited to case of a holder)		
日本国内にある事務所等 Office, etc. located in Japan	名称 Name	（事業の内容 Details of Business）
	所在地 Address	（電話番号 Telephone Number）

4　上記「3」の支払者から支払を受ける報酬・交付金等で「1」の租税条約の規定の適用を受けるものに関する事項；
Details of Remuneration, etc., received from the Payer to which the Convention mentioned in 1 above is applicable

所得の種類 Kind of Income	契約期間 Period of Contract	報酬・交付金等の支払期日 Due Date for Payment	報酬・交付金等の支払方法 Method of Payment of Remunerations, etc.	報酬・交付金等の金額及び月額・年額の区分 Amount of Remunerations, etc. (per month, year).
報酬・交付金等の支払を受ける者の資格及び提供する役務の内容 Status of Recipient of Remuneration, etc., and the Description of Services rendered				

5　上記「3」の支払者以外の者から日本国内における勤務又は人的役務の提供に関して支払を受ける報酬・給料に関する事項（注7）；
Other Remuneration, etc., paid by Persons other than 3 above for Personal Services, etc., performed in Japan (Note 7)

【裏面に続きます（Continue on the reverse）】

6　その他参考となるべき事項（注８）；
Others (Note 8)

○　代理人に関する事項　；　この届出書を代理人によって提出する場合には、次の欄に記載してください。
Details of the Agent ; If this form is prepared and submitted by the Agent, fill out the following columns.

代理人の資格 Capacity of Agent in Japan	氏名（名称） Full name		納税管理人の届出をした税務署名 Name of the Tax Office where the Tax Agent is registered
□ 納税管理人 ※ Tax Agent □ その他の代理人 Other Agent	住所（居所・所在地） Domicile (Residence or location)	(電話番号 Telephone Number)	税務署 Tax Office

※　「納税管理人」とは、日本国の国税に関する申告、申請、請求、届出、納付等の事項を処理させるため、国税通則法の規定により選任し、かつ、日本国における納税地の所轄税務署長に届出をした代理人をいいます。

※ "Tax Agent" means a person who is appointed by the taxpayer and is registered at the District Director of Tax Office for the place where the taxpayer is to pay his tax, in order to have such agent take necessary procedures concerning the Japanese national taxes, such as filing a return, applications, claims, payment of taxes, etc., under the provisions of Act on General Rules for National Taxes.

○　適用を受ける租税条約が特典条項を有する租税条約である場合；
If the applicable convention has article of limitation on benefits

特典条項に関する付表の添付
"Attachment Form for Limitation on Benefits Article" attached

□ 有Yes
□ 添付省略 Attachment not required
（特典条項に関する付表を添付して提出した租税条約に関する届出書の提出日　　年　　月　　日）
Date of previous submission of the application for income tax convention with the "Attachment Form for Limitation on Benefits Article"

演習事例25

インドネシアからの留学生に支給するアルバイト賃金

当社はインドネシアから日本の大学に留学している学生をアルバイトとして雇用しております。

中国人留学生については、租税条約により所得税は免税であることは聞いていますが、インドネシアからの留学生については、給与の支払いの際にそのような免税の取り扱いはあるのでしょうか。

インドネシアからの留学生に支払う給与については支払の際に源泉徴収の対象となりますが、日本に最初に到着した日から５課税年度は、年額60万円を超えないものは「租税条約に関する届出書」を提出することにより、免税となります。

解説

1　インドネシア留学生に対する免税に対する取扱い

インドネシア留学生のアルバイト給与については、給与所得に該当し、支払の際に源泉徴収の対象となります。

ただし、入国の直前にインドネシア国の居住者であった者が、日本国内の大学等の学生として一時的に滞在する場合に、日本国内の人的役務に対する報酬で年間60万円を超えないものは、日本に最初に到着した日から５課税年度は免税となっています。

（日インドネシア租税条約21①(C)(iv)、条約実特法省令８②）

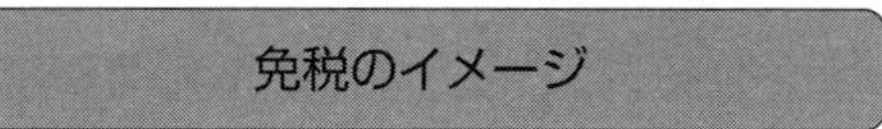

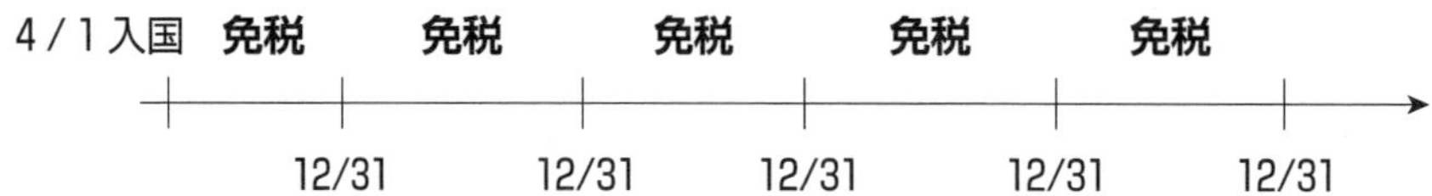

2　免税を受けるための手続き

ご質問の場合は、インドネシア留学生のアルバイト代が年間60万円を超えない場合には、入国の日以後最初にそのアルバイト代の支払を受ける日の前日までに、インドネシア留学生が貴社を通じ、貴社を所轄する税務署長に**「租税条約に関する届出書」（様式８）**と必要な添付書類を提出することにより、源泉徴収は免除となります。

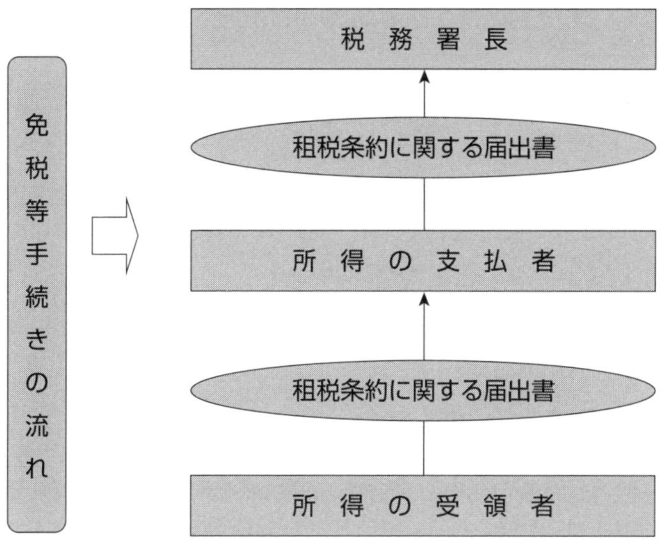

（参考）　日・インドネシア租税条約第21条1(c)（学生）……抜粋

一方の締約国を訪れる直前に他方の締約国の居住者であった個人であって、専ら当該一方の締約国内にある大学、学校その他の公認された教育機関の学生として、当該一方の締約国内に一時的に滞在するものは、当該一方の締約国に最初に到着した日から5課税事業年度を超えない期間、次のものにつき当該一方の締約国において租税を免除される。

(iv)　当該一方の締約国内における人的役務に対する報酬で、当該一方の締約国が日本国である場合にあっては年間60万円

（参考）　学生の範囲

免税となる「学生」の範囲については、「租税条約実施特例法」省令第8条で「学校教育法第1条に規定する学校の生徒」と規定されています。

演習事例26

外国人技能実習生に対する課税上の取扱いについて

当社は、「外国人技能実習制度」に基づき、ベトナムから技能実習生を３年間受け入れ予定です。受け入れに際しては、研修生と雇用契約を締結し給料を支払います。

課税上の取扱いで留意することがあれば、ご教示願います。

当社が技能実習生に支払う給与については、給与所得として所得税が課税されます。（給与支払いの際に源泉所得税を徴収する必要があります。）

また、技能実習生が国外から生計、訓練のために支払われるものは、日本とベトナムとの間の租税条約により日本では免税となります。

解説

1 「外国人技能実習制度」の概要

⑴ 外国人技能実習制度の趣旨

開発途上国等には、経済発展・産業振興の将来の担い手となる人材育成のために、我が国を含む先進国の技術、技能、知識等を修得させようとするニーズがあります。

このニーズに応えるために、諸外国の青壮年労働者を一定期間産業界に受け入れ、産業上の知識を修得してもらう趣旨です。

⑵ 外国人技能実習制度とは

技能実習制度とは、最長３年間の期間、技能実習生が雇用契約の下、日本の産業・職業上の技能等の修得・習熟をすることを内容とするものです。

受け入れる方式には、①企業単独型と②団体監理型があります。

企業単独型

本邦の企業等（実習実施機関）が海外の現地法人、合弁企業や取引先企業の職員を受け入れて技能実習を実施するもの。

団体監理型

商工会や中小企業団体等営利を目的としない団体（監理団体）が技能実習生を受け入れ、傘下の企業等（実習実施機関）で技能実習を実施するもの。

＊受け入れができる団体
① 商工会議所又は商工会
② 中小企業団体
③ 職業訓練法人
④ 農業協同組合、漁業協同組合
⑤ 公益社団法人・公益財団法人
⑥ 法務大臣が告示をもって定める監理団体

⑶ 技能実習生の処遇（団体監理型の場合）

イ 技能実習条件の書面による明示

ロ 雇用契約の適正な締結と労働条件通知書の交付

ハ 労働関係法令（労働基準法、労働安全衛生法、最低賃金法、労働者災害補償保険法、雇用保険法、健康保険法等）の遵守

ニ 賃金の適正な支払い（本人に直接その全額を毎月一定の期日に支払う……法定控除以外の費目の控除は労使協定の締結を要する。）

ホ 労働時間の取扱い（１日８時間、１週間40時間以内）

ヘ 安全衛生と保険措置

ト 労働組合等との協議

2 課税上の取扱い

⑴ 居住形態の判定（居住者か非居住者か）

外国人技能実習生は、雇用期間３年で入国することから、入国時から居住者と判定されます。

⑵ 所得の種類

外国人技能実習生は雇用契約を企業等の受入れ機関と締結することから、支払われる報酬は、給与所得として課税することになります。

⑶ 税額の計算方法

源泉所得税の計算に際しては、「給与所得者の扶養控除等申告書」を提出させる必要があります。

控除対象配偶者と控除対象扶養親族がいる場合には、生計を一にする事実と合計所得金額（48万円以下）を確認しなければなりません。

（注） 扶養控除関係資料

平成27年度の税制改正により、所得税法の一部が改正され非居住者である親族**（国外居住親族）**を所得控除（扶養、配偶者、障害者控除又は配偶者特別控除）の対象とする場合には、新たに、その非居住者に関する**「親族関係書類」**や**「送金関係書類」**を源泉徴収義務者に提出し、又は提示しなければならないことになりました。

（所法２三、所法28①、所法183①）

3 租税条約上の取扱い

⑴ 日本とベトナムの間の租税条約（第20条）

第20条

専ら教育又は訓練を受けるため一方の締約国内に滞在する学生又は事業修習者であって、現に他方の締約国の居住者であるもの又はその滞在の直前に他方の締約国の居住者であったものがその生計、教育又は訓練のために受け取る給付については、当該一方の締約国の租税を免除する。ただし、当該給付が当該一方の締約国外から支払われるものである場合に限る。

⑵ 租税条約上の取扱い

技能実習生に支給される給与は、国内法により課税されますが、日本とベトナムとの間の租税条約第20条の規定により技能実習生に国外から生計、訓練のために支払われるものは、免税となります。

演習事例27

JETプログラムにより来日した外国人英語教師に支払う報酬の取扱い

当市では、小中学生の英語能力向上のためにJETプログラムを利用し、アメリカから英語教師を2年の期間で受け入れます。

外国人英語講師には英語の講師の対価として報酬を支払い、住宅も無償で提供します。

これらの報酬と無償で提供する住宅について課税上の取り扱いを教えてください。

英語教師に支払う報酬と住宅の無償提供については、「日米租税条約」により非課税となります。

ただし、英語教師は「租税条約に関する届出書」を支払日の前日までに、支払者である市を通じて市を所轄する税務署長に提出しなければなりません。

解説

1　JETプログラムとは

⑴　JETプログラムとは、The Japan Exchange and Teaching Programme（語学指導等を行う外国青年招致事業）の略称で、地方自治体が、総務省、外務省、文部科学省及び一般財団法人自治体国際化協会の協力の下に、実施している語学指導者等の招致事業です。

⑵　事業の趣旨

地方公共団体が事業の主体となり、外国からJETプログラムの参加者を招致し、その参加者が、全国の小中学校や高校で語学指導等に従事し、各自治体の地域の住民との様々な交流を深めています。

これによりわが国の外国語教育の充実と地域レベルの草の根の国際交流の進展を図り、我が国の国際化の促進を期待するものです。

⑶　JET プログラムの仕組み

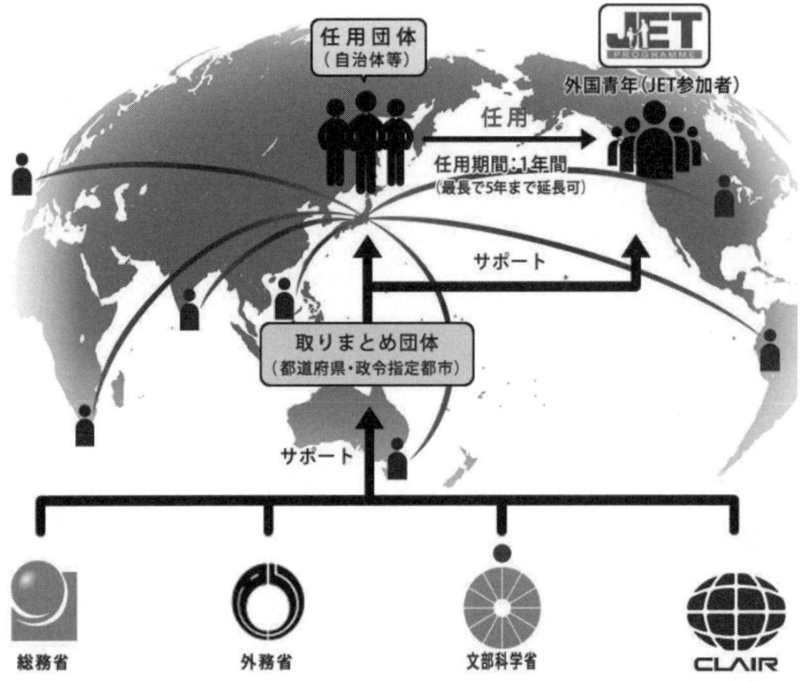

（出典：財団法人自治体国際化協会HPより）

●参加者出身国の過去の実績

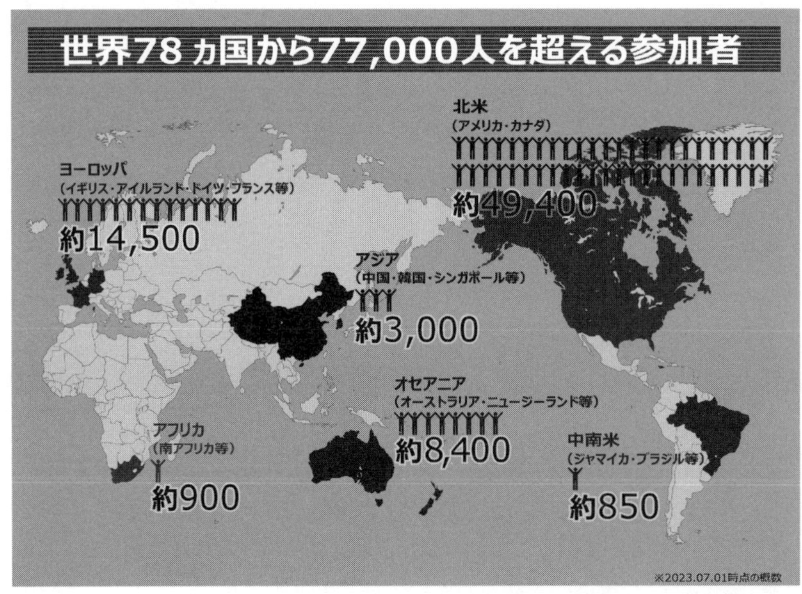

（出典：財団法人自治体国際化協会HPより）

⑷　参加者の三つの職種

㈠　外国語指導助手（ALT:Assistant Language Teacher）は教育委員会に配

属され、日本人外国語担当教員の助手として外国語授業に携わり、また、教育教材の準備や英語研究会のような課外活動に従事します。

㈺ 国際交流員（CIR：Coordinator for International Relation）

主に地方公共団体の国際交流活動に従事します。

㈧ スポーツ国際交流員（Sports Exchange Advisor）

主に地方公共団体に配属され、スポーツ指導等を行います。特定種目のスポーツ専門家として、スポーツトレーニング方法やスポーツ関連事業の立案などを通じて、国際交流活動に従事します。

⑸ 参加者のビザ

JET 参加者には3年の労働ビザが発行されます。

ALT には「教育」、CIR には「人文知識／国際業務」が発行されます。

（出典：財団法人自治体国際化協会HPより）

2 課税上の取扱い

ALT は1年以上の予定で入国することから、入国時から居住者となりますが、教育又は研究につき取得する報酬については、「日米租税条約」第20条の教授免税の条項により免税となります。

参考（教授免税とは）

租税条約の教授免税とは

大学その他の公認された教育機関において教育又は研究を行うために一時的に滞在する教授等が取得する報酬については、国内法では課税ですが、租税条約により免税とする規定です。

租税条約適用の要件

租税条約を締結している国からの教授等のみに適用されます。

「租税条約に関する届出書」を支払者経由で支払者を所轄する税務署長に支払日の前日までに提出しなければなりません。

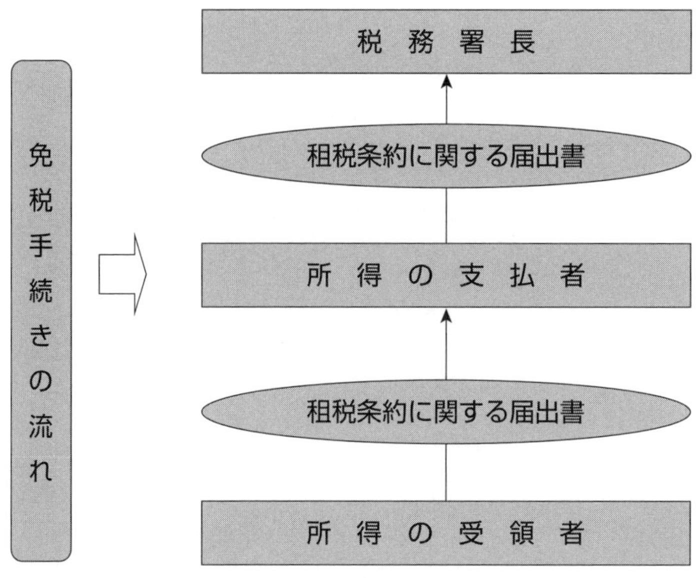

教授免税の条約締結国

主な締約国名	免除期間
アメリカ・アイルランド・インド・イタリア・イスラエル・ザンビア・韓国・スペイン・スリランカ・ソビエト連邦・タイ・ハンガリー・ドイツ・デンマーク・チェコ・スロバキア・ルーマニア・ポーランド・ブルガリア・フランス・フィンランド・フィリピン・バングラデッシュ	2年を超えない期間
中華人民共和国	3年を超えない期間
サウジアラビア	期間の規定なし

●日米租税条約（抜粋）

第20条（教授）

1　一方の締約国内にある大学、学校その他の教育機関において教育又は研究を行うために当該一方の締約国内に一時的に滞在する個人であって、他方の締約国において第四条1にいう居住者に引き続き該当するものが、教育又は研究につき取得する報酬については、当該一方の締約国に到着した日から2年を超えない期間当該一方の締約国において租税を免除する。

2　1の規定は、主として一又は二以上の特定の者の私的利益のために行われる研究から生じる所得については、適用しない。

（根拠法令等：所法2三、日米租税条約20）

[租税条約に関する届出書（教授、留学生等）・様式 8]

様式 8
FORM

租税条約に関する届出書
APPLICATION FORM FOR INCOME TAX CONVENTION

（教授等・留学生・事業等の修習者・交付金等の受領者の報酬・交付金等に対する所得税及び復興特別所得税の免除
Relief from Japanese Income Tax and Special Income Tax for Reconstruction on Remunerations, Grants, etc., Received by Professors, Students, or Business Apprentices）

この届出書の記載に当たっては、別紙の注意事項を参照してください。
See separate instructions.

（税務署整理欄
For official use only）

適用；有、無

番号確認		身元確認	

税務署受付印

＿＿＿＿税務署長殿
To the District Director, ＿＿＿＿Tax Office

1 適用を受ける租税条約に関する事項；
Applicable Income Tax Convention
日本国と＿＿＿＿との間の租税条約第＿＿条第＿＿項＿＿
The Income Tax Convention between Japan and＿＿＿＿, Article＿＿, para.＿＿

2 報酬・交付金等の支払を受ける者に関する事項；
Details of Recipient of Remuneration, etc.

氏名 Full name		
日本国内における住所又は居所 Domicile or residence in Japan		（電話番号 Telephone Number）
個人番号（有する場合のみ記入） Individual Number (Limited to case of a holder)		
入国前の住所 Domicile before entry into Japan		（電話番号 Telephone Number）
（年齢 Age）（国籍 Nationality）（入国年月日 Date of Entry）（在留期間 Authorized Period of Stay）（在留資格 Status of Residence）		
下記「4」の報酬・交付金等につき居住者として課税される国及び納税地（注6） Country where the recipient is taxable as resident on Remuneration, etc., mentioned in 4 below and the place where he is to pay tax (Note 6)		（納税者番号 Taxpayer Identification Number）
日本国において教育若しくは研究を行い又は在学し若しくは訓練を受ける学校、事業所等 School or place of business in Japan where the Recipient teaches, studies or is trained	名称 Name	
	所在地 Address	（電話番号 Telephone Number）

3 報酬・交付金等の支払者に関する事項；
Details of Payer of Remuneration, etc.

氏名又は名称 Full name		
住所（居所）又は本店（主たる事務所）の所在地 Domicile (residence) or Place of head office (main office)		（電話番号 Telephone Number）
個人番号又は法人番号（有する場合のみ記入） Individual Number or Corporate Number (Limited to case of a holder)		
日本国内にある事務所等 Office, etc. located in Japan	名称 Name	（事業の内容 Details of Business）
	所在地 Address	（電話番号 Telephone Number）

4 上記「3」の支払者から支払を受ける報酬・交付金等で「1」の租税条約の規定の適用を受けるものに関する事項；
Details of Remuneration, etc., received from the Payer to which the Convention mentioned in 1 above is applicable

所得の種類 Kind of Income	契約期間 Period of Contract	報酬・交付金等の支払期日 Due Date for Payment	報酬・交付金等の支払方法 Method of Payment of Remunerations, etc.	報酬・交付金等の金額及び月額・年額の区分 Amount of Remunerations, etc. (per month, year).
報酬・交付金等の支払を受ける者の資格及び提供する役務の内容 Status of Recipient of Remuneration, etc., and the Description of Services rendered				

5 上記「3」の支払者以外の者から日本国内における勤務又は人的役務の提供に関して支払を受ける報酬・給料に関する事項（注7）；
Other Remuneration, etc., paid by Persons other than 3 above for Personal Services, etc., performed in Japan (Note 7)

【裏面に続きます (Continue on the reverse) 】

6　その他参考となるべき事項（注８）；
Others (Note 8)

○　代理人に関する事項　；　この届出書を代理人によって提出する場合には、次の欄に記載してください。
Details of the Agent ; If this form is prepared and submitted by the Agent, fill out the following columns.

代理人の資格 Capacity of Agent in Japan	氏名（名称） Full name		納税管理人の届出をした税務署名 Name of the Tax Office where the Tax Agent is registered
□ 納税管理人 ※ Tax Agent □ その他の代理人 Other Agent	住所（居所・所在地） Domicile (Residence or location)	(電話番号 Telephone Number)	税務署 Tax Office

※　「納税管理人」とは、日本国の国税に関する申告、申請、請求、届出、納付等の事項を処理させるため、国税通則法の規定により選任し、かつ、日本国における納税地の所轄税務署長に届出をした代理人をいいます。

※ "Tax Agent" means a person who is appointed by the taxpayer and is registered at the District Director of Tax Office for the place where the taxpayer is to pay his tax, in order to have such agent take necessary procedures concerning the Japanese national taxes, such as filing a return, applications, claims, payment of taxes, etc., under the provisions of Act on General Rules for National Taxes.

○　適用を受ける租税条約が特典条項を有する租税条約である場合；
If the applicable convention has article of limitation on benefits

特典条項に関する付表の添付
"Attachment Form for Limitation on Benefits Article" attached

□有Yes
□添付省略 Attachment not required
（特典条項に関する付表を添付して提出した租税条約に関する届出書の提出日　　年　　月　　日）
Date of previous submission of the application for income tax convention with the "Attachment Form for Limitation on Benefits Article"

演習事例28

経済連携協定（EPA）に基づき受け入れる外国人看護師・介護福祉士候補者に支給する報酬の取扱い

当市は、長年、公立病院や介護施設の介護福祉士の不足に悩んでおりました。

この度、看護師や介護福祉士の不足を解消するために、EPA（日本国政府とフィリピン政府との間二国間の経済連携協定）に基づき、3年間の予定で外国人看護師と介護福祉師の候補者を受け入れる予定です。

これらの外国人の方々の日本での課税上の取り扱いはどうなるのでしょうか。

回答

EPA で日本に入国する看護師候補者と介護福祉士の候補者は、1年以上の予定で入国しますので、課税上は入国時から居住者と取り扱われることになります。

解説

1　外国看護師及び介護福祉士候補者受入の目的

看護師及び介護福祉士の不足解消のため、日本国政府とフィリピン等との二国間の経済連携協定（EPA）に基づき、外国人看護師候補者及び外国人介護福祉士候補者を日本に受け入れ、日本語研修、看護・介護研修及び病院等での就労・研修を経て、国家試験を受験させる。

合格者については、日本国内で、看護師及び介護福祉士として就労させる。

日本側の受け入れ窓口は、社団法人国際厚生事業団となっている。

病院及び介護施設等の受け入れ希望機関は、事前に外国人看護師候補者等と雇用契約を締結することとされている。

2　外国人看護師候補者等との雇用契約の内容

① 労働契約の期間（3年間）
② 就業の場所、業務内容
③ 基本給与の額、超過勤務手当の額
④ 労働時間、休暇及び休日
⑤ 日本人が従事する場合に受ける報酬と同等以上の報酬を支払うこと
⑥ 社会保険・労働保険を適用すること

3　課税上の取扱い

(1) 居住形態の判定（居住者か非居住者か）

外国人看護師候補者等は、雇用期間３年で入国することから、入国時から居住者と判定されます。

⑵　所得の種類

雇用契約を病院等の受入れ機関と締結することから、支払われる報酬は、給与所得として課税することになります。

⑶　税額の計算方法

源泉所得税の計算に際しては、「給与所得者の扶養控除等申告書」を提出させる必要があります。

控除対象配偶者と控除対象扶養親族がいる場合には、生計を一にする事実と合計所得金額（48万円以下）を確認しなければなりません。

（注）　平成27年度の税制改正により、所得税法の一部が改正され非居住者である親族**（国外居住親族）**を所得控除（扶養、配偶者、障害者控除又は配偶者特別控除）の対象とする場合には、新たに、その非居住者に関する**「親族関係書類」**や**「送金関係書類」**を源泉徴収義務者に提出し、又は提示しなければならないことになりました。

（根拠法令等：所法２三、所法28①、所法183①）

国際関係のトピック

国境を超えるEコマースと付加価値税

コロナ渦においても、日本の個人又は法人がビジネスチャンスを求めて大手のEコマースのプラットホームにテナントショップを開設し、国境を越えて事業を行っています。

EU 加盟国の顧客に対する商品の販売後、購入者から購入金額と支払金額が相違するとのクレームを受けることがあります。

EU の顧客との取引については、VAT（付加価値税）が課税されることから納税の仕組について注意が必要です。

そこで、今月は、トラブルを避けるため、クレームの原因と対策、そして、日本の事業者が、知っておくべき最新の VAT の納税方法について紹介します。

1　EU の付加価値税の納税義務者

EU 加盟国内の資産の譲渡又は役務の提供は VAT の課税対象となり、資産の譲渡又は役務の提供を行う者は VAT の納税義務者となります。

2　EU 加盟国内の付加価値税の免税措置の撤廃

EU 加盟国は、従来から VAT を各国の財源としていますが、特例として150ユーロ以下の輸入品については VAT を免税としていました。

2021年７月１日以降の輸入品については、この免税措置を撤廃することにより、輸入品のすべてについて課税対象としています。

日本の個人又は法人と EU 加盟国の顧客との間の取引品はこの輸入品に該当します。

3　顧客からのクレームの原因

日本の事業者が受けるクレームの原因は次の場合が考えられます。

⑴　購入者が2021年７月１日以降の免税措置の撤廃を理解していない場合

⑵　納品時に現地の郵便事業者等が購入者から VAT を徴収する場合

⑶　リバースチャージ方式により VAT の納税義務が商品の購入者に転嫁されている場合

4　クレーム対策と VAT 納税のための IOSS の活用

IOSS（Import One Stop Shop）とは、輸入ワンストップショップといわれるもので、EU の消費者との取引に関し発生する VAT の納税義務を簡素化できる新制度で今年の７月１日より導入されている納税方法です。商品の販売者やマーケットプレイスが販売時点でVATを徴収し、当局に納税する仕組で、商品購入者が予期せずVATを負担することがなくスムーズな取引を行うことができます。

また、リバースチャージ方式により、納税義務が商品購入者に転嫁される場合には、事前にアナウンスをすることが、クレームの防止になります。

課税実務編［米国版］

課税実務編［米国版］

ガイダンス

米国課税実務編では、我が国から米国に派遣される現地企業の社員、あるいは、留学生に対する課税関係、また、我が国の企業が米国内から取得する、利子、配当、及び使用料等に対する課税関係を演習事例より理解してもらうためのものです。

個人は外国人を居住外国人と非居住外国人に区分されています。

特に非居住外国人については、課税関係に影響を与える免税される個人とそれ以外に区分する際に、Substantial Presence Test により判断することとされるなど、やや複雑となっており、居住者と非居住者の判定及び課税範囲について正しい理解が必要です。

また、我が国の企業が、米国で投資所得を得た場合には、源泉所得税が30%課税されることとされており、源泉所得税の減免の手続きを失念してしまうと、収入金額の30%が収入金額から控除されますので、源泉所得税の対象となる所得の範囲及び源泉所得税の減免の手続きを理解することが重要になります。

1　個人に対する課税

⑴　米国に居住する外国人の課税上の分類

米国に滞在する外国人は米国の国内法上居住外国人と非居住外国人に分類されます。

居住外国人は、グリーンカード保有者とその他の外国人に分類され、その他の外国人は、Substantial Presence Test（滞在日数の計算）を行います。

非居住外国人は、Exempt individual（免税となる個人）とExempt individual（免税となる個人）以外に分類されます。

免税となる個人とは①外国政府関係者②教授・研修生③留学生④プロスポーツ競技者等に分類されます。

米国国内法

<table>
<tr><td rowspan="4">Alien
（外国人）</td><td rowspan="2">Resident Aliens
（居住外国人）</td><td colspan="2">グリーンカード保有者</td></tr>
<tr><td>Substantial Presence Test（滞在日数の計算）</td><td>3年間の滞在日数の合計が183日を超える者</td></tr>
<tr><td rowspan="2">Nonresident Aliens
（非居住外国人）</td><td>Exempt individual
Substantial Presence Testの際に滞在日数を考慮しない者</td><td>①外国政府関係者
②教授・研修生
③留学生
④プロスポーツ競技者</td></tr>
<tr><td colspan="2">Exempt individual以外</td></tr>
</table>

（参考）

⑴　Alien とは U.S.citizen（米国市民）ではない者

⑵　Resident　Aliens とは（次の①又は②に該当する者）

①　"green card"　保有者

②　Substantial Presence Test（滞在日数の計算）の結果、3年間の滞在日数の合計が183日を超える者（当該年度と前2年間の滞在日数の合計が183日を超える者（計算式＝前年は滞在日数×1/3・前々年は滞在日数×1/6）

設例（Substantial Presence Test・2022年を判定年度とする場合）

2020年，2021年，2022年の滞在日数がそれぞれ120日の場合

2020年の滞在日数…………120日×1/6＝20日

2021年の滞在日数…………120日×1/3＝40日

2022年の滞在日数……………………………120日

合計　180日

判定結果……滞在日数の合計額が180日（183日を超えない）となりNonresident Aliensに該当する

(3) Students（留学生）のvisaは“F,” “J,” “M,” 又は” Q ”であること

(4) Exempt individualに該当する場合は、Form8843をIRSに提出すること

○ 米国政府（IRS）へ留学生が提出するForm 8843について

Nonresident Aliensであることを証明するために、米国政府に対し、Form8843を確定申告書に添付し翌年4月15日まで提出する必要があります。

（確定申告の必要のない者はForm8843のみ提出する必要があります。）

＊提出先

Department of the Treasury Internal Revenue Services Center, Austin TX 73301-0215

(2) 米国における外国人の課税の範囲（非居住外国人の場合）

非居住外国人の課税所得の範囲は、米国内源泉所得と米国外源泉所得のうち資産性所得（使用料・利子・配当及び株式、資産等の譲渡損益）のみです。

課税所得の範囲

Alien（外国人）	Resident Aliens（居住外国人）	**全世界所得**
	Nonresident Aliens（非居住外国人）	**米国内源泉所得 米国外源泉所得（米国内の事業施設に関連する米国外の使用料・利子・配当及び株式、資産等の譲渡損益）**

（注） 米国外源泉所得

米国外源泉所得とは、米国内の事業施設に関連する米国外の使用料・利子・配当及び株式、資産等の譲渡損益をいいます。（上記「課税所得の範囲」参照）

（上記(1)～(2)は「U.S.Tax Guide for Alians 2022 Returns」より）

Form 8843（様式）

（免税個人と病気等により米国を離れることができない個人の申告書）

Form **8843**

Department of the Treasury
Internal Revenue Service

Statement for Exempt Individuals and Individuals With a Medical Condition

For use by alien individuals only.

Go to *www.irs.gov/Form8843* for the latest information.

For the year January 1—December 31, 2023, or other tax year beginning , 2023, and ending , 20 .

OMB No. 1545-0074

2023

Attachment Sequence No. **102**

Your first name and initial	Last name	Your U.S. taxpayer identification number (TIN), if any

Fill in your addresses only if you are filing this form by itself and not with your U.S. tax return.	Address in country of residence	Address in the United States

Part I General Information

1a Type of U.S. visa (for example, F, J, M, Q, etc.) and date you entered the United States:

b Current nonimmigrant status. If your status has changed, also enter date of change and previous status. See instructions.

2 Of what country or countries were you a citizen during the tax year?

3a What country or countries issued you a passport?

b Enter your passport number(s):

4a Enter the actual number of days you were present in the United States during:
2023 ______ 2022 ______ 2021 ______

b Enter the number of days in 2023 you claim you can exclude for purposes of the substantial presence test:

Part II Teachers and Trainees

5 For teachers, enter the name, address, and telephone number of the academic institution where you taught in 2023:

6 For trainees, enter the name, address, and telephone number of the director of the academic or other specialized program you participated in during 2023:

7 Enter the type of U.S. visa (J or Q) you held during: 2017 ______ 2018 ______
2019 ______ 2020 ______ 2021 ______ 2022 ______ . If the type of visa you held during any of these years changed, attach a statement showing the new visa type and the date it was acquired.

8 Were you exempt as a teacher, trainee, or student for any part of 2 of the preceding 6 calendar years (2017 through 2022)? . . . . . ☐ **Yes** ☐ **No**
If you checked the "Yes" box on line 8, you cannot exclude days of presence as a teacher or trainee unless you meet the *Exception* explained in the instructions.

Part III Students

9 Enter the name, address, and telephone number of the academic institution you attended during 2023:

10 Enter the name, address, and telephone number of the director of the academic or other specialized program you participated in during 2023:

11 Enter the type of U.S. visa (F, J, M, or Q) you held during: 2017 ______ 2018 ______
2019 ______ 2020 ______ 2021 ______ 2022 ______ . If the type of visa you held during any of these years changed, attach a statement showing the new visa type and the date it was acquired.

12 Were you exempt as a teacher, trainee, or student for any part of more than 5 calendar years? . . . . . ☐ **Yes** ☐ **No**
If you checked the "Yes" box on line 12, you must provide sufficient facts on an attached statement to establish that you do not intend to reside permanently in the United States.

13 During 2023, did you apply for, or take other affirmative steps to apply for, lawful permanent resident status in the United States or have an application pending to change your status to that of a lawful permanent resident of the United States? . . . . . ☐ **Yes** ☐ **No**

14 If you checked the "Yes" box on line 13, explain:

For Paperwork Reduction Act Notice, see instructions. Cat. No. 17227H Form **8843** (2023)

Form 8843（様式）

Form 8843 (2023) Page **2**

Part IV **Professional Athletes**

15 Enter the name of the charitable sports event(s) in the United States in which you competed during 2023 and the dates of competition:

16 Enter the name(s) and employer identification number(s) of the charitable organization(s) that benefited from the sports event(s):

Note: You must attach a statement to verify that all of the net proceeds of the sports event(s) were contributed to the charitable organization(s) listed on line 16.

Part V **Individuals With a Medical Condition or Medical Problem**

17a Describe the medical condition or medical problem that prevented you from leaving the United States. See instructions.

b Enter the date you intended to leave the United States prior to the onset of the medical condition or medical problem described on line 17a:

c Enter the date you actually left the United States:

18 **Physician's Statement:**

I certify that

Name of taxpayer

was unable to leave the United States on the date shown on line 17b because of the medical condition or medical problem described on line 17a and there was no indication that their condition or problem was preexisting.

Name of physician or other medical official

Physician's or other medical official's address and telephone number

Physician's or other medical official's signature Date

Sign here only if you are filing this form by itself and not with your U.S. tax return.	Under penalties of perjury, I declare that I have examined this form and the accompanying attachments, and, to the best of my knowledge and belief, they are true, correct, and complete. Your signature Date

Form **8843** (2023)

Form 8843（全訳）

Form 8843

（免税対象となる個人と病気等により米国を離れることができない個人のための申告書）

氏名・・・・・・・・　　米国の納税者番号（もしあれば）・・・・・・・

本申告書の提出が確定申告のためでない場合には、住所を記載してください。　居住している国の住所　　米国の住所

Part Ⅰ　一般的な情報

1 a　米国ビザ形態（例えば、F, J, M,Q その他）・米国への入国日

b　現状の非移民者の身分。もし、身分が変更したならば変更日と以前の身分

2　当課税年度においてどこの国の市民であるか。

3 a　あなたのパスポートの発行国はどこか。

b　パスポート番号の記入

4 a　米国での滞在日数を記入してください。

2018・・・　2017・・・　2016・・・

Part Ⅱ　教師と研修生

5　教師の場合、2018年にあなたが教鞭を執った教育施設の名称、住所及び電話番号を記入してください。

6　研修生の場合、2018年にあなたの研修プログラムの担当者の名称、住所及び電話番号を記載してください。

7　次の各年度のあなたのビザの類型（J又はQ）を記入してください。

2012____2013____2014____2015____2016____2017____

もし、それぞれの年度のビザの類型が変更となった場合には、新しいビザとその取得日を示す書類を添付してください。

8　あなたは、米国において2012年から2017年の間において、教師、研修生、又は学生でしたか。

YES □　NO □

もし、"YES" にチェックした場合には、例外の要件を満たさない限りには、教師又は研修生としての滞在日数は、滞在日数から除外することはできません。

Part Ⅲ　学生

9　あなたが、2018年に学ぶ教育機関の名称、住所及び電話番号を記載してください。

10　あなたが、2018年中に参加するプログラム及び教育機関の責任者の氏名、住所及び電話番号を記載してください。

11　次の期間のビザの類型（F,J,M 又はQ）を記入してください。

2012____2013____2014____2015____2016____2017____

Form 8843（全訳）

12　米国に過去5年間の間に、教師、研修生、又は学生として滞在していましたか。

□ Yes　□ No

もし、"Yes" にチェックした場合には、添付書類によりあなたが米国に永住する意思がない十分な事実を提供する必要があります。

13　2018年中に、あなたは、米国での適法な永久居住者のための申請、あるいは、適法な永久居住者申請のための確定的な措置を取りましたか。

または、適法な永久居住者への変更の一時保留の申請を行いましたか。

□ Yes　□ No

14　もし13が Yes であれば、その理由を記載してください。

Part Ⅳ　職業スポーツ選手

15　あなたが、2018年中に参加した慈善スポーツイベントがあれば、その名称と開催日を記入してください。

16　そのスポーツイベントから便益を受ける慈善団体のEIN(Employer Identification Number）を記入してください。

（注）　スポーツイベントの収益金のすべては、慈善団体に寄付されたことを証明する書類を添付してください。

Part Ⅴ　疾患又は医学的問題を抱える個人

17 a　米国からの帰国を妨げている病状又は医学的問題について記載してください。

b　17 a の病状又は医学的問題の発生以前にあなたが米国から帰国しようとしていた日を記載してください。

c　あなたが、実際に米国から帰国する日を記載してください。

18　主治医の診断書

わたしは証明いたします。・・・・・（納税者の氏名）・・・・・・は、以前にはなかった17 a に記載した理由により17 b に記載した日に帰国できないことを。

主治医又はその他の医師の氏名

主治医又はその他の医師の住所及び電話番号

主治医又はその他の医師の署名　　　　　　　　日付

偽証の場合には罰せられるとの下に、私はこの書類と添付書類を確認し、私の知る限りでは真実であることを宣誓いたします。

署名　　　　　　　　　　　　　　　　　　　　日付

演習事例29

留学資金の課税上の取扱い

日本人の留学生が日本の居住者から留学資金を給付される場合の米国での課税の取扱いについて、ご教示をお願いいたします。

日本人の留学生が日本から留学資金を交付される場合は、日米租税条約の規定により米国では免税になります。

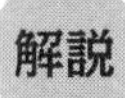

1　米国に居住する外国人（留学生）の課税上の分類

米国に滞在する外国人は米国の国内法上居住外国人と非居住外国人に分類されます。

居住外国人は、グリーンカード保有者とその他の外国人に分類され、その他の外国人は、Substantial Presence Test（滞在日数の計算）を行います。

非居住外国人は、Exempt individual（免税となる個人）とExempt individual（免税となる個人）以外に分類されます。

免税となる個人とは①外国政府関係者②教授・研修生**③留学生**④プロスポーツ競技者等に分類されます。

米国国内法

<table>
<tr><td rowspan="5">Alien
（外国人）</td><td rowspan="2">Resident Aliens
（居住外国人）</td><td colspan="2">グリーンカード保有者</td></tr>
<tr><td>Substantial Presence Test（滞在日数の計算）</td><td>3年間の滞在日数の合計が183日を超える者</td></tr>
<tr><td rowspan="3">Nonresident Aliens
（非居住外国人）</td><td>Exempt individual
Substantial Presence Testの際に滞在日数を考慮しない者</td><td>①外国政府関係者
②教授・研修生
③留学生
④プロスポーツ競技者</td></tr>
<tr><td colspan="2">Exempt individual以外</td></tr>
</table>

（参考）

⑴　Alien とは U.S.citizen（米国市民）ではない者

⑵　Resident　Aliens とは（次の①又は②に該当する者）

①　"green card" 保有者

②　Substantial Presence Test（滞在日数の計算）の結果、３年間の滞在日数の合計が183日を超える者（当該年度と前２年間の滞在日数の合計が183日を超える者（計算式＝前年は滞在日数×１/３・前々年は滞在日数×１/６）

設例（Substantial Presence Test・2016年を判定年度とする場合）

2020年、2021年、2022年の滞在日数がそれぞれ120日の場合

2020年の滞在日数…………120日×１/６＝20日

2021年の滞在日数…………120日×１/３＝40日

2022年の滞在日数……………………………120日

合計　180日

判定結果・・・滞在日数の合計額が180日（183日を超えない）となり Nonresident Aliens に該当する

⑶　Students（留学生）の visa は "F," "J," "M," 又は "Q" であること

⑷　**Exempt individual に該当する場合は、Form 8843を IRS に提出すること**

（注）外国人（政府関係者以外）は、免税の対象となる個人又は病気等により米国を離れることができない個人として、米国での滞在日数の計算から滞在日数を除外しようとする際には、**Form 8843**を提出することになります。

2　米国政府（IRS）へ留学生が提出する Form 8843について

Nonresident Aliens であることを証明するために、米国政府に対し Form 8843を確定申告書に添付し翌年４月15日まで提出する必要があります。

（確定申告の必要のない者は Form 8843のみ提出する必要があります。）

＊提出先

Department of the Treasury Internal Revenue Services Center, Austin TX 73301-0215

3　米国における外国人の課税の範囲

非居住外国人の課税所得の範囲は、米国内源泉所得と米国外源泉所得のうち資産性所得（使用料・利子・配当及び株式、資産等の譲渡損益）のみです。

課税所得の範囲

Alien （外国人）	Resident Aliens （居住外国人）	**全世界所得**
	Nonresident Aliens （非居住外国人）	**米国内源泉所得** **米国外源泉所得（米国内の事業施設に関連する米国外の使用料・利子・配当及び株式、資産等の譲渡損益）**

4　日本から送金される留学費用（奨学金、補助金等）の課税上の取扱い

日本から留学生に支給される奨学金、補助金等の**所得の源泉地**は、その奨学金等の**支払者の居住地により判断**します。

したがって、**日本から支払う留学費用等は日本国内が所得の源泉地となり、米国での課税はありません。**

> （注）　米国外源泉所得
> 米国国外源泉所得とは、米国内の事業施設に関連する米国外の使用料・利子・配当及び株式、資産等の譲渡損益をいいます。（上記「課税所得の範囲」参照）

（上記１～４は「U.S.Tax Guide for Alians 2022 Returns」より）

5　日米租税条約上の一般的な取り扱い

⑴　米国に滞在する日本のStudents（留学生）に対し、日本から送金される奨学金等（授業料、生計費等）については、免税となっています。

⑵　米国国籍を有する者が、日本の居住者として米国に留学し、日本から送金される奨学金等（授業料、生計費等）については、免税となりません。

（上記⑴～⑵は、租税条約の取扱いを解説する米国のtechnical explanationより）

6　租税条約による免税を受けるための米国政府（IRS）への提出書類について

留学生に対し海外から送金される授業料、生計費等については免税を受けるための届出等は、特に必要なし。

（「U.S.Tax Guide for Alians 2022 Returns」より）

2　外国法人に対する課税（個人と外国法人に対する源泉徴収）

⑴　米国における非居住者（個人）と外国法人等（会社等）に対する源泉徴収制度

米国の国内法では、Withholding agent（以下「源泉徴収義務者」。）は源泉徴収の対象となる所得（Fixed or determinable annual or periodical income、以下「FDAP」。）を支払う際に30%の税率により所得税を徴収します。

ただし、租税条約による税額の軽減・免除の対象となる者については、税額の軽減・免除を行います。（この場合には、租税条約の恩典を受ける者であることを証明するForm W-8BEN-E（法人の場合）の提出が必要です。）

FDAP（源泉徴収対象所得）

所得の種類	所得源泉の決定基準
①Pay for personal sevices （人的役務の提供）	人的役務の提供場所により所得源泉地を決定
②Dividends （配当）	支払者が米国法人か外国法人かにより所得源泉地を決定
③Interest （利息）	支払者の居住地により所得源泉地を決定
④Rents （賃貸料）	資産の所在地により所得源泉地を決定
⑤Royalties-Patent, Copyrights, etc （工業所有権・著作権等）	資産の使用地により所得源泉地を決定
⑥Royalties-Natural resources （ロイヤリテイ）	資産の所在地により所得源泉地を決定
⑦Pensions:Distributions Attributable to cotributios （年金）	非居住者の期間に提供された人的役務の提供地により所得源泉地を決定
⑧Pensions:Investment Earnings on contributions （年金信託）	年金信託の所在地により所得源泉地を決定
⑨Scholarships and Fellowship grants （奨学金等）	支払者の居住地により所得源泉地を決定
⑩Gurantee of indebtedness （債務保証）	①　債務者の居住地により所得源泉地を決定 ②　支払が米国の事業に密接に関連するか否かにより所得源泉を決定

⑵　源泉徴収義務者（Withholding agent）の報告義務

源泉徴収義務者は、源泉徴収した翌年の３月15日までに、源泉徴収した事績を記載した Form 1042-S（我が国の法定調書に該当）を米国の国税庁（IRS）に一部、提出し、FDAP の受領者（Recipient）に対し３部交付しなければなりません。

一部は、源泉徴収義務者が保管することになります。

Form 1042-S の提出先

CopyA ………………… IRS へ提出

CopyB～CopyD …… 受領者へ交付

CopyE ………………… 源泉徴収義務者保管

⑶　租税条約の軽減又は免税を受けるための手続き

受領者は、FDAP の支払いを受ける時までに Form W-8BEN-E（法人の場合）を源泉徴収義務者に提出し、租税条約により免税（税額なし）を受ける者であることを明示する。

⑷　源泉徴収された場合の還付手続き

①　上記２の報告期限（翌年３月15日）前の対応

源泉徴収義務者に対し Form W-8BEN-E（法人の場合）を提出し、源泉徴収義務者から徴収税額を還付してもらう。

②　上記２の報告期限（翌年３月15日）後の対応

IRS から納税者番号を取得し、Form 1120-F（法人の場合）により確定申告を行い還付を受ける。

Form 1042-S（様式）
（源泉徴収に関する法定調書）

Form **1042-S** Department of the Treasury Internal Revenue Service

Foreign Person's U.S. Source Income Subject to Withholding **2022**
▶ Go to *www.irs.gov/Form1042S* for instructions and the latest information.
UNIQUE FORM IDENTIFIER ☐ AMENDED ☐ AMENDMENT NO.

OMB No. 1545-0096
Copy A for Internal Revenue Service

1 Income code / **2** Gross income / **3** Chapter indicator. Enter "3" or "4"	**13e** Recipient's U.S. TIN, if any / **13f** Ch. 3 status code
3a Exemption code / **4a** Exemption code	**13g** Ch. 4 status code
3b Tax rate . / **4b** Tax rate .	**13h** Recipient's GIIN / **13i** Recipient's foreign tax identification number, if any / **13j** LOB code
5 Withholding allowance	
6 Net income	
7a Federal tax withheld	**13k** Recipient's account number
7b Check if federal tax withheld was not deposited with the IRS because escrow procedures were applied (see instructions) . . . . . . ☐	**13l** Recipient's date of birth (YYYYMMDD)
7c Check if withholding occurred in subsequent year with respect to a partnership interest . . . . ☐	
8 Tax withheld by other agents	**14a** Primary Withholding Agent's Name (if applicable)
9 Overwithheld tax repaid to recipient pursuant to adjustment procedures (see instructions) ( )	**14b** Primary Withholding Agent's EIN / **15** Check if pro-rata basis reporting ☐
10 Total withholding credit (combine boxes 7a, 8, and 9)	**15a** Intermediary or flow-through entity's EIN, if any / **15b** Ch. 3 status code / **15c** Ch. 4 status code
11 Tax paid by withholding agent (amounts not withheld) (see instructions)	**15d** Intermediary or flow-through entity's name
12a Withholding agent's EIN / **12b** Ch. 3 status code / **12c** Ch. 4 status code	**15e** Intermediary or flow-through entity's GIIN
12d Withholding agent's name	**15f** Country code / **15g** Foreign tax identification number, if any
12e Withholding agent's Global Intermediary Identification Number (GIIN)	**15h** Address (number and street)
12f Country code / **12g** Foreign tax identification number, if any	**15i** City or town, state or province, country, ZIP or foreign postal code
12h Address (number and street)	**16a** Payer's name / **16b** Payer's TIN
12i City or town, state or province, country, ZIP or foreign postal code	**16c** Payer's GIIN / **16d** Ch. 3 status code / **16e** Ch. 4 status code
13a Recipient's name / **13b** Recipient's country code	**17a** State income tax withheld / **17b** Payer's state tax no. / **17c** Name of state
13c Address (number and street)	
13d City or town, state or province, country, ZIP or foreign postal code	

For Privacy Act and Paperwork Reduction Act Notice, see instructions. Cat. No. 11386R Form **1042-S** (2022)

Form 1042-S（全訳）

1042-S　Foreign Person's U.S. Income Subject to Withholding　2022

1　所得コード

2　収入金額

3　適用条文“3”又は”4”

3 a　免税コード　3 b　税率　4 a　免税コード　4 b　税率

5　Withholding Allowance（1のコードが16, 17, 18, 19, 20, 42の場合に記入）

6　純利益（5を記入した場合のみ）

7 a　源泉徴収された連邦所得税

7 b　エスクロー手続きにより源泉徴収されていない場合はチェック　□

8　他の代理人による源泉徴収税額

9　調整のために受領者に返還された過大な源泉徴収税額（手引参照）

10　源泉徴収税額の合計額（7 a＋8＋9）

11　源泉徴収義務者による支払税額（源泉徴収されなかったもの）（手引参照）

12 a　源泉徴収義務者の EIN

12 b　第3章の源泉徴収義務者の区分

12 c　第4章の源泉徴収義務者の区分

12 d　源泉徴収義務者の氏名

12 e　源泉徴収義務者の Global Intermediary Identification Number（GIN）

12 f　国別コード

12 g　外国納税者番号（もしあれば）

12 h　住所（番号と通り名）

12 i　都市名、国名、郵便番号

13 a　受取人の氏名

13 b　受取人の国別コード

13 c　住所（番号と通り名）

13 d　都市名、国名、郵便番号

13 e　受取人の米国の TIN

13 f　第3章の源泉徴収義務者の区分

13 g　第4章の源泉徴収義務者の区分

13 h　受取人の GIIN

13 i　受取人の外国納税者番号（もしあれば）

13 j　LOB code

Form 1042-S（全訳）

13 k　受取人の口座番号

13 l　受取人の生年月日

14 a　主要な源泉徴収義務者の氏名（該当する場合）

14 b　主要な源泉徴収義務者の EIN

15　按分（比例）計算で報告する場合のチェック　□

15 a　中間又はパートナーシップの EIN

15 b　第 3 章の事業　15 c　第 4 章の事業

15 d　中間又はパートナーシップの氏名

15 e　中間又はパートナーシップの GIN

15 f　国別コード

15 g　外国納税者番号（もしあれば）

15 h　住所（番号と通り名）

15 i　都市名、国名、郵便番号

16 a　支払者の氏名

16 b　支払者の米国の TIN

16 c　支払者の GIIN

16 d　第 3 章の源泉徴収義務者の区分

16 e　第 4 章の源泉徴収義務者の区分

17 a　源泉徴収された州の所得税

17 b　受取人の州の所得税の納税者番号

17 c　州の名称

演習事例30

米国での源泉所得税課税、租税条約による軽減・免除と法定調書

当社は、米国の企業に子供向けの番組映像を提供していますが、今回、著作権の使用料（映像の使用料）の支払を受けました。

支払に際しては、30%の税率により源泉所得税が徴収されておりました。

米国での税金事情は詳しくわかりません。米国の源泉所得税制度についてご教示をお願いいたします。

貴社に支払われた映像の使用料は、著作権の使用料に該当し、支払の際に、30%の税率により課税が行われます。ただし、支払の前に、源泉徴収義務者に、日米租税条約に基づく条約の適用を受ける者であることを関連書類により証明した場合には、免税となり源泉徴収はされません。

解説

1　米国における非居住者（個人）と外国法人等（会社等）に対する源泉徴収制度

米国の国内法では、源泉徴収義務者（Withholding agent）は源泉徴収の対象となる所得（Fixed or determinable annual or periodicalincome・以下「FDAP」といいます。）を支払う際に30%の税率により所得税を徴収します。

ただし、租税条約による税額の軽減・免除の対象となる者については、税額の軽減・免除を行います。（この場合には、租税条約の恩典を受ける者であることを証明するForm W-8BEN-E（法人の場合）の提出が必要です。）

FDAP（源泉徴収対象所得）

所得の種類	所得源泉の決定基準
①Pay for personal sevices （人的役務の提供）	人的役務の提供場所により所得源泉地を決定
②Dividends （配当）	支払者が米国法人か外国法人かにより所得源泉地を決定
③Interest （利息）	支払者の居住地により所得源泉地を決定

④Rents （賃貸料）	資産の所在地により所得源泉地を決定
⑤Royalties-Patent, Copyrights,etc （工業所有権・著作権等）	資産の使用地により所得源泉地を決定
⑥Royalties-Nutural, resources （ロイヤリテイ）	資産の所在地により所得源泉地を決定
⑦Pensions:Distributions Attributable to cotributios （年金）	非居住者の期間に提供された人的役務の提供地により所得源泉地を決定
⑧Pensions:Investment Earnings on contributions （年金信託）	年金信託の所在地により所得源泉地を決定
⑨Scholarships and Fellowship grants （奨学金等）	支払者の居住地により所得源泉地を決定
⑩Gurantee of indebtedness （債務保証）	①　債務者の居住地により所得源泉地を決定 ②　支払が米国の事業に密接に関連するか否かにより所得源泉地を決定

2　源泉徴収義務者（Withholding agent）の報告義務

源泉徴収義務者は、源泉徴収した翌年の３月15日までに、源泉徴収した事績を記載した Form 1042-S（我が国の法定調書に該当）を米国の国税庁（IRS）に一部、提出し、FDAP の受領者（Recipient）に対し３部交付しなければなりません。

一部は、源泉徴収義務者が保管することになります。

Form 1042-S の提出先

CopyA …………………IRS へ提出

CopyB～CopyD ……受領者へ交付

CopyE …………………源泉徴収義務者保管

3　租税条約の軽減又は免税を受けるための手続き

受領者は、FDAP の支払を受ける時までに Form W-8BEN-E（法人の場合）又は Form W-8BEN（個人の場合）を源泉徴収義務者に提出し、租税条約により免税（税額なし）を受ける者であることを明示します。

Form W-8BEN-E（法人の場合）

（租税条約による軽減免除を受ける者の証明書・・一部抜粋）

Form **W-8BEN-E**

(Rev. October 2021)

Department of the Treasury
Internal Revenue Service

Certificate of Status of Beneficial Owner for United States Tax Withholding and Reporting (Entities)

▶ For use by entities. Individuals must use Form W-8BEN. ▶ Section references are to the Internal Revenue Code.
▶ Go to *www.irs.gov/FormW8BENE* for instructions and the latest information.
▶ Give this form to the withholding agent or payer. Do not send to the IRS.

OMB No. 1545-1621

Do NOT use this form for:	**Instead use Form:**
• U.S. entity or U.S. citizen or resident	W-9
• A foreign individual	W-8BEN (Individual) or Form 8233
• A foreign individual or entity claiming that income is effectively connected with the conduct of trade or business within the United States (unless claiming treaty benefits)	W-8ECI
• A foreign partnership, a foreign simple trust, or a foreign grantor trust (unless claiming treaty benefits) (see instructions for exceptions)	W-8IMY
• A foreign government, international organization, foreign central bank of issue, foreign tax-exempt organization, foreign private foundation, or government of a U.S. possession claiming that income is effectively connected U.S. income or that is claiming the applicability of section(s) 115(2), 501(c), 892, 895, or 1443(b) (unless claiming treaty benefits) (see instructions for other exceptions)	W-8ECI or W-8EXP
• Any person acting as an intermediary (including a qualified intermediary acting as a qualified derivatives dealer)	W-8IMY

Part I　Identification of Beneficial Owner

1 Name of organization that is the beneficial owner

2 Country of incorporation or organization

3 Name of disregarded entity receiving the payment (if applicable, see instructions)

4 Chapter 3 Status (entity type) (Must check one box only):
- ☐ Corporation
- ☐ Partnership
- ☐ Simple trust
- ☐ Tax-exempt organization
- ☐ Complex trust
- ☐ Foreign Government - Controlled Entity
- ☐ Central Bank of Issue
- ☐ Private foundation
- ☐ Estate
- ☐ Foreign Government - Integral Part
- ☐ Grantor trust
- ☐ Disregarded entity
- ☐ International organization

If you entered disregarded entity, partnership, simple trust, or grantor trust above, is the entity a hybrid making a treaty claim? If "Yes," complete Part III. ☐ Yes ☐ No

5 Chapter 4 Status (FATCA status) (See instructions for details and complete the certification below for the entity's applicable status.)
- ☐ Nonparticipating FFI (including an FFI related to a Reporting IGA FFI other than a deemed-compliant FFI, participating FFI, or exempt beneficial owner).
- ☐ Participating FFI.
- ☐ Reporting Model 1 FFI.
- ☐ Reporting Model 2 FFI.
- ☐ Registered deemed-compliant FFI (other than a reporting Model 1 FFI, sponsored FFI, or nonreporting IGA FFI covered in Part XII). See instructions.
- ☐ Sponsored FFI. Complete Part IV.
- ☐ Certified deemed-compliant nonregistering local bank. Complete Part V.
- ☐ Certified deemed-compliant FFI with only low-value accounts. Complete Part VI.
- ☐ Certified deemed-compliant sponsored, closely held investment vehicle. Complete Part VII.
- ☐ Certified deemed-compliant limited life debt investment entity. Complete Part VIII.
- ☐ Certain investment entities that do not maintain financial accounts. Complete Part IX.
- ☐ Owner-documented FFI. Complete Part X.
- ☐ Restricted distributor. Complete Part XI.
- ☐ Nonreporting IGA FFI. Complete Part XII.
- ☐ Foreign government, government of a U.S. possession, or foreign central bank of issue. Complete Part XIII.
- ☐ International organization. Complete Part XIV.
- ☐ Exempt retirement plans. Complete Part XV.
- ☐ Entity wholly owned by exempt beneficial owners. Complete Part XVI.
- ☐ Territory financial institution. Complete Part XVII.
- ☐ Excepted nonfinancial group entity. Complete Part XVIII.
- ☐ Excepted nonfinancial start-up company. Complete Part XIX.
- ☐ Excepted nonfinancial entity in liquidation or bankruptcy. Complete Part XX.
- ☐ 501(c) organization. Complete Part XXI.
- ☐ Nonprofit organization. Complete Part XXII.
- ☐ Publicly traded NFFE or NFFE affiliate of a publicly traded corporation. Complete Part XXIII.
- ☐ Excepted territory NFFE. Complete Part XXIV.
- ☐ Active NFFE. Complete Part XXV.
- ☐ Passive NFFE. Complete Part XXVI.
- ☐ Excepted inter-affiliate FFI. Complete Part XXVII.
- ☐ Direct reporting NFFE.
- ☐ Sponsored direct reporting NFFE. Complete Part XXVIII.
- ☐ Account that is not a financial account.

6 Permanent residence address (street, apt. or suite no., or rural route). **Do not use a P.O. box or in-care-of address** (other than a registered address).

City or town, state or province. Include postal code where appropriate. | Country

7 Mailing address (if different from above)

City or town, state or province. Include postal code where appropriate. | Country

For Paperwork Reduction Act Notice, see separate instructions.　　Cat. No. 59689N　　Form **W-8BEN-E** (Rev. 10-2021)

Form W-8BEN-E（法人の場合）

Form W-8BEN-E (Rev. 10-2021) Page **2**

Part I **Identification of Beneficial Owner** *(continued)*

8 U.S. taxpayer identification number (TIN), if required

9a GIIN	b Foreign TIN	c Check if FTIN not legally required . . . . . . ▶☐

10 Reference number(s) (see instructions)

Note: Please complete remainder of the form including signing the form in Part XXX.

Part II **Disregarded Entity or Branch Receiving Payment.** (Complete only if a disregarded entity with a GIIN or a branch of an FFI in a country other than the FFI's country of residence. See instructions.)

11 Chapter 4 Status (FATCA status) of disregarded entity or branch receiving payment

☐ Branch treated as nonparticipating FFI. ☐ Reporting Model 1 FFI. ☐ U.S. Branch.

☐ Participating FFI. ☐ Reporting Model 2 FFI.

12 Address of disregarded entity or branch (street, apt. or suite no., or rural route). **Do not use a P.O. box or in-care-of address** (other than a registered address).

City or town, state or province. Include postal code where appropriate.

Country

13 GIIN (if any) ______

Part III **Claim of Tax Treaty Benefits** (if applicable). (For chapter 3 purposes only.)

14 I certify that (check all that apply):

a ☐ The beneficial owner is a resident of ______ within the meaning of the income tax treaty between the United States and that country.

b ☐ The beneficial owner derives the item (or items) of income for which the treaty benefits are claimed, and, if applicable, meets the requirements of the treaty provision dealing with limitation on benefits. The following are types of limitation on benefits provisions that may be included in an applicable tax treaty (check only one; see instructions):

☐ Government ☐ Company that meets the ownership and base erosion test

☐ Tax-exempt pension trust or pension fund ☐ Company that meets the derivative benefits test

☐ Other tax-exempt organization ☐ Company with an item of income that meets active trade or business test

☐ Publicly traded corporation ☐ Favorable discretionary determination by the U.S. competent authority received

☐ Subsidiary of a publicly traded corporation ☐ No LOB article in treaty

☐ Other (specify Article and paragraph): ______

c ☐ The beneficial owner is claiming treaty benefits for U.S. source dividends received from a foreign corporation or interest from a U.S. trade or business of a foreign corporation and meets qualified resident status (see instructions).

15 **Special rates and conditions** (if applicable—see instructions):

The beneficial owner is claiming the provisions of Article and paragraph ______

of the treaty identified on line 14a above to claim a ______ % rate of withholding on (specify type of income): ______

Explain the additional conditions in the Article the beneficial owner meets to be eligible for the rate of withholding: ______

Part IV **Sponsored FFI**

16 Name of sponsoring entity: ______

17 **Check whichever box applies.**

☐ I certify that the entity identified in Part I:

- Is an investment entity;
- Is not a QI, WP (except to the extent permitted in the withholding foreign partnership agreement), or WT; **and**
- Has agreed with the entity identified above (that is not a nonparticipating FFI) to act as the sponsoring entity for this entity.

☐ I certify that the entity identified in Part I:

- Is a controlled foreign corporation as defined in section 957(a);
- Is not a QI, WP, or WT;
- Is wholly owned, directly or indirectly, by the U.S. financial institution identified above that agrees to act as the sponsoring entity for this entity; **and**
- Shares a common electronic account system with the sponsoring entity (identified above) that enables the sponsoring entity to identify all account holders and payees of the entity and to access all account and customer information maintained by the entity including, but not limited to, customer identification information, customer documentation, account balance, and all payments made to account holders or payees.

Form **W-8BEN-E** (Rev. 10-2021)

国際税務に関するトピック

自動的情報交換と税務調査

自動的情報交換と税務調査

平成24年度の税制改正により「国外財産調書制度」が創設され、以後、国外に5,000万円を超える財産を保有する富裕層は、毎年、日本の税務当局に、その財産の報告義務があります。

他方、当局は、どのような方法で、国外財産を把握し、活用しているのか、今月は、当局による富裕層等の海外資産把握のツールである自動的情報交換と税務調査についてのお話しです。

1　国外財産調書の提出義務

居住者（「非永住者」を除く。）は、その年の12月31日において、その価額の合計額が5,000万円を超える国外財産を有する場合には、その国外財産の種類、数量及び価額その他必要な事項を記載した**国外財産調書**を、その年の翌年の３月15日までに、住所地等の所轄税務署長に提出しなければなりません

（注）　国外財産調書に偽りの記載をして提出した場合又は国外財産調書を正当な理由がなく提出期限内に提出しなかった場合には、１年以下の懲役又は50万円以下の罰金に処されることがあります。

2　情報交換の目的

経済取引のグローバル化が進展する中で、国境を超える取引が恒常的に行われ、資産の保有・運用の形態も複雑化・多様化しています。

租税の賦課徴収を確実に行うためには、国内で入手できる情報だけでなく、国外にある情報を適切に入手することが重要となります。

国外にある情報を入手するには外国の主権（執行管轄権）により制約を受けることから、我が国を含め、各国の税務当局は租税条約等に基づき租税に関する情報を互いに提供する仕組み（情報交換）を設け、国際的な脱税及び租税回避に対処しています。

3　情報交換の形態

情報交換には、次の形態があります。

⑴　要請に基づく情報交換

課税当局が調査において課税上の問題点を把握した場合に、その問題に関連する情報の提供を求めるもの

(2) 自発的情報交換

課税当局が調査において外国における課税上の問題点を把握した場合に、その問題を提供するもの

(3) 自動的情報交換

課税当局が法定調書等から情報を収集し、大量に情報を提供するもの

4 自動的情報交換の対象となる金融機関等と口座情報

自動的情報交換とは、課税当局が金融機関等の法定調書等から情報を収集し、相互に、情報を提供するものですが、各国は、OECD 租税委員会が公表している共通報告基準（CRS:Common Reporting Standard）を適用し、情報の交換を行っています。

自動的情報交換の対象となる金融機関等と口座情報等は次とおりです。

- ➢ 金融機関等
  - ①銀行等の預金機関
  - ②生命保険会社等の特定保険会社
  - ③証券会社等の保管機関
  - ④信託等の投資事業体
- ➢ 対象となる口座
  - ①預金口座
  - ②キャッシュバリュー保険契約・年金契約
  - ③証券口座
  - ④信託受益権等の投資持分
- ➢ 口座情報
  - ①口座保有者の氏名・住所
  - ②納税者番号
  - ③口座残高
  - ④利子・配当等の年間受取総額等

（注） 共通報告基準とは

共通報告基準とは自動的情報交換の対象となる非居住者（個人・法人等）の口座の特定方法や情報の範囲等を各国で共通化する国際基準です。

5 国外財産の申告もれと税務調査

課税当局は、自動的情報交換により提供された口座情報と国外財産調書を照合することにより、国外財産の申告もれを把握し、富裕層の税務調査の端緒資料として活用しています。

還付請求実務編
［米国版］

THE
GUIDEBOOK OF
FOREIGN
TAX REFUND
FOR
PRACTITIONERS

還付請求実務編［米国版］

ガイダンス

内国法人が海外から利子、配当及び使用料等（以下「投資所得」といいます。）の支払を受ける場合には、一般的には、現地の法令により源泉所得税を課税されることになります。

ただし、我が国と租税条約を締結している国との間では、その源泉所得税の税率の軽減又は免税の手続き（以下「減免手続き」といいます。）を行うことにより、税率は軽減、又は税額は免除となります。

しかし、期限までに、減免手続きを行わない場合には、投資所得の支払の際に、現地の法令により源泉所得税を課税されることになります。

この場合に、後日、現地の源泉所得税を課税した者又は外国政府に対し、租税条約に基づく減免手続きにより源泉所得税の還付をすることができるか疑問のあるところです。

実務編では、まず、初めに、我が国との間で租税条約を締結している米国の居住者及び法人が、我が国において「減免手続き」を失念した場合の源泉所得税の還付のための手続きを説明します。

次に、米国で「減免手続き」を行わなかった場合の源泉所得税の還付の手続きを説明します。

さらに、米国で「減免手続き」を行わなかったことから、著作権の使用料に対し、現地法令の30%の税率により源泉所得税を課税された日本の法人又は居住者が、後日、米国歳入庁（Internal Revenue Service）から還付を受けるための「外国法人確定申告書」又は「非居住者確定申告書」の作成を演習事例により理解していただきます。

1　源泉所得税の還付

(1)　日本において非居住者及び外国法人が源泉所得税の還付を受ける場合の手続きと必要書類（支払先が米国の場合）

租税条約による軽減又は免除により源泉所得税の還付を受けようとする者は、支払者経由で支払者を所轄する税務署長に**「租税条約に関する届出書」（「特典条項に関する付表」・「居住者証明書を添付」を添付）**、**「租税条約に関する源泉徴収税額の還付請求書」**及び支払内容が確認できる書類の写しを提出しなければなりません。

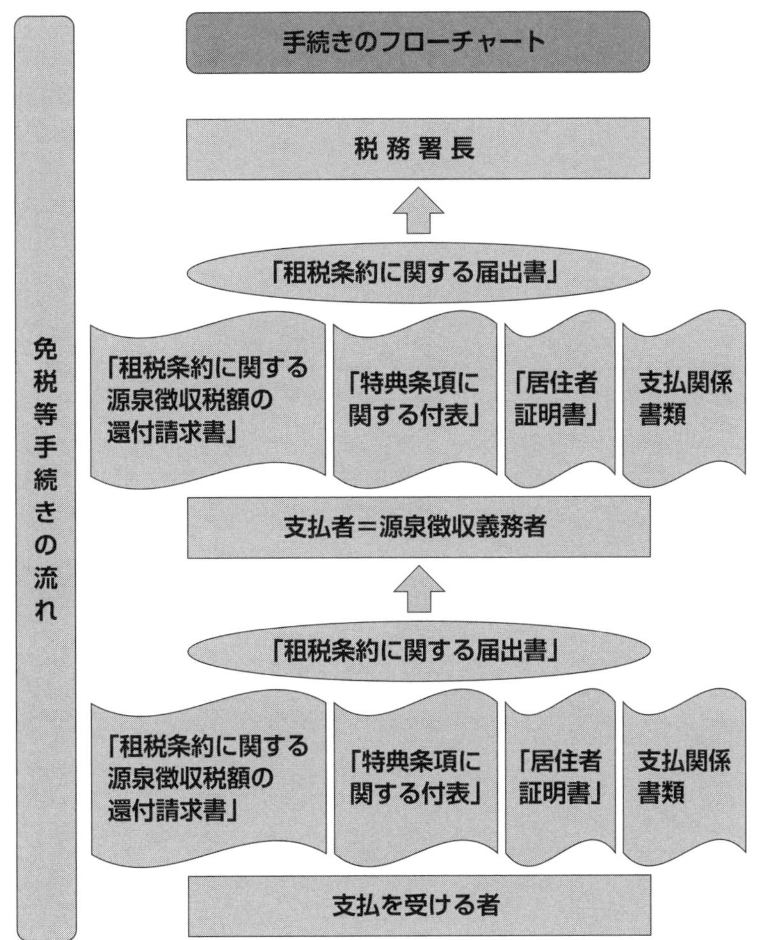

（還付請求の際の留意事項）

①　源泉所得税の還付請求のための法的根拠

租税条約に基づく軽減・免除の届出書については、租税条約等の実施に伴う特例等に関する法律（以下「実特法」。）第12条において「第二条から前条までに定めるもののほか、租税条約等の実施及びこの法律の適用に関し必要な事項は、総務省令、財務省令で定める。」と規定しています。

上記の規定を受けて租税条約に基づく軽減・免除の届出書については実特法の省令第2条①において、「……支払いを受ける日の前日までに、源泉徴収義務者を経由して、源泉徴収義務者の所轄税務署長に提出しなければならない。」と規定しています。

したがって、「租税条約に関する届出書」を提出しない場合には、支払の際に、20.42%の税率により、源泉徴収されることになります。

（実特令2①）

その後、租税条約による軽減・免除を受けるには、「租税条約に関する届出書」を後日、提出することにより、源泉徴収税額（20.42%）と限度税率（10%）の差額又は源泉徴収税額（20.42%）の還付を受けることができます。

（実特令2⑧）

② 代理人による源泉所得税の還付請求について

還付金については、原則として請求者である非居住者（個人）又は外国法人に還付されますが、代理人により還付請求することもできます（代理人に還付されます）。

その場合には、非居住者又は外国法人からの次の書類を添付しなければなりません。

① 委任状（当事者から代理人に対するもの）
② サイン証明書（委任状のサインが正当なものであるということの公的な証明）又は印鑑証明書
③ ①及び②の翻訳文

（国税庁HPタックスアンサー No.2889より）

様式３（租税条約に関する届出書）

様　式　3
FORM

税務署受付印

租税条約に関する届出書
APPLICATION FORM FOR INCOME TAX CONVENTION

（使用料に対する所得税及び復興特別所得税の軽減・免除
Relief from Japanese Income Tax and Special Income Tax for Reconstruction on Royalties）

この届出書の記載に当たっては、別紙の注意事項を参照してください。
See separate instructions.

（税務署整理欄 For official use only）

適用；有、無			
番号確認		身元確認	

□ 限度税率＿＿＿％ Applicable Tax Rate
□ 免　税（注11） Exemption (Note 11)

＿＿＿＿税務署長殿
To the District Director, ＿＿＿＿Tax Office

1　適用を受ける租税条約に関する事項；
Applicable Income Tax Convention
日本国と＿＿＿＿との間の租税条約第＿＿条第＿＿項＿＿
The Income Tax Convention between Japan and＿＿＿＿, Article＿＿, para.＿＿

2　使用料の支払を受ける者に関する事項；
Details of Recipient of Royalties

氏名又は名称 Full name		
個人番号又は法人番号（有する場合のみ記入） Individual Number or Corporate Number (Limited to case of a holder)		
個人の場合 Individual	住所又は居所 Domicile or residence	（電話番号 Telephone Number）
	国籍 Nationality	
法人その他の団体の場合 Corporation or other entity	本店又は主たる事務所の所在地 Place of head office or main office	（電話番号 Telephone Number）
	設立又は組織された場所 Place where the Corporation was established or organized	
	事業が管理・支配されている場所 Place where the business is managed and controlled	（電話番号 Telephone Number）
下記「4」の使用料につき居住者として課税される国及び納税地（注8） Country where the recipient is taxable as resident on Royalties mentioned in 4 below and the place where he is to pay tax (Note 8)		（納税者番号 Taxpayer Identification Number）
日本国内の恒久的施設の状況 Permanent establishment in Japan □有(Yes)，□無(No) If "Yes", explain:	名称 Name	
	所在地 Address	（電話番号 Telephone Number）
	事業の内容 Details of Business	

3　使用料の支払者に関する事項；
Details of Payer of Royalties

氏名又は名称 Full name		
住所（居所）又は本店（主たる事務所）の所在地 Domicile (residence) or Place of head office (main office)		（電話番号 Telephone Number）
個人番号又は法人番号（有する場合のみ記入） Individual Number or Corporate Number (Limited to case of a holder)		
日本国内にある事務所等 Office, etc. located in Japan	名称 Name	（事業の内容 Details of Business）
	所在地 Address	（電話番号 Telephone Number）

4　上記「3」の支払者から支払を受ける使用料で「1」の租税条約の規定の適用を受けるものに関する事項（注9）；
Details of Royalties received from the Payer to which the Convention mentioned in 1 above is applicable (Note 9)

使用料の内容 Description of Royalties	契約の締結年月日 Date of Contract	契約期間 Period of Contract	使用料の計算方法 Method of Computation for Royalties	使用料の支払期日 Due Date for Payment	使用料の金額 Amount of Royalties

5　その他参考となるべき事項（注10）；
Others (Note 10)

【裏面に続きます（Continue on the reverse）】

源泉所得税の還付に必要な書類

6　日本の税法上､届出書の「2」の外国法人が納税義務者とされるが､租税条約の規定によりその株主等である者（相手国居住者に限ります。）の所得として取り扱われる部分に対して租税条約の適用を受けることとされている場合の租税条約の適用を受ける割合に関する事項等（注4）；
Details of proportion of income to which the convention mentioned in 1 above is applicable, if the foreign company mentioned in 2 above is taxable as a company under Japanese tax law, and the convention is applicable to income that is treated as income of the member (limited to a resident of the other contracting country) of the foreign company in accordance with the provisions of the convention (Note 4)

届出書の「2」の外国法人の株主等で租税条約の適用を受ける者の氏名又は名称 Name of member of the foreign company mentioned in 2 above, to whom the Convention is applicable	間接保有 Indirect Ownership	持分の割合 Ratio of Ownership	受益の割合＝ 租税条約の適用を受ける割合 Proportion of benefit = Proportion for Application of Convention
	□	%	%
	□	%	%
	□	%	%
	□	%	%
	□	%	%
合計 Total		%	%

届出書の「2」の欄に記載した外国法人が支払を受ける「4」の使用料について、「1」の租税条約の相手国の法令に基づきその株主等である者の所得として取り扱われる場合には、その根拠法令及びその効力を生じる日を記載してください。
If royalties mentioned in 4 above that a foreign company mentioned in 2 above receives are treated as income of those who are its members under the law in the other contracting country of the convention mentioned in 1 above, enter the law that provides the legal basis to the above treatment and the date on which it will become effective.

根拠法令
Applicable law____________________　効力を生じる日　年　月　日
Effective date____________

7　日本の税法上､届出書の「2」の団体の構成員が納税義務者とされるが、租税条約の規定によりその団体の所得として取り扱われるものに対して租税条約の適用を受けることとされている場合の記載事項等（注5）；
Details if, while the partner of the entity mentioned in 2 above is taxable under Japanese tax law, and the convention is applicable to income that is treated as income of the entity in accordance with the provisions of the convention (Note 5)

他の全ての構成員から通知を受けこの届出書を提出する構成員の氏名又は名称____________
Full name of the partner of the entity who has been notified by all other partners and is to submit this form

届出書の「2」に記載した団体が支払を受ける「4」の使用料について、「1」の租税条約の相手国の法令に基づきその団体の所得として取り扱われる場合には、その根拠法令及びその効力を生じる日を記載してください。
If royalties mentioned in 4 above that an entity at mentioned in 2 above receives are treated as income of the entity under the law in the other contracting country of the convention mentioned in 1 above, enter the law that provides the legal basis to the above treatment and the date on which it will become effective.

根拠法令
Applicable law____________________　効力を生じる日　年　月　日
Effective date____________

○　代理人に関する事項　；　この届出書を代理人によって提出する場合には、次の欄に記載してください。
Details of the Agent　;　If this form is prepared and submitted by the Agent, fill out the following columns.

代理人の資格 Capacity of Agent in Japan	氏名（名称） Full name		納税管理人の届出をした税務署名 Name of the Tax Office where the Tax Agent is registered
□ 納税管理人 ※ Tax Agent □ その他の代理人 Other Agent	住所（居所・所在地） Domicile (Residence or location)	（電話番号 Telephone Number）	税務署 Tax Office

※　「納税管理人」とは、日本国の国税に関する申告、申請、請求、届出、納付等の事項を処理させるため、国税通則法の規定により選任し、かつ、日本国における納税地の所轄税務署長に届出をした代理人をいいます。

※ "Tax Agent" means a person who is appointed by the taxpayer and is registered at the District Director of Tax Office for the place where the taxpayer is to pay his tax, in order to have such agent take necessary procedures concerning the Japanese national taxes, such as filing a return, applications, claims, payment of taxes, etc., under the provisions of Act on General Rules for National Taxes.

○　適用を受ける租税条約が特典条項を有する租税条約である場合；
If the applicable convention has article of limitation on benefits
特典条項に関する付表の添付　□有Yes
"Attachment Form for Limitation on Benefits Article" attached　□添付省略Attachment not required
（特典条項に関する付表を添付して提出した租税条約に関する届出書の提出日　年　月　日）
Date of previous submission of the application for income tax convention with the "Attachment Form for Limitation on Benefits Article"

様式17－米（特典条項に関する付表（米））

様 式 17-米
FORM 17-US

特 典 条 項 に 関 す る 付 表（米）

ATTACHMENT FORM FOR LIMITATION ON BENEFITS ARTICLE(US)

記載に当たっては、別紙の注意事項を参照してください。
See separate instructions.

1 適用を受ける租税条約の特典条項に関する事項；
Limitation on Benefits Article of applicable Income Tax Convention
日本国とアメリカ合衆国との間の租税条約第22条
The Income Tax Convention between Japan and The United States of America, Article 22

2 この付表に記載される者の氏名又は名称；
Full name of Resident this attachment Form

	居住地国の権限ある当局が発行した居住者証明書を添付してください(注5)。 Attach Residency Certification issued by Competent Authority of Country of residence. (Note 5)

3 租税条約の特典条項の要件に関する事項；
AからCの順番に各項目の「□該当」又は「□非該当」の該当する項目に✓印を付してください。いずれかの項目に「該当」する場合には、それ以降の項目に記入する必要はありません。なお、該当する項目については、各項目ごとの要件に関する事項を記入の上、必要な書類を添付してください。(注6)
In order of sections A, B and C , check applicable box "Yes" or "No" in each line. If you check any box of "Yes", in section A to C, you need not fill the lines that follow. Applicable lines must be filled and necessary document must be attached. (Note6)

A

(1) 個人 Individual　□該当 Yes，□非該当 No

(2) 国、地方政府又は地方公共団体、中央銀行
Contracting Country, any Political Subdivision or Local Authority, Central Bank　□該当 Yes，□非該当 No

(3) 公開会社(注7)Publicly Traded Company (Note 7)　□該当 Yes，□非該当 No
(公開会社には、下表のC欄が6％未満である会社を含みません。)(注8)
("Publicly traded Company" does not include a Company for which the Figure in Column C below is less than 6%.)(Note 8)

株式の種類 Kind of Share	公認の有価証券市場の名称 Recognized Stock Exchange	シンボル又は証券コード Ticker Symbol or Security Code	発行済株式の総数の平均 Average Number of Shares outstanding	有価証券市場で取引された株式の数 Number of Shares traded on Recognized Stock Exchange	B/A(%)
			A	B	C　　%

(4) 公開会社の関連会社 Subsidiary of Publicly Traded Company　□該当 Yes，□非該当 No
(発行済株式の総数(＿＿＿＿株)の50%以上が上記(3)の公開会社に該当する5以下の法人により直接又は間接に所有されているものに限ります。)(注9)。
("Subsidiary of Publicly Traded Company" is limited to a company at least 50% of whose shares outstanding (＿＿＿＿shares) are owned directly or indirectly by 5 or fewer "Publicly Traded Companies" as defined in (3) above.)(Note 9)
＿＿年＿＿月＿＿日現在の株主の状況 State of Shareholders as of (date)＿＿/＿＿/＿＿

株主の名称 Name of Shareholder(s)	居住地国における納税地 Place where Shareholder is taxable in Country of residence	公認の有価証券市場 Recognized Stock Exchange	シンボル又は証券コード Ticker Symbol or Security Code	間接保有 Indirect Ownership	所有株式数 Number of Shares owned
1				□	
2				□	
3				□	
4				□	
5				□	
合　計 Total (持株割合 Ratio (%) of Shares owned)					(　%)

(5) 公益団体(注10)Public Service Organization (Note 10)　□該当 Yes，□非該当 No
設立の根拠法令 Law for Establishment＿＿＿＿　設立の目的 Purpose of Establishment＿＿＿＿

(6) 年金基金(注11)Pension Fund (Note 11)　□該当 Yes，□非該当 No
(直前の課税年度の終了の日においてその受益者、構成員又は参加者の50%を超える者が日本又はアメリカ合衆国の居住者である個人であるものに限ります。受益者等の50%超が、両締約国の居住者である事情を記入してください。)
"Pension Fund" is limited to one more than 50% of whose beneficiaries, members, or participants were individual residents of Japan or the United States of America as of the end of the prior taxable year. Provide below details showing that more than 50% of beneficiaries etc. are individual residents of either contracting country.

設立等の根拠法令 Law for Establishment＿＿＿＿　非課税の根拠法令 Law for Tax Exemption＿＿＿＿

Aのいずれにも該当しない場合は、Bに進んでください。If none of the lines in A applies, proceed to B.

源泉所得税の還付に必要な書類

B

次の(a)及び(b)の要件のいずれも満たす個人以外の者 Person other than an Individual, and satisfying both (a) and (b) below　□該当 Yes，□非該当 No

(a) 株式や受益に関する持分(＿＿＿＿＿＿)の 50%以上が、Aの(1)、(2)、(3)、(5)及び(6)に該当する日本又はアメリカ合衆国の居住者により直接又は間接に所有されていること(注 12)
Residents of Japan or the United States of America who fall under (1),(2),(3),(5) or (6) of A own directly or indirectly at least 50% of Shares or other beneficial Interests (＿＿＿＿＿＿) in the Person. (Note 12)
＿＿年＿＿月＿＿日現在の株主等の状況 State of Shareholders, etc. as of (date)＿＿＿＿/＿＿＿/＿＿＿

株主等の氏名又は名称 Name of Shareholders	居住地国における納税地 Place where Shareholders is taxable in Country of residence	Aの番号 Number of applicable Line in A	間接所有 Indirect Ownership	株主等の持分 Number of Shares owned
			□	
			□	
			□	
合　計 Total（持分割合 Ratio(%) of Shares owned）				(　%)

(b) 総所得のうち、課税所得の計算上控除される支出により、日本又はアメリカ合衆国の居住者に該当しない者（以下「第三国居住者」といいます。）に対し直接又は間接に支払われる金額が、50%未満であること(注 13)
Less than 50% of the person's gross income is paid or accrued directly or indirectly to persons who are not residents of Japan or the United States of America ("third country residents") in the form of payments that are deductible in computing taxable income in country of residence (Note 13)
第三国居住者に対する支払割合　Ratio of Payment to Third Country Residents　(通貨 Currency:　　　　)

	申告 Tax Return	源泉徴収税額 Withholding Tax		
	当該課税年度 Taxable Year	前々々課税年度 Taxable Year three Years prior	前々課税年度 Taxable Year two Years prior	前課税年度 Prior taxable Year
第三国居住者に対する支払 Payment to third Country Residents	A			
総所得 Gross Income	B			
A/B (%)	C　%	%	%	%

Bに該当しない場合は、Cに進んでください。If B does not apply, proceed to C.

C

次の(a)から(c)の要件を全て満たす者 Resident satisfying all of the following Conditions from (a) through (c)　□該当 Yes，□非該当 No

居住地国において従事している営業又は事業の活動の概要(注 14)；Description of trade or business in residence country (Note 14)

(a) 居住地国において従事している営業又は事業の活動が、自己の勘定のために投資を行い又は管理する活動（商業銀行、保険会社又は登録を受けた証券会社が行う銀行業、保険業又は証券業の活動を除きます。）ではないこと(注 15)：　□はい Yes，□いいえ No
Trade or business in country of residence is other than that of making or managing investments for the resident's own account (unless these activities are banking, insurance or securities activities carried on by a commercial bank, insurance company or registered securities dealer) (Note 15)　□はい Yes，□いいえ No

(b) 所得が居住地国において従事している営業又は事業の活動に関連又は付随して取得されるものであること(注 16)：
Income is derived in connection with or is incidental to that trade or business in country of residence (Note 16)

(c) （日本国内において営業又は事業の活動から所得を取得する場合）居住地国において行う営業又は事業の活動が日本国内において行う営業又は事業の活動との関係で実質的なものであること(注 17)：　□はい Yes，□いいえ No
(If you derive income from a trade or business activity in Japan) Trade or business activity carried on in the country of residence is substantial in relation to the trade or business activity carried on in Japan. (Note 17)

日本国内において従事している営業又は事業の活動の概要；Description of Trade or Business in Japan.

D　国税庁長官の認定（注 18）；
Determination by the NTA Commissioner (Note18)
国税庁長官の認定を受けている場合は、以下にその内容を記載してください。その認定の範囲内で租税条約の特典を受けることができます。なお、上記AからCまでのいずれかに該当する場合には、原則として、国税庁長官の認定は不要です。
If you have been a determination by the NTA Commissioner, describe below the determination. Convention benefits will be granted to the extent of the determination. If any of the above mentioned Lines A through to C are applicable, then in principle, determination by the NTA Commissioner is not necessary.

・認定を受けた日　Date of determination ＿＿＿年＿＿＿月＿＿＿日

・認定を受けた所得の種類
Type of income for which determination was given＿＿＿＿＿＿＿＿＿＿＿＿＿＿＿＿

様式11（租税条約に関する源泉徴収税額の還付請求書）

様 式 11
FORM

租税条約に関する源泉徴収税額の還付請求書

（発行時に源泉徴収の対象となる割引債及び芸能人等の役務提供事業の対価に係るものを除く。）

APPLICATION FORM FOR REFUND OF THE OVERPAID WITHHOLDING TAX OTHER THAN REDEMPTION OF SECURITIES WHICH ARE SUBJECT TO WITHHOLDING TAX AT THE TIME OF ISSUE AND REMUNERATION DERIVED FROM RENDERING PERSONAL SERVICES EXERCISED BY AN ENTERTAINER OR A SPORTSMAN IN ACCORDANCE WITH THE INCOME TAX CONVENTION

この還付請求書の記載に当たっては、裏面の注意事項を参照してください。
See instructions on the reverse side.

税務署受付印

（税務署整理欄 For official use only）

通 信 日付印	・ ・
確 認	
還付金；有、無	
番号確認	身元確認

＿＿＿＿税務署長殿
To the District Director, ＿＿＿＿ Tax Office

1 還付の請求をする者（所得の支払を受ける者）に関する事項；
Details of the Person claiming the Refund (Recipient of Income)

フリガナ Furigana 氏 名 又 は 名 称(注5) Full name (Note 5)	(納税者番号 Taxpayer Identification Number)
住所（居所）又は本店（主たる事務所）の所在地 Domicile (residence) or Place of head office (main office)	(電話番号 Telephone Number)
個人番号又は法人番号（有する場合のみ記入） Individual Number or Corporate Number (Limited to case of a holder)	

2 還付請求金額に関する事項；
Details of Refund

(1) 還付を請求する還付金の種類；（該当する下記の条項の□欄に✓印を付してください（注6）。）
Kind of Refund claimed; (Check applicable box below (Note 6).)

租税条約等の実施に伴う所得税法、法人税法及び地方税法の特例等に関する法律の施行に関する省令第15条第1項
Ministerial Ordinance of the Implementation of the Law concerning the Special Measures of the Income Tax Act, the Corporation Tax Act and the Local Tax Act for the Enforcement of Income Tax Conventions, paragraph 1 of Article15 ……………………

- □第1号(Subparagraph 1)
- □第3号(Subparagraph 3)
- □第5号(Subparagraph 5)
- □第7号(Subparagraph 7)

に掲げる還付金
Refund in accordance with the relevant subparagraph

(2) 還付を請求する金額；
Amount of Refund claimed　¥　　　円

(3) 還付金の受領場所等に関する希望；（該当する下記の□欄に✓印を付し、次の欄にその受領を希望する場所を記入してください。）
Options for receiving your refund; (Check the applicable box below and enter your information in the corresponding fields.)

受取希望場所 Receipt by transfer to:	銀行 Bank	支店 Branch	預金種類及び口座番号又は記号番号 Type of account and account number	口座名義人 Name of account holder
□ 日本国内の預金口座 a Japanese bank account				
□ 日本国外の預金口座(注7) a bank account outside Japan(Note 7)				
	支店住所(国名、都市名)Branch Address (Country ,City):		銀行コード(Bank Code)	送金通貨(Currency)
□ ゆうちょ銀行の貯金口座 an ordinary savings account at the Japan Post Bank		—		
□ 郵便局等の窓口受取りを希望する場合 the Japan Post Bank or the post office (receipt in person)			—	—

3 支払者に関する事項；
Details of Payer

氏 名 又 は 名 称 Full name	
住所（居所）又は本店（主たる事務所）の所在地 Domicile (residence) or Place of head office (main office)	(電話番号 Telephone Number)
個人番号又は法人番号（有する場合のみ記入） Individual Number or Corporate Number (Limited to case of a holder)	

4 源泉徴収義務者の証明事項；
Items to be certified by the withholding agent

(1) 所得の種類 Kind of Income	(2) 所得の支払期日 Due Date for Payment	(3) 所得の支払金額 Amount paid	(4)(3)の支払金額から源泉徴収した税額 Withholding Tax on (3)	(5)(4)の税額の納付年月日 Date of Payment of (4)	(6)租税条約を適用した場合に源泉徴収すべき税額 Tax Amount to be withheld under Tax Convention	(7)還付を受けるべき金額 Amount to be refunded ((4)−(6))
		円 yen	円 yen		円 yen	円 yen

上記の所得の支払金額につき、上記のとおり所得税及び復興特別所得税を徴収し、納付したことを証明します。
I hereby certify that the tax has been withheld and paid as shown above.

Date　　年　　月　　日　　源泉徴収義務者 Certifier of withholding agent ＿＿＿＿＿＿

【裏面に続きます (Continue on the reverse) 】

源泉所得税の還付に必要な書類

○ 代理人に関する事項 ；この届出書を代理人によって提出する場合には、次の欄に記載してください。
Details of the Agent ; If this form is prepared and submitted by the Agent, fill out the following columns.

代理人の資格 Capacity of Agent in Japan	氏名（名称） Full name		納税管理人の届出をした税務署名 Name of the Tax Office where the Tax Agent is registered
□ 納税管理人 ※ Tax Agent □ その他の代理人 Other Agent	住所（居所・所在地） Domicile (Residence or location)	（電話番号 Telephone Number）	税務署 Tax Office

※ 「納税管理人」については、「租税条約に関する届出書」の裏面の説明を参照してください。

※ "Tax Agent" is explained on the reverse side of the "Application Form for Income Tax Convention".

注意事項

還付請求書の提出について

1 この還付請求書は、還付を請求する税額の源泉徴収をされた所得の支払者（租税特別措置法第９条の３の２第１項に規定する利子等の支払の取扱者を含みます。以下同じです。）ごとに作成してください。

2 この還付請求書は、上記１の所得につき租税条約の規定の適用を受けるための別に定める様式（様式１～様式３、様式６～様式10及び様式19）による「租税条約に関する届出書」（その届出書に付表や書類を添付して提出することとされているときは、それらも含みます。）とともに、それぞれ正副２通を作成して所得の支払者に提出し、所得の支払者は還付請求書の「４」の欄の記載事項について証明をした後、還付請求書及び租税条約に関する届出書の正本をその支払者の所轄税務署長に提出してください。

3 この還付請求書を納税管理人以外の代理人によって提出する場合には、その委任関係を証する委任状をその翻訳文とともに添付してください。

4 この還付請求書による還付金を代理人によって受領することを希望する場合には、還付請求書にその旨を記載してください。この場合、その代理人が納税管理人以外の代理人であるときは、その委任関係を証する委任状をその翻訳文とともに添付してください。

還付請求書の記載について

5 納税者番号とは、租税の申告、納付その他の手続を行うために用いる番号、記号その他の符号でその手続をすべき者を特定することができるものをいいます。支払を受ける者の居住地である国に納税者番号に関する制度が存在しない場合や支払を受ける者が納税者番号を有しない場合には納税者番号を記載する必要はありません。

6 還付請求書の「２(1)」の条項の区分は、次のとおりです。

□第１号…… 租税条約の規定の適用を受ける人的役務の対価としての給与その他の報酬を２以上の支払者から支払を受けるため、その報酬につき「租税条約に関する届出書」を提出できなかったこと又は免税の金額基準が設けられている租税条約の規定の適用を受ける株主等対価の支払を受けるため、その対価につき「租税条約に関する届出書」を提供できなかったことに基因して源泉徴収をされた税額について還付の請求をする場合

□第３号…… 第１号及び第５号以外の場合で、租税条約の規定の適用を受ける所得につき「租税条約に関する届出書」を提出しなかったことに基因して源泉徴収をされた税額について還付の請求をする場合

□第５号…… 特定社会保険料を支払った又は控除される場合において、当該給与又は報酬につき源泉徴収をされた税額について還付の請求をする場合

□第７号…… 租税条約の規定が遡及して適用されることとなったため、当該租税条約の効力発生前に支払を受けた所得につき既に源泉徴収をされた税額について還付の請求をする場合

7 受取希望場所を「日本国外の預金口座」とした場合は、銀行コード（SWIFT コード、ABA ナンバー等）を記載し、送金通貨を指定してください。

なお、欧州向けの場合は、口座番号欄に IBAN コードを記載してください。

INSTRUCTIONS

Submission of the FORM

1 This form must be prepared separately for each Payer of Income who withheld the tax to be refunded(including Person in charge of handling payment of Interest or other payment who prescribed in paragraph 1 of Article 9-3-2 of the Act on Special Measures Concerning Taxation; the same applies below).

2 Submit this form in duplicate to the Payer of Income concerned together with the "Application Form for Income Tax Convention" (Forms 1 to 3, 6 to 10 and 19) prepared in duplicate for the application of Income Tax Convention to Income of 1 above (including attachment forms or documents if such attachment and documents are required). The Payer of the Income must certify the item in 4 on this form and then file the original of each form with the District Director of Tax Office for the place where the Payer resides.

3 An Agent other than the Tax Agent must attach a power of attorney together with its Japanese translation.

4 The applicants who wishes to receive refund through an Agent must state so on this form. If the Agent is an Agent other than a Tax Agent, a power of attorney must be attached together with its Japanese translation.

Completion of the FORM

5 The Taxpayer Identification Number is a number, code or symbol which is used for filing of return and payment of due amount and other procedures regarding tax, and which identifies a person who must take such procedures. If a system of Taxpayer Identification Number does not exist in the country where the recipient resides, or if the recipient of the payment does not have a Taxpayer Identification Number, it is not necessary to enter the Taxpayer Identification Number.

6 The distinction of the provisions of the item 2 (1) on this form is as follows:

□Subpara.1… For the refund of tax on salary or other remuneration for personal services withheld to the benefits of the Income Tax Convention which was withheld due to the failure to file the "Application Form for Income Tax Convention" because there are more than two Payers of Income. Alternatively, regarding the payment of stockholder value entitled according to the benefits of the Income Tax Convention, which provides an exemption amounts standard, the failure to file the "Application Form for Income Tax Convention" for the value.

□Subpara.3… For the refund of tax on income entitled to the benefits of the Income Tax Convention which was withheld due to the failure to file the "Application Form for Income Tax Convention" in cases other thanSubpara.1 and Subpara.5.

□Subpara.5… For the refund of tax which was withheld at the source from wages or remuneration with which designated insurance premiums were paid or from which said premiums are deducted.

□Subpara.7… For the refund of tax withheld on income paid before the coming into effect of Income Tax Convention when the Convention became applicable retroactively.

7 If you designate a "bank account outside Japan" as the place to receive of your choice, enter the bank code (Swift code, ABA number, etc.) and specify a currency for remittance.

In the case of accounts in Europe, enter IBAN code in the column for the account number.

═══ 参考・米国で「居住者証明書」を取得するための申請書類（Form 8802） ═══

○　米国で居住者証明書を取得するためにはForm 8802により申請します。

Form **8802**

(Rev. November 2018)

Department of the Treasury
Internal Revenue Service

Application for United States Residency Certification

▶ See separate instructions.

OMB No. 1545-1817

Important. For applicable user fee information, see the Instructions for Form 8802.

☐ **Additional request** (see instructions)　　☐ **Foreign claim form attached**

Electronic payment confirmation no. ▶

For IRS use only:
Pmt Amt $ ______
Deposit Date: __/__/__
Date Pmt Vrfd: __/__/__

Applicant's name	Applicant's U.S. taxpayer identification number
If a joint return was filed, spouse's name (see instructions) If a separate certification is needed for spouse, check here ▶ ☐	If a joint return was filed, spouse's U.S. taxpayer identification number

1 Applicant's name and taxpayer identification number as it should appear on the certification if different from above

2 Applicant's address during the calendar year for which certification is requested, including country and ZIP or postal code. If a P.O. box, see instructions.

3a Mail Form 6166 to the following address:

b Appointee Information (see instructions):
Appointee Name ▶ ______　CAF No. ▶ ______
Phone No. ▶ (　　) ______　Fax No. ▶ (　　) ______

4 Applicant is (check appropriate box(es)):

a ☐ Individual. Check all applicable boxes.
☐ U.S. citizen　☐ U.S. lawful permanent resident (green card holder)　☐ Sole proprietor
☐ Other U.S. resident alien. Type of entry visa ▶ ______
Current nonimmigrant status ▶ ______ and date of change (see instructions) ▶ ______
☐ Dual-status U.S. resident (see instructions). From ▶ ______ to ▶ ______
☐ Partial-year Form 2555 filer (see instructions). U.S. resident from ▶ ______ to ▶ ______

b ☐ Partnership. Check all applicable boxes.　☐ U.S.　☐ Foreign　☐ LLC

c ☐ Trust. Check if:　☐ Grantor (U.S.)　☐ Simple　☐ Rev. Rul. 81-100 Trust　☐ IRA (for Individual)
☐ Grantor (foreign)　☐ Complex　☐ Section 584　☐ IRA (for Financial Institution)

d ☐ Estate

e ☐ Corporation. If incorporated in the United States only, go to line 5. Otherwise, continue.
Check if:　☐ Section 269B　☐ Section 943(e)(1)　☐ Section 953(d)　☐ Section 1504(d)
Country or countries of incorporation ▶ ______
If a dual-resident corporation, specify other country of residence ▶ ______
If included on a consolidated return, attach page 1 of Form 1120 and Form 851.

f ☐ S corporation

g ☐ Employee benefit plan/trust. Plan number, if applicable ▶ ______
Check if:　☐ Section 401(a)　☐ Section 403(b)　☐ Section 457(b)

h ☐ Exempt organization. If organized in the United States, check all applicable boxes.
☐ Section 501(c)　☐ Section 501(c)(3)　☐ Governmental entity
☐ Indian tribe　☐ Other (specify) ▶ ______

i ☐ Disregarded entity. Check if:　☐ LLC　☐ LP　☐ LLP　☐ Other (specify) ▶ ______

j ☐ Nominee applicant (must specify the type of entity/individual for whom the nominee is acting) ▶

For Privacy Act and Paperwork Reduction Act Notice, see separate instructions.　Cat. No. 10003D　Form **8802** (Rev. 11-2018)

参考・米国で「居住者証明書」を取得するための申請書類（Form 8802）

Form 8802 (Rev. 11-2018) Page **2**

Applicant name:

5 Was the applicant required to file a U.S. tax form for the tax period(s) on which certification will be based?

Yes. Check the appropriate box for the form filed and **go to line 7.**

☐ 990 ☐ 990-T ☐ 1040 ☐ 1041 ☐ 1065 ☐ 1120 ☐ 1120S ☐ 3520-A ☐ 5227 ☐ 5500

☐ Other (specify) ▶ ____________

No. Attach explanation (see instructions). Check applicable box and go to line 6.

☐ Minor child ☐ QSub ☐ U.S. DRE ☐ Foreign DRE ☐ Section 761(a) election

☐ FASIT ☐ Foreign partnership ☐ Other ▶ ____________

6 Was the applicant's parent, parent organization or owner required to file a U.S. tax form? **(Complete this line only if you checked "No" on line 5.)**

Yes. Check the appropriate box for the form filed by the parent.

☐ 990 ☐ 990-T ☐ 1040 ☐ 1041 ☐ 1065 ☐ 1120 ☐ 1120S ☐ 5500

☐ Other (specify) ▶ ____________

Parent's/owner's name and address ▶ ____________

and U.S. taxpayer identification number ▶ ____________

No. Attach explanation (see instructions).

7 Calendar year(s) for which certification is requested.

Note. If certification is for the current calendar year or a year for which a tax return is not yet required to be filed, a penalties of perjury statement from Table 2 of the instructions must be entered on line 10 or attached to Form 8802 (see instructions).

8 Tax period(s) on which certification will be based (see instructions).

9 Purpose of certification. Must check applicable box (see instructions).

☐ Income tax ☐ VAT (specify NAICS codes) ▶ ____________

☐ Other (must specify) ▶ ____________

10 Enter penalties of perjury statements and any additional required information here (see instructions).

Sign here

Under penalties of perjury, I declare that I have examined this application and accompanying attachments, and to the best of my knowledge and belief, they are true, correct, and complete. If I have designated a third party to receive the residency certification(s), I declare that the certification(s) will be used only for obtaining information or assistance from that person relating to matters designated on line 9.

Keep a copy for your records.

Applicant's signature (or individual authorized to sign for the applicant) Applicant's daytime phone no.:

____________ Signature ____________ Date ____________

____________ Name and title (print or type)

____________ Spouse's signature. If a joint application, **both** must sign.

____________ Name (print or type)

Form **8802** (Rev. 11-2018)

参考・米国で「居住者証明書」を取得するための申請書類（Form 8802）

Form 8802 (Rev. 11-2018) **Worksheet for U.S. Residency Certification Application** Page **3**

Applicant Name	**Applicant TIN**

Appointee Name (If Applicable)

Calendar year(s) for which certification is requested (must be the same year(s) indicated on line 7)

11 Enter the number of certifications needed in the column to the right of each country for which certification is requested.
Note. If you are requesting certifications for more than one calendar year per country, enter the total number of certifications for all years for each country (see instructions).

Column A			**Column B**			**Column C**			**Column D**		
Country	**CC**	**#**	**Country**	**CC**	**#**	**Country**	**CC**	**#**	**Country**	**CC**	**#**
Armenia	AM		Finland	FI		Latvia	LG		South Africa	SF	
Australia	AS		France	FR		Lithuania	LH		Spain	SP	
Austria	AU		Georgia	GG		Luxembourg	LU		Sri Lanka	CE	
Azerbaijan	AJ		Germany	GM		Mexico	MX		Sweden	SW	
Bangladesh	BG		Greece	GR		Moldova	MD		Switzerland	SZ	
Barbados	BB		Hungary	HU		Morocco	MO		Tajikistan	TI	
Belarus	BO		Iceland	IC		Netherlands	NL		Thailand	TH	
Belgium	BE		India	IN		New Zealand	NZ		Trinidad and Tobago	TD	
Bermuda	BD		Indonesia	ID		Norway	NO		Tunisia	TS	
Bulgaria	BU		Ireland	EI		Pakistan	PK		Turkey	TU	
Canada	CA		Israel	IS		Philippines	RP		Turkmenistan	TX	
China	CH		Italy	IT		Poland	PL		Ukraine	UP	
Cyprus	CY		Jamaica	JM		Portugal	PO		United Kingdom	UK	
Czech Republic	EZ		Japan	JA		Romania	RO		Uzbekistan	UZ	
Denmark	DA		Kazakhstan	KZ		Russia	RS		Venezuela	VE	
Egypt	EG		Korea, South	KS		Slovak Republic	LO				
Estonia	EN		Kyrgyzstan	KG		Slovenia	SI				
Column A - Total			**Column B - Total**			**Column C - Total**			**Column D - Total**		

12 Enter the total number of certifications requested (add columns A, B, C, and D of line 11) . . . . ▶

Form **8802** (Rev. 11-2018)

⑵ 米国において日本の居住者及び法人が源泉所得税の還付を受ける場合の手続きと必要書類

イ Withholding agent（以下、「源泉徴収義務者」といいます。）の報告義務

源泉徴収義務者は、源泉徴収した翌年の３月15日までに、源泉徴収した事績を記載したForm 1042-S（我が国の法定調書に該当）を米国の国税庁（IRS）に一部、提出し、FDAPの受領者（Recipient）に対し３部交付しなければなりません。

一部は、源泉徴収義務者が保管することになります。

Form 1042-Sの提出先

CopyA …………………IRSへ提出（１部）

CopyB～CopyD ……受領者へ交付（３部）

CopyE …………………源泉徴収義務者保管（１部）

ロ 源泉徴収された場合の還付手続き

⑴ 上記イの報告期限（翌年３月15日）前の対応

Form 1042-Sの報告期限（翌年３月15日）前は、源泉徴収義務者に対しForm W-8BEN-E（法人の場合）を提出し、源泉徴収義務者から徴収税額を還付してもらうことになります。

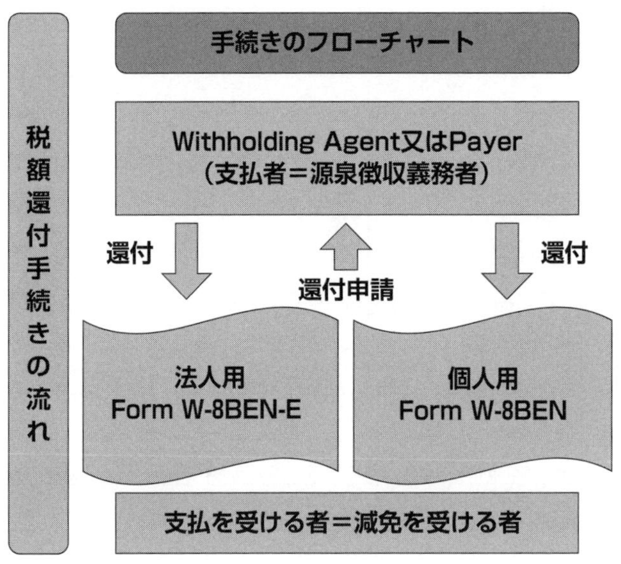

⑵　上記２の報告期限（翌年３月15日）後の対応

○　法人用

還付申請に際し米国歳入庁に対し、Form 1120-F により、Form W-BEN-E、Form 8843及び居住者証明書（日本の税務署長が発行）を添付し、確定申告により還付を受けることになります。

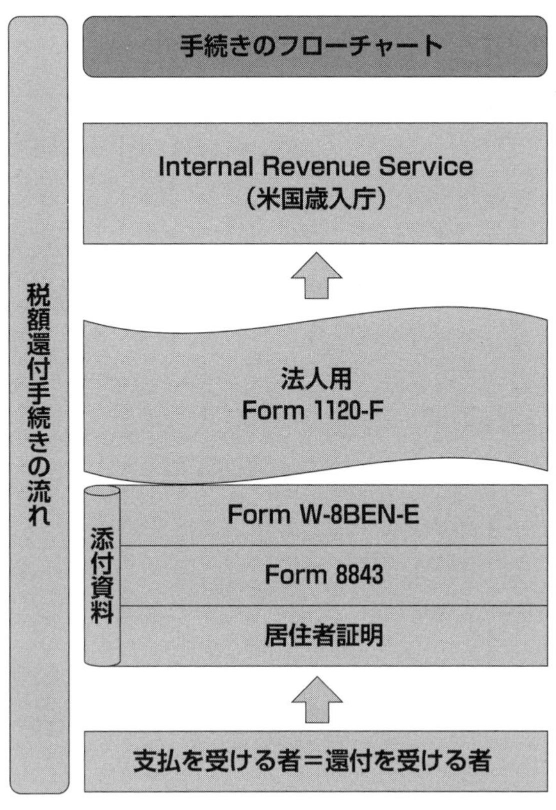

○　個人用

還付申請に際し米国歳入庁に対し、Form 1004-NR により、Form W-BEN-E、Form 8843及び居住者証明書（日本の税務署長が発行）を添付し、確定申告により還付を受けることになります。

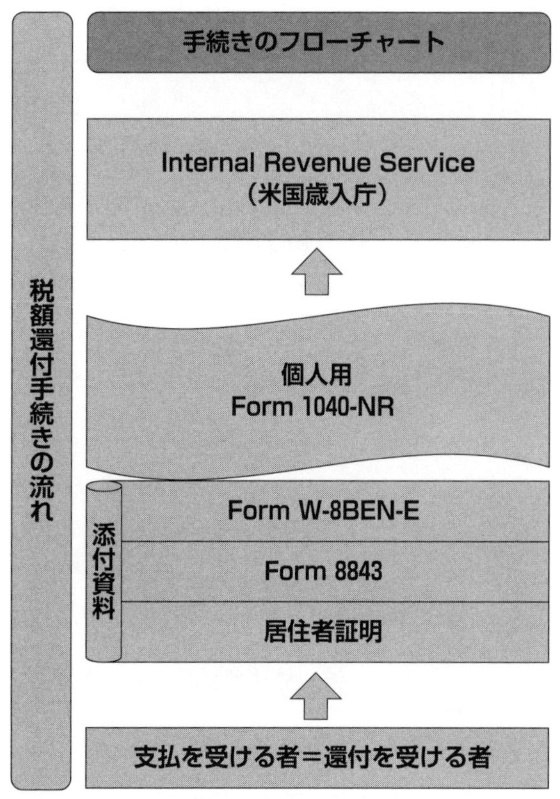

2　Form 1120-F（外国法人確定申告書）について

⑴　Form 1120-F（U.S.Income Tax Return of a Foreign Corporation）の作成目的

① 外国法人の所得申告（所得・収益・損失・控除・税額控除等）

② 米国法人税の納税債務の計算

③ 法人税の還付

④ Form 8833の通知（Treaty-Based Return Position Disclosure）

⑤ 外国法人の支店の法人税の納税額と超過利子の計算

⑵　主な申告対象者

① 米国内で事業を営む法人
（米国内の所得の源泉の有無にかかわらず、また、その事業が租税条約による免税の適用の有無にかかわらず。）

② 米国内の事業に関連する所得、譲渡益、及び損失がある法人

③ 米国内で事業を営んでいないが、米国内に所得の源泉があり、その所得について源泉所得税による課税が十分されていない法人

④ 外国法人が税額の過払分の還付を受ける場合
（米国が所得の源泉の源泉所得税の還付申請のための簡易手続きを参照）

⑤ 外国法人が所得控除及び税額控除を申請する場合

⑥ 外国法人が取得する所得に対する米国税法を無効あるいは修正する租税条約の適用を求める場合

Form 1120-F（外国法人確定申告書）・様式・2022年版

Form **1120-F** Department of the Treasury Internal Revenue Service

U.S. Income Tax Return of a Foreign Corporation

For calendar year 2022, or tax year beginning ________, 2022, and ending ________, 20____

Go to *www.irs.gov/Form1120F* for instructions and the latest information.

OMB No. 1545-0123

2022

Type or Print	Name	**Employer identification number**
	Number, street, and room or suite no. (see instructions)	**Check box(es) if:** ☐ Initial return ☐ Name or address change ☐ Final return ☐ First post-merger return ☐ Amended return ☐ Schedule M-3 attached ☐ Protective return
	City or town, state or province, country, and ZIP or foreign postal code	

A Country of incorporation ________

B Foreign country under whose laws the income reported on this return is also subject to tax ________

C Date incorporated ________

D ( ) Location of corporation's primary books and records (city, province or state, and country) ________

(2) Principal location of worldwide business ________

(3) If the corporation maintains an office or place of business in the United States, check here . . . ☐

E If the corporation had an agent in the United States at any time during the tax year, enter:

( ) Type of agent ________

(2) Name ________

(3) Address ________

F See the instructions and enter the corporation's principal:

( ) Business activity code number ________

(2) Business activity ________

(3) Product or service ________

G Check method of accounting: **( )** ☐ Cash **(2)** ☐ Accrual **(3)** ☐ Other (specify)

Computation of Tax Due or Overpayment

	Tax from Section I, line 11, page 3				
2	Tax from Section II, Schedule J, line 9, page 5		2		
3	Tax from Section III (add lines 6 and 10 on page 6)		3		
	Total tax. Add lines 1 through 3				
5a	2021 overpayment credited to 2022	5a			
b	2022 estimated tax payments	5b			
c	Less 2022 refund applied for on Form 4466	5c ( )			
d	Combine lines 5a through 5c		5d		
e	Tax deposited with Form 7004		5e		
f	Credit for tax paid on undistributed capital gains (attach Form 2439)		5f		
g	Credit for federal tax paid on fuels (attach Form 4136). See instructions		5g		
h	Reserved for future use		5h		
i	U.S. income tax paid or withheld at source (add line 12, page 3, and amounts from Forms 8288-A and 8805 (attach Forms 8288-A and 8805))		5i		
j	Total payments. Add lines 5d through 5i			5j	
6	Estimated tax penalty (see instructions). Check if Form 2220 is attached ☐			6	
7	**Amount owed.** If line 5j is smaller than the total of lines 4 and 6, enter amount owed			7	
8a	**Overpayment.** If line 5j is larger than the total of lines 4 and 6, enter amount overpaid			8a	
b	**Amount of overpayment on line 8a resulting from tax deducted and withheld under Chapters 3 and** (from Schedule W, line 7, page 8)			8b	
9	Enter portion of line 8a you want **Credited to 2023 estimated tax** . . . **Refunded**			9	

Sign Here Under penalties of perjury, I declare that I have examined this return, including accompanying schedules and statements, and to the best of my knowledge and belief, it is true, correct, and complete. Declaration of preparer (other than taxpayer) is based on all information of which preparer has any knowledge.

Signature of officer | Date | Title

May the IRS discuss this return with the preparer shown below (see instructions)? ☐ **Yes** ☐ **No**

Paid Preparer Use Only	Print/Type preparer's name	Preparer's signature	Date	Check ☐ if self-employed	PTIN
	Firm's name			Firm's EIN	
	Firm's address			Phone no.	

For Paperwork Reduction Act Notice, see separate instructions. Cat. No. 11470I Form **1120-F** (2022)

Additional Information *(continued from page 1)*

		Yes	No
H	Did the corporation's method of accounting change from the preceding tax year?		
	If "Yes," attach a statement with an explanation.		
I	Did the corporation's method of determining income change from the preceding tax year?		
	If "Yes," attach a statement with an explanation.		
J	Did the corporation file a U.S. income tax return for the preceding tax year?		
K	**(1)** At any time during the tax year, was the corporation engaged in a trade or business in the United States?		
	(2) If "Yes," is taxpayer's trade or business within the United States solely the result of a section 897 (FIRPTA) sale or disposition?		
L	Did the corporation have a permanent establishment in the United States for purposes of any applicable tax treaty between the United States and a foreign country?		
	If "Yes," enter the name of the foreign country: ______________		
M	Did the corporation have any transactions with related parties?		
	If "Yes," Form 5472 may have to be filed (see instructions).		
	Enter number of Forms 5472 attached ______________		
N	Is the corporation a controlled foreign corporation? (See section 957(a) for definition.)		
O	Is the corporation a personal service corporation? (See instructions for definition.)		
P	Enter tax-exempt interest received or accrued during the tax year (see instructions) $ ______________		
Q	At the end of the tax year, did the corporation own, directly or indirectly, 50% or more of the voting stock of a U.S. corporation? (See section 267(c) for rules of attribution.)		
	If "Yes," attach a statement showing **( )** name and EIN of such U.S. corporation; **(2)** percentage owned; and **(3)** taxable income or (loss) before NOL and special deductions of such U.S. corporation for the tax year ending with or within your tax year.		
R	If the corporation has an NOL for the tax year and is electing to forego the carryback period, check here (see instructions) . . . . ☐		
S	Enter the available NOL carryover from prior tax years. (Do not reduce it by any deduction on line 30a, page 4.) $ ______________		
T	Is the corporation a subsidiary in a parent-subsidiary controlled group?		
	If "Yes," enter the parent corporation's:		
	(1) EIN ______________		
	(2) Name ______________		
U	**(1)** Is the corporation a dealer under section 475? . .		
	(2) Did the corporation mark to market any securities or commodities other than in a dealer capacity? . .		
V	At the end of the tax year, did any individual, partnership, corporation, estate, or trust own, directly or indirectly, 50% or more of the corporation's voting stock? (See section 267 (c) for rules of attribution.)		
	If "Yes," attach a statement showing the name and identifying number. (Do not include any information already entered in item **T**.) Enter percentage owned ______________		
W	**(1)** Is the corporation taking a position on this return that a U.S. tax treaty overrules or modifies an Internal Revenue law of the United States, thereby causing a reduction of tax? .		
	If "Yes," the corporation is generally required to complete and attach Form 8833. See Form 8833 for exceptions.		
	Note: *Failure to disclose a treaty-based return position may result in a $10,000 penalty (see section 6712).*		
	(2) Is the corporation claiming treaty benefits pursuant to, or otherwise filing its return pursuant to, a Competent Authority determination or an Advance Pricing Agreement? . . .		
	If "Yes," attach a copy of the Competent Authority determination letter or Advance Pricing Agreement to your return.		
X	During the tax year, did the corporation own any entity that was disregarded as an entity separate from its owner under Regulations sections 301.7701-2 and 301.7701-3? . .		
	If "Yes," attach a statement listing the name, country under whose laws the entity was organized, and EIN (if any) of each such entity.		
Y	**(1)** Did a partnership allocate to the corporation a distributive share of income from a directly owned partnership interest, any of which is ECI or treated as ECI by the partnership or the partner?		
	If "Yes," attach Schedule P. See instructions.		
	(2) During the tax year, did the corporation own, directly or indirectly, at least a 10% interest, in any foreign partnership?		
	If "Yes," see instructions for required attachment.		
Z	**( )** Has the corporation engaged in any transactions the results of which are subject to the arm's-length standard under section 482 and its regulations?		
	(2) Has the corporation recognized any interbranch amounts? If "Yes," attach statement (see instructions)		
AA	Is the corporation required to file Schedule UTP (Form 1120), Uncertain Tax Position Statement (see instructions)?		
	If "Yes," complete and attach Schedule UTP.		
BB	During the corporation's tax year, did the corporation make any payments that would require it to file Forms 1042 and 1042-S under chapter 3 (sections 1441 through 1464) or chapter 4 (sections 1471 through 1474) of the Code? . .		
CC	Is the corporation (including the home office or any branch) a qualified derivatives dealer (QDD)?		
	( ) If "Yes," attach Schedule Q (Form 1120-F) (see instructions)		
	(2) If "Yes," enter the QI-EIN ______________		
DD	Does the corporation have gross receipts of at least $500 million in any of the 3 preceding tax years (see sections 59A(e)(2) and (3))?		
	If "Yes," complete and attach Form 8991.		
EE	During the tax year, did the corporation pay or accrue any interest or royalty for which a deduction is not allowed under section 267A (see instructions)?		
	If "Yes," enter the total amount of the disallowed deductions . . . . $		

Form **1120-F** (2022)

Form 1120-F（外国法人確定申告書）・様式・2022年版

Form 1120-F (2022) Page 3

Additional Information *(continued from page 2)*

		Yes	No
FF	Did the corporation have an election under section 163(j) for any real property trade or business or any farming business in effect during the tax year (see instructions)?		
GG	Does the corporation satisfy **one or more** of the following (see instructions)?		
	(1) The corporation owns a pass-through entity with current, or prior year carryover, excess business interest expense.		
	(2) The corporation's aggregate average annual gross receipts (determined under section 448(c)) for the 3 tax years preceding the current tax year are more than $27 million and the corporation has business interest expense.		
	(3) The corporation is a tax shelter and the corporation has business interest expense. If "Yes," to any, complete and attach Form 8990.		

		Yes	No
HH	During the tax year, did the corporation dispose of an interest in a partnership that directly or indirectly engaged in a trade or business within the United States?		
II	Is the corporation attaching Form 8996 to certify as a Qualified Opportunity Fund? . . . . If "Yes," enter amount from Form 8996, line 15 . . . . . $__________		

SECTION I—Income From U.S. Sources Not Effectively Connected With the Conduct of a Trade or Business in the United States—Do not report items properly withheld and reported on Form 1042-S. See instructions.

Report all gross transportation income subject to 4% tax on line 9. Report other column (a) income items only if not properly withheld and reported on Form 1042-S. The rate of tax on these **gross** income items is 30% or such lower rate specified by tax treaty. No deductions are allowed against these types of income. Enter treaty rates where applicable. **If the corporation is claiming a lower treaty rate, also complete item W on page 2.** If multiple treaty rates apply to a type of income (for example, subsidiary and portfolio dividends or dividends received by disregarded entities), attach a statement showing the amounts, tax rates, and withholding for each.

Name of treaty country, if any

	(a) Class of income (see instructions)	(b) Gross amount	(c) Rate of tax (%)	(d) Amount of tax liability	(e) Amount of U.S. income tax paid or withheld at the source
1	Interest				
2a	Dividends (excluding payments received by QDDs in their equity derivatives dealer capacity)				
2b	Dividend equivalents (excluding payments received by QDDs in their equity derivatives dealer capacity)				
3	Rents				
4	Royalties				
5	Annuities				
6	Gains from disposal of timber, coal, or domestic iron ore with a retained economic interest (attach supporting statement) . .				
7	Gains from sale or exchange of patents, copyrights, etc.				
8	Fiduciary distributions (attach supporting statement)				
9	Gross transportation income (see instructions)		4		
0	Other items of income				
	Total. Enter here and on line 1, page 1				
2	Total. Enter here and include on line 5i, page 1				

3 Is the corporation fiscally transparent under the laws of the foreign jurisdiction with respect to any item of income listed above? . . . . ☐ Yes ☐ No

If "Yes," attach a statement that provides the information requested above with respect to each such item of income.

Form **1120-F** (2022)

SECTION II—Income Effectively Connected With the Conduct of a Trade or Business in the United States (see instructions)

Important: *Fill in all applicable lines and schedules. If you need more space, see* ***Assembling the Return*** *in the instructions.*

Income	a	Gross receipts or sales [ ] **b** Less returns and allowances [ ] **c** Bal	c	
	2	Cost of goods sold (attach Form 1125-A)	2	
	3	Gross profit (subtract line 2 from line 1c)	3	
		Dividends (Schedule C, line 13)		
	5	Interest	5	
	6	Gross rents	6	
		Gross royalties		
	8	Capital gain net income (attach Schedule D (Form 1120))	8	
	9	Net gain or (loss) from Form 4797, Part II, line 17 (attach Form 4797)	9	
	0	Other income (see instructions—attach statement)	0	
		Total income. Add lines 3 through 10		
Deductions (See instructions for limitations on deductions.)	12	Compensation of officers (see instructions—attach Form 1125-E)	12	
	3	Salaries and wages (less employment credits)	3	
		Repairs and maintenance		
	15	Bad debts (for bad debts over $500,000, attach a list of debtors and amounts)	15	
	6	Rents	6	
		Taxes and licenses		
	18	Interest expense from Schedule I, line 25 (see instructions)	18	
	9	Charitable contributions	9	
	20	Depreciation from Form 4562 not claimed on Form 1125-A or elsewhere on return (attach Form 4562)	20	
	21	Depletion	21	
	22	Advertising	22	
	23	Pension, profit-sharing, etc., plans	23	
	24	Employee benefit programs	24	
	25	Reserved for future use	25	
	26	Deductions allocated and apportioned to ECI from Schedule H, line 20 (see instructions)	26	
	27	Other deductions (attach statement)	27	
	28	**Total deductions.** Add lines 12 through 27	28	
	29	Taxable income before NOL deduction and special deductions (subtract line 28 from line 11)	29	
	30	**Less:** **a** Net operating loss deduction (see instructions) — 30a		
		b Special deductions (Schedule C, line 14) — 30b		
		c Add lines 30a and 30b	30c	
	31	Taxable income or (loss). Subtract line 30c from line 29	31	

Form **1120-F** (2022)

Form 1120-F（外国法人確定申告書）・様式・2022年版

Form 1120-F (2022) Page **5**

SECTION II—Income Effectively Connected With the Conduct of a Trade or Business in the United States *(continued)*

Schedule C **Dividends and Special Deductions** (see instructions)

		(a) Dividends	(b) %	(c) Special deductions: (a) × (b)
1	Dividends from less-than-20%-owned domestic corporations (other than debt-financed stock)		50	
2	Dividends from 20%-or-more-owned domestic corporations (other than debt-financed stock)		65	
3	Dividends on certain debt-financed stock of domestic and foreign corporations (section 246A)		see instructions	
	Dividends on certain preferred stock of less-than-20%-owned public utilities		23.3	
5	Dividends on certain preferred stock of 20%-or-more-owned public utilities		26.7	
6	Dividends from less-than-20%-owned foreign corporations		50	
	Dividends from 20%-or-more-owned foreign corporations		65	
8	**Subtotal.** Add lines 1 through 7. See instructions for limitation		see instructions	
9	Dividends from foreign corporations not included on line 3, 6, or 7			
0	IC-DISC and former DISC dividends not included on line 1, 2, or 3 (section 246(d))			
	Other dividends			
12	Deduction for dividends paid on certain preferred stock of public utilities			
3	**Total dividends.** Add column (a), lines 8 through 11. Enter here and on line 4, page 4			
14	**Total special deductions.** Add column (c), lines 8 and 12. Enter here and on line 30b, page 4			

Schedule J **Tax Computation** (see instructions)

	Check if the corporation is a member of a controlled group (attach Schedule O (Form 1120)) ☐				
2	Income tax			2	
3	Base erosion minimum tax amount (attach Form 8991)			3	
	Add lines 2 and 3				
5a	Foreign tax credit (attach Form 1118)	5a			
b	General business credit (attach Form 3800)	5b			
c	Credit for prior year minimum tax (attach Form 8827)	5c			
d	Bond credits from Form 8912	5d			
6	**Total credits.** Add lines 5a through 5d			6	
	Subtract line 6 from line 4				
8	Other taxes. Check if from: ☐ Form 4255 ☐ Form 8611 ☐ Form 8697 ☐ Form 8866 ☐ Form 8902 ☐ Other (attach statement)			8	
9	**Total tax.** Add lines 7 and 8. Enter here and on line 2, page 1			9	

Form **1120-F** (2022)

Form 1120-F (2022) Page **6**

SECTION III—Branch Profits Tax and Tax on Excess Interest

Part I—Branch Profits Tax (see instructions)

1	Enter the amount from Section II, line 29	1	
2	Enter total adjustments to line 1 to get effectively connected earnings and profits. (Attach required statement showing the nature and amount of adjustments.) (See instructions.)	2	
3	Effectively connected earnings and profits. Combine line 1 and line 2	3	
4a	Enter U.S. net equity at the end of the current tax year. (Attach required statement.)	a	
b	Enter U.S. net equity at the end of the prior tax year. (Attach required statement.)	b	
c	Increase in U.S. net equity. If line 4a is greater than or equal to line 4b, subtract line 4b from line 4a. Enter the result here and skip to line 4e	c	
d	Decrease in U.S. net equity. If line 4b is greater than line 4a, subtract line 4a from line 4b	d	
e	Non-previously taxed accumulated effectively connected earnings and profits. Enter excess, if any, of effectively connected earnings and profits for preceding tax years beginning after 1986 over any dividend equivalent amounts for those tax years	e	
5	Dividend equivalent amount. Subtract line 4c from line 3. If zero or less, enter -0-. If no amount is entered on line 4c, add the lesser of line 4d or line 4e to line 3 and enter the total here	5	
6	**Branch profits tax.** Multiply line 5 by 30% (0.30) (or lower treaty rate if the corporation is a qualified resident or otherwise qualifies for treaty benefits). (See instructions.) Enter here and include on line 3, page 1. **Also complete item W on page 2**	6	

Part II—Tax on Excess Interest (see instructions for this Part and for Schedule I (Form 1120-F))

7a	Enter the interest from Section II, line 18	7a	
b	Enter the inverse of the total amount deferred, capitalized, and disallowed from Schedule I, line 24g (i.e., if line 24g is negative, enter as a positive number; if line 24g is positive, enter as a negative number)	b	
c	Combine lines 7a and 7b (amount must equal Schedule I, line 23)	7c	
8	**Branch Interest** (see instructions for definition): Enter the sum of Schedule I, line 9, column (c), and Schedule I, line 22. If the interest paid by the foreign corporation's U.S. trade or business was increased because 80% or more of the foreign corporation's assets are U.S. assets, check this box ☐	8	
9a	Excess interest. Subtract line 8 from line 7c. If zero or less, enter -0-	9a	
b	If the foreign corporation is a bank, enter the excess interest treated as interest on deposits (see instructions for rules for computing this amount). Otherwise, enter -0-	9b	
c	Subtract line 9b from line 9a	9c	
10	**Tax on excess interest.** Multiply line 9c by 30% (0.30) (or lower treaty rate if the corporation is a qualified resident or otherwise qualifies for treaty benefits). (See instructions.) Enter here and include on line 3, page 1. **Also complete item W on page 2**	0	

Part III—Additional Information

		Yes	No
11	Is the corporation claiming a reduction in, or exemption from, the branch profits tax due to:		
a	A complete termination of all U.S. trades or businesses?		
b	The tax-free liquidation or reorganization of a foreign corporation?		
c	The tax-free incorporation of a U.S. trade or business?		
	If **a** or **b** applies and the transferee is a domestic corporation, attach Form 8848. If **c** applies, attach the statement required by Temporary Regulations section 1.884-2T(d)(5).		

Form **1120-F** (2022)

Form 1120-F（外国法人確定申告書）・様式・2022年版

Form 1120-F (2022) Page **7**

Note: *Check if completing on* ☐ U.S. basis or ☐ Worldwide basis

Schedule L **Balance Sheets per Books**

		Beginning of tax year		End of tax year	
	Assets	(a)	(b)	(c)	(d)
	Cash				
2a	Trade notes and accounts receivable				
b	Less allowance for bad debts	( )		( )	
3	Inventories				
	U.S. government obligations				
5	Tax-exempt securities (see instructions)				
6a	Interbranch current assets*				
b	Other current non-U.S. assets*				
c	Other current U.S. assets*				
7	Loans to shareholders				
8	Mortgage and real estate loans				
9a	Other loans and investments—non-U.S. assets*				
b	Other loans and investments—U.S. assets*				
10a	Buildings and other depreciable assets				
b	Less accumulated depreciation	( )		( )	
11a	Depletable assets				
b	Less accumulated depletion	( )		( )	
12	Land (net of any amortization)				
3a	Intangible assets (amortizable only)				
b	Less accumulated amortization	( )		( )	
	Assets held in trust				
5	Other non-current interbranch assets*				
16a	Other non-current non-U.S. assets*				
b	Other non-current U.S. assets*				
17	Total assets				
	Liabilities				
18	Accounts payable				
9	Mortgages, notes, bonds payable in less than 1 year:				
a	Interbranch liabilities*				
b	Third-party liabilities*				
20	Other current liabilities*				
2	Loans from shareholders				
22	Mortgages, notes, bonds payable in 1 year or more:				
a	Interbranch liabilities*				
b	Third-party liabilities*				
23	Liabilities held in trust				
24a	Other interbranch liabilities*				
b	Other third-party liabilities*				
	Equity				
25	Capital stock: **a** Preferred stock				
	b Common stock				
26	Additional paid-in capital				
2	Retained earnings—Appropriated*				
28	Retained earnings—Unappropriated				
29	Adjustments to shareholders' equity*				
30	Less cost of treasury stock		( )		( )
3	Total liabilities and shareholders' equity				

*Attach statement—see instructions.

Form **1120-F** (2022)

Form 1120-F (2022) Page **8**

Schedule W **Overpayment Resulting From Tax Deducted and Withheld Under Chapters 3 and 4**

	Total Chapter 3 and 4 payments. Enter the amount from page 1, line 5i				
2	Enter the tax amount from page 1, line 1	2			
3	Enter the portion of the tax amount shown on page 1, line 2, pertaining to income associated with amounts deducted and withheld under sections 1445 and 1446 (see instructions for general guidelines)	3			
	Total Chapter 3 and tax. Combine lines 2 and 3				
5	**Tentative overpayment resulting from tax deducted and withheld under Chapters 3 and .** Subtract line 4 from line 1			5	
6	Enter the amount from page 1, line 8a			6	
	Overpayment resulting from tax deducted and withheld under Chapters 3 and 4. Enter the smaller of line 5 or line 6. Enter the result here and on page 1, line 8b				

Form **1120-F** (2022)

Form 1120-F（外国法人確定申告書）・和訳（一部）・2022年版

1120-F　外国法人確定申告書　2022

事業年度

会社名
所在地
都市名・郵便番号・国名

Employer identification number

チェック……………○名称又は住所変更　○当初申告
ボックス　○合併後申告　○最終申告
○Schedule M-3の添付　○修正申告
○予備申告

A　会社設立国

B　この申告書により報告される所得に対して課税が行われる国

C　会社設立年月日

D(1)　会社の主要帳簿と会計記録の保管場所
(2)　世界的事業を行う場所
(3)　米国内に事業を行う場所を有する場合にはここにチェック

E　米国内に課税期間中に代理人を有する場合には、次の事項を記載
(1)　代理人の類型
(2)　名称
(3)　所在地

F　記載要領から次の事項を記載
(1)　Business activity code number
(2)　Business activity
(3)　Product or service

G　会計処理についてチェック
(1)　現金主義
(2)　発生主義
(3)　その他

Form 1120-F（外国法人確定申告書）・和訳（一部）・2022年版

Computation of Tax Due or Overpayment（納税額又は還付税額の計算）

1　page 3の line 11の税額を記載

2　page 5の line 9の税額を記載

3　page 6の line 6と10の金額を記載

税額の集計

5 a　2022年の税額から控除する2021年の過払税金

b　2022年の見積税額

c　Form 4466により適用される2022年の還付税額

d　line 5 a～5 c までの合計

e　Form 7004による予納税額

f　未分配の譲渡益に対する税金の控除（Form 2439を添付）

g　燃料に対する連邦税の控除（Form 4136を添付）

h　Form 8827からの払戻し可能な税額控除

i　米国の所得税又は源泉徴収税額（page 3の line 12の税額と Form 8288-A と 8805の税額の合計額）

j　合計支払額（5 d から 5 i までの合計額）

6　Estimated tax penalty（Form 2220を添付）

7　納税額（line 5 j が line 4と6の合計額より小さい場合）

8 a　還付税額（line 5 j が line 4と6の合計額より大きい場合）

b　税額控除と Chapters 3及び4の規定による源泉徴収後の line 8 a の過大納付額（page 8の Schedule W の line 7から）

9　2023年の予定納税額から控除を希望する金額・**Refunded（還付税額）**

Sign Here　偽証の場合の罰則の下、私は、本件申告書、添付資料を調査し、私の知る限りでは、これらの申告書及び添付資料等は真実で、正確に完成されたものであることをここに宣言いたします。

Signature of officer（代表者の署名）

Date（日付）

Title（役職名）

IRSはこの申告書について下記の有料の作成者と検討することができるか。
YES　　NO

Paid Preparer Use Only

（有料の作成者用）

作成者の氏名	作成者の署名	日付
企業名	企業 EIN	

Form 1120-F（外国法人確定申告書）・和訳（一部）・2022年版

企業所在地　　　　　　　　　　電話番号

Page 2

追加情報（1ページから続く）

H　会社の会計処理方法は前年から変更しましたか。
　もし、Yes であれば説明書を添付してください。

I　会社の所得の計算方法は前年から変更しましたか。
　もし、Yes であれば説明書を添付してください。

J　会社は法人所得税申告書の前年分を提出していますか。

K⑴　本年の事業年度において米国で事業活動を行いましたか。

⑵　もし、Yes であれば、米国での事業活動は section 897（FIRPTA）sale あるいは disposition の結果ですか。

L　会社は米国と外国との間の租税条約が適用される恒久的施設を有していましたか。
　もし、Yes であれば、外国名を記入してください。

M　会社は related parties（関連者）と取引を行いましたか。
　もし、Yes であれば、Form 5472を添付してください。
　添付した Form 5472の番号を記入してください。

N　会社は controlled foreign corporation ですか。（定義については section957⒜参照）

O　会社は personal service corporation ですか。（定義については記載要領参照）

P　本年の事業年度において受領した又は未収の tax-exempt interest（免税利息）を記入してください。

Q　会社は事業年度末で、米国企業の議決権50%以上を直接又は間接に保有していますか。
　もし、Yes であれば、次の事項を示す書類を添付してください。

⑴　米国企業の名称と EIN

⑵　米国企業に対する議決権割合

⑶　米国企業の事業年度の営業損失と特別控除前の課税所得又は欠損金額

R　会社がその事業年度において営業損失があるが、繰り戻しを差し控える場合には、こちらにチェックしてください。

S　前年から繰り越した使用可能な営業損失を記入してください。

T　会社は親会社と子会社の関係にありますか。
　もし、Yes であれば、親会社の次の事項について記入してください。

⑴　EIN

⑵　名称

U⑴　会社は section 475のデイーラーですか。

⑵　会社はデイラー以外で、債券あるいは商品について時価評価しましたか。

V　事業年度末において、個人、パートナーシップ、会社、財団、又は信託が会社の議決権の50%以上を直接又は間接に保有していますか。

もし、Yes であれば、身分証明番号を示す書類を添付し、保有割合を記入してください。

W⑴　会社は、この申告により、租税条約に基づき米国内法を修正し、税額の減額を行うことになりますか。

もし、Yes であれば、会社は Form 8833を作成し申告書に添付してください。

（注）　a treaty-based return position を明示しない場合には $10,000の罰金が課されます。

⑵　会社は権限ある当局により租税条約の恩典を付与されていますか。

もし、Yes であれば、権限ある当局からの書面を申告書に添付してください。

X　会社は事業年度において、事業主から法的に独立したみなし事業体（disregarded entities）を有していますか。（section 301.7701－2 and 301.7701－３）

もし、Yes ならばそのみなし事業体の EIN、事業体が設立された国及び事業体の名称を記載した書類を添付してください。

Y⑴　パートナーシップは会社に対し、ECI として取り扱われるパートナーシップが直接保有する所得の distributive share（分配持分）を配分しましたか。

もし、Yes であれば、Schedule P を添付してください。

⑵　会社は事業年度中に、外国パートナーシップの持分の10%を直接又は間接に保有していますか。

もし、Yes であれば、必要書類を添付してください。

Z⑴　会社は、section 482の規定に基づく独立企業間価格による取引を行いましたか。

⑵　会社は interbranch amounts を認識しましたか。（記載要領参照）

もし、YES であれば、必要書類を添付してください。

ＡＡ　会社は Schedule UTP（Form 1120），Uncertain Tax Position Statement を提出することを要求されていますか。

もし、Yes であれば、Schedule UTP を作成し、添付してください。

ＢＢ　会社は、事業年度中、Chapter 3又は Chapter 4に基づく Form 1042と1042-S を提出することを要求される支払を行いましたか。

ＣＣ　会社（本店又は支店を含みます。）は金融派生商品を取り扱っていますか。

Form 1120-F（外国法人確定申告書）・和訳（一部）・2022年版

⑴　もし、Yes であれば所定の報告書を添付してください。（記載要領参照）

⑵　もし、YES であれば、QI-EIN を記入してください。

ＤＤ～Ⅱ　省略

Page 3

SECTION Ⅰ - 米国内の事業活動に関連しない米国源泉の所得（適正に源泉徴収され、Form 1042-S により報告された所得については記入を要しません。）

line9の４％の税率が課される運輸所得について報告します。

他の column ⒜ income で適正に源泉徴収されず、Form 1042-S において報告された所得を報告します。

税率については、総収入に対し30%の税率又は租税条約により規定された低率の税率による。これらの所得に対する税率適用に際しては、総収入から控除は認めません。

租税条約による税率が適用される場合には、その税率を適用してください。

もし、会社が租税条約による低率の税率適用を求める場合には、前ページのWを完成させてください。

もし、多様な租税条約による税率が適用される所得の場合には、金額、税率及び源泉所得税を記載した書類を添付してください。

もしあるなら租税条約の締結国名の記入

(a) 所得の種類	(b) 総収入金額	(c) 税率	(d) 税額	(e) 米国源泉所得税額
1　利息				
2　配当等				
3　賃借料				
4　ロイヤリティ				
5　年金				
6　経済的利権が付与されている材木、石炭及び鉄鉱石の処分による収益				
7　特許権、著作権等の交換又は譲渡による収益				
8　信託配当				
9　運輸収益				
10　その他の所得				
11　page 1の line 1を記入				
12　page 1の line 5 i を記入				

13　会社が上記に掲げられた所得に関し、外国の法律の下で財政的に明瞭ですか。

もし、Yesであれば、それぞれの所得に関し、要求された書面を添付してください。

Page 4

SECTION Ⅱ - 米国内の事業活動に関連する所得

省略

Page 5

SECTION Ⅱ - 米国内の事業活動に関連する所得

Schedule C 配当と特別控除

省略

Schedule J 税額計算

省略

Page 6

SECTION Ⅲ - 支店利益と超過利息に対する課税

Part Ⅰ - 支店利益課税

省略

Part Ⅱ - 超過利息に対する課税

省略

Part Ⅲ - 追加情報

省略

Page 7

Schedule L 貸借対照表

省略

Page 8

Schedule W 税額控除とChapters 3及び4の規定による源泉徴収後の過大納付額

1 Chapters 3及び4の規定による源泉徴収税額

2 page 1の line 1の税額を記入

3 page 1の line 2の税額を記入

Chapters 3及び4の規定による源泉徴収税額の合計額

5 仮の税額控除とChapters 3及び line 4の規定による仮の源泉徴収後の過大納付額

6 page 1の line 8 aの税額を記入

税額控除とChapters 3及び4の規定による源泉徴収後の過大納付額

3　Form 1040-NR（非居住者確定申告書）について

(1)　申告対象者

①　2022年に米国において事業を営んでいた非居住者外国人は、次の場合にも申告書の提出を要する。

(a)　米国における事業からの所得がない

(b)　米国源泉の所得がない

(c)　米国歳入庁の規定又は租税条約により米国での課税が免除されている

②　2022年に米国において事業を営んでいない非居住者外国人は、次の場合に申告書の提出を要する。

(a)　ScheduleNECのline 1からline 12において報告すべき米国源泉の所得を有するが、(b)当該所得に対し源泉所得税が課税されていない。

③　次の特別税を支払う義務を有している。

(a)　Alternative minimum tax（代替ミニマム税）

(b)　IRA（individual retirement arrangement）等に対する課税

(c)　Household employment taxes（家事使用人等に対する税）

(d)　雇用者に報告されていないチップ又は雇用者が源泉徴収していない給与に対するSocial security and Medicare tax

(e)　Recapture of first-time homebuyer credit（住宅取得に係る税額控除の取戻し）

(f)　その他追加の税又は取戻しの税

④　HSA（health savings accounts）、MSA（Archer Medical Savings Account）、又はMedicare Advantage MSRからの支払

⑤　事業所得の純所得が少なくとも＄400を有する事業者で、米国と社会保障協定を締結している国の居住者

⑥　本人又は被扶養者に対するPTC（Premium Tax Credit）の前払い

⑦　本人、配偶者又は被扶養者に対するHCTC（Health Coverage Tax Credit）の前払

⑧　Form 1040-NRを提出すべきであった者の代理人

⑨　Form 1040-NRを提出すべき遺産又は信託を代理する者

Form **1040-NR** Department of the Treasury—Internal Revenue Service
U.S. Nonresident Alien Income Tax Return **2022** OMB No. 1545-0074 IRS Use Only—Do not write or staple in this space.

For the year Jan. 1–Dec. 31, 2022, or other tax year beginning ______, 2022, ending ______, 20 ___ See separate instructions.

Filing Status Check only one box.
☐ Single ☐ Married filing separately (MFS) ☐ Qualifying surviving spouse (QSS) ☐ Estate ☐ Trust
If you checked the QSS box, enter the child's name if the qualifying person is a child but not your dependent:

Your first name and middle initial	Last name	**Your identifying number** (see instructions)
Home address (number and street). If you have a P.O. box, see instructions.		Apt. no.
City, town, or post office. If you have a foreign address, also complete spaces below.	State	ZIP code
Foreign country name	Foreign province/state/county	Foreign postal code

Digital Assets At any time during 2022, did you: (a) receive (as a reward, award, or payment for property or services); or (b) sell, exchange, gift, or otherwise dispose of a digital asset (or a financial interest in a digital asset)? (See instructions.) ☐ **Yes** ☐ **No**

Dependents (see instructions):
If more than four dependents, see instructions and check here ☐

(1) First name	Last name	(2) Dependent's identifying number	(3) Relationship to you	(4) Check the box if qualifies for (see inst.): Child tax credit	Credit for other dependents
				☐	☐
				☐	☐
				☐	☐
				☐	☐

Income Effectively Connected With U.S. Trade or Business

Attach Form(s) W-2, 1042-S, SSA-1042-S, RRB-1042-S, and 8288-A here. Also attach Form(s) 1099-R if tax was withheld.

If you did not get a Form W-2, see instructions.

1a	Total amount from Form(s) W-2, box 1 (see instructions)	1a	
b	Household employee wages not reported on Form(s) W-2	1b	
c	Tip income not reported on line 1a (see instructions)	1c	
d	Medicaid waiver payments not reported on Form(s) W-2 (see instructions)	1d	
e	Taxable dependent care benefits from Form 2441, line 26	1e	
f	Employer-provided adoption benefits from Form 8839, line 29	1f	
g	Wages from Form 8919, line 6	1g	
h	Other earned income (see instructions)	1h	
i	Reserved for future use — 1i		
j	Reserved for future use	1j	
k	Total income exempt by a treaty from Schedule OI (Form 1040-NR), item L, line 1(e) — 1k		
z	Add lines 1a through 1h	1z	
2a	Tax-exempt interest — 2a; **b** Taxable interest	2b	
3a	Qualified dividends — 3a; **b** Ordinary dividends	3b	
4a	IRA distributions — 4a; **b** Taxable amount	4b	
5a	Pensions and annuities — 5a; **b** Taxable amount	5b	
6	Reserved for future use	6	
7	Capital gain or (loss). Attach Schedule D (Form 1040) if required. If not required, check here ☐	7	
8	Other income from Schedule 1 (Form 1040), line 10	8	
9	Add lines 1z, 2b, 3b, 4b, 5b, 7, and 8. This is your **total effectively connected income**	9	
10	Adjustments to income:		
a	From Schedule 1 (Form 1040), line 26 — 10a		
b	Reserved for future use — 10b		
c	Reserved for future use — 10c		
d	Enter the amount from line 10a. These are your **total adjustments to income**	10d	
11	Subtract line 10d from line 9. This is your **adjusted gross income**	11	
12	**Itemized deductions** (from Schedule A (Form 1040-NR)) or, for certain residents of India, standard deduction (see instructions)	12	
13a	Qualified business income deduction from Form 8995 or Form 8995-A — 13a		
b	Exemptions for estates and trusts only (see instructions) — 13b		
c	Add lines 13a and 13b	13c	
14	Add lines 12 and 13c	14	
15	Subtract line 14 from line 11. If zero or less, enter -0-. This is your **taxable income**	15	

For Disclosure, Privacy Act, and Paperwork Reduction Act Notice, see separate instructions. Cat. No. 11364D Form **1040-NR** (2022)

Form 1040-NR（非居住者確定申告書）・様式・2022年版

Form 1040-NR (2022) Page **2**

Tax and Credits	16	**Tax** (see instructions). Check if any from Form(s): **1** ☐ 8814 **2** ☐ 4972 **3** ☐ ______		16	
	17	Amount from Schedule 2 (Form 1040), line 3		17	
	18	Add lines 16 and 17		18	
	19	Child tax credit or credit for other dependents from Schedule 8812 (Form 1040)		19	
	20	Amount from Schedule 3 (Form 1040), line 8		20	
	21	Add lines 19 and 20		21	
	22	Subtract line 21 from line 18. If zero or less, enter -0-		22	
	23a	Tax on income not effectively connected with a U.S. trade or business from Schedule NEC (Form 1040-NR), line 15	23a		
	b	Other taxes, including self-employment tax, from Schedule 2 (Form 1040), line 21	23b		
	c	Transportation tax (see instructions)	23c		
	d	Add lines 23a through 23c		23d	
	24	Add lines 22 and 23d. This is your **total tax**		24	
Payments	25	Federal income tax withheld from:			
	a	Form(s) W-2	25a		
	b	Form(s) 1099	25b		
	c	Other forms (see instructions)	25c		
	d	Add lines 25a through 25c		25d	
	e	Form(s) 8805		25e	
	f	Form(s) 8288-A		25f	
	g	Form(s) 1042-S		25g	
	26	2022 estimated tax payments and amount applied from 2021 return		26	
	27	Reserved for future use	27		
	28	Additional child tax credit from Schedule 8812 (Form 1040)	28		
	29	Credit for amount paid with Form 1040-C	29		
	30	Reserved for future use	30		
	31	Amount from Schedule 3 (Form 1040), line 15	31		
	32	Add lines 28, 29, and 31. These are your **total other payments and refundable credits**		32	
	33	Add lines 25d, 25e, 25f, 25g, 26, and 32. These are your **total payments**		33	
Refund	34	If line 33 is more than line 24, subtract line 24 from line 33. This is the amount you **overpaid**		34	
	35a	Amount of line 34 you want **refunded to you.** If Form 8888 is attached, check here ☐		35a	
Direct deposit? See instructions.	b	Routing number ______ **c** Type: ☐ Checking ☐ Savings			
	d	Account number ______			
	e	If you want your refund check mailed to an address outside the United States not shown on page 1, enter it here. ______			
	36	Amount of line 34 you want **applied to your 2023 estimated tax**	36		
Amount You Owe	37	Subtract line 33 from line 24. This is the **amount you owe.** For details on how to pay, go to *www.irs.gov/Payments* or see instructions		37	
	38	Estimated tax penalty (see instructions)	38		

Third Party Designee
Do you want to allow another person to discuss this return with the IRS? See instructions. ☐ **Yes.** Complete below. ☐ **No**
Designee's name ______ Phone no. ______ Personal identification number (PIN)

Sign Here
Under penalties of perjury, I declare that I have examined this return and accompanying schedules and statements, and to the best of my knowledge and belief, they are true, correct, and complete. Declaration of preparer (other than taxpayer) is based on all information of which preparer has any knowledge.

Your signature	Date	Your occupation	If the IRS sent you an Identity Protection PIN, enter it here (see inst.)
Phone no.	Email address		

Paid Preparer Use Only

Preparer's name	Preparer's signature	Date	PTIN	Check if: ☐ Self-employed
Firm's name			Phone no.	
Firm's address			Firm's EIN	

Go to *www.irs.gov/Form1040NR* for instructions and the latest information. Form **1040-NR** (2022)

SCHEDULE A (Form 1040-NR)

Department of the Treasury
Internal Revenue Service

Itemized Deductions

Go to *www.irs.gov/Form1040NR* for instructions and the latest information.
Attach to Form 1040-NR.
Caution: If you are claiming a net qualified disaster loss on Form 4684, see instructions for line 7.

OMB No. 1545-0074
2022
Attachment Sequence No. **7A**

Name shown on Form 1040-NR | **Your identifying number**

Taxes You Paid	1a	State and local income taxes	1a	
	b	Enter the smaller of line 1a or $10,000 ($5,000 if married filing separately)		1b
Gifts to U.S. Charities	2	Gifts by cash or check. If you made any gift of $250 or more, see instructions	2	
Caution: If you made a gift and got a benefit for it, see instructions.	3	Other than by cash or check. If you made any gift of $250 or more, see instructions. You **must** attach Form 8283 if over $500 . . .	3	
	4	Carryover from prior year	4	
	5	Add lines 2 through 4		5
Casualty and Theft Losses	6	Casualty and theft loss(es) from a federally declared disaster (other than net qualified disaster losses). Attach Form 4684 and enter the amount from line 18 of that form. See instructions		6
Other Itemized Deductions	7	Other—from list in instructions. List type and amount:		7
Total Itemized Deductions	8	Add the amounts in the far right column for lines 1b through 7. Also, enter this amount on Form 1040-NR, line 12		8

For Paperwork Reduction Act Notice, see the Instructions for Form 1040-NR. Cat. No. 72749E **Schedule A (Form 1040-NR) 2022**

Form 1040-NR（非居住者確定申告書）・様式・2022年版

SCHEDULE NEC (Form 1040-NR)
Department of the Treasury
Internal Revenue Service

Tax on Income Not Effectively Connected With a U.S. Trade or Business

Go to *www.irs.gov/Form1040NR* for instructions and the latest information.
Attach to Form 1040-NR.

OMB No. 1545-0074
2022
Attachment Sequence No. **7B**

Name shown on Form 1040-NR | **Your identifying number**

Enter **amount of income** under the appropriate rate of tax. See instructions.

	Nature of Income		**(a)** 10%	**(b)** 15%	**(c)** 30%	**(d)** Other (specify) %	%
1	Dividends and dividend equivalents:						
a	Dividends paid by U.S. corporations	1a					
b	Dividends paid by foreign corporations	1b					
c	Dividend equivalent payments received with respect to section 871(m) transactions	1c					
2	Interest:						
a	Mortgage	2a					
b	Paid by foreign corporations	2b					
c	Other	2c					
3	Industrial royalties (patents, trademarks, etc.)	3					
4	Motion picture or TV copyright royalties	4					
5	Other royalties (copyrights, recording, publishing, etc.)	5					
6	Real property income and natural resources royalties	6					
7	Pensions and annuities	7					
8	Social security benefits	8					
9	Capital gain from line 18 below	9					
10	Gambling—Residents of Canada only. Enter net income in column (c). **If zero or less, enter -0-.**						
a	Winnings						
b	Losses	10c					
11	Gambling winnings—Residents of countries other than Canada. **Note:** Losses not allowed	11					
12	Other (specify):	12					
13	Add lines 1a through 12 in columns (a) through (d)	13					
14	**Multiply line 13 by rate of tax at top of each column**	14					
15	**Tax on income not effectively connected with a U.S. trade or business.** Add columns (a) through (d) of line 14. Enter the total here and on Form 1040-NR, line 23a	15					

Capital Gains and Losses From Sales or Exchanges of Property

Enter only the capital gains and losses from property sales or exchanges that are from sources within the United States and not effectively connected with a U.S. business. Do not include a gain or loss on disposing of a U.S. real property interest; report these gains and losses on Schedule D (Form 1040).

Report property sales or exchanges that are effectively connected with a U.S. business on Schedule D (Form 1040), Form 4797, or both.

16	**(a)** Kind of property and description (if necessary, attach statement of descriptive details not shown below)	**(b)** Date acquired mm/dd/yyyy	**(c)** Date sold mm/dd/yyyy	**(d)** Sales price	**(e)** Cost or other basis	**(f) LOSS** If (e) is more than (d), subtract (d) from (e).	**(g) GAIN** If (d) is more than (e), subtract (e) from (d).
17	Add columns (f) and (g) of line 16				17	( )	
18	**Capital gain.** Combine columns (f) and (g) of line 17. Enter the net gain here and on line 9 above. If a loss, enter -0-					18	

For Paperwork Reduction Act Notice, see the Instructions for Form 1040-NR. Cat. No. 72752B **Schedule NEC (Form 1040-NR) 2022**

SCHEDULE OI (Form 1040-NR)

Department of the Treasury Internal Revenue Service

Other Information

Go to *www.irs.gov/Form1040NR* for instructions and the latest information.
Attach to Form 1040-NR.
Answer all questions.

OMB No. 1545-0074
2022
Attachment Sequence No. **7C**

Name shown on Form 1040-NR | **Your identifying number**

A Of what country or countries were you a citizen or national during the tax year? ____________

B In what country did you claim residence for tax purposes during the tax year? ____________

C Have you ever applied to be a green card holder (lawful permanent resident) of the United States? . . . . . . ☐ **Yes** ☐ **No**

D Were you ever:

1. A U.S. citizen? . . . . . . ☐ **Yes** ☐ **No**

2. A green card holder (lawful permanent resident) of the United States? . . . . . . ☐ **Yes** ☐ **No**

If you answer "Yes" to (1) or (2), see Pub. 519, chapter 4, for expatriation rules that apply to you.

E If you had a visa on the last day of the tax year, enter your visa type. If you didn't have a visa, enter your U.S. immigration status on the last day of the tax year. ____________

F Have you ever changed your visa type (nonimmigrant status) or U.S. immigration status? . . . . . . ☐ **Yes** ☐ **No**

If you answered "Yes," indicate the date and nature of the change: ____________

G List all dates you entered and left the United States during 2022. See instructions.

Note: If you're a resident of Canada or Mexico **AND** commute to work in the United States at frequent intervals, **check the box for Canada or Mexico** and skip to item H . . . . . . ☐ Canada ☐ Mexico

Date entered United States mm/dd/yy	Date departed United States mm/dd/yy	Date entered United States mm/dd/yy	Date departed United States mm/dd/yy

H Give number of days (including vacation, nonworkdays, and partial days) you were present in the United States during:
2020 ____________, 2021 ____________, and 2022 ____________.

I Did you file a U.S. income tax return for any prior year? . . . . . . ☐ **Yes** ☐ **No**

If "Yes," give the latest year and form number you filed: ____________

J Are you filing a return for a trust? . . . . . . ☐ **Yes** ☐ **No**

If "Yes," did the trust have a U.S. or foreign owner under the grantor trust rules, make a distribution or loan to a U.S. person, or receive a contribution from a U.S. person? . . . . . . ☐ **Yes** ☐ **No**

K Did you receive total compensation of $250,000 or more during the tax year? . . . . . . ☐ **Yes** ☐ **No**

If "Yes," did you use an alternative method to determine the source of this compensation? . . . . . . ☐ **Yes** ☐ **No**

L Income Exempt From Tax—If you are claiming exemption from income tax under a U.S. income tax treaty with a foreign country, complete (1) through (3) below. See Pub. 901 for more information on tax treaties.

1. Enter the name of the country, the applicable tax treaty article, the number of months in prior years you claimed the treaty benefit, and the amount of exempt income in the columns below. Attach Form 8833 if required. See instructions.

(a) Country	**(b)** Tax treaty article	**(c)** Number of months claimed in prior tax years	**(d)** Amount of exempt income in current tax year
(e) Total. Enter this amount on Form 1040-NR, line 1k. Do not enter it anywhere else on line 1 . .			

2. Were you subject to tax in a foreign country on any of the income shown in 1(d) above? . . . . . . ☐ **Yes** ☐ **No**

3. Are you claiming treaty benefits pursuant to a Competent Authority determination? . . . . . . ☐ **Yes** ☐ **No**

If "Yes," attach a copy of the Competent Authority determination letter to your return.

M Check the applicable box if:

1. This is the first year you are making an election to treat income from real property located in the United States as effectively connected with a U.S. trade or business under section 871(d). See instructions . . . . . . ☐

2. You have made an election in a previous year that has not been revoked, to treat income from real property located in the United States as effectively connected with a U.S. trade or business under section 871(d). See instructions . . . . . . ☐

For Paperwork Reduction Act Notice, see the Instructions for Form 1040-NR. Cat. No. 72756T **Schedule OI (Form 1040-NR) 2022**

Form 1040-NR・和訳（一部）

1040-NR　　米国非居住者所得税確定申告書　　2022

申告期間　2022/1/1～2022/12/31　又は他の年分

申告状況　□ Single　□ Married filling separately（MFS）
□ Qualifying surviving spouse（QSS）　□ Estate　□ Trust
もし、QSS ボックスに記入したならば、その資格を有する者があなたの扶養親族ではなく、子供である場合には、その子供の氏名を記入しなさい。

氏名　first name and middle name　（姓）　Last name　（名）
Your identifying number　（身分証明書番号）

住所・郵便番号

外国の国名　・外国の地名　・外国の郵便番号

デジタル資産

2022年中にデジタル資産の受領、売買、交換、贈与、又は譲渡はありましたか

□ YES　□ NO

扶養親族

(1) 氏名　(2) 扶養者の身分証明番号　(3) 関係　(4) 税額控除の有無

米国内の事業活動に関連する所得

1 a　Form (s)W - 2, box1の合計金額
b　Form (s)W - 2 に報告されていない家政婦及びベビーシッター等の賃金
c　1 a に含まれていないチップ
d　Form (s)W - 2 に報告されていない Medicaid waiver payments
e　Form 2441, line 26からの課税対象 dependent care benefits
f　Form 8839, line 29からの Employer - provided adoption benefits
g　Form 8919, line 6からの賃金
h　その他の所得
i　将来使用するための予備
j　将来使用するための予備
k　Schedule OI,item L,line 1(e)からの条約により免税とされている合計所得
z　line 1 a～1 h までの合計

2 a　免税利息　　2 b　課税利息
3 a　特定の配当　　3 b　普通配当
4 a　IRA（individual retirement account …個人退職金勘定）からの分配　　4 a　課税金額

Form 1040-NR・和訳（一部）

5a　年金等　　5 b 課税金額

6　将来使用するための予備

7　譲渡所得又は譲渡損失．必要ならば Schedule D（Form 1040）の添付

必要なし□

8　Schedule1（Form 1040）,line 10からのその他所得

9　1z,2b,3b,4b,5b,7及び 8 を合計（米国事業関連所得）

10　所得に対する調整

a　Schedule1（Form 1040）,line 26から　10 a

b　将来使用するための予備　10 b

c　将来使用するための予備　10 c

d　line 10 a から記入．所得に対する調整額合計

11　line 9から line 10 d を控除．調整済総所得

12　項目別控除（Schedule A（Form 1040-NR）又はインドの居住者のための基礎控除・・記載要領確認）

13a　Form 8995又は Form 8995-A からの特別事業所得控除　13 a

b　不動産と信託のための免除　13 b

c　line 13 a と line 13 b の合計

14　line 12と13 c の合計

15　line 14から line 11を控除．もしゼロ以下であれば、0 を記入．これが課税所得

16　Tax（記載要領参照）次の Form があれば確認

1 □8814　2 □4972　3 □

17　Schedule 2（Form 1040），line 3からの金額

18　line 16と17の合計額

19　Scedule 8812（Form 1040）からの子供控除又は他の扶養者の控除額

20　Schedule 3（Form 1040），line 8からの金額

21　line 19と20の合計額

22　line 18から21を控除．0以下であれば－0－を記入

23 a　Scedule NEC（Form 1040），line 15の米国外源泉所得に対する税額

b　Scedule2（Form 1040），line 21からの事業所得税を含むその他の税額

c　運送税（記載要領参照）

d　23 a から23 c を合計

24　line 22と line 23の合計額．税額の総合計

25　連邦所得税の源泉徴収税額

Form 1040-NR・和訳（一部）

a　Form (s)W - 2

b　Form (s)1099

c　その他（記載要領参照）

d　25 a から25 c を合計

e　Form (s)8805

f　Form (s)8288-A

g　Form (s)1042-S

26　2022年の予定納税と2021年申告の適用額

27　将来のための留保

28　追加の Scedule 8812（Form 1040）からの子供控除

29　Form 1040-C

30　将来のための留保

31　Schedule 3（Form 1040）、line 15からの金額

32　line 28, 29, と31の合計額．あなたのその他支払と還付金額

33　line 25d, 25e, 25f, 25g, 26と32の合計額。あなたの合計支払額

34　line 33の金額が24の金額を超える場合、33から24を控除．支払超過分

35 a　34の金額は還付額。Form 8888を添付の場合はここにチェック　□

b　Routing number　　c Type: □ Checking　□ Savings

d　Account number

e　page1に記載されていない米国外の住所宛に還付用の小切手を望む場合はここに記載

36　2023年の予定納税に充当を希望する34の金額

37　line 24から33を控除（あなたの負債）

38　予定納税のペナルティ（記載要領参照）

指名された第三者

あなたは、第三者が IRS と、この申告に関し、議論を交わすことを許可しますか。

第三者の氏名　　　　電話番号　　　　身元番号

署名欄

偽証の場合は罰則を課されることに従い、私はこの申告書と添付資料を調査したことを宣言し、私の知り得る限りでは、この申告書等は真実かつ正確であること。この申告の準備者の宣言は準備者が有する知識の情報を基礎としたものである。

あなたの署名	日付	あなたの職業	

準備者のみ使用欄

準備者の氏名	準備者の署名	日付	PTIN

事務所の名称

事務所の住所

SCHEDULE A Itemized Deductions

省略

Form 1040-NR・和訳（一部）

SCHEDULE NEC　米国内の事業活動に関連しない所得に対する税額　2022

所得の種類		(a)10%	(b)15%	(c)30%	(d)他
1　配当等と配当等の同等物 a　米国法人からの配当等	1 a				
b　外国法人からの配当等	1 b				
c　Section 871(m)に関し受領した配当等の同等物	1 c				
2　利息 a　Mortgage	2 a				
b　外国法人からの利息	2 b				
c　その他利息	2 c				
3　工業的なロイヤリティ	3				
4　映画又はテレビの著作権使用料	4				
5　その他のロイヤリティ（複写権、録音権、出版権他）	5				
6　不動産所得と自然資源ロイヤリティ	6				
7　年金等	7				
8　社会保障に関する便益	8				
9　下欄18からの譲渡所得	9				
10　ギャンブルによる所得 a　Winnings b　Losses	10 c				
11　ギャンブルによる所得・カナダ以外の居住者	11				
12　その他	12				
13　(a)欄から(d)欄までのline 1 aから12までの合計	13				
14　13に各欄の税率を掛ける	14				
15　米国の事業活動に関連しない所得に対する税額資産の交換又は譲渡から生じる譲渡益及び譲渡損失	15				

16
(a)　資産の種類　(b)　取得日　(c)　譲渡日　(d)　譲渡価額　(e)　取得価額
(f)　損失　(g)　利益

17　line 16の(f)と(g)の合計	17		
18　譲渡益（line 17の(f)と(g)の合計		18	

Form 1040-NR・和訳（一部）

SCHEDULE OI　その他情報　2022

A　課税年度においてどちらの国の市民ですか？

B　課税年度においてどちらの国の居住者ですか？

C　あなたはかつて米国のグリーンカードの保有者（法的な永久居住者）でしたか？

Yes □　No □

D　あなたは、かつて

1　米国市民でしたか？　Yes □　No □

2　米国のグリーンカードの保有者（法的な永久居住者）でしたか？

Yes □　No □

もし、YESであれば、あなたに適用される国外居住の規則に関するPub.519の⑴又は⑵を確認してください。

E　もし、課税年度の最後の日にビザを保有していたならば、ビザの種類を記入してください。もし、ビザを保有していなかった場合は、課税年度の最後の日の滞在資格を記入してください。＿＿＿＿＿＿＿＿＿＿

F　あなたは、かつて、ビザの種類又は滞在資格の変更をしましたか？

Yes □　No □

G　2022年の米国への入国日、又は、米国からの出国日を記入（記載要領参照）

（注）もし、あなたがカナダ又はメキシコの居住者で、米国で働くために通勤していた場合には、カナダ又はメキシコのどちらかにチェックし、Hへ進む。

□ Canada　□ Mexico

Date entered United Statets mm/dd/yy	Date departed United Statets mm/dd/yy

H　米国内に滞在した日数（休暇、nonworkdays、partialdaysを含む）

2020＿＿＿＿＿＿, 2021＿＿＿＿＿＿.and 2022＿＿＿＿＿＿

I　前年以前に米国所得税申告書を提出したことがありますか？　Yes □　No □

もし、YESの場合は最近の申告済の申告書の年分と申告書の書式

J　信託に係る申告を提出したことがありますか？　Yes □　No □

もし、YESの場合は、信託契約の下で、信託は米国又は外国の持分の所有者に分配したり、米国人に融資をしたり、米国人から寄付を受けていますか？

Yes □　No □

K　課税年度中に$250,000以上の報酬を受領しましたか？　Yes □　No □

もし、YESの場合は、報酬の所得源泉の決定に際し最良の方法（米国内外の所得）

Form 1040-NR・和訳（一部）

を採用しましたか？ Yes □ No □

L 免税所得＝米国と他の国との間の租税条約の下で、所得税の免税を望むならば、次の⑴から⑶の記載を要する。

⑴ 国名、租税条約の適用条文、前年において条約上の特典を受けた月数及び課税年度の免税所得の金額

(a) 国名 (b) 適用条文 (c) 特典を受けた月数 (d) 免税所得

(e) (d)の合計金額（Form 1040-NR,line 1 k に記入）

⑵ 上記 1 (d)の金額は外国において課税されましたか？ Yes □ No □

⑶ 権限ある当局の決定に従い条約の特典を受けていますか？ Yes □ No □

M 該当する場合にはボックスにチェックを入れる。

1 section 871(d)の下の米国内の事業に関連する米国に保有する不動産から生じる所得についての申告を選択した最初の年である。 □

2 section 871(d)の下の米国内の事業に関連する米国に保有する不動産から生じる所得についての申告を取消さないことを前年に選択した。 □

4 Form 8833（租税条約に基づく申告であることの開示）について

Form 8833（様式）

Form **8833**
(Rev. December 2022)
Department of the Treasury
Internal Revenue Service

Treaty-Based Return Position Disclosure
Under Section 6114 or 7701(b)
Attach to your tax return.
Go to *www.irs.gov/Form8833* for the latest information.

OMB No. 1545-1354

Attach a separate Form 8833 for each treaty-based return position taken. Failure to disclose a treaty-based return position may result in a penalty of $1,000 ($10,000 in the case of a C corporation) (see section 6712).

Name	**U.S. taxpayer identifying number**	**Reference ID number, if any (see instructions)**

Address in country of residence	Address in the United States

Check one or both of the following boxes as applicable.

- The taxpayer is disclosing a treaty-based return position as required by section 6114 . . . . ☐
- The taxpayer is a dual-resident taxpayer and is disclosing a treaty-based return position as required by Regulations section 301.7701(b)-7 . . . . ☐

Note: If the taxpayer is a dual-resident taxpayer and a long-term resident, by electing to be treated as a resident of a foreign country for purposes of claiming benefits under an applicable income tax treaty, the taxpayer will be deemed to have expatriated pursuant to section 877A. For more information, see the instructions.

Check this box if the taxpayer is a U.S. citizen or resident or is incorporated in the United States . . . . ☐

1 Enter the specific treaty position relied on:
a Treaty country
b Article(s)

2 List the Internal Revenue Code provision(s) overruled or modified by the treaty-based return position

3 Name, identifying number (if available to the taxpayer), and address in the United States of the payor of the income (if fixed or determinable annual or periodical). See instructions.

4 List the provision(s) of the limitation on benefits article (if any) in the treaty that the taxpayer relies on to qualify for benefits under the treaty

5 Is the taxpayer disclosing a treaty-based return position for which reporting is specifically required pursuant to Regulations section 301.6114-1(b)? . . . . ☐ Yes ☐ No
If "Yes," enter the specific subsection(s) of Regulations section 301.6114-1(b) requiring reporting . . . .
Also include the information requested in line 6.

6 Explain the treaty-based return position taken. Include a brief summary of the facts on which it is based. Also, list the nature and amount (or a reasonable estimate) of gross receipts, each separate gross payment, each separate gross income item, or other item (as applicable) for which the treaty benefit is claimed

For Paperwork Reduction Act Notice, see the instructions. Cat. No. 14895L Form **8833** (Rev. 12-2022)

Form 8833（全訳）

8833 **租税条約に基づく申告であることの開示**

Under Section 6114 or 7701(b)

租税条約に基づく申告であることを明確にするために、Form 8833を添付してください。

租税条約に基づく申告であることを明確にすることを怠った場合には、$1,000の罰金が課されます。（C corporation の場合には $10,000を罰金とします。Section 6712を参照）

○ 名称　○ U.S taxpayer identifying number

○ 提出者の住所　○ 米国における住所

次の事項について該当する場合は、チェックをしてください。

・納税者は Section 6114の規定による租税条約に基づく申告であることを明確にする。 ▶ □

・納税者は双方居住者であり、Section 301.7701(b) - 7 の規定による租税条約に基づく申告であることを明確にする。 ▶ □

（注） 納税者が双方居住者で、かつ、長期に滞在する居住者であるときは、租税条約の特典を受けるために外国の居住者であることを選択することによって、その納税者は Section 877 A の規定により、国外居住者とみなされます。

納税者が米国市民又は居住者、又は米国において設立された会社である場合には、次のこのボックスをチェックしてください。 ▶ □

1 条約の適用条項について

a 条約締結国

b 適用条項

2 租税条約に基づく申告により変更又は修正される米国内法

3 支払者の名称、米国における identifying number 及び所在地

4 租税条約の特典条項の適用を受けるための条項

5 納税者は、section 301.6114(b)の規定による報告のために特に要求される目的のために、租税条約に基づく申告であることを明確にするのですか。 □ YES □ NO

YES であれば、section 301.6114-1(b)の特定の subsection(s)を記入してください。

次の line 6の情報も記載してください。

6 租税条約に基づく申告を行う事情を説明してください。

総収入金額と総支払額を、所得の種類、金額ごとに記載してください。

5 Form W-8BEN-E（米国の源泉徴収に関し恩恵を受ける者の証明書＝法人用）について

Form W-8BEN-E（様式）

Form **W-8BEN-E**
(Rev. October 2021)
Department of the Treasury
Internal Revenue Service

Certificate of Status of Beneficial Owner for United States Tax Withholding and Reporting (Entities)

▶ **For use by entities. Individuals must use Form W-8BEN.** ▶ **Section references are to the Internal Revenue Code.**
▶ **Go to *www.irs.gov/FormW8BENE* for instructions and the latest information.**
▶ **Give this form to the withholding agent or payer. Do not send to the IRS.**

OMB No. 1545-1621

Do NOT use this form for: **Instead use Form:**

- U.S. entity or U.S. citizen or resident W-9
- A foreign individual . . . . . . W-8BEN (Individual) or Form 8233
- A foreign individual or entity claiming that income is effectively connected with the conduct of trade or business within the United States (unless claiming treaty benefits) W-8ECI
- A foreign partnership, a foreign simple trust, or a foreign grantor trust (unless claiming treaty benefits) (see instructions for exceptions) . . W-8IMY
- A foreign government, international organization, foreign central bank of issue, foreign tax-exempt organization, foreign private foundation, or government of a U.S. possession claiming that income is effectively connected U.S. income or that is claiming the applicability of section(s) 115(2), 501(c), 892, 895, or 1443(b) (unless claiming treaty benefits) (see instructions for other exceptions) . . . . . . W-8ECI or W-8EXP
- Any person acting as an intermediary (including a qualified intermediary acting as a qualified derivatives dealer) W-8IMY

Part I　Identification of Beneficial Owner

1 Name of organization that is the beneficial owner　　2 Country of incorporation or organization

3 Name of disregarded entity receiving the payment (if applicable, see instructions)

4 Chapter 3 Status (entity type) (Must check one box only): ☐ Corporation ☐ Partnership
☐ Simple trust ☐ Tax-exempt organization ☐ Complex trust ☐ Foreign Government - Controlled Entity
☐ Central Bank of Issue ☐ Private foundation ☐ Estate ☐ Foreign Government - Integral Part
☐ Grantor trust ☐ Disregarded entity ☐ International organization
If you entered disregarded entity, partnership, simple trust, or grantor trust above, is the entity a hybrid making a treaty claim? If "Yes," complete Part III. ☐ Yes ☐ No

5 Chapter 4 Status (FATCA status) (See instructions for details and complete the certification below for the entity's applicable status.)

☐ Nonparticipating FFI (including an FFI related to a Reporting IGA FFI other than a deemed-compliant FFI, participating FFI, or exempt beneficial owner).
☐ Participating FFI.
☐ Reporting Model 1 FFI.
☐ Reporting Model 2 FFI.
☐ Registered deemed-compliant FFI (other than a reporting Model 1 FFI, sponsored FFI, or nonreporting IGA FFI covered in Part XII). See instructions.
☐ Sponsored FFI. Complete Part IV.
☐ Certified deemed-compliant nonregistering local bank. Complete Part V.
☐ Certified deemed-compliant FFI with only low-value accounts. Complete Part VI.
☐ Certified deemed-compliant sponsored, closely held investment vehicle. Complete Part VII.
☐ Certified deemed-compliant limited life debt investment entity. Complete Part VIII.
☐ Certain investment entities that do not maintain financial accounts. Complete Part IX.
☐ Owner-documented FFI. Complete Part X.
☐ Restricted distributor. Complete Part XI.
☐ Nonreporting IGA FFI. Complete Part XII.
☐ Foreign government, government of a U.S. possession, or foreign central bank of issue. Complete Part XIII.
☐ International organization. Complete Part XIV.
☐ Exempt retirement plans. Complete Part XV.
☐ Entity wholly owned by exempt beneficial owners. Complete Part XVI.
☐ Territory financial institution. Complete Part XVII.
☐ Excepted nonfinancial group entity. Complete Part XVIII.
☐ Excepted nonfinancial start-up company. Complete Part XIX.
☐ Excepted nonfinancial entity in liquidation or bankruptcy. Complete Part XX.
☐ 501(c) organization. Complete Part XXI.
☐ Nonprofit organization. Complete Part XXII.
☐ Publicly traded NFFE or NFFE affiliate of a publicly traded corporation. Complete Part XXIII.
☐ Excepted territory NFFE. Complete Part XXIV.
☐ Active NFFE. Complete Part XXV.
☐ Passive NFFE. Complete Part XXVI.
☐ Excepted inter-affiliate FFI. Complete Part XXVII.
☐ Direct reporting NFFE.
☐ Sponsored direct reporting NFFE. Complete Part XXVIII.
☐ Account that is not a financial account.

6 Permanent residence address (street, apt. or suite no., or rural route). **Do not use a P.O. box or in-care-of address** (other than a registered address).

City or town, state or province. Include postal code where appropriate.　　Country

7 Mailing address (if different from above)

City or town, state or province. Include postal code where appropriate.　　Country

For Paperwork Reduction Act Notice, see separate instructions.　　Cat. No. 59689N　　Form **W-8BEN-E** (Rev. 10-2021)

Form W-8BEN-E（様式）

Form W-8BEN-E (Rev. 10-2021) Page **2**

Part I **Identification of Beneficial Owner** *(continued)*

8 U.S. taxpayer identification number (TIN), if required

9a GIIN

b Foreign TIN

c Check if FTIN not legally required . . . . . . ▶☐

10 Reference number(s) (see instructions)

Note: Please complete remainder of the form including signing the form in Part XXX.

Part II **Disregarded Entity or Branch Receiving Payment.** (Complete only if a disregarded entity with a GIIN or a branch of an FFI in a country other than the FFI's country of residence. See instructions.)

11 Chapter 4 Status (FATCA status) of disregarded entity or branch receiving payment

☐ Branch treated as nonparticipating FFI.
☐ Reporting Model 1 FFI.
☐ U.S. Branch.
☐ Participating FFI.
☐ Reporting Model 2 FFI.

12 Address of disregarded entity or branch (street, apt. or suite no., or rural route). **Do not use a P.O. box or in-care-of address** (other than a registered address**).**

City or town, state or province. Include postal code where appropriate.

Country

13 GIIN (if any)

Part III **Claim of Tax Treaty Benefits** (if applicable). (For chapter 3 purposes only.)

14 I certify that (check all that apply):

a ☐ The beneficial owner is a resident of ______ within the meaning of the income tax treaty between the United States and that country.

b ☐ The beneficial owner derives the item (or items) of income for which the treaty benefits are claimed, and, if applicable, meets the requirements of the treaty provision dealing with limitation on benefits. The following are types of limitation on benefits provisions that may be included in an applicable tax treaty (check only one; see instructions):

☐ Government
☐ Tax-exempt pension trust or pension fund
☐ Other tax-exempt organization
☐ Publicly traded corporation
☐ Subsidiary of a publicly traded corporation
☐ Company that meets the ownership and base erosion test
☐ Company that meets the derivative benefits test
☐ Company with an item of income that meets active trade or business test
☐ Favorable discretionary determination by the U.S. competent authority received
☐ No LOB article in treaty
☐ Other (specify Article and paragraph): ______

c ☐ The beneficial owner is claiming treaty benefits for U.S. source dividends received from a foreign corporation or interest from a U.S. trade or business of a foreign corporation and meets qualified resident status (see instructions).

15 **Special rates and conditions** (if applicable—see instructions):
The beneficial owner is claiming the provisions of Article and paragraph ______
of the treaty identified on line 14a above to claim a ______ % rate of withholding on (specify type of income): ______
Explain the additional conditions in the Article the beneficial owner meets to be eligible for the rate of withholding: ______

Part IV **Sponsored FFI**

16 Name of sponsoring entity: ______

17 **Check whichever box applies.**

☐ I certify that the entity identified in Part I:
- Is an investment entity;
- Is not a QI, WP (except to the extent permitted in the withholding foreign partnership agreement), or WT; **and**
- Has agreed with the entity identified above (that is not a nonparticipating FFI) to act as the sponsoring entity for this entity.

☐ I certify that the entity identified in Part I:
- Is a controlled foreign corporation as defined in section 957(a);
- Is not a QI, WP, or WT;
- Is wholly owned, directly or indirectly, by the U.S. financial institution identified above that agrees to act as the sponsoring entity for this entity; **and**
- Shares a common electronic account system with the sponsoring entity (identified above) that enables the sponsoring entity to identify all account holders and payees of the entity and to access all account and customer information maintained by the entity including, but not limited to, customer identification information, customer documentation, account balance, and all payments made to account holders or payees.

Form **W-8BEN-E** (Rev. 10-2021)

Part V Certified Deemed-Compliant Nonregistering Local Bank

18 ☐ I certify that the FFI identified in Part I:

- Operates and is licensed solely as a bank or credit union (or similar cooperative credit organization operated without profit) in its country of incorporation or organization;
- Engages primarily in the business of receiving deposits from and making loans to, with respect to a bank, retail customers unrelated to such bank and, with respect to a credit union or similar cooperative credit organization, members, provided that no member has a greater than 5% interest in such credit union or cooperative credit organization;
- Does not solicit account holders outside its country of organization;
- Has no fixed place of business outside such country (for this purpose, a fixed place of business does not include a location that is not advertised to the public and from which the FFI performs solely administrative support functions);
- Has no more than $175 million in assets on its balance sheet and, if it is a member of an expanded affiliated group, the group has no more than $500 million in total assets on its consolidated or combined balance sheets; **and**
- Does not have any member of its expanded affiliated group that is a foreign financial institution, other than a foreign financial institution that is incorporated or organized in the same country as the FFI identified in Part I and that meets the requirements set forth in this part.

Part VI Certified Deemed-Compliant FFI with Only Low-Value Accounts

19 ☐ I certify that the FFI identified in Part I:

- Is not engaged primarily in the business of investing, reinvesting, or trading in securities, partnership interests, commodities, notional principal contracts, insurance or annuity contracts, or any interest (including a futures or forward contract or option) in such security, partnership interest, commodity, notional principal contract, insurance contract or annuity contract;
- No financial account maintained by the FFI or any member of its expanded affiliated group, if any, has a balance or value in excess of $50,000 (as determined after applying applicable account aggregation rules); **and**
- Neither the FFI nor the entire expanded affiliated group, if any, of the FFI, have more than $50 million in assets on its consolidated or combined balance sheet as of the end of its most recent accounting year.

Part VII Certified Deemed-Compliant Sponsored, Closely Held Investment Vehicle

20 Name of sponsoring entity: ______________________

21 ☐ I certify that the entity identified in Part I:

- Is an FFI solely because it is an investment entity described in Regulations section 1.1471-5(e)(4);
- Is not a QI, WP, or WT;
- Will have all of its due diligence, withholding, and reporting responsibilities (determined as if the FFI were a participating FFI) fulfilled by the sponsoring entity identified on line 20; **and**
- 20 or fewer individuals own all of the debt and equity interests in the entity (disregarding debt interests owned by U.S. financial institutions, participating FFIs, registered deemed-compliant FFIs, and certified deemed-compliant FFIs and equity interests owned by an entity if that entity owns 100% of the equity interests in the FFI and is itself a sponsored FFI).

Part VIII Certified Deemed-Compliant Limited Life Debt Investment Entity

22 ☐ I certify that the entity identified in Part I:

- Was in existence as of January 17, 2013;
- Issued all classes of its debt or equity interests to investors on or before January 17, 2013, pursuant to a trust indenture or similar agreement; **and**
- Is certified deemed-compliant because it satisfies the requirements to be treated as a limited life debt investment entity (such as the restrictions with respect to its assets and other requirements under Regulations section 1.1471-5(f)(2)(iv)).

Part IX Certain Investment Entities that Do Not Maintain Financial Accounts

23 ☐ I certify that the entity identified in Part I:

- Is a financial institution solely because it is an investment entity described in Regulations section 1.1471-5(e)(4)(i)(A), **and**
- Does not maintain financial accounts.

Part X Owner-Documented FFI

Note: This status only applies if the U.S. financial institution, participating FFI, or reporting Model 1 FFI to which this form is given has agreed that it will treat the FFI as an owner-documented FFI (see instructions for eligibility requirements). In addition, the FFI must make the certifications below.

24a ☐ (All owner-documented FFIs check here) I certify that the FFI identified in Part I:

- Does not act as an intermediary;
- Does not accept deposits in the ordinary course of a banking or similar business;
- Does not hold, as a substantial portion of its business, financial assets for the account of others;
- Is not an insurance company (or the holding company of an insurance company) that issues or is obligated to make payments with respect to a financial account;
- Is not owned by or in an expanded affiliated group with an entity that accepts deposits in the ordinary course of a banking or similar business, holds, as a substantial portion of its business, financial assets for the account of others, or is an insurance company (or the holding company of an insurance company) that issues or is obligated to make payments with respect to a financial account;
- Does not maintain a financial account for any nonparticipating FFI; **and**
- Does not have any specified U.S. persons that own an equity interest or debt interest (other than a debt interest that is not a financial account or that has a balance or value not exceeding $50,000) in the FFI other than those identified on the FFI owner reporting statement.

Form W-8BEN-E（様式）

Form W-8BEN-E (Rev. 10-2021) Page **4**

Part X Owner-Documented FFI *(continued)*

Check box 24b or 24c, whichever applies.

b ☐ I certify that the FFI identified in Part I:

• Has provided, or will provide, an FFI owner reporting statement that contains:

(i) The name, address, TIN (if any), chapter 4 status, and type of documentation provided (if required) of every individual and specified U.S. person that owns a direct or indirect equity interest in the owner-documented FFI (looking through all entities other than specified U.S. persons);

(ii) The name, address, TIN (if any), and chapter 4 status of every individual and specified U.S. person that owns a debt interest in the owner-documented FFI (including any indirect debt interest, which includes debt interests in any entity that directly or indirectly owns the payee or any direct or indirect equity interest in a debt holder of the payee) that constitutes a financial account in excess of $50,000 (disregarding all such debt interests owned by participating FFIs, registered deemed-compliant FFIs, certified deemed-compliant FFIs, excepted NFFEs, exempt beneficial owners, or U.S. persons other than specified U.S. persons); **and**

(iii) Any additional information the withholding agent requests in order to fulfill its obligations with respect to the entity.

• Has provided, or will provide, valid documentation meeting the requirements of Regulations section 1.1471-3(d)(6)(iii) for each person identified in the FFI owner reporting statement.

c ☐ I certify that the FFI identified in Part I has provided, or will provide, an auditor's letter, signed within 4 years of the date of payment, from an independent accounting firm or legal representative with a location in the United States stating that the firm or representative has reviewed the FFI's documentation with respect to all of its owners and debt holders identified in Regulations section 1.1471-3(d)(6)(iv)(A)(2), and that the FFI meets all the requirements to be an owner-documented FFI. The FFI identified in Part I has also provided, or will provide, an FFI owner reporting statement of its owners that are specified U.S. persons and Form(s) W-9, with applicable waivers.

Check box 24d if applicable (optional, see instructions).

d ☐ I certify that the entity identified on line 1 is a trust that does not have any contingent beneficiaries or designated classes with unidentified beneficiaries.

Part XI Restricted Distributor

25a ☐ (All restricted distributors check here) I certify that the entity identified in Part I:

• Operates as a distributor with respect to debt or equity interests of the restricted fund with respect to which this form is furnished;

• Provides investment services to at least 30 customers unrelated to each other and less than half of its customers are related to each other;

• Is required to perform AML due diligence procedures under the anti-money laundering laws of its country of organization (which is an FATF-compliant jurisdiction);

• Operates solely in its country of incorporation or organization, has no fixed place of business outside of that country, and has the same country of incorporation or organization as all members of its affiliated group, if any;

• Does not solicit customers outside its country of incorporation or organization;

• Has no more than $175 million in total assets under management and no more than $7 million in gross revenue on its income statement for the most recent accounting year;

• Is not a member of an expanded affiliated group that has more than $500 million in total assets under management or more than $20 million in gross revenue for its most recent accounting year on a combined or consolidated income statement; **and**

• Does not distribute any debt or securities of the restricted fund to specified U.S. persons, passive NFFEs with one or more substantial U.S. owners, or nonparticipating FFIs.

Check box 25b or 25c, whichever applies.

I further certify that with respect to all sales of debt or equity interests in the restricted fund with respect to which this form is furnished that are made after December 31, 2011, the entity identified in Part I:

b ☐ Has been bound by a distribution agreement that contained a general prohibition on the sale of debt or securities to U.S. entities and U.S. resident individuals and is currently bound by a distribution agreement that contains a prohibition of the sale of debt or securities to any specified U.S. person, passive NFFE with one or more substantial U.S. owners, or nonparticipating FFI.

c ☐ Is currently bound by a distribution agreement that contains a prohibition on the sale of debt or securities to any specified U.S. person, passive NFFE with one or more substantial U.S. owners, or nonparticipating FFI and, for all sales made prior to the time that such a restriction was included in its distribution agreement, has reviewed all accounts related to such sales in accordance with the procedures identified in Regulations section 1.1471-4(c) applicable to preexisting accounts and has redeemed or retired any, or caused the restricted fund to transfer the securities to a distributor that is a participating FFI or reporting Model 1 FFI securities which were sold to specified U.S. persons, passive NFFEs with one or more substantial U.S. owners, or nonparticipating FFIs.

Form **W-8BEN-E** (Rev. 10-2021)

Part XII Nonreporting IGA FFI

26 ☐ I certify that the entity identified in Part I:

• Meets the requirements to be considered a nonreporting financial institution pursuant to an applicable IGA between the United States and ______________________. The applicable IGA is a ☐ Model 1 IGA or a ☐ Model 2 IGA; and is treated as a ______________________ under the provisions of the applicable IGA or Treasury regulations (if applicable, see instructions);

• If you are a trustee documented trust or a sponsored entity, provide the name of the trustee or sponsor ______________________.

The trustee is: ☐ U.S. ☐ Foreign

Part XIII Foreign Government, Government of a U.S. Possession, or Foreign Central Bank of Issue

27 ☐ I certify that the entity identified in Part I is the beneficial owner of the payment, and is not engaged in commercial financial activities of a type engaged in by an insurance company, custodial institution, or depository institution with respect to the payments, accounts, or obligations for which this form is submitted (except as permitted in Regulations section 1.1471-6(h)(2)).

Part XIV International Organization

Check box 28a or 28b, whichever applies.

28a ☐ I certify that the entity identified in Part I is an international organization described in section 7701(a)(18).

b ☐ I certify that the entity identified in Part I:

• Is comprised primarily of foreign governments;

• Is recognized as an intergovernmental or supranational organization under a foreign law similar to the International Organizations Immunities Act or that has in effect a headquarters agreement with a foreign government;

• The benefit of the entity's income does not inure to any private person; **and**

• Is the beneficial owner of the payment and is not engaged in commercial financial activities of a type engaged in by an insurance company, custodial institution, or depository institution with respect to the payments, accounts, or obligations for which this form is submitted (except as permitted in Regulations section 1.1471-6(h)(2)).

Part XV Exempt Retirement Plans

Check box 29a, b, c, d, e, or f, whichever applies.

29a ☐ I certify that the entity identified in Part I:

• Is established in a country with which the United States has an income tax treaty in force (see Part III if claiming treaty benefits);

• Is operated principally to administer or provide pension or retirement benefits; **and**

• Is entitled to treaty benefits on income that the fund derives from U.S. sources (or would be entitled to benefits if it derived any such income) as a resident of the other country which satisfies any applicable limitation on benefits requirement.

b ☐ I certify that the entity identified in Part I:

• Is organized for the provision of retirement, disability, or death benefits (or any combination thereof) to beneficiaries that are former employees of one or more employers in consideration for services rendered;

• No single beneficiary has a right to more than 5% of the FFI's assets;

• Is subject to government regulation and provides annual information reporting about its beneficiaries to the relevant tax authorities in the country in which the fund is established or operated; **and**

(i) Is generally exempt from tax on investment income under the laws of the country in which it is established or operates due to its status as a retirement or pension plan;

(ii) Receives at least 50% of its total contributions from sponsoring employers (disregarding transfers of assets from other plans described in this part, retirement and pension accounts described in an applicable Model 1 or Model 2 IGA, other retirement funds described in an applicable Model 1 or Model 2 IGA, or accounts described in Regulations section 1.1471-5(b)(2)(i)(A));

(iii) Either does not permit or penalizes distributions or withdrawals made before the occurrence of specified events related to retirement, disability, or death (except rollover distributions to accounts described in Regulations section 1.1471-5(b)(2)(i)(A) (referring to retirement and pension accounts), to retirement and pension accounts described in an applicable Model 1 or Model 2 IGA, or to other retirement funds described in this part or in an applicable Model 1 or Model 2 IGA); **or**

(iv) Limits contributions by employees to the fund by reference to earned income of the employee or may not exceed $50,000 annually.

c ☐ I certify that the entity identified in Part I:

• Is organized for the provision of retirement, disability, or death benefits (or any combination thereof) to beneficiaries that are former employees of one or more employers in consideration for services rendered;

• Has fewer than 50 participants;

• Is sponsored by one or more employers each of which is not an investment entity or passive NFFE;

• Employee and employer contributions to the fund (disregarding transfers of assets from other plans described in this part, retirement and pension accounts described in an applicable Model 1 or Model 2 IGA, or accounts described in Regulations section 1.1471-5(b)(2)(i)(A)) are limited by reference to earned income and compensation of the employee, respectively;

• Participants that are not residents of the country in which the fund is established or operated are not entitled to more than 20% of the fund's assets; **and**

• Is subject to government regulation and provides annual information reporting about its beneficiaries to the relevant tax authorities in the country in which the fund is established or operates.

Form W-8BEN-E（様式）

Part XV Exempt Retirement Plans *(continued)*

d ☐ I certify that the entity identified in Part I is formed pursuant to a pension plan that would meet the requirements of section 401(a), other than the requirement that the plan be funded by a trust created or organized in the United States.

e ☐ I certify that the entity identified in Part I is established exclusively to earn income for the benefit of one or more retirement funds described in this part or in an applicable Model 1 or Model 2 IGA, or accounts described in Regulations section 1.1471-5(b)(2)(i)(A) (referring to retirement and pension accounts), or retirement and pension accounts described in an applicable Model 1 or Model 2 IGA.

f ☐ I certify that the entity identified in Part I:

- Is established and sponsored by a foreign government, international organization, central bank of issue, or government of a U.S. possession (each as defined in Regulations section 1.1471-6) or an exempt beneficial owner described in an applicable Model 1 or Model 2 IGA to provide retirement, disability, or death benefits to beneficiaries or participants that are current or former employees of the sponsor (or persons designated by such employees); **or**
- Is established and sponsored by a foreign government, international organization, central bank of issue, or government of a U.S. possession (each as defined in Regulations section 1.1471-6) or an exempt beneficial owner described in an applicable Model 1 or Model 2 IGA to provide retirement, disability, or death benefits to beneficiaries or participants that are not current or former employees of such sponsor, but are in consideration of personal services performed for the sponsor.

Part XVI Entity Wholly Owned by Exempt Beneficial Owners

30 ☐ I certify that the entity identified in Part I:

- Is an FFI solely because it is an investment entity;
- Each direct holder of an equity interest in the investment entity is an exempt beneficial owner described in Regulations section 1.1471-6 or in an applicable Model 1 or Model 2 IGA;
- Each direct holder of a debt interest in the investment entity is either a depository institution (with respect to a loan made to such entity) or an exempt beneficial owner described in Regulations section 1.1471-6 or an applicable Model 1 or Model 2 IGA.
- Has provided an owner reporting statement that contains the name, address, TIN (if any), chapter 4 status, and a description of the type of documentation provided to the withholding agent for every person that owns a debt interest constituting a financial account or direct equity interest in the entity; **and**
- Has provided documentation establishing that every owner of the entity is an entity described in Regulations section 1.1471-6(b), (c), (d), (e), (f) and/or (g) without regard to whether such owners are beneficial owners.

Part XVII Territory Financial Institution

31 ☐ I certify that the entity identified in Part I is a financial institution (other than an investment entity) that is incorporated or organized under the laws of a possession of the United States.

Part XVIII Excepted Nonfinancial Group Entity

32 ☐ I certify that the entity identified in Part I:

- Is a holding company, treasury center, or captive finance company and substantially all of the entity's activities are functions described in Regulations section 1.1471-5(e)(5)(i)(C) through (E);
- Is a member of a nonfinancial group described in Regulations section 1.1471-5(e)(5)(i)(B);
- Is not a depository or custodial institution (other than for members of the entity's expanded affiliated group); **and**
- Does not function (or hold itself out) as an investment fund, such as a private equity fund, venture capital fund, leveraged buyout fund, or any investment vehicle with an investment strategy to acquire or fund companies and then hold interests in those companies as capital assets for investment purposes.

Part XIX Excepted Nonfinancial Start-Up Company

33 ☐ I certify that the entity identified in Part I:

- Was formed on (or, in the case of a new line of business, the date of board resolution approving the new line of business) ______________ (date must be less than 24 months prior to date of payment);
- Is not yet operating a business and has no prior operating history or is investing capital in assets with the intent to operate a new line of business other than that of a financial institution or passive NFFE;
- Is investing capital into assets with the intent to operate a business other than that of a financial institution; **and**
- Does not function (or hold itself out) as an investment fund, such as a private equity fund, venture capital fund, leveraged buyout fund, or any investment vehicle whose purpose is to acquire or fund companies and then hold interests in those companies as capital assets for investment purposes.

Part XX Excepted Nonfinancial Entity in Liquidation or Bankruptcy

34 ☐ I certify that the entity identified in Part I:

- Filed a plan of liquidation, filed a plan of reorganization, or filed for bankruptcy on ______________________________;
- During the past 5 years has not been engaged in business as a financial institution or acted as a passive NFFE;
- Is either liquidating or emerging from a reorganization or bankruptcy with the intent to continue or recommence operations as a nonfinancial entity; **and**
- Has, or will provide, documentary evidence such as a bankruptcy filing or other public documentation that supports its claim if it remains in bankruptcy or liquidation for more than 3 years.

Form **W-8BEN-E** (Rev. 10-2021)

Part XXI 501(c) Organization

35 ☐ I certify that the entity identified in Part I is a 501(c) organization that:

• Has been issued a determination letter from the IRS that is currently in effect concluding that the payee is a section 501(c) organization that is dated ______________ ; **or**

• Has provided a copy of an opinion from U.S. counsel certifying that the payee is a section 501(c) organization (without regard to whether the payee is a foreign private foundation).

Part XXII Nonprofit Organization

36 ☐ I certify that the entity identified in Part I is a nonprofit organization that meets the following requirements.

• The entity is established and maintained in its country of residence exclusively for religious, charitable, scientific, artistic, cultural or educational purposes;

• The entity is exempt from income tax in its country of residence;

• The entity has no shareholders or members who have a proprietary or beneficial interest in its income or assets;

• Neither the applicable laws of the entity's country of residence nor the entity's formation documents permit any income or assets of the entity to be distributed to, or applied for the benefit of, a private person or noncharitable entity other than pursuant to the conduct of the entity's charitable activities or as payment of reasonable compensation for services rendered or payment representing the fair market value of property which the entity has purchased; **and**

• The applicable laws of the entity's country of residence or the entity's formation documents require that, upon the entity's liquidation or dissolution, all of its assets be distributed to an entity that is a foreign government, an integral part of a foreign government, a controlled entity of a foreign government, or another organization that is described in this part or escheats to the government of the entity's country of residence or any political subdivision thereof.

Part XXIII Publicly Traded NFFE or NFFE Affiliate of a Publicly Traded Corporation

Check box 37a or 37b, whichever applies.

37a ☐ I certify that:

• The entity identified in Part I is a foreign corporation that is not a financial institution; **and**

• The stock of such corporation is regularly traded on one or more established securities markets, including ______________ (name one securities exchange upon which the stock is regularly traded).

b ☐ I certify that:

• The entity identified in Part I is a foreign corporation that is not a financial institution;

• The entity identified in Part I is a member of the same expanded affiliated group as an entity the stock of which is regularly traded on an established securities market;

• The name of the entity, the stock of which is regularly traded on an established securities market, is ______________ ; **and**

• The name of the securities market on which the stock is regularly traded is ______________ .

Part XXIV Excepted Territory NFFE

38 ☐ I certify that:

• The entity identified in Part I is an entity that is organized in a possession of the United States;

• The entity identified in Part I:

(i) Does not accept deposits in the ordinary course of a banking or similar business;

(ii) Does not hold, as a substantial portion of its business, financial assets for the account of others; **or**

(iii) Is not an insurance company (or the holding company of an insurance company) that issues or is obligated to make payments with respect to a financial account; **and**

• All of the owners of the entity identified in Part I are bona fide residents of the possession in which the NFFE is organized or incorporated.

Part XXV Active NFFE

39 ☐ I certify that:

• The entity identified in Part I is a foreign entity that is not a financial institution;

• Less than 50% of such entity's gross income for the preceding calendar year is passive income; **and**

• Less than 50% of the assets held by such entity are assets that produce or are held for the production of passive income (calculated as a weighted average of the percentage of passive assets measured quarterly) (see instructions for the definition of passive income).

Part XXVI Passive NFFE

40a ☐ I certify that the entity identified in Part I is a foreign entity that is not a financial institution (other than an investment entity organized in a possession of the United States) and is not certifying its status as a publicly traded NFFE (or affiliate), excepted territory NFFE, active NFFE, direct reporting NFFE, or sponsored direct reporting NFFE.

Check box 40b or 40c, whichever applies.

b ☐ I further certify that the entity identified in Part I has no substantial U.S. owners (or, if applicable, no controlling U.S. persons); **or**

c ☐ I further certify that the entity identified in Part I has provided the name, address, and TIN of each substantial U.S. owner (or, if applicable, controlling U.S. person) of the NFFE in Part XXIX.

Form W-8BEN-E（様式）

Form W-8BEN-E (Rev. 10-2021) Page **8**

Part XXVII Excepted Inter-Affiliate FFI

41 ☐ I certify that the entity identified in Part I:

- Is a member of an expanded affiliated group;
- Does not maintain financial accounts (other than accounts maintained for members of its expanded affiliated group);
- Does not make withholdable payments to any person other than to members of its expanded affiliated group;
- Does not hold an account (other than depository accounts in the country in which the entity is operating to pay for expenses) with or receive payments from any withholding agent other than a member of its expanded affiliated group; **and**
- Has not agreed to report under Regulations section 1.1471-4(d)(2)(ii)(C) or otherwise act as an agent for chapter 4 purposes on behalf of any financial institution, including a member of its expanded affiliated group.

Part XXVIII Sponsored Direct Reporting NFFE (see instructions for when this is permitted)

42 Name of sponsoring entity:

43 ☐ I certify that the entity identified in Part I is a direct reporting NFFE that is sponsored by the entity identified on line 42.

Part XXIX Substantial U.S. Owners of Passive NFFE

As required by Part XXVI, provide the name, address, and TIN of each substantial U.S. owner of the NFFE. Please see the instructions for a definition of substantial U.S. owner. If providing the form to an FFI treated as a reporting Model 1 FFI or reporting Model 2 FFI, an NFFE may also use this part for reporting its controlling U.S. persons under an applicable IGA.

Name	Address	TIN

Part XXX Certification

Under penalties of perjury, I declare that I have examined the information on this form and to the best of my knowledge and belief it is true, correct, and complete. I further certify under penalties of perjury that:

- The entity identified on line 1 of this form is the beneficial owner of all the income or proceeds to which this form relates, is using this form to certify its status for chapter 4 purposes, or is submitting this form for purposes of section 6050W or 6050Y;
- The entity identified on line 1 of this form is not a U.S. person;
- This form relates to: (a) income not effectively connected with the conduct of a trade or business in the United States, (b) income effectively connected with the conduct of a trade or business in the United States but is not subject to tax under an income tax treaty, (c) the partner's share of a partnership's effectively connected taxable income, or (d) the partner's amount realized from the transfer of a partnership interest subject to withholding under section 1446(f); **and**
- For broker transactions or barter exchanges, the beneficial owner is an exempt foreign person as defined in the instructions.

Furthermore, I authorize this form to be provided to any withholding agent that has control, receipt, or custody of the income of which the entity on line 1 is the beneficial owner or any withholding agent that can disburse or make payments of the income of which the entity on line 1 is the beneficial owner.

I agree that I will submit a new form within 30 days if any certification on this form becomes incorrect.

☐ **I certify that I have the capacity to sign for the entity identified on line 1 of this form.**

Sign Here ▶

Signature of individual authorized to sign for beneficial owner　　Print Name　　Date (MM-DD-YYYY)

Form **W-8BEN-E** (Rev. 10-2021)

Form W-8BEN-E・和訳（一部）

W-8BEN-E　米国の源泉徴収に関し恩恵を受ける者の証明書（法人用）

次の者はこの証明書を使用できません。

・米国の事業体、米国市民及び米国居住者
・外国の個人
・米国内の事業活動に関連する所得であることを主張する外国の個人及び事業体
・外国のパートナーシップ、単純信託及び譲渡人信託
・外国政府、国際期間、外国中央銀行、外国免税機関、外国個人基金等
・代理人として活動する者

Part I　Identification of Beneficial Owner（租税条約の恩典を受ける者の証明）

1　受益者の名称

2　受益者の所在国

3　支払を受ける事業体の名称

4　Chapter 3の事業体の類型（1のボックスにチェック）

□ Corporation　□ Disregarded entity　□ Partnership
□ Simple trust　□ Grantor trust　□ Complex trust
□ Foreign Goverment-Controlled Entity　□ Estate
□ Foreign Goverment-Integral Part　□ Central Bank of Issue
□ Tax-exempt organaization　□ Private foundation
□ International organization

もし、あなたが Disregarded entity、Partnership、Simple trust 又は Grantor trust に該当し、租税条約の恩典を受けますか。

□ YES　□ NO

恩典を受ける場合は、Part Ⅲを記載してください。

5　Chapter 4の事業体の類型

省略

6　恒久的な所在地

7　郵送先住所（上記の恒久的な所在地と異なる場合）・都市名・郵便番号・国名

8　U.S taxpayer identification number（TIN）

9 a　GIN　b　Foreign TIN　c　もし要求されたならば……

10　Reference number(s)（記載要領参照）

Part II　Disregarded Entity or Branch Receiving Payment（みなし事業体又は　Receiving Payment）

Form W-8BEN-E・和訳（一部）

省略

Part Ⅲ Claim of Tax Treaty Benefit（適用される場合）（Chapter 3にのみ使用）

14　次の事項を証明します。

a　租税条約の恩典を受ける者は、米国との間の租税条約の意味においては・・・・国の居住者である

b　租税条約の受益者は、特典の制限を規定する租税条約の条件を満たす場合には、租税条約の恩典を受ける所得を得る。以下は、租税条約の適用を受けることができる特典条項の対象となるものです。（次のいずれか１つにチェックを入れてください。）

□ Government（政府）

□ Tax exempt pension trust or fund（免税年金信託又はファンド）

□ Other tax exempt organization（その他免税団体）

□ Publicly traded corporation（上場会社）

□ Subsidiary of a publicly traded corporation（上場会社の子会社）

□ Company that meets the ownership and base erosion test（税源浸食基準テストをクリアした会社）

□ Company that meets the derivative benefits test（派生的な利益を受ける会社）

□ Company with an item of income that meets active trade or business test（能動的活動基準テストをクリアした会社）

□ Favorable discretionary determination by the U.S competent authority received（米国の権限ある当局による特別な配慮）

□ Other（specify Article and paragraph）（その他）

c　租税条約の受益者は、外国法人から受領した米国源泉の配当又は外国法人の米国の事業活動から生じた利息について租税条約の恩典の適用を要求している。

15　特別税率と条件

（上記14の条件を満たさない場合のみ使用）

Part Ⅳ～Part XXIX

省略

Part XXX Certification（証明）

罰金制度の下、私は本証明書に関する情報を確認し、私が知る限りにおいては、この情報は正確で完全なものであることを宣言します。

また、罰金制度の下、さらに、次の事項について証明いたします。

Form W-8BEN-E・和訳（一部）

・　本証明書の line1の証明された事業体は、この証明書に関連するすべての所得の受益者であり、また、この事業体は、chapter 4の類型を証明するために使用され、又はSection 6050Wの目的のために提出する事業主である。

・　本証明書の line 1の証明された事業体は、米国人でないこと。

・　本証明書に関連する所得とは、次の所得をいいます。

(a)　米国内の事業活動に関連しない所得であること。

(b)　米国内の事業活動に関連する所得であるが、租税条約の取扱いを受けない所得であること。

(c)　米国内の事業活動に関連するパートナーシップの持分の所得。

(d)　section 1446(f)の下において、源泉徴収の対象となるパートナーシップの利益の譲渡により実現したパートナーの所得。

・　仲介取引又は交換取引の場合において、租税条約の受益者は免税外国人であること。

さらに、私は、本証明書が line 1　の租税条約の受益者である会社の所得を管理、受領する源泉徴収義務者、又は line 1の租税条約の受益者である会社の所得を分配又は支払う源泉徴収義務者に提出されることを許可する。

私は、本証明書が不正確である場合には、30日以内に、新しい証明書を提出いたします。

署名　受益者のために署名する権限を与えられた者の署名・・・・・・・・・・・・・

氏名

日付

□　私は line 1において証明された事業体のために署名する権限があることを証明いたします。

6　Form W-8BEN（米国の源泉徴収に関し恩恵を受ける者の証明書＝個人用）について

Form W-8BEN-E（様式）

Form **W-8BEN**

(Rev. October 2021)

Department of the Treasury
Internal Revenue Service

Certificate of Foreign Status of Beneficial Owner for United States Tax Withholding and Reporting (Individuals)

▶ **For use by individuals. Entities must use Form W-8BEN-E.**
▶ **Go to *www.irs.gov/FormW8BEN* for instructions and the latest information.**
▶ **Give this form to the withholding agent or payer. Do not send to the IRS.**

OMB No. 1545-1621

Do NOT use this form if:	**Instead, use Form:**
• You are NOT an individual	W-8BEN-E
• You are a U.S. citizen or other U.S. person, including a resident alien individual	W-9
• You are a beneficial owner claiming that income is effectively connected with the conduct of trade or business within the United States (other than personal services)	W-8ECI
• You are a beneficial owner who is receiving compensation for personal services performed in the United States	8233 or W-4
• You are a person acting as an intermediary	W-8IMY

Note: If you are resident in a FATCA partner jurisdiction (that is, a Model 1 IGA jurisdiction with reciprocity), certain tax account information may be provided to your jurisdiction of residence.

Part I　Identification of Beneficial Owner (see instructions)

1　Name of individual who is the beneficial owner　　2　Country of citizenship

3　Permanent residence address (street, apt. or suite no., or rural route). **Do not use a P.O. box or in-care-of address.**

City or town, state or province. Include postal code where appropriate.　　Country

4　Mailing address (if different from above)

City or town, state or province. Include postal code where appropriate.　　Country

5　U.S. taxpayer identification number (SSN or ITIN), if required (see instructions)

6a　Foreign tax identifying number (see instructions)　　6b　Check if FTIN not legally required . . . . ☐

7　Reference number(s) (see instructions)　　8　Date of birth (MM-DD-YYYY) (see instructions)

Part II　Claim of Tax Treaty Benefits (for chapter 3 purposes only) (see instructions)

9　I certify that the beneficial owner is a resident of ____________ within the meaning of the income tax treaty between the United States and that country.

10　**Special rates and conditions** (if applicable—see instructions): The beneficial owner is claiming the provisions of Article and paragraph ____________ of the treaty identified on line 9 above to claim a ____ % rate of withholding on (specify type of income): ____________.

Explain the additional conditions in the Article and paragraph the beneficial owner meets to be eligible for the rate of withholding: ____________

Part III　Certification

Under penalties of perjury, I declare that I have examined the information on this form and to the best of my knowledge and belief it is true, correct, and complete. I further certify under penalties of perjury that:

- I am the individual that is the beneficial owner (or am authorized to sign for the individual that is the beneficial owner) of all the income or proceeds to which this form relates or am using this form to document myself for chapter 4 purposes;
- The person named on line 1 of this form is not a U.S. person;
- This form relates to:
  (a) income not effectively connected with the conduct of a trade or business in the United States;
  (b) income effectively connected with the conduct of a trade or business in the United States but is not subject to tax under an applicable income tax treaty;
  (c) the partner's share of a partnership's effectively connected taxable income; or
  (d) the partner's amount realized from the transfer of a partnership interest subject to withholding under section 1446(f);
- The person named on line 1 of this form is a resident of the treaty country listed on line 9 of the form (if any) within the meaning of the income tax treaty between the United States and that country; and
- For broker transactions or barter exchanges, the beneficial owner is an exempt foreign person as defined in the instructions.

Furthermore, I authorize this form to be provided to any withholding agent that has control, receipt, or custody of the income of which I am the beneficial owner or any withholding agent that can disburse or make payments of the income of which I am the beneficial owner. **I agree that I will submit a new form within 30 days if any certification made on this form becomes incorrect.**

Sign Here ▶　☐ I certify that I have the capacity to sign for the person identified on line 1 of this form.

Signature of beneficial owner (or individual authorized to sign for beneficial owner)　　Date (MM-DD-YYYY)

Print name of signer

For Paperwork Reduction Act Notice, see separate instructions.　　Cat. No. 25047Z　　Form **W-8BEN** (Rev. 10-2021)

Form W-8BEN・和訳(一部)

Form W-8BEN(米国の源泉徴収に関し恩恵を受ける者の証明書=個人用

➢ 本証明書は個人用であり、法人は Form W-8BEN-E である。

次の場合にはこの様式を使用しない。

・個人でない者

・米国市民又は米国居住外国人を含む他の米国人

・米国内の事業に関連する所得に関し恩恵を受ける受益者

・米国内の個人的な役務提供に対し受領する報酬に関し恩恵を受ける受益者

・仲介者の立場の者

Part I 恩恵を受ける受益者

1 氏名　　2 市民権を有する国

3 恒久的住所

4 郵送先住所(上記3と異なる場合)

5 米国納税者番号(SSN 又は ITIN)

6a 外国納税者番号(FTIN)　　6b 法的に FTIN が要求されない場合チェック

7 照会番号(記載要領参照)　　8 生年月日

Part II 租税条約に基づく恩典付与の要求(chapter 3にのみ適用…記載要領参照)

9 租税条約に基づく恩典を受ける者は、米国と・・・・国との間の租税条約に規定する・・・・国の居住者であることを証明する。

10 特別な税率と条件(記載要領参照):恩恵を受ける者は、特定の所得につき・・%の税率による源泉徴収を要求するために、上記9の租税条約の・・・・条の規定の適用を要求する。

源泉徴収に際し特別な税率を適用するための租税条約に規定する追加の条件の説明。

Part III 証明

罰金制度の下、私は、この情報を確認し、私が知る限りにおいては、この情報は正確で完全なものであることを宣言します。

また、罰金制度の下、私は、次の事項について証明いたします。

・ 私は、この証明書が関係するすべての所得又は収益について恩恵を受ける個人であり、又、chapter 4に関し私自身を証明するためにこの証明書を使用しています。

・ この証明書の line 1の者は米国人ではない。

・ この証明書は次に所得等に関連するものである。

(a) 米国内の事業所得に関連しない所得

(b) 米国内の事業所得に関連するが、租税条約上の所得に対する税額が適用されない

Form W-8BEN・和訳（一部）

⒞ 米国内の事業所得に関連するパートナーシップの持分

⒟ 1446⒡の規定により源泉徴収されるパートナーシップの利益の譲渡により生じるパートナーの取得金額

・ この証明書の line 1の者は、line 9の米国との間の租税条約の締結国の居住者である。

・ 販売仲介業者又は物々交換業者については、この証明書の記載上、外国人として取り扱わない

さらに、この証明者がすべての源泉徴収義務者に提供されることを許可する。

もし、この証明者の内容が正しくない場合には、30日以内に新しい証明書を提出することに同意します。

署名欄 ➢

□ 私は、この証明書の Line1の者のために署名する権限を有することを証明する。

恩恵を受ける者の署名　日付

7 Form W-7（個人の納税者番号の取得申請書）

Form W-7（様式）

Form **W-7**
(Rev. August 2019)
Department of the Treasury
Internal Revenue Service

Application for IRS Individual Taxpayer Identification Number

▶ **For use by individuals who are not U.S. citizens or permanent residents.**
▶ **See separate instructions.**

OMB No. 1545-0074

An IRS individual taxpayer identification number (ITIN) is for U.S. federal tax purposes only.
Before you begin:
• ***Don't submit*** *this form if you have, or are eligible to get, a U.S. social security number (SSN).*

Application type (check one box):
☐ Apply for a new ITIN
☐ Renew an existing ITIN

Reason you're submitting Form W-7. Read the instructions for the box you check. **Caution:** If you check box **b, c, d, e, f,** or **g, you must file a U.S. federal tax return with Form W-7 unless you meet one of the exceptions** (see instructions).

a ☐ Nonresident alien required to get an ITIN to claim tax treaty benefit
b ☐ Nonresident alien filing a U.S. federal tax return
c ☐ U.S. resident alien **(based on days present in the United States)** filing a U.S. federal tax return
d ☐ Dependent of U.S. citizen/resident alien — If **d,** enter relationship to U.S. citizen/resident alien (see instructions) ▶
e ☐ Spouse of U.S. citizen/resident alien — If **d** or **e,** enter name and SSN/ITIN of U.S. citizen/resident alien (see instructions) ▶
f ☐ Nonresident alien student, professor, or researcher filing a U.S. federal tax return or claiming an exception
g ☐ Dependent/spouse of a nonresident alien holding a U.S. visa
h ☐ Other (see instructions) ▶

Additional information for **a** and **f**: Enter treaty country ▶ and treaty article number ▶

Name (see instructions)
1a First name | Middle name | Last name

Name at birth if different . . ▶
1b First name | Middle name | Last name

Applicant's Mailing Address
2 Street address, apartment number, or rural route number. **If you have a P.O. box, see separate instructions.**
City or town, state or province, and country. Include ZIP code or postal code where appropriate.

Foreign (non-U.S.) Address (see instructions)
3 Street address, apartment number, or rural route number. **Don't use a P.O. box number.**
City or town, state or province, and country. Include postal code where appropriate.

Birth Information
4 Date of birth (month / day / year) / / | Country of birth | City and state or province (optional) | 5 ☐ Male ☐ Female

Other Information
6a Country(ies) of citizenship | 6b Foreign tax I.D. number (if any) | 6c Type of U.S. visa (if any), number, and expiration date

6d Identification document(s) submitted (see instructions) ☐ Passport ☐ Driver's license/State I.D. ☐ USCIS documentation ☐ Other
Issued by: No.: Exp. date: / / Date of entry into the United States (MM/DD/YYYY): / /

6e Have you previously received an ITIN or an Internal Revenue Service Number (IRSN)?
☐ **No/Don't know.** Skip line 6f.
☐ **Yes.** Complete line 6f. If more than one, list on a sheet and attach to this form (see instructions).

6f Enter ITIN and/or IRSN ▶ **ITIN** ☐☐☐-☐☐-☐☐☐☐ **IRSN** ☐☐☐-☐☐-☐☐☐☐ and name under which it was issued ▶
First name | Middle name | Last name

6g Name of college/university or company (see instructions) ▶
City and state ▶ Length of stay ▶

Sign Here
Keep a copy for your records.

Under penalties of perjury, I (applicant/delegate/acceptance agent) declare that I have examined this application, including accompanying documentation and statements, and to the best of my knowledge and belief, it is true, correct, and complete. I authorize the IRS to share information with my acceptance agent in order to perfect this Form W-7, Application for IRS Individual Taxpayer Identification Number.

▶ Signature of applicant (if delegate, see instructions) | Date (month / day / year) / / | Phone number
▶ Name of delegate, if applicable (type or print) | Delegate's relationship to applicant ▶ ☐ Parent ☐ Court-appointed guardian ☐ Power of attorney

Acceptance Agent's Use ONLY
▶ Signature | Date (month / day / year) / / | Phone | Fax
▶ Name and title (type or print) | Name of company | EIN | PTIN | Office code

For Paperwork Reduction Act Notice, see separate instructions. Cat. No. 10229L Form **W-7** (Rev. 8-2019)

Form W- 7 ・和訳（一部）

個人の納税者番号（ITIN）の取得申請書

➢ 申請者は米国市民でない者又は永久居住者でない者

➢ 詳細は記載要領参照

ITIN は米国連邦所得税にのみ使用

➢ 米国の社会保障番号（SSN）保有者は提出不要

申請の種類（ボックスにチェック）

☐ ITIN の申請

☐ ITIN の更新

Form W- 7 申請の理由について・・記載要領により次のボックスにチェック

注意事項：次のｂ，ｃ，ｄ，ｅ，ｆ，又はｇのボックスにチェックをした場合には、一つの例外（記載要領を確認）を除いて Form W- 7 を添付し米国連邦所得税の申告書を提出しなければならない。

a☐　租税条約に基づく恩典を受けるために ITIN を申請する非居住外国人

b☐　米国連邦所得税の申告を行う非居住外国人

c☐　米国連邦所得税の申告を行う米国居住外国人（米国内の滞在日数に基づき米国居住外国人に該当する者）

d☐　米国市民又は米国居住外国人の被扶養者

➢ ｄに該当した場合は米国市民又は米国居住外国人との関係

e☐　米国市民又は米国居住者の配偶者

➢ ｄ又はｅに該当した場合は米国市民又は米国居住外国人の SSN 又は ITIN

f☐　米国連邦所得税の申告又は当該申告の免除を希望する非居住外国人である学生、教授及び研究者

g☐　米国ビザを保有する非居住外国人の被扶養者及び配偶者

h☐　その他（記載要領参照）

ａとｆの追加情報：租税条約締結国名・・・・・・　条文・・・・・・

氏名　1ａ　First name　Middle name　Last name

住所　2

外国の住所　3

出生情報　4　生年月日　出生国　5　性別　☐ Male　☐ Female

その他情報

6ａ　市民権保有国　6ｂ　外国納税番号　6ｃ　米国ビザの種別，番号，有効期限

6ｄ　身分を証明するための提出書類

☐パスポート　☐運転免許証 /Statel.D　☐ USCIS documentation　☐その他

FormW-7・和訳(一部)

発行者：　　　　番号：　　　　有効期限：　　　　米国入国日：

6 e　ITIN 又は IRSN（Internal Revenue Service Number）を以前、取得しましたか。

□ No/Don't Know.　　　6 f の記入なし

□ Yes.　　　　　　　　6 f の記入あり

6 f　ITIN 及び IRSN の番号の記入

➢ 番号　ITIN・・・-・・-・・・・　IRSN・・・-・・-・・・・

➢ 氏名　First name・・・Middle name・・・Last name・・・

6 g　大学名及び会社名

➢ 州名と都市名

➢ 滞在期間

署名欄

罰金制度の下、私は、付随する書類を含むこの申請書を確認し、私が知る限りにおいては、この情報は正確で完全なものであることを宣言します。

私は IRS が、個人の納税者番号申請書を完成するために、私の Acceptance Agent と情報を共有することを許可する。

➢ 申請者の署名・・・・・・日付・・・・・電話番号・・・・・

➢ 代理人の署名・・・・・・申請者との関係

Acceptance Agent's の使用欄

➢ 署　名・・・・日付・・・・電話番号・・・・

➢ 氏名と職名・・・・会社名・・・・EIN・・・・PTIN・・・・

8 外国法人確定申告書（Form 1120-F）の作成手順

演習事例31

米国で源泉徴収された税金の還付方法

当社（ABC.INC）は米国の旅行代理店（DEF.INC）向けに日本の観光地の番組映像を提供し、著作権の使用料（映像の使用料）の支払いを受けておりましたが、日米租税条約に基づく免税の手続きを失念しており、30%の税率により源泉所得税が課税されていました。

なお、源泉徴収された税額は使用料の支払日の属する事業年度の損金としております。

源泉徴収された税金については、ある一定期間は、源泉徴収義務者に還付請求ができると聞きましたが、既に、その期間が経過しております。

米国の源泉所得の還付を受ける方法がありますでしょうか。

ご教示をお願いいたします。

現在、次の源泉所得税が徴収されております。

また、当社は米国に、支店や事務所などはありません。

源泉徴収税額の明細

（年度）	（収入金額）	（税率）	（源泉徴収税額）
2020	20,000ドル	30%	6,000ドル
2021	70,000ドル	30%	21,000ドル
2022	90,000ドル	30%	27,000ドル
		合計	54,000ドル

貴社に支払われた映像の使用料は、著作権の使用料に該当し、米国の国内法により支払いの際に、30%の税率により課税が行われています。

日米租税条約により著作権の使用料は免税とされていますので、ある一定期間は、源泉徴収義務者に還付請求ができますが、既に、その期間が経過している場合には、米国歳入庁（Internal Revenue Service）に対し外国法人確定申告書（Form 1120-F）を提出し還付を受けます。

解説

1　米国における外国法人等（会社等）に対する源泉徴収制度

米国の国内法では、源泉徴収義務者（Withholding agent）は源泉徴収の対象となる所得（Fixed or determinable annual or periodicalincome・以下「FDAP」といいます。）を支払う際に30%の税率により所得税を徴収します。

ただし、日米租税条約による税額の軽減・免除の対象となる者については、税額の軽減・免除を行うこととされています。

税額の軽減又は免除を受ける場合には、源泉徴収義務者に対し租税条約の恩典を受ける者であることを証明するForm W-8BEN-E（法人用）を提出する必要があります。

2　源泉徴収された税金の還付方法

⑴　源泉徴収義務者（Withholding agent）の報告義務

源泉徴収義務者は、源泉徴収した翌年の3月15日までに、源泉徴収した事績を記載したForm 1042-S（我が国の法定調書に該当）を米国の国税庁（IRS）に一部を提出し、FDAPの受領者（Recipient）に対し3部交付しなければなりません。

一部は、源泉徴収義務者が保管することになります。

Form 1042-Sの提出先

Copy A・・・・・・・・・・・IRSへ提出（1部）
Copy B～Copy D・・・・・・受領者へ交付（3部）
Copy E・・・・・・・・・・・源泉徴収義務者保管（1部）

⑵　源泉徴収義務者に対する還付手続き

IRSに対する上記⑴のForm 1042-S（我が国の法定調書に該当）の報告期限（翌年3月15日）前であれば、源泉徴収義務者に対しForm W-8BEN-E（法人用）を提出し源泉徴収義務者から徴収税額の還付を受けることができます。

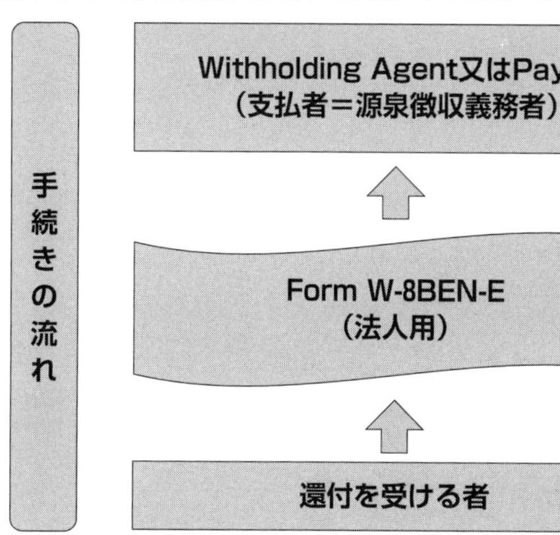

⑶　米国歳入庁（Internal Revenue Services）に対する還付請求

上記２の報告期限（翌年３月15日）後は、IRSから納税者番号を取得（米国で所得が発生する場合は既に取得済）し、Form 1120-F（外国法人確定申告書）により申告を行い還付を受けることになります。

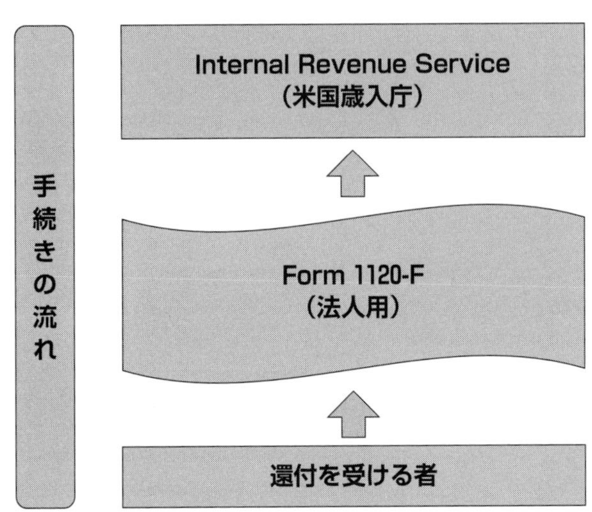

（出典）　Instruction for Form1120-F (2022): Simplified Procedure for Claiming a Return of U.S.Tax Withheld at source

……………………………………還付申告の際の留意点……………………………………

1　納税者番号（法人用）の取得

米国において確定（還付）申告を行う場合には、Employer Identification Number（納税者番号）が必要となります。

未取得の場合には、IRSに申請を行い、取得する必要があります。

2　申告書の送付先

Internal Revenue Service Center P.O.Box 409101, Ogden, UT84409

3　申告書の送付方法

送付先は私書箱であることから、いつ投函されたかが重要となります。

配送業者は日本の郵便局のEMSサービスを利用すれば、日本から約３日間で私書箱に投函されるとのことです。

4　申告書の提出期限について

還付申告書は、申告期限（12月決算の場合には、翌年の４月15日が申告期限となります。）の翌日から３年を経過する日までは提出することができますので、還付申告が過去の複数の事業年度に渡る場合には、申告期限に注意しなければなりません。

5　還付時期について

還付申告を複数年度行った場合には直近の事業年度分から還付されます。

それ以外の事業年度については、提出日から約半年で還付されます。

還付金額は、米国財務省発行の小切手が送金されます。

小切手の金額と還付申告書の還付税額を照合することにより、還付金額が正しいことを確認します。

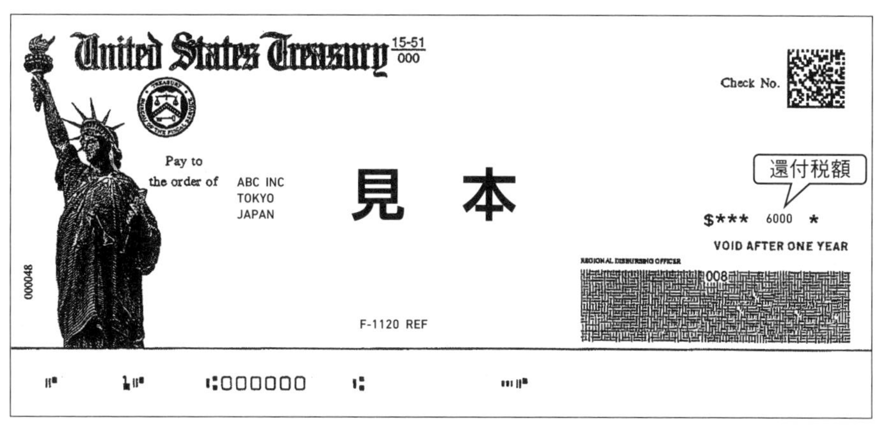

米国財務省小切手（見本）

6　還付された源泉所得税について

還付された源泉所得税については、その還付されることとなった日の属する事業年度の益金の額に算入します。

Form 1042-S（外国法人確定申告書）作成までの手続き

手続1

＝＝＝＝＝＝＝＝＝＝＝＝法定調書（源泉徴収の証明）の準備＝＝＝＝＝＝＝＝＝＝＝＝

源泉徴収義務者がIRS（米国歳入庁）に対し提出した源泉徴収の事実を証明するForm 1042-S（Foreign Person's U.S Source Income Subject to Withholding）のCopyB～CopyDを準備します。

手続2

＝＝＝＝＝＝＝＝＝＝＝＝＝＝Form W-8BEN-Eの作成＝＝＝＝＝＝＝＝＝＝＝＝＝＝

納税者が日米租税条約による恩典を受ける者であることを申告するためのForm W-8BEN-E（Certificate of Status of Beneficial O-wner for United States Tax Withholding and Reporting（Entities））を作成します。

手続3

＝＝＝＝＝＝＝＝＝＝＝＝＝＝＝Form 8833の作成＝＝＝＝＝＝＝＝＝＝＝＝＝＝＝

申告をする者が日米租税条約の適用を受けるために申告を行うものであることを明確にするためのForm 8833（Treaty-Based ReturnPosition Disclosure）を作成します。

手続4

＝＝＝＝＝＝＝＝＝＝＝＝＝＝＝居住者証明書の取得＝＝＝＝＝＝＝＝＝＝＝＝＝＝＝

申告をする者が日本の居住者であることを証明するために、所轄の税務署長宛に「居住者証明書交付請求書」を提出し、「居住者証明書」を取得します。

（注）「居住者証明書」は無料で交付されます。

手続5

＝＝＝＝＝＝＝＝＝＝＝IRS（米国歳入庁）宛のレターの作成＝＝＝＝＝＝＝＝＝＝

手続6

＝＝＝＝＝＝＝＝＝＝＝＝＝外国法人確定申告書の作成＝＝＝＝＝＝＝＝＝＝＝＝

確定申告書Form 1120-F（U.S Income Tax Return of a Foreign Corporation）を作成します。（複数年度に及ぶ場合は複数年度分）

手続1

法定調書（源泉徴収の証明）の準備

（2020年度分の Form 1042-S）

Form **1042-S** — Department of the Treasury, Internal Revenue Service

Foreign Person's U.S. Source Income Subject to Withholding — **2020**

► Go to *www.irs.gov/Form1042S* for instructions and the latest information.

UNIQUE FORM IDENTIFIER ☐ AMENDED ☐ AMENDMENT NO.

OMB No. 1545-0096

Copy B for Recipient

1 Income code: 12 / 2 Gross income: 20000	13e Recipient's U.S. TIN, if any / 13f Ch. 3 status code / 13g Ch. 4 status code
3 Chapter indicator. Enter "3" or "4": 3	13h Recipient's GIIN / 13i Recipient's foreign tax identification number, if any / 13j LOB code
3a Exemption code / 4a Exemption code	13k Recipient's account number
3b Tax rate 30 . 00 / 4b Tax rate .	13l Recipient's date of birth (YYYYMMDD)
5 Withholding allowance	14a Primary Withholding Agent's Name (if applicable)
6 Net income	14b Primary Withholding Agent's EIN
7a Federal tax withheld: 6000	15 Check if pro-rata basis reporting ☐
7b Check if federal tax withheld was not deposited with the IRS because escrow procedures were applied (see instructions) ☐	15a Intermediary or flow-through entity's EIN, if any / 15b Ch. 3 status code / 15c Ch. 4 status code
7c Check if withholding occurred in subsequent year with respect to a partnership interest ☐	15d Intermediary or flow-through entity's name
8 Tax withheld by other agents	15e Intermediary or flow-through entity's GIIN
9 Overwithheld tax repaid to recipient pursuant to adjustment procedures (see instructions) ( )	15f Country code / 15g Foreign tax identification number, if any
10 Total withholding credit (combine boxes 7a, 8, and 9): 6000	15h Address (number and street)
11 Tax paid by withholding agent (amounts not withheld) (see instructions)	15i City or town, state or province, country, ZIP or foreign postal code
12a Withholding agent's EIN: XX-XXXXXXX / 12b Ch. 3 status code: 15 / 12c Ch. 4 status code	16a Payer's name / 16b Payer's TIN
12d Withholding agent's name: DEF.INC	16c Payer's GIIN / 16d Ch. 3 status code / 16e Ch. 4 status code
12e Withholding agent's Global Intermediary Identification Number (GIIN)	17a State income tax withheld / 17b Payer's state tax no. / 17c Name of state
12f Country code / 12g Foreign tax identification number, if any	
12h Address (number and street): POBOX XX−XXXXXXX	
12i City or town, state or province, country, ZIP or foreign postal code: XX-XXXXXXX	
13a Recipient's name: ABC.INC / 13b Recipient's country code: JP	
13c Address (number and street): XXX,XXXXXX	
13d City or town, state or province, country, ZIP or foreign postal code: Tokyo, 101-0047 JAPAN	

(keep for your records) Form **1042-S** (2020)

Form **1042-S** — Department of the Treasury, Internal Revenue Service

Foreign Person's U.S. Source Income Subject to Withholding — **2020**

► Go to *www.irs.gov/Form1042S* for instructions and the latest information.

UNIQUE FORM IDENTIFIER ☐ AMENDED ☐ AMENDMENT NO.

OMB No. 1545-0096

Copy C for Recipient — Attach to any Federal tax return you file

1 Income code: 12 / 2 Gross income: 20000	13e Recipient's U.S. TIN, if any / 13f Ch. 3 status code / 13g Ch. 4 status code
3 Chapter indicator. Enter "3" or "4": 3	13h Recipient's GIIN / 13i Recipient's foreign tax identification number, if any / 13j LOB code
3a Exemption code / 4a Exemption code	13k Recipient's account number
3b Tax rate 30 . 00 / 4b Tax rate .	13l Recipient's date of birth (YYYYMMDD)
5 Withholding allowance	14a Primary Withholding Agent's Name (if applicable)
6 Net income	14b Primary Withholding Agent's EIN
7a Federal tax withheld: 6000	15 Check if pro-rata basis reporting ☐
7b Check if federal tax withheld was not deposited with the IRS because escrow procedures were applied (see instructions) ☐	15a Intermediary or flow-through entity's EIN, if any / 15b Ch. 3 status code / 15c Ch. 4 status code
7c Check if withholding occurred in subsequent year with respect to a partnership interest ☐	15d Intermediary or flow-through entity's name
8 Tax withheld by other agents	15e Intermediary or flow-through entity's GIIN
9 Overwithheld tax repaid to recipient pursuant to adjustment procedures (see instructions) ( )	15f Country code / 15g Foreign tax identification number, if any
10 Total withholding credit (combine boxes 7a, 8, and 9): 6000	15h Address (number and street)
11 Tax paid by withholding agent (amounts not withheld) (see instructions)	15i City or town, state or province, country, ZIP or foreign postal code
12a Withholding agent's EIN: XX-XXXXXXX / 12b Ch. 3 status code: 15 / 12c Ch. 4 status code	16a Payer's name / 16b Payer's TIN
12d Withholding agent's name: DEF.INC	16c Payer's GIIN / 16d Ch. 3 status code / 16e Ch. 4 status code
12e Withholding agent's Global Intermediary Identification Number (GIIN)	17a State income tax withheld / 17b Payer's state tax no. / 17c Name of state
12f Country code / 12g Foreign tax identification number, if any	
12h Address (number and street): POBOX XX-XXXXXXX	
12i City or town, state or province, country, ZIP or foreign postal code: XX-XXXXXXX	
13a Recipient's name: ABC.INC / 13b Recipient's country code: JP	
13c Address (number and street): XXX,XXXXXXX	
13d City or town, state or province, country, ZIP or foreign postal code: Tokyo, 101-0047 JAPAN	

Form **1042-S** (2020)

Form **1042-S** Department of the Treasury Internal Revenue Service

Foreign Person's U.S. Source Income Subject to Withholding **2020**

► Go to *www.irs.gov/Form1042S* for instructions and the latest information.

UNIQUE FORM IDENTIFIER ☐ AMENDED ☐ AMENDMENT NO.

OMB No. 1545-0096

Copy D for Recipient
Attach to any state tax return you file

1 Income code	12
2 Gross income	20000
3 Chapter indicator. Enter "3" or "4"	3
3a Exemption code	
3b Tax rate	30 . 00
4a Exemption code	
4b Tax rate	.
5 Withholding allowance	
6 Net income	
7a Federal tax withheld	6000
7b Check if federal tax withheld was not deposited with the IRS because escrow procedures were applied (see instructions)	☐
7c Check if withholding occurred in subsequent year with respect to a partnership interest	☐
8 Tax withheld by other agents	
9 Overwithheld tax repaid to recipient pursuant to adjustment procedures (see instructions)	( )
10 Total withholding credit (combine boxes 7a, 8, and 9)	6000
11 Tax paid by withholding agent (amounts not withheld) (see instructions)	
12a Withholding agent's EIN	XX-XXXXXXX
12b Ch. 3 status code	15
12c Ch. 4 status code	
12d Withholding agent's name	DEF.INC
12e Withholding agent's Global Intermediary Identification Number (GIIN)	
12f Country code	
12g Foreign tax identification number, if any	
12h Address (number and street)	POBOX XX-XXXXXX
12i City or town, state or province, country, ZIP or foreign postal code	XX-XXXXXX
13a Recipient's name	ABC.INC
13b Recipient's country code	
13c Address (number and street)	XXX,XXXXXXX
13d City or town, state or province, country, ZIP or foreign postal code	Tokyo,101-0047 JAPAN
13e Recipient's U.S. TIN, if any	
13f Ch. 3 status code	
13g Ch. 4 status code	
13h Recipient's GIIN	
13i Recipient's foreign tax identification number, if any	
13j LOB code	
13k Recipient's account number	
13l Recipient's date of birth (YYYYMMDD)	
14a Primary Withholding Agent's Name (if applicable)	
14b Primary Withholding Agent's EIN	
15 Check if pro-rata basis reporting	☐
15a Intermediary or flow-through entity's EIN, if any	
15b Ch. 3 status code	
15c Ch. 4 status code	
15d Intermediary or flow-through entity's name	
15e Intermediary or flow-through entity's GIIN	
15f Country code	
15g Foreign tax identification number, if any	
15h Address (number and street)	
15i City or town, state or province, country, ZIP or foreign postal code	
16a Payer's name	
16b Payer's TIN	
16c Payer's GIIN	
16d Ch. 3 status code	
16e Ch. 4 status code	
17a State income tax withheld	
17b Payer's state tax no.	
17c Name of state	

Form **1042-S** (2020)

手続1 法定調書（源泉徴収の証明）の準備 （2021年度分のForm 1042-S）

Form **1042-S** Department of the Treasury Internal Revenue Service

Foreign Person's U.S. Source Income Subject to Withholding **2021**

► Go to *www.irs.gov/Form1042S* for instructions and the latest information.

UNIQUE FORM IDENTIFIER ☐ AMENDED ☐ AMENDMENT NO.

OMB No. 1545-0096

Copy B for Recipient

1 Income code	12
2 Gross income	70000
3 Chapter indicator. Enter "3" or "4"	3
3a Exemption code	
3b Tax rate	30 . 00
4a Exemption code	
4b Tax rate	.
5 Withholding allowance	
6 Net income	
7a Federal tax withheld	21000
7b Check if federal tax withheld was not deposited with the IRS because escrow procedures were applied (see instructions)	☐
7c Check if withholding occurred in subsequent year with respect to a partnership interest	☐
8 Tax withheld by other agents	
9 Overwithheld tax repaid to recipient pursuant to adjustment procedures (see instructions)	( )
10 Total withholding credit (combine boxes 7a, 8, and 9)	21000
11 Tax paid by withholding agent (amounts not withheld) (see instructions)	
12a Withholding agent's EIN	XX-XXXXXXX
12b Ch. 3 status code	15
12c Ch. 4 status code	
12d Withholding agent's name	DEF,INC
12e Withholding agent's Global Intermediary Identification Number (GIIN)	
12f Country code	
12g Foreign tax identification number, if any	
12h Address (number and street)	POBOX XX-XXXXXXX
12i City or town, state or province, country, ZIP or foreign postal code	XX-XXXXXXXX
13a Recipient's name	ABC.INC
13b Recipient's country code	JP
13c Address (number and street)	XXX,XXXXXXXX
13d City or town, state or province, country, ZIP or foreign postal code	Tokyo, 101-0047 JAPAN
13e Recipient's U.S. TIN, if any	
13f Ch. 3 status code	
13g Ch. 4 status code	
13h Recipient's GIIN	
13i Recipient's foreign tax identification number, if any	
13j LOB code	
13k Recipient's account number	
13l Recipient's date of birth (YYYYMMDD)	
14a Primary Withholding Agent's Name (if applicable)	
14b Primary Withholding Agent's EIN	
15 Check if pro-rata basis reporting	☐
15a Intermediary or flow-through entity's EIN, if any	
15b Ch. 3 status code	
15c Ch. 4 status code	
15d Intermediary or flow-through entity's name	
15e Intermediary or flow-through entity's GIIN	
15f Country code	
15g Foreign tax identification number, if any	
15h Address (number and street)	
15i City or town, state or province, country, ZIP or foreign postal code	
16a Payer's name	
16b Payer's TIN	
16c Payer's GIIN	
16d Ch. 3 status code	
16e Ch. 4 status code	
17a State income tax withheld	0
17b Payer's state tax no.	
17c Name of state	

(keep for your records) Form **1042-S** (2021)

Form **1042-S** Department of the Treasury Internal Revenue Service

Foreign Person's U.S. Source Income Subject to Withholding **2021**

► Go to *www.irs.gov/Form1042S* for instructions and the latest information.

UNIQUE FORM IDENTIFIER ☐ AMENDED ☐ AMENDMENT NO.

OMB No. 1545-0096

Copy C for Recipient
Attach to any Federal tax return you file

1 Income code	12
2 Gross income	70000
3 Chapter indicator. Enter "3" or "4"	3
3a Exemption code	
3b Tax rate	30 . 00
4a Exemption code	
4b Tax rate	.
5 Withholding allowance	
6 Net income	
7a Federal tax withheld	21000
7b Check if federal tax withheld was not deposited with the IRS because escrow procedures were applied (see instructions)	☐
7c Check if withholding occurred in subsequent year with respect to a partnership interest	☐
8 Tax withheld by other agents	
9 Overwithheld tax repaid to recipient pursuant to adjustment procedures (see instructions)	( )
10 Total withholding credit (combine boxes 7a, 8, and 9)	21000
11 Tax paid by withholding agent (amounts not withheld) (see instructions)	
12a Withholding agent's EIN	XX-XXXXXXX
12b Ch. 3 status code	15
12c Ch. 4 status code	
12d Withholding agent's name	DEF, INC
12e Withholding agent's Global Intermediary Identification Number (GIIN)	
12f Country code	
12g Foreign tax identification number, if any	
12h Address (number and street)	POBOX XX-XXXXXXX
12i City or town, state or province, country, ZIP or foreign postal code	XX-XXXXXXX
13a Recipient's name	ABC.INC
13b Recipient's country code	JP
13c Address (number and street)	XXX,XXXXXXX
13d City or town, state or province, country, ZIP or foreign postal code	Tokyo, 101-0047 JAPAN
13e Recipient's U.S. TIN, if any	
13f Ch. 3 status code	
13g Ch. 4 status code	
13h Recipient's GIIN	
13i Recipient's foreign tax identification number, if any	
13j LOB code	
13k Recipient's account number	
13l Recipient's date of birth (YYYYMMDD)	
14a Primary Withholding Agent's Name (if applicable)	
14b Primary Withholding Agent's EIN	
15 Check if pro-rata basis reporting	☐
15a Intermediary or flow-through entity's EIN, if any	
15b Ch. 3 status code	
15c Ch. 4 status code	
15d Intermediary or flow-through entity's name	
15e Intermediary or flow-through entity's GIIN	
15f Country code	
15g Foreign tax identification number, if any	
15h Address (number and street)	
15i City or town, state or province, country, ZIP or foreign postal code	
16a Payer's name	
16b Payer's TIN	
16c Payer's GIIN	
16d Ch. 3 status code	
16e Ch. 4 status code	
17a State income tax withheld	
17b Payer's state tax no.	
17c Name of state	

Form **1042-S** (2021)

Form **1042-S** Department of the Treasury Internal Revenue Service

Foreign Person's U.S. Source Income Subject to Withholding **2021**

► Go to *www.irs.gov/Form1042S* for instructions and the latest information.

UNIQUE FORM IDENTIFIER ☐ AMENDED ☐ AMENDMENT NO.

OMB No. 1545-0096

Copy D for Recipient
Attach to any state tax return you file

1 Income code	12
2 Gross income	70000
3 Chapter indicator. Enter "3" or "4"	3
3a Exemption code	
3b Tax rate	30 . 00
4a Exemption code	
4b Tax rate	.
5 Withholding allowance	
6 Net income	
7a Federal tax withheld	21000
7b Check if federal tax withheld was not deposited with the IRS because escrow procedures were applied (see instructions)	☐
7c Check if withholding occurred in subsequent year with respect to a partnership interest	☐
8 Tax withheld by other agents	
9 Overwithheld tax repaid to recipient pursuant to adjustment procedures (see instructions)	( )
10 Total withholding credit (combine boxes 7a, 8, and 9)	21000
11 Tax paid by withholding agent (amounts not withheld) (see instructions)	
12a Withholding agent's EIN	XX-XXXXXX
12b Ch. 3 status code	15
12c Ch. 4 status code	
12d Withholding agent's name	DEF. INC
12e Withholding agent's Global Intermediary Identification Number (GIIN)	
12f Country code	
12g Foreign tax identification number, if any	
12h Address (number and street)	POBOX XX-XXXXXXX
12i City or town, state or province, country, ZIP or foreign postal code	XX-XXXXXXX
13a Recipient's name	ABC.INC
13b Recipient's country code	JP
13c Address (number and street)	XXX,XXXXXXX
13d City or town, state or province, country, ZIP or foreign postal code	Tokyo, 101-0047 JAPAN
13e Recipient's U.S. TIN, if any	
13f Ch. 3 status code	
13g Ch. 4 status code	
13h Recipient's GIIN	
13i Recipient's foreign tax identification number, if any	
13j LOB code	
13k Recipient's account number	
13l Recipient's date of birth (YYYYMMDD)	
14a Primary Withholding Agent's Name (if applicable)	
14b Primary Withholding Agent's EIN	
15 Check if pro-rata basis reporting	☐
15a Intermediary or flow-through entity's EIN, if any	
15b Ch. 3 status code	
15c Ch. 4 status code	
15d Intermediary or flow-through entity's name	
15e Intermediary or flow-through entity's GIIN	
15f Country code	
15g Foreign tax identification number, if any	
15h Address (number and street)	
15i City or town, state or province, country, ZIP or foreign postal code	
16a Payer's name	
16b Payer's TIN	
16c Payer's GIIN	
16d Ch. 3 status code	
16e Ch. 4 status code	
17a State income tax withheld	
17b Payer's state tax no.	
17c Name of state	

Form **1042-S** (2021)

手続1

法定調書（源泉徴収の証明）の準備
（2022年度分のForm 1042-S）

Form **1042-S** Department of the Treasury Internal Revenue Service

Foreign Person's U.S. Source Income Subject to Withholding **2022**

► Go to *www.irs.gov/Form1042S* for instructions and the latest information.

UNIQUE FORM IDENTIFIER ☐ AMENDED ☐ AMENDMENT NO.

OMB No. 1545-0096

Copy B for Recipient

1 Income code: 12
2 Gross income: 90000
3 Chapter indicator. Enter "3" or "4": 3
3a Exemption code
4a Exemption code
3b Tax rate: 30 . 00
4b Tax rate .
5 Withholding allowance
6 Net income
7a Federal tax withheld: 27000
7b Check if federal tax withheld was not deposited with the IRS because escrow procedures were applied (see instructions) . . . . ☐
7c Check if withholding occurred in subsequent year with respect to a partnership interest . . . . ☐
8 Tax withheld by other agents
9 Overwithheld tax repaid to recipient pursuant to adjustment procedures (see instructions) ( )
10 Total withholding credit (combine boxes 7a, 8, and 9): 27000
11 Tax paid by withholding agent (amounts not withheld) (see instructions)
12a Withholding agent's EIN: XX-XXXXXXX
12b Ch. 3 status code: 15
12c Ch. 4 status code
12d Withholding agent's name: DEF.INC
12e Withholding agent's Global Intermediary Identification Number (GIIN)
12f Country code
12g Foreign tax identification number, if any
12h Address (number and street): POBOX XX-XXXXXXX
12i City or town, state or province, country, ZIP or foreign postal code: XX-XXXXXXX
13a Recipient's name: ABC.INC
13b Recipient's country code: JP
13c Address (number and street): xxx,xxxxxxx
13d City or town, state or province, country, ZIP or foreign postal code: Tokyo,101-0047 JAPAN
13e Recipient's U.S. TIN, if any
13f Ch. 3 status code
13g Ch. 4 status code
13h Recipient's GIIN
13i Recipient's foreign tax identification number, if any
13j LOB code
13k Recipient's account number
13l Recipient's date of birth (YYYYMMDD)
14a Primary Withholding Agent's Name (if applicable)
14b Primary Withholding Agent's EIN
15 Check if pro-rata basis reporting ☐
15a Intermediary or flow-through entity's EIN, if any
15b Ch. 3 status code
15c Ch. 4 status code
15d Intermediary or flow-through entity's name
15e Intermediary or flow-through entity's GIIN
15f Country code
15g Foreign tax identification number, if any
15h Address (number and street)
15i City or town, state or province, country, ZIP or foreign postal code
16a Payer's name
16b Payer's TIN
16c Payer's GIIN
16d Ch. 3 status code
16e Ch. 4 status code
17a State income tax withheld
17b Payer's state tax no.
17c Name of state

(keep for your records)

Form **1042-S** (2022)

Form **1042-S** Department of the Treasury Internal Revenue Service

Foreign Person's U.S. Source Income Subject to Withholding **2022**

► Go to *www.irs.gov/Form1042S* for instructions and the latest information.

UNIQUE FORM IDENTIFIER ☐ AMENDED ☐ AMENDMENT NO.

OMB No. 1545-0096

Copy C for Recipient
Attach to any Federal tax return you file

1 Income code: 12
2 Gross income: 90000
3 Chapter indicator. Enter "3" or "4": 3
3a Exemption code
4a Exemption code
3b Tax rate: 30 . 00
4b Tax rate .
5 Withholding allowance
6 Net income
7a Federal tax withheld: 27000
7b Check if federal tax withheld was not deposited with the IRS because escrow procedures were applied (see instructions) . . . . ☐
7c Check if withholding occurred in subsequent year with respect to a partnership interest . . . . ☐
8 Tax withheld by other agents
9 Overwithheld tax repaid to recipient pursuant to adjustment procedures (see instructions) ( )
10 Total withholding credit (combine boxes 7a, 8, and 9): 27000
11 Tax paid by withholding agent (amounts not withheld) (see instructions)
12a Withholding agent's EIN: XX-XXXXXXX
12b Ch. 3 status code: 15
12c Ch. 4 status code
12d Withholding agent's name: DEF.INC
12e Withholding agent's Global Intermediary Identification Number (GIIN)
12f Country code
12g Foreign tax identification number, if any
12h Address (number and street): POBOX XX-XXXXXXX
12i City or town, state or province, country, ZIP or foreign postal code: XX-XXXXXXX
13a Recipient's name: ABC. INC
13b Recipient's country code
13c Address (number and street): xxx,xxxxxxx
13d City or town, state or province, country, ZIP or foreign postal code: Tokyo,101-0047 JAPAN
13e Recipient's U.S. TIN, if any
13f Ch. 3 status code
13g Ch. 4 status code
13h Recipient's GIIN
13i Recipient's foreign tax identification number, if any
13j LOB code
13k Recipient's account number
13l Recipient's date of birth (YYYYMMDD)
14a Primary Withholding Agent's Name (if applicable)
14b Primary Withholding Agent's EIN
15 Check if pro-rata basis reporting ☐
15a Intermediary or flow-through entity's EIN, if any
15b Ch. 3 status code
15c Ch. 4 status code
15d Intermediary or flow-through entity's name
15e Intermediary or flow-through entity's GIIN
15f Country code
15g Foreign tax identification number, if any
15h Address (number and street)
15i City or town, state or province, country, ZIP or foreign postal code
16a Payer's name
16b Payer's TIN
16c Payer's GIIN
16d Ch. 3 status code
16e Ch. 4 status code
17a State income tax withheld
17b Payer's state tax no.
17c Name of state

Form **1042-S** (2022)

手続１

法定調書（源泉徴収の証明）の準備

（2022年度分のForm 1042-S）

Form **1042-S** Department of the Treasury Internal Revenue Service

Foreign Person's U.S. Source Income Subject to Withholding **2022**

► Go to *www.irs.gov/Form1042S* for instructions and the latest information.

UNIQUE FORM IDENTIFIER ☐ AMENDED ☐ AMENDMENT NO.

OMB No. 1545-0096

Copy D for Recipient
Attach to any state tax return you file

1 Income code	12
2 Gross income	90000
3 Chapter indicator. Enter "3" or "4"	3
3a Exemption code	
3b Tax rate	30 . 00
4a Exemption code	
4b Tax rate	.
5 Withholding allowance	
6 Net income	
7a Federal tax withheld	27000
7b Check if federal tax withheld was not deposited with the IRS because escrow procedures were applied (see instructions)	☐
7c Check if withholding occurred in subsequent year with respect to a partnership interest	☐
8 Tax withheld by other agents	
9 Overwithheld tax repaid to recipient pursuant to adjustment procedures (see instructions)	( )
10 Total withholding credit (combine boxes 7a, 8, and 9)	27000
11 Tax paid by withholding agent (amounts not withheld) (see instructions)	
12a Withholding agent's EIN	XX-XXXXXXX
12b Ch. 3 status code	15
12c Ch. 4 status code	
12d Withholding agent's name	DEF.INC
12e Withholding agent's Global Intermediary Identification Number (GIIN)	
12f Country code	
12g Foreign tax identification number, if any	
12h Address (number and street)	POBOX XX-XXXXXXX
12i City or town, state or province, country, ZIP or foreign postal code	XX-XXXXXXX
13a Recipient's name	ABC.INC
13b Recipient's country code	JP
13c Address (number and street)	xxx,xxxxxxx
13d City or town, state or province, country, ZIP or foreign postal code	Tokyo, 101-0047 JAPAN
13e Recipient's U.S. TIN, if any	
13f Ch. 3 status code	
13g Ch. 4 status code	
13h Recipient's GIIN	
13i Recipient's foreign tax identification number, if any	
13j LOB code	
13k Recipient's account number	
13l Recipient's date of birth (YYYYMMDD)	
14a Primary Withholding Agent's Name (if applicable)	
14b Primary Withholding Agent's EIN	
15 Check if pro-rata basis reporting	☐
15a Intermediary or flow-through entity's EIN, if any	
15b Ch. 3 status code	
15c Ch. 4 status code	
15d Intermediary or flow-through entity's name	
15e Intermediary or flow-through entity's GIIN	
15f Country code	
15g Foreign tax identification number, if any	
15h Address (number and street)	
15i City or town, state or province, country, ZIP or foreign postal code	
16a Payer's name	
16b Payer's TIN	
16c Payer's GIIN	
16d Ch. 3 status code	
16e Ch. 4 status code	
17a State income tax withheld	
17b Payer's state tax no.	
17c Name of state	

Form **1042-S** (2022)

手続2

Form W-8BEN-E の作成

記入箇所は ⇦ で表示

Form **W-8BEN-E**
(Rev. October 2021)
Department of the Treasury
Internal Revenue Service

Certificate of Status of Beneficial Owner for United States Tax Withholding and Reporting (Entities)

▶ For use by entities. Individuals must use Form W-8BEN. ▶ Section references are to the Internal Revenue Code.
▶ Go to *www.irs.gov/FormW8BENE* for instructions and the latest information.
▶ Give this form to the withholding agent or payer. Do not send to the IRS.

OMB No. 1545-1621

Do NOT use this form for: **Instead use Form:**

- U.S. entity or U.S. citizen or resident W-9
- A foreign individual . . . . . W-8BEN (Individual) or Form 8233
- A foreign individual or entity claiming that income is effectively connected with the conduct of trade or business within the United States (unless claiming treaty benefits) W-8ECI
- A foreign partnership, a foreign simple trust, or a foreign grantor trust (unless claiming treaty benefits) (see instructions for exceptions) . . W-8IMY
- A foreign government, international organization, foreign central bank of issue, foreign tax-exempt organization, foreign private foundation, or government of a U.S. possession claiming that income is effectively connected U.S. income or that is claiming the applicability of section(s) 115(2), 501(c), 892, 895, or 1443(b) (unless claiming treaty benefits) (see instructions for other exceptions) . . . . . W-8ECI or W-8EXP
- Any person acting as an intermediary (including a qualified intermediary acting as a qualified derivatives dealer) W-8IMY

Part I Identification of Beneficial Owner

1 Name of organization that is the beneficial owner
ABC INC ⇦ ❶

2 Country of incorporation or organization
JAPAN ⇦ ❷

3 Name of disregarded entity receiving the payment (if applicable, see instructions)

❸

4 Chapter 3 Status (entity type) (Must check one box only):
☑ Corporation ☐ Partnership
☐ Simple trust ☐ Tax-exempt organization ☐ Complex trust ☐ Foreign Government - Controlled Entity
☐ Central Bank of Issue ☐ Private foundation ☐ Estate ☐ Foreign Government - Integral Part
☐ Grantor trust ☐ Disregarded entity ☐ International organization
If you entered disregarded entity, partnership, simple trust, or grantor trust above, is the entity a hybrid making a treaty claim? If "Yes," complete Part III. ☐ Yes ☐ No

5 Chapter 4 Status (FATCA status) (See instructions for details and complete the certification below for the entity's applicable status.)

☐ Nonparticipating FFI (including an FFI related to a Reporting IGA FFI other than a deemed-compliant FFI, participating FFI, or exempt beneficial owner).
☐ Participating FFI.
☐ Reporting Model 1 FFI.
☐ Reporting Model 2 FFI.
☐ Registered deemed-compliant FFI (other than a reporting Model 1 FFI, sponsored FFI, or nonreporting IGA FFI covered in Part XII). See instructions.
☐ Sponsored FFI. Complete Part IV.
☐ Certified deemed-compliant nonregistering local bank. Complete Part V.
☐ Certified deemed-compliant FFI with only low-value accounts. Complete Part VI.
☐ Certified deemed-compliant sponsored, closely held investment vehicle. Complete Part VII.
☐ Certified deemed-compliant limited life debt investment entity. Complete Part VIII.
☐ Certain investment entities that do not maintain financial accounts. Complete Part IX.
☐ Owner-documented FFI. Complete Part X.
☐ Restricted distributor. Complete Part XI.
☐ Nonreporting IGA FFI. Complete Part XII.
☐ Foreign government, government of a U.S. possession, or foreign central bank of issue. Complete Part XIII.
☐ International organization. Complete Part XIV.
☐ Exempt retirement plans. Complete Part XV.
☐ Entity wholly owned by exempt beneficial owners. Complete Part XVI.
☐ Territory financial institution. Complete Part XVII.
☐ Excepted nonfinancial group entity. Complete Part XVIII.
☐ Excepted nonfinancial start-up company. Complete Part XIX.
☐ Excepted nonfinancial entity in liquidation or bankruptcy. Complete Part XX.
☐ 501(c) organization. Complete Part XXI.
☐ Nonprofit organization. Complete Part XXII.
☐ Publicly traded NFFE or NFFE affiliate of a publicly traded corporation. Complete Part XXIII.
☐ Excepted territory NFFE. Complete Part XXIV.
☐ Active NFFE. Complete Part XXV.
☐ Passive NFFE. Complete Part XXVI.
☐ Excepted inter-affiliate FFI. Complete Part XXVII.
☐ Direct reporting NFFE.
☐ Sponsored direct reporting NFFE. Complete Part XXVIII.
☐ Account that is not a financial account.

6 Permanent residence address (street, apt. or suite no., or rural route). **Do not use a P.O. box or in-care-of address** (other than a registered address).
XXX.XXX.XXXXXXX ⇦ ❹

City or town, state or province. Include postal code where appropriate.
XXXX.Tokyo 101-0047 ⇦ ❹

Country
JAPAN ⇦ ❹

7 Mailing address (if different from above)

City or town, state or province. Include postal code where appropriate.

Country

For Paperwork Reduction Act Notice, see separate instructions. Cat. No. 59689N Form **W-8BEN-E** (Rev. 10-2021)

Form W-8BEN-E (Rev. 10-2021) Page **2**

Part I **Identification of Beneficial Owner** *(continued)*

8 U.S. taxpayer identification number (TIN), if required XXX.XXXX ⇦ ❺

9a GIIN | b Foreign TIN | c Check if FTIN not legally required . . . . . . ▶☐

10 Reference number(s) (see instructions)

Note: Please complete remainder of the form including signing the form in Part XXX.

Part II **Disregarded Entity or Branch Receiving Payment.** (Complete only if a disregarded entity with a GIIN or a branch of an FFI in a country other than the FFI's country of residence. See instructions.)

11 Chapter 4 Status (FATCA status) of disregarded entity or branch receiving payment

☐ Branch treated as nonparticipating FFI. ☐ Reporting Model 1 FFI. ☐ U.S. Branch.

☐ Participating FFI. ☐ Reporting Model 2 FFI.

12 Address of disregarded entity or branch (street, apt. or suite no., or rural route). **Do not use a P.O. box or in-care-of address** (other than a registered address).

City or town, state or province. Include postal code where appropriate.

Country

13 GIIN (if any)

Part III **Claim of Tax Treaty Benefits** (if applicable). (For chapter 3 purposes only.)

14 I certify that (check all that apply):

❻⇨ a ☑ The beneficial owner is a resident of JAPAN within the meaning of the income tax treaty between the United States and that country.

❼⇨ b ☑ The beneficial owner derives the item (or items) of income for which the treaty benefits are claimed, and, if applicable, meets the requirements of the treaty provision dealing with limitation on benefits. The following are types of limitation on benefits provisions that may be included in an applicable tax treaty (check only one; see instructions):

☐ Government

☐ Tax-exempt pension trust or pension fund

☐ Other tax-exempt organization

☐ Publicly traded corporation

☐ Subsidiary of a publicly traded corporation

☐ Company that meets the ownership and base erosion test

☐ Company that meets the derivative benefits test

❽⇨ ☑ Company with an item of income that meets active trade or business test

☐ Favorable discretionary determination by the U.S. competent authority received

☐ No LOB article in treaty

☐ Other (specify Article and paragraph):

c ☐ The beneficial owner is claiming treaty benefits for U.S. source dividends received from a foreign corporation or interest from a U.S. trade or business of a foreign corporation and meets qualified resident status (see instructions).

15 **Special rates and conditions** (if applicable—see instructions):

The beneficial owner is claiming the provisions of Article and paragraph Article12(1) ⇦ ❾

of the treaty identified on line 14a above to claim a 0% ⇦ ❿ % rate of withholding on (specify type of income):

Explain the additional conditions in the Article the beneficial owner meets to be eligible for the rate of withholding:

Part IV **Sponsored FFI**

16 Name of sponsoring entity:

17 **Check whichever box applies.**

☐ I certify that the entity identified in Part I:

- Is an investment entity;
- Is not a QI, WP (except to the extent permitted in the withholding foreign partnership agreement), or WT; **and**
- Has agreed with the entity identified above (that is not a nonparticipating FFI) to act as the sponsoring entity for this entity.

☐ I certify that the entity identified in Part I:

- Is a controlled foreign corporation as defined in section 957(a);
- Is not a QI, WP, or WT;
- Is wholly owned, directly or indirectly, by the U.S. financial institution identified above that agrees to act as the sponsoring entity for this entity; **and**
- Shares a common electronic account system with the sponsoring entity (identified above) that enables the sponsoring entity to identify all account holders and payees of the entity and to access all account and customer information maintained by the entity including, but not limited to, customer identification information, customer documentation, account balance, and all payments made to account holders or payees.

Form **W-8BEN-E** (Rev. 10-2021)

手続2 Form W-8BEN-E の作成手順（❶～⓭）

Form W-8BEN-E　米国の源泉徴収に関し恩恵を受ける者の証明書

次の者はこの証明書を使用できません。

・米国の事業体、米国市民及び米国居住者
・外国の個人
・米国内の事業活動に関連する所得であることを主張する外国の個人及び事業体
・外国のパートナーシップ、単純信託及び譲渡人信託
・外国政府、国際期間、外国中央銀行、外国免税機関、外国個人基金等
・代理人として活動する者

Part Ⅰ　Identification of Beneficial Owner（租税条約の恩典を受ける者の証明）

1　受益者の名称　**❶（ABC.INC と記入）**

2　受益者の所在国　**❷（JAPAN と記入）**

3　支払を受ける事業体の名称

4　Chapter 3の事業体の類型（1のボックスにチェック）

❸（Corporation にチェックします。）

□ Corporation　□ Disregarded entity　□ Partnership
□ Simple trust　□ Grantor trust　□ Complex trust
□ Foreign Goverment-Controlled Entity　□ Estate
□ Foreign Goverment-Integral Part　□ Central Bank of Issue
□ Tax-exempt organaization　□ Private foundation
□ International organization

もし、あなたが Disregarded entity、Partnership、Simple trust 又は Grantor trust に該当し、租税条約の恩典を受けますか。

□ YES　□ NO

恩典を受ける場合は、Part Ⅲを記載してください。

5　Chapter 4の事業体の類型

省略

6　恒久的な所在地**❹（日本の本店所在地を6と7に記入・国名は JAPAN と記入）**

7　郵送先住所（上記の恒久的な所在地と異なる場合）・都市名・郵便番号・国名

8　U.S taxpayer identification number（TIN）**❺（米国での納税者番号を記入）**

9 a　GIN　　b　Foreign TIN　　c　Check if

10　Reference number(s)（記載要領参照）

手続2　Form W-8BEN-E の作成手順（❶〜⓭）

Part Ⅱ Disregarded Entity or Branch Receiving Payment（みなし事業体又はReceiving Payment）

省略

Part Ⅲ Claim of Tax Treaty Benefit（適用される場合）（Chapter 3にのみ使用）

14　次の事項を証明します。

a　租税条約の恩典を受ける者は、米国との間の租税条約の意味においては・・・・国の居住者である。**❻（aの■にチェックし空欄にJAPANと記入）**

b　租税条約の受益者は、特典の制限を規定する租税条約の条件を満たす場合には、租税条約の恩典を受ける所得を得る。以下は、特典の制限に関する類型は、適用される租税に含まれます。（次のいずれか一つにチェックを入れてください。）

❼（bの■にチェック）

□ Government（政府）

□ Tax exempt pension trust or fund（免税年金信託又はファンド）

□ Other tax exempt organization（その他免税団体）

□ Publicly traded corporation（上場会社）

□ Subsidiary of a publicly traded corporation（上場会社の子会社）

□ Company that meets the ownership and base erosion test（税源浸食基準テストをクリアした会社）

□ Company that meets the derivative benefits test（派生的な恩恵を受けるためのテストをクリアした会社）

■ Company with an item of income that meets active trade or business test（能動的活動基準テストをクリアした会社）**❽（この■にチェック）**

□ Favorable discretionary determination by the U.S competent authority received（

□ No LOB article in treaty

□ Other（specify Article and paragraph）（

c　租税条約の受益者は、外国法人から受領した米国源泉の配当又は外国法人の米国の事業活動から生じた利息について租税条約の恩典の適用を要求している。

15　特別税率と条件（該当する場合）

租税条約の受益者は、・・% **❿（0%と記入）**の源泉徴収税率の適用を要求するために、上記14aに規定する租税条約…**❾（Article12⑴と記入）**の適用を要求する。

手続２ Form W-8BEN-E の作成

Form W-8BEN-E (Rev. 10-2021) Page **3**

Part V **Certified Deemed-Compliant Nonregistering Local Bank**

18 ☐ I certify that the FFI identified in Part I:

• Operates and is licensed solely as a bank or credit union (or similar cooperative credit organization operated without profit) in its country of incorporation or organization;

• Engages primarily in the business of receiving deposits from and making loans to, with respect to a bank, retail customers unrelated to such bank and, with respect to a credit union or similar cooperative credit organization, members, provided that no member has a greater than 5% interest in such credit union or cooperative credit organization;

• Does not solicit account holders outside its country of organization;

• Has no fixed place of business outside such country (for this purpose, a fixed place of business does not include a location that is not advertised to the public and from which the FFI performs solely administrative support functions);

• Has no more than $175 million in assets on its balance sheet and, if it is a member of an expanded affiliated group, the group has no more than $500 million in total assets on its consolidated or combined balance sheets; **and**

• Does not have any member of its expanded affiliated group that is a foreign financial institution, other than a foreign financial institution that is incorporated or organized in the same country as the FFI identified in Part I and that meets the requirements set forth in this part.

Part VI **Certified Deemed-Compliant FFI with Only Low-Value Accounts**

19 ☐ I certify that the FFI identified in Part I:

• Is not engaged primarily in the business of investing, reinvesting, or trading in securities, partnership interests, commodities, notional principal contracts, insurance or annuity contracts, or any interest (including a futures or forward contract or option) in such security, partnership interest, commodity, notional principal contract, insurance contract or annuity contract;

• No financial account maintained by the FFI or any member of its expanded affiliated group, if any, has a balance or value in excess of $50,000 (as determined after applying applicable account aggregation rules); **and**

• Neither the FFI nor the entire expanded affiliated group, if any, of the FFI, have more than $50 million in assets on its consolidated or combined balance sheet as of the end of its most recent accounting year.

Part VII **Certified Deemed-Compliant Sponsored, Closely Held Investment Vehicle**

20 Name of sponsoring entity: ____________________

21 ☐ I certify that the entity identified in Part I:

• Is an FFI solely because it is an investment entity described in Regulations section 1.1471-5(e)(4);

• Is not a QI, WP, or WT;

• Will have all of its due diligence, withholding, and reporting responsibilities (determined as if the FFI were a participating FFI) fulfilled by the sponsoring entity identified on line 20; **and**

• 20 or fewer individuals own all of the debt and equity interests in the entity (disregarding debt interests owned by U.S. financial institutions, participating FFIs, registered deemed-compliant FFIs, and certified deemed-compliant FFIs and equity interests owned by an entity if that entity owns 100% of the equity interests in the FFI and is itself a sponsored FFI).

Part VIII **Certified Deemed-Compliant Limited Life Debt Investment Entity**

22 ☐ I certify that the entity identified in Part I:

• Was in existence as of January 17, 2013;

• Issued all classes of its debt or equity interests to investors on or before January 17, 2013, pursuant to a trust indenture or similar agreement; **and**

• Is certified deemed-compliant because it satisfies the requirements to be treated as a limited life debt investment entity (such as the restrictions with respect to its assets and other requirements under Regulations section 1.1471-5(f)(2)(iv)).

Part IX **Certain Investment Entities that Do Not Maintain Financial Accounts**

23 ☐ I certify that the entity identified in Part I:

• Is a financial institution solely because it is an investment entity described in Regulations section 1.1471-5(e)(4)(i)(A), **and**

• Does not maintain financial accounts.

Part X **Owner-Documented FFI**

Note: This status only applies if the U.S. financial institution, participating FFI, or reporting Model 1 FFI to which this form is given has agreed that it will treat the FFI as an owner-documented FFI (see instructions for eligibility requirements). In addition, the FFI must make the certifications below.

24a ☐ (All owner-documented FFIs check here) I certify that the FFI identified in Part I:

• Does not act as an intermediary;

• Does not accept deposits in the ordinary course of a banking or similar business;

• Does not hold, as a substantial portion of its business, financial assets for the account of others;

• Is not an insurance company (or the holding company of an insurance company) that issues or is obligated to make payments with respect to a financial account;

• Is not owned by or in an expanded affiliated group with an entity that accepts deposits in the ordinary course of a banking or similar business, holds, as a substantial portion of its business, financial assets for the account of others, or is an insurance company (or the holding company of an insurance company) that issues or is obligated to make payments with respect to a financial account;

• Does not maintain a financial account for any nonparticipating FFI; **and**

• Does not have any specified U.S. persons that own an equity interest or debt interest (other than a debt interest that is not a financial account or that has a balance or value not exceeding $50,000) in the FFI other than those identified on the FFI owner reporting statement.

Form **W-8BEN-E** (Rev. 10-2021)

Form W-8BEN-E (Rev. 10-2021) Page **4**

Part X **Owner-Documented FFI** *(continued)*

Check box 24b or 24c, whichever applies.

b ☐ I certify that the FFI identified in Part I:

- Has provided, or will provide, an FFI owner reporting statement that contains:

  (i) The name, address, TIN (if any), chapter 4 status, and type of documentation provided (if required) of every individual and specified U.S. person that owns a direct or indirect equity interest in the owner-documented FFI (looking through all entities other than specified U.S. persons);

  (ii) The name, address, TIN (if any), and chapter 4 status of every individual and specified U.S. person that owns a debt interest in the owner-documented FFI (including any indirect debt interest, which includes debt interests in any entity that directly or indirectly owns the payee or any direct or indirect equity interest in a debt holder of the payee) that constitutes a financial account in excess of $50,000 (disregarding all such debt interests owned by participating FFIs, registered deemed-compliant FFIs, certified deemed-compliant FFIs, excepted NFFEs, exempt beneficial owners, or U.S. persons other than specified U.S. persons); **and**

  (iii) Any additional information the withholding agent requests in order to fulfill its obligations with respect to the entity.

- Has provided, or will provide, valid documentation meeting the requirements of Regulations section 1.1471-3(d)(6)(iii) for each person identified in the FFI owner reporting statement.

c ☐ I certify that the FFI identified in Part I has provided, or will provide, an auditor's letter, signed within 4 years of the date of payment, from an independent accounting firm or legal representative with a location in the United States stating that the firm or representative has reviewed the FFI's documentation with respect to all of its owners and debt holders identified in Regulations section 1.1471-3(d)(6)(iv)(A)(2), and that the FFI meets all the requirements to be an owner-documented FFI. The FFI identified in Part I has also provided, or will provide, an FFI owner reporting statement of its owners that are specified U.S. persons and Form(s) W-9, with applicable waivers.

Check box 24d if applicable (optional, see instructions).

d ☐ I certify that the entity identified on line 1 is a trust that does not have any contingent beneficiaries or designated classes with unidentified beneficiaries.

Part XI **Restricted Distributor**

25a ☐ (All restricted distributors check here) I certify that the entity identified in Part I:

- Operates as a distributor with respect to debt or equity interests of the restricted fund with respect to which this form is furnished;
- Provides investment services to at least 30 customers unrelated to each other and less than half of its customers are related to each other;
- Is required to perform AML due diligence procedures under the anti-money laundering laws of its country of organization (which is an FATF-compliant jurisdiction);
- Operates solely in its country of incorporation or organization, has no fixed place of business outside of that country, and has the same country of incorporation or organization as all members of its affiliated group, if any;
- Does not solicit customers outside its country of incorporation or organization;
- Has no more than $175 million in total assets under management and no more than $7 million in gross revenue on its income statement for the most recent accounting year;
- Is not a member of an expanded affiliated group that has more than $500 million in total assets under management or more than $20 million in gross revenue for its most recent accounting year on a combined or consolidated income statement; **and**
- Does not distribute any debt or securities of the restricted fund to specified U.S. persons, passive NFFEs with one or more substantial U.S. owners, or nonparticipating FFIs.

Check box 25b or 25c, whichever applies.

I further certify that with respect to all sales of debt or equity interests in the restricted fund with respect to which this form is furnished that are made after December 31, 2011, the entity identified in Part I:

b ☐ Has been bound by a distribution agreement that contained a general prohibition on the sale of debt or securities to U.S. entities and U.S. resident individuals and is currently bound by a distribution agreement that contains a prohibition of the sale of debt or securities to any specified U.S. person, passive NFFE with one or more substantial U.S. owners, or nonparticipating FFI.

c ☐ Is currently bound by a distribution agreement that contains a prohibition on the sale of debt or securities to any specified U.S. person, passive NFFE with one or more substantial U.S. owners, or nonparticipating FFI and, for all sales made prior to the time that such a restriction was included in its distribution agreement, has reviewed all accounts related to such sales in accordance with the procedures identified in Regulations section 1.1471-4(c) applicable to preexisting accounts and has redeemed or retired any, or caused the restricted fund to transfer the securities to a distributor that is a participating FFI or reporting Model 1 FFI securities which were sold to specified U.S. persons, passive NFFEs with one or more substantial U.S. owners, or nonparticipating FFIs.

Form **W-8BEN-E** (Rev. 10-2021)

手続２ Form W-8BEN-E の作成

Form W-8BEN-E (Rev. 10-2021) Page **5**

Part XII Nonreporting IGA FFI

26 ☐ I certify that the entity identified in Part I:

• Meets the requirements to be considered a nonreporting financial institution pursuant to an applicable IGA between the United States and ______________________. The applicable IGA is a ☐ Model 1 IGA or a ☐ Model 2 IGA; and is treated as a ______________________ under the provisions of the applicable IGA or Treasury regulations (if applicable, see instructions);

• If you are a trustee documented trust or a sponsored entity, provide the name of the trustee or sponsor ______________________.
The trustee is: ☐ U.S. ☐ Foreign

Part XIII Foreign Government, Government of a U.S. Possession, or Foreign Central Bank of Issue

27 ☐ I certify that the entity identified in Part I is the beneficial owner of the payment, and is not engaged in commercial financial activities of a type engaged in by an insurance company, custodial institution, or depository institution with respect to the payments, accounts, or obligations for which this form is submitted (except as permitted in Regulations section 1.1471-6(h)(2)).

Part XIV International Organization

Check box 28a or 28b, whichever applies.

28a ☐ I certify that the entity identified in Part I is an international organization described in section 7701(a)(18).

b ☐ I certify that the entity identified in Part I:

• Is comprised primarily of foreign governments;

• Is recognized as an intergovernmental or supranational organization under a foreign law similar to the International Organizations Immunities Act or that has in effect a headquarters agreement with a foreign government;

• The benefit of the entity's income does not inure to any private person; **and**

• Is the beneficial owner of the payment and is not engaged in commercial financial activities of a type engaged in by an insurance company, custodial institution, or depository institution with respect to the payments, accounts, or obligations for which this form is submitted (except as permitted in Regulations section 1.1471-6(h)(2)).

Part XV Exempt Retirement Plans

Check box 29a, b, c, d, e, or f, whichever applies.

29a ☐ I certify that the entity identified in Part I:

• Is established in a country with which the United States has an income tax treaty in force (see Part III if claiming treaty benefits);

• Is operated principally to administer or provide pension or retirement benefits; **and**

• Is entitled to treaty benefits on income that the fund derives from U.S. sources (or would be entitled to benefits if it derived any such income) as a resident of the other country which satisfies any applicable limitation on benefits requirement.

b ☐ I certify that the entity identified in Part I:

• Is organized for the provision of retirement, disability, or death benefits (or any combination thereof) to beneficiaries that are former employees of one or more employers in consideration for services rendered;

• No single beneficiary has a right to more than 5% of the FFI's assets;

• Is subject to government regulation and provides annual information reporting about its beneficiaries to the relevant tax authorities in the country in which the fund is established or operated; **and**

(i) Is generally exempt from tax on investment income under the laws of the country in which it is established or operates due to its status as a retirement or pension plan;

(ii) Receives at least 50% of its total contributions from sponsoring employers (disregarding transfers of assets from other plans described in this part, retirement and pension accounts described in an applicable Model 1 or Model 2 IGA, other retirement funds described in an applicable Model 1 or Model 2 IGA, or accounts described in Regulations section 1.1471-5(b)(2)(i)(A));

(iii) Either does not permit or penalizes distributions or withdrawals made before the occurrence of specified events related to retirement, disability, or death (except rollover distributions to accounts described in Regulations section 1.1471-5(b)(2)(i)(A) (referring to retirement and pension accounts), to retirement and pension accounts described in an applicable Model 1 or Model 2 IGA, or to other retirement funds described in this part or in an applicable Model 1 or Model 2 IGA); **or**

(iv) Limits contributions by employees to the fund by reference to earned income of the employee or may not exceed $50,000 annually.

c ☐ I certify that the entity identified in Part I:

• Is organized for the provision of retirement, disability, or death benefits (or any combination thereof) to beneficiaries that are former employees of one or more employers in consideration for services rendered;

• Has fewer than 50 participants;

• Is sponsored by one or more employers each of which is not an investment entity or passive NFFE;

• Employee and employer contributions to the fund (disregarding transfers of assets from other plans described in this part, retirement and pension accounts described in an applicable Model 1 or Model 2 IGA, or accounts described in Regulations section 1.1471-5(b)(2)(i)(A)) are limited by reference to earned income and compensation of the employee, respectively;

• Participants that are not residents of the country in which the fund is established or operated are not entitled to more than 20% of the fund's assets; **and**

• Is subject to government regulation and provides annual information reporting about its beneficiaries to the relevant tax authorities in the country in which the fund is established or operates.

Form **W-8BEN-E** (Rev. 10-2021)

Part XV **Exempt Retirement Plans** *(continued)*

d ☐ I certify that the entity identified in Part I is formed pursuant to a pension plan that would meet the requirements of section 401(a), other than the requirement that the plan be funded by a trust created or organized in the United States.

e ☐ I certify that the entity identified in Part I is established exclusively to earn income for the benefit of one or more retirement funds described in this part or in an applicable Model 1 or Model 2 IGA, or accounts described in Regulations section 1.1471-5(b)(2)(i)(A) (referring to retirement and pension accounts), or retirement and pension accounts described in an applicable Model 1 or Model 2 IGA.

f ☐ I certify that the entity identified in Part I:

• Is established and sponsored by a foreign government, international organization, central bank of issue, or government of a U.S. possession (each as defined in Regulations section 1.1471-6) or an exempt beneficial owner described in an applicable Model 1 or Model 2 IGA to provide retirement, disability, or death benefits to beneficiaries or participants that are current or former employees of the sponsor (or persons designated by such employees); **or**

• Is established and sponsored by a foreign government, international organization, central bank of issue, or government of a U.S. possession (each as defined in Regulations section 1.1471-6) or an exempt beneficial owner described in an applicable Model 1 or Model 2 IGA to provide retirement, disability, or death benefits to beneficiaries or participants that are not current or former employees of such sponsor, but are in consideration of personal services performed for the sponsor.

Part XVI **Entity Wholly Owned by Exempt Beneficial Owners**

30 ☐ I certify that the entity identified in Part I:

• Is an FFI solely because it is an investment entity;

• Each direct holder of an equity interest in the investment entity is an exempt beneficial owner described in Regulations section 1.1471-6 or in an applicable Model 1 or Model 2 IGA;

• Each direct holder of a debt interest in the investment entity is either a depository institution (with respect to a loan made to such entity) or an exempt beneficial owner described in Regulations section 1.1471-6 or an applicable Model 1 or Model 2 IGA.

• Has provided an owner reporting statement that contains the name, address, TIN (if any), chapter 4 status, and a description of the type of documentation provided to the withholding agent for every person that owns a debt interest constituting a financial account or direct equity interest in the entity; **and**

• Has provided documentation establishing that every owner of the entity is an entity described in Regulations section 1.1471-6(b), (c), (d), (e), (f) and/or (g) without regard to whether such owners are beneficial owners.

Part XVII **Territory Financial Institution**

31 ☐ I certify that the entity identified in Part I is a financial institution (other than an investment entity) that is incorporated or organized under the laws of a possession of the United States.

Part XVIII **Excepted Nonfinancial Group Entity**

32 ☐ I certify that the entity identified in Part I:

• Is a holding company, treasury center, or captive finance company and substantially all of the entity's activities are functions described in Regulations section 1.1471-5(e)(5)(i)(C) through (E);

• Is a member of a nonfinancial group described in Regulations section 1.1471-5(e)(5)(i)(B);

• Is not a depository or custodial institution (other than for members of the entity's expanded affiliated group); **and**

• Does not function (or hold itself out) as an investment fund, such as a private equity fund, venture capital fund, leveraged buyout fund, or any investment vehicle with an investment strategy to acquire or fund companies and then hold interests in those companies as capital assets for investment purposes.

Part XIX **Excepted Nonfinancial Start-Up Company**

33 ☐ I certify that the entity identified in Part I:

• Was formed on (or, in the case of a new line of business, the date of board resolution approving the new line of business) ______________ (date must be less than 24 months prior to date of payment);

• Is not yet operating a business and has no prior operating history or is investing capital in assets with the intent to operate a new line of business other than that of a financial institution or passive NFFE;

• Is investing capital into assets with the intent to operate a business other than that of a financial institution; **and**

• Does not function (or hold itself out) as an investment fund, such as a private equity fund, venture capital fund, leveraged buyout fund, or any investment vehicle whose purpose is to acquire or fund companies and then hold interests in those companies as capital assets for investment purposes.

Part XX **Excepted Nonfinancial Entity in Liquidation or Bankruptcy**

34 ☐ I certify that the entity identified in Part I:

• Filed a plan of liquidation, filed a plan of reorganization, or filed for bankruptcy on ______________________;

• During the past 5 years has not been engaged in business as a financial institution or acted as a passive NFFE;

• Is either liquidating or emerging from a reorganization or bankruptcy with the intent to continue or recommence operations as a nonfinancial entity; **and**

• Has, or will provide, documentary evidence such as a bankruptcy filing or other public documentation that supports its claim if it remains in bankruptcy or liquidation for more than 3 years.

Form **W-8BEN-E** (Rev. 10-2021)

手続2

Form W-8BEN-E の作成

Form W-8BEN-E (Rev. 10-2021) Page **7**

Part XXI 501(c) Organization

35 ☐ I certify that the entity identified in Part I is a 501(c) organization that:

• Has been issued a determination letter from the IRS that is currently in effect concluding that the payee is a section 501(c) organization that is dated ________________ ; **or**

• Has provided a copy of an opinion from U.S. counsel certifying that the payee is a section 501(c) organization (without regard to whether the payee is a foreign private foundation).

Part XXII Nonprofit Organization

36 ☐ I certify that the entity identified in Part I is a nonprofit organization that meets the following requirements.

• The entity is established and maintained in its country of residence exclusively for religious, charitable, scientific, artistic, cultural or educational purposes;

• The entity is exempt from income tax in its country of residence;

• The entity has no shareholders or members who have a proprietary or beneficial interest in its income or assets;

• Neither the applicable laws of the entity's country of residence nor the entity's formation documents permit any income or assets of the entity to be distributed to, or applied for the benefit of, a private person or noncharitable entity other than pursuant to the conduct of the entity's charitable activities or as payment of reasonable compensation for services rendered or payment representing the fair market value of property which the entity has purchased; **and**

• The applicable laws of the entity's country of residence or the entity's formation documents require that, upon the entity's liquidation or dissolution, all of its assets be distributed to an entity that is a foreign government, an integral part of a foreign government, a controlled entity of a foreign government, or another organization that is described in this part or escheats to the government of the entity's country of residence or any political subdivision thereof.

Part XXIII Publicly Traded NFFE or NFFE Affiliate of a Publicly Traded Corporation

Check box 37a or 37b, whichever applies.

37a ☐ I certify that:

• The entity identified in Part I is a foreign corporation that is not a financial institution; **and**

• The stock of such corporation is regularly traded on one or more established securities markets, including ____________________ (name one securities exchange upon which the stock is regularly traded).

b ☐ I certify that:

• The entity identified in Part I is a foreign corporation that is not a financial institution;

• The entity identified in Part I is a member of the same expanded affiliated group as an entity the stock of which is regularly traded on an established securities market;

• The name of the entity, the stock of which is regularly traded on an established securities market, is ____________________ ; **and**

• The name of the securities market on which the stock is regularly traded is ____________________ .

Part XXIV Excepted Territory NFFE

38 ☐ I certify that:

• The entity identified in Part I is an entity that is organized in a possession of the United States;

• The entity identified in Part I:

(i) Does not accept deposits in the ordinary course of a banking or similar business;

(ii) Does not hold, as a substantial portion of its business, financial assets for the account of others; **or**

(iii) Is not an insurance company (or the holding company of an insurance company) that issues or is obligated to make payments with respect to a financial account; **and**

• All of the owners of the entity identified in Part I are bona fide residents of the possession in which the NFFE is organized or incorporated.

Part XXV Active NFFE

39 ☐ I certify that:

• The entity identified in Part I is a foreign entity that is not a financial institution;

• Less than 50% of such entity's gross income for the preceding calendar year is passive income; **and**

• Less than 50% of the assets held by such entity are assets that produce or are held for the production of passive income (calculated as a weighted average of the percentage of passive assets measured quarterly) (see instructions for the definition of passive income).

Part XXVI Passive NFFE

40a ☐ I certify that the entity identified in Part I is a foreign entity that is not a financial institution (other than an investment entity organized in a possession of the United States) and is not certifying its status as a publicly traded NFFE (or affiliate), excepted territory NFFE, active NFFE, direct reporting NFFE, or sponsored direct reporting NFFE.

Check box 40b or 40c, whichever applies.

b ☐ I further certify that the entity identified in Part I has no substantial U.S. owners (or, if applicable, no controlling U.S. persons); **or**

c ☐ I further certify that the entity identified in Part I has provided the name, address, and TIN of each substantial U.S. owner (or, if applicable, controlling U.S. person) of the NFFE in Part XXIX.

Form **W-8BEN-E** (Rev. 10-2021)

Form W-8BEN-E (Rev. 10-2021) Page **8**

Part XXVII Excepted Inter-Affiliate FFI

41 ☐ I certify that the entity identified in Part I:

- Is a member of an expanded affiliated group;
- Does not maintain financial accounts (other than accounts maintained for members of its expanded affiliated group);
- Does not make withholdable payments to any person other than to members of its expanded affiliated group;
- Does not hold an account (other than depository accounts in the country in which the entity is operating to pay for expenses) with or receive payments from any withholding agent other than a member of its expanded affiliated group; **and**
- Has not agreed to report under Regulations section 1.1471-4(d)(2)(ii)(C) or otherwise act as an agent for chapter 4 purposes on behalf of any financial institution, including a member of its expanded affiliated group.

Part XXVIII Sponsored Direct Reporting NFFE (see instructions for when this is permitted)

42 Name of sponsoring entity:

43 ☐ I certify that the entity identified in Part I is a direct reporting NFFE that is sponsored by the entity identified on line 42.

Part XXIX Substantial U.S. Owners of Passive NFFE

As required by Part XXVI, provide the name, address, and TIN of each substantial U.S. owner of the NFFE. Please see the instructions for a definition of substantial U.S. owner. If providing the form to an FFI treated as a reporting Model 1 FFI or reporting Model 2 FFI, an NFFE may also use this part for reporting its controlling U.S. persons under an applicable IGA.

Name	Address	TIN

Part XXX Certification

Under penalties of perjury, I declare that I have examined the information on this form and to the best of my knowledge and belief it is true, correct, and complete. I further certify under penalties of perjury that:

- The entity identified on line 1 of this form is the beneficial owner of all the income or proceeds to which this form relates, is using this form to certify its status for chapter 4 purposes, or is submitting this form for purposes of section 6050W or 6050Y;
- The entity identified on line 1 of this form is not a U.S. person;
- This form relates to: (a) income not effectively connected with the conduct of a trade or business in the United States, (b) income effectively connected with the conduct of a trade or business in the United States but is not subject to tax under an income tax treaty, (c) the partner's share of a partnership's effectively connected taxable income, or (d) the partner's amount realized from the transfer of a partnership interest subject to withholding under section 1446(f); **and**
- For broker transactions or barter exchanges, the beneficial owner is an exempt foreign person as defined in the instructions.

Furthermore, I authorize this form to be provided to any withholding agent that has control, receipt, or custody of the income of which the entity on line 1 is the beneficial owner or any withholding agent that can disburse or make payments of the income of which the entity on line 1 is the beneficial owner.

I agree that I will submit a new form within 30 days if any certification on this form becomes incorrect.

☑ **I certify that I have the capacity to sign for the entity identified on line 1 of this form.**

Sign Here ⑪ ⇨ ______ Signature of individual authorized to sign for beneficial owner | XXXXX-XXXXX Print Name | ______ Date (MM-DD-YYYY)

Form **W-8BEN-E** (Rev. 10-2021)

手続2

Form W- 8 BEN-E の作成手順（❶～⓭）

Part Ⅳ～Part XXIX

省略

Part XXX Certification（証明）

罰金制度の下、私は本証明書に関する情報を確認し、私が知る限りにおいては、この情報は正確で完全なものであることを宣言します。

また、罰金制度の下、さらに、次の事項について証明いたします。

・本証明書の line 1の証明された事業体は、この証明書に関連するすべての所得の受益者であり、また、この事業体は、chapter 4の類型を証明するために使用され、又は Section 6050W or 6050Y の目的のために提出する商店主である。

・本証明書の line 1の証明された事業体は、米国人でないこと。

・本証明書に関連する所得とは、次の所得をいます。

(a)　米国内の事業活動に関連しない所得であること。

(b)　米国内の事業活動に関連する所得であるが、租税条約の取扱いを受けない所得であること。

(c)　米国内の事業活動に関連するパートナーシップの持分の所得

(d)　section 1446(f)の下において、源泉徴収の対象となるパートナーシップの利益の譲渡により実現したパートナーの所得。

・　仲介取引又は交換取引の場合において、租税条約の受益者は免税外国人であること。

さらに、私は、本証明書が line 1の者が受益者である所得の受領者、管理者である源泉徴収義務者に提供されることを許可する。また、源泉徴収義務者が line 1の受益者の所得を支払うをことも許可する。

私は、本証明書が不正確である場合には、30日以内に、新しい証明書を提出いたします。

署名　受益者のために署名する権限を与えられた者の署名　**⓫（代表者の署名）**

氏名　**⓬（氏名を活字体で記入）**

日付　**⓭（作成日を記入）**

手続 3

Form 8833の作成

記入箇所は ⇦ で表示

Form **8833**
(Rev. December 2022)
Department of the Treasury
Internal Revenue Service

Treaty-Based Return Position Disclosure Under Section 6114 or 7701(b)

Attach to your tax return.
Go to *www.irs.gov/Form8833* for the latest information.

OMB No. 1545-1354

Attach a separate Form 8833 for each treaty-based return position taken. Failure to disclose a treaty-based return position may result in a penalty of $1,000 ($10,000 in the case of a C corporation) (see section 6712).

Name	U.S. taxpayer identifying number	Reference ID number, if any (see instructions)
ABC.INC ❶	XX-XXXXXXX ❷	
Address in country of residence	Address in the United States	
❸ XX,XXXXXXXX,XXXXXX		

Check one or both of the following boxes as applicable.
- The taxpayer is disclosing a treaty-based return position as required by section 6114 . . . . ❹ ☑
- The taxpayer is a dual-resident taxpayer and is disclosing a treaty-based return position as required by Regulations section 301.7701(b)-7 . . . . ☐

Note: If the taxpayer is a dual-resident taxpayer and a long-term resident, by electing to be treated as a resident of a foreign country for purposes of claiming benefits under an applicable income tax treaty, the taxpayer will be deemed to have expatriated pursuant to section 877A. For more information, see the instructions.

Check this box if the taxpayer is a U.S. citizen or resident or is incorporated in the United States . . . . ☐

1 Enter the specific treaty position relied on:
- **a** Treaty country JAPAN ❺
- **b** Article(s) 12(1) ❻

2 List the Internal Revenue Code provision(s) overruled or modified by the treaty-based return position SECTION 1441 ❼

3 Name, identifying number (if available to the taxpayer), and address in the United States of the payor of the income (if fixed or determinable annual or periodical). See instructions.
DEF.INC. TIN XX-XXXXXXX
XXX,XXXXXX,XXXXXXXXXX ❽

4 List the provision(s) of the limitation on benefits article (if any) in the treaty that the taxpayer relies on to qualify for benefits under the treaty 22(2) ❾

5 Is the taxpayer disclosing a treaty-based return position for which reporting is specifically required pursuant to Regulations section 301.6114-1(b)? . . . . ☐ Yes ☑ No
If "Yes," enter the specific subsection(s) of Regulations section 301.6114-1(b) requiring reporting . . . . ❿
Also include the information requested in line 6.

6 Explain the treaty-based return position taken. Include a brief summary of the facts on which it is based. Also, list the nature and amount (or a reasonable estimate) of gross receipts, each separate gross payment, each separate gross income item, or other item (as applicable) for which the treaty benefit is claimed

For Paperwork Reduction Act Notice, see the instructions. Cat. No. 14895L Form **8833** (Rev. 12-2022)

手続３ Form 8833の作成手順（❶～❿）

8833　**租税条約に基づく申告であることの開示**

Under Section 6114 or 7701(b)

租税条約に基づく申告であることを明確にするために、Form 8833を添付してください。

租税条約に基づく申告であることを明確にすることを怠った場合には、$1,000の罰金が課されます。(C corporation の場合には $10,000を罰金とします。Section 6712を参照)

○ 名称 **❶（ABC.INC と記入）**

○ U.S taxpayer identifying number **❷（米国の納税者番号を記入）**

○ 提出者の住所 **❸（日本の本店所在地を記入）** ○ 米国における住所

次の事項について該当する場合は、チェックをしてください。

・納税者は section 6114の規定による租税条約に基づく申告であることを明確にする。

❹（右記の□にチェック） □

・納税者は双方居住者であり、section 301.7701(b)-7の規定による租税条約に基づく申告であることを明確にする。 ▶□

（注） 納税者が双方居住者で、かつ、長期に滞在する居住者であるときは、租税条約の特典を受けるために外国の居住者であることを選択することによって、その納税者は section 877Aの規定mにより、国外居住者とみなされます。

納税者が米国市民又は居住者、又は米国において設立された会社である場合には、次のこのボックスをチェックしてください。 ▶□

1 条約の適用条項について

a 条約締結国 **❺（JAPAN と記入）**

b 適用条項 **❻（12(1)）と記入）**

SECTION 1441とは外国人と外国法人等に対する源泉徴収の規定です。

2 租税条約に基づく申告により変更又は修正される米国内法 **❼（SECTION 1441と記入）**

3 支払者の名称、米国における identifying number 及び所在地

❽（DEF INC.・DEF INC の納税者番号・DEF INC の所在地を記入）

4 租税条約の特典条項の適用を受けるための条項 **❾（22(2) と記入）**

5 納税者は、section 301.6114(b)の規定による報告のために特に要求される目的のために、租税条約に基づく申告であることを明確にするのですか。 YES NO □

YES であれば、section 301.6114-1(b)の特定の subsection (s)を記入してください。

次の line 6の情報も記載してください。　**⑩（NOの□にチェック）**

6　租税条約に基づく申告を行う事情を説明してください。

総収入金額と総支払額を、所得の種類、金額ごとに記載してください。

手続4　居住者証明書の取得

記入箇所は ⇐ で表示

※租税条約等締結国用様式

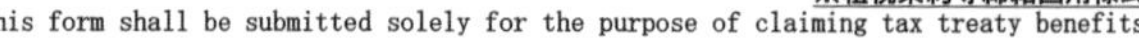
This form shall be submitted solely for the purpose of claiming tax treaty benefits

国税庁
National Tax Agency

日本国居住者記載欄
For use by a resident of Japan

居住者証明書交付請求書

APPLICATION FOR CERTIFICATE OF RESIDENCE IN JAPAN

記載に当たっては留意事項・記載要領を参照してください。

＿＿＿＿＿＿＿＿税務署長　あて

請求日　Date of request:　＿＿＿＿年＿＿月＿＿日

【代理人記入欄】Information on the agent
※代理人の方のみ記入してください。
住所　Address

氏名　Name

（電話番号 Telephone number　　　　　　）

※代理人の方が請求される場合は代理の権限を有することを証明する書類が必要です。

Information on the applicant:

住所（納税地）Address	※日本語及び英語で記入してください。
（フリガナ）氏名又は法人名及び代表者氏名 Name or corporation name and representative name	※日本語及び英語で記入してください。 （電話番号 Telephone number :　　　　　）

租税条約上の特典を得る目的で、下記のとおり居住者証明書の交付を請求します。

For the purpose of obtaining benefits under the Income Tax Convention, I hereby request the issuance of certificate of residence as follows:

記

提出先の国名等 Name of the State to which this certificate is submitted	※日本語及び英語で記入してください。	
対象期間 Period concerned (Optional)		
申述事項 Declaration	以下の事項を申述します。 □ 請求者は租税の適用上日本国の居住者であること □ 当該請求は専ら居住性の証明のためになされること □ 本請求書の情報は真正かつ正確であること □	I hereby declare that: The applicant is the resident of Japan for tax purposes; This application is made only for the purpose of residency certification; and The information in this application is true and correct.
証明書の請求枚数 Requested number of copies	枚	※本交付請求書は、居住者証明書の必要部数＋１部を提出してください。　整理番号 Reference number (Optional)

国税庁
National Tax Agency

税務署記載欄
For use by Tax Office

居住者証明書

CERTIFICATE OF RESIDENCE IN JAPAN

当方の知り得る限りにおいて、上記の請求者は、日本国と（相手国）との間の租税条約上、日本国居住者であることをここに証明します。

I, the undersigned acting as District Director of the Tax Office of the National Tax Agency, hereby certify that, to the best of my knowledge, the above applicant is the resident of Japan within the meaning of the Income Tax Convention between Japan and ＿＿＿＿＿＿＿＿＿＿＿＿.

- 証明日
  Date of certification: ＿＿＿＿＿＿＿＿
- 証明番号
  Certificate number: ＿＿＿＿＿＿＿＿
- 税務署名及び役職名
  Name of Tax Office and title: ＿＿＿＿＿＿＿＿
- 氏名
  Print Name : ＿＿＿＿＿＿＿＿

官印　Official Stamp

手続4

居住者証明書の取得（記載要領等）

「居住者証明書交付請求書・居住者証明書」（留意事項・記載要領）

1　居住者証明書交付請求書の種類

税務署で、居住者証明書の交付を請求する場合には、提出先・用途に応じて次の居住者証明書交付請求書を使用してください。

①　居住者証明書交付請求書・居住者証明書（租税条約等締結国用様式）

租税条約等の締結国（地域）に対して、租税条約等に基づく居住者証明書を提出する必要があるときに使用してください。

②　居住者証明書交付請求書・居住者証明書（その他用様式）

租税条約等の締結国（地域）以外の国等に対して、付加価値税の還付又は租税の減免等の目的で居住者証明書を提出する必要があるときに使用してください。

（注）提出先の国等に定められた様式があるときは、原則としてそちらを使用してください。

また、任意で作成した様式を使用することも可能ですが、記載内容によっては証明書を発行できないことがありますのでご注意ください。

2　居住者証明書を請求する際に必要なもの

居住者証明書の請求に当たっては、次のものを持参していただく必要があります。

⑴　居住者証明書交付請求書・居住者証明書

記載要領をご参照の上、必要事項を記入して**2部**持参してください。

※　複数部必要な場合は、必要部数＋１部を持参してください。

⑵　本人（法人の場合は代表者本人）又は代理人本人であることを確認できる書類

運転免許証、写真付き住民基本台帳カード、パスポート、国又は地方公共団体の機関が発行した顔写真付きの身分・資格証明書等を持参してください。

※　顔写真付きでない身分・資格証明書等の場合は、２通（枚）を提示していただく必要があります。詳しくは、所轄の税務署にお尋ねください。

⑶　代理の権限を有することを証明した書類（代理人の場合）

代理人の方（家族、代表者以外の役員、従業員を含みます。）が請求される場合に必要となります。

⑷　返信用封筒・切手（郵送で請求する場合）

原則としてご本人又は法人の住所（納税地）に送付することになりますので、あらかじめご了承ください。

3　記載要領

①　「住所・氏名又は法人名及び代表者氏名」欄

居住者証明書を請求する個人又は法人の住所（納税地）及び氏名（法人名・代表者氏名）を記入してください。

②　「提出先の国名等」欄

居住者証明書を提出する国名（地域名）を日本語及び英語で記入してください。

③　「請求目的」欄【その他用様式】

該当するものにチェックしてください。

その他にチェックをした場合は、内容を日本語及び英語で記入してください。

④　「対象期間」欄【任意項目】

対象期間の指定がある場合は、暦年又は事業年度等を記入してください。

⑤　「申述事項」欄

内容を確認し、上から３つのチェックボックスを必ずチェックしてください。

また、他に申述が必要な事項があれば、空欄に日本語と英語で記入してください。

（例）「請求者は相手国内に恒久的施設を有しないこと」

⑥　「証明書の請求枚数」欄

居住者証明書の必要部数を記入してください。

※　居住者証明書交付請求書・居住者証明書は、居住者証明書の必要部数＋１部を提出してください。

⑦　「整理番号」欄【任意項目】

必要があるときは記入してください。

⑧　「居住者証明書」欄【租税条約等締結国用様式】

提出先の国名（地域名）を英語で記入してください。

4　その他

証明書の発行には日数が掛かることがありますので、あらかじめご了承ください。

その他、ご不明な点は税務署（管理運営部門）までお尋ねください。

手続5　IRS（米国歳入庁）宛のレターの作成

ABC.INC
・・・・・・・・・・・・・・・
・・・・・・・・・・・・・・・
TOKYO　　　　　　JAPAN
Telephone（+81）3-・・・・・
Fax　　　（+81）3-・・・・・
Mailto:・・・・・・・・・・・

April 20,20××

送付先

Internal Revenue Service Center
P.O.Box 409101, Ogden, UT84409

Dear sirs（拝啓）

Subject:U.S Income Tax Return of a Foreign Corporation for the refund of the tax withheld（源泉徴収された税額の還付のための外国法人の申告について）

We are Japanese company, and has been receiving royalty from DEF Inc. as the consideration of use of our copyright.
（当社は、日本の企業です。米国のDEFインクから著作権の対価としてロイヤリティを受け取っております。）

We know that foreign company is subject to U.S. tax on its U.S. source income, and the income is subject to U.S. tax of 30%.
（米国においては、外国企業が米国を源泉とする所得の支払を受ける際には、30%の税率により課税されることを承知しております。）

The tax on the following royalty from 2020 to 2022was whithheld at 30%tax rate because of no documentary evidence which identify beneficial owner under tax treaty between Japan and United States.
（次の2020年から2022年までのロイヤリティについては、当社が日米租税条約の適用を受ける者であることを証明する証拠書類がないことから、30%の税率により源泉所得税が課税されておりました。）

手続5　IRS（米国歳入庁）宛のレターの作成

Beneficial Owner is exempt from withholding tax under the tax treaty. Therefore, this time, we want make a procedure to receive the refund of the following tax withheld by the way of filing U.S. Income Tax Return of a Foreign corporation.

（日米租税条約の適用を受ける者は源泉所得税を免除されております。今回、外国法人の確定申告の方法により源泉徴収された税額の還付を受けるための手続きを行うことを希望します。）

(year) （年度）	(gross income) （収入金額）	(tax rate) （税率）	(tax withheld) （源泉徴収税額）
2020	20,000	30%	6,000
2021	70,000	30%	21,000
2022	90,000	30%	27,000
		Total（合計）	54,000

We attached the following Form and Certification to identify that we are beneficial owner of Tax Treaty between Japan and United States.

（当社が日米租税条約の適用を受ける者であることを証明する次の書類を添付します。）

① Form 1120-F　U.S Income Tax Return of a Foreign Corporation (Year 2020, Year2021, Year2022)

② Form 1042-S　(issued by DEF Inc.) (Year 2020, Year2021, Year2022

③ Form 8833

④ Form W-8BEN-E

⑤ Certification of Japanese corporation (issued by Tax administration in Japan)

If you have any question and necessary documents or certification concerning the refund of tax withheld, please contact the following person in charge of tax refund.

（源泉所得税の還付に関する必要な書類又はご質問があれば、次の連絡先にお願い申しあげます。）

(Name)　　　　・・・・・・・・・・

(E-mail)　　　　・・・・・・・・・・

(Telephone)　(+81) 3-・・・・・・・

(Fax)　　　　(+81) 3-・・・・・・・

Sincerely.

ABC INC.　　　　　　　　　　President ・・・・・・・・・・・

手続 6

外国法人確定申告書・2020年分の作成

記入箇所は ⇦ で表示

Form **1120-F** Department of the Treasury Internal Revenue Service

U.S. Income Tax Return of a Foreign Corporation ❶ ❶

For calendar year 2020, or tax year beginning Jan1, 2020, and ending DECEM31, 20 20

▶ Go to *www.irs.gov/Form1120F* for instructions and the latest information.

OMB No. 1545-0123

2020

Type or Print

Name: ABC.INC ❷

Number, street, and room or suite no. (see instructions): XXX,XXXXXX,XXXXXXX ❸

City or town, state or province, country, and ZIP or foreign postal code: Tokyo 101-0047 JAPAN ❹

Employer identification number: XX-XXXXXX ❺ ❻

Check box(es) if: ☐ Name or address change ☐ First post-merger return ☐ Schedule M-3 attached ☑ Initial return ☐ Final return ☐ Amended return ☐ Protective return

A Country of incorporation JAPAN ❼

B Foreign country under whose laws the income reported on this return is also subject to tax JAPAN ❽

C Date incorporated Jan1.20 ❾

D (1) Location of corporation's primary books and records (city, province or state, and country) Tokyo JAPAN ❿

(2) Principal location of worldwide business Tokyo JAPAN ⓫

(3) If the corporation maintains an office or place of business in the United States, check here . . . ▶ ☐

E If the corporation had an agent in the United States at any time during the tax year, enter:

(1) Type of agent

(2) Name

(3) Address

F See the instructions and enter the corporation's principal:

(1) Business activity code number ▶ 511190 ⓬

(2) Business activity ▶ Publising ⓭

(3) Product or service ▶

G Check method of accounting: (1) ☐ Cash (2) ☑ Accrual (3) ☐ Other (specify) ▶ ⓮

Computation of Tax Due or Overpayment

1	Tax from Section I, line 11, page 3	1	⓯ 0		
2	Tax from Section II, Schedule J, line 9, page 5	2			
3	Tax from Section III (add lines 6 and 10 on page 6)	3			
4	**Total tax.** Add lines 1 through 3 511190			4	⓰ 0
5a	2019 overpayment credited to 2020	5a			
b	2020 estimated tax payments	5b			
c	Less 2020 refund applied for on Form 4466	5c	( )		
d	Combine lines 5a through 5c	5d			
e	Tax deposited with Form 7004	5e			
f	Credit for tax paid on undistributed capital gains (attach Form 2439)	5f			
g	Credit for federal tax paid on fuels (attach Form 4136). See instructions	5g			
h	Reserved for future use	5h			
i	U.S. income tax paid or withheld at source (add line 12, page 3, and amounts from Forms 8288-A and 8805 (attach Forms 8288-A and 8805))	5i	⓱ 6000		
j	Total payments. Add lines 5d through 5i			5j	⓲ 6000
6	Estimated tax penalty (see instructions). Check if Form 2220 is attached ▶☐			6	
7	**Amount owed.** If line 5j is smaller than the total of lines 4 and 6, enter amount owed			7	
8a	**Overpayment.** If line 5j is larger than the total of lines 4 and 6, enter amount overpaid			8a	⓳ 6000
b	**Amount of overpayment on line 8a resulting from tax deducted and withheld under Chapters 3 and 4** (from Schedule W, line 7, page 8)			8b	⓴ 6000
9	Enter portion of line 8a you want **Credited to 2021 estimated tax** ▶ **Refunded** ▶			9	㉑ 6000

Sign Here

Under penalties of perjury, I declare that I have examined this return, including accompanying schedules and statements, and to the best of my knowledge and belief, it is true, correct, and complete. Declaration of preparer (other than taxpayer) is based on all information of which preparer has any knowledge.

▶ ㉒ Signature of officer | ㉓ Date | ▶ ㉔ Title

May the IRS discuss this return with the preparer shown below (see instructions)? ☐ Yes ☑ No

Paid Preparer Use Only

Print/Type preparer's name	Preparer's signature	Date	Check ☐ if self-employed	PTIN ㉕
Firm's name ▶			Firm's EIN ▶	
Firm's address ▶			Phone no.	

For Paperwork Reduction Act Notice, see separate instructions. Cat. No. 11470I Form **1120-F** (2020)

手続6　外国法人確定申告書・2020年分の作成手順（❶〜㊴）

1120-F　外国法人確定申告書　2020

事業年度　**❶（1/1〜12/31の事業年度を記入）**

会社名　**❷（ABC.INC と記入）**
所在地　**❸（日本の本店所在地を記入）**
都市名・郵便番号・国名　**❹（都市名・郵便番号・JAPAN と記入）**

Employer identification number
❺　納税者番号の記入
□当初申告
□名称・住所変更　□最終申告
□合併後申告　□修正申告
□ Schedule M-3の添付　□予備申告
❻（当初申告の□にチェック）

A　会社設立国　**❼（JAPAN と記入）**
B　この申告書により報告される所得に対して課税が行われる国　**❽（JAPAN と記入）**
C　会社設立年月日　**❾（会社設立年月日を記入）**
D⑴　会社の主要帳簿と会計記録の保管場所　**❿（都市名と JAPAN と記入）**
⑵　世界的事業を行う場所　**⓫（都市名と JAPAN と記入）**
⑶　米国内に事業を行う場所を有する場合にはここにチェック　□
E　米国内に課税期間中に代理人を有する場合には、次の事項を記載
⑴　代理人の類型
⑵　名称
⑶　所在地
F　記載要領から次の事項を記載
⑴　Business activity code number　**⓬（記載要領を参照）**
⑵　Business activity　**⓭（記載要領を参照）**
⑶　Product or Service
G　会計処理についてチェック　**⓮（⑵の□にチェック）**
⑴　現金主義　□
⑵　発生主義　□
⑶　その他　□

Computation of Tax Due or Overpayment（納税額又は還付税額の計算）

1　page 3の line 11の税額を記載　**⓯（0を記入）**

2　page 5の line 9の税額を記載

3　page 6の line 6と10の合計金額を記載

4　税額の集計（1〜3）　**⓰（0を記入）**

5 a　2020年の税額から控除する2019年の過払税金

b　2020年の見積税額

c　Form 4466により適用される2017年の還付税額

d　line 5a〜5cまでの合計

e　Form 7004による予納税額

f　未分配の譲渡益に対する税金の控除（Form 2439を添付）

g　燃料に対する連邦税の控除（Form 4136を添付）

h　将来のための予備（備蓄）

i　米国の所得税又は源泉徴収税額（page 3の line 12の税額と Form 8288-Aと8805の税額の合計額）　**⓱（6000を記入）**

j　5d〜5iまでの支払額合計　**⓲（6000を記入）**

6　Estimated tax penalty（チェック Form 2220を添付している場合）□

7　納税額（line 5jが line 4と6の合計額より小さい場合）

8 a　還付税額（line 5jが line 4と6の合計額より大きい場合）　**⓳（6000を記入）**

b　税額控除と Chapters 3及び4の規定による源泉徴収後の line 8aの過大納付額（page 8の Schedule Wの line 7から）　**⓴（6000を記入）**

9　2021年の予定納税額から控除を希望する金額・**Refunded（還付税額）**

㉑（6000を記入）

Sign Here　偽証の場合の罰則の下、私は、本件申告書、添付資料を調査し、私の知る限りでは、これらの申告書及び添付資料等は真実で、正確に完成されたものであることを、ここに宣言いたします。

Signature of officer（代表者の署名）　**㉒（署名）**

Date（日付）　**㉓（作成日を記入）**

Title（役職名）　**㉔（役職名を記入）**

IRSはこの申告書について下記の有料の作成者と検討することができるか。
YES　　NO

㉕（NOの□にチェック）

外国法人確定申告書・2020年分の作成手順（❶～㊴）

Paid Preparer Use Only

（有料の作成者用）

作成者の氏名	作成者の署名	日付
企業名	企業 EIN	
企業所在地	電話番号	

Form 1120-F (2020) Page **2**

Additional Information *(continued from page 1)*

		Yes	No
H	Did the corporation's method of accounting change from the preceding tax year? If "Yes," attach a statement with an explanation.		✓
I	Did the corporation's method of determining income change from the preceding tax year? If "Yes," attach a statement with an explanation.		✓
J	Did the corporation file a U.S. income tax return for the preceding tax year?		✓
K	**(1)** At any time during the tax year, was the corporation engaged in a trade or business in the United States?		✓
	(2) If "Yes," is taxpayer's trade or business within the United States solely the result of a section 897 (FIRPTA) sale or disposition?		
L	Did the corporation have a permanent establishment in the United States for purposes of any applicable tax treaty between the United States and a foreign country? If "Yes," enter the name of the foreign country:		✓
M	Did the corporation have any transactions with related parties? If "Yes," Form 5472 may have to be filed (see instructions). Enter number of Forms 5472 attached ▶		✓
N	Is the corporation a controlled foreign corporation? (See section 957(a) for definition.)		✓
O	Is the corporation a personal service corporation? (See instructions for definition.)		✓
P	Enter tax-exempt interest received or accrued during the tax year (see instructions) ▶ $		
Q	At the end of the tax year, did the corporation own, directly or indirectly, 50% or more of the voting stock of a U.S. corporation? (See section 267(c) for rules of attribution.) If "Yes," attach a statement showing **(1)** name and EIN of such U.S. corporation; **(2)** percentage owned; and **(3)** taxable income or (loss) before NOL and special deductions of such U.S. corporation for the tax year ending with or within your tax year.		✓
R	If the corporation has an NOL for the tax year and is electing to forego the carryback period, check here (see instructions) ▶ ☐		
S	Enter the available NOL carryover from prior tax years. (Do not reduce it by any deduction on line 30a, page 4.) ▶ $		
T	Is the corporation a subsidiary in a parent-subsidiary controlled group? If "Yes," enter the parent corporation's: **(1)** EIN ▶ **(2)** Name ▶		✓
U	**(1)** Is the corporation a dealer under section 475?		✓
	(2) Did the corporation mark to market any securities or commodities other than in a dealer capacity?		✓
V	At the end of the tax year, did any individual, partnership, corporation, estate, or trust own, directly or indirectly, 50% or more of the corporation's voting stock? (See section 267 (c) for rules of attribution.) If "Yes," attach a statement showing the name and identifying number. (Do not include any information already entered in item **T**.) Enter percentage owned ▶		✓
W	**(1)** Is the corporation taking a position on this return that a U.S. tax treaty overrules or modifies an Internal Revenue law of the United States, thereby causing a reduction of tax? If "Yes," the corporation is generally required to complete and attach Form 8833. See Form 8833 for exceptions. **Note:** *Failure to disclose a treaty-based return position may result in a $10,000 penalty (see section 6712).*	✓	㉖
	(2) Is the corporation claiming treaty benefits pursuant to, or otherwise filing its return pursuant to, a Competent Authority determination or an Advance Pricing Agreement? If "Yes," attach a copy of the Competent Authority determination letter or Advance Pricing Agreement to your return.		✓
X	During the tax year, did the corporation own any entity that was disregarded as an entity separate from its owner under Regulations sections 301.7701-2 and 301.7701-3? If "Yes," attach a statement listing the name, country under whose laws the entity was organized, and EIN (if any) of each such entity.		✓
Y	**(1)** Did a partnership allocate to the corporation a distributive share of income from a directly owned partnership interest, any of which is ECI or treated as ECI by the partnership or the partner? If "Yes," attach Schedule P. See instructions.		✓
	(2) During the tax year, did the corporation own, directly or indirectly, at least a 10% interest, in any foreign partnership? If "Yes," see instructions for required attachment.		✓
Z	**(1)** Has the corporation engaged in any transactions the results of which are subject to the arm's-length standard under section 482 and its regulations?		✓
	(2) Has the corporation recognized any interbranch amounts? If "Yes," attach statement (see instructions)		✓
AA	Is the corporation required to file Schedule UTP (Form 1120), Uncertain Tax Position Statement (see instructions)? If "Yes," complete and attach Schedule UTP.		✓
BB	During the corporation's tax year, did the corporation make any payments that would require it to file Forms 1042 and 1042-S under chapter 3 (sections 1441 through 1464) or chapter 4 (sections 1471 through 1474) of the Code?		✓
CC	Is the corporation (including the home office or any branch) a qualified derivatives dealer (QDD)? **(1)** If "Yes," attach Schedule Q (Form 1120-F) (see instructions) **(2)** If "Yes," enter the QI-EIN ▶		✓
DD	Does the corporation have gross receipts of at least $500 million in any of the 3 preceding tax years (see sections 59A(e)(2) and (3))? If "Yes," complete and attach Form 8991.		✓
EE	During the tax year, did the corporation pay or accrue any interest or royalty for which a deduction is not allowed under section 267A (see instructions)? If "Yes," enter the total amount of the disallowed deductions ▶ $		✓

Form **1120-F** (2020)

外国法人確定申告書・2020年分の作成

Form 1120-F (2020) Page **3**

Additional Information *(continued from page 2)*

		Yes	No
FF	Did the corporation have an election under section 163(j) for any real property trade or business or any farming business in effect during the tax year (see instructions)?		✓
GG	Does the corporation satisfy **one or more** of the following (see instructions)?		✓
	(1) The corporation owns a pass-through entity with current, or prior year carryover, excess business interest expense.		
	(2) The corporation's aggregate average annual gross receipts (determined under section 448(c)) for the 3 tax years preceding the current tax year are more than $26 million and the corporation has business interest expense.		
	(3) The corporation is a tax shelter and the corporation has business interest expense. If "Yes," to any, complete and attach Form 8990.		
HH	During the tax year, did the corporation dispose of an interest in a partnership that directly or indirectly engaged in a trade or business within the United States?		✓
II	Is the corporation attaching Form 8996 to certify as a Qualified Opportunity Fund?		✓
	If "Yes," enter amount from Form 8996, line 15 ▶ $		

SECTION I—Income From U.S. Sources Not Effectively Connected With the Conduct of a Trade or Business in the United States—Do not report items properly withheld and reported on Form 1042-S. See instructions.

Report all gross transportation income subject to 4% tax on line 9. Report other column (a) income items only if not properly withheld and reported on Form 1042-S. The rate of tax on these **gross** income items is 30% or such lower rate specified by tax treaty. No deductions are allowed against these types of income. Enter treaty rates where applicable. **If the corporation is claiming a lower treaty rate, also complete item W on page 2.** If multiple treaty rates apply to a type of income (for example, subsidiary and portfolio dividends or dividends received by disregarded entities), attach a statement showing the amounts, tax rates, and withholding for each.

Name of treaty country, if any ▶ **JAPAN** ⬅ ㉘

	(a) Class of income (see instructions)	(b) Gross amount	(c) Rate of tax (%)	(d) Amount of tax liability	(e) Amount of U.S. income tax paid or withheld at the source
1	Interest				
2a	Dividends (excluding payments received by QDDs in their equity derivatives dealer capacity)				
2b	Dividend equivalents (excluding payments received by QDDs in their equity derivatives dealer capacity)	㉙	㉚	㉛	㉜
3	Rents				
4	Royalties	20000	0	0	6000
5	Annuities				
6	Gains from disposal of timber, coal, or domestic iron ore with a retained economic interest (attach supporting statement)				
7	Gains from sale or exchange of patents, copyrights, etc.				
8	Fiduciary distributions (attach supporting statement)				
9	Gross transportation income (see instructions)		4		
10	Other items of income				
11	Total. Enter here and on line 1, page 1 ▶			0	
12	Total. Enter here and include on line 5i, page 1 ▶				6000

13 Is the corporation fiscally transparent under the laws of the foreign jurisdiction with respect to any item of income listed above? ☐ Yes ☑ No ㉝
If "Yes," attach a statement that provides the information requested above with respect to each such item of income.

Form **1120-F** (2020)

追加情報　　　　　　　　　　Yes又はNoにチェック

H　会社の会計処理方法は前年から変更しましたか。
　もし、Yes であれば説明書を添付してください。

I　会社の所得の計算方法は前年から変更しましたか。
　もし、Yes であれば説明書を添付してください。

J　会社は法人所得税申告書の前年分を提出していますか。

K(1)　本年の事業年度において米国で事業活動を行いましたか。

(2)　もし、Yes であれば、米国での事業活動は section 897（FIRPTA）sale あるいは disposition の結果ですか。

L　会社は米国と外国との間の租税条約が適用される恒久的施設を有していましたか。
　もし、Yes であれば、外国名を記入してください。

M　会社は related parties（関連者）と取引を行いましたか。
　もし、Yes であれば、Form 5472を添付してください。添付した Form 5472の番号を記入してください。

（上記のHからMはすべて、NO の□にチェック）

N　会社は controlled foreign corporation ですか。（定義については section 957参照）

O　会社は personal service corporation ですか。（定義については記載要領参照）

P　本年の事業年度において受領した又は未収の tax-exempt interest（免税利息）を記入してください。

Q　会社は事業年度末で、米国企業の議決権50%以上を直接又は間接に保有していますか。
　もし、Yes であれば、次の事項を示す書類を添付してください

(1)　米国企業の名称と EIN の

(2)　米国企業に対する議決権割合

(3)　米国企業の事業年度の繰越欠損金と特別控除の控除前の課税所得又は欠損金額

R　会社がその事業年度において繰越欠損金があるが、適用を差し控える場合には、こちらにチェックしてください。　□

S　前年から繰り越した使用可能な繰越欠損金を記入してください。

T　会社は親会社と子会社の関係にありますか。
　もし、Yes であれば、親会社の次の事項について記入してください。

(1)　EIN（納税者番号）

(2)　名称

外国法人確定申告書・2020年分の作成手順（❶〜㊴）

U⑴　会社は section 475の証券等の取引業者ですか。

⑵　証券等の取引業者以外で時価会計を適用していますか。

V　事業年度末において、個人、パートナーシップ、会社、財団、又は信託が会社の議決権の50%以上を直接又は間接に保有していますか。

もし、Yes であれば、身分証明番号を示す書類を添付し保有割合を記入してください。

W⑴　会社は、この申告により、租税条約に基づき米国内法を修正し、税額の減額を行うことになりますか。**㉖（Wの YES の□にチェック）**

もし、Yes であれば、会社は Form 8833を作成し申告書に添付してください。

（注）　a treaty-based return position を明示しない場合には $10,000の罰金が課されます。

⑵　会社は、権限ある当局の決定又は Advance Pricing Agreement により、租税条約上の恩典を受けますか。

もし、Yes であれば、権限ある当局の決定書又は Advance Pricing Agreement を添付してください。

X　会社は事業年度において、事業主から法的に独立したみなし事業体（disregarded entities）を有していますか。（section 301.7701-2 and 301.7701-3）

もし、Yes ならばそのみなし事業体の EIN、事業体が設立された国及び事業体の名称を記載した書類を添付してください。

Y⑴　パートナーシップは会社に対し、ECI として取り扱われるパートナーシップが直接保有する所得の distributive share（分配持分）を配分しましたか。

もし、Yes であれば、Schedule P を添付してください。

⑵　会社は事業年度中に、外国パートナーシップの持分の10%を直接又は間接に保有していますか。

もし、Yes であれば、必要書類を添付してください。

Z⑴　会社は、section 482の規定に基づく独立企業間価格による取引を行いましたか。

⑵　会社は interbranch amounts を認識しましたか。（記載要領参照）

AA　会社は Schedule UTP（Form 1120）, Uncertain Tax Position Statement を提出することを要求されていますか。

もし、Yes であれば、Schedule UTP を作成し、添付してください。

㉗（N〜Y及びX〜AAの NO の□にチェック）

BB〜Ⅱ　省略（BB〜ⅡのNOの□にチェック）

SECTION Ⅰ－米国内の事業活動に関連しない米国源泉の所得（適正に源泉徴収され、Form 1042-S により報告された所得については記入を要しません。）

line 9の4％の税率が課される運輸所得について報告します。

他の column ⒜ income で適正に源泉徴収されず、Form 1042-S において報告された所得を報告します。

税率については、総収入に対し30%の税率又は租税条約により規定された低率の税率による。これらの所得に対する税率適用に際しては、総収入から控除は認めません。

租税条約による税率が適用される場合には、その税率を適用してください。

もし、会社が租税条約による低率の税率適用を求める場合には、前ページのWを完成させてください。

もし、多様な租税条約による税率が適用される所得の場合には、金額、税率及び源泉所得税を記載した書類を添付してください。

もしあるなら租税条約の締結国名の記入　**㉘（JAPANを記入）**

	(a) 所得の種類	(b) 総収入金額	(c) 税率	(d) 税額	(e) 米国源泉所得税額
1	利息				
2 a	配当				
2 b	配当				
3	賃借料				
4	ロイヤリティ	**㉙（20000）**	**㉚ 0**	**㉛ 0**	**㉜6000**
5	年金				
6	経済的利権が付与されている材木、石炭及び鉄鉱石の処分による収益				
7	特許権、著作権等の交換又は譲渡による収益				
8	信託配当				
9	運輸収益				
10	その他の所得				
11	page1の line 1を記入				
12	page1の line 5i を記入				

13　会社が上記に掲げられた所得に関し、外国の法律の下で財政的に透明ですか。
もし、Yesであれば、それぞれの所得に関し、要求された書面を添付してください。

Yes □　No □

㉝（NOの□にチェック）

外国法人確定申告書・2020年分の作成

Form 1120-F (2020) Page **4**

SECTION II—Income Effectively Connected With the Conduct of a Trade or Business in the United States (see instructions)

Important: *Fill in all applicable lines and schedules. If you need more space, see* ***Assembling the Return*** *in the instructions.*

Income	**1a**	Gross receipts or sales [ ] **b** Less returns and allowances [ ] **c** Bal ▶	**1c**	
	2	Cost of goods sold (attach Form 1125-A)	**2**	
	3	Gross profit (subtract line 2 from line 1c)	**3**	
	4	Dividends (Schedule C, line 13)	**4**	
	5	Interest	**5**	
	6	Gross rents	**6**	
	7	Gross royalties	**7**	
	8	Capital gain net income (attach Schedule D (Form 1120))	**8**	
	9	Net gain or (loss) from Form 4797, Part II, line 17 (attach Form 4797)	**9**	
	10	Other income (see instructions—attach statement)	**10**	
	11	**Total income.** Add lines 3 through 10 ▶	**11**	
Deductions (See instructions for limitations on deductions.)	**12**	Compensation of officers (see instructions—attach Form 1125-E)	**12**	
	13	Salaries and wages (less employment credits)	**13**	
	14	Repairs and maintenance	**14**	
	15	Bad debts (for bad debts over $500,000, attach a list of debtors and amounts)	**15**	
	16	Rents	**16**	
		Taxes and licenses		
	8	Interest expense from Schedule I, line 25 (see instructions)	**8**	
	9	Charitable contributions	**9**	
	20	Depreciation from Form 4562 not claimed on Form 1125-A or elsewhere on return (attach Form 4562)	**20**	
	2	Depletion	**2**	
	22	Advertising	**22**	
	23	Pension, profit-sharing, etc., plans	**23**	
	2	Employee benefit programs	**2**	
	25	Reserved for future use	**25**	
	26	Deductions allocated and apportioned to ECI from Schedule H, line 20 (see instructions)	**26**	
	2	Other deductions (attach statement)	**2**	
	28	**Total deductions.** Add lines 12 through 27 ▶	**28**	
	29	Taxable income before NOL deduction and special deductions (subtract line 28 from line 11) ▶	**29**	
	30	**Less: a** Net operating loss deduction (see instructions) [**30a**]		
		b Special deductions (Schedule C, line 14) [**30b**]		
		c Add lines 30a and 30b	**30c**	
	3	Taxable income or (loss). Subtract line 30c from line 29	**3**	

Form **1120-F** (2020)

Form 1120-F (2020) Page **5**

SECTION II—Income Effectively Connected With the Conduct of a Trade or Business in the United States *(continued)*

Schedule C Dividends and Special Deductions (see instructions)

		(a) Dividends	(b) %	(c) Special deductions: (a) × (b)
1	Dividends from less-than-20%-owned domestic corporations (other than debt-financed stock)		50	
2	Dividends from 20%-or-more-owned domestic corporations (other than debt-financed stock)		65	
3	Dividends on certain debt-financed stock of domestic and foreign corporations (section 246A)		see instructions	
4	Dividends on certain preferred stock of less-than-20%-owned public utilities		23.3	
5	Dividends on certain preferred stock of 20%-or-more-owned public utilities		26.7	
6	Dividends from less-than-20%-owned foreign corporations		50	
7	Dividends from 20%-or-more-owned foreign corporations		65	
8	**Subtotal.** Add lines 1 through 7. See instructions for limitation		see instructions	
9	Dividends from foreign corporations not included on line 3, 6, or 7			
10	IC-DISC and former DISC dividends not included on line 1, 2, or 3 (section 246(d))			
11	Other dividends			
12	Deduction for dividends paid on certain preferred stock of public utilities			
3	**Total dividends.** Add column (a), lines 8 through 11. Enter here and on line 4, page 4			
	Total special deductions. Add column (c), lines 8 and 12. Enter here and on line 30b, page 4 ▶			

Schedule J Tax Computation (see instructions)

	Check if the corporation is a member of a controlled group (attach Schedule O (Form 1120)) ▶ ☐				
2	Income tax			2	
3	Base erosion minimum tax amount (attach Form 8991)			3	
	Add lines 2 and 3				
5a	Foreign tax credit (attach Form 1118)	5a			
b	General business credit (attach Form 3800)	5b			
c	Credit for prior year minimum tax (attach Form 8827)	5c			
d	Bond credits from Form 8912	5d			
6	**Total credits.** Add lines 5a through 5d			6	
	Subtract line 6 from line 4				
8	Other taxes. Check if from: ☐ Form 4255 ☐ Form 8611 ☐ Form 8697 ☐ Form 8866 ☐ Form 8902 ☐ Other (attach statement)			8	
9	**Total tax.** Add lines 7 and 8. Enter here and on line 2, page 1			9	

Form **1120-F** (2020)

外国法人確定申告書・2020年分の作成

Form 1120-F (2020) Page **6**

SECTION III—Branch Profits Tax and Tax on Excess Interest

Part I—Branch Profits Tax (see instructions)

1	Enter the amount from Section II, line 29	1	
2	Enter total adjustments to line 1 to get effectively connected earnings and profits. (Attach required statement showing the nature and amount of adjustments.) (See instructions.)	2	
3	Effectively connected earnings and profits. Combine line 1 and line 2	3	
4a	Enter U.S. net equity at the end of the current tax year. (Attach required statement.)	4a	
b	Enter U.S. net equity at the end of the prior tax year. (Attach required statement.)	4b	
c	Increase in U.S. net equity. If line 4a is greater than or equal to line 4b, subtract line 4b from line 4a. Enter the result here and skip to line 4e	4c	
d	Decrease in U.S. net equity. If line 4b is greater than line 4a, subtract line 4a from line 4b	4d	
e	Non-previously taxed accumulated effectively connected earnings and profits. Enter excess, if any, of effectively connected earnings and profits for preceding tax years beginning after 1986 over any dividend equivalent amounts for those tax years	4e	
5	Dividend equivalent amount. Subtract line 4c from line 3. If zero or less, enter -0-. If no amount is entered on line 4c, add the lesser of line 4d or line 4e to line 3 and enter the total here	5	
6	**Branch profits tax.** Multiply line 5 by 30% (0.30) (or lower treaty rate if the corporation is a qualified resident or otherwise qualifies for treaty benefits). (See instructions.) Enter here and include on line 3, page 1. **Also complete item W on page 2**	6	

Part II—Tax on Excess Interest (see instructions for this Part and for Schedule I (Form 1120-F))

a	Enter the interest from Section II, line 18	a	
b	Enter the inverse of the total amount deferred, capitalized, and disallowed from Schedule I, line 24d (i.e., if line 24d is negative, enter as a positive number; if line 24d is positive, enter as a negative number)	b	
c	Combine lines 7a and 7b (amount must equal Schedule I, line 23)	c	
8	**Branch Interest** (see instructions for definition): Enter the sum of Schedule I, line 9, column (c), and Schedule I, line 22. If the interest paid by the foreign corporation's U.S. trade or business was increased because 80% or more of the foreign corporation's assets are U.S. assets, check this box ▶ ☐	8	
9a	Excess interest. Subtract line 8 from line 7c. If zero or less, enter -0-	9a	
b	If the foreign corporation is a bank, enter the excess interest treated as interest on deposits (see instructions for rules for computing this amount). Otherwise, enter -0-	9b	
c	Subtract line 9b from line 9a	9c	
0	**Tax on excess interest.** Multiply line 9c by 30% (0.30) (or lower treaty rate if the corporation is a qualified resident or otherwise qualifies for treaty benefits). (See instructions.) Enter here and include on line 3, page 1. **Also complete item W on page 2**	0	

Part III—Additional Information

	Yes	No
Is the corporation claiming a reduction in, or exemption from, the branch profits tax due to:		
a A complete termination of all U.S. trades or businesses?		
b The tax-free liquidation or reorganization of a foreign corporation?		
c The tax-free incorporation of a U.S. trade or business?		
If **a** or **b** applies and the transferee is a domestic corporation, attach Form 8848. If **c** applies, attach the statement required by Temporary Regulations section 1.884-2T(d)(5).		

Form **1120-F** (2020)

Form 1120-F (2020) Page **7**

Note: *Check if completing on* ▶ ☐ U.S. basis or ☐ Worldwide basis

Schedule L Balance Sheets per Books

		Beginning of tax year		End of tax year	
	Assets	(a)	(b)	(c)	(d)
1	Cash				
2a	Trade notes and accounts receivable				
b	Less allowance for bad debts	( )		( )	
3	Inventories				
4	U.S. government obligations				
5	Tax-exempt securities (see instructions)				
6a	Interbranch current assets*				
b	Other current non-U.S. assets*				
c	Other current U.S. assets*				
7	Loans to shareholders				
8	Mortgage and real estate loans				
9a	Other loans and investments—non-U.S. assets*				
b	Other loans and investments—U.S. assets*				
10a	Buildings and other depreciable assets				
b	Less accumulated depreciation	( )		( )	
a	Depletable assets				
b	Less accumulated depletion	( )		( )	
2	Land (net of any amortization)				
3a	Intangible assets (amortizable only)				
b	Less accumulated amortization	( )		( )	
	Assets held in trust				
5	Other non-current interbranch assets*				
6a	Other non-current non-U.S. assets*				
b	Other non-current U.S. assets*				
	Total assets				
	Liabilities				
8	Accounts payable				
9	Mortgages, notes, bonds payable in less than 1 year:				
a	Interbranch liabilities*				
b	Third-party liabilities*				
20	Other current liabilities*				
2	Loans from shareholders				
22	Mortgages, notes, bonds payable in 1 year or more:				
a	Interbranch liabilities*				
b	Third-party liabilities*				
23	Liabilities held in trust				
2 a	Other interbranch liabilities*				
b	Other third-party liabilities*				
	Equity				
25	Capital stock: **a** Preferred stock				
	b Common stock				
26	Additional paid-in capital				
2	Retained earnings—Appropriated*				
28	Retained earnings—Unappropriated				
29	Adjustments to shareholders' equity*				
30	Less cost of treasury stock		( )		( )
31	Total liabilities and shareholders' equity				

*Attach statement—see instructions.

Form **1120-F** (2020)

外国法人確定申告書・2020年分の作成手順（❶～㊴）

Form 1120-F (2020) Page 8

Schedule W Overpayment Resulting From Tax Deducted and Withheld Under Chapters 3 and 4

1	**Total Chapter 3 and 4 payments.** Enter the amount from page 1, line 5i			1	㉞ 6000
2	Enter the tax amount from page 1, line 1	2	㉟ 0		
3	Enter the portion of the tax amount shown on page 1, line 2, pertaining to income associated with amounts deducted and withheld under sections 1445 and 1446 (see instructions for general guidelines)	3			
4	**Total Chapter 3 and 4 tax.** Combine lines 2 and 3			4	㊱ 6000
5	**Tentative overpayment resulting from tax deducted and withheld under Chapters 3 and 4.** Subtract line 4 from line 1			5	㊲ 0
6	Enter the amount from page 1, line 8a			6	㊳ 6000
7	**Overpayment resulting from tax deducted and withheld under Chapters 3 and 4.** Enter the smaller of line 5 or line 6. Enter the result here and on page 1, line 8b			7	㊴ 6000

Form **1120-F** (2020)

Schedule W 税額控除とChapters 3及び4の規定による源泉徴収後の過大納付額

1 Chapters 3及び4の規定による源泉徴収税額 **㉞（6000を記入）**

2 Page 1のline 1の税額を記入 **㉟（0を記入）**

3 Page 1のline 2の税額を記入

4 Chapters 3及び4の規定による源泉徴収税額の合計額 **㊱（6000を記入）**

5 仮の税額控除とChapters 3及び4の規定による仮の源泉徴収後の課題納付額 **㊲（0を記入）**

6 Page 1のline 8aの税額を記入 **㊳（6000を記入）**

7 税額控除とChapters 3及び4の規定による源泉徴収後の課題納付額 **㊴（6000を記入）**

手続 6

外国法人確定申告書・2021年分の作成

記入箇所は ⇦ で表示

Form **1120-F** Department of the Treasury Internal Revenue Service

U.S. Income Tax Return of a Foreign Corporation ❶ ❶

For calendar year 2021, or tax year beginning Jan1 , 2021, and ending DECEM31 , 20 21

▶ Go to *www.irs.gov/Form1120F* for instructions and the latest information.

OMB No. 1545-0123 **2021**

Type or Print	
Name	ABC. INC ❷
Number, street, and room or suite no. (see instructions)	XXX,XXXXX,XXXXXXX ❸
City or town, state or province, country, and ZIP or foreign postal code	Tokyo 101-0047 JAPAN ❹

Employer identification number XX-XXXXXX ❺ ❻

Check box(es) if: ☑ Initial return ☐ Name or address change ☐ Final return ☐ First post-merger return ☐ Amended return ☐ Schedule M-3 attached ☐ Protective return

A Country of incorporation JAPAN ❼

B Foreign country under whose laws the income reported on this return is also subject to tax JAPAN ❽

C Date incorporated Jan1.2000 ❾

D (1) Location of corporation's primary books and records (city, province or state, and country) Tokyo JAPAN ❿

(2) Principal location of worldwide business Tokyo JAPAN ⓫

(3) If the corporation maintains an office or place of business in the United States, check here . . . ▶ ☐

E If the corporation had an agent in the United States at any time during the tax year, enter:

(1) Type of agent

(2) Name

(3) Address

F See the instructions and enter the corporation's principal:

(1) Business activity code number ▶ 511190 ⓬

(2) Business activity ▶ Publising ⓭

(3) Product or service ▶

G Check method of accounting: (1) ☐ Cash (2) ☑ Accrual (3) ☐ Other (specify) ▶ ⓮

Computation of Tax Due or Overpayment

1	Tax from Section I, line 11, page 3	1	⓯ 0		
2	Tax from Section II, Schedule J, line 9, page 5	2			
3	Tax from Section III (add lines 6 and 10 on page 6)	3			
4	**Total tax.** Add lines 1 through 3			4	⓰ 0
5a	2020 overpayment credited to 2021	5a			
b	2021 estimated tax payments	5b			
c	Less 2021 refund applied for on Form 4466	5c	( )		
d	Combine lines 5a through 5c	5d			
e	Tax deposited with Form 7004	5e			
f	Credit for tax paid on undistributed capital gains (attach Form 2439)	5f			
g	Credit for federal tax paid on fuels (attach Form 4136). See instructions	5g			
h	Reserved for future use	5h			
i	U.S. income tax paid or withheld at source (add line 12, page 3, and amounts from Forms 8288-A and 8805 (attach Forms 8288-A and 8805))	5i	⓱ 21000		
j	Total payments. Add lines 5d through 5i			5j	⓲ 21000
6	Estimated tax penalty (see instructions). Check if Form 2220 is attached ▶ ☐			6	
7	**Amount owed.** If line 5j is smaller than the total of lines 4 and 6, enter amount owed			7	
8a	**Overpayment.** If line 5j is larger than the total of lines 4 and 6, enter amount overpaid			8a	⓳ 21000
b	**Amount of overpayment on line 8a resulting from tax deducted and withheld under Chapters 3 and 4** (from Schedule W, line 7, page 8)			8b	⓴ 21000
9	Enter portion of line 8a you want **Credited to 2022 estimated tax** ▶ **Refunded** ▶			9	㉑ 21000

Sign Here Under penalties of perjury, I declare that I have examined this return, including accompanying schedules and statements, and to the best of my knowledge and belief, it is true, correct, and complete. Declaration of preparer (other than taxpayer) is based on all information of which preparer has any knowledge.

㉒ Signature of officer ㉓ Date ㉔ Title

May the IRS discuss this return with the preparer shown below (see instructions)? ☐ Yes ☑ No ㉕

Paid Preparer Use Only	Print/Type preparer's name	Preparer's signature	Date	Check ☐ if self-employed	PTIN
	Firm's name ▶			Firm's EIN ▶	
	Firm's address ▶			Phone no.	

For Paperwork Reduction Act Notice, see separate instructions. Cat. No. 11470I Form **1120-F** (2021)

手続6　**外国法人確定申告書・2021年分の作成手順（❶〜㊴）**

1120-F　外国法人確定申告書　2021

事業年度　**❶（1/1〜12/31の事業年度を記入）**

会社名　**❷（ABC.INC と記入）**
所在地　**❸（日本の本店所在地を記入）**
都市名・郵便番号・国名　**❹（都市名・郵便番号・JAPAN と記入）**

Employer identification number
❺　納税者番号の記入
□当初申告
□名称・住所変更　□最終申告
□合併後申告　□修正申告
□ Schedule M- 3の添付　□予備申告
❻（当初申告の□にチェック）

A　会社設立国　**❼（JAPAN と記入）**
B　この申告書により報告される所得に対して課税が行われる国　**❽（JAPAN と記入）**
C　会社設立年月日　**❾（会社設立年月日を記入）**
D(1)　会社の主要帳簿と会計記録の保管場所　**❿（都市名と JAPAN と記入）**
(2)　世界的事業を行う場所　**⓫（都市名と JAPAN と記入）**
(3)　米国内に事業を行う場所を有する場合にはここにチェック　□
E　米国内に課税期間中に代理人を有する場合には、次の事項を記載
(1)　代理人の類型
(2)　名称
(3)　所在地
F　記載要領から次の事項を記載
(1)　Business activity code number　**⓬（記載要領を参照）**
(2)　Business activity　**⓭（記載要領を参照）**
(3)　Product or service
G　会計処理についてチェック　**⓮（(2)の□にチェック）**
(1)　現金主義　□
(2)　発生主義　□
(3)　その他　□

Computation of Tax Due or Overpayment(納税額又は還付税額の計算)

1 page 3の line 11の税額を記載 **⑮(0を記入)**

2 page 5の line 9の税額を記載

3 page 6の line 6と10の合計金額を記載

4 税額の集計(1〜3) **⑯(0を記入)**

5 a 2020年の税額から控除する2019年の過払税金

b 2021年の見積税額

c Form 4466により適用される2021年の還付税額

d line 5a〜5cまでの合計

e Form 7004による予納税額

f 未分配の譲渡益に対する税金の控除(Form 2439を添付)

g 燃料に対する連邦税の控除(Form 4136を添付)

h 将来使用のための予備(備蓄)

i 米国の所得税又は源泉徴収税額(page 3の line 12の税額と Form 8288-A と 8805の税額の合計額) **⑰(21000を記入)**

j 5d〜5iまでの支払額合計 **⑱(21000を記入)**

6 Estimated tax penalty(チェック Form 2220を添付している場合) □

7 納税額(line 5j が line 4と6の合計額より小さい場合)

8 a 還付税額(line 5j が line 4と6の合計額より大きい場合) **⑲(21000を記入)**

b 税額控除と Chapters 3及び4の規定による源泉徴収後の line 8aの過大納付額(page 8の Schedule W の line 7から) **⑳(21000を記入)**

9 2022年の予定納税額から控除を希望する金額・Refunded(還付税額)

㉑(21000を記入)

Sign Here 偽証の場合の罰則の下、私は、本件申告書、添付資料を調査し、私の知る限りでは、これらの申告書及び添付資料等は真実で、正確に完成されたものであることを、ここに宣言いたします。

Signature of officer(代表者の署名) **㉒(署名)**

Date(日付) **㉓(作成日を記入)**

Title(役職名) **㉔(役職名を記入)**

IRSはこの申告書について下記の有料の作成者と検討することができるか。
YES NO

㉕(NOの□にチェック)

外国法人確定申告書・2021年分の作成手順（❶〜㊴）

Paid Preparer Use Only

（有料の作成者用）

作成者の氏名	作成者の署名　　日付
企業名	企業 EIN
企業所在地	電話番号

Form 1120-F (2021) Page **2**

Additional Information *(continued from page 1)*

		Yes	No
H	Did the corporation's method of accounting change from the preceding tax year?		✓
	If "Yes," attach a statement with an explanation.		
I	Did the corporation's method of determining income change from the preceding tax year?		✓
	If "Yes," attach a statement with an explanation.		
J	Did the corporation file a U.S. income tax return for the preceding tax year?		✓
K	**(1)** At any time during the tax year, was the corporation engaged in a trade or business in the United States?		✓
	(2) If "Yes," is taxpayer's trade or business within the United States solely the result of a section 897 (FIRPTA) sale or disposition?		✓
L	Did the corporation have a permanent establishment in the United States for purposes of any applicable tax treaty between the United States and a foreign country?		✓
	If "Yes," enter the name of the foreign country:		
M	Did the corporation have any transactions with related parties?		✓
	If "Yes," Form 5472 may have to be filed (see instructions).		
	Enter number of Forms 5472 attached ▶		
N	Is the corporation a controlled foreign corporation? (See section 957(a) for definition.)		✓
O	Is the corporation a personal service corporation? (See instructions for definition.)		✓
P	Enter tax-exempt interest received or accrued during the tax year (see instructions) ▶ $		
Q	At the end of the tax year, did the corporation own, directly or indirectly, 50% or more of the voting stock of a U.S. corporation? (See section 267(c) for rules of attribution.)		✓
	If "Yes," attach a statement showing **(1)** name and EIN of such U.S. corporation; **(2)** percentage owned; and **(3)** taxable income or (loss) before NOL and special deductions of such U.S. corporation for the tax year ending with or within your tax year.		
R	If the corporation has an NOL for the tax year and is electing to forego the carryback period, check here (see instructions) . . . . ▶ ☐		
S	Enter the available NOL carryover from prior tax years. (Do not reduce it by any deduction on line 30a, page 4.) ▶ $		
T	Is the corporation a subsidiary in a parent-subsidiary controlled group?		✓
	If "Yes," enter the parent corporation's:		
	(1) EIN ▶		
	(2) Name ▶		
U	**(1)** Is the corporation a dealer under section 475? . .		✓
	(2) Did the corporation mark to market any securities or commodities other than in a dealer capacity? . .		✓

		Yes	No
V	At the end of the tax year, did any individual, partnership, corporation, estate, or trust own, directly or indirectly, 50% or more of the corporation's voting stock? (See section 267 (c) for rules of attribution.)		✓
	If "Yes," attach a statement showing the name and identifying number. (Do not include any information already entered in item **T.**) Enter percentage owned ▶		
W	**(1)** Is the corporation taking a position on this return that a U.S. tax treaty overrules or modifies an Internal Revenue law of the United States, thereby causing a reduction of tax? .	✓ ⇦ 26	
	If "Yes," the corporation is generally required to complete and attach Form 8833. See Form 8833 for exceptions.		
	Note: *Failure to disclose a treaty-based return position may result in a $10,000 penalty (see section 6712).*		
	(2) Is the corporation claiming treaty benefits pursuant to, or otherwise filing its return pursuant to, a Competent Authority determination or an Advance Pricing Agreement? . . .		✓
	If "Yes," attach a copy of the Competent Authority determination letter or Advance Pricing Agreement to your return.		
X	During the tax year, did the corporation own any entity that was disregarded as an entity separate from its owner under Regulations sections 301.7701-2 and 301.7701-3? . .		✓
	If "Yes," attach a statement listing the name, country under whose laws the entity was organized, and EIN (if any) of each such entity.		
Y	**(1)** Did a partnership allocate to the corporation a distributive share of income from a directly owned partnership interest, any of which is ECI or treated as ECI by the partnership or the partner?		✓
	If "Yes," attach Schedule P. See instructions.		
	(2) During the tax year, did the corporation own, directly or indirectly, at least a 10% interest, in any foreign partnership?		✓
	If "Yes," see instructions for required attachment.		
Z	**(1)** Has the corporation engaged in any transactions the results of which are subject to the arm's-length standard under section 482 and its regulations?		✓
	(2) Has the corporation recognized any interbranch amounts? If "Yes," attach statement (see instructions)		✓
AA	Is the corporation required to file Schedule UTP (Form 1120), Uncertain Tax Position Statement (see instructions)?		✓
	If "Yes," complete and attach Schedule UTP.		
BB	During the corporation's tax year, did the corporation make any payments that would require it to file Forms 1042 and 1042-S under chapter 3 (sections 1441 through 1464) or chapter 4 (sections 1471 through 1474) of the Code? . .		✓
CC	Is the corporation (including the home office or any branch) a qualified derivatives dealer (QDD)?		✓
	(1) If "Yes," attach Schedule Q (Form 1120-F) (see instructions)		
	(2) If "Yes," enter the QI-EIN ▶		
DD	Does the corporation have gross receipts of at least $500 million in any of the 3 preceding tax years (see sections 59A(e)(2) and (3))?		✓
	If "Yes," complete and attach Form 8991.		
EE	During the tax year, did the corporation pay or accrue any interest or royalty for which a deduction is not allowed under section 267A (see instructions)?		✓
	If "Yes," enter the total amount of the disallowed deductions . . . ▶ $		

Form **1120-F** (2021)

外国法人確定申告書・2021年分の作成

Form 1120-F (2021) Page 3

Additional Information *(continued from page 2)*

	Yes	No
FF Did the corporation have an election under section 163(j) for any real property trade or business or any farming business in effect during the tax year (see instructions)?		✓
GG Does the corporation satisfy **one or more** of the following (see instructions)?		✓
(1) The corporation owns a pass-through entity with current, or prior year carryover, excess business interest expense.		
(2) The corporation's aggregate average annual gross receipts (determined under section 448(c)) for the 3 tax years preceding the current tax year are more than $26 million and the corporation has business interest expense.		
(3) The corporation is a tax shelter and the corporation has business interest expense. If "Yes," to any, complete and attach Form 8990.		
HH During the tax year, did the corporation dispose of an interest in a partnership that directly or indirectly engaged in a trade or business within the United States?		✓
II Is the corporation attaching Form 8996 to certify as a Qualified Opportunity Fund?		✓
If "Yes," enter amount from Form 8996, line 15 ▶ $		

SECTION I—Income From U.S. Sources Not Effectively Connected With the Conduct of a Trade or Business in the United States—Do not report items properly withheld and reported on Form 1042-S. See instructions.

Report all gross transportation income subject to 4% tax on line 9. Report other column (a) income items only if not properly withheld and reported on Form 1042-S. The rate of tax on these **gross** income items is 30% or such lower rate specified by tax treaty. No deductions are allowed against these types of income. Enter treaty rates where applicable. **If the corporation is claiming a lower treaty rate, also complete item W on page 2.** If multiple treaty rates apply to a type of income (for example, subsidiary and portfolio dividends or dividends received by disregarded entities), attach a statement showing the amounts, tax rates, and withholding for each.

Name of treaty country, if any ▶ JAPAN ㉘

	(a) Class of income (see instructions)	(b) Gross amount	(c) Rate of tax (%)	(d) Amount of tax liability	(e) Amount of U.S. income tax paid or withheld at the source
1	Interest				
2a	Dividends (excluding payments received by QDDs in their equity derivatives dealer capacity)				
2b	Dividend equivalents (excluding payments received by QDDs in their equity derivatives dealer capacity)	㉙	㉚	㉛	㉜
3	Rents				
4	Royalties	70000	0	0	21000
5	Annuities				
6	Gains from disposal of timber, coal, or domestic iron ore with a retained economic interest (attach supporting statement)				
7	Gains from sale or exchange of patents, copyrights, etc.				
8	Fiduciary distributions (attach supporting statement)				
9	Gross transportation income (see instructions)		4		
10	Other items of income				
11	Total. Enter here and on line 1, page 1 ▶			0	
12	Total. Enter here and include on line 5i, page 1 ▶				21000

13 Is the corporation fiscally transparent under the laws of the foreign jurisdiction with respect to any item of income listed above? ☐ Yes ☑ No ㉝
If "Yes," attach a statement that provides the information requested above with respect to each such item of income.

Form **1120-F** (2021)

追加情報　　　　　　　　　Yes又はNoにチェック

H　会社の会計処理方法は前年から変更しましたか。
　もし、Yes であれば説明書を添付してください。

I　会社の所得の計算方法は前年から変更しましたか。
　もし、Yes であれば説明書を添付してください。

J　会社は法人所得税申告書の前年分を提出していますか。

K⑴　本年の事業年度において米国で事業活動を行いましたか。

⑵　もし、Yes であれば、米国での事業活動は section 897（FIRPTA）sale あるいは disposition の結果ですか。

L　会社は米国と外国との間の租税条約が適用される恒久的施設を有していましたか。
　もし、Yes であれば、外国名を記入してください。

M　会社は related parties（関連者）と取引を行いましたか。
　もし、Yes であれば、Form 5472を添付してください。
　添付した Form 5472の番号を記入してください。

（上記のHからMはすべて、NO の□にチェック）

N　会社は controlled foreign corporation ですか。（定義については section 957参照）

O　会社は personal service corporation ですか。（定義については記載要領参照）

P　本年の事業年度において受領した又は未収の tax-exempt interest（免税利息）を記入してください。

Q　会社は事業年度末で、米国企業の議決権50%以上を直接又は間接に保有していますか。
　もし、Yes であれば、次の事項を示す書類を添付してください

⑴　米国企業の名称と EIN の

⑵　米国企業に対する議決権割合

⑶　米国企業の事業年度の繰越欠損金と特別控除の控除前の課税所得又は欠損金額

R　会社がその事業年度において繰越欠損金があるが、適用を差し控える場合には、こちらにチェックしてください。　□

S　前年から繰り越した使用可能な繰越欠損金を記入してください。

T　会社は親会社と子会社の関係にありますか。
　もし、Yes であれば、親会社の次の事項について記入してください。

⑴　EIN（納税者番号）

⑵　名称

外国法人確定申告書・2021年分の作成手順（❶〜㊴）

U⑴　会社はsection 475の証券等の取引業者ですか。

⑵　証券等の取引業者以外で時価会計を適用していますか。

V　事業年度末において、個人、パートナーシップ、会社、財団、又は信託が会社の議決権の50%以上を直接又は間接に保有していますか。

もし、Yesであれば、身分証明番号を示す書類を添付し保有割合を記入してください。

W⑴　会社は、この申告により、租税条約に基づき米国内法を修正し、税額の減額を行うことになりますか。 **㉖（WのYESの□にチェック）**

もし、Yesであれば、会社はForm 8833を作成し申告書に添付してください。

（注）a teaty-based return positionを明示しない場合には$10,000の罰金が課されます。

⑵　会社は、権限ある当局の決定又はAdvance Pricing Agreementにより、租税条約上の恩典を受けますか。

もし、Yesであれば、権限ある当局の決定書又はAdvance Pricing Agreementを添付してください。

X　会社は事業年度において、事業主から法的に独立したみなし事業体（disregarded entities）を有していますか。（section 301.7701-2 and 301.7701-3）

もし、Yesならばそのみなし事業体のEIN、事業体が設立された国及び事業体の名称を記載した書類を添付してください。

Y⑴　パートナーシップは会社に対し、ECIとして取り扱われるパートナーシップが直接保有する所得のdistributive share（分配持分）を配分しましたか。

もし、Yesであれば、Schedule Pを添付してください。

⑵　会社は事業年度中に、外国パートナーシップの持分の10%を直接又は間接に保有していますか。

もし、Yesであれば、必要書類を添付してください。

Z⑴　会社は、section 482の規定に基づく独立企業間価格による取引を行いましたか。

⑵　会社はinterbranch amountsを認識しましたか。（記載要領参照）

ＡＡ　会社はSchedule UTP（Form 1120）, Uncertain Tax Position Statementを提出することを要求されていますか。

もし、Yesであれば、Schedule UTPを作成し、添付してください。

㉗（N〜Y及びX〜ＡＡのNOの□にチェック）

ＢＢ〜Ⅱ　省略（ＢＢ〜ⅡのNOの□にチェック）

SECTION Ⅰ－米国内の事業活動に関連しない米国源泉の所得（適正に源泉徴収され、Form 1042-S により報告された所得については記入を要しません。）

line 9の4%の税率が課される運輸所得について報告します。

他の column ⒜ income で適正に源泉徴収されず、Form 1042-S において報告された所得を報告します。

税率については、総収入に対し30%の税率又は租税条約により規定された低率の税率によります。これらの所得に対する税率適用に際しては、総収入から控除は認めません。

租税条約による税率が適用される場合には、その税率を適用してください。

もし、会社が租税条約による低率の税率適用を求める場合には、前ページのWを完成させてください。

もし、多様な租税条約による税率が適用される所得の場合には、金額、税率及び源泉所得税を記載した書類を添付してください。

もしあるなら租税条約の締結国名の記入　**㉘（JAPAN を記入）**

(a) 所得の種類	(b) 総収入金額	(c) 税率	(d) 税額	(e) 米国源泉所得税額
1　利息				
2 a　配当				
2 b　配当				
3　賃借料				
4　ロイヤリティ	**㉙（70000）**	**㉚ 0**	**㉛ 0**	**㉜21000**
5　年金				
6　経済的利権が付与されている材木、石炭及び鉄鉱石の処分による収益				
7　特許権、著作権等の交換又は譲渡による収益				
8　信託配当				
9　運輸収益				
10　その他の所得				
11　page 1の line 1を記入				
12　page 1の line 5i を記入				

13　会社が上記に掲げられた所得に関し、外国の法律の下で財政的に透明ですか。
もし、Yesであれば、それぞれの所得に関し、要求された書面を添付してください。

Yes □　No □

㉝（NO の□にチェック）

外国法人確定申告書・2021年分の作成手順（❶～㊴）

SECTION I ―米国内の事業活動に関連しない米国源泉の所得（適正に源泉徴収され、Form 1042-S により報告された所得については記入を要しません。）

line 9の4％の税率が課される運輸所得について報告します。

他の column ⒜ income で適正に源泉徴収されず、Form 1042-S において報告された所得を報告します。

税率については、総収入に対し30％の税率又は租税条約により規定された低率の税率による。これらの所得に対する税率適用に際しては、総収入から控除は認めません。

租税条約による税率が適用される場合には、その税率を適用してください。

もし、会社が租税条約による低率の税率適用を求める場合には、前ページのWを完成させてください。

もし、多様な租税条約による税率が適用される所得の場合には、金額、税率及び源泉所得税を記載した書類を添付してください。

もしあるなら租税条約の締結国名の記入　**㉘（JAPAN を記入）**

	(a) 所得の種類	(b) 総収入金額	(c) 税率	(d) 税額	(e) 米国源泉所得税額
1	利息				
2	配当				
3	賃借料				
4	ロイヤリティ	**㉙（70000）**	**㉚ 0**	**㉛ 0**	**㉜21000**
5	年金				
6	経済的利権が付与されている材木、石炭及び鉄鉱石の処分による収益				
7	特許権、著作権等の交換又は譲渡による収益				
8	信託配当				
9	運輸収益				
10	その他の所得				
11	page 1の line 1を記入				
12	page 1の line 5iを記入				

13　会社が上記に掲げられた所得に関し、外国の法律の下で財政的に明瞭ですか。
もし、Yesであれば、それぞれの所得に関し、要求された書面を添付してください。

Yes □　No □

㉝（NO の□にチェック）

Form 1120-F (2021) Page **4**

SECTION II—Income Effectively Connected With the Conduct of a Trade or Business in the United States (see instructions)

Important: *Fill in all applicable lines and schedules. If you need more space, see* ***Assembling the Return*** *in the instructions.*

Income	**1a**	Gross receipts or sales ______ **b** Less returns and allowances ______ **c** Bal ▶	**1c**	
	2	Cost of goods sold (attach Form 1125-A)	**2**	
	3	Gross profit (subtract line 2 from line 1c)	**3**	
	4	Dividends (Schedule C, line 13)	**4**	
	5	Interest	**5**	
	6	Gross rents	**6**	
	7	Gross royalties	**7**	
	8	Capital gain net income (attach Schedule D (Form 1120))	**8**	
	9	Net gain or (loss) from Form 4797, Part II, line 17 (attach Form 4797)	**9**	
	10	Other income (see instructions—attach statement)	**10**	
	11	**Total income.** Add lines 3 through 10 ▶	**11**	
Deductions (See instructions for limitations on deductions.)	**12**	Compensation of officers (see instructions—attach Form 1125-E)	**12**	
	13	Salaries and wages (less employment credits)	**13**	
	14	Repairs and maintenance	**14**	
	15	Bad debts (for bad debts over $500,000, attach a list of debtors and amounts)	**15**	
	16	Rents	**16**	
		Taxes and licenses		
	8	Interest expense from Schedule I, line 25 (see instructions)	**8**	
	9	Charitable contributions	**9**	
	20	Depreciation from Form 4562 not claimed on Form 1125-A or elsewhere on return (attach Form 4562)	**20**	
	2	Depletion	**2**	
	22	Advertising	**22**	
	23	Pension, profit-sharing, etc., plans	**23**	
	2	Employee benefit programs	**2**	
	25	Reserved for future use	**25**	
	26	Deductions allocated and apportioned to ECI from Schedule H, line 20 (see instructions)	**26**	
	2	Other deductions (attach statement)	**2**	
	28	**Total deductions.** Add lines 12 through 27 ▶	**28**	
	29	Taxable income before NOL deduction and special deductions (subtract line 28 from line 11) ▶	**29**	
	30	**Less: a** Net operating loss deduction (see instructions) **30a**		
		b Special deductions (Schedule C, line 14) **30b**		
		c Add lines 30a and 30b	**30c**	
	3	Taxable income or (loss). Subtract line 30c from line 29	**3**	

Form **1120-F** (2021)

外国法人確定申告書・2021年分の作成

Form 1120-F (2021) Page 5

SECTION II—Income Effectively Connected With the Conduct of a Trade or Business in the United States *(continued)*

Schedule C Dividends and Special Deductions (see instructions)

		(a) Dividends	(b) %	(c) Special deductions: (a) × (b)
1	Dividends from less-than-20%-owned domestic corporations (other than debt-financed stock)		50	
2	Dividends from 20%-or-more-owned domestic corporations (other than debt-financed stock)		65	
3	Dividends on certain debt-financed stock of domestic and foreign corporations (section 246A)		see instructions	
4	Dividends on certain preferred stock of less-than-20%-owned public utilities		23.3	
5	Dividends on certain preferred stock of 20%-or-more-owned public utilities		26.7	
6	Dividends from less-than-20%-owned foreign corporations		50	
7	Dividends from 20%-or-more-owned foreign corporations		65	
8	**Subtotal.** Add lines 1 through 7. See instructions for limitation		see instructions	
9	Dividends from foreign corporations not included on line 3, 6, or 7			
10	IC-DISC and former DISC dividends not included on line 1, 2, or 3 (section 246(d))			
11	Other dividends			
12	Deduction for dividends paid on certain preferred stock of public utilities			
13	**Total dividends.** Add column (a), lines 8 through 11. Enter here and on line 4, page 4			
14	**Total special deductions.** Add column (c), lines 8 and 12. Enter here and on line 30b, page 4 ▶			

Schedule J Tax Computation (see instructions)

1	Check if the corporation is a member of a controlled group (attach Schedule O (Form 1120)) ▶ ☐				
2	Income tax			2	
3	Base erosion minimum tax amount (attach Form 8991)			3	
4	Add lines 2 and 3			4	
5a	Foreign tax credit (attach Form 1118)	5a			
b	General business credit (attach Form 3800)	5b			
c	Credit for prior year minimum tax (attach Form 8827)	5c			
d	Bond credits from Form 8912	5d			
6	**Total credits.** Add lines 5a through 5d			6	
7	Subtract line 6 from line 4			7	
8	Other taxes. Check if from: ☐ Form 4255 ☐ Form 8611 ☐ Form 8697 ☐ Form 8866 ☐ Form 8902 ☐ Other (attach statement)			8	
9	**Total tax.** Add lines 7 and 8. Enter here and on line 2, page 1			9	

Form **1120-F** (2021)

Form 1120-F (2021) Page 6

SECTION III—Branch Profits Tax and Tax on Excess Interest

Part I—Branch Profits Tax (see instructions)

1	Enter the amount from Section II, line 29	1	
2	Enter total adjustments to line 1 to get effectively connected earnings and profits. (Attach required statement showing the nature and amount of adjustments.) (See instructions.)	2	
3	Effectively connected earnings and profits. Combine line 1 and line 2	3	
4a	Enter U.S. net equity at the end of the current tax year. (Attach required statement.)	4a	
b	Enter U.S. net equity at the end of the prior tax year. (Attach required statement.)	4b	
c	Increase in U.S. net equity. If line 4a is greater than or equal to line 4b, subtract line 4b from line 4a. Enter the result here and skip to line 4e	4c	
d	Decrease in U.S. net equity. If line 4b is greater than line 4a, subtract line 4a from line 4b	4d	
e	Non-previously taxed accumulated effectively connected earnings and profits. Enter excess, if any, of effectively connected earnings and profits for preceding tax years beginning after 1986 over any dividend equivalent amounts for those tax years	4e	
5	Dividend equivalent amount. Subtract line 4c from line 3. If zero or less, enter -0-. If no amount is entered on line 4c, add the lesser of line 4d or line 4e to line 3 and enter the total here	5	
6	**Branch profits tax.** Multiply line 5 by 30% (0.30) (or lower treaty rate if the corporation is a qualified resident or otherwise qualifies for treaty benefits). (See instructions.) Enter here and include on line 3, page 1. **Also complete item W on page 2**	6	

Part II—Tax on Excess Interest (see instructions for this Part and for Schedule I (Form 1120-F))

a	Enter the interest from Section II, line 18	a	
b	Enter the inverse of the total amount deferred, capitalized, and disallowed from Schedule I, line 24g (i.e., if line 24g is negative, enter as a positive number; if line 24g is positive, enter as a negative number)	b	
c	Combine lines 7a and 7b (amount must equal Schedule I, line 23)	c	
8	**Branch Interest** (see instructions for definition): Enter the sum of Schedule I, line 9, column (c), and Schedule I, line 22. If the interest paid by the foreign corporation's U.S. trade or business was increased because 80% or more of the foreign corporation's assets are U.S. assets, check this box ▶ ☐	8	
9a	Excess interest. Subtract line 8 from line 7c. If zero or less, enter -0-	9a	
b	If the foreign corporation is a bank, enter the excess interest treated as interest on deposits (see instructions for rules for computing this amount). Otherwise, enter -0-	9b	
c	Subtract line 9b from line 9a	9c	
0	**Tax on excess interest.** Multiply line 9c by 30% (0.30) (or lower treaty rate if the corporation is a qualified resident or otherwise qualifies for treaty benefits). (See instructions.) Enter here and include on line 3, page 1. **Also complete item W on page 2**	0	

Part III—Additional Information

	Yes	No
Is the corporation claiming a reduction in, or exemption from, the branch profits tax due to:		
a A complete termination of all U.S. trades or businesses?		
b The tax-free liquidation or reorganization of a foreign corporation?		
c The tax-free incorporation of a U.S. trade or business?		
If **a** or **b** applies and the transferee is a domestic corporation, attach Form 8848. If **c** applies, attach the statement required by Temporary Regulations section 1.884-2T(d)(5).		

Form **1120-F** (2021)

外国法人確定申告書・2021年分の作成

Form 1120-F (2021) Page **7**

Note: *Check if completing on* ▶ ☐ U.S. basis or ☐ Worldwide basis

Schedule L **Balance Sheets per Books**

	Assets	**Beginning of tax year**		**End of tax year**	
		(a)	**(b)**	**(c)**	**(d)**
1	Cash				
2a	Trade notes and accounts receivable				
b	Less allowance for bad debts	( )		( )	
3	Inventories				
4	U.S. government obligations				
5	Tax-exempt securities (see instructions)				
6a	Interbranch current assets*				
b	Other current non-U.S. assets*				
c	Other current U.S. assets*				
7	Loans to shareholders				
8	Mortgage and real estate loans				
9a	Other loans and investments—non-U.S. assets*				
b	Other loans and investments—U.S. assets*				
10a	Buildings and other depreciable assets				
b	Less accumulated depreciation	( )		( )	
a	Depletable assets				
b	Less accumulated depletion	( )		( )	
2	Land (net of any amortization)				
3a	Intangible assets (amortizable only)				
b	Less accumulated amortization	( )		( )	
	Assets held in trust				
5	Other non-current interbranch assets*				
6a	Other non-current non-U.S. assets*				
b	Other non-current U.S. assets*				
	Total assets				
	Liabilities				
8	Accounts payable				
9	Mortgages, notes, bonds payable in less than 1 year:				
a	Interbranch liabilities*				
b	Third-party liabilities*				
20	Other current liabilities*				
2	Loans from shareholders				
22	Mortgages, notes, bonds payable in 1 year or more:				
a	Interbranch liabilities*				
b	Third-party liabilities*				
23	Liabilities held in trust				
2 a	Other interbranch liabilities*				
b	Other third-party liabilities*				
	Equity				
25	Capital stock: **a** Preferred stock				
	b Common stock				
26	Additional paid-in capital				
2	Retained earnings—Appropriated*				
28	Retained earnings—Unappropriated				
29	Adjustments to shareholders' equity*				
30	Less cost of treasury stock		( )		( )
31	Total liabilities and shareholders' equity				

*Attach statement—see instructions.

Form **1120-F** (2021)

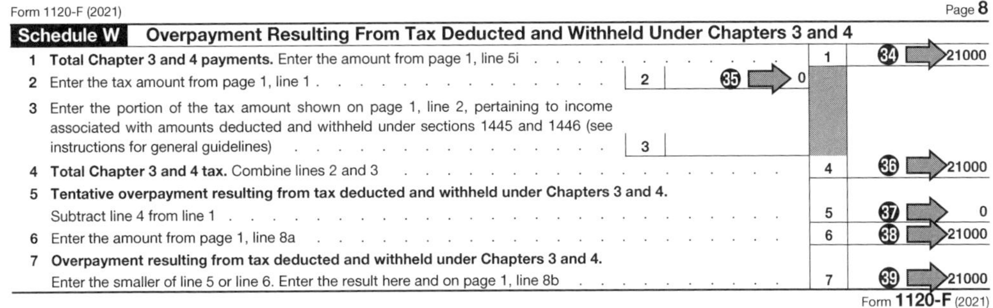

Form 1120-F (2021) Page 8

Schedule W **Overpayment Resulting From Tax Deducted and Withheld Under Chapters 3 and 4**

1	**Total Chapter 3 and 4 payments.** Enter the amount from page 1, line 5i		1	㉞ 21000
2	Enter the tax amount from page 1, line 1	2 ㉟ 0		
3	Enter the portion of the tax amount shown on page 1, line 2, pertaining to income associated with amounts deducted and withheld under sections 1445 and 1446 (see instructions for general guidelines)	3		
4	**Total Chapter 3 and 4 tax.** Combine lines 2 and 3		4	㊱ 21000
5	**Tentative overpayment resulting from tax deducted and withheld under Chapters 3 and 4.** Subtract line 4 from line 1		5	㊲ 0
6	Enter the amount from page 1, line 8a		6	㊳ 21000
7	**Overpayment resulting from tax deducted and withheld under Chapters 3 and 4.** Enter the smaller of line 5 or line 6. Enter the result here and on page 1, line 8b		7	㊴ 21000

Form **1120-F** (2021)

Schedule W 税額控除とChapters 3及び4の規定による源泉徴収後の過大納付額

1　Chapters 3及び4の規定による源泉徴収税額　**㉞（21000を記入）**

2　page 1の line 1の税額を記入　**㉟（0を記入）**

3　page 1の line 2の税額を記入

4　Chapters 3及び4の規定による源泉徴収税額の合計額　**㊱（21000を記入）**

5　仮の税額控除とChapters 3及び4の規定による仮の源泉徴収後の課題納付額

㊲（0を記入）

6　page 1の line 8aの税額を記入　**㊳（21000を記入）**

7　税額控除とChapters 3及び4の規定による源泉徴収後の課題納付額

㊴（21000を記入）

手続6 外国法人確定申告書・2022年分の作成

記入箇所は ⇦ で表示

Form **1120-F** Department of the Treasury Internal Revenue Service

U.S. Income Tax Return of a Foreign Corporation ❶

For calendar year 2022, or tax year beginning Jan1 ❶, 2022, and ending DECEM31, 20 22 ❶

Go to *www.irs.gov/Form1120F* for instructions and the latest information.

OMB No. 1545-0123 **2022**

Type or Print	
Name	ABC.INC ⇦ ❷
Number, street, and room or suite no. (see instructions)	XXX,XXXX,XXXXXX ⇦ ❸
City or town, state or province, country, and ZIP or foreign postal code	Tokyo 101-0047 JAPAN ⇦ ❹

Employer identification number XX-XXXXXX ⇦ ❺

Check box(es) if: ☑ Initial return ⇦ ❻ ☐ Name or address change ☐ Final return ☐ First post-merger return ☐ Amended return ☐ Schedule M-3 attached ☐ Protective return

A Country of incorporation JAPAN ⇦ ❼

B Foreign country under whose laws the income reported on this return is also subject to tax JAPAN ⇦ ❽

C Date incorporated Jan1.2000 ⇦ ❾

D (1) Location of corporation's primary books and records (city, province or state, and country) Tokyo JAPAN ⇦ ❿

(2) Principal location of worldwide business Tokyo JAPAN ⇦ ⓫

(3) If the corporation maintains an office or place of business in the United States, check here ☐

E If the corporation had an agent in the United States at any time during the tax year, enter:
(1) Type of agent
(2) Name
(3) Address

F See the instructions and enter the corporation's principal:
(1) Business activity code number 511190 ⇦ ⓬
(2) Business activity Publising ⇦ ⓭
(3) Product or service

G Check method of accounting: (1) ☐ Cash (2) ☑ Accrual ⇧ ⓮ (3) ☐ Other (specify)

Computation of Tax Due or Overpayment

1	Tax from Section I, line 11, page 3	1	⓯ ⇨ 0
2	Tax from Section II, Schedule J, line 9, page 5	2	
3	Tax from Section III (add lines 6 and 10 on page 6)	3	
4	**Total tax.** Add lines 1 through 3	4	⓰ ⇨ 0
5a	2021 overpayment credited to 2022	5a	
b	2022 estimated tax payments	5b	
c	Less 2022 refund applied for on Form 4466	5c	( )
d	Combine lines 5a through 5c	5d	
e	Tax deposited with Form 7004	5e	
f	Credit for tax paid on undistributed capital gains (attach Form 2439)	5f	
g	Credit for federal tax paid on fuels (attach Form 4136). See instructions	5g	
h	Reserved for future use	5h	
i	U.S. income tax paid or withheld at source (add line 12, page 3, and amounts from Forms 8288-A and 8805 (attach Forms 8288-A and 8805))	5i	⓱ ⇨ 27000
j	Total payments. Add lines 5d through 5i	5j	⓲ ⇨ 27000
6	Estimated tax penalty (see instructions). Check if Form 2220 is attached ☐	6	
7	**Amount owed.** If line 5j is smaller than the total of lines 4 and 6, enter amount owed	7	
8a	**Overpayment.** If line 5j is larger than the total of lines 4 and 6, enter amount overpaid	8a	⓳ ⇨ 27000
b	**Amount of overpayment on line 8a resulting from tax deducted and withheld under Chapters 3 and 4** (from Schedule W, line 7, page 8)	8b	⓴ ⇨ 27000
9	Enter portion of line 8a you want **Credited to 2023 estimated tax** ... Refunded	9	㉑ ⇨ 27000

Sign Here Under penalties of perjury, I declare that I have examined this return, including accompanying schedules and statements, and to the best of my knowledge and belief, it is true, correct, and complete. Declaration of preparer (other than taxpayer) is based on all information of which preparer has any knowledge.

㉒ ⇨ Signature of officer　⇩ ㉓ Date　⇦ ㉔ Title

May the IRS discuss this return with the preparer shown below (see instructions)? ☐ Yes ☑ No

Paid Preparer Use Only

Print/Type preparer's name	Preparer's signature	Date	Check ☐ if self-employed	PTIN ⇧ ㉕
Firm's name			Firm's EIN	
Firm's address			Phone no.	

For Paperwork Reduction Act Notice, see separate instructions. Cat. No. 11470I Form **1120-F** (2022)

1120-F　外国法人確定申告書　2022

事業年度 **❶（1/1～12/31の事業年度を記入）**

会社名 **❷（ABC.INC と記入）** 所在地 **❸（日本の本店所在地を記入）** 都市名・郵便番号・国名 **❹（都市名・郵便番号・JAPAN と記入）**	Employer identification number **❺ 納税者番号の記入** □当初申告 □名称・住所変更　□最終申告 □合併後申告　□修正申告 □ Schedule M-3の添付　□予備申告 **❻（当初申告の□にチェック）**

A　会社設立国　**❼（JAPAN と記入）**

B　この申告書により報告される所得に対して課税が行われる国　**❽（JAPAN と記入）**

C　会社設立年月日　**❾（会社設立年月日を記入）**

D(1)　会社の主要帳簿と会計記録の保管場所　**❿（都市名と JAPAN と記入）**

(2)　世界的事業を行う場所　**⓫（都市名と JAPAN と記入）**

(3)　米国内に事業を行う場所を有する場合にはここにチェック　□

E　米国内に課税期間中に代理人を有する場合には、次の事項を記載

(1)　代理人の類型

(2)　名称

(3)　所在地

F　記載要領から次の事項を記載

(1)　Business activity code number　**⓬（記載要領を参照）**

(2)　Business activity　**⓭（記載要領を参照）**

(3)　Product or Service

G　会計処理についてチェック **⓮　((2)の□にチェック)**

(1)　現金主義　□

(2)　発生主義　□

(3)　その他　□

外国法人確定申告書・2022年分の作成手順（❶～㊴）

Computation of Tax Due or Overpayment（納税額又は還付税額の計算）

1　page 3のline 11の税額を記載　**⓯（0を記入）**

2　page 5のline 9の税額を記載

3　page 6のline 6と10の合計金額を記載

4　税額の集計（1～3）　**⓰（0を記入）**

5 a　2022年の税額から控除する2021年の過払税金

b　2022年の見積税額

c　Form 4466により適用される2017年の還付税額

d　line 5a～5cまでの合計

e　Form 7004による予納税額

f　未分配の譲渡益に対する税金の控除（Form 2439を添付）

g　燃料に対する連邦税の控除（Form 4136を添付）

h　将来使用のための予備（備蓄）

i　米国の所得税又は源泉徴収税額（page 3のline 12の税額とForm 8288-Aと8805の税額の合計額）**⓱（27000を記入）**

j　5d～5iまでの支払額合計　**⓲（27000を記入）**

6　Estimated tax penalty（チェックForm 2220を添付している場合）□

7　納税額（line 5jがline 4と6の合計額より小さい場合）

8 a　還付税額（line 5jがline 4と6の合計額より大きい場合）**⓳（27000を記入）**

b　税額控除とChapters 3及び4の規定による源泉徴収後のline 8aの過大納付額（page 8のSchedule Wのline 7から）**⓴（27000を記入）**

9　2023年の予定納税額から控除を希望する金額・Refunded（還付税額）

㉑（27000を記入）

Sign Here　偽証の場合の罰則の下、私は、本件申告書、添付資料を調査し、私の知る限りでは、これらの申告書及び添付資料等は真実で、正確に完成されたものであることを、ここに宣言いたします。

Signature of officer（代表者の署名）**㉒（署名）**

Date（日付）**㉓（作成日を記入）**

Title（役職名）**㉔（役職名を記入）**

IRSはこの申告書について下記の有料の作成者と検討することができるか。
YES　　NO

㉕（NOの□にチェック）

Paid Preparer Use Only

（有料の作成者用）

作成者の氏名	作成者の署名　　日付
企業名	企業 EIN
企業所在地	電話番号

外国法人確定申告書・2022年分の作成

Form 1120-F (2022) Page **2**

Additional Information *(continued from page 1)*

		Yes	No
H	Did the corporation's method of accounting change from the preceding tax year? If "Yes," attach a statement with an explanation.		✓
I	Did the corporation's method of determining income change from the preceding tax year? If "Yes," attach a statement with an explanation.		✓
J	Did the corporation file a U.S. income tax return for the preceding tax year?		✓
K	**(1)** At any time during the tax year, was the corporation engaged in a trade or business in the United States?		✓
	(2) If "Yes," is taxpayer's trade or business within the United States solely the result of a section 897 (FIRPTA) sale or disposition?		✓
L	Did the corporation have a permanent establishment in the United States for purposes of any applicable tax treaty between the United States and a foreign country? If "Yes," enter the name of the foreign country: ________		✓
M	Did the corporation have any transactions with related parties? If "Yes," Form 5472 may have to be filed (see instructions). Enter number of Forms 5472 attached ________		✓
N	Is the corporation a controlled foreign corporation? (See section 957(a) for definition.)		✓
O	Is the corporation a personal service corporation? (See instructions for definition.)		✓
P	Enter tax-exempt interest received or accrued during the tax year (see instructions) $ ________		
Q	At the end of the tax year, did the corporation own, directly or indirectly, 50% or more of the voting stock of a U.S. corporation? (See section 267(c) for rules of attribution.) If "Yes," attach a statement showing **(1)** name and EIN of such U.S. corporation; **(2)** percentage owned; and **(3)** taxable income or (loss) before NOL and special deductions of such U.S. corporation for the tax year ending with or within your tax year.		✓
R	If the corporation has an NOL for the tax year and is electing to forego the carryback period, check here (see instructions) ☐		
S	Enter the available NOL carryover from prior tax years. (Do not reduce it by any deduction on line 30a, page 4.) $ ________		
T	Is the corporation a subsidiary in a parent-subsidiary controlled group? If "Yes," enter the parent corporation's: **(1)** EIN ________ **(2)** Name ________		✓
U	**(1)** Is the corporation a dealer under section 475?		✓
	(2) Did the corporation mark to market any securities or commodities other than in a dealer capacity?		✓
V	At the end of the tax year, did any individual, partnership, corporation, estate, or trust own, directly or indirectly, 50% or more of the corporation's voting stock? (See section 267 (c) for rules of attribution.) If "Yes," attach a statement showing the name and identifying number. (Do not include any information already entered in item **T**.) Enter percentage owned ________		✓
W	**(1)** Is the corporation taking a position on this return that a U.S. tax treaty overrules or modifies an Internal Revenue law of the United States, thereby causing a reduction of tax? If "Yes," the corporation is generally required to complete and attach Form 8833. See Form 8833 for exceptions. **Note:** *Failure to disclose a treaty-based return position may result in a $10,000 penalty (see section 6712).*	✓ ⇦ 26	
	(2) Is the corporation claiming treaty benefits pursuant to, or otherwise filing its return pursuant to, a Competent Authority determination or an Advance Pricing Agreement? If "Yes," attach a copy of the Competent Authority determination letter or Advance Pricing Agreement to your return.		✓
X	During the tax year, did the corporation own any entity that was disregarded as an entity separate from its owner under Regulations sections 301.7701-2 and 301.7701-3? If "Yes," attach a statement listing the name, country under whose laws the entity was organized, and EIN (if any) of each such entity.		✓
Y	**(1)** Did a partnership allocate to the corporation a distributive share of income from a directly owned partnership interest, any of which is ECI or treated as ECI by the partnership or the partner? If "Yes," attach Schedule P. See instructions.		✓
	(2) During the tax year, did the corporation own, directly or indirectly, at least a 10% interest, in any foreign partnership? If "Yes," see instructions for required attachment.		✓
Z	**(1)** Has the corporation engaged in any transactions the results of which are subject to the arm's-length standard under section 482 and its regulations?		✓
	(2) Has the corporation recognized any interbranch amounts? If "Yes," attach statement (see instructions)		✓
AA	Is the corporation required to file Schedule UTP (Form 1120), Uncertain Tax Position Statement (see instructions)? If "Yes," complete and attach Schedule UTP.		✓
BB	During the corporation's tax year, did the corporation make any payments that would require it to file Forms 1042 and 1042-S under chapter 3 (sections 1441 through 1464) or chapter 4 (sections 1471 through 1474) of the Code?		✓
CC	Is the corporation (including the home office or any branch) a qualified derivatives dealer (QDD)? **(1)** If "Yes," attach Schedule Q (Form 1120-F) (see instructions) **(2)** If "Yes," enter the QI-EIN ________		✓
DD	Does the corporation have gross receipts of at least $500 million in any of the 3 preceding tax years (see sections 59A(e)(2) and (3))? If "Yes," complete and attach Form 8991.		✓
EE	During the tax year, did the corporation pay or accrue any interest or royalty for which a deduction is not allowed under section 267A (see instructions)? If "Yes," enter the total amount of the disallowed deductions $		✓

Form **1120-F** (2022)

Form 1120-F (2022) Page **3**

Additional Information *(continued from page 2)*

		Yes	No
FF	Did the corporation have an election under section 163(j) for any real property trade or business or any farming business in effect during the tax year (see instructions)?		✓
GG	Does the corporation satisfy **one or more** of the following (see instructions)?		✓
	(1) The corporation owns a pass-through entity with current, or prior year carryover, excess business interest expense.		
	(2) The corporation's aggregate average annual gross receipts (determined under section 448(c)) for the 3 tax years preceding the current tax year are more than $27 million and the corporation has business interest expense.		
	(3) The corporation is a tax shelter and the corporation has business interest expense. If "Yes," to any, complete and attach Form 8990.		
HH	During the tax year, did the corporation dispose of an interest in a partnership that directly or indirectly engaged in a trade or business within the United States?		✓
II	Is the corporation attaching Form 8996 to certify as a Qualified Opportunity Fund?		✓
	If "Yes," enter amount from Form 8996, line 15 . . . . . $		

SECTION I—Income From U.S. Sources Not Effectively Connected With the Conduct of a Trade or Business in the United States—Do not report items properly withheld and reported on Form 1042-S. See instructions.

Report all gross transportation income subject to 4% tax on line 9. Report other column (a) income items only if not properly withheld and reported on Form 1042-S. The rate of tax on these **gross** income items is 30% or such lower rate specified by tax treaty. No deductions are allowed against these types of income. Enter treaty rates where applicable. **If the corporation is claiming a lower treaty rate, also complete item W on page 2.** If multiple treaty rates apply to a type of income (for example, subsidiary and portfolio dividends or dividends received by disregarded entities), attach a statement showing the amounts, tax rates, and withholding for each.

Name of treaty country, if any **JAPAN** ㉘

	(a) Class of income (see instructions)	(b) Gross amount ㉙	(c) Rate of tax (%) ㉚	(d) Amount of tax liability ㉛	(e) Amount of U.S. income tax paid or withheld at the source ㉜
1	Interest				
2a	Dividends (excluding payments received by QDDs in their equity derivatives dealer capacity)				
2b	Dividend equivalents (excluding payments received by QDDs in their equity derivatives dealer capacity)				
3	Rents				
4	Royalties	90000	0	0	27000
5	Annuities				
6	Gains from disposal of timber, coal, or domestic iron ore with a retained economic interest (attach supporting statement)				
7	Gains from sale or exchange of patents, copyrights, etc.				
8	Fiduciary distributions (attach supporting statement)				
9	Gross transportation income (see instructions)		4		
10	Other items of income				
11	Total. Enter here and on line 1, page 1			0	
12	Total. Enter here and include on line 5i, page 1				27000

13 Is the corporation fiscally transparent under the laws of the foreign jurisdiction with respect to any item of income listed above? ☐ Yes ☑ No ㉝

If "Yes," attach a statement that provides the information requested above with respect to each such item of income.

Form **1120-F** (2022)

外国法人確定申告書・2022年分の作成手順（❶～㊴）

追加情報　　　　　　　Yes又はNoにチェック

H　会社の会計処理方法は前年から変更しましたか。
　もし、Yes であれば説明書を添付してください。

I　会社の所得の計算方法は前年から変更しましたか。
　もし、Yes であれば説明書を添付してください。

J　会社は法人所得税申告書の前年分を提出していますか。

K⑴　本年の事業年度において米国で事業活動を行いましたか。
　⑵　もし、Yes であれば、米国での事業活動は section 897（FIRPTA）sale あるいは disposition の結果ですか。

L　会社は米国と外国との間の租税条約が適用される恒久的施設を有していましたか。
　もし、Yes であれば、外国名を記入してください。

M　会社は related parties（関連者）と取引を行いましたか。
　もし、Yes であれば、Form 5472を添付してください。
　添付した Form 5472の番号を記入してください。

（上記のHからMはすべて、NO の□にチェック）

N　会社は controlled foreign corporation ですか。（定義については section 957参照）

O　会社は personal service corporation ですか。（定義については記載要領参照）

P　本年の事業年度において受領した又は未収の tax-exempt interest（免税利息）を記入してください。

Q　会社は事業年度末で、米国企業の議決権50%以上を直接又は間接に保有していますか。
　もし、Yes であれば、次の事項を示す書類を添付してください
　⑴　米国企業の名称と EIN の
　⑵　米国企業に対する議決権割合
　⑶　米国企業の事業年度の繰越欠損金と特別控除の控除前の課税所得又は欠損金額

R　会社がその事業年度において繰越欠損金があるが、適用を差し控える場合には、こちらにチェックしてください。　□

S　前年から繰り越した使用可能な繰越欠損金を記入してください。

T　会社は親会社と子会社の関係にありますか。
　もし、Yes であれば、親会社の次の事項について記入してください。
　⑴　EIN（納税者番号）
　⑵　名称

U(1)　会社は section 475の証券等の取引業者ですか。

(2)　証券等の取引業者以外で時価会計を適用していますか。

V　事業年度末において、個人、パートナーシップ、会社、財団、又は信託が会社の議決権の50%以上を直接又は間接に保有していますか。

もし、Yes であれば、身分証明番号を示す書類を添付し保有割合を記入してください。

W(1)　会社は、この申告により、租税条約に基づき米国内法を修正し、税額の減額を行うことになりますか。 **㉖（Wの YES の□にチェック）**

もし、Yes であれば、会社は Form 8833を作成し申告書に添付してください。

（注）　a treaty-based return position を明示しない場合には $10,000の罰金が課されます。

(2)　会社は、権限ある当局の決定又は Advance Pricing Agreement により、租税条約上の恩典を受けますか。

もし、Yes であれば、権限ある当局の決定書又は Advance Pricing Agreement を添付してください。

X　会社は事業年度において、事業主から法的に独立したみなし事業体（disregarded entities）を有していますか。（section 301.7701-2 and 301.7701-３）

もし、Yes ならばそのみなし事業体の EIN、事業体が設立された国及び事業体の名称を記載した書類を添付してください。

Y(1)　パートナーシップは会社に対し、ECI として取り扱われるパートナーシップが直接保有する所得の distributive share（分配持分）を配分しましたか。

もし、Yes であれば、Schedule P を添付してください。

(2)　会社は事業年度中に、外国パートナーシップの持分の10%を直接又は間接に保有していますか。

もし、Yes であれば、必要書類を添付してください。

Z(1)　会社は、section 482の規定に基づく独立企業間価格による取引を行いましたか。

(2)　会社は interbranch amounts を認識しましたか。（記載要領参照）

ＡＡ　会社は Schedule UTP（Form 1120），Uncertain Tax Position Statement を提出することを要求されていますか。

もし、Yes であれば、Schedule UTP を作成し、添付してください。

㉗（N～Y及びX～AA の NO の□にチェック）

ＢＢ～Ⅱ　省略（ＢＢ～ⅡのNO の□にチェック）

外国法人確定申告書・2022年分の作成手順（❶～㊴）

SECTION Ⅰ－米国内の事業活動に関連しない米国源泉の所得（適正に源泉徴収され、Form 1042-S により報告された所得については記入を要しません）

line 9の4%の税率が課される運輸所得について報告します。

他の column ⓐ income で適正に源泉徴収されず、Form 1042-S において報告された所得を報告します。

税率については、総収入に対し30%の税率又は租税条約により規定された低率の税率による。これらの所得に対する税率適用に際しては、総収入から控除は認めません。

租税条約による税率が適用される場合には、その税率を適用してください。

もし、会社が租税条約による低率の税率適用を求める場合には、前ページのWを完成させてください。

もし、多様な租税条約による税率が適用される所得の場合には、金額、税率及び源泉所得税を記載した書類を添付してください。

もしあるなら租税条約の締結国名の記入　**㉘（JAPAN を記入）**

	(a) 所得の種類	(b) 総収入金額	(c) 税率	(d) 税額	(e) 米国源泉所得税額
1	利息				
2 a	配当				
2 b	配当				
3	賃借料				
4	ロイヤリティ	**㉙（90000）**	**㉚ 0**	**㉛ 0**	**㉜27000**
5	年金				
6	経済的利権が付与されている材木、石炭及び鉄鉱石の処分による収益				
7	特許権、著作権等の交換又は譲渡による収益				
8	信託配当				
9	運輸収益				
10	その他の所得				
11	page 1の line 1を記入				
12	page 1の line 5 i を記入				

13　会社が上記に掲げられた所得に関し、外国の法律の下で財政的に透明ですか。
もし、Yesであれば、それぞれの所得に関し、要求された書面を添付してください。

Yes □　No □

㉝（NO の□にチェック）

Form 1120-F (2022) Page **4**

SECTION II—Income Effectively Connected With the Conduct of a Trade or Business in the United States (see instructions)

Important: *Fill in all applicable lines and schedules. If you need more space, see* ***Assembling the Return*** *in the instructions.*

Income	a	Gross receipts or sales ______ b Less returns and allowances ______ c Bal	c	
	2	Cost of goods sold (attach Form 1125-A)	2	
	3	Gross profit (subtract line 2 from line 1c)	3	
		Dividends (Schedule C, line 13)		
	5	Interest	5	
	6	Gross rents	6	
		Gross royalties		
	8	Capital gain net income (attach Schedule D (Form 1120))	8	
	9	Net gain or (loss) from Form 4797, Part II, line 17 (attach Form 4797)	9	
	0	Other income (see instructions—attach statement)	0	
		Total income. Add lines 3 through 10		
Deductions (See instructions for limitations on deductions.)	12	Compensation of officers (see instructions—attach Form 1125-E)	12	
	3	Salaries and wages (less employment credits)	3	
		Repairs and maintenance		
	15	Bad debts (for bad debts over $500,000, attach a list of debtors and amounts)	15	
	6	Rents	6	
		Taxes and licenses		
	18	Interest expense from Schedule I, line 25 (see instructions)	18	
	9	Charitable contributions	9	
	20	Depreciation from Form 4562 not claimed on Form 1125-A or elsewhere on return (attach Form 4562)	20	
	21	Depletion	21	
	22	Advertising	22	
	23	Pension, profit-sharing, etc., plans	23	
	24	Employee benefit programs	24	
	25	Reserved for future use	25	
	26	Deductions allocated and apportioned to ECI from Schedule H, line 20 (see instructions)	26	
	27	Other deductions (attach statement)	27	
	28	**Total deductions.** Add lines 12 through 27	28	
	29	Taxable income before NOL deduction and special deductions (subtract line 28 from line 11)	29	
	30	**Less:** **a** Net operating loss deduction (see instructions) — 30a		
		b Special deductions (Schedule C, line 14) — 30b		
		c Add lines 30a and 30b	30c	
	31	Taxable income or (loss). Subtract line 30c from line 29	31	

Form **1120-F** (2022)

外国法人確定申告書・2022年分の作成

Form 1120-F (2022) Page 5

SECTION II—Income Effectively Connected With the Conduct of a Trade or Business in the United States *(continued)*

Schedule C Dividends and Special Deductions (see instructions)

		(a) Dividends	(b) %	(c) Special deductions: (a) × (b)
1	Dividends from less-than-20%-owned domestic corporations (other than debt-financed stock)		50	
2	Dividends from 20%-or-more-owned domestic corporations (other than debt-financed stock)		65	
3	Dividends on certain debt-financed stock of domestic and foreign corporations (section 246A)		see instructions	
	Dividends on certain preferred stock of less-than-20%-owned public utilities		23.3	
5	Dividends on certain preferred stock of 20%-or-more-owned public utilities		26.7	
6	Dividends from less-than-20%-owned foreign corporations		50	
	Dividends from 20%-or-more-owned foreign corporations		65	
8	**Subtotal.** Add lines 1 through 7. See instructions for limitation		see instructions	
9	Dividends from foreign corporations not included on line 3, 6, or 7			
0	IC-DISC and former DISC dividends not included on line 1, 2, or 3 (section 246(d))			
	Other dividends			
12	Deduction for dividends paid on certain preferred stock of public utilities			
3	**Total dividends.** Add column (a), lines 8 through 11. Enter here and on line 4, page 4			
14	**Total special deductions.** Add column (c), lines 8 and 12. Enter here and on line 30b, page 4			

Schedule J Tax Computation (see instructions)

	Check if the corporation is a member of a controlled group (attach Schedule O (Form 1120)) ☐				
2	Income tax			2	
3	Base erosion minimum tax amount (attach Form 8991)			3	
	Add lines 2 and 3				
5a	Foreign tax credit (attach Form 1118)	5a			
b	General business credit (attach Form 3800)	5b			
c	Credit for prior year minimum tax (attach Form 8827)	5c			
d	Bond credits from Form 8912	5d			
6	**Total credits.** Add lines 5a through 5d			6	
	Subtract line 6 from line 4				
8	Other taxes. Check if from: ☐ Form 4255 ☐ Form 8611 ☐ Form 8697 ☐ Form 8866 ☐ Form 8902 ☐ Other (attach statement)			8	
9	**Total tax.** Add lines 7 and 8. Enter here and on line 2, page 1			9	

Form **1120-F** (2022)

Form 1120-F (2021) Page **6**

SECTION III—Branch Profits Tax and Tax on Excess Interest

Part I—Branch Profits Tax (see instructions)

1	Enter the amount from Section II, line 29	1	
2	Enter total adjustments to line 1 to get effectively connected earnings and profits. (Attach required statement showing the nature and amount of adjustments.) (See instructions.)	2	
3	Effectively connected earnings and profits. Combine line 1 and line 2	3	
4a	Enter U.S. net equity at the end of the current tax year. (Attach required statement.)	4a	
b	Enter U.S. net equity at the end of the prior tax year. (Attach required statement.)	4b	
c	Increase in U.S. net equity. If line 4a is greater than or equal to line 4b, subtract line 4b from line 4a. Enter the result here and skip to line 4e	4c	
d	Decrease in U.S. net equity. If line 4b is greater than line 4a, subtract line 4a from line 4b	4d	
e	Non-previously taxed accumulated effectively connected earnings and profits. Enter excess, if any, of effectively connected earnings and profits for preceding tax years beginning after 1986 over any dividend equivalent amounts for those tax years	4e	
5	Dividend equivalent amount. Subtract line 4c from line 3. If zero or less, enter -0-. If no amount is entered on line 4c, add the lesser of line 4d or line 4e to line 3 and enter the total here	5	
6	**Branch profits tax.** Multiply line 5 by 30% (0.30) (or lower treaty rate if the corporation is a qualified resident or otherwise qualifies for treaty benefits). (See instructions.) Enter here and include on line 3, page 1. **Also complete item W on page 2**	6	

Part II—Tax on Excess Interest (see instructions for this Part and for Schedule I (Form 1120-F))

a	Enter the interest from Section II, line 18	a	
b	Enter the inverse of the total amount deferred, capitalized, and disallowed from Schedule I, line 24g (i.e., if line 24g is negative, enter as a positive number; if line 24g is positive, enter as a negative number)	b	
c	Combine lines 7a and 7b (amount must equal Schedule I, line 23)	c	
8	**Branch Interest** (see instructions for definition): Enter the sum of Schedule I, line 9, column (c), and Schedule I, line 22. If the interest paid by the foreign corporation's U.S. trade or business was increased because 80% or more of the foreign corporation's assets are U.S. assets, check this box ▶ ☐	8	
9a	Excess interest. Subtract line 8 from line 7c. If zero or less, enter -0-	9a	
b	If the foreign corporation is a bank, enter the excess interest treated as interest on deposits (see instructions for rules for computing this amount). Otherwise, enter -0-	9b	
c	Subtract line 9b from line 9a	9c	
0	**Tax on excess interest.** Multiply line 9c by 30% (0.30) (or lower treaty rate if the corporation is a qualified resident or otherwise qualifies for treaty benefits). (See instructions.) Enter here and include on line 3, page 1. **Also complete item W on page 2**	0	

Part III—Additional Information

		Yes	No
	Is the corporation claiming a reduction in, or exemption from, the branch profits tax due to:		
a	A complete termination of all U.S. trades or businesses?		
b	The tax-free liquidation or reorganization of a foreign corporation?		
c	The tax-free incorporation of a U.S. trade or business?		
	If a or b applies and the transferee is a domestic corporation, attach Form 8848. If c applies, attach the statement required by Temporary Regulations section 1.884-2T(d)(5).		

Form **1120-F** (2021)

外国法人確定申告書・2022年分の作成

Form 1120-F (2022) Page **7**

Note: *Check if completing on* ☐ U.S. basis or ☐ Worldwide basis

Schedule L **Balance Sheets per Books**

		Beginning of tax year		End of tax year	
	Assets	(a)	(b)	(c)	(d)
	Cash				
2a	Trade notes and accounts receivable				
b	Less allowance for bad debts	( )		( )	
3	Inventories				
	U.S. government obligations				
5	Tax-exempt securities (see instructions)				
6a	Interbranch current assets*				
b	Other current non-U.S. assets*				
c	Other current U.S. assets*				
7	Loans to shareholders				
8	Mortgage and real estate loans				
9a	Other loans and investments—non-U.S. assets*				
b	Other loans and investments—U.S. assets*				
10a	Buildings and other depreciable assets				
b	Less accumulated depreciation	( )		( )	
11a	Depletable assets				
b	Less accumulated depletion	( )		( )	
12	Land (net of any amortization)				
3a	Intangible assets (amortizable only)				
b	Less accumulated amortization	( )		( )	
	Assets held in trust				
5	Other non-current interbranch assets*				
16a	Other non-current non-U.S. assets*				
b	Other non-current U.S. assets*				
17	Total assets				
	Liabilities				
18	Accounts payable				
9	Mortgages, notes, bonds payable in less than 1 year:				
a	Interbranch liabilities*				
b	Third-party liabilities*				
20	Other current liabilities*				
2	Loans from shareholders				
22	Mortgages, notes, bonds payable in 1 year or more:				
a	Interbranch liabilities*				
b	Third-party liabilities*				
23	Liabilities held in trust				
24a	Other interbranch liabilities*				
b	Other third-party liabilities*				
	Equity				
25	Capital stock: **a** Preferred stock				
	b Common stock				
26	Additional paid-in capital				
2	Retained earnings—Appropriated*				
28	Retained earnings—Unappropriated				
29	Adjustments to shareholders' equity*				
30	Less cost of treasury stock		( )		( )
3	Total liabilities and shareholders' equity				

*Attach statement—see instructions.

Form **1120-F** (2022)

Form 1120-F (2022) Page 8

Schedule W	Overpayment Resulting From Tax Deducted and Withheld Under Chapters 3 and 4				
1	**Total Chapter 3 and 4 payments.** Enter the amount from page 1, line 5i			1	㉞ 27000
2	Enter the tax amount from page 1, line 1	2	㉟ 0		
3	Enter the portion of the tax amount shown on page 1, line 2, pertaining to income associated with amounts deducted and withheld under sections 1445 and 1446 (see instructions for general guidelines)	3			
4	**Total Chapter 3 and 4 tax.** Combine lines 2 and 3			4	㊱ 27000
5	**Tentative overpayment resulting from tax deducted and withheld under Chapters 3 and 4.** Subtract line 4 from line 1			5	㊲ 0
6	Enter the amount from page 1, line 8a			6	㊳ 27000
7	**Overpayment resulting from tax deducted and withheld under Chapters 3 and 4.** Enter the smaller of line 5 or line 6. Enter the result here and on page 1, line 8b			7	㊴ 27000

Form **1120-F** (2022)

Schedule W 税額控除とChapters 3及び4の規定による源泉徴収後の過大納付額

1 Chapters 3及び4の規定による源泉徴収税額 ㉞ **（27000を記入）**

2 Page 1のline 1の税額を記入 ㉟ **（0を記入）**

3 Page 1のline 2の税額を記入

4 Chapters 3及び4の規定による源泉徴収税額の合計額 ㊱ **（27000を記入）**

5 仮の税額控除とChapters 3及び4の規定による仮の源泉徴収後の課題納付額 ㊲ **（0を記入）**

6 Page 1のline 8aの税額を記入 ㊳ **（27000を記入）**

7 税額控除とChapters 3及び4の規定による源泉徴収後の課題納付額 ㊴ **（27000を記入）**

その他資料（⑫と⑬を記入する際の資料）
（Business activity code numberとBusiness activity）

Principal Business Activity Codes

This list of principal business activities and their associated codes is designed to classify an enterprise by the type of activity in which it is engaged to facilitate the administration of the Internal Revenue Code. These principal business activity codes are based on the North American Industry Classification System.

Using the list of activities and codes below, determine from which activity the company derives the largest percentage of its "total receipts." Total receipts is defined as the sum of gross receipts or sales (page 1, line 1a) plus all other income (page 1, lines 4 through 10). If the company purchases raw materials and supplies them to a subcontractor to produce the finished product, but retains title to the product, the company is considered a manufacturer and must use one of the manufacturing codes (311110–339900).

Once the principal business activity is determined, entries must be made on Form 1120, Schedule K, lines 2a, 2b, and 2c. On line 2a, enter the six-digit code selected from the list below. On line 2b, enter the company's business activity. On line 2c, enter a brief description of the principal product or service of the company.

Agriculture, Forestry, Fishing, and Hunting

Crop Production

111100 Oilseed & Grain Farming
111210 Vegetable & Melon Farming (including potatoes & yams)
111300 Fruit & Tree Nut Farming
111400 Greenhouse, Nursery, & Floriculture Production
111900 Other Crop Farming (including tobacco, cotton, sugarcane, hay, peanut, sugar beet, & all other crop farming)

Animal Production

112111 Beef Cattle Ranching & Farming
112112 Cattle Feedlots
112120 Dairy Cattle & Milk Production
112210 Hog & Pig Farming
112300 Poultry & Egg Production
112400 Sheep & Goat Farming
112510 Aquaculture (including shellfish & finfish farms & hatcheries)
112900 Other Animal Production

Forestry and Logging

113110 Timber Tract Operations
113210 Forest Nurseries & Gathering of Forest Products
113310 Logging

Fishing, Hunting, and Trapping

114110 Fishing
114210 Hunting & Trapping

Support Activities for Agriculture and Forestry

115110 Support Activities for Crop Production (including cotton ginning, soil preparation, planting, & cultivating)
115210 Support Activities for Animal Production (including farriers)
115310 Support Activities for Forestry

Mining

211120 Crude Petroleum Extraction
211130 Natural Gas Extraction
212110 Coal Mining
212200 Metal Ore Mining
212310 Stone Mining & Quarrying
212320 Sand, Gravel, Clay, & Ceramic & Refractory Minerals Mining & Quarrying
212390 Other Nonmetallic Mineral Mining & Quarrying
213110 Support Activities for Mining

Utilities

221100 Electric Power Generation, Transmission & Distribution
221210 Natural Gas Distribution
221300 Water, Sewage & Other Systems
221500 Combination Gas & Electric

Construction

Construction of Buildings

236110 Residential Building Construction
236200 Nonresidential Building Construction

Heavy and Civil Engineering Construction

237100 Utility System Construction
237210 Land Subdivision
237310 Highway, Street, & Bridge Construction
237990 Other Heavy & Civil Engineering Construction

Specialty Trade Contractors

238100 Foundation, Structure, & Building Exterior Contractors (including framing carpentry, masonry, glass, roofing, & siding)
238210 Electrical Contractors
238220 Plumbing, Heating, & Air-Conditioning Contractors
238290 Other Building Equipment Contractors
238300 Building Finishing Contractors (including drywall, insulation, painting, wallcovering, flooring, tile, & finish carpentry)
238900 Other Specialty Trade Contractors (including site preparation)

Manufacturing

Food Manufacturing

311110 Animal Food Mfg
311200 Grain & Oilseed Milling
311300 Sugar & Confectionery Product Mfg
311400 Fruit & Vegetable Preserving & Specialty Food Mfg
311500 Dairy Product Mfg
311610 Animal Slaughtering and Processing
311710 Seafood Product Preparation & Packaging
311800 Bakeries, Tortilla & Dry Pasta Mfg
311900 Other Food Mfg (including coffee, tea, flavorings & seasonings)

Beverage and Tobacco Product Manufacturing

312110 Soft Drink & Ice Mfg
312120 Breweries
312130 Wineries
312140 Distilleries
312200 Tobacco Manufacturing

Textile Mills and Textile Product Mills

313000 Textile Mills
314000 Textile Product Mills

Apparel Manufacturing

315100 Apparel Knitting Mills
315210 Cut & Sew Apparel Contractors
315250 Cut & Sew Apparel Mfg (except Contractors)
315990 Apparel Accessories & Other Apparel Mfg

Leather and Allied Product Manufacturing

316110 Leather & Hide Tanning & Finishing
316210 Footwear Mfg (including rubber & plastics)
316990 Other Leather & Allied Product Mfg

Wood Product Manufacturing

321110 Sawmills & Wood Preservation
321210 Veneer, Plywood, & Engineered Wood Product Mfg
321900 Other Wood Product Mfg

Paper Manufacturing

322100 Pulp, Paper, & Paperboard Mills
322200 Converted Paper Product Mfg

Printing and Related Support Activities

323100 Printing & Related Support Activities

Petroleum and Coal Products Manufacturing

324110 Petroleum Refineries (including integrated)
324120 Asphalt Paving, Roofing, & Saturated Materials Mfg
324190 Other Petroleum & Coal Products Mfg

Chemical Manufacturing

325100 Basic Chemical Mfg
325200 Resin, Synthetic Rubber, & Artificial & Synthetic Fibers & Filaments Mfg
325300 Pesticide, Fertilizer, & Other Agricultural Chemical Mfg
325410 Pharmaceutical & Medicine Mfg
325500 Paint, Coating, & Adhesive Mfg
325600 Soap, Cleaning Compound, & Toilet Preparation Mfg
325900 Other Chemical Product & Preparation Mfg

Plastics and Rubber Products Manufacturing

326100 Plastics Product Mfg
326200 Rubber Product Mfg

Nonmetallic Mineral Product Manufacturing

327100 Clay Product & Refractory Mfg
327210 Glass & Glass Product Mfg
327300 Cement & Concrete Product Mfg
327400 Lime & Gypsum Product Mfg
327900 Other Nonmetallic Mineral Product Mfg

Primary Metal Manufacturing

331110 Iron & Steel Mills & Ferroalloy Mfg
331200 Steel Product Mfg from Purchased Steel
331310 Alumina & Aluminum Production & Processing
331400 Nonferrous Metal (except Aluminum) Production & Processing
331500 Foundries

Fabricated Metal Product Manufacturing

332110 Forging & Stamping
332210 Cutlery & Handtool Mfg
332300 Architectural & Structural Metals Mfg
332400 Boiler, Tank, & Shipping Container Mfg
332510 Hardware Mfg
332610 Spring & Wire Product Mfg
332700 Machine Shops; Turned Product; & Screw, Nut, & Bolt Mfg
332810 Coating, Engraving, Heat Treating, & Allied Activities
332900 Other Fabricated Metal Product Mfg

Machinery Manufacturing

333100 Agriculture, Construction, & Mining Machinery Mfg
333200 Industrial Machinery Mfg
333310 Commercial & Service Industry Machinery Mfg
333410 Ventilation, Heating, Air-Conditioning, & Commercial Refrigeration Equipment Mfg
333510 Metalworking Machinery Mfg
333610 Engine, Turbine & Power Transmission Equipment Mfg
333900 Other General Purpose Machinery Mfg

Computer and Electronic Product Manufacturing

334110 Computer & Peripheral Equipment Mfg
334200 Communications Equipment Mfg
334310 Audio & Video Equipment Mfg
334410 Semiconductor & Other Electronic Component Mfg
334500 Navigational, Measuring, Electromedical, & Control Instruments Mfg
334610 Manufacturing & Reproducing Magnetic & Optical Media

Electrical Equipment, Appliance, and Component Manufacturing

335100 Electric Lighting Equipment Mfg
335200 Household Appliance Mfg
335310 Electrical Equipment Mfg
335900 Other Electrical Equipment & Component Mfg

Transportation Equipment Manufacturing

336100 Motor Vehicle Mfg
336210 Motor Vehicle Body & Trailer Mfg
336300 Motor Vehicle Parts Mfg
336410 Aerospace Product & Parts Mfg
336510 Railroad Rolling Stock Mfg
336610 Ship & Boat Building
336990 Other Transportation Equipment Mfg

Furniture and Related Product Manufacturing

337000 Furniture & Related Product Manufacturing

Miscellaneous Manufacturing

339110 Medical Equipment & Supplies Mfg
339900 Other Miscellaneous Manufacturing

Wholesale Trade

Merchant Wholesalers, Durable Goods

423100 Motor Vehicle & Motor Vehicle Parts & Supplies
423200 Furniture & Home Furnishings
423300 Lumber & Other Construction Materials
423400 Professional & Commercial Equipment & Supplies
423500 Metal & Mineral (except Petroleum)
423600 Household Appliances and Electrical & Electronic Goods
423700 Hardware, Plumbing, & Heating Equipment & Supplies
423800 Machinery, Equipment, & Supplies
423910 Sporting & Recreational Goods & Supplies
423920 Toy & Hobby Goods & Supplies
423930 Recyclable Materials
423940 Jewelry, Watch, Precious Stone, & Precious Metals
423990 Other Miscellaneous Durable Goods

Merchant Wholesalers, Nondurable Goods

424100 Paper & Paper Products
424210 Drugs & Druggists' Sundries
424300 Apparel, Piece Goods, & Notions
424400 Grocery & Related Products
424500 Farm Product Raw Materials
424600 Chemical & Allied Products
424700 Petroleum & Petroleum Products
424800 Beer, Wine, & Distilled Alcoholic Beverages
424910 Farm Supplies
424920 Book, Periodical, & Newspapers
424930 Flower, Nursery Stock, & Florists' Supplies
424940 Tobacco Products & Electronic Cigarettes
424950 Paint, Varnish, & Supplies
424990 Other Miscellaneous Nondurable Goods

WholesaleTrade Agents and Brokers

425120 Wholesale Trade Agents & Brokers

Retail Trade

Motor Vehicle and Parts Dealers

441110 New Car Dealers
441120 Used Car Dealers
441210 Recreational Vehicle Dealers
441222 Boat Dealers
441227 Motorcycle, ATV, and All Other Motor Vehicle Dealers
441300 Automotive Parts, Accessories, & Tire Retailers

Furniture and Home Furnishings Retailers

449110 Furniture Retailers
449121 Floor Covering Retailers
449122 Window Treatment Retailers
449129 All Other Home Furnishings Retailers

Electronics and Appliance Retailers

449210 Electronics & Appliance Retailers (including Computers)

Building Material and Garden Equipment and Supplies Dealers

444110 Home Centers
444120 Paint & Wallpaper Retailers
444140 Hardware Retailers

その他資料（⓬と⓭を記入する際の資料）

（Business activity code numberとBusiness activity）

Principal Business Activity Codes *(Continued)*

444180 Other Building Material Dealers
444200 Lawn & Garden Equipment & Supplies Retailers

Food and Beverage Retailers

445110 Supermarkets and Other Grocery Retailers (except Convenience)
445131 Convenience Retailers
445132 Vending Machine Operators
445230 Fruit & Vegetable Markets
445240 Meat Retailers
445250 Fish & Seafood Retailers
445291 Baked Goods Retailers
445292 Confectionery & Nut Retailers
445298 All Other Specialty Food Retailers
445320 Beer, Wine, & Liquor Retailers

Health and Personal Care Retailers

456110 Pharmacies & Drug Retailers
456120 Cosmetics, Beauty Supplies, & Perfume Retailers
456130 Optical Goods Retailers
456190 Other Health & Personal Care Retailers

Gasoline Stations & Fuel Dealers

457100 Gasoline Stations (including convenience stores with gas)
457210 Fuel Dealers (including Heating Oil and Liquefied Petroleum)

Clothing and Accessories Retailers

458110 Clothing and Clothing Accessories Retailers
458210 Shoe Retailers
458310 Jewelry Retailers
458320 Luggage & Leather Goods Retailers

Sporting Goods, Hobby, Book, Musical Instrument and Miscellaneous Retailers

459110 Sporting Goods Retailers
459120 Hobby, Toy, & Game Retailers
459130 Sewing, Needlework, & Piece Goods Retailers
459140 Musical Instrument & Supplies Retailers
459210 Book Retailers & News Dealers (including newsstands)
459310 Florists
459410 Office Supplies & Stationery Retailers
459420 Gift, Novelty, & Souvenir Retailers
459510 Used Merchandise Retailers
459910 Pet & Pet Supplies Retailers
459920 Art Dealers
459930 Manufactured (Mobile) Home Dealers
459990 All Other Miscellaneous Retailers (including tobacco, candle, & trophy retailers)

General Merchandise Retailers

455110 Department Stores
455210 Warehouse Clubs, Supercenters, & Other General Merch. Retailers

Nonstore Retailers

Nonstore retailers sell all types of merchandise using such methods as Internet, mail-order catalogs, interactive television, or direct sales. These types of Retailers should select the PBA associated with their primary line of products sold. For example, establishments primarily selling prescription and non-prescription drugs, select PBA code 456110 Pharmacies & Drug Retailers

Transportation and Warehousing

Air, Rail, and Water Transportation

481000 Air Transportation
482110 Rail Transportation
483000 Water Transportation

Truck Transportation

484110 General Freight Trucking, Local
484120 General Freight Trucking, Long-distance
484200 Specialized Freight Trucking

Transit and Ground Passenger Transportation

485110 Urban Transit Systems
485210 Interurban & Rural Bus Transportation
485310 Taxi and Ridesharing Services
485320 Limousine Service
485410 School & Employee Bus Transportation
485510 Charter Bus Industry
485990 Other Transit & Ground Passenger Transportation

Pipeline Transportation

486000 Pipeline Transportation

Scenic & Sightseeing Transportation

487000 Scenic & Sightseeing Transportation

Support Activities for Transportation

488100 Support Activities for Air Transportation
488210 Support Activities for Rail Transportation
488300 Support Activities for Water Transportation
488410 Motor Vehicle Towing
488490 Other Support Activities for Road Transportation
488510 Freight Transportation Arrangement
488990 Other Support Activities for Transportation

Couriers and Messengers

492110 Couriers & Express Delivery Services
492210 Local Messengers & Local Delivery

Warehousing and Storage

493100 Warehousing & Storage (except lessors of miniwarehouses & self-storage units)

Information

Motion Picture and Sound Recording Industries

512100 Motion Picture & Video Industries (except video rental)
512200 Sound Recording Industries

Publishing Industries

513110 Newspaper Publishers
513120 Periodical Publishers
513130 Book Publishers
513140 Directory & Mailing List Publishers
513190 Other Publishers
513210 Software Publishers

Broadcasting, Content Providers, and Telecommunications

516100 Radio & Television Broadcasting Stations
516210 Media Streaming, Social Networks, & Other Content Providers
517000 Telecommunications (including Wired, Wireless, Satellite, Cable & Other Program Distribution, Resellers, Agents, Other Telecommunications, & Internet Service Providers)

Data Processing, Web Search Portals, & Other Information Services

518210 Computing Infrastructure Providers, Data Processing, Web Hosting, & Related Services
519200 Web Search Portals, Libraries, Archives, & Other Info. Services

Finance and Insurance

Depository Credit Intermediation

522110 Commercial Banking
522130 Credit Unions
522180 Savings Institutions & Other Depository Credit Intermediation

Nondepository Credit Intermediation

522210 Credit Card Issuing
522220 Sales Financing
522291 Consumer Lending
522292 Real Estate Credit (including mortgage bankers & originators)
522299 Intl, Secondary Market, & Other Nondepos. Credit Intermediation

Activities Related to Credit Intermediation

522300 Activities Related to Credit Intermediation (including loan brokers, check clearing, & money transmitting)

Securities, Commodity Contracts, and Other Financial Investments and Related Activities

523150 Investment Banking & Securities Intermediation
523160 Commodity Contracts Intermediation
523210 Securities & Commodity Exchanges
523900 Other Financial Investment Activities (including portfolio management & investment advice)

Insurance Carriers and Related Activities

524110 Direct Life, Health, & Medical Insurance Carriers
524120 Direct Insurance (except Life, Health, & Medical) Carriers
524210 Insurance Agencies & Brokerages
524290 Other Insurance Related Activities (including third-party administration of insurance and pension funds)

Funds, Trusts, and Other Financial Vehicles

525100 Insurance & Employee Benefit Funds
525910 Open-End Investment Funds (Form 1120-RIC)
525920 Trusts, Estates, & Agency Accounts
525990 Other Financial Vehicles (including mortgage REITs & closed-end investment funds) "Offices of Bank Holding Companies" and "Offices of Other Holding Companies" are located under **Management of Companies (Holding Companies)**, later.

Real Estate and Rental and Leasing

Real Estate

531110 Lessors of Residential Buildings & Dwellings (including equity REITs)
531120 Lessors of Nonresidential Buildings (except Miniwarehouses) (including equity REITs)
531130 Lessors of Miniwarehouses & Self-Storage Units (including equity REITs)
531190 Lessors of Other Real Estate Property (including equity REITs)
531210 Offices of Real Estate Agents & Brokers
531310 Real Estate Property Managers
531320 Offices of Real Estate Appraisers
531390 Other Activities Related to Real Estate

Rental and Leasing Services

532100 Automotive Equipment Rental & Leasing
532210 Consumer Electronics & Appliances Rental
532281 Formal Wear & Costume Rental
532282 Video Tape & Disc Rental
532283 Home Health Equipment Rental
532284 Recreational Goods Rental
532289 All Other Consumer Goods Rental
532310 General Rental Centers
532400 Commercial & Industrial Machinery & Equipment Rental & Leasing

Lessors of Nonfinancial Intangible Assets (except copyrighted works)

533110 Lessors of Nonfinancial Intangible Assets (except copyrighted works)

Professional, Scientific, and Technical Services

Legal Services

541110 Offices of Lawyers
541190 Other Legal Services

Accounting, Tax Preparation, Bookkeeping, and Payroll Services

541211 Offices of Certified Public Accountants
541213 Tax Preparation Services
541214 Payroll Services
541219 Other Accounting Services

Architectural, Engineering, and Related Services

541310 Architectural Services
541320 Landscape Architecture Services
541330 Engineering Services
541340 Drafting Services
541350 Building Inspection Services
541360 Geophysical Surveying & Mapping Services
541370 Surveying & Mapping (except Geophysical) Services
541380 Testing Laboratories & Services

Specialized Design Services

541400 Specialized Design Services (including interior, industrial, graphic, & fashion design)

Computer Systems Design and Related Services

541511 Custom Computer Programming Services
541512 Computer Systems Design Services
541513 Computer Facilities Management Services
541519 Other Computer Related Services

Other Professional, Scientific, and Technical Services

541600 Management, Scientific, & Technical Consulting Services
541700 Scientific Research & Development Services
541800 Advertising, Public Relations, & Related Services
541910 Marketing Research & Public Opinion Polling
541920 Photographic Services
541930 Translation & Interpretation Services
541940 Veterinary Services
541990 All Other Professional, Scientific, & Technical Services

Management of Companies (Holding Companies)

551111 Offices of Bank Holding Companies
551112 Offices of Other Holding Companies

Administrative and Support and Waste Management and Remediation Services

Administrative and Support Services

561110 Office Administrative Services
561210 Facilities Support Services
561300 Employment Services
561410 Document Preparation Services
561420 Telephone Call Centers
561430 Business Service Centers (including private mail centers & copy shops)
561440 Collection Agencies
561450 Credit Bureaus
561490 Other Business Support Services (including repossession services, court reporting, & stenotype services)
561500 Travel Arrangement & Reservation Services
561600 Investigation & Security Services
561710 Exterminating & Pest Control Services
561720 Janitorial Services
561730 Landscaping Services
561740 Carpet & Upholstery Cleaning Services
561790 Other Services to Buildings & Dwellings
561900 Other Support Services (including packaging & labeling services, & convention & trade show organizers)

Waste Management and Remediation Services

562000 Waste Management & Remediation Services

Educational Services

611000 Educational Services (including schools, colleges, & universities)

Health Care and Social Assistance

Offices of Physicians and Dentists

621111 Offices of Physicians (except mental health specialists)
621112 Offices of Physicians, Mental Health Specialists
621210 Offices of Dentists

その他資料（⑫と⑬を記入する際の資料）
（Business activity code numberとBusiness activity）

Principal Business Activity Codes *(Continued)*

Offices of Other Health Practitioners
621310 Offices of Chiropractors
621320 Offices of Optometrists
621330 Offices of Mental Health Practitioners (except Physicians)
621340 Offices of Physical, Occupational & Speech Therapists, & Audiologists
621391 Offices of Podiatrists
621399 Offices of All Other Miscellaneous Health Practitioners

Outpatient Care Centers
621410 Family Planning Centers
621420 Outpatient Mental Health & Substance Abuse Centers
621491 HMO Medical Centers
621492 Kidney Dialysis Centers
621493 Freestanding Ambulatory Surgical & Emergency Centers
621498 All Other Outpatient Care Centers

Medical and Diagnostic Laboratories
621510 Medical & Diagnostic Laboratories

Home Health Care Services
621610 Home Health Care Services

Other Ambulatory Health Care Services
621900 Other Ambulatory Health Care Services (including ambulance services & blood & organ banks)

Hospitals
622000 Hospitals

Nursing and Residential Care Facilities
623000 Nursing & Residential Care Facilities

Social Assistance
624100 Individual & Family Services
624200 Community Food & Housing, & Emergency & Other Relief Services
624310 Vocational Rehabilitation Services
624410 Childcare Services

Arts, Entertainment, and Recreation

Performing Arts, Spectator Sports, and Related Industries
711100 Performing Arts Companies
711210 Spectator Sports (including sports clubs & racetracks)
711300 Promoters of Performing Arts, Sports, & Similar Events
711410 Agents & Managers for Artists, Athletes, Entertainers, & Other Public Figures
711510 Independent Artists, Writers, & Performers

Museums, Historical Sites, and Similar Institutions
712100 Museums, Historical Sites, & Similar Institutions

Amusement, Gambling, and Recreation Industries
713100 Amusement Parks & Arcades
713200 Gambling Industries
713900 Other Amusement & Recreation Industries (including golf courses, skiing facilities, marinas, fitness centers, & bowling centers)

Accommodation and Food Services

Accommodation
721110 Hotels (except Casino Hotels) & Motels
721120 Casino Hotels
721191 Bed & Breakfast Inns
721199 All Other Traveler Accommodation
721210 RV (Recreational Vehicle) Parks & Recreational Camps
721310 Rooming & Boarding Houses, Dormitories, & Workers' Camps

Food Services and Drinking Places
722300 Special Food Services (including food service contractors & caterers)
722410 Drinking Places (Alcoholic Beverages)
722511 Full-Service Restaurants
722513 Limited-Service Restaurants
722514 Cafeterias, Grill Buffets, and Buffets
722515 Snack and Non-alcoholic Beverage Bars

Other Services

Repair and Maintenance
811110 Automotive Mechanical & Electrical Repair & Maintenance
811120 Automotive Body, Paint, Interior, & Glass Repair
811190 Other Automotive Repair & Maintenance (including oil change & lubrication shops & car washes)
811210 Electronic & Precision Equipment Repair & Maintenance
811310 Commercial & Industrial Machinery & Equipment (except Automotive & Electronic) Repair & Maintenance
811410 Home & Garden Equipment & Appliance Repair & Maintenance
811420 Reupholstery & Furniture Repair
811430 Footwear & Leather Goods Repair
811490 Other Personal & Household Goods Repair & Maintenance

Personal and Laundry Services
812111 Barber Shops
812112 Beauty Salons
812113 Nail Salons
812190 Other Personal Care Services (including diet & weight reducing centers)
812210 Funeral Homes & Funeral Services
812220 Cemeteries & Crematories
812310 Coin-Operated Laundries & Drycleaners
812320 Drycleaning & Laundry Services (except Coin-Operated)
812330 Linen & Uniform Supply
812910 Pet Care (except Veterinary) Services
812920 Photofinishing
812930 Parking Lots & Garages
812990 All Other Personal Services

Religious, Grantmaking, Civic, Professional, and Similar Organizations
813000 Religious, Grantmaking, Civic, Professional, & Similar Organizations (including condominium and homeowners associations)

Other
999000 Unclassified Establishments (unable to classify)

国際税務に関するトピック

国際的なシェアリングエコノミーと自動的情報交換

国際的なシェアリングエコノミーと自動的情報交換

国税庁はシェアリングエコノミー等新分野の経済活動への的確な対応について、令和元年6月にアナウンスしたところですが、経済取引のグローバル化が進展する中で、海外のプラットフォーマーを仲介人とし国境を超える国際的なシェアリングエコノミー取引が恒常的に行われ、複雑化・多様化していることから、当該取引から生じる所得に対し適正公平な課税を行うために、納税者の情報収集のための諸外国との自動的情報交換を活用することが予想されています。

1　シェアリングエコノミーとは

シェアリングエコノミーとは、物・サービス・場所などを多くの人と共有・交換して利用する社会的な仕組みで、共有型経済といわれるものです。

シェアリングエコノミーのサービスはプラットフォーマー（シェア事業者）、サービス提供者、サービス利用者の三者から構成されておりシェア事業者を介してサービスの提供が行われます。

[シェアリングエコノミーのイメージ]

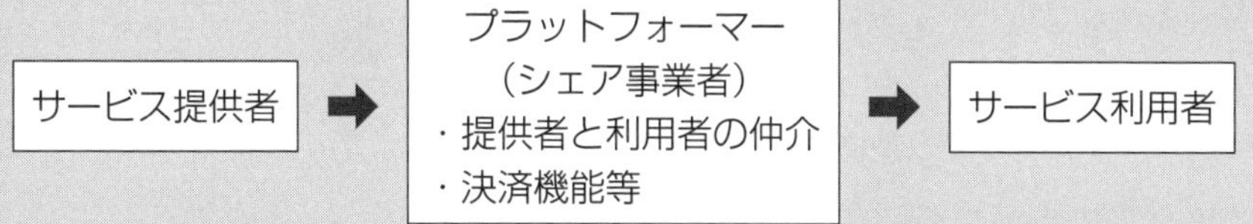

シェアリングエコノミーのサービスには、ネットオークションやフリマーケットアプリを利用した売買などを始めとして、次の取引があります。

(1)　衣類・雑貨・家電などの資産の売買

(2)　自家用車・不動産などの貸付

(3)　ベビーシッターや家庭教師などの派遣等

(4)　民泊施設の賃貸

2　国税庁とシェアリングエコノミー

国税庁はシェアリングエコノミーは次の特徴を有していると分析しており、国内のみならず、国際的にも、適正課税の確保に向けた取組や制度的対応の必要性が課題であるとして適正申告のための環境作りと、情報収集を拡充しています。

⑴　広域的・国際的な取引が比較的容易である

⑵　足が速い

⑶　無店舗形態の取引やヒト・モノの移動を伴わない取引も存在するなど外観上、取引の実態が分かりにくい

⑷　申告手続等に馴染みのない方も参入が容易である

3　国際的なシェアリングエコノミーに対する情報収集

経済取引のグローバル化が進展する中で、海外のプラットフォーマー（シェア事業者）を仲介人とし国境を超える国際的なシェアリングエコノミー取引が恒常的に行われ、複雑化・多様化しています。

国税庁は、国際的なシェアリングエコノミーから生じる所得に対する租税の賦課徴収を確実に行うためには、国内で入手できる情報だけでなく、国外にある情報を適切に入手することが重要となります。

特に、海外のプラットフォーマー事業者を介して行われる取引に関する我が国の所得者の情報を入手する必要があります。

国外にある情報を入手するには外国の主権（執行管轄権）により制約を受けることから、我が国を含め、各国の税務当局は租税条約等に基づき租税に関する情報を互いに提供する仕組み（情報交換）により、売主に関する情報の入手を行うことになります。

4　今後想定される情報交換の活用

情報交換には、次の⑴〜⑶の形態がありますが、経済協力開発機構（OECD）租税委員会による国際的なモデルルールの策定、また、昨年の政府税制調査会の議論から⑶の自動的情報交換の活用が予想されています。

国内はもちろんのこと海外のプラットフォーマーを利用して所得を得た納税者は、今後、適正な申告が求められます。

⑴　要請に基づく情報交換

課税当局が調査において課税上の問題点を把握した場合に、その問題に関連する情報の提供を求めるもの

⑵　自発的情報交換

課税当局が調査において外国における課税上の問題点を把握した場合に、その問題を提供するもの

⑶　自動的情報交換

課税当局が法定調書等から情報を収集し、大量に情報を提供するもの

9　非居住者確定申告書（Form 1040-NR）の作成手順

演習事例32

米国で源泉徴収された税金の還付方法

私は個人でゲームソフトの制作を行っており、米国のゲームソフト販売会社（ABC.INC）にゲームソフトを提供し、同販売会社から著作権の使用料（ゲームソフトの使用料）の支払いを受けておりました。

しかし、日米租税条約に基づく免税の手続きを失念しており、ゲームソフトの使用料支払いの際に、30%の税率により源泉所得税が課税されました。

なお、源泉徴収された税額は使用料の支払日の年分の費用としております。

源泉徴収された税金については、ある一定期間は、源泉徴収義務者に還付請求ができると聞きましたが、既に、その期間が経過しております。

米国の源泉所得の還付を受ける方法がありますでしょうか。

ご教示をお願いいたします。

また、私は米国に、事業を行う事務所等はありません。

現在、次の源泉所得税が徴収されております。

源泉徴収税額の明細

（年度）	（収入金額）	（税率）	（源泉徴収税額）
2022	150,000ドル	30%	45,000ドル
		合計	45,000ドル

回答

貴方に支払われた映像の使用料は、著作権の使用料に該当し、米国の国内法により支払いの際に、30%の税率により課税が行われています。

日米租税条約により著作権の使用料は免税とされていますので、ある一定期間は、源泉徴収義務者に還付請求ができますが、既に、その期間が経過している場合には、米国歳入庁（Internal Revenue Service）に対し非居住者確定申告書（Form 1040-NR）を提出し還付を受けます。

解説

1　米国における非居住者（個人）と外国法人等（会社等）に対する源泉徴収制度

米国の国内法では、源泉徴収義務者（Withholding agent）は源泉徴収の対象となる所得（Fixed or determinable annual or periodicalincome・以下「FDAP」と

いいます。）を支払う際に30%の税率により所得税を徴収します。

ただし、日米租税条約による税額の軽減・免除の対象となる者については、税額の軽減・免除を行うこととされています。

税額の軽減又は免除を受ける場合には、源泉徴収義務者に対し租税条約の恩典を受ける者であることを証明するForm W-8BEN（個人用）を提出する必要があります。

2　源泉徴収された税金の還付方法

⑴　源泉徴収義務者（Withholding agent）の報告義務

源泉徴収義務者は、源泉徴収した翌年の3月15日までに、源泉徴収した事績を記載したForm 1042-S（我が国の法定調書に該当）を米国の国税庁（IRS）に一部を提出し、FDEPの受領者（Recipient）に対し3部交付しなければなりません。

一部は、源泉徴収義務者が保管することになります。

Form 1042-Sの提出先

Copy A・・・・・・・・・・・ IRSへ提出（1部）

Copy B〜Copy D・・・・・・受領者へ交付（3部）

Copy E・・・・・・・・・・・ 源泉徴収義務者保管（1部）

⑵　源泉徴収義務者に対する還付手続き

上記⑴のForm 1042-S（我が国の法定調書に該当）の報告期限（翌年3月15日）前であれば、源泉徴収義務者に対しForm W-8BEN（個人の場合）を提出し源泉徴収義務者から徴収税額の還付を受けます。

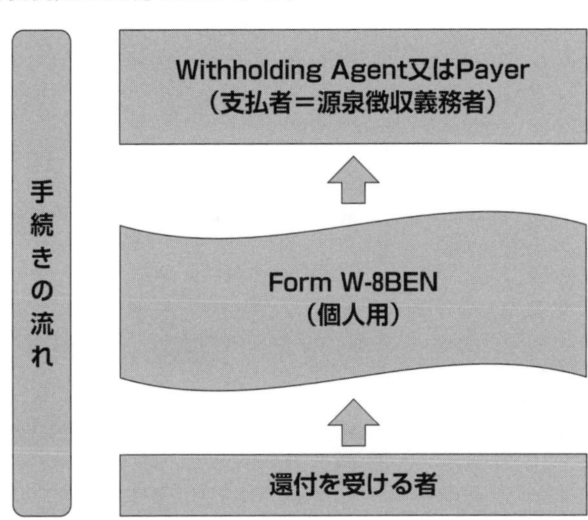

⑶　米国歳入庁（Internal Revenue Services）に対する還付請求

上記2の報告期限（翌年3月15日）後は、IRSから納税者番号を取得（米国で所得が発生する場合は既に取得済）し、Form 1120-Fにより確定申告を行い還付を受けることになります。

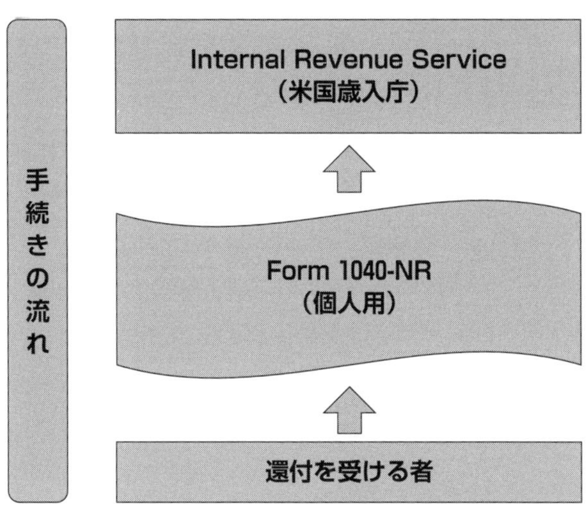

（出典） Instruction for Form 1040-NR (2022): Simplified Procedure for Claiming Certain Refunds

還付申告の際の留意点

1　納税者番号（個人用）の取得

米国において確定（還付）申告を行う場合には、Individual Tax Payer Identification Number（納税者番号）が必要となります。

未取得の場合には、IRS に申請を行い、取得する必要があります。

2　申告書の送付先

Department of the Treasury Internal Revenue Service Austin, TX 73301-0215 U.S.A

3　申告書の送付方法

送付先は私書箱であることから、いつ投函されたかが重要となります。

配送業者は日本の郵便局の EMS サービスを利用すれば、日本から約 3 日間で私書箱に投函されるとのことです。

4　申告書の提出期限について

還付申告書は、申告期限の翌日から三年を経過する日までは提出することができますので、還付申告が過去の複数の事業年度にわたる場合には、申告期限に注意しなければなりません。

5　還付時期について

還付金額は、米国財務省発行の小切手が送金されます。

小切手の金額と還付申告書の還付税額を照合することにより、還付金額が正しいことを確認します。

6　還付された源泉所得税について

還付された源泉所得税については、その還付されることとなった日の属する年分の収入とします。

Form 1042-NR（非居住者確定申告書）作成までの手続き

手続1

＝＝＝＝＝＝＝＝＝＝＝＝法定調書（源泉徴収の証明）の準備＝＝＝＝＝＝＝＝＝＝＝＝

源泉徴収義務者がIRS（米国歳入庁）に対し提出した源泉徴収の事実を証明するForm 1042-S（Foreign Person's U.S Source Income Subject to Withholding）のCopyB～CopyDを準備します。

手続2

＝＝＝＝＝＝＝＝＝＝＝＝＝＝Form W-8BENの作成＝＝＝＝＝＝＝＝＝＝＝＝＝＝

納税者が日米租税条約による恩典を受ける者であることを申告するためのForm W-8BEN（Certificate of Foreign Status of Beneficial Owner for United States Tax Withholding and Reporting（Induvidual））を作成します。

手続3

＝＝＝＝＝＝＝＝＝＝＝＝＝＝＝Form 8833の作成＝＝＝＝＝＝＝＝＝＝＝＝＝＝＝

申告をする者が日米租税条約の適用を受けるために申告を行うものであることを明確にするためのForm 8833（Treaty-Based Return Position Disclosure）を作成します。

手続4

＝＝＝＝＝＝＝＝＝＝＝＝＝＝＝居住者証明書の取得＝＝＝＝＝＝＝＝＝＝＝＝＝＝＝

申告をする者が日本の居住者であることを証明するために、所轄の税務署長宛に「居住者証明書交付請求書」を提出し、「居住者証明書」を取得します。

（注）「居住者証明書」は無料で交付されます。

手続5

＝＝＝＝＝＝＝＝＝＝＝米国歳入庁（IRS）宛のレターの作成＝＝＝＝＝＝＝＝＝＝

手続6

＝＝＝＝＝＝＝＝＝＝＝＝＝非居住者確定申告書の作成＝＝＝＝＝＝＝＝＝＝＝＝

確定申告書Form 1040-NR（U.S Nonresident Alian Income Tax Return）を作成します。（複数年度に及ぶ場合は複数年度分）

手続1

法定調書（源泉徴収の証明）の準備
（2022年度分の Form 1042-S）

Form **1042-S** Department of the Treasury Internal Revenue Service

Foreign Person's U.S. Source Income Subject to Withholding **2022**

▶ Go to *www.irs.gov/Form1042S* for instructions and the latest information.

UNIQUE FORM IDENTIFIER ☐ AMENDED ☐ AMENDMENT NO.

OMB No. 1545-0096

Copy B for Recipient

1 Income code	12
2 Gross income	150000
3 Chapter indicator. Enter "3" or "4"	3
3a Exemption code	
3b Tax rate	30 . 00
4a Exemption code	
4b Tax rate	.
5 Withholding allowance	
6 Net income	
7a Federal tax withheld	45000
7b Check if federal tax withheld was not deposited with the IRS because escrow procedures were applied (see instructions)	☐
7c Check if withholding occurred in subsequent year with respect to a partnership interest	☐
8 Tax withheld by other agents	
9 Overwithheld tax repaid to recipient pursuant to adjustment procedures (see instructions)	( )
10 Total withholding credit (combine boxes 7a, 8, and 9)	45000
11 Tax paid by withholding agent (amounts not withheld) (see instructions)	
12a Withholding agent's EIN	XX-XXXXXXX
12b Ch. 3 status code	15
12c Ch. 4 status code	
12d Withholding agent's name	ABC.INC
12e Withholding agent's Global Intermediary Identification Number (GIIN)	
12f Country code	
12g Foreign tax identification number, if any	
12h Address (number and street)	POBOX XX-XXXXXXX
12i City or town, state or province, country, ZIP or foreign postal code	XX-XXXXXXX
13a Recipient's name	YAMADA・・・・・
13b Recipient's country code	JP
13c Address (number and street)	xxx,xxxxxxx
13d City or town, state or province, country, ZIP or foreign postal code	Tokyo,101-0047 JAPAN
13e Recipient's U.S. TIN, if any	
13f Ch. 3 status code	
13g Ch. 4 status code	
13h Recipient's GIIN	
13i Recipient's foreign tax identification number, if any	
13j LOB code	
13k Recipient's account number	
13l Recipient's date of birth (YYYYMMDD)	
14a Primary Withholding Agent's Name (if applicable)	
14b Primary Withholding Agent's EIN	
15 Check if pro-rata basis reporting	☐
15a Intermediary or flow-through entity's EIN, if any	
15b Ch. 3 status code	
15c Ch. 4 status code	
15d Intermediary or flow-through entity's name	
15e Intermediary or flow-through entity's GIIN	
15f Country code	
15g Foreign tax identification number, if any	
15h Address (number and street)	
15i City or town, state or province, country, ZIP or foreign postal code	
16a Payer's name	
16b Payer's TIN	
16c Payer's GIIN	
16d Ch. 3 status code	
16e Ch. 4 status code	
17a State income tax withheld	0
17b Payer's state tax no.	
17c Name of state	

(keep for your records) Form **1042-S** (2022)

手続1

法定調書（源泉徴収の証明）の準備
（2022年度分の Form 1042-S）

Form **1042-S** Department of the Treasury Internal Revenue Service

Foreign Person's U.S. Source Income Subject to Withholding **2022**

► Go to *www.irs.gov/Form1042S* for instructions and the latest information.

UNIQUE FORM IDENTIFIER ☐ AMENDED ☐ AMENDMENT NO.

OMB No. 1545-0096

Copy C for Recipient

Attach to any Federal tax return you file

1 Income code	2 Gross income	3 Chapter indicator. Enter "3" or "4"	3
		3a Exemption code	4a Exemption code
12	150000	3b Tax rate 30 . 00	4b Tax rate .

5 Withholding allowance

6 Net income

7a Federal tax withheld 45000

7b Check if federal tax withheld was not deposited with the IRS because escrow procedures were applied (see instructions) . . . . . . ☐

7c Check if withholding occurred in subsequent year with respect to a partnership interest . . . . ☐

8 Tax withheld by other agents

9 Overwithheld tax repaid to recipient pursuant to adjustment procedures (see instructions)

( )

10 Total withholding credit (combine boxes 7a, 8, and 9) 45000

11 Tax paid by withholding agent (amounts not withheld) (see instructions)

12a Withholding agent's EIN	12b Ch. 3 status code	12c Ch. 4 status code
XX-XXXXXXX	15	

12d Withholding agent's name

ABC. INC

12e Withholding agent's Global Intermediary Identification Number (GIIN)

12f Country code	12g Foreign tax identification number, if any

12h Address (number and street)

POBOX XX-XXXXXXX

12i City or town, state or province, country, ZIP or foreign postal code

XX-XXXXXXX

13a Recipient's name	13b Recipient's country code
YAMADA・・・・・	

13c Address (number and street)

xxx,xxxxxxx

13d City or town, state or province, country, ZIP or foreign postal code

Tokyo,101-0047 JAPAN

13e Recipient's U.S. TIN, if any	13f Ch. 3 status code
	13g Ch. 4 status code

13h Recipient's GIIN	13i Recipient's foreign tax identification number, if any	13j LOB code

13k Recipient's account number

13l Recipient's date of birth (YYYYMMDD)

☐☐☐☐☐☐☐☐

14a Primary Withholding Agent's Name (if applicable)

14b Primary Withholding Agent's EIN

15 Check if pro-rata basis reporting ☐

15a Intermediary or flow-through entity's EIN, if any	15b Ch. 3 status code	15c Ch. 4 status code

15d Intermediary or flow-through entity's name

15e Intermediary or flow-through entity's GIIN

15f Country code	15g Foreign tax identification number, if any

15h Address (number and street)

15i City or town, state or province, country, ZIP or foreign postal code

16a Payer's name	16b Payer's TIN

16c Payer's GIIN	16d Ch. 3 status code	16e Ch. 4 status code

17a State income tax withheld	17b Payer's state tax no.	17c Name of state
0		

Form **1042-S** (2022)

手続１

法定調書（源泉徴収の証明）の準備（2022年度分の Form 1042-S）

Form **1042-S** Department of the Treasury Internal Revenue Service

Foreign Person's U.S. Source Income Subject to Withholding **2022**
▶ Go to *www.irs.gov/Form1042S* for instructions and the latest information.

OMB No. 1545-0096
Copy D for Recipient
Attach to any state tax return you file

UNIQUE FORM IDENTIFIER ☐ AMENDED ☐ AMENDMENT NO.

1 Income code	12
2 Gross income	150000
3 Chapter indicator. Enter "3" or "4"	3
3a Exemption code	
3b Tax rate	30 . 00
4a Exemption code	
4b Tax rate	.
5 Withholding allowance	
6 Net income	
7a Federal tax withheld	45000
7b Check if federal tax withheld was not deposited with the IRS because escrow procedures were applied (see instructions)	☐
7c Check if withholding occurred in subsequent year with respect to a partnership interest	☐
8 Tax withheld by other agents	
9 Overwithheld tax repaid to recipient pursuant to adjustment procedures (see instructions)	( )
10 Total withholding credit (combine boxes 7a, 8, and 9)	45000
11 Tax paid by withholding agent (amounts not withheld) (see instructions)	
12a Withholding agent's EIN	XX-XXXXXXX
12b Ch. 3 status code	15
12c Ch. 4 status code	
12d Withholding agent's name	ABC.INC
12e Withholding agent's Global Intermediary Identification Number (GIIN)	
12f Country code	
12g Foreign tax identification number, if any	
12h Address (number and street)	POBOX XX-XXXXXXX
12i City or town, state or province, country, ZIP or foreign postal code	XX-XXXXXXX
13a Recipient's name	YAMADA・・・・・
13b Recipient's country code	JP
13c Address (number and street)	xxx,xxxxxxx
13d City or town, state or province, country, ZIP or foreign postal code	Tokyo, 101-0047 JAPAN
13e Recipient's U.S. TIN, if any	
13f Ch. 3 status code	
13g Ch. 4 status code	
13h Recipient's GIIN	
13i Recipient's foreign tax identification number, if any	
13j LOB code	
13k Recipient's account number	
13l Recipient's date of birth (YYYYMMDD)	
14a Primary Withholding Agent's Name (if applicable)	
14b Primary Withholding Agent's EIN	
15 Check if pro-rata basis reporting	☐
15a Intermediary or flow-through entity's EIN, if any	
15b Ch. 3 status code	
15c Ch. 4 status code	
15d Intermediary or flow-through entity's name	
15e Intermediary or flow-through entity's GIIN	
15f Country code	
15g Foreign tax identification number, if any	
15h Address (number and street)	
15i City or town, state or province, country, ZIP or foreign postal code	
16a Payer's name	
16b Payer's TIN	
16c Payer's GIIN	
16d Ch. 3 status code	
16e Ch. 4 status code	
17a State income tax withheld	0
17b Payer's state tax no.	
17c Name of state	

Form **1042-S** (2022)

手続1

法定調書（源泉徴収の証明）の準備
（2022年度分の Form 1042-S）

Form **1042-S** Department of the Treasury Internal Revenue Service

Foreign Person's U.S. Source Income Subject to Withholding **2022**

▶ Go to *www.irs.gov/Form1042S* for instructions and the latest information.

UNIQUE FORM IDENTIFIER ☐ AMENDED ☐ AMENDMENT NO.

OMB No. 1545-0096

Copy E for Withholding Agent

1 Income code	12
2 Gross income	150000
3 Chapter indicator. Enter "3" or "4"	3
3a Exemption code	
4a Exemption code	
3b Tax rate	30 . 00
4b Tax rate	.
5 Withholding allowance	
6 Net income	
7a Federal tax withheld	45000
7b Check if federal tax withheld was not deposited with the IRS because escrow procedures were applied (see instructions)	☐
7c Check if withholding occurred in subsequent year with respect to a partnership interest	☐
8 Tax withheld by other agents	
9 Overwithheld tax repaid to recipient pursuant to adjustment procedures (see instructions)	( )
10 Total withholding credit (combine boxes 7a, 8, and 9)	45000
11 Tax paid by withholding agent (amounts not withheld) (see instructions)	
12a Withholding agent's EIN	XX-XXXXXXX
12b Ch. 3 status code	15
12c Ch. 4 status code	
12d Withholding agent's name	ABC.INC
12e Withholding agent's Global Intermediary Identification Number (GIIN)	
12f Country code	
12g Foreign tax identification number, if any	
12h Address (number and street)	POBOX XX-XXXXXXX
12i City or town, state or province, country, ZIP or foreign postal code	XX-XXXXXXX
13a Recipient's name	YAMADA・・・・・
13b Recipient's country code	JP
13c Address (number and street)	xxx,xxxxxxx
13d City or town, state or province, country, ZIP or foreign postal code	Tokyo, 101-0047 JAPAN
13e Recipient's U.S. TIN, if any	
13f Ch. 3 status code	
13g Ch. 4 status code	
13h Recipient's GIIN	
13i Recipient's foreign tax identification number, if any	
13j LOB code	
13k Recipient's account number	
13l Recipient's date of birth (YYYYMMDD)	
14a Primary Withholding Agent's Name (if applicable)	
14b Primary Withholding Agent's EIN	
15 Check if pro-rata basis reporting	☐
15a Intermediary or flow-through entity's EIN, if any	
15b Ch. 3 status code	
15c Ch. 4 status code	
15d Intermediary or flow-through entity's name	
15e Intermediary or flow-through entity's GIIN	
15f Country code	
15g Foreign tax identification number, if any	
15h Address (number and street)	
15i City or town, state or province, country, ZIP or foreign postal code	
16a Payer's name	
16b Payer's TIN	
16c Payer's GIIN	
16d Ch. 3 status code	
16e Ch. 4 status code	
17a State income tax withheld	0
17b Payer's state tax no.	
17c Name of state	

For Privacy Act and Paperwork Reduction Act Notice, see instructions. Form **1042-S** (2022)

手続２ Form W-8BEN の作成

記入箇所は ⇦ で表示

Form W-8BEN
(Rev. October 2021)
Department of the Treasury
Internal Revenue Service

Certificate of Foreign Status of Beneficial Owner for United States Tax Withholding and Reporting (Individuals)

▶ For use by individuals. Entities must use Form W-8BEN-E.
▶ Go to *www.irs.gov/FormW8BEN* for instructions and the latest information.
▶ Give this form to the withholding agent or payer. Do not send to the IRS.

OMB No. 1545-1621

Do NOT use this form if:	**Instead, use Form:**
• You are NOT an individual	W-8BEN-E
• You are a U.S. citizen or other U.S. person, including a resident alien individual	W-9
• You are a beneficial owner claiming that income is effectively connected with the conduct of trade or business within the United States (other than personal services)	W-8ECI
• You are a beneficial owner who is receiving compensation for personal services performed in the United States	8233 or W-4
• You are a person acting as an intermediary	W-8IMY

Note: If you are resident in a FATCA partner jurisdiction (that is, a Model 1 IGA jurisdiction with reciprocity), certain tax account information may be provided to your jurisdiction of residence.

Part I Identification of Beneficial Owner (see instructions)

1 Name of individual who is the beneficial owner
・・・・・・YAMADA ⇦ ❶

2 Country of citizenship
JAPAN ⇦ ❷

3 Permanent residence address (street, apt. or suite no., or rural route). **Do not use a P.O. box or in-care-of address.**

City or town, state or province. Include postal code where appropriate. | Country

4 Mailing address (if different from above)

City or town, state or province. Include postal code where appropriate. | Country

5 U.S. taxpayer identification number (SSN or ITIN), if required (see instructions)
XXX−XX−XX ⇦ ❸

6a Foreign tax identifying number (see instructions)

6b Check if FTIN not legally required . . . . ☐

7 Reference number(s) (see instructions)

8 Date of birth (MM-DD-YYYY) (see instructions)
YYYY−YY−YY ⇦ ❹

Part II Claim of Tax Treaty Benefits (for chapter 3 purposes only) (see instructions)

9 I certify that the beneficial owner is a resident of JAPAN ⇦ ❺ within the meaning of the income tax treaty between the United States and that country.

10 **Special rates and conditions** (if applicable—see instructions): The beneficial owner is claiming the provisions of Article and paragraph 12（1）⇦ ❻ of the treaty identified on line 9 above to claim a 0 % rate of withholding on (specify type of income): Royalties ⇦ ❼ ⇧ ❽ .
Explain the additional conditions in the Article and paragraph the beneficial owner meets to be eligible for the rate of withholding:

Part III Certification

Under penalties of perjury, I declare that I have examined the information on this form and to the best of my knowledge and belief it is true, correct, and complete. I further certify under penalties of perjury that:

- I am the individual that is the beneficial owner (or am authorized to sign for the individual that is the beneficial owner) of all the income or proceeds to which this form relates or am using this form to document myself for chapter 4 purposes;
- The person named on line 1 of this form is not a U.S. person;
- This form relates to:
  (a) income not effectively connected with the conduct of a trade or business in the United States;
  (b) income effectively connected with the conduct of a trade or business in the United States but is not subject to tax under an applicable income tax treaty;
  (c) the partner's share of a partnership's effectively connected taxable income; or
  (d) the partner's amount realized from the transfer of a partnership interest subject to withholding under section 1446(f);
- The person named on line 1 of this form is a resident of the treaty country listed on line 9 of the form (if any) within the meaning of the income tax treaty between the United States and that country; and
- For broker transactions or barter exchanges, the beneficial owner is an exempt foreign person as defined in the instructions.

Furthermore, I authorize this form to be provided to any withholding agent that has control, receipt, or custody of the income of which I am the beneficial owner or any withholding agent that can disburse or make payments of the income of which I am the beneficial owner. **I agree that I will submit a new form within 30 days if any certification made on this form becomes incorrect.**

Sign Here ▶ ☐ I certify that I have the capacity to sign for the person identified on line 1 of this form.

Signature of beneficial owner (or individual authorized to sign for beneficial owner)

⇩ ❾
XX XX
Date (MM-DD-YYYY)

XXXXXXXX ⇦ ❿
Print name of signer

For Paperwork Reduction Act Notice, see separate instructions. Cat. No. 25047Z Form **W-8BEN** (Rev. 10-2021)

手続2

Form W-8BEN の作成

記入箇所は ⇐ で表示

Form W-8BEN（米国の源泉徴収に関し恩恵を受ける者の証明書＝個人用）

Form W-8BEN（訳）

➢ 本証明書は個人用であり、法人は Form W-8BEN-E である。

次の場合にはこの様式を使用しない。

・個人でない者

・米国市民又は米国居住外国人を含む他の米国人

・米国内の事業に関連する所得に関し恩恵を受ける受益者

・米国内の個人的な役務提供に対し受領する報酬に関し恩恵を受ける受益者

・仲介者の立場の者

Part Ⅰ を受ける受益者

1　氏名　❶（氏名を記入）　　2　市民権を有する国　❷（JAPAN と記入）

3　恒久的住所

4　郵送先住所（上記3と異なる場合）

5　米国納税者番号（SSN 又は ITIN）❸（納税者番号を記入）

6a　外国納税者番号（FTIN）　6b　法的に FTIN が要求されない場合チェック□

7　照会番号（記載要領参照）　8　生年月日　❹（生年月日記入）

Part Ⅱ 租税条約に基づく恩典付与の要求（chapter 3にのみ適用…記載要領参照）

9　租税条約に基づく恩典を受ける者は、米国との間の租税条約に規定する❺（JAPAN と記入）の居住者であることを証明する。

10　特別な税率と条件（記載要領参照）：恩恵を受ける者は、上記9の租税条約条約の❻（12⑴と記入）の規定に基づく❼（Royalities と記入）につき❽税率0％と記入）の適用による源泉徴収の適用を要求する。

源泉徴収に際し特別な税率を適用するための租税条約に規定する追加の条件の説明。

Part Ⅲ 証明

罰金制度の下、私は、この情報を確認し、私が知る限りにおいては、この情報は正確で完全なものであることを宣言します。

また、罰金制度の下、私は、次の事項について証明致します。

・　私は、この証明書が関係するすべての所得又は収益について恩恵を受ける個人であり、又、chapter 4に関し私自身を証明するためにこの証明書を使用しています。

・　この証明書の line 1の者は米国人ではない。

・　この証明書は次に所得等に関連するものである。

(a) 米国内の事業所得に関連しない所得
(b) 米国内の事業所得に関連するが、租税条約上の所得に対する税額が適用されない
(c) 米国内の事業所得に関連するパートナーシップの持分
(d) 1446(f)の規定により源泉徴収されるパートナーシップの利益の譲渡により生じるパートナーの取得金額

・ この証明書の line 1の者は、line 9の米国との間の租税条約の締結国の居住者である。

・ 販売仲介業者又は物々交換業者については、この証明書の記載上、外国人として取り扱わない。

さらに、この証明者がすべての源泉徴収義務者に提供されることを許可する。

もし、この証明者の内容が正しくない場合には、30日以内に新しい証明書を提出することに同意します。

署名欄 ➢

□ 私は、この証明書の line1の者のために署名する権限を有することを証明する。

日付 ❾（日付記入）

恩恵を受ける者の署名

❿（署名）

手続2

Form 8833の作成

記入箇所は ⇐ で表示

Form **8833**
(Rev. December 2022)
Department of the Treasury
Internal Revenue Service

Treaty-Based Return Position Disclosure Under Section 6114 or 7701(b)

Attach to your tax return.
Go to *www.irs.gov/Form8833* for the latest information.

OMB No. 1545-1354

Attach a separate Form 8833 for each treaty-based return position taken. Failure to disclose a treaty-based return position may result in a penalty of $1,000 ($10,000 in the case of a C corporation) (see section 6712).

Name	U.S. taxpayer identifying number	Reference ID number, if any (see instructions)
ABC.INC ⇐ ❶	XX-XXXXXXX ⇐ ❷	
Address in country of residence ⇓ ❸ XX,XXXXXXXX,XXXXXX	Address in the United States	

Check one or both of the following boxes as applicable.
- The taxpayer is disclosing a treaty-based return position as required by section 6114 . . . . ❹ ⇒ ☑
- The taxpayer is a dual-resident taxpayer and is disclosing a treaty-based return position as required by Regulations section 301.7701(b)-7 . . . . ☐

Note: If the taxpayer is a dual-resident taxpayer and a long-term resident, by electing to be treated as a resident of a foreign country for purposes of claiming benefits under an applicable income tax treaty, the taxpayer will be deemed to have expatriated pursuant to section 877A. For more information, see the instructions.

Check this box if the taxpayer is a U.S. citizen or resident or is incorporated in the United States . . . . ☐

1 Enter the specific treaty position relied on:
a Treaty country JAPAN ⇐ ❺
b Article(s) 12(1) ⇐ ❻

2 List the Internal Revenue Code provision(s) overruled or modified by the treaty-based return position
SECTION 1441 ⇐ ❼

3 Name, identifying number (if available to the taxpayer), and address in the United States of the payor of the income (if fixed or determinable annual or periodical). See instructions.
DEF.INC. TIN XX-XXXXXXX
XXX,XXXXXX,XXXXXXXXXX ⇐ ❽

4 List the provision(s) of the limitation on benefits article (if any) in the treaty that the taxpayer relies on to qualify for benefits under the treaty 22(2) ⇐ ❾

5 Is the taxpayer disclosing a treaty-based return position for which reporting is specifically required pursuant to Regulations section 301.6114-1(b)? . . . . ☐ Yes ☑ No
If "Yes," enter the specific subsection(s) of Regulations section 301.6114-1(b) requiring reporting . . . . ❿ ⇑
Also include the information requested in line 6.

6 Explain the treaty-based return position taken. Include a brief summary of the facts on which it is based. Also, list the nature and amount (or a reasonable estimate) of gross receipts, each separate gross payment, each separate gross income item, or other item (as applicable) for which the treaty benefit is claimed

For Paperwork Reduction Act Notice, see the instructions. Cat. No. 14895L Form **8833** (Rev. 12-2022)

手続3 **Form 8833の作成手順（❶～❿）**

8833 **租税条約に基づく申告であることの開示**

Under Section 6114 or 7701(b)

租税条約に基づく申告であることを明確にするために、Form 8833を添付してください。

租税条約に基づく申告であることを明確にすることを怠った場合には、$1,000の罰金が課されます。（C corporation の場合には $10,000を罰金とします。Section 6712を参照）

○ 名称 **❶（YAMADAXXXX と記入）**

○ U.S taxpayer identifying number **❷（米国の納税者番号を記入）**

○ 提出者の住所 **❸（日本の住所を記入）** ○ 米国における住所

次の事項について該当する場合は、チェックをしてください。

・納税者は Section 6114の規定による租税条約に基づく申告であることを明確にする。

❹（右記の□にチェック） □

・納税者は双方居住者であり、Section 301.7701(b) - 7 の規定による租税条約に基づく申告であることを明確にする。 ▶□

（注） 納税者が双方居住者で、かつ、長期に滞在する居住者であるときは、租税条約の特典を受けるために外国の居住者であることを選択することによって、その納税者は Section 877Aの規定mにより、国外居住者とみなされます。

納税者が米国市民又は居住者、又は米国において設立された会社である場合には、次のこのボックスをチェックしてください。 ▶□

1 条約の適用条項について

a 条約締結国 **❺（JAPAN と記入）**

b 適用条項 **❻（12(1)）と記入）**

SECTION 1441とは外国人と外国法人等に対する源泉徴収の規定です。

2 租税条約に基づく申告により変更又は修正される米国内法 **❼（SECTION 1441と記入）**

3 支払者の名称、米国における identifying number 及び所在地

❽（ABC INC.・ABC INC の納税者番号・所在地を記入）

4 租税条約の特典条項の適用を受けるための条項 **❾（22(2)と記入）**＿

5 納税者は、section 301.6114(b)の規定による報告のために特に要求される目的のために、租税条約に基づく申告であることを明確にするのですか。 YES NO □

YES であれば、section 301.6114-1(b)の特定の subsection (s)を記入してください。

次の line 6の情報も記載してください。 **⓾（NO の□にチェック）**

6　租税条約に基づく申告を行う事情を説明してください。

総収入金額と総支払金額を、所得の種類、金額ごとに記載してください。

手続 4 居住者証明書の取得

記入箇所は ⇐ で表示

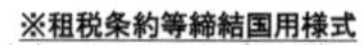
※租税条約等締結国用様式

This form shall be submitted solely for the purpose of claiming tax treaty benefits

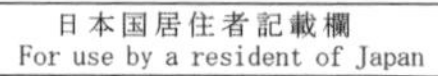
日本国居住者記載欄
For use by a resident of Japan

国税庁
National Tax Agency

居住者証明書交付請求書

APPLICATION FOR CERTIFICATE OF RESIDENCE IN JAPAN

記載に当たっては留意事項・記載要領を参照してください。

＿＿＿＿＿＿＿＿ 税務署長　あて

請求日　Date of request: ＿＿＿＿＿ 年　　月　　日

【代理人記入欄】Information on the agent
※代理人の方のみ記入してください。
住所　Address

氏名　Name

（電話番号 Telephone number　　　　　　　　）

※代理人の方が請求される場合は代理の権限を有することを証明する書類が必要です。

Information on the applicant:

住所（納税地）Address	※日本語及び英語で記入してください。
（フリガナ）氏名又は法人名及び代表者氏名 Name or corporation name and representative name	※日本語及び英語で記入してください。 （電話番号 Telephone number :　　　　　　）

租税条約上の特典を得る目的で、下記のとおり居住者証明書の交付を請求します。

For the purpose of obtaining benefits under the Income Tax Convention, I hereby request the issuance of certificate of residence as follows:

記

提出先の国名等 Name of the State to which this certificate is submitted	※日本語及び英語で記入してください。	
対象期間 Period concerned (Optional)		
申述事項 Declaration	以下の事項を申述します。 □ 請求者は租税の適用上日本国の居住者であること □ 当該請求は専ら居住性の証明のためになされること □ 本請求書の情報は真正かつ正確であること □	I hereby declare that: The applicant is the resident of Japan for tax purposes; This application is made only for the purpose of residency certification; and The information in this application is true and correct.
証明書の請求枚数 Requested number of copies	枚　※本交付請求書は、居住者証明書の必要部数＋１部を提出してください。	整理番号 Reference number (Optional)

国税庁
National Tax Agency

税務署記載欄
For use by Tax Office

居住者証明書

CERTIFICATE OF RESIDENCE IN JAPAN

当方の知り得る限りにおいて、上記の請求者は、日本国と（相手国）との間の租税条約上、日本国居住者であることをここに証明します。

I, the undersigned acting as District Director of the Tax Office of the National Tax Agency, hereby certify that, to the best of my knowledge, the above applicant is the resident of Japan within the meaning of the Income Tax Convention between Japan and ＿＿＿＿＿＿＿＿＿＿＿＿＿＿.

- 証明日
  Date of certification: ＿＿＿＿＿＿＿＿
- 証明番号
  Certificate number: ＿＿＿＿＿＿＿＿
- 税務署名及び役職名
  Name of Tax Office and title: ＿＿＿＿＿＿＿＿
- 氏名
  Print Name : ＿＿＿＿＿＿＿＿

官印 Official Stamp

手続4

居住者証明書の取得（記載要領等）

「居住者証明書交付請求書・居住者証明書」（留意事項・記載要領）

1　居住者証明書交付請求書の種類

税務署で、居住者証明書の交付を請求する場合には、提出先・用途に応じて次の居住者証明書交付請求書を使用してください。

①　居住者証明書交付請求書・居住者証明書（租税条約等締結国用様式）

租税条約等の締結国（地域）に対して、租税条約等に基づく居住者証明書を提出する必要があるときに使用してください。

②　居住者証明書交付請求書・居住者証明書（その他用様式）

租税条約等の締結国（地域）以外の国等に対して、付加価値税の還付又は租税の減免等の目的で居住者証明書を提出する必要があるときに使用してください。

（注）提出先の国等に定められた様式があるときは、原則としてそちらを使用してください。

また、任意で作成した様式を使用することも可能ですが、記載内容によっては証明書を発行できないことがありますのでご注意ください。

2　居住者証明書を請求する際に必要なもの

居住者証明書の請求に当たっては、次のものを持参していただく必要があります。

⑴　居住者証明書交付請求書・居住者証明書

記載要領をご参照の上、必要事項を記入して**2部**持参してください。

※　複数部必要な場合は、必要部数＋１部を持参してください。

⑵　本人（法人の場合は代表者本人）又は代理人本人であることを確認できる書類

運転免許証、写真付き住民基本台帳カード、パスポート、国又は地方公共団体の機関が発行した顔写真付きの身分・資格証明書等を持参してください。

※　顔写真付きでない身分・資格証明書等の場合は、２通（枚）を提示していただく必要があります。詳しくは、所轄の税務署にお尋ねください。

⑶　代理の権限を有することを証明した書類（代理人の場合）

代理人の方（家族、代表者以外の役員、従業員を含みます。）が請求される場合に必要となります。

⑷　返信用封筒・切手（郵送で請求する場合）

原則としてご本人又は法人の住所（納税地）に送付することになりますので、あらかじめご了承ください。

3　記載要領

①　「住所・氏名又は法人名及び代表者氏名」欄

居住者証明書を請求する個人又は法人の住所（納税地）及び氏名（法人名・代表者氏名）を記入してください。

②　「提出先の国名等」欄

居住者証明書を提出する国名（地域名）を日本語及び英語で記入してください。

③　「請求目的」欄【その他用様式】

該当するものにチェックしてください。

その他にチェックをした場合は、内容を日本語及び英語で記入してください。

④　「対象期間」欄【任意項目】

対象期間の指定がある場合は、暦年又は事業年度等を記入してください。

⑤　「申述事項」欄

内容を確認し、上から３つのチェックボックスを必ずチェックしてください。

また、他に申述が必要な事項があれば、空欄に日本語と英語で記入してください。

（例）「請求者は相手国内に恒久的施設を有しないこと」

⑥　「証明書の請求枚数」欄

居住者証明書の必要部数を記入してください。

※　居住者証明書交付請求書・居住者証明書は、居住者証明書の必要部数＋１部を提出してください。

⑦　「整理番号」欄【任意項目】

必要があるときは記入してください。

⑧　「居住者証明書」欄【租税条約等締結国用様式】

提出先の国名（地域名）を英語で記入してください。

4　その他

証明書の発行には日数が掛かることがありますので、あらかじめご了承ください。

その他、ご不明な点は税務署（管理運営部門）までお尋ねください。

手続５ IRS（米国歳入庁）宛のレターの作成

YAMADA XXXXX
・・・・・・・・・・・・・・
・・・・・・・・・・・・・・
TOKYO JAPAN
Telephone（+81）3-・・・・・
Fax （+81）3-・・・・・
Mailto:・・・・・・・・・・・

April 20,20××

送付先

Department of the Treasury Internal Revenue Service Austin
TX 73301-0215 U.S.A

Dear sirs（拝啓）

Subject:U.S Nonresident Alien Income Tax Return of for the refund of the tax withheld（源泉徴収された税額の還付のための非居住者の確定申告について）

We are Japanese , and has been receiving royalty from ABC Inc. as the consideration of use of our copyright.
（私は、日本人です。米国の ABC インクから著作権の対価としてロイヤリティを受け取っております。）

We know that foreign company is subject to U.S. tax on its U.S. source income, and the income is subject to U.S. tax of 30%.
（米国においては、非居住者が米国を源泉とする所得の支払を受ける際には、30%の税率により課税されることを承知しております。）

The tax on the following royalty of 2022 was whithheld at 30%tax rate because of no documentary evidence which identify beneficial owner under tax treaty between Japan and United States.
（次の2022のロイヤリティについては、当社が日米租税条約の適用を受ける者であることを証明する証拠書類がないことから、30%の税率により源泉所得税が課税されておりました。）

手続５ IRS（米国歳入庁）宛のレターの作成

Beneficial Owner is exempt from withholding tax under the tax treaty. Therefore, this time, we want make a procedure to receive the refund of the following tax withheld by the way of filing U.S. Income Tax Return of a Foreign corporation.
（日米租税条約の適用を受ける者は源泉所得税を免除されております。今回、外国法人の確定申告の方法により源泉徴収された税額の還付を受けるための手続きを行うことを希望します。）

(year) （年度）	(gross income) （収入金額）	(tax rate) （税率）	(tax withheld) （源泉徴収税額）
2022	$150,000	30%	$45,000

We attached the following Form and Certification to identify that we are beneficial owner of Tax Treaty between Japan and United States.
（私が日米租税条約の適用を受ける者であることを証明する次の書類を添付します。）

① Form 1040-NR　U.S Nonresident Alian Income Tax Return (Year 2022)
② Form 1042-S　(issued by ABC Inc.Year 2022)
③ Form 8833
④ Form W-8BEN
⑤ Certification of Japanese corporation (issued by Tax administration in Japan)

If you have any question and necessary documents or certification concerning the refund of tax withheld, please contact the following person in charge of tax refund.
（源泉所得税の還付に関する必要な書類又はご質問があれば、次の連絡先にお願い申しあげます。

(Name)　・・・・・・・・・・・
(E-mail)　・・・・・・・・・・・
(Telephone)　(+81) 3-・・・・・・・
(Fax)　(+81) 3-・・・・・・・

Sincerely.
YAMADA XXXXXX

手続 6

非居住者確定申告書の作成

Form **1040-NR** Department of the Treasury—Internal Revenue Service **U.S. Nonresident Alien Income Tax Return** **2022** OMB No. 1545-0074 IRS Use Only—Do not write or staple in this space.

For the year Jan. 1–Dec. 31, 2022, or other tax year beginning ________, 2022, ending ________, 20 ___ See separate instructions.

Filing Status Check only one box. ❶ ☑ Single ☐ Married filing separately (MFS) ☐ Qualifying surviving spouse (QSS) ☐ Estate ☐ Trust
If you checked the QSS box, enter the child's name if the qualifying person is a child but not your dependent: ________

Your first name and middle initial	Last name	Your identifying number (see instructions)
XXXXX ❷	YAMADA ❸	

Home address (number and street). If you have a P.O. box, see instructions.	Apt. no.

City, town, or post office. If you have a foreign address, also complete spaces below.	State	ZIP code
XXXX XX XXXX Tokyo Japan ❹		

Foreign country name	Foreign province/state/county	Foreign postal code
JAPAN ❺	TOKYO ❻	XXX−XX−XX ❼

Digital Assets At any time during 2022, did you: (a) receive (as a reward, award, or payment for property or services); or (b) sell, exchange, gift, or otherwise dispose of a digital asset (or a financial interest in a digital asset)? (See instructions.) ☐ Yes ☑ No

Dependents (see instructions): If more than four dependents, see instructions and check here ☐

(1) First name Last name	(2) Dependent's identifying number	(3) Relationship to you	(4) Check the box if qualifies for (see inst.): ❽ Child tax credit	Credit for other dependents
			☐	☐
			☐	☐
			☐	☐
			☐	☐

Income Effectively Connected With U.S. Trade or Business

Attach Form(s) W-2, 1042-S, SSA-1042-S, RRB-1042-S, and 8288-A here. Also attach Form(s) 1099-R if tax was withheld.

If you did not get a Form W-2, see instructions.

1a	Total amount from Form(s) W-2, box 1 (see instructions)	1a	
b	Household employee wages not reported on Form(s) W-2	1b	
c	Tip income not reported on line 1a (see instructions)	1c	
d	Medicaid waiver payments not reported on Form(s) W-2 (see instructions)	1d	
e	Taxable dependent care benefits from Form 2441, line 26	1e	
f	Employer-provided adoption benefits from Form 8839, line 29	1f	
g	Wages from Form 8919, line 6	1g	
h	Other earned income (see instructions)	1h	
i	Reserved for future use — 1i		
j	Reserved for future use	1j	
k	Total income exempt by a treaty from Schedule OI (Form 1040-NR), item L, line 1(e) — 1k ❾ 150000		
z	Add lines 1a through 1h	1z	
2a	Tax-exempt interest — 2a ___ b Taxable interest	2b	
3a	Qualified dividends — 3a ___ b Ordinary dividends	3b	
4a	IRA distributions — 4a ___ b Taxable amount	4b	
5a	Pensions and annuities — 5a ___ b Taxable amount	5b	
6	Reserved for future use	6	
7	Capital gain or (loss). Attach Schedule D (Form 1040) if required. If not required, check here ☐	7	
8	Other income from Schedule 1 (Form 1040), line 10	8	
9	Add lines 1z, 2b, 3b, 4b, 5b, 7, and 8. This is your **total effectively connected income**	9	
10	Adjustments to income:		
a	From Schedule 1 (Form 1040), line 26 — 10a		
b	Reserved for future use — 10b		
c	Reserved for future use — 10c		
d	Enter the amount from line 10a. These are your **total adjustments to income**	10d	
11	Subtract line 10d from line 9. This is your **adjusted gross income**	11	
12	**Itemized deductions** (from Schedule A (Form 1040-NR)) or, for certain residents of India, standard deduction (see instructions)	12	
13a	Qualified business income deduction from Form 8995 or Form 8995-A — 13a		
b	Exemptions for estates and trusts only (see instructions) — 13b		
c	Add lines 13a and 13b	13c	
14	Add lines 12 and 13c	14	
15	Subtract line 14 from line 11. If zero or less, enter -0-. This is your **taxable income**	15	

For Disclosure, Privacy Act, and Paperwork Reduction Act Notice, see separate instructions. Cat. No. 11364D Form **1040-NR** (2022)

Form 1040-NR (2022) Page 2

Tax and Credits	16	**Tax** (see instructions). Check if any from Form(s): 1 ☐ 8814 2 ☐ 4972 3 ☐			16	
	17	Amount from Schedule 2 (Form 1040), line 3			17	
	18	Add lines 16 and 17			18	
	19	Child tax credit or credit for other dependents from Schedule 8812 (Form 1040)			19	
	20	Amount from Schedule 3 (Form 1040), line 8			20	
	21	Add lines 19 and 20			21	
	22	Subtract line 21 from line 18. If zero or less, enter -0-			22	
	23a	Tax on income not effectively connected with a U.S. trade or business from Schedule NEC (Form 1040-NR), line 15	23a	⑩ 0		
	b	Other taxes, including self-employment tax, from Schedule 2 (Form 1040), line 21	23b			
	c	Transportation tax (see instructions)	23c			
	d	Add lines 23a through 23c			23d	⑪ 0
	24	Add lines 22 and 23d. This is your **total tax**			24	⑫ 0
Payments	25	Federal income tax withheld from:				
	a	Form(s) W-2	25a			
	b	Form(s) 1099	25b			
	c	Other forms (see instructions)	25c			
	d	Add lines 25a through 25c			25d	
	e	Form(s) 8805			25e	
	f	Form(s) 8288-A			25f	
	g	Form(s) 1042-S			25g	⑬ 45000
	26	2022 estimated tax payments and amount applied from 2021 return			26	
	27	Reserved for future use	27			
	28	Additional child tax credit from Schedule 8812 (Form 1040)	28			
	29	Credit for amount paid with Form 1040-C	29			
	30	Reserved for future use	30			
	31	Amount from Schedule 3 (Form 1040), line 15	31			
	32	Add lines 28, 29, and 31. These are your **total other payments and refundable credits**			32	
	33	Add lines 25d, 25e, 25f, 25g, 26, and 32. These are your **total payments**			33	⑭ 45000
Refund	34	If line 33 is more than line 24, subtract line 24 from line 33. This is the amount you **overpaid**			34	⑮ 45000
	35a	Amount of line 34 you want **refunded to you.** If Form 8888 is attached, check here ☐			35a	⑯ 45000
Direct deposit? See instructions.	b	Routing number　　c Type: ☐ Checking ☐ Savings				
	d	Account number				
	e	If you want your refund check mailed to an address outside the United States not shown on page 1, enter it here.				
	36	Amount of line 34 you want **applied to your 2023 estimated tax**	36			
Amount You Owe	37	Subtract line 33 from line 24. This is the **amount you owe.** For details on how to pay, go to *www.irs.gov/Payments* or see instructions			37	
	38	Estimated tax penalty (see instructions)	38			

Third Party Designee
Do you want to allow another person to discuss this return with the IRS? See instructions. ☐ **Yes.** Complete below. ☐ **No**
Designee's name　Phone no.　Personal identification number (PIN)

Sign Here
Under penalties of perjury, I declare that I have examined this return and accompanying schedules and statements, and to the best of my knowledge and belief, they are true, correct, and complete. Declaration of preparer (other than taxpayer) is based on all information of which preparer has any knowledge.

Your signature	Date	Your occupation	If the IRS sent you an Identity Protection PIN, enter it here (see inst.)
⑰	⑱	⑲	
Phone no. ⑳	Email address ㉑		

Paid Preparer Use Only

Preparer's name	Preparer's signature	Date	PTIN	Check if: ☐ Self-employed
Firm's name			Phone no.	
Firm's address			Firm's EIN	

Go to *www.irs.gov/Form1040NR* for instructions and the latest information.　Form **1040-NR** (2022)

手続6 非居住者確定申告書の作成

1040-NR　非居住者確定申告書の作成　2022

申告期間　2022/1/1～2022/12/31　又は他の年分

申告形態　□ Single ❶（Single にチェック）　□ Married filing separately（MFS）
□ Qualifying surviving spouse（QSS）　□ Estate　□ Trust

氏名　❷（First name（名）を記入）　❸（Last name（姓）を記入）

住所　❹（日本の住所を記入）

外国の国名　❺（Japanを記入）・外国の地名 ❻（都市名を記入）・❼（郵便番号を記入）

デジタル資産

2022年中にデジタル資産の受領、売買、交換、贈与、又は譲渡はありましたか

YES □　NO □❽（NO にチェック）

扶養親族

(1) 氏名　(2) 扶養者の身分証明番号　(3) 関係　(4) 税額控除の有無

米国内の事業活動に関連する所得

1 a　Form (s)W -2,box1の合計金額

b　Form (s)W - 2 に報告されていない家政婦及びベビーシッター等の賃金

c　1 a に含まれていないチップ

d　Form (s)W - 2 に報告されていない Medicaid waiver payments

e　Form 2441, line 26からの課税対象 dependent care benefits

f　Form 8339, line 29からの Employer-provided adoption benefits

g　Form 8919, line 6 からの賃金

h　その他の所得

i　将来使用するための予備

j　将来使用するための予備

k　Schedule OI, itemL, line 1(e)からの条約により免税とされている合計所得

❾（150000を記入）

z　1 a～1 h までの合計

2 a　免税利息　　2 b　課税利息

3 a　特定の配当　　3 b　普通配当

4 a　IRA（individual retirement account・・個人退職金勘定）からの分配　　4 b　課税金額

5 a　年金等　　5 b　課税金額

6　将来使用するための予備

7　譲渡所得又は譲渡損失．必要ならば Schedule D（Form 1040）の添付必要なし□

8　Schedule 1（Form 1040）,line 10からのその他所得

9　1 z，2 b，3 b，4 b，5 b，7及び8を合計（米国事業関連所得）

10　所得に対する調整

a　Schedule 1（Form 1040），line 26から　　10 a

b　将来使用するための予備　　10 b

c　将来使用するための予備　　10 c

d　line 10 a から記入．所得に対する調整額合計

11　line 9から line 10 d を控除．調整済総所得

12　項目別控除（Schedule A（Form 1040-NR）又はインドの居住者のための基礎控除…記載要領確認）

13a　Form 8995又は Form 8995-A からの特別事業所得控除　　13 a

b　不動産と信託のための免除　　13 b

c　line13 a と line13 b の合計

14　line 12と13 c の合計

15　line 11から line 14を控除．もしゼロ以下であれば、0を記入．これが課税所得

税額と税額控除

16　Tax（記載要領参照）次の Form があれば確認

1□8814　2□4972　3□

17　Schedule 2（Form 1040），line 3からの金額

18　16と17の合計額

19　Scedule 8812（Form 1040）からの子供控除又は他の扶養者の控除額

20　Schedule 3（Form 1040），line 8からの金額

21　19と20の合計額

22　18から21を控除．0以下であれば0を記入

23 a　Schedule NEC（Form 1040-NR），line 15からの税額　❿（0を記入）

b　Scedule 2（Form 1040），line 21からの事業所得税を含むその他の税額

c　運送税（記載要領参照）

d　23 a から23 c を合計　⓫（0を記入）

24　22と23 d の合計額．税額の総合計　⓬（0を記入）

源泉徴収税額等

25　連邦所得税の源泉徴収税額

a　Form (s)W - 2

b　Form (s)1099

c　その他（記載要領参照）

d　25ａから25ｃを合計

e　Form (s)8805

f　Form (s)8288-A

g　Form (s)1042-S　⓭（45000を記入）

26　2022年の予定納税と2021年申告の適用額

27　将来のための留保

28　追加の Scedule 8812（Form 1040）からの子供控除

29　Form 1040-C

30　将来のための留保

31　Schedule 3（Form 1040）,line15からの金額

32　28, 29, と31の合計額 . あなたのその他支払と還付金額

33　25ｄ，25ｅ，25ｆ，25ｇ，26と32の合計額. あなたの合計支払額

⓮（45000を記入）

還付税額

34　33の金額が24の金額を超える場合、33から24を控除 . 支払超過分

⓯（45000を記入）

35ａ　還付額⓰（45000を記入）Form 8888を添付の場合はここにチェック　□

b　Routing number　　c Type: □ Checking □ Savings

d　Account number

e　page 1に記載されていない米国外の住所宛に還付用の小切手を望む場合はここに記載

36　2023年の予定納税に充当を希望する34の金額

37　24から33を控除（あなたの負債）

38　予定納税のペナルティ（記載要領参照）

指名された第三者

あなたは、第三者が IRS と、この申告に関し、議論を交わすことを許可しますか。

第三者の氏名　　電話番号　　身元番号

署名欄

偽証の場合は罰則を課されることに従い、私はこの申告書と添付資料を調査したことを宣言し、私の知り得る限りでは、この申告書等は真実かつ正確である。

この申告の準備者の宣言は準備者が有する知識の情報を基礎としたものである。

⓱（署　名）　⓲（日付を記入）　⓳（職業を記入）

⓴（電話番号を記入）　㉑（メールアドレスを記入）

準備者のみ使用欄

準備者の氏名　準備者の署名　日付　PTIN

事務所の名称

事務所の住所

手続 6

非居住者確定申告書の作成

SCHEDULE A (Form 1040-NR) Department of the Treasury Internal Revenue Service	**Itemized Deductions** Go to *www.irs.gov/Form1040NR* for instructions and the latest information. Attach to Form 1040-NR. **Caution:** If you are claiming a net qualified disaster loss on Form 4684, see instructions for line 7.	OMB No. 1545-0074 2022 Attachment Sequence No. **7A**

Name shown on Form 1040-NR	Your identifying number

Taxes You Paid	1a	State and local income taxes	1a			
	b	Enter the smaller of line 1a or $10,000 ($5,000 if married filing separately)			1b	
Gifts to U.S. Charities	2	Gifts by cash or check. If you made any gift of $250 or more, see instructions	2			
Caution: If you made a gift and got a benefit for it, see instructions.	3	Other than by cash or check. If you made any gift of $250 or more, see instructions. You **must** attach Form 8283 if over $500 . . .	3			
	4	Carryover from prior year	4			
	5	Add lines 2 through 4			5	
Casualty and Theft Losses	6	Casualty and theft loss(es) from a federally declared disaster (other than net qualified disaster losses). Attach Form 4684 and enter the amount from line 18 of that form. See instructions			6	
Other Itemized Deductions	7	Other—from list in instructions. List type and amount:			7	
Total Itemized Deductions	8	Add the amounts in the far right column for lines 1b through 7. Also, enter this amount on Form 1040-NR, line 12			8	

For Paperwork Reduction Act Notice, see the Instructions for Form 1040-NR. Cat. No. 72749E **Schedule A (Form 1040-NR) 2022**

SCHEDULE NEC (Form 1040-NR)
Department of the Treasury Internal Revenue Service

Tax on Income Not Effectively Connected With a U.S. Trade or Business

Go to *www.irs.gov/Form1040NR* for instructions and the latest information.
Attach to Form 1040-NR.

OMB No. 1545-0074
2022
Attachment Sequence No. 7B

Name shown on Form 1040-NR | Your identifying number

Enter **amount of income** under the appropriate rate of tax. See instructions.

	Nature of Income		(a) 10%	(b) 15%	(c) 30%	(d) Other (specify) ㉒ 0 %	%
1	Dividends and dividend equivalents:						
a	Dividends paid by U.S. corporations	1a					
b	Dividends paid by foreign corporations	1b					
c	Dividend equivalent payments received with respect to section 871(m) transactions	1c					
2	Interest:						
a	Mortgage	2a					
b	Paid by foreign corporations	2b					
c	Other	2c					
3	Industrial royalties (patents, trademarks, etc.)	3					
4	Motion picture or TV copyright royalties	4					
5	Other royalties (copyrights, recording, publishing, etc.)	5				㉓ 150000	
6	Real property income and natural resources royalties	6					
7	Pensions and annuities	7					
8	Social security benefits	8					
9	Capital gain from line 18 below	9					
10	Gambling—Residents of Canada only. Enter net income in column (c). **If zero or less, enter -0-.**						
a	Winnings						
b	Losses	10c					
11	Gambling winnings—Residents of countries other than Canada. **Note:** Losses not allowed	11					
12	Other (specify):	12					
13	Add lines 1a through 12 in columns (a) through (d)	13				㉔ 150000	
14	**Multiply line 13 by rate of tax at top of each column**	14				0 ㉕	
15	**Tax on income not effectively connected with a U.S. trade or business.** Add columns (a) through (d) of line 14. Enter the total here and on Form 1040-NR, line 23a	15					0 ㉖

Capital Gains and Losses From Sales or Exchanges of Property

Enter only the capital gains and losses from property sales or exchanges that are from sources within the United States and not effectively connected with a U.S. business. Do not include a gain or loss on disposing of a U.S. real property interest; report these gains and losses on Schedule D (Form 1040).

Report property sales or exchanges that are effectively connected with a U.S. business on Schedule D (Form 1040), Form 4797, or both.

16	(a) Kind of property and description (if necessary, attach statement of descriptive details not shown below)	(b) Date acquired mm/dd/yyyy	(c) Date sold mm/dd/yyyy	(d) Sales price	(e) Cost or other basis	(f) LOSS If (e) is more than (d), subtract (d) from (e).	(g) GAIN If (d) is more than (e), subtract (e) from (d).
17	Add columns (f) and (g) of line 16				17	( )	
18	**Capital gain.** Combine columns (f) and (g) of line 17. Enter the net gain here and on line 9 above. If a loss, enter -0-					18	

For Paperwork Reduction Act Notice, see the Instructions for Form 1040-NR. Cat. No. 72752B **Schedule NEC (Form 1040-NR) 2022**

手続6 **非居住者確定申告書の作成**

SCHEDULE NEC　米国内の事業活動に関連しない所得に対する税額　2022

所得の種類		(a)10%	(b)15%	(c)30%	(d) 0 % ❷❷
1　配当等と配当等の同等物 a　米国法人からの配当等	1 a				
b　外国法人からの配当	1 b				
c　Section 871(m)に関し受領した配当等の同等物	1 c				
2　利息 a　Mortgage	2 a				
b　外国法人からの利息	2 b				
c　その他利息	2 c				
3　工業的なロイヤリティ	3				
4　映画又はテレビの著作権使用料	4				
5　その他のロイヤリティ（複写権、録音権、出版権他）	5				❷❸ 150000
6　不動産所得と自然資源ロイヤリティ	6				
7　年金等	7				
8　社会保障に関する便益	8				
9　下欄18からの譲渡所得	9				
10　ギャンブルによる所得 a　Winnings b　Losses	10 c				
11　ギャンブルによる所得・カナダ以外の居住者	11				
12　その他	12				
13　(a)欄から(d)欄までの 1 a から12までの合計	13				❷❹ 150000
14　13に各欄の税率を掛ける	14				❷❺　0
15　米国の事業活動に関連しない所得に対する税額					15 ❷❻　0

資産の交換又は譲渡から生じる譲渡益及び譲渡損失
資産の譲渡又は交換からの利益又は損失

16　(3)　資産の種類	(b)取得日	(c)譲渡日	(d)譲渡価額	(e)取得価額	(f)損失	(g)利益
17　16の(f)と(g)の合計				17		
18　譲渡益（17の(f)と(g)の合計					18	

SCHEDULE OI (Form 1040-NR)

Department of the Treasury Internal Revenue Service

Other Information

Go to *www.irs.gov/Form1040NR* for instructions and the latest information.
Attach to Form 1040-NR.
Answer all questions.

OMB No. 1545-0074
2022
Attachment Sequence No. 7C

Name shown on Form 1040-NR: XXX-XXX ㉗ | Your identifying number

A Of what country or countries were you a citizen or national during the tax year? JAPAN ㉘

B In what country did you claim residence for tax purposes during the tax year? JAPAN ㉙

C Have you ever applied to be a green card holder (lawful permanent resident) of the United States? . . . . . ☐ Yes ☑ No ㉚

D Were you ever:

1. A U.S. citizen? . . . ☐ Yes ☑ No ㉛

2. A green card holder (lawful permanent resident) of the United States? . . . ☐ Yes ☑ No ㉜

If you answer "Yes" to (1) or (2), see Pub. 519, chapter 4, for expatriation rules that apply to you.

E If you had a visa on the last day of the tax year, enter your visa type. If you didn't have a visa, enter your U.S. immigration status on the last day of the tax year. ______

F Have you ever changed your visa type (nonimmigrant status) or U.S. immigration status? . . . ☐ Yes ☐ No

If you answered "Yes," indicate the date and nature of the change: ______

G List all dates you entered and left the United States during 2022. See instructions.

Note: If you're a resident of Canada or Mexico **AND** commute to work in the United States at frequent intervals, **check the box for Canada or Mexico** and skip to item H . . . ☐ Canada ☐ Mexico

Date entered United States mm/dd/yy	Date departed United States mm/dd/yy	Date entered United States mm/dd/yy	Date departed United States mm/dd/yy

H Give number of days (including vacation, nonworkdays, and partial days) you were present in the United States during: 2020 ______, 2021 ______, and 2022 ______.

I Did you file a U.S. income tax return for any prior year? . . . ☐ Yes ☑ No ㉝

If "Yes," give the latest year and form number you filed: ______

J Are you filing a return for a trust? . . . ☐ Yes ☑ No ㉞

If "Yes," did the trust have a U.S. or foreign owner under the grantor trust rules, make a distribution or loan to a U.S. person, or receive a contribution from a U.S. person? . . . ☐ Yes ☐ No

K Did you receive total compensation of $250,000 or more during the tax year? . . . ☐ Yes ☑ No ㉟

If "Yes," did you use an alternative method to determine the source of this compensation? . . . ☐ Yes ☐ No

L Income Exempt From Tax—If you are claiming exemption from income tax under a U.S. income tax treaty with a foreign country, complete (1) through (3) below. See Pub. 901 for more information on tax treaties.

1. Enter the name of the country, the applicable tax treaty article, the number of months in prior years you claimed the treaty benefit, and the amount of exempt income in the columns below. Attach Form 8833 if required. See instructions.

(a) Country	**(b)** Tax treaty article	**(c)** Number of months claimed in prior tax years	**(d)** Amount of exempt income in current tax year
JAPAN ㊱	12(1) ㊲		㊳ 150000
(e) Total. Enter this amount on Form 1040-NR, line 1k. Do not enter it anywhere else on line 1 . .			㊴ 150000

2. Were you subject to tax in a foreign country on any of the income shown in 1(d) above? . . . ☐ Yes ☑ No ㊵

3. Are you claiming treaty benefits pursuant to a Competent Authority determination? . . . ☐ Yes ☑ No ㊶

If "Yes," attach a copy of the Competent Authority determination letter to your return.

M Check the applicable box if:

1. This is the first year you are making an election to treat income from real property located in the United States as effectively connected with a U.S. trade or business under section 871(d). See instructions . . . ☐

2. You have made an election in a previous year that has not been revoked, to treat income from real property located in the United States as effectively connected with a U.S. trade or business under section 871(d). See instructions . . . ☐

For Paperwork Reduction Act Notice, see the Instructions for Form 1040-NR. Cat. No. 72756T **Schedule OI (Form 1040-NR) 2022**

手続 6

非居住者確定申告書の作成

SCHEDULE OI　その他情報　2022

氏名　㉗（氏名記入）　　　　　　　　　　　　　　　　　　　身分証明書番号

A　課税年度においてどちらの国の市民ですか？　　　㉘（Japan を記入）

B　課税年度においてどちらの国の居住者ですか？　　㉙（Japan を記入）

C　あなたはかつて米国のグリーンカードの保有者（法的な永久居住者）でしたか？

Yes □　No □

㉚（No にチェック）

D　あなたは、かつて

1．米国市民でしたか？　　Yes □　No □

㉛（No にチェック）

2　米国のグリーンカードの保有者（法的な永久居住者）でしたか？

Yes □　No □

㉜（No にチェック）

もし、YES であれば、あなたに適用される国外居住の規則に関する Pub.519の⑴又は⑵を確認してください。

E　もし、課税年度の最後の日にビザを保有していたならば、ビザの種類を記入して下さい。もし、ビザを保有していなかった場合は、課税年度の最後の日の滞在資格を記入して下さい。

F　あなたは、かつて、ビザの種類又は滞在資格の変更をしましたか？

Yes □　No □

G　2022年の米国への入国日、又は、米国からの出国日を記入（記載要領参照）

（注）もし、あなたがカナダ又はメキシコの居住者で、米国で働くために通勤していた場合には、カナダ又はメキシコのどちらかにチェックし、Hへ進む。

□ Canada　□ Mexico

Date entered United Statets mm/dd/yy	Date departed United Statets mm/dd/yy

H　米国内に滞在した日数（休暇、nonworkdays、partial days を含む）

2020＿＿＿＿＿＿＿, 2021＿＿＿＿＿＿＿,and 2022＿＿＿＿＿＿＿.

I　前年以前に米国所得税申告書を提出したことがありますか？　　Yes □　No □

㉝（No にチェック）

もし、Yes の場合は最近の申告済の申告書の年分と申告書の書式

J　信託に係る申告を提出したことがありますか？　　Yes □　No □

❸❹（No にチェック）

もし、Yes の場合は、信託契約の下で、信託は米国又は外国の持分の所有者に分配したり、米国人に融資をしたり、米国人から寄付を受けていますか？

Yes □　No □

K　課税年度中に $250,000以上の報酬を受領しましたか？　　Yes □　No □

❸❺（No にチェック）

もし、Yes の場合は、報酬の所得源泉の決定に際し最良の方法（米国内外の所得）を採用しましたか？　　Yes □　No □

L　免税所得＝米国と他の国との間の租税条約の下で、所得税の免税を望むならば、次の(1)から(3)の記載を要する。

(1)　国名、租税条約の適用条文、前年において条約上の特典を受けた月数及び課税年度の免税所得の金額

(a)　国名❸❻（Japan を記入）　　(b)　適用条文❸❼（12(1)）を記入

(c)　特典を受けた月数　　(d)　免税所得❸❽（150000を記入）

(e)　(d)の合計金額（Form 1040-NR, line 1k に記入）❸❾（150000を記入）

(2)　上記(1)(d)の金額は外国において課税されましたか？　　Yes □　No □

❹⓪（No にチェック）

(3)　権限ある当局の決定に従い条約の特典を受けていますか？　　Yes □　No □

❹❶（No にチェック）

M　該当する場合にはボックスにチェックを入れる。

1．Section 871(d)の下の米国内の事業に関連する米国に保有する不動産から生じる所得についての申告を選択した最初の年である。　□

2．Section 871(d)の下の米国内の事業に関連する米国に保有する不動産から生じる所得についての申告を取消さないことを前年に選択した。　□

国際税務に関するトピック

米国におけるJoint accountと日本における相続税法上のJoint accountに関する取扱い

米国における Joint account と日本における相続税法上の Joint account に関する取扱い

米国及びその他の国々においては、配偶者と共同で開設する Joint account（夫婦共同名義預金口座）が存在する。

当該預金口座は、一般的に、一方の配偶者の死亡により、その所有権が他方の配偶者に自動的に移転することから、海外に居住していた被相続人の日本における相続税の申告に際し、申告もれが発生する可能性がある。

今回は、米国の Joint account（夫婦共同名義預金口座）について、その内容と相続税法上の取扱いについてお話します。

1　米国における Joint account とは

米国で預金を開設する際に、配偶者を有する場合には、Joint account（夫婦共同名義預金口座）を開設するのが一般的である。

複数の当事者の名義で開設できることから、Multiple parties account とも呼ばれている。

2　Joint account 開設のメリット

Joint account（夫婦共同名義預金口座）開設は次のメリットを有する。

第1のメリットは、夫婦それぞれが預金を引き出す権限があり、夫婦それぞれが小切手を作成することにより出金することができる利便性がある。

第2のメリットは、夫婦の一方の財産管理能力の喪失又は死亡に備えて Joint account を開設することである。

日本においては、相続人である配偶者は、被相続人の死亡後、即座に、被相続人の預金を解約又は出金することはできないが、米国においては一方の配偶者の死亡により、Joint account の所有権が他方の配偶者に自動的に移転することから、他方の配偶者は、自由に Joint account を利用することができる。

第3のメリットは、遺言代替方法としての Joint account を開設することである。

夫婦の一方が相手に預金口座の利益を与えたいが、自分が死亡した時に与えたいケースである。

すなわち、自分が生存中は預金口座を支配するが、自分が死亡した時点で、当該預金口座の残額について、裁判所を通しての相続手続きを経ずに、自動的に他方に移転させることができる。

また、当該預金口座は相続財産に入らず、他方の配偶者に預金の利益を与えることができる。

3　日本における相続税法上のJoint account（夫婦共同名義預金口座）に関する取扱いについて

⑴　相続の効力

相続人は、相続開始の時から、被相続人の財産に属した一切の権利義務を承継する。（民法896条）

⑵　相続税の納税義務者

相続により財産を取得した者は相続税を納める義務がある。（相法１の３）

⑶　相続税の課税財産の範囲

相続により取得した財産の全部に対し、相続税を課する。（相法２）

⑷　相続税法上のJoint accountに関する取扱い

米国においては、共同名義者は、預金者の死亡により、生残者として口座の管理権も所有権も承継することが認められているが、日本の民法上は、当該承継は、預金者の死亡が原因であることから、配偶者が共同名義者である場合には、相続人（配偶者）が被相続人の財産（Joint account）に属した権利義務を承継すること（民法896条該当）である。

したがって、日本の相続税法上は、当該Joint accountのうち、被相続人に帰属する部分は、配偶者が相続により取得した財産に該当し、配偶者は相続財産として申告しなければならない。（相法１の３、相法２該当）

10　ハワイにおける不動産譲渡時の源泉所得税課税と還付手続き

演習事例32

ハワイの不動産譲渡に課税された源泉所得税の還付方法

私はハワイに不動産を保有していましたが、この度、譲渡しました。

不動産譲渡の際に、不動産譲渡価額に対し、ハワイ州政府から7.25%の税率により、源泉所得税の課税を受けました。

ハワイ州政府による不動産譲渡価額に対する源泉所得税は、その一部は申請により還付されると聞いております。

還付方法についてご教示をお願い致します。

ハワイにおいて、不動産を所有するのみで、事業等は行っていません。

なお、不動産の譲渡価額及び購入価額等は次のとおりです。

1．不動産譲渡価額　US$1,000,000
2．購入価額　US$　600,000
3．修繕費用　US$　50,000
4．譲渡費用　US$　100,000
5．減価償却費　US$　80,000
6．源泉所得税　US$　72,500（1,000,000×7.25%）

非居住者である譲渡人のハワイの所得が、不動産の譲渡による所得のみの場合には、ハワイ州政府に対し還付申請書（APPLICATION FOR TENTATIVE REFUND OF WITHHOLDING ON DISPOSITIONS BY NONRESIDENT PERSONS OF HAWAII REAL PROPERTY INTERESTS）を提出することにより、源泉徴収された税額の一部について、還付を受けることができます。

解説

⑴　不動産譲渡時の源泉所得税の課税と納税

非居住者（譲渡人）がハワイにおいて不動産を譲渡した場合には、譲受人は譲渡価額に対しハワイ州の法律により、7.25%の税率により源泉所得税を課税し、その源泉所得税をハワイ州政府に対し納付しなければなりません。

⑵　源泉税の還付手続き

源泉所得税は譲渡価額に源泉徴収税率（7.25%）を乗じて計算されていることから、譲渡人は譲渡価額から不動産の取得価額、譲渡費用等を控除し、譲渡所得を算定、税額を計算し、本来の納税額を確定させ、ハワイ州政府に対し不動産譲渡時の源泉税と本来の納税額との差額の還付申請を行います。

還付申請に際しては、ハワイ州政府に対し還付申請書（APPLICATION FORTENTATIVE REFUND OF WITHHOLDING ON DISPOSITIONS BY NONRESIDENT PERSONS OF HAWAII REAL PROPERTY INTERESTS）を作成し提出することになります。

⑶　不動産譲渡時の課税と還付手続きまでの具体的な流れ

①　不動産売却

②　譲受人は不動産譲渡価額から7.25%の税率による源泉税を控除し譲渡代金を支払う

③　不動産譲受人は、ハワイ州政府に対し、Form N-288［HAWAII WITHHOLDING TAX RETURN FOR DISPOSITION BY NONRESIDENT PERSONS OF HAWAII REAL PROPERTY INTERESTS（非居住者による不動産譲渡に係る源泉所得税課税申告書）］とForm N-288A（Copy A）［Statement of Withholding on Dispositions By Nonresident Persons Of Hawaii Real Property Interests］を提出し、非居住者から不動産の購入及び源泉所得税の課税を行った旨申告する。

④　不動産譲受人は、ハワイ州当局者に対し、源泉所得税を納付する。

⑤　不動産譲受人は、譲渡人に対し、Form N-288A（Copy B）［Statement of With-holding on Dispositions By Nonresident Persons Of Hawaii Real Property Interests］を交付し、Form N-288A（Copy C）を控えとして保管する。

⑥　ハワイ州政府は、譲渡人に対し、NOTICE OF TAXES WITHHELD ON THE SALE OF REAL PROPERTY IN HAWAII（不動産譲渡に係る源泉税徴収済通知）を交付。

⑦　不動産譲渡人は、ハワイ州政府に対し、APPLICATION FOR TENTATIVE REFUND OF WITHHOLDING ON DISPOSITIONS BY NONRESIDENT PERSONS OF HAWAII REAL PROPERTY INTERESTS（非居住者による不動産譲渡に係る源泉所得税の還付のための申請書）を提出し源泉税の一部の還付を受ける。

[ハワイの不動産譲渡とハワイ州政府に対する源泉所得税の還付までの流れ]

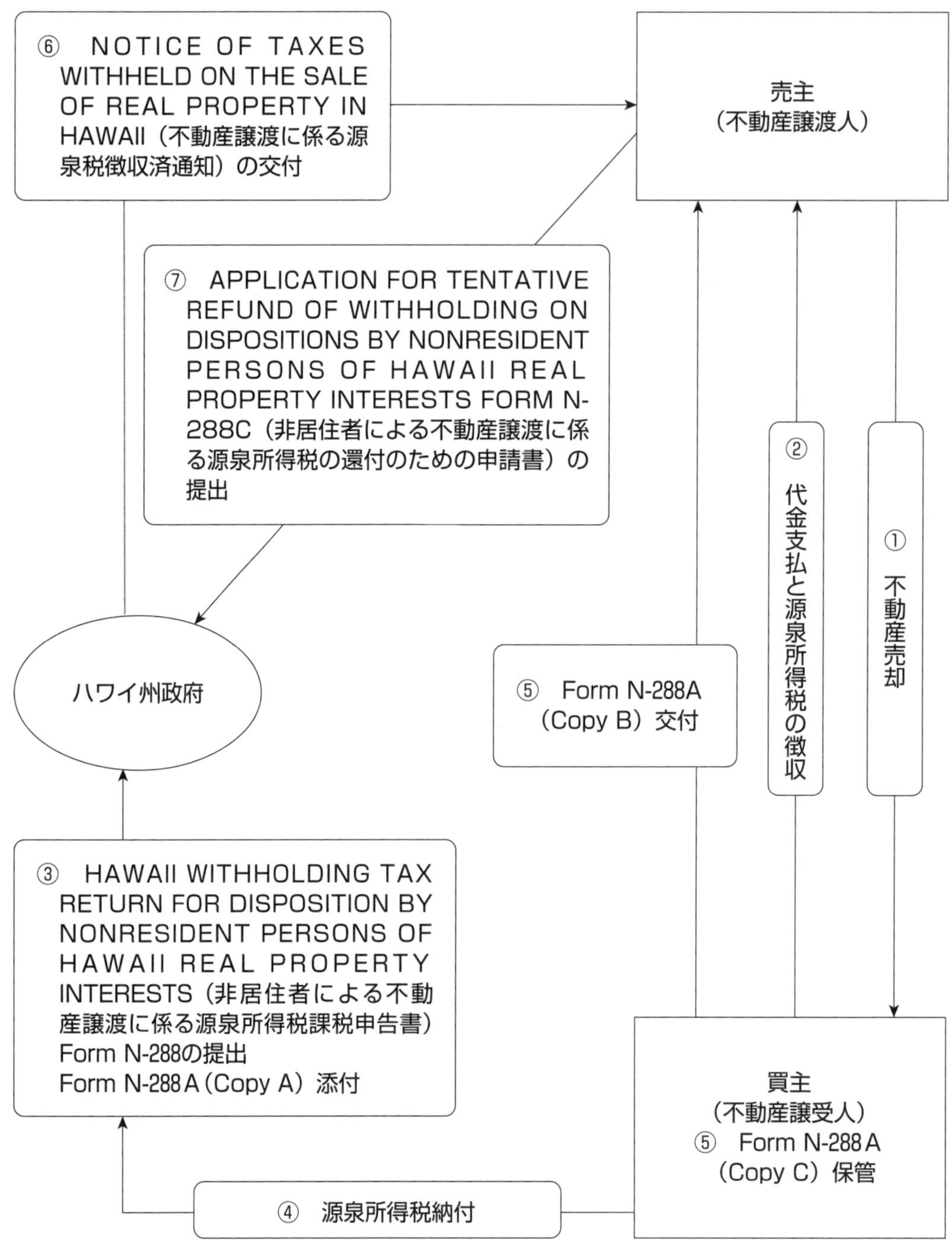

⑷ ハワイの源泉所得税還付申請書（Form N-288C）の作成手順

Form N-288C（源泉所得税還付申請書）作成までの手続き

手続1

============法定調書（源泉徴収の証明）の確認============

源泉徴収義務者がハワイ州に対し提出した源泉徴収の事実を証明するForm N-288、Form N-288A-Copy A、Form N-288A-Copy B、Form N-288A-Copy C、及びForm N-288Cを確認します。

手続2

=========法定調書（源泉徴収の証明・譲渡人交付用）の準備=========

Form N-288C（源泉所得税還付申請書）作成のために、Form N-288A-Copy B（譲渡人用）を準備します。

手続3

========Form N-288C（源泉所得税還付申請書）の作成========

Form N-288C（源泉所得税還付申請書）の作成を行います。

手続１

法定調書（源泉徴収の証明）の確認

(1) Form N-288［非居住者の不動産譲渡に係る源泉所得税課税申告書］

○ 作成者・・・譲受人

○ 用途・・・・ハワイ州政府提出用（非居住者の不動産取引に係る申告）

FORM **N-288** (REV. 2022)

STATE OF HAWAII — DEPARTMENT OF TAXATION

HAWAII WITHHOLDING TAX RETURN FOR DISPOSITIONS BY NONRESIDENT PERSONS OF HAWAII REAL PROPERTY INTERESTS

(NOTE: References to "married" and "spouse" are also references to "in a civil union" and "civil union partner," respectively.)

2023

N288_I 2022A 01 VID01

Copy A of Form(s) N-288A and your check or money order MUST be attached.

• ATTACH YOUR CHECK OR MONEY ORDER HERE •

To Be Completed by the Transferee/Buyer Required to Withhold
Complete Lines 1 - 6.

1 Name of Transferee/Buyer			Transferee/Buyer's SSN or FEIN
Address (Number and Street)			
City, State, and Postal/ZIP Code (Province, Postal Code, and Country)			
2 Description and Location of Property Acquired (Include Tax Map Key Number)			
3 Date of Transfer	4 Number of Forms N-288A Attached	5 Total Amount Realized on the Transfer	6 Total Amount Withheld

Please Sign Here

I hereby declare under penalties provided by section 231-36, HRS, that I have examined this return and accompanying attachments, and, to the best of my knowledge and belief, they are true, correct, and complete. Declaration of preparer (other than individual, partner or member, fiduciary, or corporate officer) is based on all information of which preparer has any knowledge.

➤ Signature of Transferee/Buyer (Individual, Partner or Member, Fiduciary, or Corporate Officer) | Title (if applicable) | Date

Paid Preparer's Use Only

Preparer's signature Print preparer's name ➤	Date	Check if If-employed ➤ ☐	Preparer's Identification Number
Firm's name (or yours if self-employed), address, and Postal/ZIP Code ➤		Federal E.I. No. ➤	
		Phone No. ➤	

手続1

法定調書（源泉徴収の証明）の確認

(2) Form N-288A-Copy A［不動産取引の明細と源泉徴収税額］

- ○ Form N-288の添付資料
- ○ 作成者・・・譲受人
- ○ 用途・・・・ハワイ州政府提出用（不動産取引の明細と源泉徴収税額の報告）

FORM
N-288A
(REV. 2022)

N288A_I 2022A 01 VID01

STATE OF HAWAII—DEPARTMENT OF TAXATION
Statement of Withholding on Dispositions By Nonresident Persons of Hawaii Real Property Interests

Calendar Year 2023

THIS SPACE FOR DATE RECEIVED STAMP

Copy A — Submit to the State of Hawaii - Department of Taxation. *See Copy C for Instructions*

1. Description and Location of Property Transferred *(Include tax map key number)*	2. Transferor/Seller's Share of Amount Realized	3. Date of Transfer OR ☐ Installment Payment Date

4. Transferor/Seller is an: ☐ Individual or RLT ☐ Partnership ☐ Corporation ☐ S corporation ☐ Trust or Estate	5. Transferor/Seller's Hawaii Income Tax Withheld

6. Transferor/Seller's Business Name				6a. Transferor/Seller's FEIN
7. Transferor/Seller's First Name	M.I.	Last Name	Suffix	7a. Transferor/Seller's SSN
8. Transferor/Seller's Street Address				
9. City or Province	State	Postal/ZIP code	Non U.S.A. Country	
10. Transferee/Buyer's Name				11. Transferee/Buyer's FEIN
12. Transferee/Buyer's Street Address				13. Transferee/Buyer's SSN
14. City or Province	State	Postal/ZIP code	Non U.S.A. Country	

THIS FORM IS TO BE USED FOR TRANSFERS OR PAYMENTS MADE IN 2023 ONLY.

ATTACH THIS COPY OF FORM(S) N-288A AND YOUR CHECK OR MONEY ORDER TO FORM N-288 (Payable to "Hawaii State Tax Collector")

288AC0S1　　ID NO 01　　**FORM N-288A (REV. 2022)**

手続１ 法定調書（源泉徴収の証明）の確認

(3) Form N-288A-Copy B［不動産取引の明細と源泉徴収税額］

○ 用途・・・譲渡者交付用

FORM **N-288A** (REV. 2022)

STATE OF HAWAII—DEPARTMENT OF TAXATION
Statement of Withholding on Dispositions By Nonresident Persons of Hawaii Real Property Interests

Calendar Year 2023

THIS SPACE FOR DATE RECEIVED STAMP

Copy B

Send to Transferor/Seller. This information is being furnished to the State of Hawaii, Department of Taxation. *See Instructions on back of this copy.*

1. Description and Location of Property Transferred *(Include tax map key number)*	2. Transferor/Seller's Share of Amount Realized	3. Date of Transfer OR ☐ Installment Payment Date
4. Transferor/Seller is an: ☐ Individual or RLT ☐ Partnership ☐ Corporation ☐ S corporation ☐ Trust or Estate	5. Transferor/Seller's Hawaii Income Tax Withheld	
6. Transferor/Seller's Business Name		6a. Transferor/Seller's FEIN
7. Transferor/Seller's First Name / M.I. / Last Name / Suffix		7a. Transferor/Seller's SSN
8. Transferor/Seller's Street Address		
9. City or Province / State / Postal/ZIP code / Non U.S.A. Country		
10. Transferee/Buyer's Name		
12. Transferee/Buyer's Street Address		
14. City or Province / State / Postal/ZIP code / Non U.S.A. Country		

THIS FORM IS TO BE USED FOR TRANSFERS OR PAYMENTS MADE IN 2023 ONLY.

FORM N-288A (REV. 2022)

(4) Form N-288A-Copy C ［不動産取引の明細と源泉徴収税額］

○ 用途・・・譲受者控用

FORM **N-288A** (REV. 2022)

STATE OF HAWAII—DEPARTMENT OF TAXATION
Statement of Withholding on Dispositions By Nonresident Persons of Hawaii Real Property Interests

Calendar Year 2023

THIS SPACE FOR DATE RECEIVED STAMP

Copy C

For Transferee's/Buyer's Records.

1. Description and Location of Property Transferred *(Include tax map key number)*	2. Transferor/Seller's Share of Amount Realized	3. Date of Transfer OR ☐ Installment Payment Date

4. Transferor/Seller is an: ☐ Individual or RLT ☐ Partnership ☐ Corporation ☐ S corporation ☐ Trust or Estate	5. Transferor/Seller's Hawaii Income Tax Withheld

6. Transferor/Seller's Business Name				
7. Transferor/Seller's First Name	M.I.	Last Name	Suffix	
8. Transferor/Seller's Street Address				
9. City or Province	State	Postal/ZIP code	Non U.S.A. Country	
10. Transferee/Buyer's Name				11. Transferee/Buyer's FEIN
12. Transferee/Buyer's Street Address				13. Transferee/Buyer's SSN
14. City or Province	State	Postal/ZIP code	Non U.S.A. Country	

THIS FORM IS TO BE USED FOR TRANSFERS OR PAYMENTS MADE IN 2023 ONLY.

FORM N-288A (REV. 2022)

手続1 法定調書（源泉徴収の証明）の確認

(5) Form N-288C［暫定の源泉徴収税額の還付申請書］

○ 作成者・・・譲渡者

○ 用途・・・・ハワイ州政府提出用（源泉所得税の一部の還付を申請）

FORM **N-288C** (REV. 2022)

STATE OF HAWAII—DEPARTMENT OF TAXATION

APPLICATION FOR TENTATIVE REFUND OF WITHHOLDING ON DISPOSITIONS BY NONRESIDENT PERSONS OF HAWAII REAL PROPERTY INTERESTS

THIS SPACE FOR DATE RECEIVED STAMP

For Tax Year Ending

(NOTE: References to "married" and "spouse" are also references to "in a civil union" and "civil union partner," respectively.)

NOTE: DO NOT file this form unless you have received notification from the Department of Taxation that we have received your withholding payment.

Check only ONE box: Individual Corporation Trust Partnership Estate

● Name	Last Name	Suffix	● Your Social Security Number
● Spouse's Name	Spouse's Last Name	Suffix	● Spouse's Social Security Number
● Name (Corporation, Partnership, Trust, or Estate)			● Federal Employer I.D. No.
● Trade Name/Doing Business As (DBA) Name or C/O			Daytime Phone No. ( )
● Mailing Address (number and street)			
● City or Province	State	Postal/ZIP Code	Country

Description of Hawaii real property transaction:

a. Date of transfer (mm dd yyyy)

b. Location and general description of property

c. Tax map key number

d. County where property is located

Was the property used at anytime as a rental? **Yes** **No** If yes, enter your Hawaii Tax I.D. Number: **GE** ___-___-_____-__

and indicate the start date and end date of the rental activity: (month, day, year) ______ to (month, day, year) ______

1. Enter the amount withheld on Form N-288A. (Attach a copy of Form N-288A)			1 ●	
2. Sales price (Attach final sales statement)			2	
3. Purchase price of property (Attach final purchase statement)		3		
4. Improvements (Attach schedule)	4			
5. Selling expenses	5			
6. Other (Attach list and schedule)	6			
7. **Total Additions** — Add lines 4 thru 6.		7		
8. Depreciation (Attach schedule)	8			
9. Other (Attach list and schedule)	9			
10. **Total Subtractions** — Add lines 8 and 9.		10		
11. Adjusted basis of property. (Line 3 plus line 7, minus line 10)			11	
12. Gain. Line 2 minus line 11 (See Instructions for installment sales)			12	
13. Enter the tentative tax on the gain (See Instructions)			13 ●	
14. **REFUND** of amount withheld. Line 1 minus line 13. **(This line MUST be filled in.)**			14 ●	

Please Sign Here

I hereby declare under penalties provided by section 231-36, HRS, that I have examined this application and accompanying attachments, and, to the best of my knowledge and belief, they are true, correct, and complete.

● Signature Title (If applicable) Date

● Signature Title (If applicable) Date

N288C_I 2022A 01 VID01

288CE3T4 ID NO 01

FORM N-288C (REV. 2022)

Form N-288C〔源泉徴収税額の還付申請書〕・・・・・・和訳

N-288C APPLICATION FOR TENTATIVE REFUND OF WITHHOLDING ON DISPOSITIONS BY NONRESIDENT PERSONS OF HAWAII REAL PROPERTY INTERESTS〔暫定の源泉徴収税額の還付申請書〕

課税年度最終日

（注） ハワイ州政府から源泉所得税の納付があった旨の通知がない場合には、この申請書は提出できない。

ボックスの１つをチェック：□個人　□法人　□信託　□パートナーシップ　□遺産

氏名	社会保障番号
配偶者の氏名	社会保障番号（配偶者）
名称（法人、信託等）	FE I.D.
商号	電話番号
住所	

都市名　州名　郵便番号　国名

ハワイの不動産取引の内容

a．譲渡年月日　　b．不動産の所在地と状況

c．Tax map key number　　d．郡名

不動産は賃貸用として使用していましたか？　Yes □　No □

もし、Yes であれば、Hawaii Tax I.D. 番号を記入、・・・・・・・・・・・・・・・

さらに、賃貸期間を記入・・・・・・・・・・・・・・・・・・・

1．Form N-288 A に記載されている源泉所得税を記入			1
2．譲渡価額			2
3．購入価額		3	
4．修繕費等	4		
5．譲渡費用	5		
6．その他費用	6		
7．合計額（4＋5＋6）		7	

8．減価償却費	8		
9．その他費用	9		
10. 合計額（8＋9）		10	
11. 調整価額（3＋7－10）			11
12. 譲渡所得（2－11）			12
13. 暫定税額			13
14. 還付金額（1－13）			14

署名欄

署名　　　　職名　　　　日付

署名　　　　職名　　　　日付

法定調書（源泉徴収の証明・譲渡人交付用）の準備

FORM
N-288A
(REV. 2022)

STATE OF HAWAII—DEPARTMENT OF TAXATION
Statement of Withholding on Dispositions By Nonresident Persons of Hawaii Real Property Interests

Calendar Year **2023**

THIS SPACE FOR DATE RECEIVED STAMP

Copy B

Send to Transferor/Seller. This information is being furnished to the State of Hawaii, Department of Taxation. *See Instructions on back of this copy.*

1. Description and Location of Property Transferred *(Include tax map key number)*	2. Transferor/Seller's Share of Amount Realized	3. Date of Transfer OR ☐ Installment Payment Date

4. Transferor/Seller is an: ☐ Individual or RLT ☐ Partnership ☐ Corporation ☐ S corporation ☐ Trust or Estate	5. Transferor/Seller's Hawaii Income Tax Withheld 72500.00

6. Transferor/Seller's Business Name				6a. Transferor/Seller's FEIN
7. Transferor/Seller's First Name XXXX	M.I.	Last Name DDDD	Suffix	7a. Transferor/Seller's SSN
8. Transferor/Seller's Street Address XXXX XXX XXXX				
9. City or Province	State	Postal/ZIP code	Non U.S.A. Country	
10. Transferee/Buyer's Name AAA BBB				
12. Transferee/Buyer's Street Address XXXX-XX-XXXX				
14. City or Province	State	Postal/ZIP code	Non U.S.A. Country	

THIS FORM IS TO BE USED FOR TRANSFERS OR PAYMENTS MADE IN 2023 ONLY.

FORM N-288A (REV. 2022)

手続 3　Form N-288C（源泉所得税還付申請書）の作成

Clear Form

FORM **N-288C** (REV. 2022)

STATE OF HAWAII—DEPARTMENT OF TAXATION

APPLICATION FOR TENTATIVE REFUND OF WITHHOLDING ON DISPOSITIONS BY NONRESIDENT PERSONS OF HAWAII REAL PROPERTY INTERESTS

THIS SPACE FOR DATE RECEIVED STAMP

For Tax Year Ending 12-31-2022 ❶

(NOTE: References to "married" and "spouse" are also references to "in a civil union" and "civil union partner," respectively.)

NOTE: DO NOT file this form unless you have received notification from the Department of Taxation that we have received your withholding payment.

Check only ONE box: Individual ☑ ❷ Corporation Trust Partnership Estate

● Name	Last Name	Suffix	● Your Social Security Number
XXXXX ❸	XXXX ❸		❹
● Spouse's Name	Spouse's Last Name	Suffix	● Spouse's Social Security Number
● Name (Corporation, Partnership, Trust, or Estate)			● Federal Employer I.D. No.
● Trade Name/Doing Business As (DBA) Name or C/O			Daytime Phone No. ( )
● Mailing Address (number and street) XXX-XX-XXXX ❺			
● City or Province HONOLULU ❻	State ❼	Postal/ZIP Code	Country

Description of Hawaii real property transaction:

a. Date of transfer (mm dd yyyy) ❽

b. Location and general description of property XXXXXX ❾

c. Tax map key number ❿

d. County where property is located ⓫

Was the property used at anytime as a rental? **Yes** **No** ⓬ If yes, enter your Hawaii Tax I.D. Number: **GE** ___ - ____ - ______ - ___ and indicate the start date and end date of the rental activity: (month, day, year) ________ to (month, day, year) ________

1.	Enter the amount withheld on Form N-288A. (Attach a copy of Form N-288A)			1 •	72500 ⓭
2.	Sales price (Attach final sales statement)			2	1000000 ⓮
3.	Purchase price of property (Attach final purchase statement)		3	⓯ 600000	
4.	Improvements (Attach schedule)	4	⓰ 50000		
5.	Selling expenses	5	⓱ 100000		
6.	Other (Attach list and schedule)	6			
7.	**Total Additions** — Add lines 4 thru 6.		7	⓲ 150000	
8.	Depreciation (Attach schedule)	8	⓳ 80000		
9.	Other (Attach list and schedule)	9			
10.	**Total Subtractions** — Add lines 8 and 9.		10	⓴ 80000	
11.	Adjusted basis of property. (Line 3 plus line 7, minus line 10)			11	㉑ 670000
12.	Gain. Line 2 minus line 11 (See Instructions for installment sales)			12	㉒ 330000
13.	Enter the tentative tax on the gain (See Instructions)			13 •	㉓ 23539
14.	**REFUND** of amount withheld. Line 1 minus line 13. **(This line MUST be filled in.)**			14 •	㉔ 48961

Please Sign Here

I hereby declare under penalties provided by section 231-36, HRS, that I have examined this application and accompanying attachments, and, to the best of my knowledge and belief, they are true, correct, and complete.

● ________ Signature ________ Title (If applicable) ________ Date

● ________ Signature ________ Title (If applicable) ________ Date

N288C_I 2022A 01 VID01

288CE3T4 ID NO 01

FORM N-288C (REV. 2022)

手続3 **FormN-288C（源泉所得税還付申請書）の作成**

N-288C　APPLICATION FOR TENTATIVE REFUND OF WITHHOLDING ON DISPOSITIONS BY NONRESIDENT PERSONS OF HAWAII REAL PROPERTY INTERESTS［源泉徴収税額の還付申請書］

課税年度最終日　12-31-20XX ❶（最終日を記入）

（注）ハワイ州政府から源泉所得税の納付があった旨の通知がない場合には、この申請書は提出できない。

❷（個人にチェック）

ボックスの1つをチェック：☑個人　□法人　□信託　□パートナーシップ　□遺産	
氏名　XXXX　❸（氏名を記入）	社会保障番号　XXXX　❹（番号を記入）
配偶者の氏名	社会保障番号（配偶者）
名称（法人、信託等）	FE I.D.
商号	電話番号
住所　❺（住所を記入）	
都市名　HONOLULU ❻（ホノルルを記入）　州名　HI ❼（HI を記入）　郵便番号　国名	

ハワイの不動産取引の内容

a．譲渡年月日❽（譲渡年月日を記入）　b．不動産の所在地等❾（所在地等を記入）

c．Tax map key number❿（番号を記入）　d．郡名HONOLULU⓫（ホノルルを記入）

不動産は賃貸用として使用していましたか？

Yes □　No ☑　⓬（No にチェック）

もし、Yes であれば、Hawaii Tax I.D. 番号を記入、・・・・・・・・・・・・・・・・・・

さらに、賃貸期間を記入・・・・・・・・・・・・・・・・・・・・

1．Form N-288Aに記載されている源泉所得税を記入			1　72500 ⓭
2．譲渡価額			2　1000000 ⓮
3．購入価額		3　600000 ⓯	
4．修繕費等	4　50000 ⓰		
5．譲渡費用	5　100000 ⓱		

6．その他費用	6		
7．合計額（4＋5＋6）		7　150000 ⓲	
8．減価償却費	8　80000 ⓳		
9．その他費用	9		
10．合計額（8＋9）		10　80000 ⓴	
11．調整価額（3＋7－10）			11　670000 ㉑
12．譲渡所得（2－11）			12　330000 ㉒
13．税額（$1,354+（330,000－24,000）×7.25%） ［税額計算はSingle individual；Over$24,000を適用］			13　23539 ㉓
14．還付金額（1－13）			14　48961 ㉔

署名欄

署名　　　　職名　　　　日付

署名　　　　職名　　　　日付

（参考）税額表

Tax Rate Schedules

Schedule I

SINGLE INDIVIDUALS AND MARRIED INDIVIDUALS FILING SEPARATE RETURNS

If the taxable income is:	The tax shall be:
Not over $2,400	1.40% of taxable income
Over $2,400 but not over $4,800	$34.00 plus 3.20% over $2,400
Over $4,800 but not over $9,600	$110.00 plus 5.50% over $4,800
Over $9,600 but not over $14,400	$374.00 plus 6.40% over $9,600
Over $14,400 but not over $19,200	$682.00 plus 6.80% over $14,400
Over $19,200 but not over $24,000	$1,008.00 plus 7.20% over $19,200
Over $24,000	$1,354.00 plus 7.25% over $24,000

Schedule II

MARRIED INDIVIDUALS FILING JOINT RETURNS AND CERTAIN WIDOWS AND WIDOWERS

If the taxable income is:	The tax shall be:
Not over $4,800	1.40% of taxable income
Over $4,800 but not over $9,600	$67.00 plus 3.20% over $4,800
Over $9,600 but not over $19,200	$221.00 plus 5.50% over $9,600
Over $19,200 but not over $28,800	$749.00 plus 6.40% over $19,200
Over $28,800 but not over $38,400	$1,363.00 plus 6.80% over $28,800
Over $38,400 but not over $48,000	$2,016.00 plus 7.20% over $38,400
Over $48,000	$2,707.00 plus 7.25% over $48,000

Schedule III

HEAD OF HOUSEHOLD

If the taxable income is:	The tax shall be:
Not over $3,600	1.40% of taxable income
Over $3,600 but not over $7,200	$50.00 plus 3.20% over $3,600
Over $7,200 but not over $14,400	$166.00 plus 5.50% over $7,200
Over $14,400 but not over $21,600	$562.00 plus 6.40% over $14,400
Over $21,600 but not over $28,800	$1,022.00 plus 6.80% over $21,600
Over $28,800 but not over $36,000	$1,512.00 plus 7.20% over $28,800
Over $36,000	$2,030.00 plus 7.25% over $36,000

（出典） STAYE OF HAWAII-DEPARTMENT OF HAWAII: Instruction for Form N-288C

参考法令等

THE
GUIDEBOOK OF
FOREIGN
TAX REFUND
FOR
PRACTITIONERS

（所得税法）

（給与所得）

第二十八条　給与所得とは、俸給、給料、賃金、歳費及び賞与並びにこれらの性質を有する給与（以下この条において「給与等」という。）に係る所得をいう。

2　給与所得の金額は、その年中の給与等の収入金額から給与所得控除額を控除した残額とする。

3　前項に規定する給与所得控除額は、次の各号に掲げる場合の区分に応じ当該各号に定める金額とする。

一　前項に規定する収入金額が百八十万円以下である場合　当該収入金額の百分の四十に相当する金額（当該金額が六十五万円に満たない場合には、六十五万円）

二　前項に規定する収入金額が百八十万円を超え三百六十万円以下である場合　七十二万円と当該収入金額から百八十万円を控除した金額の百分の三十に相当する金額との合計額

三　前項に規定する収入金額が三百六十万円を超え六百六十万円以下である場合　百二十六万円と当該収入金額から三百六十万円を控除した金額の百分の二十に相当する金額との合計額

四　前項に規定する収入金額が六百六十万円を超え千万円以下である場合　百八十六万円と当該収入金額から六百六十万円を控除した金額の百分の十に相当する金額との合計額

五　前項に規定する収入金額が千万円を超える場合　二百二十万円

4　その年中の給与等の収入金額が六百六十万円未満である場合には、当該給与等に係る給与所得の金額は、前二項の規定にかかわらず、当該収入金額を別表第五の給与等の金額として、同表により当該金額に応じて求めた同表の給与所得控除後の給与等の金額に相当する金額とする。

第二款　所得金額の計算の通則

（収入金額）

第三十六条　その年分の各種所得の金額の計算上収入金額とすべき金額又は総収入金額に算入すべき金額は、別段の定めがあるものを除き、その年において収入すべき金額（金銭以外の物又は権利その他経済的な利益をもつて収入する場合には、その金銭以外の物又は権利その他経済的な利益の価額）とする。

2　前項の金銭以外の物又は権利その他経済的な利益の価額は、当該物若しくは権利を取得し、又は当該利益を享受する時における価額とする。

3　無記名の公社債の利子、無記名の株式（無記名の公募公社債等運用投資信託以外の公社債等運用投資信託の受益証券及び無記名の社債的受益権に係る受益証券を含む。第百六十九条第二号（分離課税に係る所得税の課税標準）、第二百二十四条第一項及び第二項（利子、配当等の受領者の告知）並びに第二百二十五条第一項及び第二項（支払調書及び支払通知書）において「無記名株式等」という。）の剰余金の配当（第二十四条第一項（配当所得）に規定する剰余金の配当をいう。）又は無記名の貸付信託、投資信託若しくは特定受益証券発行信託の受益証券に係る収益の分配については、その年分の利子所得の金額又は配当所得の金額の計算上収入金額とすべき金額は、第一項の規定にかかわらず、その年において支払を受けた金額とする。

第三編　非居住者及び法人の納税義務

第一章　国内源泉所得

（国内源泉所得）

第百六十一条　この編において「国内源泉所得」とは、次に掲げるものをいう。

一　非居住者が恒久的施設を通じて事業を行う場合において、当該恒久的施設が当該非居住者から独立して事業を行う事業者であるとしたならば、当該恒久的施設が果たす機能、当該恒久的施設において使用する資産、当該恒久的施設と当該非居住者の事業場等（当該非居住者の事業に係る事業場その他これに準ずるものとして政令で定めるものであつて当該恒久的施設以外のものをいう。次項及び次条第二項において同じ。）との間の内部取引その他の状況を勘案して、当該恒久的施設に帰せられるべき所得（当該恒久的施設の譲渡により生ずる所得を含む。）

二　国内にある資産の運用又は保有により生ずる所得（第八号から第十六号までに該当するものを除く。）

三　国内にある資産の譲渡により生ずる所得として政令で定めるもの

四　民法第六百六十七条第一項（組合契約）に規定する組合契約（これに類するものとして政令で定める契約を含む。以下この号において同じ。）に基づいて恒久的施設を通じて行う事業から生ずる利益で当該組合契約に基づいて配分を受けるもののうち政令で定めるもの

五　国内にある土地若しくは土地の上に存する権利又は建物及びその附属設備若しくは構築物の譲渡による対価（政令で定めるものを除く。）

六　国内において人的役務の提供を主たる内容とする事業で政令で定めるものを行う者が受ける当該人的役務の提供に係る対価

七　国内にある不動産、国内にある不動産の上に存する権利若しくは採石法（昭和二十五年法律第二百九十一号）の規定による採石権の貸付け（地上権又は採石権の設定その他他人に不動産、不動産の上に存する権利又は採石権を使用させる一切の行為を含む。）、鉱業法（昭和二十五年法律第二百八十九号）の規定による租鉱権の設定又は居住者若しくは内国法人に対する船舶若しくは航空機の貸付けによる対価

八　第二十三条第一項（利子所得）に規定する利子等のうち次に掲げるもの

イ　日本国の国債若しくは地方債又は内国法人の発行する債券の利子

ロ　外国法人の発行する債券の利子のうち当該外国法人の恒久的施設を通じて行う事業に係るもの

ハ　国内にある営業所、事務所その他これらに準ずるもの（以下この編において「営業所」という。）に預け入れられた預貯金の利子

ニ　国内にある営業所に信託された合同運用信託、公社債投資信託又は公募公社債等運用投資信託の収益の分配

九　第二十四条第一項（配当所得）に規定する配当等のうち次に掲げるもの

イ　内国法人から受ける第二十四条第一項に規定する剰余金の配当、利益の配当、剰余金の分配、金銭の分配又は基金利息

ロ　国内にある営業所に信託された投資信託（公社債投資信託及び公募公社債等運用投資信託を除く。）又は特定受益証券発行信託の収益の分配

十　国内において業務を行う者に対する貸付金（これに準ずるものを含む。）で当該業務に係るものの利子（政令で定める利子を除き、債券の買戻又は売戻条件付売買取引として政令で定めるものから生ずる差益として政令で定めるものを含む。）

十一　国内において業務を行う者から受ける次に掲げる使用料又は対価で当該業務に係るもの

イ　工業所有権その他の技術に関する権利、特別の技術による生産方式若しくはこれらに準ずるものの使用料又はその譲渡による対価

ロ　著作権（出版権及び著作隣接権その他これに準ずるものを含む。）の使用料又はその譲渡による対価

ハ　機械、装置その他政令で定める用具の使用料

十二　次に掲げる給与、報酬又は年金

イ　俸給、給料、賃金、歳費、賞与又はこれらの性質を有する給与その他人的役務の提供に対する報酬のうち、国内において行う勤務その他の人的役務の提供（内国法人の役員として国外において行う勤務その他の政令で定める人的役務の提供を含む。）に基因するもの

ロ　第三十五条第三項（公的年金等の定義）に規定する公的年金等（政令で定めるものを除く。）

ハ　第三十条第一項（退職所得）に規定する退職手当等のうちその支払を受ける者が居住者であつた期間に行つた勤務その他の人的役務の提供（内国法人の役員として非居住者であつた期間に行つた勤務その他の政令で定める人的役務の提供を含む。）に基因するもの

十三　国内において行う事業の広告宣伝のための賞金として政令で定めるもの

十四　国内にある営業所又は国内において契約の締結の代理をする者を通じて締結した保険業法第二条第三項（定義）に規定する生命保険会社又は同条第四項に規定する損害保険会社の締結する保険契約その他の年金に係る契約で政令で定めるものに基づいて受ける年金（第二百九条第二号（源泉徴収を要しない年金）に掲げる年金に該当するものを除く。）で第十二号ロに該当するもの以外のもの（年金の支払の開始の日以後に当該年金に係る契約に基づき分配を受ける剰余金又は割戻しを受ける割戻金及び当該契約に基づき年金に代えて支給される一時金を含む。）

十五　次に掲げる給付補塡金、利息、利益又は差益

イ　第百七十四条第三号（内国法人に係る所得税の課税標準）に掲げる給付補塡金のうち国内にある営業所が受け入れた定期積金に係るもの

ロ　第百七十四条第四号に掲げる給付補塡金のうち国内にある営業所が受け入れた同号に

規定する掛金に係るもの
ハ　第百七十四条第五号に掲げる利息のうち国内にある営業所を通じて締結された同号に規定する契約に係るもの
ニ　第百七十四条第六号に掲げる利益のうち国内にある営業所を通じて締結された同号に規定する契約に係るもの
ホ　第百七十四条第七号に掲げる差益のうち国内にある営業所が受け入れた預貯金に係るもの
ヘ　第百七十四条第八号に掲げる差益のうち国内にある営業所又は国内において契約の締結の代理をする者を通じて締結された同号に規定する契約に係るもの
十六　国内において事業を行う者に対する出資につき、匿名組合契約（これに準ずる契約として政令で定めるものを含む。）に基づいて受ける利益の分配
十七　前各号に掲げるもののほかその源泉が国内にある所得として政令で定めるもの
2　前項第一号に規定する内部取引とは、非居住者の恒久的施設と事業場等との間で行われた資産の移転、役務の提供その他の事実で、独立の事業者の間で同様の事実があつたとしたならば、これらの事業者の間で、資産の販売、資産の購入、役務の提供その他の取引（資金の借入れに係る債務の保証、保険契約に係る保険責任についての再保険の引受けその他これらに類する取引として政令で定めるものを除く。）が行われたと認められるものをいう。
3　恒久的施設を有する非居住者が国内及び国外にわたつて船舶又は航空機による運送の事業を行う場合には、当該事業から生ずる所得のうち国内において行う業務につき生ずべき所得として政令で定めるものをもつて、第一項第一号に掲げる所得とする。

（租税条約に異なる定めがある場合の国内源泉所得）

第百六十二条　日本国が締結した所得に対する租税に関する二重課税防止のための条約（以下この条において「租税条約」という。）において国内源泉所得につき前条の規定と異なる定めがある場合には、その租税条約の適用を受ける者については、同条の規定にかかわらず、国内源泉所得は、その異なる定めがある限りにおいて、その租税条約に定めるところによる。この場合において、その租税条約が同条第一項第六号から第十六号までの規定に代わつて国内源泉所得を定めているときは、この法律中これらの号に規定する事項に関する部分の適用については、その租税条約により国内源泉所得とされたものをもつてこれに対応するこれらの号に掲げる国内源泉所得とみなす。
2　恒久的施設を有する非居住者の前条第一項第一号に掲げる所得を算定する場合において、当該非居住者の恒久的施設と事業場等との間の同号に規定する内部取引から所得が生ずる旨を定める租税条約以外の租税条約の適用があるときには、同号に規定する内部取引には、当該非居住者の恒久的施設と事業場等との間の利子（これに準ずるものとして政令で定めるものを含む。）の支払に相当する事実その他政令で定める事実は、含まれないものとする。

（国内源泉所得の範囲の細目）

第百六十三条　前二条に定めるもののほか、国内源泉所得の範囲に関し必要な事項は、政令で定める。

（源泉徴収義務）

第二百十二条　非居住者に対し国内において第百六十一条第一項第四号から第十六号まで（国内源泉所得）に掲げる国内源泉所得（政令で定めるものを除く。）の支払をする者又は外国法人に対し国内において同項第四号から第十一号まで若しくは第十三号から第十六号までに掲げる国内源泉所得（第百八十条第一項（恒久的施設を有する外国法人の受ける国内源泉所得に係る課税の特例）又は第百八十条の二第一項若しくは第二項（信託財産に係る利子等の課税の特例）の規定に該当するもの及び政令で定めるものを除く。）の支払をする者は、その支払の際、これらの国内源泉所得について所得税を徴収し、その徴収の日の属する月の翌月十日までに、これを国に納付しなければならない。

2　前項に規定する国内源泉所得の支払が国外において行われる場合において、その支払をする者が国内に住所若しくは居所を有し、又は国内に事務所、事業所その他これらに準ずるものを有するときは、その者が当該国内源泉所得を国内において支払うものとみなして、同項の規定を適用する。この場合において、同項中「翌月十日まで」とあるのは、「翌月末日まで」とする。

3　内国法人に対し国内において第百七十四条各号（内国法人に係る所得税の課税標準）に掲げる利子等、配当等、給付補塡金、利息、利益、差益、利益の分配又は賞金（これらのうち第百七十六条第一項又は第二項（信託財産に係る利子等の課税の特例）の規定に該当するものを除く。）の支払をする者は、その支払の際、当該利子等、配当等、給付補塡金、利息、利益、差益、利益の分配又は賞金について所得税を徴収し、その徴収の日の属する月の翌月十日までに、これを国に納付しなければならない。

4　第百八十一条第二項（配当等の支払があつたものとみなす場合）の規定は第一項又は前項の規定を適用する場合について、第百八十三条第二項（賞与の支払があつたものとみなす場合）の規定は第一項の規定を適用する場合についてそれぞれ準用する。

5　第百六十一条第一項第四号に規定する配分を受ける同号に掲げる国内源泉所得については、同号に規定する組合契約を締結している組合員（これに類する者で政令で定めるものを含む。）である非居住者又は外国法人が当該組合契約に定める計算期間その他これに類する期間（これらの期間が一年を超える場合は、これらの期間をその開始の日以後一年ごとに区分した各期間（最後に一年未満の期間を生じたときは、その一年未満の期間）。以下この項において「計算期間」という。）において生じた当該国内源泉所得につき金銭その他の資産（以下この項において「金銭等」という。）の交付を受ける場合には、当該配分をする者を当該国内源泉所得の支払をする者とみなし、当該金銭等の交付をした日（当該計算期間の末日の翌日から二月を経過する日までに当該国内源泉所得に係る金銭等の交付がされない場合には、同日）においてその支払があつたものとみなして、この法律の規定を適用する。

（所得税法施行令）

（国内に住所を有する者と推定する場合）

第十四条　国内に居住することとなつた個人が次の各号のいずれかに該当する場合には、その者は、国内に住所を有する者と推定する。

一　その者が国内において、継続して一年以上居住することを通常必要とする職業を有すること。

二　その者が日本の国籍を有し、かつ、その者が国内において生計を一にする配偶者その他の親族を有することその他国内におけるその者の職業及び資産の有無等の状況に照らし、その者が国内において継続して一年以上居住するものと推測するに足りる事実があること。

2　前項の規定により国内に住所を有する者と推定される個人と生計を一にする配偶者その他その者の扶養する親族が国内に居住する場合には、これらの者も国内に住所を有する者と推定する。

（国内に住所を有しない者と推定する場合）

第十五条　国外に居住することとなつた個人が次の各号のいずれかに該当する場合には、その者は、国内に住所を有しない者と推定する。

一　その者が国外において、継続して一年以上居住することを通常必要とする職業を有すること。

二　その者が外国の国籍を有し又は外国の法令によりその外国に永住する許可を受けており、かつ、その者が国内において生計を一にする配偶者その他の親族を有しないことその他国内におけるその者の職業及び資産の有無等の状況に照らし、その者が再び国内に帰り、主として国内に居住するものと推測するに足りる事実がないこと。

2　前項の規定により国内に住所を有しない者と推定される個人と生計を一にする配偶者その他その者の扶養する親族が国外に居住する場合には、これらの者も国内に住所を有しない者と推定する。

（国内に源泉がある給与、報酬又は年金の範囲）

第二百八十五条　法第百六十一条第一項第十二号イ（国内源泉所得）に規定する政令で定める人的役務の提供は、次に掲げる勤務その他の人的役務の提供とする。

一　内国法人の役員としての勤務で国外において行うもの（当該役員としての勤務を行う者が同時にその内国法人の使用人として常時勤務を行う場合の当該役員としての勤務を除く。）

二　居住者又は内国法人が運航する船舶又は航空機において行う勤務その他の人的役務の提供（国外における寄航地において行われる一時的な人的役務の提供を除く。）

2　法第百六十一条第一項第十二号ロに規定する政令で定める公的年金等は、第七十二条第三項第八号（退職手当等とみなす一時金）に規定する制度に基づいて支給される年金（これに類する給付を含む。）とする。

3　法第百六十一条第一項第十二号ハに規定する政令で定める人的役務の提供は、第一項各号に掲げる勤務その他の人的役務の提供で当該勤務その他の人的役務の提供を行う者が非居住者であつた期間に行つたものとする。

（所得税基本通達）

（住所の意義）

2－1　法に規定する住所とは各人の生活の本拠をいい、生活の本拠であるかどうかは客観的事実によって判定する。

（注）　国の内外にわたって居住地が異動する者の住所が国内にあるかどうかの判定に当たっては、令第14条《国内に住所を有する者と推定する場合》及び第15条《国内に住所を有しない者と推定する場合》の規定があることに留意する。

（再入国した場合の居住期間）

2－2　国内に居所を有していた者が国外に赴き再び入国した場合において、国外に赴いていた期間（以下この項において「在外期間」という。）中、国内に、配偶者その他生計を一にする親族を残し、再入国後起居する予定の家屋若しくはホテルの一室等を保有し、又は生活用動産を預託している事実があるなど、明らかにその国外に赴いた目的が一時的なものであると認められるときは、当該在外期間中も引き続き国内に居所を有するものとして、法第2条第1項第3号及び第4号の規定を適用する。

（国内に居住する者の非永住者等の区分）

2－3　国内に居住する者については、次により非居住者、非永住者等の区分を行うことに留意する。（平18課個2－7、課資3－2、課審4－89改正）

(1)　入国後1年を経過する日まで住所を有しない場合　　入国後1年を経過する日までの間は非居住者、1年を経過する日の翌日以後は居住者

(2)　入国直後には国内に住所がなく、入国後1年を経過する日までの間に住所を有することとなった場合　　住所を有することとなった日の前日までの間は非居住者、住所を有することとなった日以後は居住者

(3)　日本の国籍を有していない居住者で、過去10年以内において国内に住所又は居所を有していた期間の合計が5年を超える場合　　5年以内の日までの間は非永住者、その翌日以後は非永住者以外の居住者

（居住期間の計算の起算日）

2－4　法第2条第1項第3号に規定する「1年以上」の期間の計算の起算日は、入国の日の翌日となることに留意する。（平18課個2－7、課資3－2、課審4－89改正）

（過去10年以内の計算）

2－4の2　法第2条第1項第4号に規定する「過去10年以内」とは、判定する日の10年前の同日から、判定する日の前日までをいうことに留意する。（平18課個2－7、課資3－2、

課審４－89追加）

（国内に住所又は居所を有していた期間の計算）

２－４の３　法第２条第１項第４号に規定する「国内に住所又は居所を有していた期間」は、暦に従って計算し、１月に満たない期間は日をもって数える。

また、当該期間が複数ある場合には、これらの年数、月数及び日数をそれぞれ合計し、日数は30日をもって１月とし、月数は12月をもって１年とする。

なお、過去10年以内に住所又は居所を有することとなった日（以下この項において「入国の日」という。）と住所又は居所を有しないこととなった日（以下この項において「出国の日」という。）がある場合には、当該期間は、入国の日の翌日から出国の日までとなることに留意する。（平18課個２－７、課資３－２、課審４－89追加）

（国内に居住することとなった者等の住所の推定）

３－３　国内又は国外において事業を営み若しくは職業に従事するため国内又は国外に居住することとなった者は、その地における在留期間が契約等によりあらかじめ１年未満であることが明らかであると認められる場合を除き、それぞれ令第14条第１項第１号又は第15条第１項第１号の規定に該当するものとする。

〔使用料等の所得（第11号関係）〕

（当該業務に係るものの意義）

161－33　法第161条第１項第11号に掲げる「当該業務に係るもの」とは、国内において業務を行う者に対し提供された同号イ、ロ又はハに規定する資産の使用料又は対価で、当該資産のうち国内において行う業務の用に供されている部分に対応するものをいう。したがって、例えば、居住者又は内国法人が非居住者又は外国法人から提供を受けた工業所有権等を国外において業務を行う他の者（以下この項において「再実施権者」という。）の当該国外における業務の用に提供することにより当該非居住者又は外国法人に対して支払う使用料のうち、再実施権者の使用に係る部分の使用料（当該居住者又は内国法人が再実施権者から受領する使用料の額を超えて支払う場合には、その受領する使用料の額に達するまでの部分の金額に限る。）は、同号に掲げる使用料に該当しないことに留意する（平28課２－４、課法11－８、課審５－５改正）。

（工業所有権等の意義）

161－34　法第161条第１項第11号イに規定する「工業所有権その他の技術に関する権利、特別の技術による生産方式若しくはこれらに準ずるもの」（以下第161条関係において「工業所有権等」という。）とは、特許権、実用新案権、意匠権、商標権の工業所有権及びその実施権等のほか、これらの権利の目的にはなっていないが、生産その他業務に関し繰り返し使用し得るまでに形成された創作、すなわち、特別の原料、処方、機械、器具、工程によるなど独自の考案又は方法を用いた生産についての方式、これに準ずる秘けつ、秘伝その他特別に技術的価値を有する知識及び意匠等をいう。したがって、ノーハウはもちろん、機械、設備等の設計及び図面等に化体された生産方式、デザインもこれに含まれるが、海外における技術の動向、製品の販路、特定の品目の生産高等の情報又は機械、装置、原材料等の材質等の鑑定若しくは性能の調査、検査等は、これに該当しない（平28課２－４、課法11－８、課審５－５追加）。

（使用料の意義）

161－35　法第161条第１項第11号イの工業所有権等の使用料とは、工業所有権等の実施、使用、採用、提供若しくは伝授又は工業所有権等に係る実施権若しくは使用権の設定、許諾若しくはその譲渡の承諾につき支払を受ける対価の一切をいい、同号ロの著作権の使用料とは、著作物（著作権法第２条第１項第１号（(定義)）に規定する著作物をいう。以下この項において同じ。）の複製、上演、演奏、放送、展示、上映、翻訳、編曲、脚色、映画化その他著作物の利用又は出版権の設定につき支払を受ける対価の一切をいうのであるから、これらの使用料には、契約を締結するに当たって支払を受けるいわゆる頭金、権利金等のほか、これらのものを提供し、又は伝授するために要する費用に充てるものとして支払を受けるものも含まれることに留意する（平28課２－４、課法11－８、課審５－５改正）。

（図面、人的役務等の提供の対価として支払を受けるものが使用料に該当するかどうかの判定）

161－36　工業所有権等を提供し又は伝授するために図面、型紙、見本等の物又は人的役務を提供し、かつ、当該工業所有権等の提供又は伝授の対価の全てを当該提供した物又は人的役務の対価として支払を受ける場合には、当該対価として支払を受けるもののうち、次のいずれかに該当するものは法第161条第１項第11号イに掲げる使用料に該当するものとし、その他のものは当該物又は人的役務の提供の対価に該当するものとする（平28課２－４、課法11－８、課審５－５改正）。

⑴　当該対価として支払を受ける金額が、当該提供し又は伝授した工業所有権等を使用した回数、期間、生産高又はその使用による利益の額に応じて算定されるもの

⑵　⑴に掲げるもののほか、当該対価として支払を受ける金額が、当該図面その他の物の作成又は当該人的役務の提供のために要した経費の額に通常の利潤の額（個人が自己の作成した図面その他の物を提供し、又は自己の人的役務を提供した場合には、その者がその物の作成又は人的役務の提供につき通常受けるべき報酬の額を含む。）を加算した金額に相当する金額を超えるもの

（注）　上記により物又は人的役務の提供の対価に該当するとされるものは、通常その図面等が作成された地又は人的役務の提供が行われた地に源泉がある所得と

なる。

なお、これらの所得のうち、国内源泉所得とされるものは、同項第1号、第6号又は第12号に掲げる所得に該当する。

（使用料に含まれないもの）

161－37　工業所有権等又は著作権の提供契約に基づき支払を受けるもののうち次に掲げる費用又は代金で、当該契約の目的である工業所有権等又は著作権の使用料として支払を受ける金額と明確に区分されているものは、161－35及び161－36にかかわらず、法第161条第1項第11号イ又はロに掲げる使用料に該当しないものとする（平28課2－4、課法11－8、課審5－5改正）。

(1)　工業所有権等の提供契約に基づき、工業所有権等の提供者が自ら又は技術者を派遣して国内において人的役務を提供するために要する費用（例えば、派遣技術者の給与及び通常必要と認められる渡航費、国内滞在費、国内旅費）

(2)　工業所有権等の提供契約に基づき、工業所有権等の提供者のもとに技術習得のために派遣された技術者に対し技術の伝授をするために要する費用

(3)　工業所有権等の提供契約に基づき提供する図面、型紙、見本等の物の代金で、その作成のための実費の程度を超えないと認められるもの

(4)　映画フィルム、テレビジョン放送用のフィルム又はビデオテープの提供契約に基づき、これらの物とともに提供するスチール写真等の広告宣伝用材料の代金で、その作成のための実費の程度を超えないと認められるもの

（法人税法）

（法人税額から控除する外国税額の損金不算入）

第四十一条　内国法人が第六十九条第一項（外国税額の控除）に規定する控除対象外国法人税の額につき同条又は第七十八条第一項（所得税額等の還付）若しくは第百三十三条第一項（更正等による所得税額等の還付）の規定の適用を受ける場合には、当該控除対象外国法人税の額は、その内国法人の各事業年度の所得の金額の計算上、損金の額に算入しない。

（外国税額の控除）

第六十九条　内国法人が各事業年度において外国法人税（外国の法令により課される法人税に相当する税で政令で定めるものをいう。以下この項及び第十二項において同じ。）を納付することとなる場合には、当該事業年度の所得の金額につき第六十六条第一項から第三項まで（各事業年度の所得に対する法人税の税率）の規定を適用して計算した金額のうち当該事業年度の国外所得金額（国外源泉所得に係る所得のみについて各事業年度の所得に対する法人税を課するものとした場合に課税標準となるべき当該事業年度の所得の金額に相当するものとして政令で定める金額をいう。第十四項において同じ。）に対応するものとして政令で定めるところにより計算した金額（以下この条において「控除限度額」という。）を限度として、その外国法人税の額（その所得に対する負担が高率な部分として政令で定める外国法人税の額、内国法人の通常行われる取引と認められないものとして政令で定める取引に基因して生じた所得に対して課される外国法人税の額、内国法人の法人税に関する法令の規定により法人税が課されないこととなる金額を課税標準として外国法人税に関する法令により課されるものとして政令で定める外国法人税の額その他政令で定める外国法人税の額を除く。以下この条において「控除対象外国法人税の額」という。）を当該事業年度の所得に対する法人税の額から控除する。

2　内国法人が各事業年度において納付することとなる控除対象外国法人税の額が当該事業年度の控除限度額、地方法人税法第十二条第一項（外国税額の控除）に規定する地方法人税控除限度額及び地方税控除限度額として政令で定める金額の合計額を超える場合において、前三年内事業年度（当該事業年度開始の日前三年以内に開始した各事業年度をいう。以下この条において同じ。）の控除限度額のうち当該事業年度に繰り越される部分として政令で定める金額（以下この項及び第二十六項において「繰越控除限度額」という。）があるときは、政令で定めるところにより、その繰越控除限度額を限度として、その超える部分の金額を当該事業年度の所得に対する法人税の額から控除する。

3　内国法人が各事業年度において納付することとなる控除対象外国法人税の額が当該事業年度の控除限度額に満たない場合において、その前三年内事業年度において納付することとなつた控除対象外国法人税の額のうち当該事業年度に繰り越される部分として政令で定める金額（以下この項及び第二十六項において「繰越控除対象外国法人税額」という。）があるときは、政令で定めるところにより、当該控除限度額から当該事業年度において納付することとなる控除対象外国法人税の額を控除した残額を限度として、その繰越控除対象外国法人税額を当該事業年度の所得に対する法人税の額から控除する。

4　第一項に規定する国外源泉所得とは、次に掲げるものをいう。

一　内国法人が国外事業所等（国外にある恒久的施設に相当するものその他の政令で定めるものをいう。以下この条において同じ。）を通じて事業を行う場合において、当該国外事業所等が当該内国法人から独立して事業を行う事業者であるとしたならば、当該国外事業所等が果たす機能、当該国外事業所等において使用する資産、当該国外事業所等と当該内国法人の本店等（当該内国法人の本店、支店、工場その他これらに準ずるものとして政令で定めるものであつて当該国外事業所等以外のものをいう。以下この条において同じ。）との間の内部取引その他の状況を勘案して、当該国外事業所等に帰せられるべき所得（当該国外事業所等の譲渡により生ずる所得を含み、第十四号に該当するものを除く。）

二　国外にある資産の運用又は保有により生ずる所得

三　国外にある資産の譲渡により生ずる所得として政令で定めるもの

四　国外において人的役務の提供を主たる内容とする事業で政令で定めるものを行う法人が受ける当該人的役務の提供に係る対価

五　国外にある不動産、国外にある不動産の上に存する権利若しくは国外における採石権の貸付け（地上権又は採石権の設定その他他人に不動産、不動産の上に存する権利又は採石権を使用させる一切の行為を含む。）、国外における租鉱権の設定又は所得税法第二条第一項第五号（定義）に規定する非居住者若しくは外国法人に対する船舶若しくは航空機の貸付けによる対価

六　所得税法第二十三条第一項（利子所得）に規定する利子等及びこれに相当するもののうち次に掲げるもの

イ　外国の国債若しくは地方債又は外国法人の発行する債券の利子

ロ　国外にある営業所、事務所その他これらに準ずるもの（以下この項において「営業所」という。）に預け入れられた預貯金（所得税法第二条第一項第十号に規定する政令で定めるものに相当するものを含む。）の利子

ハ　国外にある営業所に信託された合同運用信託若しくはこれに相当する信託、公社債投資信託又は公募公社債等運用投資信託（所得税法第二条第一項第十五号の三に規定する公募公社債等運用投資信託をいう。次号ロにおいて同じ。）若しくはこれに相当する信託の収益の分配

七　所得税法第二十四条第一項（配当所得）に規定する配当等及びこれに相当するもののうち次に掲げるもの

イ　外国法人から受ける所得税法第二十四条第一項に規定する剰余金の配当、利益の配当若しくは剰余金の分配又は同項に規定する金銭の分配若しくは基金利息に相当するもの

ロ　国外にある営業所に信託された所得税法第二条第一項第十二号の二に規定する投資信託（公社債投資信託並びに公募公社債等運用投資信託及びこれに相当する信託を除く。）

又は第二条第二十九号ハ（定義）に規定する特定受益証券発行信託若しくはこれに相当する信託の収益の分配

ハ　国外において業務を行う者に対する貸付金（これに準ずるものを含む。）で当該業務に係るものの利子（債券の買戻又は売戻条件付売買取引として政令で定めるものから生ずる差益として政令で定めるものを含む。）

九　国外において業務を行う者から受ける次に掲げる使用料又は対価で当該業務に係るもの

イ　工業所有権その他の技術に関する権利、特別の技術による生産方式若しくはこれらに準ずるものの使用料又はその譲渡による対価

ロ　著作権（出版権及び著作隣接権その他これに準ずるものを含む。）の使用料又はその譲渡による対価

ハ　機械、装置その他政令で定める用具の使用料

十　国外において行う事業の広告宣伝のための賞金として政令で定めるもの

十一　国外にある営業所又は国外において契約の締結の代理をする者を通じて締結した保険業法第二条第六項（定義）に規定する外国保険業者の締結する保険契約その他の年金に係る契約で政令で定めるものに基づいて受ける年金（年金の支払の開始の日以後に当該年金に係る契約に基づき分配を受ける剰余金又は割戻しを受ける割戻金及び当該契約に基づき年金に代えて支給される一時金を含む。）

十二　次に掲げる給付補塡金、利息、利益又は差益

イ　所得税法第百七十四条第三号（内国法人に係る所得税の課税標準）に掲げる給付補塡金のうち国外にある営業所が受け入れた定期積金に係るもの

ロ　所得税法第百七十四条第四号に掲げる給付補塡金に相当するもののうち国外にある営業所が受け入れた同号に規定する掛金に相当するものに係るもの

ハ　所得税法第百七十四条第五号に掲げる利息に相当するもののうち国外にある営業所を通じて締結された同号に規定する契約に相当するものに係るもの

ニ　所得税法第百七十四条第六号に掲げる利益のうち国外にある営業所を通じて締結された同号に規定する契約に係るもの

ホ　所得税法第百七十四条第七号に掲げる差益のうち国外にある営業所が受け入れた預貯金に係るもの

ヘ　所得税法第百七十四条第八号に掲げる差益に相当するもののうち国外にある営業所又は国外において契約の締結の代理をする者を通じて締結された同号に規定する契約に相当するものに係るもの

十三　国外において事業を行う者に対する出資につき、匿名組合契約（これに準ずる契約として政令で定めるものを含む。）に基づいて受ける利益の分配

十四　国内及び国外にわたつて船舶又は航空機による運送の事業を行うことにより生ずる所得のうち国外において行う業務につき生ずべき所得として政令で定めるもの

十五　第二条第十二号の十九ただし書に規定する条約（以下この号及び第六項から第八項までにおいて「租税条約」という。）の規定により当該租税条約の我が国以外の締約国又は

締約者（第七項及び第八項において「相手国等」という。）において租税を課することができることとされる所得のうち政令で定めるもの

十六　前各号に掲げるもののほかその源泉が国外にある所得として政令で定めるもの

5　前項第一号に規定する内部取引とは、内国法人の国外事業所等と本店等との間で行われた資産の移転、役務の提供その他の事実で、独立の事業者の間で同様の事実があつたとしたならば、これらの事業者の間で、資産の販売、資産の購入、役務の提供その他の取引（資金の借入れに係る債務の保証、保険契約に係る保険責任についての再保険の引受けその他これらに類する取引として政令で定めるものを除く。）が行われたと認められるものをいう。

6　租税条約において国外源泉所得（第一項に規定する国外源泉所得をいう。以下この項において同じ。）につき前二項の規定と異なる定めがある場合には、その租税条約の適用を受ける内国法人については、これらの規定にかかわらず、国外源泉所得は、その異なる定めがある限りにおいて、その租税条約に定めるところによる。

7　内国法人の第四項第一号に掲げる所得を算定する場合において、当該内国法人の国外事業所等が、租税条約（当該内国法人の同号に掲げる所得に対して租税を課することができる旨の定めのあるものに限るものとし、同号に規定する内部取引から所得が生ずる旨の定めのあるものを除く。）の相手国等に所在するときは、同号に規定する内部取引には、当該内国法人の国外事業所等と本店等との間の利子（これに準ずるものとして政令で定めるものを含む。以下この項において同じ。）の支払に相当する事実（政令で定める金融機関に該当する内国法人の国外事業所等と本店等との間の利子の支払に相当する事実を除く。）その他政令で定める事実は、含まれないものとする。

8　内国法人の国外事業所等が、租税条約（内国法人の国外事業所等が本店等のために棚卸資産を購入する業務及びそれ以外の業務を行う場合に、その棚卸資産を購入する業務から生ずる所得が、その国外事業所等に帰せられるべき所得に含まれないとする定めのあるものに限る。）の相手国等に所在し、かつ、当該内国法人の国外事業所等が本店等のために棚卸資産を購入する業務及びそれ以外の業務を行う場合には、当該国外事業所等のその棚卸資産を購入する業務から生ずる第四項第一号に掲げる所得は、ないものとする。

9　内国法人が適格合併、適格分割又は適格現物出資（以下この項及び第十二項において「適格合併等」という。）により被合併法人、分割法人又は現物出資法人（同項において「被合併法人等」という。）である他の内国法人から事業の全部又は一部の移転を受けた場合には、当該内国法人の当該適格合併等の日の属する事業年度以後の各事業年度における第二項及び第三項の規定の適用については、次の各号に掲げる適格合併等の区分に応じ当該各号に定める金額は、政令で定めるところにより、当該内国法人の前三年内事業年度の控除限度額及び当該内国法人が当該前三年内事業年度において納付することとなつた控除対象外国法人税の額とみなす。

一　適格合併　当該適格合併に係る被合併法人の合併前三年内事業年度（適格合併の日前三年以内に開始した各事業年度をいう。）の控除限度額及び控除対象外国法人税の額

二　適格分割又は適格現物出資（以下第十一項までにおいて「適格分割等」という。）　当該

適格分割等に係る分割法人又は現物出資法人（次項及び第十一項において「分割法人等」という。）の分割等前三年内事業年度（適格分割等の日の属する事業年度開始の日前三年以内に開始した各事業年度をいう。同項において同じ。）の控除限度額及び控除対象外国法人税の額のうち、当該適格分割等により当該内国法人が移転を受けた事業に係る部分の金額として政令で定めるところにより計算した金額

10　前項の規定は、適格分割等により当該適格分割等に係る分割法人等である他の内国法人から事業の移転を受けた内国法人にあつては、当該内国法人が当該適格分割等の日以後三月以内に当該内国法人の前三年内事業年度の控除限度額及び控除対象外国法人税の額とみなされる金額その他の財務省令で定める事項を記載した書類を納税地の所轄税務署長に提出した場合に限り、適用する。

11　適格分割等に係る分割承継法人又は被現物出資法人（以下この項において「分割承継法人等」という。）が第九項の規定の適用を受ける場合には、当該適格分割等に係る分割法人等の当該適格分割等の日の属する事業年度以後の各事業年度における第二項及び第三項の規定の適用については、当該分割法人等の分割等前三年内事業年度の控除限度額及び控除対象外国法人税の額のうち、第九項の規定により当該分割承継法人等の前三年内事業年度の控除限度額とみなされる金額及び同項の規定により当該分割承継法人等が当該前三年内事業年度において納付することとなつた控除対象外国法人税の額とみなされる金額は、ないものとする。

12　内国法人が納付することとなつた外国法人税の額につき第一項から第三項まで又は第十八項（第二十四項において準用する場合を含む。）の規定の適用を受けた事業年度（以下この項において「適用事業年度」という。）開始の日後七年以内に開始する当該内国法人の各事業年度において当該外国法人税の額が減額された場合（当該内国法人が適格合併等により被合併法人等である他の内国法人から事業の全部又は一部の移転を受けた場合にあつては、当該被合併法人等が納付することとなつた外国法人税の額のうち当該内国法人が移転を受けた事業に係る所得に基因して納付することとなつた外国法人税の額に係る当該被合併法人等の適用事業年度開始の日後七年以内に開始する当該内国法人の各事業年度において当該外国法人税の額が減額された場合を含む。）における第一項から第三項までの規定の適用については、政令で定めるところによる。

13　前各項の規定は、内国法人である公益法人等又は人格のない社団等が収益事業以外の事業又はこれに属する資産から生ずる所得について納付する控除対象外国法人税の額については、適用しない。

14　通算法人の第一項の各事業年度（当該通算法人に係る通算親法人の事業年度終了の日に終了するものに限る。以下この項において「通算事業年度」という。）の第一項の控除限度額は、当該通算法人の当該通算事業年度の所得の金額につき第六十六条第一項、第三項及び第六項の規定を適用して計算した金額並びに当該通算事業年度終了の日において当該通算法人との間に通算完全支配関係がある他の通算法人の当該終了の日に終了する各事業年度の所得の金額につき同条第一項、第三項及び第六項の規定を適用して計算した金額の合計額のうち、当該通算法人の当該通算事業年度の国外所得金額に対応するものとして政令で定めるところ

により計算した金額とする。

15　第一項から第三項までの規定を適用する場合において、通算法人の第一項から第三項までの各事業年度（当該通算法人に係る通算親法人の事業年度終了の日に終了するものに限るものとし、被合併法人の合併の日の前日の属する事業年度、残余財産の確定の日の属する事業年度及び公益法人等に該当することとなつた日の前日の属する事業年度を除く。以下第十七項までにおいて「適用事業年度」という。）の税額控除額（当該適用事業年度における第一項から第三項までの規定による控除をされるべき金額をいう。以下この条において同じ。）が、当初申告税額控除額（当該適用事業年度の第七十四条第一項（確定申告）の規定による申告書に添付された書類に当該適用事業年度の税額控除額として記載された金額をいう。以下この項及び第十七項において同じ。）と異なるときは、当初申告税額控除額を税額控除額とみなす。

16　前項の通算法人の適用事業年度について、次に掲げる場合のいずれかに該当する場合には、当該適用事業年度については、同項の規定は、適用しない。

一　通算法人又は当該通算法人の適用事業年度終了の日において当該通算法人との間に通算完全支配関係がある他の通算法人が、適用事業年度における税額控除額の計算の基礎となる事実の全部又は一部を隠蔽し、又は仮装して税額控除額を増加させることによりその法人税の負担を減少させ、又は減少させようとする場合

二　第六十四条の五第八項（損益通算）の規定の適用がある場合

17　適用事業年度について前項（第一号に係る部分に限る。）の規定を適用して修正申告書の提出又は更正がされた後における第十五項の規定の適用については、前項の規定にかかわらず、当該修正申告書又は当該更正に係る国税通則法第二十八条第二項（更正又は決定の手続）に規定する更正通知書に添付された書類に当該適用事業年度の税額控除額として記載された金額を当初申告税額控除額とみなす。

18　通算法人（通算法人であつた内国法人（公益法人等に該当することとなつた内国法人を除く。）を含む。以下第二十一項までにおいて同じ。）の各事業年度（以下第二十二項までにおいて「対象事業年度」という。）において、過去適用事業年度（当該対象事業年度開始の日前に開始した各事業年度で第十五項の規定の適用を受けた事業年度をいう。以下この項及び第二十一項において同じ。）における税額控除額（当該対象事業年度開始の日前に開始した各事業年度（以下この項において「対象前各事業年度」という。）において当該過去適用事業年度に係る税額控除額につきこの項又は次項の規定の適用があつた場合には、同項の規定により当該対象前各事業年度の法人税の額に加算した金額の合計額からこの項の規定により当該対象前各事業年度の法人税の額から控除した金額の合計額を減算した金額を加算した金額。以下この項及び次項において「調整後過去税額控除額」という。）が過去当初申告税額控除額（当該過去適用事業年度の第七十四条第一項の規定による申告書に添付された書類に当該過去適用事業年度の第一項から第三項までの規定による控除をされるべき金額として記載された金額（当該過去適用事業年度について前項の規定の適用を受けた場合には、その適用に係る修正申告書又は更正に係る国税通則法第二十八条第二項に規定する更正通知書に添

付された書類のうち、最も新しいものに当該過去適用事業年度の第一項から第三項までの規定による控除をされるべき金額として記載された金額）をいう。以下この項及び次項において同じ。）を超える場合には、税額控除不足額相当額（当該調整後過去税額控除額から当該過去当初申告税額控除額を控除した金額に相当する金額をいう。第二十項から第二十二項までにおいて同じ。）を当該対象事業年度の所得に対する法人税の額から控除する。

19　通算法人の対象事業年度において過去当初申告税額控除額が調整後過去税額控除額を超える場合には、当該対象事業年度の所得に対する法人税の額は、第六十六条第一項から第三項まで及び第六項の規定にかかわらず、これらの規定により計算した法人税の額に、税額控除超過額相当額（当該過去当初申告税額控除額から当該調整後過去税額控除額を控除した金額に相当する金額をいう。次項から第二十二項までにおいて同じ。）を加算した金額とする。

20　前二項の規定を適用する場合において、通算法人の対象事業年度の税額控除不足額相当額又は税額控除超過額相当額が当初申告税額控除不足額相当額又は当初申告税額控除超過額相当額（それぞれ当該対象事業年度の第七十四条第一項の規定による申告書に添付された書類に当該対象事業年度の税額控除不足額相当額又は税額控除超過額相当額として記載された金額をいう。以下この項及び第二十二項において同じ。）と異なるときは、当初申告税額控除不足額相当額又は当初申告税額控除超過額相当額を当該対象事業年度の税額控除不足額相当額又は税額控除超過額相当額とみなす。

21　前項の通算法人の対象事業年度について、次に掲げる場合のいずれかに該当する場合には、当該対象事業年度については、同項の規定は、適用しない。

一　税額控除不足額相当額又は税額控除超過額相当額の計算の基礎となる事実の全部又は一部を隠蔽し、又は仮装して、当該税額控除不足額相当額を増加させ、又は当該税額控除超過額相当額を減少させることによりその法人税の負担を減少させ、又は減少させようとする場合

二　対象事業年度において第十八項の規定により法人税の額から控除した税額控除不足額相当額又は第十九項の規定により法人税の額に加算した税額控除超過額相当額に係る過去適用事業年度について第十六項の規定の適用がある場合

三　対象事業年度（第三十二項又は第三十三項の規定による説明が行われた日の属するものに限る。以下この号において同じ。）の第七十四条第一項の規定による申告書に添付された書類に当該対象事業年度の税額控除不足額相当額又は税額控除超過額相当額として記載された金額及びその計算の根拠が第三十二項又は第三十三項の規定による説明の内容と異なる場合

22　対象事業年度について前項の規定を適用して修正申告書の提出又は更正がされた後における第二十項の規定の適用については、前項の規定にかかわらず、当該修正申告書又は当該更正に係る国税通則法第二十八条第二項に規定する更正通知書に添付された書類に当該対象事業年度の税額控除不足額相当額又は税額控除超過額相当額として記載された金額を当初申告税額控除不足額相当額又は当初申告税額控除超過額相当額とみなす。

23　第十八項及び第十九項の規定は、通算法人（通算法人であつた内国法人を含む。以下この

項及び次項において同じ。）が合併により解散した場合又は通算法人の残余財産が確定した場合について準用する。この場合において、次の表の上欄に掲げる規定中同表の中欄に掲げる字句は、それぞれ同表の下欄に掲げる字句に読み替えるものとする。

第十八項	の各事業年度（以下第二十二項までにおいて「対象事業年度」という。）において、過去適用事業年度（当該対象事業年度	が合併により解散した場合又は通算法人の残余財産が確定した場合において、その合併の日以後又はその残余財産の確定の日の翌日以後に、過去適用事業年度（最終事業年度（その合併の日の前日又はその残余財産の確定の日の属する事業年度をいう。以下この項及び次項において同じ。）
	税額控除額（当該対象事業年度	税額控除額（当該最終事業年度
	超える場合には	超えるときは
	を当該対象事業年度	を当該最終事業年度
第十九項	の対象事業年度において	が合併により解散した場合又は通算法人の残余財産が確定した場合において、その合併の日以後又はその残余財産の確定の日の翌日以後に
	場合には、当該対象事業年度	ときは、最終事業年度

24　第十八項及び第十九項の規定は、通算法人が公益法人等に該当することとなつた場合について準用する。この場合において、次の表の上欄に掲げる規定中同表の中欄に掲げる字句は、それぞれ同表の下欄に掲げる字句に読み替えるものとする。

第十八項	の各事業年度（以下第二十二項までにおいて「対象事業年度」という。）において、過去適用事業年度（当該対象事業年度	が公益法人等に該当することとなつた場合において、その該当することとなつた日以後に、過去適用事業年度（最終事業年度（その該当することとなつた日の前日の属する事業年度をいう。以下この項及び次項において同じ。）
	税額控除額（当該対象事業年度	税額控除額（当該最終事業年度
	超える場合には	超えるときは
	を当該対象事業年度	を当該最終事業年度
第十九項	の対象事業年度において	が公益法人等に該当することとなつた場合において、その該当することとなつた日以後に
	場合には、当該対象事業年度	ときは、最終事業年度

25　第一項の規定は、確定申告書、修正申告書又は更正請求書（次項、第二十七項及び第三十一項において「申告書等」という。）に第一項の規定による控除を受けるべき金額及びその計算に関する明細を記載した書類並びに控除対象外国法人税の額の計算に関する明細その他の財務省令で定める事項を記載した書類（以下この項において「明細書」という。）の添付があり、かつ、控除対象外国法人税の額を課されたことを証する書類その他の財務省令で定める書類を保存している場合に限り、適用する。この場合において、第一項の規定による控

除をされるべき金額の計算の基礎となる控除対象外国法人税の額その他の財務省令で定める金額は、税務署長において特別の事情があると認める場合を除くほか、当該明細書に当該金額として記載された金額を限度とする。

26　第二項及び第三項の規定は、繰越控除限度額又は繰越控除対象外国法人税額に係る事業年度のうち最も古い事業年度以後の各事業年度の申告書等に当該各事業年度の控除限度額及び当該各事業年度において納付することとなつた控除対象外国法人税の額を記載した書類の添付があり、かつ、これらの規定の適用を受けようとする事業年度の申告書等にこれらの規定による控除を受けるべき金額を記載した書類及び繰越控除限度額又は繰越控除対象外国法人税額の計算の基礎となるべき事項その他の財務省令で定める事項を記載した書類の添付があり、かつ、これらの規定による控除を受けるべき金額に係る控除対象外国法人税の額を課されたことを証する書類その他の財務省令で定める書類を保存している場合に限り、適用する。この場合において、これらの規定による控除をされるべき金額の計算の基礎となる当該各事業年度の控除限度額及び当該各事業年度において納付することとなつた控除対象外国法人税の額その他の財務省令で定める金額は、税務署長において特別の事情があると認める場合を除くほか、当該各事業年度の申告書等にこの項前段の規定により添付された書類に当該計算の基礎となる金額として記載された金額を限度とする。

27　第十八項（第二十三項及び第二十四項において準用する場合を含む。以下第三十項までにおいて同じ。）の規定は、申告書等に第十八項の規定による控除を受けるべき金額及びその計算に関する明細を記載した書類その他の財務省令で定める事項を記載した書類（以下この項において「明細書」という。）の添付があり、かつ、第十八項の規定による控除を受けるべき金額に係る控除対象外国法人税の額を課されたことを証する書類その他の財務省令で定める書類を保存している場合に限り、適用する。この場合において、同項の規定による控除をされるべき金額の計算の基礎となる控除対象外国法人税の額その他の財務省令で定める金額は、税務署長において特別の事情があると認める場合を除くほか、当該明細書に当該金額として記載された金額を限度とする。

28　税務署長は、第一項から第三項まで又は第十八項の規定による控除をされるべきこととなる金額の全部又は一部につき前三項に規定する財務省令で定める書類の保存がない場合においても、その書類の保存がなかつたことについてやむを得ない事情があると認めるときは、その書類の保存がなかつた金額につき第一項から第三項まで又は第十八項の規定を適用することができる。

29　第一項から第三項まで又は第十八項の規定の適用を受ける内国法人は、当該内国法人が他の者との間で行つた取引のうち、当該内国法人の各事業年度の第一項に規定する国外所得金額の計算上、当該取引から生ずる所得が当該内国法人の国外事業所等に帰せられるものについては、財務省令で定めるところにより、当該国外事業所等に帰せられる取引に係る明細を記載した書類その他の財務省令で定める書類を作成しなければならない。

30　第一項から第三項まで又は第十八項の規定の適用を受ける内国法人は、当該内国法人の本店等と国外事業所等との間の資産の移転、役務の提供その他の事実が第四項第一号に規定する内部取引に該当するときは、財務省令で定めるところにより、当該事実に係る明細を記載した書類その他の財務省令で定める書類を作成しなければならない。

31　第十九項（第二十三項及び第二十四項において準用する場合を含む。以下この項において同じ。）の規定の適用を受ける通算法人（通算法人であつた内国法人を含む。次項及び第三十三項において同じ。）は、申告書等に第十九項の規定により法人税の額に加算されるべき金額及びその計算に関する明細を記載した書類その他の財務省令で定める事項を記載した書類（以下この項において「明細書」という。）を添付し、かつ、第十九項の規定により加算されるべき金額に係る控除対象外国法人税の額を課されたことを証する書類その他の財務省令で定める書類を保存しなければならない。この場合において、同項の規定により加算されるべき金額の計算の基礎となる控除対象外国法人税の額その他の財務省令で定める金額は、税務署長において特別の事情があると認める場合を除くほか、当該明細書に当該金額として記載された金額を限度とする。

32　法人税に関する調査を行つた結果、通算法人の各事業年度（第七十四条第一項の規定による申告書の提出期限が到来していないものに限る。）において第十八項又は第十九項の規定を適用すべきと認める場合には、国税庁、国税局又は税務署の当該職員は、当該通算法人に対し、その調査結果の内容（第十八項又は第十九項の規定を適用すべきと認めた金額及びその理由を含む。）を説明するものとする。

33　実地の調査により国税通則法第七十四条の九第一項（納税義務者に対する調査の事前通知等）に規定する質問検査等を行つた通算法人について同条第三項第二号に規定する税務代理人がある場合において、当該通算法人の同法第七十四条の十一第四項（調査の終了の際の手続）の同意があるときは、当該通算法人への前項に規定する説明に代えて、当該税務代理人への同項に規定する説明を行うことができる。

34　第十二項、第十三項及び第二十五項から前項までに定めるもののほか、第一項から第十一項まで及び第十四項から第二十四項までの規定の適用に関し必要な事項は、政令で定める。

（法人税法施行令）

（外国税額控除の対象とならない外国法人税の額）

第百四十二条の二　法第六十九条第一項（外国税額の控除）に規定するその所得に対する負担が高率な部分として政令で定める外国法人税の額（次項及び第三項において「所得に対する負担が高率な部分の金額」という。）は、同条第一項に規定する内国法人が納付することとなる外国法人税の額のうち当該外国法人税を課す国又は地域において当該外国法人税の課税標準とされる金額に百分の三十五を乗じて計算した金額を超える部分の金額とする。

2　次の各号に掲げる内国法人が納付することとなる法第六十九条第四項第六号及び第八号に掲げる国外源泉所得（以下この項において「利子等」という。）の収入金額を課税標準として所得税法第二条第一項第四十五号（定義）に規定する源泉徴収の方法に類する方法により課される外国法人税（当該外国法人税が課される国又は地域において、当該外国法人税以外の外国法人税の額から控除されるものを除く。）については、前項の規定にかかわらず、当該外国法人税の額のうち当該利子等の収入金額の百分の十に相当する金額を超える部分の金額が所得に対する負担が高率な部分の金額に該当するものとする。ただし、当該内国法人の所得率（次の各号に掲げる内国法人の区分に応じ、当該各号に定める割合をいう。以下この項において同じ。）が百分の十を超え百分の二十以下であるときは、当該外国法人税の額のうち当該利子等の収入金額の百分の十五に相当する金額を超える部分の金額が所得に対する負担が高率な部分の金額に該当するものとし、当該所得率が百分の二十を超えるときは、当該外国法人税の額のうち所得に対する負担が高率な部分の金額はないものとする。

一　金融業（金融商品取引法第二条第八項（定義）に規定する金融商品取引業を含む。）を主として営む内国法人　当該外国法人税を納付することとなる事業年度（以下この項において「納付事業年度」という。）及び納付事業年度開始の日前二年以内に開始した各事業年度（以下この項において「前二年内事業年度」という。）の調整所得金額の合計額を納付事業年度及び前二年内事業年度の総収入金額（当該総収入金額のうちに有価証券及び固定資産（以下この号において「資産」という。）の譲渡に係る収入金額がある場合には、当該収入金額から当該資産の譲渡の直前の帳簿価額を控除した残額を当該資産の譲渡に係る収入金額とみなして、当該総収入金額を算出するものとする。第四号において同じ。）の合計額で除して計算した割合

二　生命保険業を主として営む内国法人　納付事業年度及び前二年内事業年度の調整所得金額の合計額を前号に規定する総収入金額の合計額に相当する金額として財務省令で定める金額で除して計算した割合

三　損害保険業を主として営む内国法人　納付事業年度及び前二年内事業年度の調整所得金額の合計額を第一号に規定する総収入金額の合計額に相当する金額として財務省令で定める金額で除して計算した割合

四　前三号に掲げる事業以外の事業を主として営む内国法人（納付事業年度及び前二年内事

業年度の利子等の収入金額の合計額を当該合計額にこれらの事業年度の売上総利益の額の合計額として財務省令で定める金額を加算した金額で除して計算した割合が百分の二十以上である内国法人に限る。）　納付事業年度及び前二年内事業年度の調整所得金額の合計額をこれらの事業年度の総収入金額の合計額から当該これらの事業年度の売上総原価の額の合計額として財務省令で定める金額を控除した残額で除して計算した割合

3　外国法人税の額に我が国が租税条約（法第二条第十二号の十九ただし書（定義）に規定する条約をいう。以下この項及び第八項第五号において同じ。）を締結している条約相手国等（租税条約の我が国以外の締約国又は締約者をいう。以下この項及び同号において同じ。）の法律又は当該租税条約の規定により軽減され、又は免除された当該条約相手国等の租税の額で当該租税条約の規定により内国法人が納付したものとみなされるものの額（以下この項において「みなし納付外国法人税の額」という。）が含まれているときは、当該外国法人税の額のうち所得に対する負担が高率な部分の金額は、まずみなし納付外国法人税の額から成るものとする。

4　第二項各号に規定する調整所得金額とは、第七十三条第二項第一号及び第三号から第二十六号まで（一般寄附金の損金算入限度額）に掲げる規定並びに法第二十三条（受取配当等の益金不算入）、第二十三条の二（外国子会社から受ける配当等の益金不算入）、第三十七条（寄附金の損金不算入）、第三十九条の二（外国子会社から受ける配当等に係る外国源泉税等の損金不算入）及び第六十四条の八（通算法人の合併等があつた場合の欠損金の損金算入）並びに租税特別措置法第六十六条の四第三項（国外関連者との取引に係る課税の特例）、第六十六条の八第一項、第三項、第七項及び第九項（内国法人の外国関係会社に係る所得の課税の特例）並びに第六十六条の九の四第一項、第三項、第六項及び第八項（特殊関係株主等である内国法人に係る外国関係法人に係る所得の課税の特例）の規定を適用しないで計算した場合における所得の金額に外国法人税の額（損金経理をしたものに限るものとし、第七項第一号及び第二号に掲げるものを除く。）を加算した金額をいう。

5　法第六十九条第一項に規定する政令で定める取引は、次に掲げる取引とする。

一　内国法人が、当該内国法人が金銭の借入れをしている者又は預入を受けている者と特殊の関係のある者に対し、その借り入れられ、又は預入を受けた金銭の額に相当する額の金銭の貸付けをする取引（当該貸付けに係る利率その他の条件が、その借入れ又は預入に係る利率その他の条件に比し、特に有利な条件であると認められる場合に限る。）

二　貸付債権その他これに類する債権を譲り受けた内国法人が、当該債権に係る債務者（当該内国法人に対し当該債権を譲渡した者（以下この号において「譲渡者」という。）と特殊の関係のある者に限る。）から当該債権に係る利子の支払を受ける取引（当該内国法人が、譲渡者に対し、当該債権から生ずる利子の額のうち譲渡者が当該債権を所有していた期間に対応する部分の金額を支払う場合において、その支払う金額が、次に掲げる額の合計額に相当する額であるときに限る。）

イ　当該債権から生ずる利子の額から当該債務者が住所又は本店若しくは主たる事務所を有する国又は地域において当該内国法人が当該利子につき納付した外国法人税の額を控

除した額のうち、譲渡者が当該債権を所有していた期間に対応する部分の額

ロ　当該利子に係る外国法人税の額（第三項に規定するみなし納付外国法人税の額を含む。）のうち、譲渡者が当該債権を所有していた期間に対応する部分の額の全部又は一部に相当する額

6　前項に規定する特殊の関係のある者とは、次に掲げる者をいう。

一　第四条（同族関係者の範囲）に規定する個人又は法人

二　次に掲げる事実その他これに類する事実が存在することにより二の者のいずれか一方の者が他方の者の事業の方針の全部又は一部につき実質的に決定できる関係にある者

イ　当該他方の者の役員の二分の一以上又は代表する権限を有する役員が、当該一方の者の役員若しくは使用人を兼務している者又は当該一方の者の役員若しくは使用人であつた者であること。

ロ　当該他方の者がその事業活動の相当部分を当該一方の者との取引に依存して行つていること。

ハ　当該他方の者がその事業活動に必要とされる資金の相当部分を当該一方の者からの借入れにより、又は当該一方の者の保証を受けて調達していること。

三　その者の前項に規定する内国法人に対する債務の弁済につき、同項第一号に規定する内国法人が金銭の借入れをしている者若しくは預入を受けている者が保証をしている者又は同項第二号に規定する譲渡者が保証をしている者

7　法第六十九条第一項に規定する内国法人の法人税に関する法令の規定により法人税が課されないこととなる金額を課税標準として外国法人税に関する法令により課されるものとして政令で定める外国法人税の額は、次に掲げる外国法人税の額とする。

一　法第二十四条第一項各号（配当等の額とみなす金額）に掲げる事由により交付を受ける金銭の額及び金銭以外の資産の価額に対して課される外国法人税の額（当該交付の基因となつた同項に規定する法人の株式又は出資の取得価額を超える部分の金額に対して課される部分を除く。）

二　法人の所得の金額が租税条約等の実施に伴う所得税法、法人税法及び地方税法の特例等に関する法律（昭和四十四年法律第四十六号）第七条第一項（租税条約に基づく合意があつた場合の更正の特例）（外国居住者等の所得に対する相互主義による所得税等の非課税等に関する法律（昭和三十七年法律第百四十四号）第三十二条第二項（国税庁長官の確認があつた場合の更正の請求の特例等）において準用する場合を含む。）の規定により減額される場合において、租税条約等の実施に伴う所得税法、法人税法及び地方税法の特例等に関する法律第七条第三項に規定する相手国居住者等に支払われない金額又は外国居住者等の所得に対する相互主義による所得税等の非課税等に関する法律第三十二条第四項に規定する外国居住者等に支払われない金額に対し、これらを法第二十三条第一項第一号に掲げる金額に相当する金銭の支払とみなして課される外国法人税の額

三　法第二十三条の二第一項に規定する外国子会社から受ける同項に規定する剰余金の配当等の額（以下この号において「剰余金の配当等の額」といい、同条第二項の規定の適用を

受ける部分の金額を除く。）に係る外国法人税の額（剰余金の配当等の額を課税標準として課される外国法人税の額に限るものとし、剰余金の配当等の額（同条第二項の規定の適用を受ける部分の金額を除く。）の計算の基礎となつた同条第一項に規定する外国子会社の所得のうち内国法人に帰せられるものとして計算される金額を課税標準として当該内国法人に対して課される外国法人税の額を含む。）

四　国外事業所等（法第六十九条第四項第一号に規定する国外事業所等をいう。以下この号及び第六号において同じ。）から本店等（同項第一号に規定する本店等をいう。第六号において同じ。）への支払につき当該国外事業所等の所在する国又は地域において当該支払に係る金額を課税標準として課される外国法人税の額

五　内国法人が有する株式又は出資を発行した外国法人の本店又は主たる事務所の所在する国又は地域の法令に基づき、当該外国法人に係る租税の課税標準等（国税通則法第二条第六号イからハまで（定義）に掲げる事項をいう。）又は税額等（同号ニからヘまでに掲げる事項をいう。）につき更正又は決定（同法第二十五条（決定）の規定による決定をいう。）に相当する処分（当該内国法人との間の取引に係るものを除く。）があつた場合において、当該処分が行われたことにより増額された当該外国法人の所得の金額に相当する金額に対し、これを法第二十三条第一項第一号に掲げる金額に相当する金銭の支払とみなして課される外国法人税の額その他の他の者の所得の金額に相当する金額に対し、これを内国法人（当該内国法人と当該他の者との間に当該内国法人が当該他の者（法人に限る。）の株式又は出資を直接又は間接に保有する関係その他の財務省令で定める関係がある場合における当該内国法人に限る。）の所得の金額とみなして課される外国法人税の額

六　内国法人の国外事業所等の所在する国又は地域（以下この号において「国外事業所等所在地国」という。）において課される外国法人税（当該国外事業所等所在地国において当該内国法人の国外事業所等（当該国外事業所等所在地国に所在するものに限る。以下この号において同じ。）を通じて行う事業から生ずる所得に対して課される他の外国法人税の課税標準となる所得の金額に相当する金額に、当該内国法人の国外事業所等から当該内国法人と他の者との間に当該他の者が当該内国法人の議決権の総数の百分の二十五以上の数を有する関係その他の財務省令で定める関係がある場合における当該他の者（当該国外事業所等所在地国に住所若しくは居所、本店若しくは主たる事務所その他これらに類するもの又は当該国外事業所等所在地国の国籍その他これに類するものを有するものを除く。）及び当該内国法人の本店等（当該国外事業所等所在地国に所在するものを除く。）（以下この号において「関連者等」という。）への支払に係る金額並びに当該内国法人の国外事業所等が当該内国法人の関連者等から取得した資産に係る償却費の額のうち当該他の外国法人税の課税標準となる所得の金額の計算上損金の額に算入される金額を加算することその他これらの金額に関する調整を加えて計算される所得の金額につき課されるものに限る。）の額（当該他の外国法人税の課税標準となる所得の金額に相当する金額に係る部分を除く。）

8　法第六十九条第一項に規定するその他政令で定める外国法人税の額は、次に掲げる外国法

人税の額とする。

一　外国法人（租税特別措置法第六十六条の八第一項又は第七項に規定する外国法人に限る。以下この号において同じ。）から受けるこれらの規定に規定する剰余金の配当等の額（以下この号において「剰余金の配当等の額」といい、これらの規定の適用を受ける部分の金額に限る。）に係る外国法人税の額（剰余金の配当等の額を課税標準として課される外国法人税の額及び剰余金の配当等の額の計算の基礎となつた外国法人の所得のうち内国法人に帰せられるものとして計算される金額を課税標準として当該内国法人に対して課される外国法人税の額に限る。）

二　外国法人から受ける租税特別措置法第六十六条の八第三項又は第九項に規定する剰余金の配当等の額（以下この号において「剰余金の配当等の額」といい、これらの規定の適用を受ける部分の金額に限る。）に係る外国法人税の額（剰余金の配当等の額を課税標準として課される外国法人税の額及び剰余金の配当等の額の計算の基礎となつた外国法人の所得のうち内国法人に帰せられるものとして計算される金額を課税標準として当該内国法人に対して課される外国法人税の額に限る。）

三　外国法人（租税特別措置法第六十六条の九の四第一項又は第六項に規定する外国法人に限る。以下この号において同じ。）から受けるこれらの規定に規定する剰余金の配当等の額（以下この号において「剰余金の配当等の額」といい、これらの規定の適用を受ける部分の金額に限る。）に係る外国法人税の額（剰余金の配当等の額を課税標準として課される外国法人税の額及び剰余金の配当等の額の計算の基礎となつた外国法人の所得のうち内国法人に帰せられるものとして計算される金額を課税標準として当該内国法人に対して課される外国法人税の額に限る。）

四　外国法人から受ける租税特別措置法第六十六条の九の四第三項又は第八項に規定する剰余金の配当等の額（以下この号において「剰余金の配当等の額」といい、これらの規定の適用を受ける部分の金額に限る。）に係る外国法人税の額（剰余金の配当等の額を課税標準として課される外国法人税の額及び剰余金の配当等の額の計算の基礎となつた外国法人の所得のうち内国法人に帰せられるものとして計算される金額を課税標準として当該内国法人に対して課される外国法人税の額に限る。）

五　我が国が租税条約を締結している条約相手国等又は外国（外国居住者等の所得に対する相互主義による所得税等の非課税等に関する法律第二条第三号（定義）に規定する外国をいい、同法第五条各号（相互主義）のいずれかに該当しない場合における当該外国を除く。以下この号において同じ。）において課される外国法人税の額のうち、当該租税条約の規定（当該外国法人税の軽減又は免除に関する規定に限る。）により当該条約相手国等において課することができることとされる額を超える部分に相当する金額若しくは免除することとされる額に相当する金額又は当該外国において、同条第一号に規定する所得税等の非課税等に関する規定により当該外国に係る同法第二条第三号に規定する外国居住者等の同法第五条第一号に規定する対象国内源泉所得に対して所得税若しくは法人税を軽減し、若しくは課さないこととされる条件と同等の条件により軽減することとされる部分に相当す

る金額若しくは免除することとされる額に相当する金額

（租税条約等の実施に伴う所得税法、法人税法及び地方税法の特例等に関する法律）

（定義）

第二条　この法律において、次の各号に掲げる用語の意義は、当該各号に定めるところによる。

一　租税条約　我が国が締結した所得に対する租税に関する二重課税の回避又は脱税の防止のための条約をいう。

二　租税条約等　租税条約及び租税相互行政支援協定（租税条約以外の我が国が締結した国際約束で、租税の賦課若しくは徴収に関する情報を相互に提供すること、租税の徴収の共助若しくは徴収のための財産の保全の共助をすること又は租税に関する文書の送達の共助をすることを定める規定を有するものをいう。）をいう。

三　相手国等　租税条約等の我が国以外の締約国又は締約者をいう。

四　相手国居住者等　所得税法第二条第一項第五号に規定する非居住者（以下「非居住者」という。）又は同項第七号に規定する外国法人（同項第八号に規定する人格のない社団等（以下「人格のない社団等」という。）を含む。以下「外国法人」という。）で、租税条約の規定により当該租税条約の相手国等の居住者又は法人とされるものをいう。

五　限度税率　租税条約において相手国居住者等に対する課税につき一定の税率又は一定の割合で計算した金額を超えないものとしている場合におけるその一定の税率又は一定の割合をいう。

（配当等に対する源泉徴収に係る所得税の税率の特例等）

第三条の二　相手国居住者等が支払を受ける配当等（租税条約に規定する配当、利子若しくは使用料（当該租税条約においてこれらに準ずる取扱いを受けるものを含む。）又はその他の所得で、所得税法の施行地にその源泉があるものをいう。以下同じ。）のうち、当該相手国居住者等に係る相手国等との間の租税条約の規定において、当該相手国等においてその法令に基づき当該相手国居住者等の所得として取り扱われるものとされるもの（次項において「相手国居住者等配当等」という。）であつて限度税率を定める当該租税条約の規定の適用があるものに対する同法第百七十条、第百七十九条若しくは第二百十三条第一項又は租税特別措置法第三条第一項、第八条の二第一項、第三項若しくは第四項、第九条の三、第九条の三の二第一項、第四十一条の九第一項から第三項まで、第四十一条の十第一項、第四十一条の十二第一項若しくは第二項若しくは第四十一条の十二の二第一項から第三項までの規定の適用については、当該限度税率が当該配当等に適用されるこれらの規定に規定する税率以上である場合を除き、これらの規定に規定する税率に代えて、当該租税条約の規定により当該配当等につきそれぞれ適用される限度税率によるものとする。

2　相手国居住者等が支払を受ける相手国居住者等配当等であつて所得税の免除を定める租税条約の規定の適用があるものについては、所得税法第七条第一項第三号及び第五号、第百六十四条第二項、第百六十九条、第百七十条、第百七十八条、第百七十九条並びに第二百十二条第一項及び第二項並びに租税特別措置法第三条第一項、第八条の二第一項、第九条の三の二第一項、第四十一条の九第一項から第三項まで、第四十一条の十第一項、第四十一条の十二第一項及び第二項並びに第四十一条の十二の二第一項から第三項までの規定の適用はないものとする。

3　外国法人が支払を受ける配当等のうち、租税条約の規定において、当該租税条約の相手国等においてその法令に基づき当該外国法人の株主等である者（当該租税条約の規定により当該租税条約の相手国等の居住者とされる者に限る。）の所得として取り扱われるものとされる部分（次項において「株主等配当等」という。）であつて限度税率を定める当該租税条約の規定の適用があるものに対する所得税法第百七十九条若しくは第二百十三条第一項又は租税特別措置法第八条の二第三項若しくは第四項、第九条の三、第九条の三の二第一項、第四十一条の九第二項若しくは第三項、第四十一条の十二第二項若しくは第四十一条の十二の二第一項から第三項までの規定の適用については、当該限度税率が当該配当等に適用されるこれらの規定に規定する税率以上である場合を除き、これらの規定に規定する税率に代えて、当該租税条約の規定により当該配当等につきそれぞれ適用される限度税率によるものとする。

4　外国法人が支払を受ける株主等配当等であつて所得税の免除を定める租税条約の規定の適用があるものについては、所得税法第七条第一項第五号、第百七十八条、第百七十九条並びに第二百十二条第一項及び第二項並びに租税特別措置法第九条の三の二第一項、第四十一条の九第二項及び第三項、第四十一条の十二第二項並びに第四十一条の十二の二第一項から第三項までの規定の適用はないものとする。

（租税条約等の実施に伴う所得税法、法人税法及び地方税法の特例等に関する法律の施行に関する省令）

（定義）

第一条　この省令において、次の各号に掲げる用語の意義は、当該各号に定めるところによる。

一　法　租税条約等の実施に伴う所得税法、法人税法及び地方税法の特例等に関する法律（昭和四十四年法律第四十六号）をいう。

二　租税条約　法第二条第一号に規定する租税条約をいう。

三　相手国等　法第二条第三号に規定する相手国等をいう。

四　相手国居住者等　法第二条第四号に規定する相手国居住者等をいう。

五　源泉徴収義務者　所得税法（昭和四十年法律第三十三号）第四編第一章から第六章まで並びに租税特別措置法（昭和三十二年法律第二十六号）第九条の三の二第一項、第三十七条の十一の四第一項、第四十一条の九第三項、第四十一条の十二第三項、第四十一条の十二の二第二項及び第三項並びに第四十一条の二十二第一項の規定により所得税を徴収し及び納付すべき者をいう。

六　国内　所得税法の施行地をいう。

七　国外　所得税法の施行地外の地域をいう。

八　租税　租税条約が適用される租税をいう。

九　みなし外国税額　相手国等の法律の規定又は当該相手国等との間の租税条約の規定により軽減され又は免除された当該相手国等の租税の額で、当該租税条約の規定に基づき納付したものとみなされるものをいう。

（相手国居住者等配当等に係る所得税の軽減又は免除を受ける者の届出等）

第二条　相手国居住者等は、その支払を受ける法第三条の二第一項に規定する相手国居住者等配当等（以下この条において「相手国居住者等配当等」という。）につき所得税法第二百十二条第一項若しくは第二項又は租税特別措置法第九条の三の二第一項、第三十七条の十一の四第一項、第四十一条の九第三項若しくは第四十一条の十二の二第二項若しくは第三項の規定により徴収されるべき所得税について当該相手国居住者等に係る相手国等との間の租税条約の規定に基づき軽減又は免除を受けようとする場合には、当該相手国居住者等配当等に係る源泉徴収義務者ごとに、次に掲げる事項を記載した届出書を、当該租税条約の効力発生の日以後最初にその支払を受ける日の前日まで（その支払を受ける相手国居住者等配当等が無記名の株式、出資若しくは受益証券に係るもの若しくは無記名の債券に係るもの又は所得税法施行令（昭和四十年政令第九十六号）第二百八十一条第一項第四号ロに掲げる所得に該当するもの（次項において「無記名配当等」という。）である場合にあつては、その支払を受ける都度、当該支払を受ける時）に、当該源泉徴収義務者を経由して、当該源泉徴収義務者の納税地の所轄税務署長に提出しなければならない。

一　当該相手国居住者等配当等の支払を受ける者の氏名、国籍及び住所若しくは居所（個人番号を有する者にあつては、氏名、国籍、住所又は居所及び個人番号）又は名称、本店若しくは主たる事務所の所在地及びその事業が管理され、かつ、支配されている場所の所在地（法人番号を有する者にあつては、名称、本店又は主たる事務所の所在地、その事業が管理され、かつ、支配されている場所の所在地及び法人番号）

二　当該相手国居住者等配当等の支払を受ける者の当該相手国居住者等配当等に係る当該相手国等における納税地及び当該支払を受ける者が当該相手国等において納税者番号を有する場合には、当該納税者番号

三　当該相手国居住者等配当等につき当該租税条約の規定に基づき租税の軽減又は免除を受けることができる事情の詳細

四　当該相手国居住者等配当等の支払者の氏名及び住所若しくは居所又は名称及び本店若しくは主たる事務所の所在地

五　次に掲げる場合の区分に応じそれぞれ次に掲げる事項

イ　当該相手国居住者等配当等である配当（租税条約に規定する配当（当該租税条約においてこれに準ずる取扱いを受けるものを含む。）で、国内にその源泉があるものをいう。以下第二条の五までにおいて同じ。）の支払を受ける場合　当該配当に係る株式（投資信託及び投資法人に関する法律（昭和二十六年法律第百九十八号）第二条第十四項に規定する投資口を含む。以下第二条の五までにおいて同じ。）、出資、基金又は受益権の銘柄又は名称、種類及び数量並びにその取得の日

ロ　当該相手国居住者等配当等である利子（租税条約に規定する利子（当該租税条約においてこれに準ずる取扱いを受けるものを含む。）で、国内にその源泉があるものをいう。以下第二条の五までにおいて同じ。）で債券に係るものの支払を受ける場合　当該債券の種類、名称、額面金額及び数量並びにその取得の日

ハ　当該相手国居住者等配当等である利子で債券に係るもの以外のものの支払を受ける場合　当該利子の支払の基因となつた契約の締結の日、契約金額及び契約期間並びに当該契約期間において支払われる当該利子の金額及びその支払期日

ニ　当該相手国居住者等配当等である使用料（租税条約に規定する使用料（当該租税条約においてこれに準ずる取扱いを受けるものを含む。）で、国内にその源泉があるものをいう。以下第二条の五までにおいて同じ。）の支払を受ける場合　当該使用料の支払の基因となつた契約の締結の日及び契約期間並びに当該契約期間において支払われる当該使用料の金額及びその支払期日

ホ　当該相手国居住者等配当等であるその他の所得（租税条約に規定するその他の所得で、国内にその源泉があるものをいう。以下第二条の五までにおいて同じ。）の支払を受ける場合　当該その他の所得の種類、金額、支払方法、支払期日及び支払の基因となつた契約の内容

ヘ　当該相手国居住者等配当等である譲渡収益（法第三条の二第一項に規定する譲渡収益をいう。第三項において同じ。）で株式又は出資に係るものの支払を受ける場合　当該株式又は出資の銘柄、種類及び数量並びにその取得の日

六　当該相手国居住者等配当等の支払を受ける者が国税通則法第百十七条第二項の規定による納税管理人の届出をしている場合には、当該納税管理人の氏名及び住所又は居所

七　その他参考となるべき事項

2　前項に規定する届出書（無記名配当等に係るものを除く。）を提出した者は、その記載事項について異動を生じた場合には、当該異動を生じた事項、当該異動を生じた日その他参考となるべき事項を記載した届出書を、当該異動を生じた日以後最初に当該届出書に係る相手国居住者等配当等の支払を受ける日の前日までに、当該相手国居住者等配当等に係る源泉徴収義務者を経由して、当該源泉徴収義務者の納税地の所轄税務署長に提出しなければならない。

3　前項の場合において、同項に規定する異動を生じた事項が第一項第五号に規定する事項（当該異動を生じた事項が特定利子配当等以外の相手国居住者等配当等に係るものである場合には、同号イに規定する数量、同号ロに規定する額面金額、同号ハに規定する契約金額又は同号ヘに規定する数量（これらに類する事項を含む。））のみであるとき（これらの事項の異動により当該事項に係る相手国居住者等配当等である配当、利子、その他の所得又は譲渡収益につき、当該異動前に適用される租税条約の規定と異なる定めがある当該租税条約の規定が適用されることとなる場合を除く。）は、前項の規定にかかわらず、同項の届出書の提出を省略することができる。

4　前項に規定する特定利子配当等とは、所得税法第百六十一条第一項に規定する国内源泉所得（同法第百六十二条第一項の規定により国内源泉所得とみなされるものを含む。）又は法人税法（昭和四十年法律第三十四号）第百三十八条第一項に規定する国内源泉所得（同法第百三十九条第一項の規定により国内源泉所得とみなされるものを含む。）のうち次に掲げるものをいう。

一　所得税法第百六十一条第一項第八号イに掲げる国債若しくは地方債又は内国法人の発行する債券の利子（当該債券の発行が金融商品取引法（昭和二十三年法律第二十五号）第二条第三項に規定する有価証券の私募（これに相当するものを含む。次号において「有価証券の私募」という。）によるものに係るものを除く。）

二　所得税法第百六十一条第一項第八号ロに掲げる外国法人の発行する債券の利子（当該債券の発行が有価証券の私募によるものに係るものを除く。）

三　所得税法第百六十一条第一項第八号ハに掲げる預貯金の利子

四　所得税法第百六十一条第一項第八号ニに掲げる合同運用信託、公社債投資信託又は公募公社債等運用投資信託の収益の分配

五　所得税法第百六十一条第一項第九号に規定する配当等で、租税特別措置法第九条の三第一号に規定する株式等の配当等に該当するもの（内国法人からその支払がされる当該配当等の支払に係る基準日（当該配当等が所得税法第二十五条第一項の規定により剰余金の配当、利益の配当、剰余金の分配又は金銭の分配とみなされるものに係る配当等である場合には、同号に規定する政令で定める日）においてその内国法人の発行済株式（投資信託及び投資法人に関する法律第二条第十二項に規定する投資法人にあつては、発行済みの投資

ロ）又は出資の総数又は総額の百分の五以上に相当する数又は金額の株式又は出資を有する者が支払を受けるものを除く。）

六　所得税法第百六十一条第一項第九号に規定する配当等で、租税特別措置法第九条の三第二号から第五号までに掲げるものに該当するもの

七　所得税法第百六十一条第一項第十五号に掲げる給付補塡金、利息、利益又は差益

八　所得税法第百六十一条第一項第二号に掲げる所得で、租税特別措置法第四十一条の九第一項に規定する懸賞金付預貯金等の懸賞金等に該当するもの

九　所得税法第百六十一条第一項第三号に掲げる所得で、第五号又は第六号に掲げる配当等の基因となる株式又は出資の譲渡による所得に該当するもの

5　相手国居住者等は、その支払を受ける相手国居住者等配当等である配当又は利子につき所得税法第二百十二条第一項若しくは第二項又は租税特別措置法第九条の三の二第一項、第四十一条の九第三項若しくは第四十一条の十二の二第二項若しくは第三項の規定により徴収されるべき所得税について第一項に規定する租税条約の規定に基づき免除を受けようとする場合には、同項又は第二項の規定により提出する届出書に、当該租税条約の相手国等の権限ある当局のその者が当該配当又は利子につき租税の免除を定める当該租税条約の規定の適用を受けることができる相手国等における居住者であることを証明する書類を添付しなければならない。

6　前項の場合において、同項の相手国等の権限ある当局が同項に規定する証明する書類の発行又は発給をすることができないときは、同項の相手国居住者等は、当該書類に代えて、同項に規定する租税の免除を定める租税条約の規定に定める要件を満たすことを明らかにする書類（当該書類が外国語で作成されている場合には、その翻訳文を含む。）及び当該相手国等の権限ある当局の当該相手国居住者等の居住者証明書を同項の届出書に添付しなければならない。ただし、当該租税条約の規定の適用開始日（租税条約の規定が最初に適用されることとなる日をいう。以下同じ。）が平成十六年四月一日前である場合には、この限りでない。

7　相手国居住者等は、その支払を受ける相手国居住者等配当等である使用料につき所得税法第二百十二条第一項又は第二項の規定により徴収されるべき所得税について第一項に規定する租税条約の規定に基づき免除を受けようとする場合には、同項又は第二項の規定により提出する届出書（同項の届出書にあつては、同項に規定する異動を生じた事項が当該使用料に係る事項である場合に提出するものに限る。）に、当該使用料の支払の基因となつた契約の内容を記載した書類及び当該租税条約の相手国等の権限ある当局の当該相手国居住者等の居住者証明書を添付しなければならない。ただし、当該租税条約の規定の適用開始日が平成十六年四月一日前である場合には、この限りでない。

8　相手国居住者等は、所得税法第二百十二条第一項若しくは第二項又は租税特別措置法第九条の三の二第一項、第三十七条の十一の四第一項、第四十一条の九第三項若しくは第四十一条の十二の二第二項若しくは第三項の規定（以下この項において「相手国居住者等の相手国居住者等配当等に関する規定」という。）の適用がある相手国居住者等配当等の支払を受けた場合において、第一項に規定する租税条約の規定の適用を受けなかつたことにより当該相

手国居住者等配当等につき相手国居住者等の相手国居住者等配当等に関する規定により徴収された所得税について、当該租税条約の規定に基づき軽減又は免除を受けようとするときは、次の各号に掲げる場合の区分に応じ当該各号に定める金額の還付を請求することができる。

一　租税条約の規定により当該相手国居住者等配当等について所得税が軽減される場合　当該相手国居住者等配当等に対する源泉徴収による所得税の額から当該相手国居住者等配当等の額に当該相手国居住者等配当等に対して適用される法第三条の二第一項に規定する限度税率を乗じて計算した金額を控除した残額に相当する金額

二　租税条約の規定により当該相手国居住者等配当等について所得税が免除される場合　当該相手国居住者等配当等に対する源泉徴収による所得税の額

9　前項の規定による所得税の還付の請求をしようとする者は、第一項各号に掲げる事項並びにその還付を受けようとする所得税の額及びその計算に関して必要な事項を記載した還付請求書（第五項から第七項までに規定する場合に該当するときは、これらの規定により添付すべき書類の添付があるものに限る。）を、当該所得税に係る源泉徴収義務者を経由して、当該源泉徴収義務者の納税地の所轄税務署長に提出しなければならない。

10　相手国居住者等で、その支払を受ける相手国居住者等配当等（租税特別措置法第九条の三の二第一項に規定する上場株式等の配当等（同項に規定する利子等を除く。）に限る。以下この条において「相手国居住者等上場株式等配当等」という。）につき同項の規定により徴収されるべき所得税について当該相手国居住者等に係る相手国等との間の租税条約の規定に基づき軽減又は免除を受けようとするものが、次に掲げる事項を記載した届出書（以下この条において「特例届出書」という。）を、当該相手国居住者等上場株式等配当等の支払の取扱者（同項の規定の適用を受ける同項に規定する支払の取扱者をいい、次項の届出をした者に限る。以下この条において同じ。）を経由して、当該支払の取扱者の納税地の所轄税務署長に提出した場合には、当該相手国居住者等は、その提出の日以後当該支払の取扱者から交付を受ける相手国居住者等上場株式等配当等につき第一項の規定による届出書の提出をしたものとみなす。

一　相手国居住者等上場株式等配当等の支払を受ける者の氏名、国籍及び住所若しくは居所（個人番号を有する者にあつては、氏名、国籍、住所又は居所及び個人番号）又は名称、本店若しくは主たる事務所の所在地及びその事業が管理され、かつ、支配されている場所の所在地（法人番号を有する者にあつては、名称、本店又は主たる事務所の所在地、その事業が管理され、かつ、支配されている場所の所在地及び法人番号）

二　相手国居住者等上場株式等配当等の支払を受ける者の相手国居住者等上場株式等配当等に係る当該相手国等における納税地及び当該支払を受ける者が当該相手国等において納税者番号を有する場合には、当該納税者番号

三　相手国居住者等上場株式等配当等に係る当該租税条約の名称

四　相手国居住者等上場株式等配当等の支払の取扱者の名称及び本店又は主たる事務所の所在地

五　相手国居住者等上場株式等配当等の支払を受ける者が国税通則法第百十七条第二項の規

定による納税管理人の届出をしている場合には、当該納税管理人の氏名及び住所又は居所
六　その他参考となるべき事項
11　租税特別措置法第九条の三の二第一項の規定の適用を受ける同項に規定する支払の取扱者は、平成二十六年一月一日以後最初に前項の規定により提出される特例届出書を受理しようとするときは、あらかじめ、その旨を書面により当該支払の取扱者の納税地の所轄税務署長に届け出なければならない。
12　第二項の規定は、第十項の規定により提出した特例届出書の記載事項について異動が生じた場合について準用する。
13　特例届出書を提出した者は、当該特例届出書に係る支払の取扱者から交付を受ける相手国居住者等上場株式等配当等の支払者ごとに、次に掲げる事項を、当該特例届出書の提出の日以後最初にその支払を受ける日の前日までに、当該支払の取扱者に通知しなければならない。
一　当該相手国居住者等上場株式等配当等につき当該相手国居住者等上場株式等配当等に係る租税条約の規定に基づき租税の軽減又は免除を受けることができる事情の詳細
二　当該相手国居住者等上場株式等配当等の支払者の名称及び本店又は主たる事務所の所在地
三　当該相手国居住者等上場株式等配当等に係る株式、出資又は受益権の銘柄又は名称、種類及び数量並びにその取得の日
四　その他参考となるべき事項
14　前項の規定による通知をした者は、その通知をした事項について異動を生じた場合には、当該異動を生じた事項、当該異動を生じた日その他参考となるべき事項を、当該異動を生じた日以後最初に当該通知に係る相手国居住者等上場株式等配当等の支払を受ける日の前日までに、同項の支払の取扱者に通知しなければならない。
15　特例届出書を提出した者は、当該特例届出書に係る支払の取扱者から交付を受ける相手国居住者等上場株式等配当等につき租税特別措置法第九条の三の二第一項の規定により徴収されるべき所得税について第十項に規定する租税条約の規定に基づき免除を受けようとする場合には、当該相手国居住者等上場株式等配当等の支払者ごとに、同項第一号及び第二号に掲げる事項を記載した書面に、当該租税条約の相手国等の権限ある当局のその者が当該相手国居住者等上場株式等配当等につき租税の免除を定める当該租税条約の規定の適用を受けることができる相手国等における居住者であることを証明する書類を添付して、これを、当該特例届出書の提出の日以後最初にその支払を受ける日の前日までに、当該支払の取扱者を経由して、当該支払の取扱者の納税地の所轄税務署長に提出しなければならない。
16　前項の場合において、同項の相手国等の権限ある当局が同項に規定する証明する書類の発行又は発給をすることができないときは、同項の特例届出書を提出した者は、当該書類に代えて、同項に規定する租税の免除を定める租税条約の規定に定める要件を満たすことを明らかにする書類（当該書類が外国語で作成されている場合には、その翻訳文を含む。）及び当該相手国等の権限ある当局の当該特例届出書を提出した者の居住者証明書を同項の書面に添付しなければならない。ただし、当該租税条約の規定の適用開始日が平成十六年四月一日前

である場合には、この限りでない。

17 特例届出書を提出した者に対し相手国居住者等上場株式等配当等の交付をする支払の取扱者は、当該特例届出書を提出した者の各人別に、次に掲げる事項を、その交付をした日の属する月の翌月十日までに、当該事項を記録した光ディスク又は磁気ディスクを提出する方法により当該支払の取扱者の納税地の所轄税務署長に提供しなければならない。この場合において、その月中に相手国居住者等上場株式等配当等の交付がなかつたときは、その旨を当該所轄税務署長に通知しなければならない。

一 当該相手国居住者等上場株式等配当等の支払を受ける者の氏名及び住所若しくは居所（個人番号を有する者にあつては、氏名、住所又は居所及び個人番号）又は名称及び本店若しくは主たる事務所の所在地（法人番号を有する者にあつては、名称、本店又は主たる事務所の所在地及び法人番号）並びに当該支払を受ける者が当該相手国居住者等上場株式等配当等に係る相手国等において納税者番号を有する場合には、当該納税者番号

二 当該相手国居住者等上場株式等配当等につき当該相手国居住者等上場株式等配当等に係る租税条約の規定に基づき租税の軽減又は免除を受けることができる事情の詳細

三 当該相手国居住者等上場株式等配当等の支払者の名称及び本店又は主たる事務所の所在地

四 当該相手国居住者等上場株式等配当等に係る株式、出資又は受益権の銘柄又は名称、種類及び数量並びにその取得の日

五 当該相手国居住者等上場株式等配当等の金額及びその交付の日

六 前号の金額につき源泉徴収をされる所得税の額

七 その他参考となるべき事項

18 特例届出書を提出した者がその提出前に当該特例届出書に係る支払の取扱者から交付を受ける相手国居住者等上場株式等配当等につき第一項又は第二項に規定する届出書を提出しているときは、当該特例届出書の提出の日以後においては、当該届出書の提出がなかつたものとみなし、特例届出書を提出した者がその提出後に当該特例届出書に係る支払の取扱者から交付を受ける相手国居住者等上場株式等配当等につき第一項に規定する届出書を提出したときは、当該届出書の提出の日以後においては、当該特例届出書の提出がなかつたものとみなす。

19 次の各号に掲げる者が個人番号又は法人番号を有する場合には、当該各号に定める書類にその者の個人番号又は法人番号を付記するものとする。

一 第一項若しくは第二項の規定により提出する届出書又は第九項の規定により提出する還付請求書を受理したこれらの規定に規定する源泉徴収義務者　これらの届出書又は還付請求書

二 第十項の規定により提出する特例届出書、第十二項において準用する第二項の規定により提出する届出書又は第十五項の規定により提出する書面を受理したこれらの規定に規定する支払の取扱者　これらの届出書又は書面

（自由職業者、芸能人及び短期滞在者等の届出等）

第四条　相手国居住者等は、その支払を受ける所得税法第百六十一条第一項第六号に掲げる対価（法第三条第一項の規定の適用を受ける対価を除く。）又は所得税法第百六十一条第一項第十二号イに掲げる報酬につき同法第二百十二条第一項若しくは第二項又は租税特別措置法第四十一条の二十二第一項の規定の適用がある場合において、当該対価又は報酬につき、その者が恒久的施設（租税条約に規定する恒久的施設のうち国内にあるものをいう。以下この項において同じ。）若しくは固定的施設（租税条約に規定する固定的施設のうち国内にあるものをいう。以下この条において同じ。）を有しないこと若しくはその者が有する恒久的施設若しくは固定的施設に帰せられないこと又は一定の金額を超えないことを要件とする租税の免除を定める租税条約の規定の適用を受けようとするとき（当該租税条約の規定が当該対価又は報酬につき一定の金額を超えないことを要件としている場合にあつては、当該対価又は報酬に係る源泉徴収義務者が一である場合に限る。）は、第三項、第五項又は第八条第二項の規定により届出書を提出すべき場合を除くほか、当該対価又は報酬に係る源泉徴収義務者ごとに、次に掲げる事項を記載した届出書を、入国の日（所得税法第百六十一条第一項第六号に規定する事業を行う者にあつては、国内において当該事業を開始した日とし、当該入国の日又は国内において当該事業を開始した日が当該租税条約の効力発生の日前であるときは、当該効力発生の日とする。）以後最初にその支払を受ける日の前日までに、当該源泉徴収義務者を経由して、当該源泉徴収義務者の納税地の所轄税務署長に提出しなければならない。

一　当該対価又は報酬の支払を受ける者の氏名、国籍、住所、国内における居所（個人番号を有する者にあつては、氏名、国籍、住所、国内における居所及び個人番号）、在留期間及び在留資格又は名称、本店若しくは主たる事務所の所在地及びその事業が管理され、かつ、支配されている場所の所在地（法人番号を有する者にあつては、名称、本店又は主たる事務所の所在地、その事業が管理され、かつ、支配されている場所の所在地及び法人番号）並びに入国の日（所得税法第百六十一条第一項第六号に規定する事業を行う者にあつては、国内において当該事業を開始した日）

二　当該対価又は報酬の支払を受ける者の当該対価又は報酬に係る租税条約の相手国等における納税地及び当該支払を受ける者が当該相手国等において納税者番号を有する場合には、当該納税者番号

三　当該対価又は報酬につき租税条約の規定により所得税の免除を受けることができる事情の詳細

四　当該対価又は報酬の種類、金額、支払方法、支払期日及び支払の基因となつた契約の内容

五　当該対価又は報酬の支払者の氏名及び住所若しくは居所又は名称及び本店若しくは主たる事務所の所在地

六　当該対価又は報酬の支払を受ける者が国税通則法第百十七条第二項の規定による納税管理人の届出をしている場合には、当該納税管理人の氏名及び住所又は居所

七　その他参考となるべき事項

2　相手国居住者等は、その支払を受ける所得税法第百六十一条第一項第六号に掲げる対価又は同項第十二号イに掲げる報酬につき同法第二百十二条第一項若しくは第二項又は租税特別措置法第四十一条の二十二第一項の規定の適用がある場合において、当該対価又は報酬につき、その者の役務が文化交流を目的とする我が国政府と相手国等の政府との間の特別の計画（以下この項において「政府間の特別の計画」という。）に基づいて行われること又はその者の役務がいずれかの締約国若しくは締約者若しくはその地方公共団体の公的資金その他これに類する資金（以下この項において「政府の公的資金等」という。）から全面的若しくは実質的に援助を受けて行われることを要件とする租税の免除を定める租税条約の規定の適用を受けようとするときは、当該対価又は報酬に係る源泉徴収義務者ごとに、第一号から第七号までに掲げる事項を記載した届出書に第八号に掲げる書類を添付して、これを、入国の日（所得税法第百六十一条第一項第六号に規定する事業を行う者にあつては、国内において当該事業を開始した日とし、当該入国の日又は国内において当該事業を開始した日が当該租税条約の効力発生の日前であるときは、当該効力発生の日とする。）以後最初にその支払を受ける日の前日までに、当該源泉徴収義務者を経由して、当該源泉徴収義務者の納税地の所轄税務署長に提出しなければならない。

一　当該対価又は報酬の支払を受ける者の氏名、国籍、住所、国内における居所（個人番号を有する者にあつては、氏名、国籍、住所、国内における居所及び個人番号）、在留期間及び在留資格又は名称、本店若しくは主たる事務所の所在地及びその事業が管理され、かつ、支配されている場所の所在地（法人番号を有する者にあつては、名称、本店又は主たる事務所の所在地、その事業が管理され、かつ、支配されている場所の所在地及び法人番号）並びに入国の日（所得税法第百六十一条第一項第六号に規定する事業を行う者にあつては、国内において当該事業を開始した日）

二　当該対価又は報酬の支払を受ける者の当該対価又は報酬に係る租税条約の相手国等における納税地及び当該支払を受ける者が当該相手国等において納税者番号を有する場合には、当該納税者番号

三　当該対価又は報酬につき租税条約の規定により所得税の免除を受けることができる事情の詳細

四　当該対価又は報酬の種類、金額、支払方法、支払期日及び支払の基因となつた契約の内容

五　当該対価又は報酬の支払者の氏名及び住所若しくは居所又は名称及び本店若しくは主たる事務所の所在地

六　当該対価又は報酬の支払を受ける者が国税通則法第百十七条第二項の規定による納税管理人の届出をしている場合には、当該納税管理人の氏名及び住所又は居所

七　その他参考となるべき事項

八　その者の役務が政府間の特別の計画に基づいて行われること又は政府の公的資金等から全面的若しくは実質的に援助を受けて行われることを証明する書類

3　相手国居住者等である個人は、その支払を受ける所得税法第百六十一条第一項第十二号イに掲げる給与又は報酬につき同法第二百十二条第一項若しくは第二項又は租税特別措置法第四十一条の二十二第一項の規定の適用がある場合において、当該給与又は報酬につき国内での滞在が年間又は継続する十二月の期間中百八十三日又はそれより短い一定の期間を超えないことを要件とする租税の免除を定める租税条約の規定の適用を受けようとするとき（当該租税条約の規定が当該給与又は報酬につき一定の金額を超えないことをも要件としている場合にあつては、当該給与又は報酬に係る源泉徴収義務者が一である場合に限る。）は、次項又は第五項の規定により届出書を提出すべき場合を除くほか、当該源泉徴収義務者ごとに、次に掲げる事項を記載した届出書を、入国の日（その日が当該租税条約の効力発生の日前であるときは、当該効力発生の日）以後最初にその支払を受ける日の前日までに、当該源泉徴収義務者を経由して、当該源泉徴収義務者の納税地の所轄税務署長に提出しなければならない。

一　当該給与又は報酬の支払を受ける者の氏名、国籍、住所、国内における居所（個人番号を有する者にあつては、氏名、国籍、住所、国内における居所及び個人番号）、入国の日、在留期間及び在留資格

二　当該給与又は報酬の支払を受ける者の当該給与又は報酬に係る租税条約の相手国等における納税地及び当該支払を受ける者が当該相手国等において納税者番号を有する場合には、当該納税者番号

三　当該給与又は報酬につき租税条約の規定に基づき所得税の免除を受けることができる事情の詳細

四　当該給与又は報酬の種類、金額、支払方法、支払期日及び支払の基因となつた契約の内容

五　当該給与又は報酬の支払者の氏名及び住所若しくは居所又は名称及び本店若しくは主たる事務所の所在地

六　当該給与又は報酬の支払を受ける者が国税通則法第百十七条第二項の規定による納税管理人の届出をしている場合には、当該納税管理人の氏名及び住所又は居所

七　その他参考となるべき事項

4　相手国居住者等である個人は、その支払を受ける所得税法第百六十一条第一項第十二号イに掲げる給与につき同法第二百十二条第一項又は第二項の規定の適用がある場合において、当該給与につき国際運輸（租税条約に規定する国際運輸をいう。次項において同じ。）の用に供される船舶又は航空機において行う勤務に基因するものであることを要件とする租税の免除を定める当該租税条約の規定の適用を受けようとするときは、次項の規定により届出書を提出すべき場合を除くほか、当該給与に係る源泉徴収義務者ごとに、次に掲げる事項を記載した届出書を、当該租税条約の効力発生の日以後最初にその支払を受ける日の前日までに、当該源泉徴収義務者を経由して、当該源泉徴収義務者の納税地の所轄税務署長に提出しなければならない。

一　当該給与の支払を受ける者の氏名、国籍、住所及び国内における居所（個人番号を有す

る者にあつては、氏名、国籍、住所、国内における居所及び個人番号）

二　当該給与の支払を受ける者の当該給与に係る租税条約の相手国等における納税地及び当該支払を受ける者が当該相手国等において納税者番号を有する場合には、当該納税者番号

三　当該給与につき租税条約の規定に基づき所得税の免除を受けることができる事情の詳細

四　当該給与の種類、金額、支払方法、支払期日及び支払の基因となつた契約の内容

五　当該給与の支払者の氏名及び住所若しくは居所又は名称及び本店若しくは主たる事務所の所在地

六　当該給与の支払を受ける者が国税通則法第百十七条第二項の規定による納税管理人の届出をしている場合には、当該納税管理人の氏名及び住所又は居所

七　その他参考となるべき事項

5　相手国居住者等である個人は、非居住者又は外国法人で国内において所得税法第百六十一条第一項第六号に規定する事業を行うものから同項第十二号イに掲げる給与又は報酬の支払を受ける場合（当該非居住者又は外国法人が支払を受ける同項第六号に掲げる対価で当該給与又は報酬に係るものにつき同法第二百十二条第一項若しくは第二項又は租税特別措置法第四十一条の二十二第一項の規定の適用がある場合に限る。）において、当該給与又は報酬につき、当該相手国居住者等が固定的施設を有しないこと若しくはその者が有する固定的施設に帰せられないこと、国内での滞在が年間若しくは継続する十二月の期間中百八十三日若しくはそれより短い一定の期間を超えないこと又は国際運輸の用に供される船舶若しくは航空機において行う勤務に基因するものであることを要件とする租税の免除を定める租税条約の規定の適用を受けようとするとき（当該租税条約の規定が当該給与又は報酬につき一定の金額を超えないことをも要件としている場合にあつては、当該給与又は報酬に係る源泉徴収義務者が一である場合に限る。）は、第三項各号に掲げる事項に準ずる事項を記載した届出書を、当該非居住者又は外国法人が当該租税条約の効力発生の日以後最初に当該対価の支払を受ける日の前日までに、当該非居住者又は外国法人及び当該対価の支払者を経由して、当該対価の支払者の納税地の所轄税務署長に提出しなければならない。

6　前項に規定する届出書が提出された場合には、当該届出書の提出の際に経由した同項に規定する非居住者又は外国法人が支払を受ける所得税法第百六十一条第一項第六号に掲げる対価のうち、当該届出書に記載された前項に規定する給与又は報酬で同項に規定する租税の免除を定める租税条約の規定の適用があるものに相当する部分の金額については、同法第二百十二条第一項及び第二項並びに租税特別措置法第四十一条の二十二第一項の規定は、適用しない。

7　相手国居住者等である個人は、所得税法第二百十二条第一項若しくは第二項又は租税特別措置法第四十一条の二十二第一項の規定の適用がある第一項又は第三項に規定する対価、給与又は報酬を二以上の支払者から支払を受けた場合において、第一項、第三項又は第五項に規定する租税の免除を定める租税条約の規定の適用を受けられなかつたことにより当該対価、給与又は報酬につき所得税法第二百十二条第一項若しくは第二項又は租税特別措置法第四十一条の二十二第一項の規定により徴収された所得税について、これらの租税条約の規定に基

づき免除を受けようとするときは、その徴収された所得税の額の還付を請求することができる。

8　前項の規定による所得税の還付の請求をしようとする者は、第一項各号若しくは第三項各号に掲げる事項又は第五項に規定する第三項各号に掲げる事項に準ずる事項並びにその還付を受けようとする所得税の額及びその計算に関して必要な事項を記載した還付請求書を、当該所得税に係る源泉徴収義務者を経由して、当該源泉徴収義務者の納税地の所轄税務署長に提出しなければならない。

9　第二条第二項の規定は、第一項から第五項までに規定する届出書を提出した者について準用する。

10　相手国居住者等は、所得税法第二百十二条第一項若しくは第二項又は租税特別措置法第四十一条の二十二第一項の規定の適用がある第一項から第五項までに規定する対価、給与又は報酬の支払を受けた場合において、第一項から第五項までに規定する租税の免除を定める租税条約の規定の適用を受けなかつたことにより当該対価、給与又は報酬につき所得税法第二百十二条第一項若しくは第二項又は租税特別措置法第四十一条の二十二第一項の規定により徴収された所得税について、これらの租税条約の規定に基づき免除を受けようとするとき（当該相手国居住者等が当該対価、給与又は報酬につき第七項の規定の適用を受けているときを除く。）は、その徴収された所得税の額の還付を請求することができる。

11　前項の規定による所得税の還付の請求をしようとする者は、第一項各号、第二項第一号から第七号まで、第三項各号若しくは第四項各号に掲げる事項又は第五項に規定する第三項各号に掲げる事項に準ずる事項並びにその還付を受けようとする所得税の額及びその計算に関して必要な事項を記載した還付請求書（第二項に規定する場合に該当するときは、同項第八号に掲げる書類の添付があるものに限る。）を、当該所得税に係る源泉徴収義務者を経由して、当該源泉徴収義務者の納税地の所轄税務署長に提出しなければならない。

12　外国法人は、その支払を受ける所得税法第百六十一条第一項第六号に掲げる対価（租税条約の規定において当該外国法人の株主等である者（当該租税条約の規定により当該租税条約の相手国等の居住者とされる者に限る。）の所得として取り扱われる部分に限るものとし、法第三条第一項の規定の適用を受ける対価を除く。以下この条において「株主等対価」という。）につき所得税法第二百十二条第一項又は第二項の規定により徴収されるべき所得税について当該租税条約の規定に基づき免除を受けようとする場合（当該租税条約の規定が当該株主等対価につき一定の金額を超えないことを要件としている場合を除く。）には、当該株主等対価に係る源泉徴収義務者ごとに、第一号から第八号までに掲げる事項を記載した届出書に第九号から第十一号までに掲げる書類を添付して、これを、当該租税条約の効力発生の日以後最初にその支払を受ける日の前日までに、当該源泉徴収義務者を経由して、当該源泉徴収義務者の納税地の所轄税務署長に提出しなければならない。

一　当該株主等対価に係る所得税法第百六十一条第一項第六号に掲げる対価の支払を受ける外国法人の名称、本店又は主たる事務所の所在地及びその事業が管理され、かつ、支配されている場所の所在地（法人番号を有する外国法人にあつては、名称、本店又は主たる事務所の所在地、その事業が管理され、かつ、支配されている場所の所在地及び法人番号）並びに当該外国法人が納税者番号を有する場合には、当該納税者番号

二　前号の対価が当該租税条約の相手国等の法令に基づき当該外国法人の株主等である者の所得として取り扱われる場合には、その事情の詳細

三　第一号の外国法人の株主等である者の各人別に、その者の氏名及び住所若しくは居所又は名称、本店若しくは主たる事務所の所在地及びその事業が管理され、かつ、支配されている場所の所在地並びに同号の対価のうち、当該租税条約の規定においてその者の所得として取り扱われる部分の金額及び当該金額のうち当該租税条約の規定の適用を受けようとする金額

四　当該株主等対価につき当該租税条約の規定に基づき所得税の免除を受けることができる事情の詳細

五　第一号の対価の種類、金額、支払方法、支払期日及び支払の基因となつた契約の内容

六　第一号の対価の支払者の氏名及び住所若しくは居所又は名称及び本店若しくは主たる事務所の所在地

七　第一号の対価の支払を受ける者が国税通則法第百十七条第二項の規定による納税管理人の届出をしている場合には、当該納税管理人の氏名及び住所又は居所

八　その他参考となるべき事項

九　第二号に規定する場合には、同号に掲げる事情の詳細を明らかにする書類（当該書類が外国語で作成されている場合には、その翻訳文を含む。次号において同じ。）

十　第三号に規定する株主等である者（同号の租税条約の規定の適用に係るものに限る。）が第一号の外国法人の株主等であることを明らかにする書類

十一　当該相手国等の権限ある当局の前号の株主等である者の居住者証明書

13　前項の届出書を提出した外国法人は、その記載事項について異動を生じた場合には、当該異動を生じた事項、当該異動を生じた日その他参考となるべき事項を記載した届出書に同項第九号から第十一号までに掲げる書類（以下この項及び第十五項において「確認書類」という。）を添付して、これを、当該異動を生じた日以後最初に当該届出書に係る株主等対価の支払を受ける日の前日までに、当該株主等対価に係る源泉徴収義務者を経由して、当該源泉徴収義務者の納税地の所轄税務署長に提出しなければならない。この場合において、当該異動を生じた事項が確認書類に係る記載事項以外の記載事項である場合には、当該届出書に係る確認書類の添付は要しないものとする。

14　外国法人は、所得税法第二百十二条第一項又は第二項の規定の適用がある株主等対価の支払を受ける場合において、当該株主等対価につき租税条約の規定により免除を受けようとするとき（第十二項の規定により届出書を提出している場合を除く。）は、同条第一項又は第二項の規定により徴収された所得税の額の還付を請求することができる。

15　前項の規定による所得税の還付の請求をしようとする者は、第十二項第一号から第八号までに掲げる事項に準ずる事項並びにその還付を受けようとする所得税の額及びその計算に関して必要な事項を記載した還付請求書に確認書類を添付して、これを、当該所得税に係る源

泉徴収義務者を経由して、当該源泉徴収義務者の納税地の所轄税務署長に提出しなければならない。

16　第一項から第五項までの規定により提出する届出書、第八項の規定により提出する還付請求書、第九項において準用する第二条第二項の規定により提出する届出書、第十一項の規定により提出する還付請求書、第十二項若しくは第十三項の規定により提出する届出書又は前項の規定により提出する還付請求書を受理したこれらの規定に規定する源泉徴収義務者が個人番号又は法人番号を有する場合には、これらの届出書又は還付請求書に、その者の個人番号又は法人番号を付記するものとする。

（源泉徴収に係る所得税につき特典条項に係る規定の適用を受ける者の届出等）

第九条の五　相手国居住者等は、その支払を受ける国内源泉所得につき所得税法第二百十二条第一項若しくは第二項又は租税特別措置法第九条の三の二第一項、第三十七条の十一の四第一項、第四十一条の九第三項若しくは第四十一条の十二の二第二項若しくは第三項の規定により徴収されるべき所得税について当該相手国居住者等に係る相手国等との間の租税条約の特定規定に基づき軽減又は免除を受けようとする場合には、第二条、第四条第一項から第五項まで、第五条、第六条及び第七条から第九条までの規定にかかわらず、当該国内源泉所得に係る源泉徴収義務者ごとに、これらの規定（第二条第十項の規定を除く。）に規定する届出書（これらの規定により添付すべき書類がある場合には当該書類の添付があるものに限る。以下この条において「条約届出書等」という。）に第九条の二第一項第三号及び第九号に掲げる事項を記載した書類（同項第十号及び第十一号に掲げる書類の添付があるものに限る。以下この条において「特典条項関係書類等」という。）を添付した書類（以下この条において「特典条項条約届出書等」という。）を、当該租税条約の効力発生の日以後その支払を受ける都度、その支払を受ける日の前日まで（その支払を受ける国内源泉所得が無記名配当等（第二条第一項に規定する無記名配当等をいう。次項において同じ。）である場合にあつては、その支払を受ける時）に、当該源泉徴収義務者を経由して、当該源泉徴収義務者の納税地の所轄税務署長に提出しなければならない。

2　相手国居住者等で、その支払を受ける国内源泉所得（無記名配当等を除く。以下この項及び第五項において「対象国内源泉所得」という。）につき所得税法第二百十二条第一項若しくは第二項又は租税特別措置法第九条の三の二第一項、第三十七条の十一の四第一項、第四十一条の九第三項若しくは第四十一条の十二の二第二項若しくは第三項の規定により徴収されるべき所得税について前項に規定する租税条約の特定規定に基づき軽減又は免除を受けようとするものが、当該対象国内源泉所得の支払を受ける日の前日以前三年内（その者が第九条の二第五項各号に掲げる規定に係る者である場合には、一年内。以下第九条の九までにおいて同じ。）のいずれかの時において、その支払を受けた国内源泉所得（当該国内源泉所得に係る資産、契約その他その所得の基因となるものが当該対象国内源泉所得に係るものと同一であるものに限る。）につき当該国内源泉所得に係る源泉徴収義務者を経由して前項の所轄税務署長に対し条約届出書等（特典条項関係書類等の添付があるものに限る。以下この項において「提出済条約届出書等」という。）を提出している場合には、前項の規定にかかわらず、その支払を受ける対象国内源泉所得に係る特典条項条約届出書等の提出は省略することができる。ただし、当該特典条項条約届出書等の記載事項が提出済条約届出書等の記載事項と異なるときは、この限りでない。

3　前項ただし書の場合において、同項ただし書に規定する提出済条約届出書等の記載事項と異なる記載事項が同項の特典条項関係書類等に係る記載事項以外の記載事項であるときは、同項ただし書の規定により提出すべき特典条項条約届出書等に係る当該特典条項関係書類等の添付を要しないものとする。

4　第二条第三項の規定は、第二項ただし書の規定により提出すべきこととされる特典条項条約届出書等（同条第一項に規定する相手国居住者等配当等につき提出すべきこととされるものに限る。）について準用する。

5　相手国居住者等で、その支払を受ける対象国内源泉所得（第二条第四項に規定する特定利子配当等（以下第九条の九までにおいて「特定利子配当等」という。）に該当するものに限る。以下この項において「特定国内源泉所得」という。）につき所得税法第二百十二条第一項若しくは第二項又は租税特別措置法第九条の三の二第一項、第三十七条の十一の四第一項若しくは第四十一条の九第三項の規定により徴収されるべき所得税について第一項に規定する租税条約の特定規定に基づき軽減又は免除を受けようとするものが、既に支払を受けた特定国内源泉所得につき当該特定国内源泉所得に係る源泉徴収義務者を経由して同項の所轄税務署長に対し条約届出書等（特典条項関係書類等の添付があるものに限る。以下この項において「提出済条約届出書等」という。）を提出している場合には、第一項又は第二項の規定にかかわらず、その支払を受ける特定国内源泉所得に係る特典条項条約届出書等の提出は省略することができる。ただし、当該特典条項条約届出書等の記載事項が提出済条約届出書等の記載事項と異なるときは、この限りでない。

6　第三項及び第二条第三項の規定は、前項に規定する相手国居住者等が同項ただし書の規定により提出すべき特典条項条約届出書等について準用する。

7　第一項の場合において、相手国居住者等が第二条第十項に規定する支払の取扱者から交付を受ける同項に規定する相手国居住者等上場株式等配当等（第九項において「相手国居住者等上場株式等配当等」という。）につき租税特別措置法第九条の三の二第一項の規定により徴収されるべき所得税について第一項に規定する租税条約の特定規定に基づき軽減又は免除を受けようとするときは、当該相手国居住者等は、特典条項条約届出書等に代えて、第二条第十項に規定する特例届出書に特典条項関係書類等を添付した書類（次項及び第九項において「特典条項特例届出書等」という。）を提出することができる。

8　前項の規定により特典条項特例届出書等を提出する場合には、第二項中「当該国内源泉所得に係る資産、契約その他その所得の基因となるものが当該対象国内源泉所得に係るものと同一であるもの」とあるのは「第二条第十項に規定する相手国居住者等上場株式等配当等」と、「条約届出書等（」とあるのは「第七項に規定する特例届出書（」と、「提出済条約届出書等」とあるのは「提出済特例届出書等」と、「係る特典条項条約届出書等」とあるのは

「係る第七項に規定する特典条項特例届出書等」と、「当該特典条項条約届出書等」とあるのは「当該特典条項特例届出書等」と、第三項中「提出済条約届出書等」とあるのは「提出済特例届出書等」と、「特典条項条約届出書等」とあるのは「特典条項特例届出書等」とし、第四項から第六項までの規定は適用しない。

9　第二条第十三項から第十八項までの規定は、相手国居住者等上場株式等配当等の支払を受ける相手国居住者等が当該相手国居住者等上場株式等配当等につき第七項の規定により特典条項特例届出書等を提出した場合について準用する。この場合において、同条第十八項中「第一項又は第二項に規定する届出書」とあるのは「第九条の五第一項に規定する特典条項条約届出書等」と、「当該届出書」とあるのは「当該特典条項条約届出書等」と、「第一項に規定する届出書」とあるのは「同項に規定する特典条項条約届出書等」と読み替えるものとする。

10　第一条の二第一項に規定する免税相手国居住者等は、その支払を受ける同項に規定する対価（同項に規定する租税条約の規定が特定規定であるものに限る。）につき法第三条第二項の規定による所得税の還付を受けようとする場合には、第一条の二第一項の規定にかかわらず、同項に規定する還付請求書（同項第十一号及び第十二号に掲げる書類の添付があるものに限る。）に特典条項関係書類等を添付して、これを、同項に規定する所轄税務署長に提出しなければならない。

11　相手国居住者等は、その支払を受けた第二条第一項に規定する相手国居住者等配当等（同項に規定する租税条約の規定が特定規定であるものに限る。）につき同条第八項の規定による所得税の還付の請求をしようとする場合には、同条第九項の規定にかかわらず、同項に規定する還付請求書（同項の規定により添付すべき書類がある場合には、当該書類の添付があるものに限る。）に特典条項関係書類等を添付して、これを、同項に規定する源泉徴収義務者を経由して、当該源泉徴収義務者の納税地の所轄税務署長に提出しなければならない。

12　相手国居住者等は、その支払を受ける第三条の四第一項に規定する償還差益（法第三条の三第一項に規定する償還差益に対する所得税の軽減又は免除を定める租税条約の規定が特定規定であるものに限る。）につき法第三条の三第一項の規定による所得税の還付を受けようとする場合には、第三条の四第一項の規定にかかわらず、同項に規定する還付請求書（同項又は同条第二項若しくは第三項の規定による書類の添付があるものに限る。）に特典条項関係書類等を添付して、これを、同条第一項に規定する源泉徴収義務者を経由して、当該源泉徴収義務者の納税地の所轄税務署長に提出しなければならない。

13　相手国居住者等である個人は、その支払を受けた第四条第七項に規定する対価、給与又は報酬（同項に規定する租税条約の規定が特定規定であるものに限る。）につき同項の規定による所得税の還付の請求をしようとする場合には、同条第八項の規定にかかわらず、同項に規定する還付請求書に特典条項関係書類等を添付して、これを、同項に規定する源泉徴収義務者を経由して、当該源泉徴収義務者の納税地の所轄税務署長に提出しなければならない。

14　相手国居住者等は、その支払を受けた第四条第一項から第五項までに規定する対価、給与又は報酬（これらの規定に規定する租税条約の規定が特定規定であるものに限る。）につき同条第十項の規定による所得税の還付の請求をしようとする場合には、同条第十一項の規定にかかわらず、同項に規定する還付請求書（同項の規定により添付すべき書類がある場合には、当該書類の添付があるものに限る。）に特典条項関係書類等を添付して、これを、同項に規定する源泉徴収義務者を経由して、当該源泉徴収義務者の納税地の所轄税務署長に提出しなければならない。

15　相手国居住者等である個人は、その支払を受けた第五条第一項に規定する退職年金等（同項に規定する租税条約の規定が特定規定であるものに限る。）につき同条第三項の規定による所得税の還付の請求をしようとする場合には、同条第四項の規定にかかわらず、同項に規定する還付請求書に特典条項関係書類等を添付して、これを、同項に規定する源泉徴収義務者を経由して、当該源泉徴収義務者の納税地の所轄税務署長に提出しなければならない。

16　相手国居住者等である個人は、その支払を受けた第六条第一項に規定する保険年金（同項に規定する租税条約の規定が特定規定であるものに限る。）につき同条第三項の規定による所得税の還付の請求をしようとする場合には、同条第四項において準用する第五条第四項の規定にかかわらず、第六条第四項において準用する第五条第四項に規定する還付請求書に特典条項関係書類等を添付して、これを、第六条第四項において準用する第五条第四項に規定する源泉徴収義務者を経由して、当該源泉徴収義務者の納税地の所轄税務署長に提出しなければならない。

17　相手国居住者等である個人又は居住者は、その支払を受けた第七条第一項に規定する報酬（同項に規定する租税条約の規定が特定規定であるものに限る。）につき同条第三項の規定による所得税の還付の請求をしようとする場合には、同条第四項において準用する第五条第四項の規定にかかわらず、第七条第四項において準用する第五条第四項に規定する還付請求書に特典条項関係書類等を添付して、これを、第七条第四項において準用する第五条第四項に規定する源泉徴収義務者を経由して、当該源泉徴収義務者の納税地の所轄税務署長に提出しなければならない。

18　第八条第一項に規定する留学生等（次項及び第二十項において「留学生等」という。）は、その支払を受けた同条第二項に規定する報酬（同項に規定する租税条約の規定が特定規定であるものに限る。）につき同条第三項の規定による所得税の還付の請求をしようとする場合には、同条第四項の規定にかかわらず、同項に規定する還付請求書（同項に規定する書類の添付があるものに限る。）に特典条項関係書類等を添付して、これを、同項に規定する源泉徴収義務者を経由して、当該源泉徴収義務者の納税地の所轄税務署長に提出しなければならない。

19　留学生等は、その支払を受けた第八条第一項に規定する給付、送金又は交付金等（同項に規定する租税条約の規定が特定規定であるものに限る。）につき同条第六項の規定による所得税の還付の請求をしようとする場合には、同条第七項において準用する同条第四項の規定にかかわらず、同条第七項において準用する同条第四項に規定する還付請求書（同条第七項において準用する同条第四項に規定する書類の添付があるものに限る。）に特典条項関係書類等を添付して、これを、同条第七項において準用する同条第四項に規定する源泉徴収義務者を経由して、当該源泉徴収義務者の納税地の所轄税務署長に提出しなければならない。

20　留学生等は、その支払を受けた第八条第二項に規定する報酬（同項に規定する租税条約の規定が特定規定であるものに限る。）につき同条第八項の規定による所得税の還付の請求をしようとする場合には、同条第九項において準用する同条第四項の規定にかかわらず、同条第九項において準用する同条第四項に規定する還付請求書（同条第九項において準用する同条第四項に規定する書類の添付があるものに限る。）に特典条項関係書類等を添付して、これを、同条第九項において準用する同条第四項に規定する源泉徴収義務者を経由して、当該源泉徴収義務者の納税地の所轄税務署長に提出しなければならない。

21　相手国居住者等は、その支払を受けた第九条第一項に規定する国内源泉所得（同項に規定する租税条約の規定が特定規定であるものに限る。）につき同条第三項の規定による所得税の還付の請求をしようとする場合には、同条第四項において準用する第五条第四項の規定にかかわらず、第九条第四項において準用する第五条第四項に規定する還付請求書に特典条項関係書類等を添付して、これを、第九条第四項において準用する第五条第四項に規定する源泉徴収義務者を経由して、当該源泉徴収義務者の納税地の所轄税務署長に提出しなければならない。

22　次の各号に掲げる者が個人番号又は法人番号を有する場合には、当該各号に定める書類にその者の個人番号又は法人番号を付記するものとする。

一　第一項の規定により提出する特典条項条約届出書等又は第十一項から前項までの規定により提出する還付請求書を受理したこれらの規定に規定する源泉徴収義務者　これらの特典条項条約届出書等又は還付請求書

二　第七項の規定により提出する特典条項特例届出書等又は第九項において準用する第二条第十五項の規定により提出する書面を受理したこれらの規定に規定する支払の取扱者　当該特典条項特例届出書等又は当該書面

（居住者証明書の提出の特例）

第九条の十　非居住者若しくは外国法人又は居住者若しくは内国法人（以下この項及び次項において「非居住者等」という。）がその支払を受ける国内源泉所得に対する所得税につき租税条約の規定に基づき軽減又は免除を受けるため、第二条第一項及び第二項（同条第六項又は第七項の規定の適用を受ける場合に限る。）並びに同条第十五項（同条第十六項の規定の適用を受ける場合に限り、第九条の五第九項において準用する場合を含む。）、第二条の二第一項、第二項前段（同条第十一項において準用する場合を含む。）及び第九項、第二条の三第一項、第二項前段（同条第十項において準用する場合を含む。）及び第八項、第二条の四第一項、第二項前段（同条第十項において準用する場合を含む。）及び第八項、第二条の五第一項、第二項前段（同条第十一項において準用する場合を含む。）及び第九項、第三条の四第一項（同条第三項の規定の適用を受ける場合に限る。）及び第四項、第四条第十一項、第十二項前段及び第十四項（同項の規定にあつては、同条第十一項の規定により届出書を提出すべき場合を除く。）並びに第九条の五第一項（同条第七項の規定の適用を受ける場合を含む。)、第十三項、第十四項及び第十九項の規定に基づいてこれらの規定に規定する届出書、書面又は還付請求書をこれらの規定に規定する源泉徴収義務者又は支払の取扱者(以下この条において「源泉徴収義務者」という。)を経由して、これらの規定に規定する所轄税務署長に対し提出する場合において、当該非居住者等が居住者証明書を当該源泉徴収義務者に提示をして、当該届出書、書面又は還付請求書に記載されている氏名又は名称及び住所若しくは居所又は本店若しくは主たる事務所の所在地若しくはその事業が管理され、かつ、支配されている場所の所在地について確認を受けたとき(当該届出書、書面又は還付請求書にその確認をした旨の記載がある場合に限る。)は、これらの規定にかかわらず、当該届出書、書面又は還付請求書への当該居住者証明書の添付は省略することができる。

2　前項に規定する源泉徴収義務者は、同項の規定の適用を受けようとする非居住者等から居住者証明書の提示を受けた場合には、当該居住者証明書の写しを作成し、これを国内にある事務所、事業所その他これらに準ずるものの所在地においてその提示を受けた日から五年間保存しなければならない。

3　前二項に規定する居住者証明書とは、第二条第六項、第七項及び第十六項、第二条の二第一項第十一号及び第九項第十号、第二条の三第一項第十一号及び第八項第十号、第二条の四第一項第十一号及び第八項第十号、第二条の五第一項第十号及び第九項第九号、第三条の四第三項及び第四項第十三号並びに第四条第十一項第十一号に規定する居住者証明書(同条第十四項の規定により同項に規定する還付請求書に添付することとされている同号に掲げる書類並びに第九条の五第一項、第七項、第十三項、第十四項及び第十九項の規定により同条第一項に規定する特典条項関係書類等として同項、同条第七項、第十三項、第十四項又は第十九項に規定する条約届出書等、特例届出書又は還付請求書に添付することとされている第九条の二第一項第十号に掲げる書類を含む。)で、第一項に規定する提示の日前一年以内に作成されたものをいう。

【索　引】

英　数

か　行

さ　行

た　行

な　行

は　行

ま　行

【著者紹介】

髙橋 幸之助（たかはし・こうのすけ）

中央大学商学部卒業。
東京国税局調査部、都内各税務署勤務後、平成26年8月髙橋幸之助税理士事務所開設。
現在、税理士・研修・セミナー等の講師。
著書に『三訂版 源泉所得税の誤りが多い事例と判断に迷う事例Q&A』『新訂版 科目別 実務上誤りが多い事例と判断に迷う事例Q&A』『中小企業者の誤りが多い事例と判断に迷う事例 Q&A』（いずれも大蔵財務協会）、『改訂版 実務家のための図解によるタックス・ヘイブン対策税制』（法令出版）がある。

改訂版 実務家のための外国税額還付の手引書

令和６年１月12日　初版印刷
令和６年１月30日　初版発行

著　者　髙　橋　幸之助

（一財）大蔵財務協会　理事長
発行者　木　村　幸　俊

発行所　一般財団法人　大　蔵　財　務　協　会
〔郵便番号　130-8585〕
東京都墨田区東駒形1丁目14番1号
（販　売　部）TEL03（3829）4141・FAX03（3829）4001
（出版編集部）TEL03（3829）4142・FAX03（3829）4005
http：//www.zaikyo.or.jp

印刷　恵友社
ISBN978-4-7547-3183-0